Cindy Cumfer & Kay Sohl

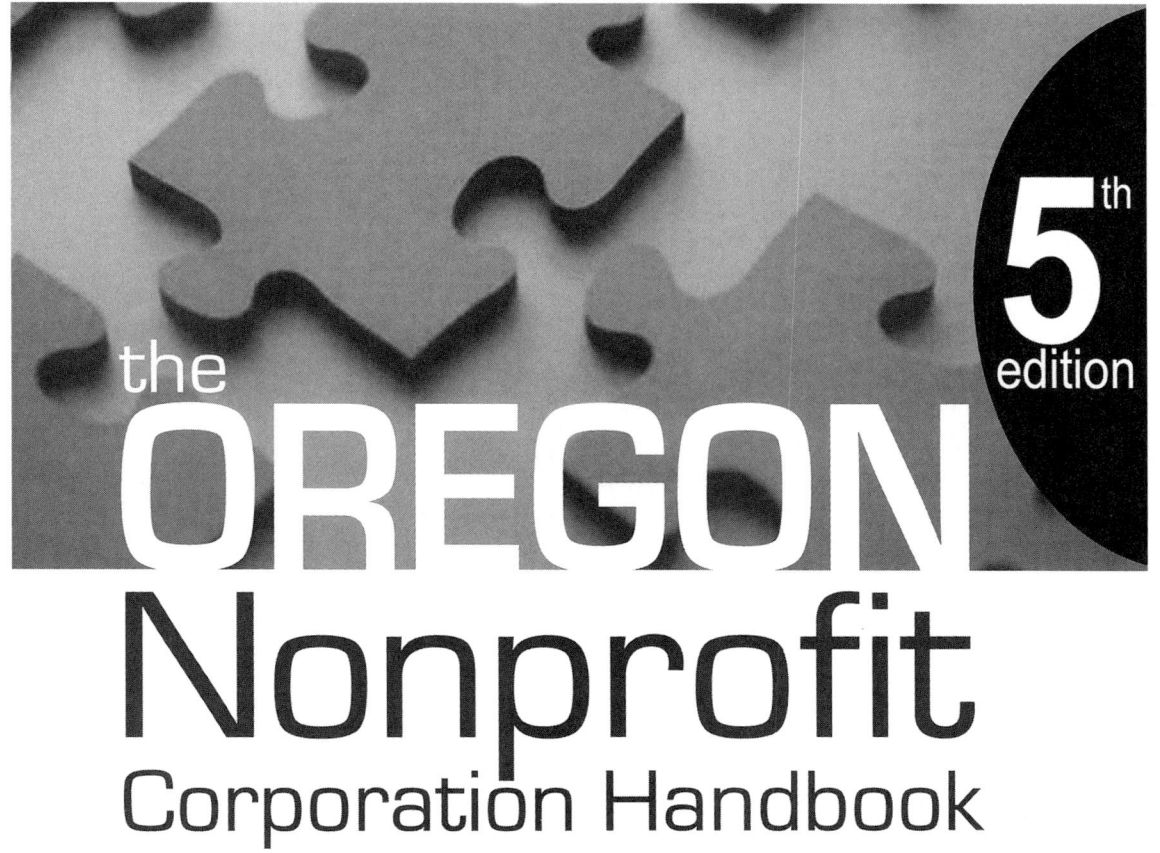

the OREGON Nonprofit Corporation Handbook

5th edition

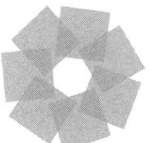

THE NONPROFIT
ASSOCIATION OF
OREGON

Published by:
The Nonprofit Association of Oregon
www.nonprofitoregon.org
5100 SW Macadam Avenue, Suite 360, Portland, OR 97239
503.239.4001   fax 503.236.8313

THE NONPROFIT
ASSOCIATION OF
OREGON

Copyright © 2012, 2005, 2001, 1996, 1993 by Cynthia Cumfer and Kay Sohl. All rights reserved. Printed in the United States of America. No part of this publication may be reproduced, stored in a retrieval system, or transmitted, in any form or by any means, electronic, mechanical, photocopying, recording or otherwise, without the prior written permission of Cynthia Cumfer and Kay Sohl.

Cover design by Marcia Barrentine.

To order a copy of *The Oregon Nonprofit Corporation Handbook*, visit *www.nonprofit oregon.org* or call Nonprofit Association of Oregon (formerly Technical Assistance for Community Services) at 503.239.4001 to place your order over the telephone. Visit our website or call NAO for pricing and shipping information. If you are ordering bulk quantities, special discounts may apply.

We have done our best to produce accurate information, forms, and samples.
Laws are subject to differing interpretations and can change, and each group
has its own unique facts. Neither the authors nor publisher assumes liability
in connection with the use of the information, forms, and samples in this book.
You should have an attorney or accountant review your paperwork
and the decisions you make based on this book.

To my parents with love

DONALD A. CUMFER

(1924–2007)

Thanks, Dad, for your sense of ethics, your faith in me, your kind heart, your good business and common sense, and your hard-headed stubbornness that sees a difficult project through from beginning to end.

WINCY CUMFER

(1925–2011)

Thanks, Mom, for your respect for all people, your terrific sense of humor, your wonderful modeling of how to listen with your heart, and your amazing organizational skills that keep a large book from looking like spaghetti.

Cindy

To my daughter, MORGAN SOHL, and my longtime friend, CHRIS ARTHUR

Thank you for accepting the Oregon Nonprofit Corporation Handbook as a demanding member of our family and enduring the creation of five editions.

Kay

Table of Contents

Acknowledgments	xxiii
How to Use this Book	xxiv
What's New in this Book	xxv
How to Find an Attorney or an Accountant	xxvii

I GETTING STARTED 1

1. Should Your Organization Be a Nonprofit Corporation?	3
2. The Structure and Types of Oregon Nonprofit Corporations	18
3. Setting Up Your Nonprofit Corporation	32
4. Writing Bylaws	52

II THE TAX-EXEMPT ORGANIZATION 89

5. Federal Tax-Exempt Status	91
6. Filling Out Tax Exempt Applications	119
7. Publicly Supported Organizations and Fee/Activity Supported Organizations (PSOs and FASOs)	145
8. Political Activity and Lobbying by Tax-Exempt Organizations	172
9. Business Activities by Tax-Exempt Organizations	203
10. Fiscal Sponsorship	219
11. State and Local Tax Exemptions	238
12. Tax Returns for Tax-Exempt Organizations	246

III SUCCESSFUL FUNCTIONING: BOARD OF DIRECTORS 263

13. What the Board Does	265
14. How the Board Manages the Corporation	289
15. Who Sits on the Board	305
16. How the Board Manages Itself	321
17. Protection of the Board	352

IV SUCCESSFUL FUNCTIONING: PEOPLE 365

18. Members and Membership Corporations	367
19. Employees	393
20. Independent Contractors	427
21. Volunteers	444

V SUCCESSFUL FUNCTIONING: MONEY, RECORDS, AND RULES 469

22. Funding: Obtaining Resources for Your Organization	471
23. Understanding Financial Management	507
24. Making a Budget	518
25. Protecting Your Nonprofit from Fraud and Errors	546
26. Keeping Books and Preparing Financial Reports	571
27. Payroll and Fringe Benefits	613
28. Evaluating Your Organization's Financial Health	632
29. Electioneering and Lobbying Rules for All Nonprofit Corporations	651
30. Compliance: Ongoing Maintenance of Your Nonprofit	676

VI CHANGING YOUR CORPORATION 709

31. Reviewing and Changing Your Articles and Bylaws	711
32. Merging with Another Corporation or Selling Your Assets	730
33. Dissolving Your Nonprofit Corporation	745

APPENDICES

1. Source Material	757
2. List of Tax and Regulatory Agencies	757

FORMS

INDEX

Expanded Table of Contents

Acknowledgments   xxiii
How to Use this Book   xxiv
What's New in this Book   xxv
How to Find an Attorney or an Accountant   xxvii

PART I
GETTING STARTED   1

1 Should Your Organization Be a Nonprofit Corporation? 3

Types of Nonprofit Organizations 4
- Nonprofit Corporation 4
- Trusts 5
- Unincorporated Associations 6

Other Types of Business Organizations 8
- Cooperative 8
- Profit (Business) Corporations 9
- General Partnerships 9
- Limited Partnerships 10
- Limited Liability Companies 10
- Sole Proprietorships 11

Advantages and Disadvantages of Being a Nonprofit Organization 12
- Advantages of the Nonprofit Organization 12
- Disadvantages of the Nonprofit Organization 12

Which Nonprofit Structure Is Best for You? 13

Making a Business Plan 14

2 The Structure and Types of Oregon Nonprofit Corporations 18

The Board of Directors 19
- Powers and Duties 19
- Qualifications of Directors 20
- Number of Directors 20
- Election, Designation and Appointment of Directors 21
- Composition of Board 21
- Terms of Directors 22
- Multiple Roles by Directors 22
- Standard of Conduct for Directors 23
- Committees of the Board 24

Officers 25
- Standard of Conduct for Officers 25

Membership or Nonmembership Corporations 25

Types of Oregon Nonprofit Corporations 27
- Which Type Is Your Nonprofit? 27
- Major Features of Each Type 28

Nonprofit Corporations Connected with Governmental Agencies 29
- Issues 30

3 Setting Up Your Nonprofit Corporation 32

Choosing and Reserving a Name 33
- Corporations Sole 33

Filling Out and Filing the Articles of Incorporation 34
- Filling Out the Articles of Incorporation 35
- Other "Additional Provisions" to Consider for Your Articles 39

Filing Your Articles of Incorporation 41

Writing Your Bylaws 42

Holding the Organizational Meeting 45
Setting Your Fiscal Year 45
Loans by Founders 46

Establishing a Board Policy Manual 46

Registering with the Department of Justice 47

Applying for a Federal Tax ID Number 47

Registering in Other States 49

Doing Business Under Another Name 49

Obtaining Licenses and Permits 50

Applying for Postal Benefits 50

Roadmap for Running Your Nonprofit Corporation 50

4 Writing Bylaws 52

How Bylaws Fit with Other Rules 53
Articles of Incorporation 54
Bylaws 54
Board Policies 54

Tips for Drafting Bylaws 54
Consistent with Laws 55
Consistent with Your Articles 55
Internally Consistent 55
Focus on Governance, Not Management 55
Understandability and Utility 56
Completeness 56
Using Bylaws to Handle Conflict 57

Bylaws for Nonmembership Corporations 57
Article I: Purpose 57
Article II: Nonmembership 58
Article III: Board of Directors 58

Article IV: Committees 65
Article V: Officers 67
Article VI: Corporate Indemnity 69
Article VII: Amendments to Bylaws 70

Bylaws for Membership Corporations 70
Article I: Purpose 71
Article II: Members 71
Article III: Board of Directors 75
Article IV: Committees 82
Article V: Officers 84
Article VI: Corporate Indemnity 86
Article VII: Amendments to Bylaws 87

PART II THE TAX-EXEMPT ORGANIZATION 89

5 Federal Tax-Exempt Status 91

Tax Exemption: Do You Want It? 92

§501(c)(3): Public Benefit and Religious Organizations 93
Who Qualifies for §501(c)(3) Exemption 93
Classifications of §501(c)(3) Groups 99
Who Must File the Application 107
Effective Date of the Exemption 107
Cost of Applying 109

§501(c)(4): Civic Leagues and Social Welfare Organizations 109

Other Exempt Groups 110
Labor, Agricultural and Horticultural Organizations—(c)(5) 110
Business Leagues—(c)(6) 110
Social Clubs—(c)(7) 111
Fraternal Societies—(c)(8) and (c)(10) 111

    Veterans Organizations—(c)(19) 112
    Political Organizations—§527   112
    Miscellaneous Exempt Groups   112

Affiliated Organizations 113

General Information For Organizations Seeking Any Type of Tax Exemption   115
    Cost of Applying   115
    Annual Returns 116
    Public Inspection of Application and Annual Returns 116
    Unrelated Business Income   117
    Group Exemption   117
    Time for IRS Response 118

6 Filling Out Tax Exempt Applications   119

Filling Out Form 1023   120
    Part I – Identification of Applicant 121
    Part II—Organizational Structure 123
    Part III—Required Provisions   124
    Part IV—Narrative Description   124
    Part V—Compensation and Financial Arrangements   128
    Part VI—Your Members and Others You Benefit   131
    Part VII—History   132
    Part VIII—Specific Activities   133
    Part IX—Financial Data 137
    Part X—Public Charity or Private Foundation Status   138
    Part XI—User Fee Information   139
    Signature Line 139
    Form 1023 Checklist   142

Filling Out Form 1024   143

Questions Back From the IRS   144

7 Publicly Supported Organizations and Fee/Activity Supported Organizations (PSOs and FASOs)   145

Support Requirements for PSO's and FASO's   146

How to Calculate the Total Support Base   148
    1. Contributions, Grants and Membership Fees.   148
    2. Gross Receipts from Related Business Activities   149
    3. Net Income from Unrelated Business Activities   149
    4. Gross Investment Income   150
    5. Certain Tax Revenues   150
    6. Certain Services and Facilities Furnished by the Government   151

Summary of the Formulas   151

How to Calculate Your Support from Qualified Sources for the PSO Test   152
    The Mechanical Test (or One-Third Support Test)   152
    Facts and Circumstances Test   159

How to Calculate Your Support from Qualified Sources for the FASO Test   162
    One-Third Support Test 162
    One-Third Gross Investment Income Test   164

The Normalcy Period   165
    General Rule   165

Recordkeeping Issues   165

8 Political Activity and Lobbying by Tax-Exempt Organizations 172

Who Should Read This Chapter? 173

Political Activity and §501(c)(3) Groups   173
    Prohibited Activities for (c)(3)s 174
    Permissible Activities for (c)(3)s 174

Lobbying and §501(c)(3) Groups:

ix

Two Tests   180
  Lobbying Tests 181

Understanding the Lobbying Election: What Lobbying Is   182
  What Is Lobbying   182
  What Is Not Lobbying   187

The Lobbying Election Computations   188
  Lobbying Expenditures 188
  Exempt Purpose Expenditures (EPE) 189
  Making the Calculations 189
  Special Rules for Affiliated Organizations   190
  Consequences of Exceeding Your Lobbying Limits 191
  Calculating the Lobbying Expenditures and Taxes–An Example 192

Making the Lobbying Election   193
  Choosing to Come Under the Lobbying Election   193
  How to Make the Election   194

Proving Compliance with the Lobbying Rules   194
  Keep Good Records   194

Political Activity and Lobbying by Non-(c)(3) Exempt Groups   198
  §501(c)(4) Organizations   198
  §501(c)(5) and (6) Organizations 199
  Limits on Political Activity by Non-(c)(3) Groups   199
  Deductibility of Dues Used for Lobbying   199

Affiliated Organizations 200

Other Laws Concerning Political Activity and Lobbying   202

9 Business Activities by Tax-Exempt Organizations 203

Running a Business as a Nonprofit 204

  Creating a Business Plan   205

Unrelated Business Income   206
  Trade or Business   207
  Regularly Carried On   208
  Substantially Related to Exempt Purpose   208

Examples of Unrelated Business Income   212
  Services   212
  Sales of Goods 212

Exceptions to the Unrelated Business Income Rules 213

The Unrelated Business Income Tax 215
  Who is Subject to the Unrelated Business Income Tax (UBIT)?   215
  How to Calculate and Pay the Unrelated Business Income Tax 215

Protecting Your Tax-Exempt Status 216
  When Does Unrelated Business Income Threaten Your Tax Exemption?   216
  Forming a New Corporation   217

Joint Ventures   218

10 Fiscal Sponsorship 219

Proper Uses of Fiscal Sponsorships   220
  New and Small Projects 221
  Projects of Limited Duration   221
  Ongoing Project with a Major Donor/Funder 221
  Assistance to Qualified Individuals   222

Fiscal Sponsorship Alternatives 222
  Programs of the Sponsor   222
  Administrative Assistance for Another §501(c)(3) Organization   223

Misuses of Fiscal Sponsorships 223
  Pass-Through Donations and Grants   223

Conduit for Gifts or Grants to
Individuals   224
Conduit to Nonexempt Organizations
224
Avoidance of the Public Support Test
224
Avoidance of the Lobbying Excise
Tax by Private Foundations   225
Consequences of the Misuse of Fiscal
Sponsorships   225

**Issues in the Fiscal
Sponsor Relationship   225**
Characterizing the Use of Project
Funds   225
Control   228
Internal Accounting of the Project
Funds   229
Ownership of Property   230
Payments to the Sponsor   230
Liabilities   230
Public Relations 231
Protecting the Sponsor's Funding
Sources 231
Special Issues for the Sponsor   231

**How to Structure a Fiscal
Sponsorship Agreement 232**
Phase 1: Handling the Initial
Contribution or Grant   232
Phase 2: Funding the Project   234
Drafting an Agreement   236

11 State and Local Tax Exemptions   238

State Income Tax Exemption   239
Who is Covered by the Exemption?
239
How to Apply for the Exemption
239
Other Forms You Must File   239

**Tri-Met and Lane Transit
District Taxes   240**

**County Business Tax Exemption
240**

**County Property Tax Exemption
240**

Whether to Apply for the Exemption
241
What Groups Are Covered by the
Exemption   241
How to Apply for the Exemption
243
Leases and Lease Options   244

Local Business License Fees   244

12 Tax Returns for Tax-Exempt Organizations 246

Filing Federal Returns   247
Who Must File Form 990, Form 990
EZ and Form 990N   247
Revocation of Tax-Exempt Status for
Failure to File Returns   248
What Is Schedule 990A and Who
Must File It?   249
When and Where to File Form 990
or 990 EZ and Schedule 990A   249
How to Deal with 990, 990 EZ and
Schedule 990A Late Filing Penalties
249
What Is the Accounting Period for
Form 990, 990 EZ and Schedule
990A?   250
How to Change Your Fiscal Year 250
What Are the Acceptable Accounting
Methods for the 990, 990EZ and
Schedule 990A?   251
How Do You Change Your Method of
Accounting?   252
Public Inspection of Your 990, 990
EZ and Schedule 990A   252
How to Complete the 990, 990EZ,
and Schedule 990A   253
Form 990 Part VI Governance
Questions   254
Most Common 990 Mistakes and
Problems   255

Filing State Returns   261
Who Must File Form CT-12 and
When Is It Due?   261
Filling Out Form CT-12   262

Filling Out the Inventory

and Personal Property Assessment 262

PART III
SUCCESSFUL FUNCTIONING: BOARD OF DIRECTORS 263

13 What the Board Does 265

Establishing the Corporation's Purpose 267

Determining Your Management Type 267

Direct Management Corporations 269
Management Tasks 269
Recordkeeping 270
Protecting the Corporate Status 271
Independent Contractors 271
Founders 271
Members 272

Delegated Management Corporations 272
When to Delegate 272
Terms of the Delegation 273
Limitations on the Delegation 275
Choosing an Executive Director 276
Oversight 278
Suspicious Circumstances 284
Members 285
Special Concerns of Smaller Delegated Management Corporations 285

14 How the Board Manages the Corporation 289

Setting Up a Management Structure 290
Direct Management Corporations 291
Delegated Management Corporations 291

Getting Informed 292
Information about Your Corporation's Governance 292
Information about Your Corporation's Operations 294

Participation 296

Standards of Conduct 297
Duty of Follow the Corporate Purpose 298
Duty to Act with Due Care 298
Duty to Be Loyal to the Corporation 299
Protecting Your Directors 304

15 Who Sits on the Board 305

Recruiting and Retaining the Directors Your Organization Needs 306

Diversity 308

Staff as Directors 310

Board Orientation 311

Clarifying Board Expectations 312

Key Board Transitions 313
Board Transitions for Community-Based Nonprofits 313
Board Transitions for Institutional Spin-off Nonprofits 315

Replacing Directors and Officers 316
Expiration of Terms of Office of Directors 316
Resignation of Directors 316
Removal of Directors 316
Vacancy on the Board 319
Resignation and Removal of Officers 319

Conclusion 319

16 How the Board Manages Itself 321

Board Meetings and Decision-Making 322
    Why Have Meetings? 322
    Types of Meetings 323
    Before the Meeting 324
    At the Meeting 325
    Minutes 330
    Holding Effective Meetings 332
    Decisions Without a Meeting 335
    Committees that Exercise Board Authority 336
    Board Committees that Don't Exercise Board Authority 338
    Separate Advisory Boards and Committees 340
    Board Member Responsibilities for Board Committee Work 340

Board Officers 341
    President 341
    Secretary 342
    Treasurer 342
    Executive Director as Officer 343
    Other Officers 344
    Standard of Conduct for Officers 344
    Training the Next Officers 344
    Resignations 345

Board Policies 345
    Board Policies for Direct Management Corporations 346
    Board Policies for Delegated Management Corporations 347
    Board Policy Manuals 350

Evaluating the Effectiveness of Your Board 350

Perpetuating Institutional Memory 351

17 Protection of the Board 352

Personal Liability of Your Directors and Officers 353
    When You Are Personally Liable 353
    Who Can Sue You 355
    Which Boards Are Most Vulnerable to Being Sued 356

Protection of Your Directors and Officers 357
    Educate Your Board 357
    Maintain Proof of Correct Behavior 357
    Reliance on Reports 358
    Proper Handling of Conflicts of Interest 358
    Create an Advisory Board 358
    Limited Liability of Directors and Officers 359
    Reimbursement by the Corporation When You Are Sued 360
    Insurance 362
    Final Note 363

PART IV SUCCESSFUL FUNCTIONING: PEOPLE 365

18 Members and Membership Corporations 367

Admission of Members 369
    Criteria for Admission 369
    Consent of Members 370

Rights, Obligations, and Liabilities of Members 371
    Classes of Members 371
    Members' Rights and Obligations 371
    Liability of Members 372
    Membership Dues 373

Notice of Meetings 373
    Who Gets Notice? 373
    Contents of Notice 373
    How Notice Is Given 374
    Notice of Adjournment of Meetings 374

Waiver of Notice 374
Record Date 375

Meetings of Members 376
Who Attends the Membership Meetings 376
Types of Members' Meetings 377
Conduct of Meeting 378
Minutes 378
Action Without Meeting 378
Delegates 379

Voting by Members 379
Quorum Requirements 379
Voting Requirements at Meetings 380
Voting by Proxy 380
Voting By Written Ballot (Vote by Mail) 381
Voting and Vote Splitting 381
Corporation's Acceptance of Votes 382

Election and Removal of the Board 383
Election of Directors 383
Vacancy on the Board 383
Removal of Directors 383

Inspection of Your Records by Members 384
Records Subject to Inspection Without a Reason by the Members 385
Inspections That Require a Proper Purpose 386
Restrictions on Members' Rights to Inspect and Copy 387

Resignation and Termination of Members 387
Resignation 387
Expulsion, Suspension, or Termination 387

Special Rights of Members in Mutual Benefit Corporations 389
Voting on Conflicts of Interest 389
Right to Assets on Dissolution 389

Change from Membership to Nonmembership Corporation 390
Making Changes When You Have Members 390
Making Changes When You Have No Members 391

19 Employees 393

Wage and Hour Laws 394
Who Is Subject to the Laws 394
Exempt and Nonexempt Employees 395
Overtime and Volunteer Time 395
"Comp"Time 396
Attendance at Trainings, Conferences and Staff Meetings 397
Enforcement of Wage and Hour Laws—the Real Whammy 397

Discrimination and Harassment Issues 398

Unionization 399

Personnel Policies and Employee Handbooks 399
Developing Personnel Policies 400
Your Approach to Personnel Policies 401
What to Include in Your Personnel Policies 403
Creating an Employee Handbook 420
Amendments to Personnel Policies and Employee Handbooks 421
Distribution of the Employee Handbook 422
Administering Personnel Policies and the Employee Handbook 423

Dismissal or Termination of Employees 423

Excessive Compensation 424

Evaluating the Executive Director 424

Independent Contractors and Volunteers as Employees 426
Independent Contractors 426
Volunteers Who Are Paid 426

20 Independent Contractors   427

Who Is an Independent Contractor?   428

Federal Income Tax and Social Security Issues   429

State Income Tax Issues   432

State Unemployment Issues   434

Workers' Compensation Issues   435
Your Service Providers   435
Workers for Those With Whom You Subcontract   437

Federal and State Wage and Hour Laws   438
Federal Law   438
State Law   438

The Importance of Complying with the Laws   439

Danger Signals   439

Protections for Your Nonprofit Organization   440
Expert Opinion in Writing   441
Ask the IRS—Form SS-8   441
Assessing and Limiting Your Exposure   441
Independent Contractor Agreement   442

21 Volunteers   444

Recruiting, Screening, and Placing Volunteers in Your Organization   445
Recruiting Volunteers   445
Screening Volunteers   447
Placing Volunteers in the Right Spot in Your Organization   448

Orienting, Training, Supervising and Evaluating Volunteers   449
Orienting Volunteers   449
Training 450
Supervising Volunteers 451
Evaluating Volunteers   451

Recognizing and Rewarding Volunteers   452

Volunteers Who Are Really Employees   453
Federal and State Wage and Hours Laws   453
State Unemployment and Worker Compensation   455

Volunteers and Liability 456
Assessing the Risk of Harm by Volunteers   456

When Your Volunteers Face Personal Liability   457

When Your Organization is Liable for the Actions of Your Volunteers   458
When Your Nonprofit Is Negligent   458
When Your Nonprofit Is Not Negligent but Liable   459

When Your Volunteer Is Injured   460
Assessing the Risk of Harm to Volunteers   461

Protection for Your Volunteers and Your Organization   461
Federal and State Law Protections   461
Preventive Actions   462
Damage Control   462
Protection for Your Nonprofit Organization and Your Volunteer When Your Volunteer Is Injured 465

PART V SUCCESSFUL FUNCTIONING: MONEY, RECORDS, AND RULES   469

22 Funding: Obtaining Resources for Your

Organization   471

How Are Nonprofits Funded?   472

Foundation Grants   473
Foundation Funding Preferences   475

Corporate and Other Business Giving   477
Business Giving Contrasts with Foundation Giving   478

Individual Contributions   478
Repeat Giving   480
Key Numbers   480
Do People Need to Get Something in Return for Giving $ to Your Nonprofit?   481
Donor Acknowledgement   481
Gift Acceptance Policy   482

Fundraising Events   482
Determining the Purpose of the Event   482
Projecting the Income and Expenses for the Event   482
Considering the True Cost of the Event   483
Is It Worth It?   483

Membership Fees   483

Civic and Religious Organizations as Funders   485
Civic Organizations   485
Religious Organizations   486

Bingo, Raffles, and Other Gaming   487
Exceptions to Licensing   487
Getting A License   488
Is Bingo the Best Strategy for Your Nonprofit?   489

Government Grants and Contracts for Services   490
Government Grants   490
Government Contracts   491

Program Service Fees   492

Sales of Products Related to Your Mission   494

Internet Sales of Goods and Services   495

Social Enterprise and Business Ventures   495
Can Social Enterprise or Providing Goods and Services Threaten Our Tax-exempt Status ?   496

Investment Income   497
Components of an Investment Policy   497
Who Makes Investment Decisions?   498

In-Kind Contributions   499

Using the Internet and Social Media to Raise Funds   500
Solicitations Across State Line   500
Other Social Media Issues   501
Email Promotions   501

Ethical and Legal Issues in Fundraising   502
Ethical Fundraising   502
Unethical Fundraising   503
Cautions When Working with Professional Fundraising Firms   504
Rules on Solicitation for Non-(c)(3) Exempt Groups 505

Final Tips 506

23 Understanding Financial Management 507

Signs of Good Financial Management   508
Achieving Your Mission 508
Solvency—Staying in the Black 508
Liquidity—Having the Cash You Need When You Need It   508
Documenting the Compliance with Restrictions   508

The Big Picture   509
Planning   509
Execution   509
Recording   510
Reporting   510

Monitoring　510

Timing for the Financial Management Cycle　511

Financial Management Check-up　511

24 Making a Budget　518

Budget Terminology　519

Why Have a Budget?　519

Basic Budgeting Guidelines for Nonprofit Organizations　520
　Budgeting for Funds from Prior Years　521

Budget Development Steps　522
　Projecting Income　522
　Projecting Expenses　526

Fixed and Variable Costs　530
　The Effect of Volume of Services and Activities on Costs　530

Functional Budgeting　530
　Management Costs　531
　Fundraising Costs　532
　Cost Allocation　532
　Direct Costs　534
　Shared Costs　534
　Choosing a Cost Allocation Method　535
　Allocating Management (Administration) Costs　535
　Cost Allocation Plans　536

Budgets for Grants　537
　Start with Your Annual Operating Budget:　537
　Budgets When Funders Support Only New Projects　538
　Grant Budget Notes　538

Budgeting for Restricted Funds　539

Capital Budgets　540

Cash Flow Projections　541

Your Budget Process　543

Boards and Budgets　544

25 Protecting Your Nonprofit from Fraud and Errors　546

Who Should Do What? Developing Financial Policies and Procedures　547
　Sample Table of Contents for Fiscal Policies and Procedures Manual　548

Key Banking Issues　551
　Opening Your Checking Account 551
　Common Bank Account Set-up Mistakes　551
　Check Choices　552
　Keep Unused Check Stock Under Control 553
　Protect Your Account from Unauthorized Checks　553
　Never Permit Blank Checks to Be Signed 554
　Should We Require Two Signatures on Each Check? 554
　Should We Use On-line Payment Features?　555
　Bank Deposits　555
　Do We Need to Get Our Processed Checks Returned with Our Bank Statement?　556
　Should We Use Positive Pay?　557
　Bank Reconciliations Are Essential 557
　Dealing with Multiple Bank Accounts 558

Petty Cash Funds　559

Processing Payments　560
　Reimbursing Expenses 561
　Travel Expense Reimbursements: 562
　Corporate Credit Cards 563
　Debit Cards　564

Handling Cash Receipts 564

Should We Accept Credit Card Payment for Donations or Purchases?　565

xvii

In-Kind Contributions   566

Risk Management
and Insurance   566
   Insurance   567

What Your Board Must Do
to Protect Your Nonprofit   569

Checklists of Key Controls   569

26 Keeping Books and Preparing Financial Reports   571

What is Accounting?   572
   Sample Chart of Accounts   573
   Functional Cost Centers: 574
   Funding Source Cost Center: 574

Big Choices for Your
Accounting System   575
   Should You Use the Cash or the Accrual Method?   575
   Do You Need to Track Multiple Programs
   or Multiple Funding Sources?   577
   How Will You Meet IRS Reporting Requirements?   578
   Do You Want or Need to Use Generally Accepted Accounting Principles (GAAP)?   578

Nonprofit Accounting Requires More Than Tracking Revenues and Expenses   580

Double-Entry Accounting Is Essential   581

Very Small Nonprofits: Basic Accounting and Reporting   582

Dealing with Carry-over Funds   583

How is Nonprofit Accounting Different from Business Accounting?   584
   Classification of Contributions   585
   Distinguishing Contributions from Purchases of Services or Goods   586
   Three Classes of Net Assets   586
   Board Directions Are Designations, Not Restrictions   587
   Fulfilling Restrictions   587
   Unrestricted Expenses   587
   Recording Promises to Give   588
   Multi-year Grant Commitments   589
   Program Fees Received in Advance   589
   Using Deferred Revenue to Track Grant Income   590
   Government Grants and Contracts   590
   Cost Allocation   591
   Accounting for Fundraising Costs   591
   Accounting for In-Kind Contributions   592
   Gains and Losses on Investments   593
   Accounting for Land, Building, and Equipment   594

Government Funds Accounting Requirements   596

Whatever Happened to Fund Accounting?   597

Financial Statements   598
   Statement of Financial Position   598
   Statement of Activities   598
   Statement of Functional Expenses   601
   Statement of Cash Flows   602
   Key Connection Between Financial Statements   603

Tips for Useful Financial Reports   604

Accounting Software Choices   606

Tips for QuickBooks® Users   608

Who Should Do Your Nonprofit's Accounting?   609
   Small Organizations   610
   Mid-sized or Small Nonprofits with Multiple Programs or Multiple Restricted Funding Sources   610
   Larger or Complex Nonprofits   611

27 Payroll and Fringe Benefits 613

Payroll Terms 614
Federal Employer Identification Number (EIN) 614
State of Oregon Employer Identification Number 614
Gross Wages 614
Employer Taxes 614
Mandatory Payroll Withholdings 615
Workers Compensation Insurance: 615
Voluntary Payroll Deductions 615
Net Pay 616
Draws or Payroll Advances 616
Payroll Direct Deposits 616
Payroll Tax Deposits 616
Payroll Tax Reports 617
Payroll Software 617
Payroll Services 617
Fringe Benefits 617

Payroll Basics 618

Employer Taxes 619
Employers' Share of Social Security and Medicare Taxes (FICA) 619
Unemployment 620
SAIF or Workers' Compensation 621
Local Governmental Unit Employer Taxes 622

Preparing Your Own Payroll 622
Setting Up Your Payroll System 622
Payroll Withholding Tax Tables 623
Payroll Records 623
Payroll Processing Procedures 624

Payroll Tax Deposit Requirements 625

Payroll Tax Reporting Requirements 626

Fringe Benefit Basics 627
Paid Time Off 628
Health, Dental and Disability Insurance 628
Other Plans to Help Employees Meet Expenses with Pre-Tax Dollars 630
Retirement Plans 630

28 Evaluating Your Organization's Financial Health 632

How to Ask the Right Questions about Your Financial Statements 633
How Financially Strong is This Organization? 633
Can the Organization Meet Its Obligations on Time? 633
Are There Limitations on What the Organization Can Do With Its Resources? 634
How Can I Tell if the Organization is Complying with Restrictions on the Use of Funds? 637
Is the Organization "Breaking Even"? 637
Is the Organization Using Its Resources Wisely? 638
Are the Books In Balance? 639
How Do We Know the Financial Statements Are "Right"? 640

The Manager's Role in Monitoring Financial Performance 640
Steps to Be Sure the Reports Are Accurate: 640
Steps to Determine Whether Action is Needed to Protect the Organization's Financial Health 641

Should Your Nonprofit Have an Independent Audit or Review? 642
Audits 643
Reviews 644
Choosing Your Auditor 644

Understanding and Preparing for Audits and Fiscal Monitoring 645
Types of Audits 645
Preparing for an Audit 646

Will Your Organization Need an A-133 Federal Funds Audit? 647
The Nonprofit Organization's Responsibilities 648
The Auditor's Responsibilities 648
The Focus of the A-133 Audit 649

Steps to Prepare for A-133 Audits   650

29 Electioneering and Lobbying Rules for All Nonprofit Corporations   651

Spaghetti Rules   652

Federal Election Rules   653
Endorsing or Opposing Candidates   654
Contributions to Federal Candidates and Political Parties by Nonprofit Corporations   654
Advocating for Candidates or Political Parties by Nonprofit Corporations   655
Voter Activities   661

Federal Lobbying Rules   663
Lobbying by (c)(3) Organizations   664

Oregon Rules Governing Political Campaigns   664
Independent Expenditures   665
Political Committees   666
Electioneering Conduct   669
(c)(3) Organizations   669

Oregon Lobbying Rules   670

Local Political and Lobbying Rules   672

Use of Federal Funds for Political and Lobbying Activities   672

Political Expenditure Tax   673

30 Compliance: Ongoing Maintenance of Your Nonprofit   676

Books and Records   677
What Books and Records Should You Keep?   677
How Long Should You Keep Them?   678
Who Can See or Copy Your Books and Records   680
What Records Can and Must Be Protected   682

Reports and Registrations   682
Secretary of State (Corporation Commissioner)   682
Department of Justice (Attorney General)   683
Other State and Local Licenses and Filings   683

Confidential Information   684
Identity Theft   684
Medical Information   685

Notices   685
Personal and Newspaper Notice   685
Notice by Email   685
Effective Date of Notice   686
Address for Notice   686

Releases   686

Terrorism Laws   687
Actions that Aid Suspected Terrorists   688
Sanctions for Aiding Suspected Terrorists   688
Treasury Department's Voluntary Guidelines   689
What Should You Do?   690
Government Lists of Suspected Terrorists   691

Tax-Exempt Groups: Operational Rules   692
Public Inspection and Copying of Papers   692
Charitable Contributions   694
Solicitations by Exempt Organizations Other Than §501(c)(3)   699
Member Notification Regarding Lobbying   699
Changes in Activities   699
Group Exemptions   699
Special Requirements for Schools   699
Excess Benefits Transactions   700

PART VI CHANGING YOUR CORPORATION 709

31 Reviewing and Changing Your Articles and Bylaws 711

Reviewing Your Articles of Incorporation 712

Changing Your Registered Agent or Registered Office 712

Amending Your Articles of Incorporation 713
- Amendment by Corporations with No Members or No Members with Voting Rights on Amendments 713
- Corporations With Voting Members 714
- Filing of Amendment 717
- Tax-Exempt Organizations 717

Restating Your Articles of Incorporation 718

Reviewing Your Bylaws 718
- Understanding the Hierarchy 719
- Tips for Reviewing Bylaws 720
- Common Pitfalls in Bylaws 722

Amending Your Bylaws 728
- Amendment by Corporations with No Members or No Members with Voting Rights on Amendments 728
- Corporations With Voting Members on the Bylaws 728
- Approval by a Third Party 729
- Tax-Exempt Organizations 729

32 Merging with Another Corporation or Selling Your Assets 730

Mergers 731
- Why Nonprofits Decide to Merge 731
- Some Merger Terminology 731
- Limitations on Mergers by Public Benefit or Religious Corporations 732
- Alternatives to Mergers 732
- An Overview of the Merger Process 733
- The Steps of the Merger 734
- The Effect of a Merger 740
- Accounting for Mergers and Take-Overs 741
- Special Note for Tax-Exempt Corporations 741

Sale of Most of the Assets of Your Corporation 741
- In the Usual Course of Your Activities 742
- Not in the Usual Course of Your Activities 742
- §501(c)(3) Groups 743
- Creditors 743

33 Dissolving Your Nonprofit Corporation 745

Voluntary Dissolution 746
- Issues to Consider 746
- Overview of the Dissolution Procedure 748
- Claims Against a Dissolved Corporation 751
- Effect of a Dissolution/Winding Up Affairs 753

Involuntary Dissolution 753
- Administrative Dissolution 753
- Judicial Dissolution 755

Activities After Dissolution 755

Special Note for Tax-Exempt Corporations That Are Voluntarily or Involuntarily Dissolved 756

APPENDICES 757

1 Source Material   759

2 List of Tax and Regulatory Agencies   789

FORMS

INDEX

Acknowledgments

We would like to thank our families, Valerie and Kiera, and Chris and Morgan for putting up with us while we have put out this book five times. We would also like to acknowledge that our parents played significant roles in the development of our shared passion for nonprofit organizations. Kay's mother and father, Carol George Sohl and William A. Sohl, defined their lives through civic activism and building nonprofit organizations. Cindy's parents started, ran and served on the Boards of a number of nonprofits. On so many levels, this book would not exist without all these special people.

A book, like a successful nonprofit, is the work of many people. We are very grateful to Karin Guenther, an employment attorney, for her review and updating of Chapter 19. A tip of the hat to Gary McGee, a nonprofit accountant who very knowledgeably discussed with us some of the tax and accounting issues we cover in this book. Oregon is very fortunate to have an excellent Assistant Attorney General, Elizabeth Grant, in charge of the Department of Justice's Charitable Activities Section that oversees public benefit nonprofits. We thank Liz for her help with several important issues in this book and for her true dedication to the prevention of problems in nonprofits as well as her work with nonprofits in trouble.

Many thanks to Marcia Barrentine for her terrific design skills that you see reflected in the cover and book design and her expert assistance with desktop publishing. Marcia is a very talented designer who has more patience than Job. We know because we tested her. We thank John Laursen of Press-22 Book Design & Production for his time and expertise that pointed us to a path that made this book possible. A fifth toast to Ruth Gundle of Eighth Mountain Press for guidance (again) in the intricacies of selecting a printer. We appreciate Carrie Hoops and Alice Forbes of the Nonprofit Association of Oregon for their help with the production of this book and Abe Conway of NAO for his computer know-how.

As always, we want to thank the people who start and run nonprofit organizations. Nonprofits have been an amazingly important and largely overlooked force in American public life since the American Revolution and before. Over the past 35 years we have each been privileged to meet many very dedicated and able people who often make great sacrifices of time and money for an organization that they do not "own." Although American culture is often portrayed as very individualistic and materialistic, these people reaffirm that we Americans care about our communities and our world. We all owe them a debt of gratitude.

How to Use this Book

This is a large book. We've been told that we should call it *The Oregon Nonprofit Corporation Two-Hands Book* or *The Oregon Nonprofit Corporation Handtruck Book*. It is unlikely that any group will need ALL the information in this book, so don't be daunted by the size. We have written this book for beginners, for those who are working in or volunteering for nonprofits, and for nonprofit professionals. If you are new to the nonprofit arena and are using this book to get started, you should look at Chapter 3 and the **ROADMAP** at the end of Chapter 3 for help in negotiating this book. You will also find that in many places we tell you sections and chapters you can skip. The parts that you do read are not meant to be read all at once—for instance, it's unlikely that you will need to know how to incorporate and how to dissolve in the same month. (At least we hope not!) Keep this as your reference book over time.

This book has an improved **INDEX** located at the very end of the book. If you are looking for information on a specific topic, you may want to check the index first. We have learned that preparing an index is one of the great challenges of producing a book of this size. If you don't find the topic you are looking for in the index, you may want to check the **EXPANDED TABLE OF CONTENTS** as well.

There are **FORMS** near the end of the book. In order to make them more usable, the forms do not have page numbers on them. In the book, we refer to the forms by name and the forms are alphabetized by name so that you can find the form you want more easily. In many cases, you can get (possibly updated) electronic copies of the forms under the Resources tab at Cindy Cumfer's website at *www.cumfer.net*. The Forms section does not include forms that you can get from the government on-line. Because government forms change from time to time and are now so accessible, we refer you to the websites where you can obtain them. If you don't have access to the web, you can get copies by contacting the appropriate agency. Appendix 2 provides a list of the agencies and their contact information and web addresses.

If you are a technical person—a lawyer, accountant, or similar professional—Appendix 1 contains a list of **SOURCE MATERIALS** that we rely on in each chapter. The Sources section includes citations to statutes, administrative regulations and rulings, cases, generally accepted accounting principles, and general reference material to assist you. We've also included some references in Appendix 1 to materials accessible to and of interest to all readers. We alert you to these materials at the end of each chapter as appropriate.

If you want to obtain additional copies of this book, contact the Nonprofit Association of Oregon (NAO). NAO, the publisher of this book, is a §501(c)(3) nonprofit organization that is an excellent training and consulting resource for nonprofits. NAO maintains a website at *www.nonprofitoregon.org*. Author Cindy Cumfer maintains a website at *www.cumfer.net* which includes periodic updates on issues of interest to nonprofits, sample forms and policies, and items about nonprofit history that tickle her fancy. Author Kay Sohl has a website at *www.kaysohlconsulting.net*. You should check these websites for updated information about matters in this book.

What's New in this Book

The Fifth Edition contains some exciting additions and updating. Among the most important are these:

- An extensive revision and expansion of our discussion of the role and operation of the **Board of Directors**. What used to be Chapter 13 is now 5 chapters comprising Part III on the Board. This revision introduces a new approach to understanding Board duties. We move away from the common approach that talks about Board duties as the duties of due care and loyalty. We now describe *what* the Board's job is—to manage the corporation. We then recognize two approaches to nonprofit corporate management—direct management and delegated management. The duties of the Board are different depending on which approach to management the Board is using and we describe the duties of the Board for organizations using each approach. This more targeted description allows your Directors to have a crisper understanding of what it is they actually do, given the type of corporation they manage. We explain the duty of due care and the duty of loyalty as the standards of conduct that every Board must observe as it carries out its duty to manage the corporation. Other chapters give much more specific information about *how* the Board goes about managing the corporation, depending again on which type of management style the Board uses, *who* sits on the Board, and *how* the Board manages itself. This is a very original approach that we now utilize in our trainings and find is much more practical and helpful to Boards.

- A more comprehensive guide to **fundraising**, including new discussions of earned income strategies and social enterprises in Chapter 22.

- A stronger focus on **key accounting choices** your organization must make and the factors you should consider in making them in Chapter 26.

- An emphasis on **sustainability strategies** you can adopt to enhance your long-term success in Chapters 9, 22, and 28.

- More coverage throughout of the almost universal failure of smaller nonprofits to have good **financial controls** and an explanation of what these nonprofits need to do to institute good controls, as well as a new sample Financial Controls Policies and Procedures for Small Nonprofits in the Forms section.

- A discussion of the changes on the **Form 990** informational return related to governance in Chapter 12 and six new policies in the Forms section that allow you to comply with the IRS governance concerns.

- A more comprehensive **Conflicts of Interest** and Executive Compensation Policy in the Forms section and a discussion of the rules underlying that policy in Chapters 14 and 30.

- More discussion about the **Internet and social media**, especially as these vehicles are used by organizations who solicit for donations on the web in Chapter 22.

- New material about **business planning by nonprofits** in Chapters 1 and 9.

- An improved explanation in Chapter 6 of how to fill out **Form 1023**, the §501(c)(3) exemption application, particularly Part IV on how to write your narrative statement.

- Updates on **employee** issues, including a new discussion of harassment in the workplace in Chapter 19 and a new discussion of fringe benefits in Chapter 27.

- An updated Chapter 20 on **independent contractors**, an area currently under scrutiny by the IRS and the Oregon Department of Revenue.

- A more comprehensive guidance to **cost allocation techniques** in budgeting in Chapter 24.

- An expanded discussion throughout of the importance of **Board policies**, particularly Board governance policies.

- A new discussion about **membership corporations that change to non-membership corporations** in Chapter 18.

- An update in Chapter 29 on the dramatic changes made by the U.S. Supreme Court to **federal campaign finance reform laws** that change the type and scope of involvement by nonprofit (and for-profit) corporations and unions in federal elections campaigns.

How to Find an Attorney or an Accountant

"What?" you may be saying, "I bought this book so I wouldn't have to see an accountant or an attorney." With this book, you may be able to do much of your accounting and legal work yourself. At the least, it will provide you with a lot of information that should cut down on how much time (and money) you have to spend on a professional.

Still, there are a variety of circumstances when you may need to get help:

- You may have special problems or issues that this book does not address.

- You should get an accountant's help to get your books set up properly, so that your financial information can be easily conveyed to the forms that are required for nonprofit and tax exempt groups.

- You should have a professional review your papers before you submit them to the state or federal government to be sure they are correct.

- You should run any significant decisions you make by a professional to be sure you are doing everything properly.

There are a number of ways to choose an attorney or accountant. Keep in mind that nonprofit law and accounting are quite specialized areas within their fields and most attorneys and accountants know little or nothing about it. The Nonprofit Association of Oregon operates the Nonprofit Organization Information and Referral Helpline. The Helpline is a free service providing referrals to qualified professionals with experience assisting nonprofits. This is probably your best place to start. You can reach the Helpline at 503.233.9240 or 888.206.3076 (toll-free) or by email at *helpline@ nonprofit.org*.

If you already know a professional that you feel is competent and trustworthy, you could ask that person if they do nonprofit work or can recommend someone who does. If you don't know an attorney or accountant you feel is good and the Helpline can't help you, ask around among other nonprofit groups to see who they use and like. For an attorney, you can also call the Oregon State Bar–Lawyer Referral Services. You might also ask the Bar for the names of attorneys who are members of the Nonprofit Law Section in your geographical area. For accountants, call the Oregon Society of CPA's and tell them you are looking for an accountant who does nonprofit work. As a last resort, you could call an attorney or accountant in the phone book, but your odds of finding someone who knows much about nonprofits are probably less than 1 in 100.

Before you actually call an accountant or an attorney, it is a good idea to make a list of questions. These questions might include:

- Are you familiar with nonprofits? How much of your practice is with nonprofits? How long have you been working with nonprofits?

- Have you worked with our type of nonprofit?

- Are you comfortable with working with a group that wants to do as much of its own work as possible?

- How much will you charge?

PART I
GETTING STARTED

1

SHOULD YOUR ORGANIZATION BE A NONPROFIT CORPORATION?

THIS CHAPTER COVERS

- Types of Nonprofit Organizations
- Other Types of Business Organizations
- Advantages and Disadvantages of Being a Nonprofit Organization
- Which Nonprofit Structure Is Best for You?
- Making a Business Plan

Your group has decided to provide a particular service, educate your community, bring the arts alive, or to make or sell a product. Now you are faced with the question of how to organize yourself to do this in the face of all the bewildering legal, accounting, tax, and licensing requirements. The first decision you must make is what legal structure best suits your needs. If you already know that you want to be a nonprofit corporation, you can skip this chapter. However, you should read this chapter if you are not certain that you want to be nonprofit and want an overview of other possible structures, if you want to be sure you understand the implications of being nonprofit, or if you want to be nonprofit but are not certain that you want to incorporate.

We start this chapter with a discussion about what structures, both nonprofit and profit, are possibilities for carrying on activities. Then we'll get you started on considering the advantages and disadvantages of becoming a nonprofit corporation.

If you are considering beginning a group that will operate for motives other than to make a profit, you will first need to determine what type of organization you want to be. Following are brief descriptions of some of the more commonly used organizational forms, beginning with those that are used by nonprofit organizations. Since you are reading this book, it is very possible that the form most likely to meet your needs is the Nonprofit Corporation.

Types of Nonprofit Organizations

In this section we'll contrast three different types of legal structure used by nonprofit organizations—nonprofit corporations, trusts, and unincorporated associations.

Nonprofit Corporation

A Nonprofit Corporation is an artificial entity created by law. It has no owners. In a sense, it's "owned" by the public at large or by its members. If it makes a "profit," that excess of income over expenses cannot be paid to anyone (the way a profit entity could pay it to its owners or shareholders) but must be used for nonprofit purposes. In most cases, when the nonprofit corporation dissolves, the assets that are left over after the debts are paid must be distributed to other nonprofit corporations or to its members. The nonprofit corporation is governed by a Board of Directors, who in larger organizations will usually hire an Executive Director to run the organization, who, in turn, will usually hire other employees.

Setting your corporation up as nonprofit does not mean you are exempt from paying taxes or will qualify to receive grants or tax-deductible contributions.

A nonprofit corporation can be set up for any lawful purpose and has all the powers a profit corporation has, such as owning property, conducting a business, and making charitable contributions.

Setting your corporation up as nonprofit does not mean you are exempt from paying taxes or will qualify to receive grants or tax-deductible contributions. Becoming a nonprofit corporation is the first (and easiest) step in that direction. If you want to be tax-exempt, in most cases you must apply for and qualify for tax-exempt status from the federal, state, regional, and county governments (see Part II). If you do not qualify for tax exemption, you will pay taxes just like a profit corporation and you will not be eligible for grants or tax-deductible contributions.

Formation

A nonprofit corporation is formed by filing Nonprofit Articles of Incorporation with the Corporation Division of Oregon's Secretary of State.

Liability

The Board of Directors, members, officers, and employees of the nonprofit corporation, as a usual rule, are not personally liable for the debts of the nonprofit corporation. This means that, with some exceptions described in Chapter 17, their personally-owned property cannot be taken by the corporation's creditors.

Control

The Board of Directors has final authority over the nonprofit corporation. If the nonprofit corporation has members, they have the power to elect some or all of the Board.

Continued Existence

The Board of Directors, officers, employees, and members of the nonprofit corporation can die or leave the nonprofit corporation and the nonprofit corporation will continue its existence without interruption.

Registrations, Books and Records

The nonprofit corporation must file an annual report with the state. It must file annual tax returns with the federal and state governments. If the nonprofit corporation receives tax exemption, then it will file different reports with the federal and state governments. Some nonprofits must register with the Attorney General's office. If the nonprofit has employees, it must file federal and state payroll tax reports and Unemployment and Workers' Compensation reports. The nonprofit corporation also has to maintain a variety of other records to meet legal requirements.

Tax Consequences

The nonprofit corporation pays taxes on its corporate income just as does a profit corporation, unless the nonprofit corporation gets tax exemption from the federal and state governments. The nonprofit corporation may have to pay county property and business taxes, unless the nonprofit corporation gets an exemption from the county government.

Trusts

A trust is an entity set up by a Trustor, who supplies money or property to be managed by a Trustee, for the benefit of those described as the beneficiaries in the document creating the trust. The provisions for the management and distribution of the trust's property are set out in the trust document, and are interpreted and administered by the Trustee.

Many trusts are nonprofit. This structure is commonly used when an individual or family wishes to donate money for a nonprofit purpose and to provide some conditions for how it is to be administered. The procedures for setting up a trust are beyond the scope of this book. If you feel that this is a form you might be interested in, you should consult an attorney.

Formation

The trust is typically formed when a trust document is signed by a Trustor and property is transferred to the trust.

Liability

In many cases, the Trustee is personally liable for her or his negligent acts that cause loss to the trust or to a third party. The trust is liable for judgments involving it.

Control

The Trustor in the document setting up the trust sets out the terms under which the trust operates. The Trustee makes the decisions about how to carry out these terms. The Trustor can keep the power to amend or revoke the trust.

Continued Existence

The Trustor and Trustee can die or lose interest in the trust and the trust will continue its existence unless the Trustor has the power to, and does, revoke the trust.

Registrations, Books and Records

The trust must file annual tax returns with the federal and state government on its income. If the trust receives tax exemption, then it will file different reports with the federal and state government. Charitable trusts must register with the Attorney General. If the trust has employees, it must file federal and state payroll tax reports. If it is nonprofit, it must maintain a variety of other records to meet legal requirements.

Tax Consequences

The nonprofit trust pays taxes on its trust income just as a profit trust, unless the nonprofit trust gets tax exemptions from the federal and state governments. The nonprofit trust may have to pay county property and business taxes, unless it gets an exemption from the county.

Unincorporated Associations

An association is a group of people who come together for some purpose other than to do business (for example, a computer club, a cancer support group, or a labor union). If your organization has already begun a nonprofit project and you are not incorporated, you are an association. If your organization will handle substantial income and output, an association may not be appropriate for you. A group that has the word "Association" in its title is not necessarily an association. It may be a corporation.

Formation

There are no papers that are necessary to file to establish an association. Some groups, especially those planning to seek tax exemption, will write a charter or Articles of Association, similar to the Articles of Incorporation used by corporations. However, the charter or Articles are not filed with the state.

Liability

The decision makers for the association are generally personally liable for the debts of the association and the members of the association may also be personally liable. This means that if the assets of the association are not sufficient to pay what the association owes, the association's creditors may be able to seize the personally-owned assets of the members.

Control

The association has a great deal of flexibility as to how it is controlled and managed. Many smaller groups are run by the members through voting. Associations with a written charter may provide for a different method of management. For example, the members might elect managers, or, if the association is a branch of some larger group, the larger group might choose the managers.

Continued Existence

The association has great flexibility in changing members. Unless the association's rules provide differently, members can come and go at will. The death or resignation of one member will not affect the association's existence.

Registrations, Books and Records

The association does not have to register with the state in order to exist. The association must keep whatever books are necessary for tax purposes and may have to file tax returns. If the association has employees, it must file federal and state payroll tax reports, Unemployment and Workers' Compensation reports.

Tax Consequences

The association may be treated like a general partnership or like a corporation for tax purposes. The IRS decides which way to treat it depending upon whether the association functions more like a partnership or more like a corporation. The IRS looks at whether the association's members have limited liability, whether ownership is freely transferable, how much the management is centralized, and whether the association's duration appears indefinite. Associations can receive tax exemption from the federal, state, and county governments.

THE OREGON NONPROFIT CORPORATION HANDBOOK

Other Types of Business Organizations

Cooperative

A cooperative is an artificial entity created by law. It is owned by the people or groups that buy stock in it, called stockholders or shareholders. The stock may or may not be owned by members. The major decisions about the cooperative are made by the Board of Directors, elected by its members. The cooperative may have officers, such as a President, who manage the cooperative.

Oregon has a special cooperative law covering manufactured homeowner cooperatives. This statute allows the homeowners who live in manufactured home parks to band together and form a cooperative which can buy the land on which their homes sit. While this is a cooperative, some of the features are different from the cooperatives described in this section. If you are interested in a manufactured homeowner cooperative, you will need to get legal advice.

Major Features

In almost all cases, the members and stockholders are not liable for the cooperative's debts, except for the money the members agree to put in for membership fees or stock, and except for the money the stockholders agree to put in for the stock.

- The Board of Directors, which is elected by the members, has final authority over the business affairs of the cooperative.

- Members of the cooperative split the profits that are not reinvested in the coop at the end of the year.

- Stockholders can leave the cooperative at will, as long as they can find someone to buy their stock. Stockholders can join at will if they can find stock to buy. Some cooperatives may choose to limit how freely their stock may be bought or sold, but the law generally puts no restriction on its sale. Members can also leave the cooperative at will. The conditions for becoming a member are defined by the cooperative. The business continues without interruption through stock transfers and membership changes.

- The cooperative pays federal and state income tax on its income. It may also pay property, inventory and other taxes. Shareholders pay personal income tax on the dividends received from the cooperative. These dividends are paid with dollars which have already been taxed as income to the cooperative.

Profit (Business) Corporations

A profit corporation is an artificial entity created by law. It is owned by the people or groups that buy stock in it, called stockholders or shareholders. The major decisions about the profit corporation are made by a Board of Directors, elected by the stockholders. The profit corporation may have a CEO or person who holds another title who manages the corporation.

Major Features

- In almost all cases, the stockholders of the profit corporation are not liable for the corporation debts, except for the money the stockholder has put in to buy stock. This means that the stockholder's personal assets are safe from the corporation's creditors. The same is true (with a few exceptions) for the Board of Directors.

- The Board of Directors, which is elected by the stockholders, has final authority over the business affairs of the corporation.

- Stockholders can leave the corporation at will, as long as they find someone to buy their stock. Stockholders can also join at will, as long as they can find stock to buy. Some corporations may choose to limit how freely their stock can be bought or sold, but the law generally puts no such restrictions on the sale of stock. The business continues without interruption when stock is bought and sold.

- The corporation pays income tax on its corporate income. When the corporate net income is distributed to the stockholders in the form of dividends, the stockholders pay income tax on this money. The corporation also pays property and business taxes.

General Partnerships

Two or more people who carry on a business for profit and who do not incorporate are considered to be partners.

Major Features

- Partners may have a written agreement that makes them partners, but this is not necessary. A verbal agreement, or even conduct in acts showing that they are carrying on a business for profit together, can be enough to create a partnership. A general partnership does not have to file anything with the state in order to create a partnership, although the partners may have to file their business name and may have to get licenses and permits in order to operate a business.

- Each partner is personally liable for all the debts of the partnership. This means that if the assets of the partnership are insufficient to pay what the partnership owes, the partnership's creditors can seize the personally-owned assets of the partners. Even if the debt was incurred by one of the other partners, all of the partners are personally liable for all debt validly incurred by the partnership.

- Each partner, regardless of how much of the profits she or he takes, shares equally in the management and business decisions. The only thing that changes this is a written agreement by the partners that provides for different rules.

- Each partner must report her/his share of the net profit or loss figures shown on the partnership informational return on their individual tax returns. The partners must report these amounts and pay taxes on them even though the money was not withdrawn from the business.

Limited Partnerships

A limited partnership is a partnership in which some of the partners take no part in the control or management of the partnership but are entitled to a share of the profits (or losses) because they have invested money in the partnership. Those partners who take no part in the control of the management of the partnership are called limited partners. At least one of the partners must be responsible for control and management of the partnership, and this partner is called a general partner.

Major Features

- In Oregon, the limited partnership must file a certificate of limited partnership with the appropriate state agency before it will be recognized as a limited partnership.

- Each general partner is personally liable for all the debts of the partnership. The limited partners are only liable for the money they put into the partnership. The partnership's creditors can only seize the limited partner's personal assets (l) when her/his name appears in the partnership name; (2) when she or he engages in management activities in the partnership; or (3) to the extent that she or he has withdrawn the initial funds she or he contributed.

- The general partners in the limited partnership have nearly total control in management of the business. If a limited partner tries to intervene or participate in the management of the business, she or he may lose the freedom from personal liability she or he enjoys.

Limited Liability Companies

Limited liability companies are a cross between partnerships and corporations. This structure allows one or more people (called "members") to do business without incorporating but gives them the protection from liability that a corporation offers. A limited liability company may function as a nonprofit organization, although there are a limited number of circumstances where this is desirable. If you are a nonprofit that is setting up a related nonprofit entity that you will control, you may want to consider the LLC structure. You will need legal assistance to structure this kind of arrangement.

Major Features

- In almost all cases, the members are not personally liable for the LLC's debts.

- The members run the business affairs of the LLC, or they can hire managers.

- The members can leave at will, as long as they find someone to buy their interests. The business continues without interruption.

- The LLC is usually taxed like a partnership. However, if the LLC is a nonprofit entity whose member or members are all tax-exempt under the same section of the tax code, then the LLC has the same tax exemption as its member or members. This means that if the LLC is a sole member LLC and the sole member of the LLC is a tax-exempt organization, the LLC will be considered to have the same exemption as its member. This is quite common in the affordable housing arena and this strategy is occasionally used by other tax-exempt entities as well.

Sole Proprietorships

A sole proprietorship is a business completely and directly owned by a single person. It may or may not have employees.

Major Features

- No formalities are required to form a sole proprietorship.

- The owner is personally liable for all of the debts of the sole proprietorship.

- The sole proprietorship is controlled by its owner.

- If the owner dies or decides to withdraw from the business, the business is dissolved. The owner can sell the business to another sole proprietor, partnership, corporation, or other entity.

Advantages and Disadvantages of Being a Nonprofit Organization

To assist you in making the decision about your group structure, you should first decide whether you want your group to be profit or nonprofit. You can start by making a list of the advantages and disadvantages of choosing the nonprofit structure. What follows is a list of the most common considerations.

Advantages of the Nonprofit Organization

Tax Advantages

Organizing as a nonprofit group may allow you to get exemptions from a variety of federal, state, and local taxes. See Chapters 5 and 11.

Funding

As a nonprofit organization, you are in the best position to attract grants and donations. In order to do this, you will probably be required to go the further step of obtaining a §501(c)(3) tax exemption. Not all groups will qualify to get a §501(c)(3) exemption, so if this is important to your decision, check to see if you will qualify. See Chapter 5 for more details.

Public Profile

People are more likely to be supportive of a group that is nonprofit rather than profit. You will generally find that the nonprofit form is more likely to encourage donations and volunteers.

Postal Benefits

Being a nonprofit organization may make it easier for you to get special postal rates. See Chapter 3.

Disadvantages of the Nonprofit Organization

Financial Drawbacks

The income made by the group must be used for its nonprofit purposes. You can pay reasonable salaries, but cannot use any "extra" for the personal gain of the employees or members of the group. In most cases, when your group dissolves, it will have to turn over any excess funds (after the debts are paid) to another nonprofit group with similar purposes, or to your members if you are a Mutual Benefit nonprofit corporation. You or other founders and key staff cannot own the "business" nor can you "sell" it for personal gain. There are also start-up and maintenance costs for being nonprofit. You may need legal advice to run a nonprofit. If you decide to apply for tax exemption, the government has fees associated with the filings.

Paperwork

Setting up and maintaining a nonprofit structure requires a certain amount of paperwork. You must prepare organizational documents and keep minutes of your meetings, as well as maintain a variety of other records. Most profit forms that you might choose will also require paperwork. However, funders may require additional accounting records that are more detailed than those that profit businesses must keep.

Which Nonprofit Structure Is Best for You?

If you have decided that your project is nonprofit, before you go further you may want to consider whether you want to incorporate your program into an existing nonprofit rather than to set up a new nonprofit organization. You will want to investigate what groups may already be doing what you want to do and explore whether one of those organizations might take on your project as a program. If you do this, you will lose the ability to completely control your project but will avoid the administrative demands and fundraising responsibilities of running your own organization. Read Chapter 10 to learn more about the possibility of working with an existing organization through a fiscal sponsorship relationship. Or consider a much less elaborate approach and simply volunteer your time and energy to help an existing organization implement your good ideas to meet community needs.

If you do want your group to be a separate nonprofit organization, you then need to decide if you are going to be a nonprofit corporation, a charitable trust, or a nonprofit association. Individuals with a large sum of money to donate that want to exercise control over the organization often use the charitable trust. Most other groups will choose between the unincorporated association and the nonprofit corporation. In some very restricted cases, you may want to consider the limited liability company.

The unincorporated association is often preferred by newer and smaller groups engaged in safe activities that do not want to take on the paperwork and rules that come with being incorporated. In some cases, groups with members that do not fit within or want to comply with the rules for membership corporations (see pp. 25-26) may choose to remain unincorporated.

There are significant disadvantages to this form. If the group is sued, its leaders and possibly members generally are personally liable for any judgment. This means that you each pay from your own pockets. Also, if your association has a bank account or property, the account or property cannot be held in the association's name. Even if the bank account has the association's name on the statement, an individual is actually the account's owner. This can create difficulties for the group and the individual. If the unincorporated association obtains an exemption from federal income tax (discussed in Chapter 5) and later incorporates, it must reapply for exemption as a corporation. Your association may have more difficulty getting insurance, particularly directors and officers insurance. See pp. 362-363.

The nonprofit corporation is preferred by most groups primarily because of the limited liability it offers. It is also used because the corporate model provides a more stable existence. The corporation can own property. It is also easier to attract funding, buy property and obtain insurance as a corporation.

The nonprofit corporation is preferred by most groups primarily because of the limited liability it offers.

The nonprofit corporation has some disadvantages. There is more paperwork associated with it than with an unincorporated association. The state regulates how you can do things more closely than it does for unincorporated associations, so you will need to become familiar with and follow more rules about how you govern yourself.

Making a Business Plan

Simply choosing the best legal form for your efforts won't ensure that you will actually be able to move forward with your ideas. To move from ideas to successful action, you need to create a realistic plan for how you will get the resources you need and use them wisely to build an effective organization and carry out your mission.

You will want to develop a business plan that fits your circumstances. A business plan allows you to clarify your goals and develop specific strategies to get and use resources, including the financial and human resources you'll need to build a sustainable organization that really serves your community.

If you are just starting your organization, you will want to focus your business plan on the next 2 or 3 years rather than trying to see far into the future.

Your plan should include:

1. *Your Mission*

Your mission statement is a clear description of what will be different as a result of the creation of your organization

SHOULD YOUR ORGANIZATION BE A NONPROFIT CORPORATION?

> For example: Our organization will organize volunteers to help low income families obtain the fresh fruits and vegetables needed for a healthy diet.

2. *Community Needs /Market Niche*

Identify the most significant needs your organization will work to address in the first 2-3 years. Identify the other organizations or efforts are already underway that are addressing these or related needs. Show how will your work differ from or work in partnership with those efforts.

> For example: Low income families cannot stretch their food stamps or other resources to meet the high cost of fresh produce and frequently live in neighborhoods in which stores do not offer fresh produce. The food pantries serving our community do not have enough fresh produce to meet the needs of the families they serve.

3. *Program Strategies*:

Create the primary strategies you will use to accomplish your mission:

> For example: In the first year, we will:

- Recruit and train volunteers to care for and harvest fruit trees.
- Reach agreements with property owners to allow our volunteers to care for and harvest fruit trees
- Donate one half of the fruit harvested to our local food pantries with the remaining half of the harvest being divided between the volunteers and the property owners.

> In the second year, we will:

- Expand volunteer recruitment to encourage participation by low income individuals.
- Increase the number of participating property owners.
- Study the feasibility of increasing the amount and variety of food we make available to low income families by utilizing volunteers to cultivate fresh produce on donated land.

4. *Infrastructure Strategies*

What are the major steps you will need to take to build the Board and the financial, communication, risk management, and other capacities your organization will need to be sure that it operates responsibly and can sustain its efforts?

> For example:
>
> Year 1:
> - Complete application for tax exempt status

- Obtain insurance
- Establish Board recruitment and orientation process and develop sound Board procedures
- Set up accounting system
- Establish website, database, logo, and basic communications materials and strategies
- Complete all required corporate reports

Year 2:
- Maintain systems established in year 1
- Establish payroll system
- Establish structure to supervise employee
- Improve volunteer recruitment and management systems
- Review risks and improve risk management

5. *Financial Strategies*

How will you get the funds you need to accomplish your program and infrastructure strategies?

For example:

Year 1:

- Board members will volunteer their time to conduct all the program strategies described above.
- Our Board chair will allow us to use her home as an office without charge.
- Board members will contribute funds and ask their friends to make small contributions in order to obtain the cash needed to pay for minimal operating expenses.
- Board members will identify and contact foundations and businesses that might be interested in supporting our work.
- We will apply for a Vista or Americorps volunteer staff position

Year 2:

- We will obtain a Vista/Americorp volunteer position to coordinate volunteers.
- We will increase the number of individual donors and the average gift size.
- We will obtain at least 2 foundation grants and support from at least 3 businesses.

6. *Budget/Financial Projections*

Project your organization's income and expenses for each of the first two years. Identify each source of income and how much you expect to obtain from it during each year. Show each type

SHOULD YOUR ORGANIZATION BE A NONPROFIT CORPORATION?

of expense and how much it will cost in each year. Be sure to consider your start-up expenses including fees to obtain tax exempt status, software, etc.

Determine when you will need to have cash available to meet your expenses and how you will be sure that it will be available. Chapter 24 will help you make your budget. Chapter 22 will help you be realistic about raising funds.

If you are planning on selling goods or services, see the discussion about business plans for nonprofit businesses in Chapter 9 for some additional ideas. The Small Business Administration works with nonprofits and can assist you with developing a business plan. See Appendix 2 for contact information.

After your group has discussed your draft plan, seek out other organizations in your community that have recently gone through the start up process. Ask them to review your plan and alert you to areas in which your assumptions about implementing your program goals or raising funds may be incomplete or unrealistic. They will almost certainly remind you that just getting tax exempt status does not result in individuals, businesses, or foundations deciding to make contributions to your organization. Your board will have to be ready to ask for support and to give support themselves. And, as you'll read in Chapter 21, volunteers are never free. Finding, preparing and using volunteers effectively will require investment of substantial time and energy.

Is it worth it? Almost certainly! You and those working with you have the opportunity to truly change the lives of individuals, families, and your community. Along the way, you will almost certainly change your own lives as you learn how to work together, manage, and generate support for your organization. The rest of this book is devoted to providing the tools you will need to operate legally and effectively. We and thousands of Oregon nonprofit leaders are rooting for your success.

Consult Appendix 1 if you would like information about source material related to this Chapter.

If your group has decided to become a nonprofit corporation, the remainder of this book is written for you. Your next step is to learn about the structure and types of nonprofit corporations.

THE STRUCTURE AND TYPES OF OREGON NONPROFIT CORPORATIONS

THIS CHAPTER COVERS

- The Board of Directors
- Officers
- Membership or Nonmembership Corporations
- Types of Oregon Nonprofit Corporations
- Nonprofit Corporations Connected with Governmental Agencies

If you have decided to become an Oregon nonprofit corporation, you need to become familiar with the general structure and types of nonprofit corporations.

Generally, a nonprofit corporation is governed by its Board of Directors. The Board may, but does not have to, appoint committees to exercise Board functions. In most cases, the corporation is also required to have a President and Secretary, who may be the same individual. The corporation may or may not have members.

This chapter will not try to tell you everything you need to know about your Board, officers, and members. Later chapters will cover each of these components in more detail. This chapter will orient you so that you have an idea about how to start thinking about your structure and how to fill in some structural details.

Oregon law recognizes three types of nonprofit corporations. It's important to understand the variations so that you can make an informed decision as to which kind of nonprofit corporation you will be.

THE STRUCTURE AND TYPES OF OREGON NONPROFIT CORPORATIONS

> **A note on terminology:**
>
> There are four terms that sound similar and may cause confusion.
>
> - Director
> - Board member
> - Member
> - Executive Director
>
> **Director** and **Board member** mean the same thing – someone who is on the Board of Directors. In this book, we will generally use the term **Director** to refer to someone on the Board.
>
> **Member** is a person or entity with voting power in a membership corporation. This is a different role than Board member. A member may also be a Board member but does not have to be. In most membership corporations, most or all of the Board members will also be members but they do not have to be unless the corporation requires it.
>
> **Executive Director** (sometimes called Director in the working world) is the person hired (usually by the Board) to oversee the operations of the corporation. The Executive Director is not normally a Board member.

The Board of Directors

Powers and Duties

Your Board of Directors must manage the business affairs of your corporation, unless your Articles of Incorporation provide differently. This means that your Board makes all the major decisions about your corporation. Every nonprofit corporation must have a Board of Directors, except for certain types of Religious Corporations. You may call your Board of Directors by another name, such as Board of Trustees or Steering Committee. Regardless of the name, the group is that is empowered to make the manage the affairs of your corporation will be treated as your Board of Directors for legal purposes. Chapter 13 describes in more detail *what* the Board does to manage the corporation, Chapters 14 describes *how* the Board manages the corporation, and Chapter 16 discusses how the Board manages *itself*.

Your corporation may allow someone or some group other than your Board (or a committee composed entirely of Directors) to make some or all major corporate decisions. These decision-makers may be your members, a Governance Committee (that has some non-Directors on it), or some other designated individuals. This must be set out in your Articles of Incorporation. Putting this provision in the Bylaws without putting it in your Articles is not enough. To the extent that your Articles do this, your Directors are relieved from those responsibilities.

Example: The Ross Neighborhood Association is a nonprofit membership corporation that requires that its budget and all land-use issues be approved by its members. These provisions must be in its Articles.

Your corporation may allow someone or some group other than your Board (or a committee composed entirely of Directors) to make some or all major corporate decisions. This must be set out in your Articles of Incorporation.

The most common model in the nonprofit field is the Board-run corporation. Oregon law is built around this assumption which is why exceptions must be written into your Articles. The decision to set up your corporation to be run by someone other than the Board may have some significant consequences. You may have a hard time getting §501(c) status. You may also have difficulty getting funding. Your members who make the decision in place of the Board may be personally liable if they are sued for their decisions in the same circumstances that a Board member would be personally liable. See Chapter 17 for the Board's personal liability. You may get questions from the Attorney General's office. You should explore this decision with an attorney.

Qualifications of Directors

All Directors must be individuals—they can't be legal entities like corporations. They do not have to be Oregon residents or U.S. citizens. If you want to establish other qualifications, your Articles, Bylaws, or Board policies should set them out. Minors (people under 18 years old) may be Directors, though they may have limitations in some areas, such as signing contracts.

Number of Directors

You should plan to have enough Directors on your Board so that your Board can carry out your mission, but not so many people as to make your functioning unwieldy or impossible.

The minimum number of Directors required by law depends on what type of nonprofit corporation you are (the various types are explained on pages 27-29). Public Benefit Corporations must have at least three Directors, and Religious and Mutual Benefit Corporations may have only one. Beyond that, your Articles or Bylaws will fix the number. Your Articles or Bylaws may establish a variable range for the size of the Board by fixing a minimum and maximum number of Directors. Many, perhaps most, nonprofit corporations have variable Boards. If this is done, the number may be fixed or changed periodically within a range you set, by the Board or, in some cases, by the members. The drawback with having a variable-range Board is that it can make calculating a quorum (the number needed to hold a valid meeting) tricky. See pp. 327-28.

Election, Designation and Appointment of Directors

Initially, your incorporator or incorporators name your Directors. After that, your corporation may acquire its Directors by one of three methods:

- election;
- appointment by some other person or entity; or
- designation in the Articles or Bylaws.

Elected Directors

If your corporation has elected Directors, these Directors are elected by the members or by the Board of Directors:

Membership Corporations: If your corporation is a membership corporation, you must have members who are entitled to vote for some or all of the Directors. (See page 25). These Directors are elected at the first annual meeting of members. The Directors continue to be elected at each annual meeting after that, unless the Articles or Bylaws provide differently.

Nonmember Corporations: If your corporation does not have members entitled to vote for Directors but does have elected Directors, these Directors are elected by the Board of Directors.

Appointed Directors

Your corporation has appointed Directors if your Directors are named by someone outside of your corporation. A governmental agency may have the right to appoint some of your Directors. Some nonprofits are coalitions of nonprofit groups in which each constituent group has the right to name a representative to the Board. Some national organizations appoint some or all of the Directors of their local chapters.

Designated Directors

Your Articles or Bylaws may designate Board members. For example, your Bylaws may name a founder as a Director for his/her lifetime. Some bylaws designate a Director by providing that the retiring Board President serves as an *ex officio* voting or nonvoting Director. Nonprofits with a governmental link may provide that the person holding a particular governmental position (such as the mayor of the city) is automatically a Director of the nonprofit.

Composition of Board

To the extent that your corporation is in a position to choose Directors, you should give some thought to the composition of your Board of Directors. Several key issues should be considered:

- The Board has final legal authority over the corporation. The Board composition should assure that basic organizational goals and philosophies will be maintained.

- Board composition can have a significant impact on funding and community relations. Particularly in new organizations, potential funders may look to the Directors for evidence of stability, credibility, responsibility and expertise in the field.

- Directors may be asked to contribute significant amounts of volunteer time to the organization.

- Directors may be needed to play a major role in fundraising, particularly in the cultivation of individual donors and planning and promotion of special events.

- Directors can provide significant expertise (legal, accounting, finance, program) which the corporation may not be able to afford to purchase. For some professionals, the "honor" (recognition and potential business contacts) of serving on a Board is a fair trade for sharing professional skills.

- Grassroots programs which are committed to serving and involving the entire community, including various ethnic and racial groups, low income individuals, and others traditionally denied access to resources, may want to specifically involve members of these groups on the Board of Directors. This may be done to insure that commitments will be honored and to provide continuous monitoring of programming efforts in relation to these communities.

Chapter 15 discusses the topic of finding and selecting Directors in more detail.

Terms of Directors

Your Articles or Bylaws may specify the terms of Directors. You should provide for terms that are long enough to permit your Directors to become familiar with their roles and to operate effectively in them, and with enough turnover to bring in "new blood." Except for those who are designated or appointed Directors, the terms of your Directors may not exceed five years. If your Articles or Bylaws don't spell out a term, the term of each Director will be one year. Directors can be re-elected. Despite the expiration of a Director's term, your Director continues to serve until her or his successor is elected, designated or appointed, or until there is an official decrease in the number of Directors.

Your Articles or Bylaws may provide for staggering the terms of Directors by dividing them into groups. The terms of office of the several groups do not have to be uniform. Staggering is a good idea for many groups because it avoids the situation in which a Board loses all it members at once.

Multiple Roles by Directors

Your Directors can hold any other position in your corporation (employee, officer, etc.) and can be your corporation's registered agent or incorporator. You should exercise caution in having Directors who are paid staff members. Some funders are reluctant to fund a nonprofit corporation whose staff members are also Directors. The IRS often questions this. Staff members who are also Directors are in the position of having a conflict of interest over issues such as salaries, and the Board must follow special rules in dealing with these conflicts. (See pages 310-11 for a discussion of this issue).

Standard of Conduct for Directors

There is a myth in some parts of the nonprofit world that a person can simply list her or his name as a Director of an Oregon nonprofit corporation without taking on any responsibility. This is false. The law expects your Directors to act in accordance with certain standards of conduct. Your Directors take on both a duty of care and a duty of loyalty to the corporation.

> *There is a myth in some parts of the nonprofit world that a person can simply list her/his name as a Director of an Oregon nonprofit corporation without taking on any responsibility. This is false.*

In order to meet the duty of care, each Director must act with the care an ordinarily prudent person in a like position would exercise under similar circumstances. Each Director should use the same care in running your corporation as she or he would use in running her or his own business. Your Board may delegate its responsibilities to officers or committees as long as the Board oversees what is done. Each Director must keep current with what is going on in the corporation by going to Board meetings and requiring operational information from your President, Executive Director, or similar responsible person; financial information from your Secretary, Treasurer, or bookkeeper; and any other information needed to run your corporation.

The duty of loyalty means that your Board must act in good faith and in the manner each Director reasonably believes to be in the best interests of the corporation. Your Board must be faithful to the mission of your corporation. Your Board must exercise care in conflict of interest situations. A conflict of interest situation could arise when the Board discusses salaries for the staff, if some Directors are also staff members. It could also arise if one of your Directors has an interest in an outside business that is doing business with your nonprofit corporation. See pp. 299-303 for more information on conflict of interest situations.

The duty of loyalty means your Directors cannot exploit corporate opportunities or misuse insider information. For example, a Director of a childcare center cannot use her or his Board position to obtain a list of parents with children in the center and solicit the parents to place their children with her or him in home-care.

Under special circumstances a Director can be forced to pay a judgment out of her or his pocket. Chapter 17 contains a more detailed discussion about the potential personal liability of Directors.

Committees of the Board

The Board often forms committees when the whole Board does not have the time to manage all the necessary details of its work. The committees may be standing committees or ad hoc committees.

Standing Committees

Standing committees are ongoing committees that handle permanent or long-range tasks for the Board—for example, an Executive Committee, Finance Committee or Nomination Committee. Handling business between Board meetings, overseeing the financial affairs of the corporation, and finding potential new Board members are permanent tasks almost every nonprofit must manage. Bylaws or Board policies will generally establish standing committees and describe the charges to the committees and how committee members will be selected.

Ad hoc Committees

Ad hoc committees are committees that the Board establishes to handle a specific short-term project. For example, an organization planning an auction may have an Auction Committee. These committees are often established by a Board decision but generally not included in the Bylaws or Board policies because they come and go. The Board decides how ad hoc committee members are chosen. In some Boards, the President of the Board names the members to the committee. In others, the entire Board must approve committee appointments.

Committees Exercising Authority of the Board

You need to be aware that Oregon law has a different way of looking at committees. The law distinguishes between a committee that actually makes major decisions that the Board would otherwise be required to make and all other committees that do not exercise Board authority. This distinction applies to both standing and ad hoc committees. That is to say, some standing committees may exercise Board authority while others do not and the same is true of ad hoc committees. It is important that you determine which of your standing and ad hoc committees, if any, exercise Board authority because these committees are subject to special rules.

If any standing or ad hoc committee exercises the power of the Board by making Board-level decisions, the Board must appoint the Directors to serve on committees or designate the method of selecting committee members. Each committee must consist of two or more Directors, who serve at the pleasure of the Board. All voting members of the committee should be Board members (unless your Articles allow otherwise). The creation of the committee and the appointment of Directors or method of selection of the committee members must be approved by the majority of all Directors in office when the action is taken. If your Articles or Bylaws require a larger majority than this to take action (for example, all actions must be taken by consensus), then you must follow your documents. A common example of a standing committee that exercises Board authority is the Executive Committee. An ad hoc committee that exercises Board authority might be a Capital Campaign Committee that is given the final power to decide donor strategies and naming opportunities for the campaign.

Officers

Your corporation must have a President and a Secretary (unless you are a Religious Corporation Sole described on pp. 33-34). Your Articles or Bylaws may designate other titles instead of President and Secretary. Generally, your President is responsible for overseeing the operations of the entire corporation. In many groups the President is also the Chair of the Board. Your Secretary is usually responsible for keeping the corporate records, seeing that minutes are taken at all Board, committee, and members' meetings, and keeping the books and finances. The same individual can simultaneously hold more than one office in the corporation.

Your group can appoint additional officers besides President and Secretary, who may perform other functions or who may share the functions described above. For example, most groups will want a treasurer who handles or oversees finances.

Standard of Conduct for Officers

Each of your officers must act in good faith, with the care an ordinarily careful person in a like position would exercise under similar circumstances and in a manner your officer reasonably believes to be in the best interest of the corporation. Your officer is entitled to rely on reports prepared by competent people.

Membership or Nonmembership Corporations

Your corporation may have members or it may be a nonmembership corporation. Most nonprofits think of members as people who support the organization, pay dues, and perhaps get a newsletter. Oregon law defines a membership corporation differently. Members are people or other entities (like corporations) who are given the right in your Articles or Bylaws to vote on more than one occasion for at least one member of the Board of Directors. Members may be permitted to vote on a number of other major issues. See pp. 371-72. Members may be permitted to vote for some purposes and not others—such as to elect Directors but not to amend the Bylaws—depending on what the law and your Articles or Bylaws provide. Be aware that if you have any person or group in your corporation (other than your Board or committee composed of Directors) who can vote on more than one occasion for Directors, these people are probably "members," regardless of what you call them. Your corporation will need to comply with all the membership laws. You should talk to an attorney about this.

While your members must be allowed to vote for at least one of your Directors and may vote for certain other purposes, your members *cannot* make management decisions for your corporation (such as approving the budget, hiring staff, etc.) unless your Articles allow this. This is the Board's job, as discussed on page 19.

You may want some of your members to have different rights with respect to voting, dissolution of the corporation, and redemption and transfer (two ways of conveying your membership shares to someone else). If so, you can set up different classes of members.

Members are people or other entities (like corporations) who are given the right in your Articles or Bylaws to vote on more than one occasion for at least one member of the Board of Directors.

Some thought should be given before setting up a membership corporation. A major concern is whether your members are really committed to being involved in electing Directors over the long haul. A serious problem for membership organizations is that members lose interest in governing over time. In many cases, the organization fails to amend its Articles to reflect that it is no longer a membership organization, but the Board begins to replace Directors whose terms expire because members are not interested enough to meet. The organization is now operating illegally with no easy way to correct the problem. Another consideration is whether your members are capable of recognizing and choosing good Board members. Do they and will they in the future know the people running for the Board? Will they understand or will they take an interest in being educated about what the Board needs?

If you do have members, the members must consent to be members. This means that you cannot designate members by some criterion (such as, "Members are all those people who live or have a business in the area bounded by 6th and 26th Streets and Main and River Roads") which does not include the consent of the members. A vote by your members may be required for a range of decisions, including election of the Board, amendments or restatements to the Articles, mergers, sale of the corporate assets, and dissolution, unless you limit this. You must have a membership meeting every year (and provide notice of that meeting) and special membership meetings as explained in Chapter 18. If you are a Public Benefit or Mutual Benefit Corporation, you cannot terminate, expel, or suspend your members without following the procedure given in the statute.

There are many other technical membership rules. Membership corporations (especially those that provide significant benefits to their members) may have difficulty getting some types of tax exemption. See Chapter 18 to get an idea of how involved having members can get, before you make the decision to be a membership corporation. You may want to see a professional for help.

If you have do not have members who vote for the Board but whom you want to call members, you need to state in your Articles of Incorporation that you are not a membership corporation (which by definition means that some members vote). In your Bylaws, you should say that you are not a membership corporation as that term is defined by Oregon law, but you have members for other purposes. See the suggested language for the Bylaws on p. 58. Alternatively, you can call your members by another name, such as "Friends" or "Sustainers."

Types of Oregon Nonprofit Corporations

There are three types of nonprofit corporations in Oregon. Prior to incorporation, you must decide which type of nonprofit corporation you are.

A **Public Benefit Corporation** is a corporation that is tax-exempt under Internal Revenue Code §501(c)(3) (see Chapter 5) or is organized for a public or charitable purpose. Upon dissolution it must distribute its assets to an organization organized for public or charitable purposes, a Religious Corporation, the United States, a state, or an entity recognized as tax-exempt under §501(c)(3).

> *Examples*: social service agencies, schools, foundations, theatres, charities, scientific and research groups.

A **Religious Corporation** is one that is organized primarily or exclusively for religious purposes. These corporations may also be tax-exempt under §501(c)(3).

> *Examples*: synagogues, churches, Buddhist meditation groups.

A **Mutual Benefit Corporation** is a nonprofit corporation that does not come within the definition of a Religious or Public Benefit Corporation. These corporations are not tax-exempt under §501(c)(3) but may be tax-exempt under some other section of the law. Generally, they are organized to provide benefits for their members or a small group of people.

> *Examples*: social clubs, business leagues, veterans groups, unions.

Which Type Is Your Nonprofit?

The majority of the readers of this book can figure out from the description above which type of nonprofit corporation describes your organization. You may want to skim this chapter to get some basic information on your type of corporation and to be sure that you are not putting yourself in a category that is not what you want.

Many groups have characteristics of two or even all three types of nonprofit corporation. For example, your group may be organized as a social club for your members and may also engage in charitable projects. In order to decide which type of nonprofit corporation you are, you should clarify your primary purpose and use this to make your choice. Before you select your type, you may want to read the next section carefully to be sure that you are making the most appropriate choice for your organization. If you have questions, you should see an attorney.

Major Features of Each Type

Public Benefit Corporations

Public Benefit Corporations have these features:

- The Public Benefit Corporation is the most heavily regulated corporation. Public Benefit Corporations must register with the Attorney General's office. The Attorney General has oversight authority and at times must approve actions by Public Benefit Corporations.

- The other rules governing Public Benefit Corporations are also somewhat more restrictive, because these corporations hold themselves out as serving the public.

- Public Benefit Corporations must have at least three people on the Board of Directors.

- If you want to be tax-exempt under §501(c)(3), you must register as a Public Benefit Corporation (unless you are a Religious Corporation).

- Public Benefit Corporations that are membership corporations can restrict, to some extent, its members' rights to inspect its records.

- When you dissolve, you must give your assets to another public benefit type of nonprofit corporation.

Religious Corporations

Important information about Religious Corporations is as follows:

- Religious Corporations are also subject to some oversight and regulation. However, because of constitutional requirements concerning government regulation of Religious Corporations, they have more freedom than Public Benefit Corporations.

- A Religious Corporation generally does not have to register with the Attorney General's office, although if the organization solicits the public for contributions the Attorney General's office may require registration.

- Religious Corporations can have as few as one person on the Board of Directors, or can be set up without a Board in some cases.

- Religious Corporations can qualify for exemption under §501(c)(3).

- A Religious Corporation can restrict its members' rights to inspect its records.

- Oregon law does not restrict who gets this corporation's assets when it dissolves. If it does get a §501(c)(3) exemption, its assets must be given to another §501(c)(3) group.

Mutual Benefit Corporations

General features of Mutual Benefit Corporations include:

- Mutual Benefit Corporations are the least regulated of the Oregon nonprofit corporations.

- A Religious Corporation generally does not have to register with the Attorney General's office.

- Mutual Benefit Corporations can have as few as one person on the Board of Directors.

- Mutual Benefit Corporations are not exempt under §501(c)(3).

- A Mutual Benefit Corporation cannot restrict its members' rights to inspect its records that the law opens for membership inspection.

- You may give your assets on dissolution to whomever you want. Often Mutual Benefit Corporation gives them to its members or the people it serves.

If you still have questions, you should consult an attorney.

Nonprofit Corporations Connected with Governmental Agencies

Not all governmental work is done by the government. The various governmental agencies often seek recommendations and input through governmental commissions, act through quasi-public nonprofit corporations, or work with private nonprofit corporations to carry out governmental functions.

Commissions and Advisory Bodies. In some cases, the government appoints a commissions or advisory bodies to provide assistance to the government. These commissions often study a problem and offer suggestions to the legislature about how the problem could be handled. An example is the Warren Commission, that investigated President Kennedy's assassination.

Public Corporations. Some groups are established directly by the government as public corporations. The voters may elect a public corporation's governing body or the government may appoint it. Public corporations operate somewhat outside the traditional governmental structure. For example, some water districts are set up like this.

Private nonprofit corporations. Some private nonprofit corporations are closely connected with governmental agencies, often working hand-in-hand with the government to perform what is essentially a governmental function. In some cases, these corporations were set up in response to a specific statute enacted by the legislature or a local government. Examples are economic development corporations that were set up to improve various local economies and local watershed associations that work with the federal and state governments to promote fish habitats and water quality. In other cases, the connection between the nonprofit corporation and the government is a common desire to perform a public service and sometimes a contract that sets out how the private nonprofit will do it. One example is a Friends of the Library group that assists in maintaining and raising funds for public libraries.

If your group is a private nonprofit corporation that is working with the government, you should check to see if there is a special statute that mandates how you should operate. If there is such a statute, it will usually set out some of the terms about your operation. Often, it will include some requirements about the composition of your Board. If a specific statute does govern you, you must follow the terms of that statute.

To the extent that the law does not place specific requirements on you, you are subject to the same laws as all other nonprofit corporations. You should also review the terms of any contract you have with the government, because that may set some limits on what you can do.

Issues

Close connections between a nonprofit and the government raises some important questions. Because the organization has one foot in the world of government and the other in the world of private corporations, these questions do not have definite answers.

One concern has to do with liability. In many situations, the law places limits on suing governmental entities and employees, and when they are sued the government usually handles the claim. The issue for the nonprofit is whether this preferential treatment will apply to them. This is quite a gray area, and may depend on the facts of each case. However, your nonprofit, if it is contracting with a governmental agency, should consider negotiating with the government to see if the government would agree to handle and pay any claims made against you.

Another gray area has to do with the Public Meeting and Public Record Laws. Most governmental agencies are required to give notice of their meetings, make decisions at the meeting and not outside of the meeting, and follow certain procedures so that the public has access to decision making. The Public Records Law similarly gives the public access to many governmental records. If your group is exercising governmental functions, does this mean you must observe and follow these laws? In some cases, it does.

THE STRUCTURE AND TYPES OF OREGON NONPROFIT CORPORATIONS

Employment is another area. Governmental employees are protected by more Constitutional guarantees than are employees in the private sphere. In some cases, the courts have held that employees of private nonprofit corporations that have significant governmental connection are entitled to the protections afforded governmental employees. A related employment issue has to do with benefits. If your nonprofit is very closely connected with the government, you may be required to provide your employees the same benefits they would receive if they were employed by the government. This is determined on a case by case basis.

As you can see, private nonprofit corporations with strong governmental links do have some special issues. Some governmental agencies may also have government-mandated restrictions on what its nonprofits can do. Check out co-author Cindy Cumfer's website at *www.cumfer.net* under the Resources tab for more information on these groups. Except for these special areas, however, these corporations are subject to the same rules as all other nonprofit corporations. This book describes those rules.

Consult Appendix 1 if you would like information about source material related to this Chapter.

Once you have decided which type of corporation you are, you are ready to begin setting up your Oregon nonprofit corporation.

SETTING UP YOUR NONPROFIT CORPORATION

THIS CHAPTER COVERS

- Choosing and Reserving a Name
- Filling Out and Filing the Articles of Incorporation
- Writing Your Bylaws
- Holding the Organizational Meeting
- Establishing a Board Policy Manual
- Registering with the Department of Justice
- Applying for a Federal Tax ID Number
- Registering in Other States
- Doing Business Under Another Name
- Obtaining Licenses and Permits
- Applying for Postal Benefits
- Roadmap for Running Your Nonprofit

There are several steps involved in setting up an Oregon nonprofit corporation. We will go through them in order, giving you the information and instructions you need to either complete the steps yourself or to intelligently participate in the process with a professional in the field. You can use the topics covered in this chapter as a step-by-step guide to organizing your group and the topics in the remainder of the book to run your nonprofit. Check off each of the tasks below (that apply to you) as you complete them. Because Bylaws are such an important topic, this topic is covered in more depth in Chapter 4.

SETTING UP YOUR OREGON NONPROFIT CORPORATION

Choosing and Reserving a Name

Before you can file with the state as a nonprofit corporation, you must choose a name. You can choose any name you want, subject to a few restrictions:

- The name can't state or imply that your organization is other than nonprofit or is organized for a purpose other than the purpose stated in your Articles of Incorporation;

- You cannot use the word "cooperative" or "limited partnership";

- The name must be written in the English alphabet but may contain Arabic or Roman numerals and incidental punctuation;

- It must be distinguishable from other names on record with the state; and

- It cannot imply that your corporation is organized for any purpose other than that permitted by law and your Articles.

If your name contains the words "trust," "bank" or similar words that sound like the corporation might be in the banking or financial business, the Secretary of State has the discretion to refuse to accept the filing until you get a waiver from the Department of Consumer and Business Services. For example, if your name contains the words "land trust" or "exchange bank" you might run into this bump.

You can reserve your name so that no one else takes it before you file your Articles of Incorporation. To do so, you must submit an application to the Office of the Secretary of State. This will hold your name for 120 days. After that, you may reapply for it on the same basis as everyone else. Most groups don't bother to reserve a name, but you may want to do so if you have one that is very important to you. Once you file your Articles, that will reserve the name for you as long as you are incorporated.

If you want to reserve your name on a national basis, to protect your right to use your name and to prevent someone else from using it elsewhere in the United States, you will need to obtain trademark recognition for your name. You will need to see an attorney who works in the trademark area.

Corporations Sole

A Corporation Sole is a one-person corporation in which the corporate property passes on the death of that person to a successor who becomes the sole person in the corporation. In Oregon, a nonprofit Corporation Sole must be a Religious Corporation and is created by an individual in conformity with the constitution, canons, rules, regulations, and disciplines of a religion. A Corporation Sole allow a religious office holder—for example, a bishop—to hold church property in his or her corporation which, on the bishop's death, passes not to the bishop's heirs but to the next bishop. Unlike other Religious Corporations, a Corporation Sole has no Board of Directors and does not need to have officers or Bylaws. It is managed by the sole Director who is the individual constituting the corporation and who is its incorporator (or the successor of the incorporator). If the corporation has no officers, the Director may perform the duties of the officers. The name of the corporation is the same as the office within the religious denomination (e.g. "Reverend," "Bishop," or "Rinpoche") held by the incorporator and must be followed by the words "and successors, a corporation sole." (For example, "Reverend Maria Martinez and her successors, a corporation sole.") The Director pays taxes on his/her income just as an other taxpayer in his/her position. If you are considering this form of corporation, you should get legal advice. The IRS has identified this as an area that is rife with fraud, closely monitors these exemptions, and will pursue penalties against those misusing it.

Filling Out and Filing the Articles of Incorporation

The most important document your group will have is its Articles of Incorporation. You start your corporation by filing Articles. They contain some major provisions about your corporation. The provisions in the Articles govern all other corporate documents.

Your Bylaws are next in your hierarchy of governance documents. They contain the rules and procedures by which the corporation will be run. The provisions in the Bylaws govern over all other corporate documents, except those in the Articles.

For most matters, the law has rules that will govern your nonprofit corporation, but the law usually gives you the choice to provide something different in your Articles or Bylaws. Many provisions that you may want to make for how your organization will function can go into either your Articles or Bylaws. In some cases, the law says that you must put certain provisions in your Articles if you want them to apply. You can add provisions not mentioned by the law to your Articles and Bylaws, as long as the provisions are not illegal.

In choosing between whether to put a provisions in your Articles or Bylaws, keep in mind that the Articles are usually somewhat harder to change than the Bylaws. Most groups prefer to keep their Articles simple and to include the details about how they are run in their Bylaws.

Your Board will want to enact Board policies from time to time to supplement the provisions in your Bylaws related to board governance and to provide for its management of the corporation's activities. Board policies (which include Board procedures) fall under the Bylaws in the hierarchy of governance documents.

Filling Out the Articles of Incorporation

The Articles must contain certain provisions. You can get a blank "Articles of Incorporation" from the Secretary of State's website which include everything that must be in the Articles. (See Appendix 2.) The instructions below are keyed to that form.

The Secretary of State also allows you to apply for Articles online. This procedure does save time. However, there is one disadvantage. The online application requires you to choose a "Business Activity Type" for your corporation. Unfortunately, the list is primarily for for-profit corporations and the categories related to nonprofits are very specific and most nonprofits will have difficulty finding a good fit. Many will be forced into something like "Civic and Social" under the "Other Services" or a "social advocacy" listing. This category description may appear on your final Articles (which is not the case if you file offline using the state form). If you are applying for a (c)(3) exemption, a statement on your Articles that you are a civic or social organization may throw the IRS examiner off, since civic and advocacy groups are (c)(4) groups and social groups are (c)(7) groups. You may want to file off-line to avoid this possibility.

> *If you apply for exemption under 501(c)(3) and do not have the language referred to in Articles 5 and 8 (or similar language) in your Articles, the IRS will return your application with instructions to amend your Articles.*

If your corporation is planning to apply for tax exemption be sure to read Chapter 5 before you fill out the Articles form, because you will need to know under what section you will be applying in order to fill out your Articles. If you apply for exemption under §501(c)(3) and do not have the language referred to in Articles 5 and 8 (or similar language) in your Articles, the IRS will refuse to grant your request for exemption until you amend your Articles. If you file online, the state has a separate attachment that contains this language, so be sure to include it if you plan to apply for (c)(3) exemption.

Article 1. Name of Corporation. Fill in the name of the corporation. See page 33 for a discussion about names.

Article 2. Registered Agent. Your registered agent is the person upon whom all legal papers, notices, and demands upon the corporation will be served. The registered agent does not respond in any way to the legal papers but turns them over to your corporation. The registered agent may also receive a yearly notice from the state that the annual fee to remain a nonprofit corporation is due. The registered agent must be someone who resides in Oregon, an Oregon business or nonprofit corporation with offices in Oregon, or a foreign business or nonprofit corporation authorized to transact business in Oregon with an office in Oregon. This person should be responsible enough to notify the corporation that he or she has received any legal papers or the annual notice, because the corporation may need to get an attorney, and must pay its annual fees.

Article 3. Address of Registered Agent. The address for the registered agent should be the business office of the registered agent. The registered agent and address must be in Oregon. It should be a reasonably permanent address. The address cannot be a post office box, because in some cases the registered agent has to be served personally with papers. The corporation must notify the Secretary of State if it changes its registered agent or the address of its registered agent. (See pp. 682-83)

Article 4. Address for Mailing Notices. Much of what the state sends you can be done by mail. Fill in the address where you want to receive mail. For many corporations, this may be a different address than your registered agent's, often an office address. This can be a post office box. This address can be anywhere in the world.

Article 5. Optional Provisions. There are a variety of optional provisions that you should consider putting in your Articles. Put them on a separate sheet of paper called "Article 5."

If you are planning to apply for a tax exemption under §501(c)(3) (see Chapter 5), the Internal Revenue Service requires that you include substantially the following provisions in your Articles. If you are using the Articles form from the state's website, the state supplies this information on a separate sheet included as an Attachment, so be sure that you include the Attachment. For those putting these provisions in Article 5, here they are:

1. "This corporation is organized exclusively for charitable, religious, educational, and scientific purposes, including, for such purposes, the making of distributions to such organizations that qualify as exempt organizations under §501(c)(3) of the Internal Revenue Code, or the corresponding section of any future federal tax code."

2. "No part of the net earnings of the corporation shall inure to the benefit of, or be distributable to its members, directors, trustees, officers, or other private persons, except that the corporation shall be authorized and empowered to pay reasonable compensation for services rendered and to make payments and distributions in furtherance of the purposes of this corporation.

3. No substantial part of the activities of the corporation shall be the carrying on of propaganda, or otherwise attempting to influence legislation, and the corporation shall not participate in, or intervene in (including the publishing or distribution of statements) any political campaign on behalf of or in opposition to any candidate for public office. Notwithstanding any other provision of these articles, the corporation shall not carry on any other activities not permitted to be carried on (a) by a corporation exempt from federal income tax under §501(c)(3) of the Internal Revenue Code, or the corresponding section of any future federal tax code, or (b) by a corporation, contributions to which are deductible under 170(c)(2) of the Internal Revenue Code, or the corresponding section of any future federal tax code."

If you are using the state's form for Articles, the form allows you to check whether you want to indemnify your directors, officers, employees, and agents for liability and related expenses under ORS 65.387-65.414. Indemnity is discussed on pp. 360-362. We generally recommend including the indemnity provision in the Bylaws, where it can be more easily amended and we include an indemnity provision in our sample Bylaws in this book. If you are going to do that, do not check this provision. It may cause problems later if your Board amends the indemnity provision in your Bylaws and forgets this provision is also in your Articles (a very common occurrence).

However, what you do need to consider including in your Articles is a provision limiting the liability of your directors to the corporation itself. See page 359. If you want this provision, it must be in your Articles. Putting it in your Bylaws is not sufficient. Article 5 is a good place to insert this provision. If you are applying online, you can insert this or other optional provisions on the screen that contains the indemnification election.

On pages 39-41 we discuss other additional optional provisions you may want to consider.

Article 6. Type of Corporation. Oregon recognizes three types of nonprofit corporations: Religious Corporations, Public Benefit Corporations, and Mutual Benefit Corporations. The type of corporation you select will have important consequences for how your corporation is run and what the law will allow your corporation to do. It may also determine whether or not you can qualify for tax exemption under §501(c)(3) of the Internal Revenue Code. Chapter 2 describes in detail the implications of selecting each of these types of corporations. You should read that very carefully before making your selection.

Article 7. Will the Corporation Have Members? You should only answer "yes" if your members elect some or all of your Board. See pages 25-26 and Chapter 18 for a discussion about members.

Article 8. Distribution of Assets on Dissolution. Here you are required to describe your provisions for the distribution of the assets of your corporation upon dissolution or final liquidation (in other words, when the corporation closes down). "Assets" refers to all the money and property (of all kinds) that the corporation owns. Pages 28-29 explain the options your type of nonprofit has in this situation. If you are not applying for exemption under §501(c)(3), you may need legal help in how deciding to distribute your assets on dissolution and how to word this properly. This is particularly the case for Mutual Benefit Corporations.

If you are using the forms on the state's website, the state's addendum for §501(c)(3) corporations contains the language below in its attachment. Be sure you include this attachment with your Articles. If you are not using the state's attachment, and you are a corporations applying for tax exemption under §501(c)(3) (see Chapter 5), you should put this provision in your Articles:

"Upon the dissolution of the corporation, assets shall be distributed for one or more exempt purposes within the meaning of §501(c)(3) of the Internal Revenue Code, or the corresponding section of any future federal tax code, or shall be distributed to the federal government, or to a state or local government, for a public purpose. Any such assets not so disposed of shall be disposed of by the court of appropriate jurisdiction of the county in which the principal office of the corporation is then located, exclusively for such purposes or to such organization or organizations, as that court shall determine, which are organized and operated exclusively for such purposes."

If you are applying for tax exemption under §501(c)(3), you can name a specific organization to receive your assets as long as it is a (c)(3). However, you must state that it can only receive your assets if it is a (c)(3) at the time of your dissolution and you must make an alternative provision for disposal of your assets if it is not. Your clause might read:

"Upon the dissolution of the corporation, assets shall be distributed to [name of corporation], a nonprofit corporation organized in the state of [name the state where it is incorporated], if such corporation is exempt from taxation under §501(c)(3) of the Internal Revenue Code, or the corresponding section of any future federal tax code. If it is not exempt, assets shall be distributed for one or more exempt purposes within the meaning of §501(c)(3) of the Internal Revenue Code, or the corresponding section of any future federal tax code, or shall be distributed to the federal government, or to a state or local government, for a public purpose. Any such assets not so disposed of shall be disposed of by the court of appropriate jurisdiction of the county in which the principal office of the corporation is then located, exclusively for such purposes or to such organization or organizations, as that court shall determine, which are organized and operated exclusively for such purposes."

Article 9. Incorporator. Your incorporator is the person (or persons) who signs the Articles, sees that they are filed, and arranges for the organizational meeting of the

Board (pages 45-46) to be held. The incorporator can be a person over the age of 18, a corporation, a partnership, or an association.

Your incorporator needs to fill in her or his name and address here. You may have more than one incorporator and, if so, you should list the appropriate information for all of them.

Article 10. Execution. All of your incorporators sign here and print their names.

Article 11. Contact Name. The person to contact about the filing may but does not have to be an incorporator. The contact person can be any responsible individual who is willing to deal with the State about this filing.

Other "Additional Provisions" to Consider for Your Articles

Whether or not you are applying for tax exemption under §501(c)(3), there are a variety of provisions that the law says must be in your Articles if you want them to apply to you. Any of these provisions that you want to include should be written in under Article 5. Before reviewing these provisions you may find it helpful to read Chapter 17 since a good deal of what is discussed below is explained in that chapter. You may need to consult an attorney for help in wording any of these additional provisions. We have placed the items most likely to be of interest in the first and second sections below.

Notice that you do not have to list your Board members in your Articles. Many organizations haven't assembled their full Board at the time of filing and this allows them to get started while still organizing a Board. You can choose to list your Board in the Articles if you want, but if you do, then a majority of the Board must get together to call the first Board meeting. If you do not list the Board, the incorporator calls the first Board meeting. Most corporations prefer the latter method.

Item of Interest to Almost All Nonprofits

Limiting Liability of Directors and Officers. Your Articles may eliminate or limit the personal liability of a Director or uncompensated officer of the corporation or its members for claims relating to their conduct as a Director, officer, or member. This limitation on liability applies only to actions *by the corporation or its members* against the Director, officer, or members and does not apply to actions by parties outside of the corporation. (See Chapter 17 for a discussion of personal liability and under what circumstances the corporation may want to sue its Directors and officers.) This provision cannot eliminate or limit liability for:

- acts or omissions before the date the provisions became effective;
- a breach of the duty of loyalty;
- acts or omissions not in good faith or that involve intentional misconduct or knowing violations of the law;

- unlawful distributions (See page 282);
- any transaction in which the Director or officer got an improper personal benefit;
- any act or omission that violates the conflict of interest laws (See pp. 299-303);
- illegal loans to or guarantees for Directors and officers (See page 303); or
- actions brought by a person or entity other than the corporation itself.

Despite its many exceptions, many consider a provision limiting liability to be a very important provision to be added to the Articles in order to attract Directors. Knowledgeable Directors will look for this provision in your Articles. On the other hand, your corporation may not want to prevent the corporation or its members from suing Directors who are grossly negligent. Most nonprofit corporations will want to at least consider whether to add this provision.

Despite its many exceptions, many consider a provision limiting liability to be a very important provision to be added to the Articles in order to attract Directors.

If you are interested in protecting your Directors, officers, and members (if any) from claims by the nonprofit corporation, you should consider adding one of the clauses described below that limit the liability of Directors and uncompensated officers to the fullest extent possible. Put this language in your Articles of Incorporation under Article 5 as Additional Provisions:

FOR NONMEMBERSHIP CORPORATIONS:

"The personal liability to the corporation, for monetary or other damages, of each member of the Board of Directors and each uncompensated officer of the corporation for conduct as a director or officer shall be eliminated to the fullest extent permitted by current or future law."

FOR MEMBERSHIP CORPORATIONS:

"The personal liability to the corporation or its members, for monetary or other damages, of each member of the Board of Directors and each uncompensated officer of the corporation for conduct as a director or officer shall be eliminated to the fullest extent permitted by current or future law."

Items of Greater Interest to Many Nonprofits

Limitations on Board's Powers. If you want to limit the power of your Board to exercise corporate powers, you must do so through a provision in your Articles. Your Articles may authorize one or more people (or the manner of designating a person or persons) to exercise some or all of the powers which would otherwise be exercised by the Board. For example, if your members (or a committee that has some members who are not Directors) have the right to veto Board actions, approve the budget, or otherwise participate in the management of the corporation (other than electing the Board and approving conflict of interest transactions, amendments to Articles or Bylaws, sale of substantially all the assets, mergers, and dissolutions), you must put these rights in the Articles.

Amendments to Bylaws (Membership Corporations only). Generally, the Board in membership corporations is entitled to amend or repeal the corporation's Bylaws. Your members may or may not also have the right to amend the Bylaws, depending on what powers you give your members. If you want to provide that *only* the members can amend the Bylaws and that the Board cannot amend them, the simplest way to do this is to provide in your Articles of Incorporation that the power to amend Bylaws is reserved to the members exclusively. You must put it in your Articles; putting it in your Bylaws is not enough.

Size of Board (Membership Corporations only). If your corporation has members entitled to vote for Directors, and you want to be sure that only the members can change the range or the size of the Board (if you have a variable-range Board) or can change from a fixed or a variable-range sized Board, your Articles must establish a fixed or variable-range size of the Board. If the Articles do this, only the members may make the change.

Removal of Directors for Cause (Membership Corporations only). If your Public Benefit or Mutual Benefit Corporation has Directors elected by members, and you want to provide that the members must have reasons (called "cause") to remove the Directors (rather than removing them with or without cause), you must so provide in your Articles. Otherwise, the members can remove a Director they elect with or without cause.

Access to Records (Membership Corporations Only). If you are a Public Benefit Corporation organized primarily for political or social action (such as political or social advocacy, education, litigation or a combination of these purposes), your members have the right to inspect and copy certain of your records (see pages 384-87). Some advocacy organizations have donors or members who want their identity to be protected. This may particularly be true if it is very easy for anyone to become a member, which means that someone from the opposition or the press could join your organization.

If you are the type of Public Benefit Corporation described above, you may limit or abolish the right of your members to obtain from the corporation information as to the identity of its contributors. You may also limit or abolish the right of your members or a member's agent or attorney to inspect or copy your membership list. If you do limit or abolish any of these rights, the corporation must provide a reasonable means for the member making the request to mail communications to the other members through the corporation at her or his expense. If you wish to do this, you must include this limitation in your Articles.

Filing Your Articles of Incorporation

Your corporation is officially set up when the incorporator:

- Signs your "Articles of Incorporation" (in this book called the Articles); and
- Files the Articles (along with a filing fee) with the Secretary of State; and
- The State accepts the filing.

The Secretary's office is very helpful to nonprofits. If you want to speed up the process by several weeks, you can have someone from your group hand-deliver the original with the filing fee to the above address. You can file online, though that may have problems as discussed on page 42. You can also fax the Articles with a VISA or Mastercard payment and request a return "as soon as possible." If you mail documents and use a credit card for payment, you will also speed the process.

The state has a form, called "Articles of Incorporation—Nonprofit" which can be obtained free of charge from the Secretary of State, Corporation Division or their website. You can get the street and web address for the Secretary of State from Appendix 2. You may also draw up your own form, if you prefer.

If the Articles you file comply with the law, the Corporation Commissioner will stamp "Filed" and the date filed on the Articles. On that date (unless you specified a later date in your Articles), the corporation is officially in existence. The Articles may specify a delayed effective date as long as the date is within ninety days of the filing.

For a small fee, the Corporation Commissioner will send one copy of the "filed" Articles back to the incorporators, or give it to your messenger if you arrange to have the Articles personally delivered. You can save the copy fee by going to the Corporation Division's Name Registry on the Secretary of State's website (see Appendix 2) and entering your corporation's name into the registry. If you follow the links to your corporate information, you will find an entry that shows the date your Articles of Incorporation were filed. An icon next to that entry allows you to see and copy a copy of your filed Articles.

You need a copy of your filed Articles for your corporate records. You also need a copy if you are applying for an IRS exemption, because the IRS will want a copy of the filed Articles, showing they were filed. The IRS does not require that the copy be certified by the state.

Once the Articles have been filed, your corporation is like a car without a driver. Your Board is the driver. In order for your corporation to function legally, after the filing of the Articles a majority of incorporators must call an organizational meeting of the Board of Directors named in the Articles. Since the Board usually adopts its Bylaws at this meeting, the Bylaws are often drafted before this meeting.

Writing Your Bylaws

The Bylaws contain the rules and procedures by which the corporation is run. The first Bylaws generally are adopted by the Board of Directors at its organizational meeting.

There is no particular form that you must follow in drawing up Bylaws, and you don't have to file them with the Corporation Commissioner (where you file your Articles of Incorporation) unless you want to. (Most corporations do not.) If you are a Public Benefit Corporation, you will have to file the Bylaws with the Attorney General's office. (See page 47). All nonprofits have to file them with the IRS if you apply for tax-exempt status.

Typically, a corporation will want to consider putting these items in its Bylaws:

ARTICLE I   Purposes

ARTICLE II   Members (if applicable)

    Section 1   Classes and Voting

    Section 2   Qualifications

    Section 3   Termination

    Section 4   Annual Meeting

    Section 5   Special Meetings

    Section 6   Notice of Meeting

    Section 7   Quorum and Voting

    Section 8   Proxy Voting

    Section 9   Action by Consent

ARTICLE III   Board of Directors

    Section 1   Duties

    Section 2   Number

    Section 3   Terms and Election

    Section 4   Removal

    Section 5   Vacancies

    Section 6   Quorum and Action

    Section 7   Regular Meetings

    Section 8   Special Meetings

    Section 9   Meeting by Telecommunication or Computer

    Section 10   Action by Consent

ARTICLE IV   Committees

    Section 1   Executive Committee

    Section 2   Other Committees

    Section 3   Composition of Committees Exercising Board Functions

        Section 4   Quorum and Actions

        Section 5   Limitations on Powers

ARTICLE V   Officers

        Section 1   Titles

        Section 2   Election

        Section 3   Vacancy

        Section 4   Other Officers

        Section 5   President

        Section 6   Secretary

        Section 7   Treasurer

ARTICLE VI   Corporate Indemnity

ARTICLE VII   Amendments to Bylaws

Do not assume that you can simply copy or modify someone else's Bylaws. Using the cut-and-paste method, especially with Bylaws found on the Internet, is the most common mistake that organizations make in preparing Bylaws.

Because writing Bylaws is an involved process, it is covered in detail in Chapter 4. You should turn to Chapter 4 for help in drafting Bylaws. Do not assume that you can simply copy or modify someone else's Bylaws. Using the cut-and-paste method, especially with Bylaws found on the Internet, is the most common mistake that organizations make in preparing Bylaws. State nonprofit statutes that are the basis for Bylaws vary widely from state to state and very few people who draft Bylaws you may borrow or find online are familiar with Oregon's statute. You should also read Chapter 4 because it contains important additional information about how membership and nonmembership corporations are run.

After you have read Chapter 4 and have developed your set of Bylaws, remember to return to this chapter to complete the remaining steps in order to finish setting up your corporation.

Holding the Organizational Meeting

After your Articles of Incorporation have been filed with the state, your corporation must hold an organizational meeting. If initial Directors are named in the Articles of Incorporation, the initial Directors must hold an organizational meeting at the call of the majority of the Directors with notice as described on page 64 for special meetings. If initial Directors are not named in the Articles, the incorporator or a majority of the incorporators name the Directors and call the meeting with the same notice as described on page 64 for special meetings. The notice of the meeting does not have to be given if all the Directors sign a waiver of this notice. See the "Waiver of Notice of Meeting of Directors" in the Forms section of this book.

The purpose of the meeting is to complete the organization of the corporation. If initial Directors were not named in the Articles, the incorporators elect the Directors. Once the corporation has Directors, the Directors complete the organizational meeting by appointing officers, adopting Bylaws, and carrying on other business brought before the meeting. Such business may include selecting a bank and signers on the account; authorizing borrowing; adopting a budget; setting salaries; ratifying acts previously taken on behalf of the corporation; and taking care of other business needs. If you will be applying for tax exemption status under §501(c)(3), you will want to adopt a conflict of interest policy to include with the application. (See p. 130.)

Many groups have already agreed on these items before the organizational meeting so that the meeting is just a formality. It is important to hold it, however, so that the organization's decisions can be officially adopted and made a part of the Board's minutes. "Minutes of First Meeting of Board of Directors" is included in the Forms section as sample minutes of the organizational meeting which your group can modify to meet your needs. After this meeting has occurred, your corporation is officially set up.

The organizational meeting does not need to be held if *each* incorporator or Director signs a written statement consenting to the action taken as described on page 325. A "Consent to Corporate Action without a Meeting by the Board of Directors" is in the Forms section.

Setting Your Fiscal Year

One important item on the agenda at the organizational meeting is a determination of the corporation's fiscal year. The fiscal year is the twelve-month cycle used by the organization for financial management purposes. You will report this year to taxing agencies on any filings you make with them. Once you set it, you will need the permission of the IRS to change it.

Generally, you should choose the calendar year as your fiscal year, unless there is a good reason to vary it. The calendar year is the one most familiar to people in your organization. Your individual donors will be on a calendar year, so your fiscal year will sync up with their giving patterns at the end of the calendar year.

There are several factors that may persuade you to set a different fiscal year. First, examine your primary sources of funding. If your major funders are and will continue to be the state or local governments, consider setting your fiscal year to run concurrently with theirs from July to June. The federal government's cycle is October through September. If your programs follow an annual cycle that is different from the calendar year, you may want to adopt this cycle as your fiscal year so that all of your receipts and costs that are related to the program are captured in one cycle. For example, schools may chose a fiscal year from July until June. Generally, unless there is a compelling reason to break the rule, you will want to end on a calendar quarter (March, June, September, or December) if you are audited. Failing to do so creates extra work for your auditor and, thus, expense for you. Talk over your choice with your accountant, if you have one.

Loans by Founders

Another item that deserves special attention at the organizational meeting is whether any of the founders loaned money to the corporation to get it started. This is particularly important to address if that individual is now on the Board. If someone has advanced money that the corporation is to repay, you should have a written acknowledgment of this in some form, along with a receipt showing what the money was spent for. One option would be to have the corporation sign a promissory note (a legal I.O.U.), setting out the amount of the loan and the terms of repayment. One possible form is the "Promissory Note" found in the Forms section in this book. If that one doesn't fit, you can get others from a legal stationery store, on-line, or from an attorney.

Establishing a Board Policy Manual

The Board will from time to time enact Board policies. This topic is addressed on pages 345-50. If your Board adopted any policies in its first meeting, now is a good time to get in the habit of creating and using a Board Policy Manual. This can be as simple as a folder or notebook into which you insert every Board policy that the Board enacts, along with the date it was enacted. The policy should also be in your meeting minutes. Your conflicts of interest policy, especially if you are applying for tax exemption (see p. 130), may be your first Board policy.

Putting your Board policies in a manual makes them accessible to the Board in the future, to new Board members, to the Executive Director, and to auditors. If you leave them in the minutes, they tend to be lost and forgotten.

SETTING UP YOUR OREGON NONPROFIT CORPORATION

Registering with the Department of Justice

The Charitable Activities Section of the Attorney General's office (in the Department of Justice) is the state office that is responsible for ensuring that nonprofit corporations comply with the law. Oregon is very fortunate to have an excellent and helpful Attorney General's office.

If you stated in your Articles of Incorporation that you are a Public Benefit Corporation and you plan to become exempt under §501(c)(3), you must register with the Attorney General's office. If you are a Public Benefit Corporation and you do not plan to apply for exemption under that section, you should send in the registration form. It is possible that the Attorney General's office will contact you to tell you that you don't need to register. If you are a Religious Corporation that is not a place of worship or an organization formed to provide religious teachings and you are organized to offer programs that are similar to those offered by Public Benefit Corporations, you may need to register. For example, if your nonprofit operates a program offering meals for the homeless based on your Christian principles of feeding the poor as Jesus did, you may classify yourself as a Religious Corporation but the Attorney General's office may want you to register, particularly if you plan to solicit for funds. Contact the Attorney General's office at the address in Appendix 2 to see if you should register. If you are not a Public Benefit Corporation or this type of Religious Corporation, you don't have to register.

You can obtain the Registration of Charitable Corporation form with instructions from the Attorney General's office. We've listed the contact information in Appendix 2. The form is available on-line and changes fairly frequently so we have not included it in the Forms section. Registration is free; however, every year you must update your registration and pay a fee based on the receipts and assets of your organization.

Applying for a Federal Tax ID Number

All groups that incorporate are going to need a federal tax identification number, also known as the Employer Identification Number and called the EIN (and sometimes TIN). Typically, your group will encounter its first requirement for this number when you try to open a bank account. You will also need this number if you apply for tax exemption and when you file tax forms. You need the EIN whether or not you have employees. If you want to obtain the EIN before the first board meeting and the Articles did not name your Board members, you as incorporator can name yourself the President of the corporation for the period prior to the first board meeting. If you obtain the EIN after the first board meeting, the President or other officer must obtain the EIN.

Obtaining your EIN number is free and is relatively easy. You can obtain your tax identification number most quickly by going online to the IRS website at *http://www.irs.gov/businesses/small* and clicking on the link for EINs.

Obtaining your EIN number is free. Be wary about getting to the IRS online by typing an EIN request into a general search engine. A number of companies have addresses that appear to be IRS addresses but are not.

Be wary about getting to the IRS online by typing an EIN request into a general search engine. A number of companies have addresses that appear to be IRS addresses but are not. The web address should begin with *www.irs.gov*. If you are asked to pay a fee, you are not on the IRS line. More seriously, you will need to give an officer's social security number to get an EIN and you don't want to give this number to anyone but the IRS. Check the web address to be sure that you have the real IRS when you use the online service to get an EIN.

Once you are at the IRS's website to get an EIN, here is a general guide as to how to answer the IRS questions. The EIN form is used mostly by for-profit businesses and was designed with those businesses in mind, so it can be a little awkward for nonprofits to answer the questions. The IRS changes the questions from time to time, so use this as it is appropriate.

- You are a "nonprofit/ tax-exempt organization." Stay with this answer for three screens.

- You are starting a new business. (See what we mean about awkward?)

- You are an individual who is the responsible party. If the Board has not yet met, you as incorporator having named yourself President until the Board meets can file for the EIN as President. If the Board has met, a corporate officer should be obtaining this number.

- Be sure to fill in the correct corporate address.

- Fill in the corporate name, exactly as it appears on the Articles. However, you will need to omit special characters. Start with everything and redo if the system rejects your name.

- The Articles were filed in Oregon (if you used this book).

- The date you started is the month and year stamped on your Articles. The EIN is for this corporation and not for any activities you may have engaged in before you incorporated.

- Your fiscal year is your financial year. See pp. 45-46.

- On the questions about your business, you do not file the Form 720 (an excise tax form for businesses). Answer the question about employees "yes" if you plan to have employees in the next year.

- When you are asked what business you do, be sure that your answer reflects your nonprofit mission, as much as you can. This is particularly important if you are applying for tax exemption. If you are applying for recognition under §501(c)(3), you may call yourself a "charity," a word that has a much broader definition than the more common one in the nonprofit community. Be sure that whatever description you choose matches what you plan to tell the IRS in your tax exemption application.

Check the Confirmation screen for accuracy and hit Confirm to receive your number. Print it for your records.

If you can't or don't want to get the number online, contact the IRS office or go to the IRS website and obtain Form SS-4. Read the instructions and fill the form out. You can then telephone the IRS and give the information to the operator who will give you a number or you can fax it in or mail it in. The telephone methods is faster than mailing the form in. If you fax the form in, you should get a number in a few days. If you mail in the form, you should get your number in 2-4 weeks. Regardless of which method you use, be sure to save your number in a safe place. Appendix 2 provides you with contact information to obtain Form SS-4 and to each the IRS using these various methods.

Registering in Other States

You may need to register your corporation in a state other than Oregon. State laws require this if you are doing business in that state. In some cases, engaging in activity on the Internet (such as soliciting members or donations or selling products) may constitute doing business in other states. You'll have to check with an attorney to determine if you are required to register.

Doing Business Under Another Name

If your corporation wants to do business under a name other than or in addition to the one listed in its Articles, you can do so by submitting an assumed business name form to the Secretary of State. You can get these forms at the Corporation Division's website (see Appendix 2) or at legal stationery stores.

Obtaining Licenses and Permits

The state and each local government has their own rules about business licenses and requirements for doing business. The state maintains a website with the state licenses and permits and many of the local licenses and permits. The website is at *http://licenseinfo.oregon.gov*. In addition, the nature of your activity may subject you to special licensing, registration, or reporting requirements—for example, schools and hospitals. In some cases, your fundraising activities may require that you get special permits—for example, bingo games. (See Chapter 22.)

Applying for Postal Benefits

The Postal Services gives permits for reduced standard mailing rates to certain nonprofit organizations. These permits give you much lower mailing rates. Generally, nonprofits that would qualify as exempt under §501(c)(3) will be eligible for these benefits. Other types of nonprofits—such as agricultural, labor, veterans, and fraternal organizations—are also eligible. Some nonprofits are specifically excluded, including business leagues, civic improvement associations and service, social and hobby clubs. The postal service has an extensive set of regulations governing nonprofit preferential mailing rates that includes rules about what types of mailings and what content in the mailings are permissible. You can get Publication 417, *Nonprofit Standard Mail Eligibility*, that has more complete information, from the postal service. These publications are available on-line at *www.usps.com,* where you can type "Publication 417" into the search engine, or you can contact the United States Postal Service for copies.

Roadmap for Running Your Nonprofit Corporation

The remainder of this book is designed to help you run your nonprofit corporation. We want to offer you a roadmap so that you can use this book most efficiently. You will, of course, be pursing many of these courses simultaneously. For example, while you are waiting for your fundraising to pay off, you should be setting up your financial controls and financial management system.

- *Tax Exemption*. If you are interested in tax exemption, see chapters 5-12. These chapters describe how to get and keep federal, state, and local tax exemptions.

- *Governance*. All nonprofit corporations are run by a Board of Directors (though you can call this group of people by another name). Chapters 13-17 give your Board information that it needs to operate properly. If your nonprofit has voting members electing your Board, you will also need to understand the rules for voting membership corporations. See Chapter 18.

- *Personnel*. In some small nonprofits, the Board may handle everything. Most nonprofits rely on non-Board members to help run the corporation and its programs. The people who actually perform these jobs are either employees, independent contractors, or volunteers. See Chapters 19-21 for information you need to know about your relationship with these different groups of people.

- *Fundraising*. For most Boards, a big concern is often how to raise money so that you can begin your activities. Go to Chapter 22 for ideas.

- *Financial Management*. As you raise and spend funds, you need to set up accounting systems to track and report your activities. Chapters 23-28 will help you with this.

- *Lobbying and Political Activities*. Some nonprofits get involved with lobbying and political campaigning. There are a myriad of rules that apply to these organizations. See Chapter 8 for the IRS rules relating to certain tax-exempt organizations and Chapter 29 for electioneering and lobbying rules that apply to all nonprofits engaged in these activities.

- *Compliance with Laws*. As a part of running your corporation and your programs, you need to be concerned with complying with the various laws that regulate nonprofits, including keeping records, protecting confidential information, and others. Chapters 7-12 explains to tax-exempt organizations how to comply with many of the IRS rules concerning exempt organizations. Chapter 30 guides exempt and non-exempt organizations through some additional requirements.

- *Changes*. At various points, you may need to change your internal governance by amending your Articles or Bylaws. You may rearrange your corporate structure by merging with another organization or you may decide to dissolve your corporation. Chapters 31-33 cover these topics.

Consult Appendix 1 if you would like information about source material related to this Chapter.

Chapter 4 covers how to draft your Bylaws.

WRITING BYLAWS

THIS CHAPTER COVERS

- How Bylaws Fit With Other Rules
- Tips for Drafting Bylaws
- Bylaws for Nonmembership Corporations
- Bylaws for Membership Corporations

One of the most important tasks in setting up a nonprofit corporation is to develop your Bylaws. Bylaws are the rules about how the corporation is *governed* (run)—generally by the Board and, in membership corporations, with involvement from the members. The Board then *manages* the corporation. Typically, the Bylaws describe the basic rules of corporate governance, not corporate management.

If you don't write out the rules you use for your basic governance structure, you are operating with verbal Bylaws. It is very important to get your procedures in writing. A good set of Bylaws can be used by your Board as a guidebook for the major procedures for governing the corporation.

The consequences of failing to write good Bylaws can range from the annoying to the disastrous. Lack of good internal procedures can subject your group to needless squabbles, as individuals with differing agendas use your procedural defects to further their own causes. If your Bylaws conflict with the law, you may be operating illegally. This means that Board decisions may not be valid. In the worst case, noncompliance could subject the Board and everyone involved with the corporation to personal liability if a court should decide that you are so out of compliance with the law that it will treat you as though you are not incorporated.

This chapter will take you step-by-step through a procedure that will help you draft Bylaws that are legal and useful.

The process of drafting Bylaws requires some care on your part. In 1989, the Oregon legislature dramatically changed the law covering nonprofit corporations in Oregon. The law is now quite detailed and contains some pitfalls that most nonprofits would not expect in terms of how nonprofit corporations are to be governed.

WRITING BYLAWS 4

Many groups put together their Bylaws by the "cut and paste" method. The group assembles the Bylaws by getting sample copies of Bylaws from several different groups and/or from the Internet and picking and choosing the provisions that it wants in its own Bylaws. These provisions are then cut and pasted into a new set of Bylaws.

This method is a terrible way to assemble a your Bylaws. There are several reasons for this. Often, you have no way of knowing whether the Bylaws you are using comply with Oregon law. They may have come from another state (and no state has a nonprofit statute exactly like Oregon's); they may have been written before 1989, under Oregon's old statute; or they may not have been drafted by someone who knew what they were doing. Even if the samples you are using are all in compliance with Oregon law, in the process of cutting and pasting you may build in inconsistencies and ambiguities without realizing it. Furthermore, organizations tend to put lots of provisions in their Bylaws that would better be enacted as Board policies.

> *Many groups put together their Bylaws by the "cut and paste" method. This method is a terrible way to assemble your Bylaws.*

In this chapter we will help you to draft Bylaws that are legal and useful. We will begin by explaining where Bylaws fit in the legal hierarchy of rules. We will then give you some drafting tips so that you can get a feel for what you are trying to do in designing Bylaws. Finally, we will examine section by section two complete sets of Bylaws—one for nonmembership corporations and one for membership corporations. We will use the sample sets of Bylaws that appear in the Forms section. For each section, we will print the section from our sample set and will let you know how you can modify it if you want to do so, and in what ways you cannot change it. To get the maximum benefit from this approach, avoid cutting and pasting from a number of sets of Bylaws and then trying to compare it to the ones in this book. Instead, you may want to bring your ideas from those Bylaws but start with our samples and amend them to fit what you want to do to the extent you can legally do that.

If at all possible, you should have an attorney review your Bylaws after you have followed the suggestions of this chapter and come up with your best product. Your Bylaws are a critically important document and you should be sure that you have drafted them correctly.

How Bylaws Fit with Other Rules

The legal workings of your nonprofit corporation are found in a variety of sources—the law, your Articles of Incorporation, your Bylaws, and your Board policies. These sources exist as a hierarchy: those above in the hierarchy control those below. In this hierarchy, the law controls all of your organizational documents and actions (Articles, Bylaws, policies). In many situations, state law allows your Articles and Bylaws to control the governance of your corporation and only steps in if you don't provide differently in your Articles or Bylaws. Your Articles then control your Bylaws, and your Bylaws control any policies of your Board.

Articles of Incorporation

The most important corporate document you have is your Articles of Incorporation (and amendments to it). Your Articles are typically very short and establish basic items like your name, office address, type of nonprofit corporation you are, whether you have members, and distribution of assets upon dissolution. They may include other provisions you add. Your Articles and its amendments are like your corporation's constitution. If your other organizational documents conflict with your Articles, your Articles prevail. This means that you must read your Articles and amendments or restatements along with your Bylaws when you draft your Bylaws because your Bylaws cannot contradict your Articles.

Bylaws

Your next most important corporate document is your Bylaws. The purpose of Bylaws is to provide the structure for how your Board operates as your governing body. The Bylaws should contain the provisions about how the Board is selected, how Board decisions are made, how members (if any) participate in governance, how the Board functions through its officers and committees, and provisions for amending the Bylaws. We recommend that the Board put provisions about how the Board manages the corporation (such as the fiscal year, who signs contracts, etc.) in Board policies, rather than the Bylaws.

Board Policies

The Board should make policies that provide more details about how the Board operates as a governing body and all the details about how the Board carries out its management of the corporation, as long as the policies don't conflict with the Articles or Bylaws. These policies are a way of establishing consistency for recurring events. For example, the Board may have a policy that its regular Board meetings are set for the first Tuesday of the month. The Board may have a policy that it must approve personnel policies or authorize the establishment of any bank account. We discuss Board policies in more detail on pages 345-350.

Tips for Drafting Bylaws

As you draft your Bylaws, keep these guidelines in mind.

Consistent with Laws

Your Bylaws must be consistent with the law. The discussion beginning on page 57 will describe the laws that apply to each section of your Bylaws.

Consistent with Your Articles

Your Bylaws must be consistent with your Articles. Begin drafting your Bylaws by reading your Articles of Incorporation and all of its amendments. If your Articles have been restated (which means your prior Articles and amendments have been canceled and replaced), you can start with the Restatement and read forward in time. If your Bylaws conflict with any of these documents, your Articles prevail. For example, if your Articles say that your Board is composed of 7 people and your Bylaws say your Board has 9 members, then your Board can only be composed of 7 members. If you need to change your Articles, see Chapter 31.

> *Your Bylaws must be consistent with your Articles. Begin drafting your Bylaws by reading your Articles of Incorporation and all of its amendments.*

There are subjects that must be in your Articles. See pages 35-41 for a discussion of these items. For example, if some group other than your Board of Directors or a committee composed only of Directors makes Board-level decisions for your corporation, you must include this in your Articles. If you have these provisions in your Bylaws and not in your Articles, these provisions are very likely not valid.

Internally Consistent

Each provision in your Bylaws must be consistent with the other provisions in your Bylaws. Be careful as you include each provision that your provision does not conflict with other provisions. When you have completed your first draft, read it carefully to see if there are inconsistencies. For example, if your Bylaws provide in one section that your officers are a President and Secretary, and in another provide duties for a Treasurer, you need to harmonize these sections.

Focus on Governance, Not Management

The Board has two jobs—to manage corporate governance and to manage corporate operations. (See Chapter 13.) We recommend that Bylaws focus on the governance responsibilities and leave management of the corporation to Board and administrative policies. In most corporations, this means that the Bylaws will be concerned with how the Board functions—how it is selected, how it makes valid decisions, etc. In membership corporations, since members elect at least one Board member and may make other governance decisions, the Board needs to be concerned with who is a voting member, how members make proper decisions, and what voting rights members have. Items related to corporate management, like the fiscal year and who has authority to sign contracts, are best handled as policies. This allows managers more flexibility, since Bylaws are harder to change, and safeguards the corporation, since future managers are unlikely to think about consulting the Bylaws for management matters and may inadvertently operate in violation of the Bylaws.

Understandability and Utility

Your Bylaws should be written so they are easily understandable. They should strike a balance between being detailed enough so that your organization knows how you are run but not so detailed that they stifle whatever flexibility you need. Items typically covered by Bylaws are listed on pages 42-44. Items like the authority to sign checks and grievance procedures are usually better handled by a Board policy than by inclusion in the Bylaws. If you put these kinds of items in your Bylaws, you have to amend your Bylaws when you want to change them.

Be cautious about including in your Bylaws a provision that requires the Board to follow outside documents like Robert's Rules of Order. Robert's Rules comes in many versions (including a Robert's Rules for Dummies) and in many editions. Some of the editions are more than 600 pages. If you are going to require that the Board follow Robert's Rules, the Bylaws will need to specify which version and edition you are to follow and someone who has read the book will need to be on hand to ensure that the Board follows it. If your Bylaws require that you run your meetings using some parliamentary system and you fail to do so, it is possible that your decisions are invalid.

Be cautious about including in your Bylaws a provision that requires the Board to follow outside documents like Robert's Rules of Order.

For most organizations, it is a better idea to consider whether you need any kind of manual or formal procedure. Most groups do just fine with a chair who moderates the discussion, calls for a vote when everyone has had a chance to be heard, and states clearly what it is that is being decided. In smaller groups, there is generally no need for motions, seconds, and all the other rules that accompany discussions about amendments, etc.

If your Board does feel that it needs to follow Robert's Rules or some other outside document, consider enacting this decision as a Board policy and leaving it out of the Bylaws. This will allow the Board the flexibility to set the rules aside if a circumstance arises where the Board does not want to follow that much procedure. If your Bylaws require Robert's Rules, you will have to amend your Bylaws (see Chapter 31) if you want to set Robert's Rules aside.

Completeness

Be sure in preparing your Bylaws that you notice what is not in them as well as what is there. Make certain that you have covered items about voting, quorums, meetings, notice, and officers. Compare your Bylaws to the Bylaws in the Forms section for nonmembership corporations or membership corporations to be sure everything essential to governance is covered. For example, it is not uncommon for Bylaws to fail to provide for how they are to be amended or what voting rights members have.

Using Bylaws to Handle Conflict

Some groups approach their Bylaws as an instrument to manage all of the group's conflict. While a good set of Bylaws should provide a clear mechanism for dealing with governance, you should not approach the Bylaws as a cure-all for organizational disagreements. If you find that your group is focusing extensive amounts of attention on the Bylaws in an effort to settle or prevent conflict, you may want to address the issue directly or to consult a mediator.

Bylaws for Nonmembership Corporations

In this section, we will examine the "Bylaws of a Nonmembership Corporation" found in the Forms section. This section will first present the language from that sample in italics, then provide information that should be helpful for you in deciding whether this sample fits your situation and, if not, what the permissible modifications are.

Article I: Purpose

This corporation shall be organized and operated exclusively for charitable, scientific, literary, religious, and educational purposes. Subject to the limitations stated in the Articles of Incorporation, the purposes of this corporation shall be to engage in any lawful activities, none of which are for profit, for which corporations may be organized under Chapter 65 of the Oregon Revised Statutes (or its corresponding future provisions) and Section 501(c)(3) of the Internal Revenue Code (or its corresponding future provisions).

This corporation's primary purpose shall be _____.

Discussion: The reason for writing this section so broadly is to permit your §501(c)(3) corporation to operate for any legal purpose. Some corporations do not include the first paragraph and simply state their current purpose. If you do this, you are restricted to operating only for that purpose. If you later change slightly what you do, you will need to remember to amend your Bylaws. Many groups that adopt restrictive language forget to amend it when they change their purpose and operate illegally because they are then operating outside their purpose.

That said, the statement of your primary purpose is a directive to your Board about how to use your corporation's resources. If the Board is going to substantially change your primary purpose, it will need to amend the Bylaws.

If your organization is not a Public Benefit or Religious Corporation planning to be exempt under §501(c)(3), you will need to amend the first paragraph. At a minimum, you will want to provide:

Subject to the limitations stated in the Articles of Incorporation, the purposes of this corporation shall be to engage in any lawful activities, none of which are for profit, for which corporations may be organized under Chapter 65 of the Oregon Revised Statutes (or its corresponding future provisions).

This corporation's primary purpose shall be _____.

Article II: Nonmembership

This corporation shall have no members.

Discussion: As discussed in Chapter 18, members have the right to vote, inspect records, and other rights. Many Oregon nonprofits want to have "members" who pay dues and perhaps receive a newsletter but who do not vote or have other significant rights. You are better off from a legal viewpoint calling these people something besides "members," in order to distinguish them from members who by law have the rights referred to above. For example, you might call them "contributors," "angels," "friends," or "sustainers."

There are often nonlegal reasons for calling these supporters "members." If you feel you want to use the "member" designation, your Articles of Incorporation should reflect that you are *not* a membership organization, since the members do not vote. This section of your Bylaws should still be titled "Nonmembership," but might read something like this:

"This corporation shall have no members as that term is defined by Oregon Revised Statutes Chapter 65, but shall have members for other purposes. These members shall have none of the rights or duties described in ORS Chapter 65 (or any corresponding future statute)."

Article III: Board of Directors

Section 1. Duties.

The affairs of the corporation shall be managed by the Board of Directors.

Discussion: The law requires that your affairs be managed by your Board in a nonmembership corporation. Your Board can delegate some of its authority to committees of the Board if done properly. See page 336-38. If your corporation allows major decisions to be made by anyone other than the Board or a committee of the Board, you must state this in your Articles of Incorporation. If you have done this, then the Bylaws in the Forms section will probably not apply to your group. You will need to see an attorney for help in drafting your Bylaws. You should be aware that, if you are applying for tax exemption, this unusual structure may create problems for your application.

Section 2. Number and Qualifications.

The number of Directors may vary between a minimum of three and a maximum of fifteen.

Discussion: If you are a Public Benefit Corporation, you must have at least three Directors. If you are a Mutual Benefit or Religious Corporation, you can have as few as one. There is no legal ceiling on how many Directors you can have.

This section of your Bylaws can specify the exact number of Directors, which is called a *fixed number* (for example, "The number of Directors shall be five."). Alternatively, as above, this section can set a *variable number* of Directors. One reason for a variable number is to allow the Board to expand or contract within the limits you set without going through the procedure to amend the Bylaws. Many organizations like the variable number provision because of the flexibility it gives them.

If you decide on a variable number of Directors, you need to be aware that it is often important to know the specific size of your Board at a particular point in time. For example, this figure is used in calculating a quorum and in calculating how many votes are needed to set up a committee that exercises Board functions. You have two choices about how to set the official size of your Board for these purposes—prescribing it or winging it. Your Board at a meeting can prescribe (set) the specific number of Directors and reflect this in the minutes. For example, the Board may make a decision to have eleven Directors. Later, if it adds or subtracts members, it can reset the number at a meeting and reflect that in the minutes. This is then the figure from which quorum and committee calculations are made. There may be a difference between the prescribed number of Directors and the actual number of Directors. For example, the Board may have decided to have eleven positions and filled them; later, two Directors resigned and were not replaced. Your prescribed size is still eleven, and this is the number (and not nine) that should be used for calculations involving Board size, such as setting a quorum.

The second method you can use to set Board size is to wing it—that is, simply elect Directors without setting a number, as long as you stay within the range stated in the Bylaws. If that is what you do, your Board size is the number of Directors in office immediately before the meeting.

The sample section above does not set out any particular qualifications for Directors. All Directors must be individuals, as opposed to corporations or some other legal entity. They can live anywhere in the world. They can be under the age of 18, although there may be some limitations on what they as a minor can do. You can set out any other qualifications that you want. If you do, you should change the heading to read "Number and Qualifications."

One area of some interest is whether you can discriminate in setting the qualifications for your Board. For example, an organization devoted to helping Vietnamese immigrants may want to provide that some or all of its Board consist of people of Vietnamese ancestry. The law is somewhat unclear in this area, but in most cases it appears that you can write in these types of qualifications. You should get legal advice for your own situation.

Section 3. Term and Election.

The term of office for Directors shall be one year. A Director may be reelected without limitation on the number of terms s/he may serve. The Board shall elect its own members, except that a Director shall not vote on that member's own position.

Discussion: The maximum term of office in Oregon for *elected* Directors is five years. Your Bylaws should not provide that a Director is elected until replaced, without setting a limit on the term, because this could violate the five year rule. A Director can be re-elected without limitation, although you may choose to limit the number of terms a Director may serve. Many Boards do this to assure new leadership.

Many organizations who have longer Board terms want to provide for staggered terms for their Directors, so that the Board always has some experienced members in place. One way to do this is to divide the total number of Directors into groups and elect each group at different times. For example:

Except for the initial adjustments of shorter terms needed in order to create staggered terms, the term of office for Directors shall be two years. The Board shall make provisions to stagger the terms of Directors so that each year the terms of as close as possible to one-half of the Directors shall expire. A Director may be reelected without limitation on the number of terms she or he may serve. The board shall elect its own members, except that a Director shall not vote on that member's own position.

If you have a variable size Board, you can accomplish staggering without this awkward language in your Bylaws. You can do this by setting your Board size the first year at one-half of what you eventually want, and the next year add the other one-half of the Directors.

If you have a group within your organization other than the existing Board who will be electing Directors, then you probably have some version of a membership corporation. You should check your Articles of Incorporation to see if you incorporated as a membership corporation and, if so, look at the Bylaws for membership corporations later in this chapter. If you have any question about which you are, you should get legal advice.

Some corporations have some or all Directors who are appointed or designated, rather than elected. The five-year term limit rule does not apply to these Directors. Those situations are outside the scope of these Bylaws. If you want to provide for this, you should review page 21 and get legal advice.

Occasionally, an organization will provide that a Director whose term has ended (often the President) will remain on the Board in an *ex officio* capacity. *Ex officio* means "by virtue of one's office," in this case, the office of President. Simply stating that the Board member holds the office in an *ex officio* capacity does not indicate whether the Board member has the right to vote. Organizations go both ways on whether the Director can vote, so it is vital to clarify if the Director is a "voting, *ex officio* Director" or a "non-voting *ex officio* Director."

Section 4. Removal.

Any Director may be removed, with or without cause, by a vote of two-thirds of the Directors then in office.

Discussion: Although it sounds harsh, many corporations opt to permit removal of Directors with or without cause. This means that you do not need to have a reason to remove a Director. If you try to limit removal only to certain circumstances, you run a serious risk that a situation will arise that you did not anticipate that requires removal of a Director and that is not spelled out in your reasons for removal. You are then stuck with a Director you don't want. Alternatively, the Board may vote to terminate the Director and the Director then has grounds for a lawsuit.

Many groups feel that if two-thirds of the entire Board is willing to vote for removal, it makes no sense to leave that person on the Board. If you do decide to specify reasons for removal, you should get some legal help. These Bylaws are drafted on the assumption that the Director can be removed without the corporation having to prove its reason for removal.

If you are going to remove an elected Director under Bylaws that provide you can do so with or without cause, state law requires that you must do so by at least a two-thirds majority of all Directors *in office* (not just at the meeting). You cannot require a lower number than this, such as a majority at the meeting.

Some organizations want to include a provision in the Bylaws requiring that a Director that has missed a certain number of meetings is removed from the Board. If you are considering that type of provision, review the discussion on page 319.

If you are going to remove an elected Director with or without cause, you must do so by at least a two-thirds majority of all Directors in office (not just at the meeting). You cannot require a lower number than this, such as a majority at the meeting.

A Religious Corporation may require a different procedures by which the Board or any person can remove (with or without cause) a Director elected by the Board. A Religious Corporation can even limit or prohibit the ability of a court to remove Directors.

Section 5. Vacancies.

Vacancies on the Board of Directors and newly created Board positions shall be filled by a majority vote of the Directors then on the Board of Directors.

Discussion: Notice that this wording requires the vote of a majority of all Directors in office, not just a majority of those at the meeting, to fill a vacancy. You could word your Bylaws to allow the Board to fill a vacancy with a majority at the meeting; however, if the directors remaining in office are not enough to constitute a quorum, the law requires that they can fill the vacancy only by a majority vote of all the directors remaining in office. To keep it simple, we suggest that you use only one approach, which will work no matter what your situation is.

If you wish, your Bylaws can make different provisions than the one above for filling vacancies. For example, your President could appoint Directors to fill the vacancies.

Section 6. Quorum and Action.

A quorum at a Board meeting shall be a majority of the number of Directors prescribed by the Board, or if no number is prescribed, a majority of the number in office immediately before the meeting begins. If a quorum is present, action is taken by a majority vote of the Directors present, except as otherwise provided by these Bylaws. Where the law requires a majority vote of the Directors in office to establish committees to exercise Board functions, to amend the Articles of Incorporation, to sell assets not in the regular course of business, to merge, or to dissolve, or for other matters, such action is taken by that majority as required by law.

Discussion: A **quorum** is the number of Directors who must be present at a Board meeting in order for it to be held. If fewer Directors than the number set as a quorum show up, the Board cannot do any business and must reschedule the meeting. This is discussed on pages 327-28. A quorum has to be at least one-third of the Directors.

The calculation of the number of Directors needed to make a quorum is complicated by the fact that the Bylaws of some nonprofit corporations provide for a fixed number of Directors and some have a variable number.

If your Bylaws have a *fixed number of Directors*, then you should modify the wording in the sample clause above to state that the quorum is a majority (or some other percentage greater than one-third) of the fixed number of Directors. Be aware that if the actual number of Directors falls below the number fixed by your Bylaws (which can happen when a Director resigns or the term ends and she or he is not replaced or through some other cause), you still use the number fixed by your Bylaws (and not the number of Directors in office) in calculating whether you have a quorum. For example, if your Bylaws state that you have seven Directors and that your quorum is a majority of the Directors, you must have four Directors for a quorum, even if at that point you only have five Directors in office because of vacancies. You could clarify this for future Board by stating in your Bylaws that your quorum was four Directors.

If your Bylaws provide that you have a *variable Board size*, then you must determine how you set the actual number of your Directors before you can figure out your quorum rules. See the discussion above under Article III, Section 2 about deciding the Board number by prescribing it or by winging it. The rather awkward wording in the sample clause above is wording that could be used by any corporation that has a variable size Board. It is important to keep this wording in the Bylaws even if your Board for now has decided whether it will or will not prescribe Directors. This type of decision is rarely passed on to future Boards and the Bylaw provision may alert a future Board to the complexities of this issue.

You can increase the number of Directors required for a quorum to be more than the majority stated above. You can lower it to be as little as one-third of the fixed or prescribed Directors as described above. You cannot set the quorum at less than one-third. Many groups feel that one-third is too few Directors to conduct a meeting. The sample Bylaw above follows the common practice of setting the quorum at a majority of the Board.

Voting: Once a quorum is present, action must be taken by at least a majority vote of the Directors present. You can require more than a majority vote but not less.

WRITING BYLAWS 4

There are two traps to avoid here. First, avoid using the phrase "present and voting" when describing the majority needed to take action. The majority must be of the Directors *present*, and not just the Directors *voting*. Consequently, if 11 Directors are present but only 9 vote (because 2 abstain), you need 6 votes, not 5, to decide on an action. It is a good idea to spell this out in your Bylaws, as the sample clause above does.

There are two traps to avoid. Avoid using the phrase "present and voting" and avoid replacing the word "majority" with "50% plus 1."

Avoid replacing the word "majority" with "50% plus 1" as some Bylaws do. These are not the same thing. A majority means any number more than half, including 50.01. 50% plus 1 means one half plus one. So if you have 13 Directors at your meeting, a majority is 7, which is what most people will understand. 50% of 13 = 6½ + 1 = 7½. 7 is less than 7½ and so is not enough to constitute 50% + 1. The Board of 13 Directors at this meeting will need 8 Directors to take action. Some drafters use "50% plus 1" because they want to be clear that if there are an even number of people voting, more than half must vote for the action in order to pass it. However, the phrase "majority" means more than half, so there is no reason to use the misleading "50% plus 1."

There are some types of action (described in the sample clause above) which require the vote of a majority of Directors *in office* in order to be effective. These circumstances are put into the Bylaws so that you are sure to know the proper vote needed in those circumstances.

Section 7. Regular Meetings.

Regular meetings of the Board of Directors shall be held at the time and place to be determined by the Board of Directors. No other notice of the date, time, place, or purpose of these meetings is required.

Discussion: Regular meetings are those in which the time and place is regularly scheduled by the Board (for example, the first Monday of the month at 7:00 p.m. at the corporation's office). The law does not require additional notice of these meetings. If you change the time or place, this will make the meeting a special meeting, and you must give the notice you require for special meetings.

If you want, your Bylaws can require that you give notice of your regular meetings. The drawback is that, if your Bylaws require you to give notice and you don't, the action taken at the meeting may be invalid. Your Board may choose to give notice of regular meetings without such notice being required in your Bylaws.

Section 8. Special Meetings.

Special meetings of the Board of Directors shall be held at the time and place to be determined by the Board of Directors. Notice of such meetings, describing the date, time, place, and purpose of the meeting, shall be delivered to each Director personally or by telephone or by mail not less than two days prior to the special meeting. Written notice, if mailed postpaid and correctly addressed to the Director at the address shown in the corporate records, is effective when mailed.

Discussion: Special meetings are all meetings that are not regular meetings. If your Bylaws don't provide for a longer or shorter period for notice for special meetings, the law provides that notice is to be not less than two days. There are only certain circumstances in which you are required to state the purpose of special meetings and your Bylaws could require that only in those cases do you need to state the purpose in your special meeting notice. Rather than lengthen the Bylaws with this kind of detail, these sample Bylaws provide that you will always state the purpose of a special meeting. Your meeting will then by limited to the purposes stated. If you want to avoid this result, you will need to check with an attorney to be sure that you can consider the items you want to talk about without giving notice of them.

The presiding officer of the Board, the President, or twenty percent of the Directors then in office may call and give notice of the meeting of the Board. You can make different provisions than this in your Bylaws if you wish.

The law that provides for notice was drafted in 1989 before the advent of the Internet and it is not clear whether the statute allows electronic notice. In spite of this, many organizations use email for notice. If you decide to take the risk that your notice is improper and use email for notice, consult the discussion on page 685 for how to minimize your risk.

Section 9. Meeting by Telecommunication or Computer.

Any regular or special meeting of the Board of Directors may be held by telephone, telecommunications or electronic means, as long as all Directors can hear or read each other's communications during the meeting or all communications during the meeting are immediately transmitted to each participating Director, and each participating Director is able to immediately send messages to all other participating Directors. All participating Directors shall be informed that a meeting is taking place at which official business may be transacted.

Discussion: You can hold a Board meeting by conference call or in a computer conference-type setting as long as everyone can hear or simultaneously communicate each other. The idea is that a meeting is a setting in which dissenters or those with questions about an action have the opportunity to communicate with everyone at once, so that the issue can be hashed out in a group setting.

A "meeting" by email does not meet this requirement, since email communication is not simultaneous and someone is often away from their email and responds later. Similarly, you cannot hold a Board meeting by phone by simply calling each Director individually and polling them. If your email communication or phone calls reveal that all Directors are in agreement, however, you can take action by consent without a meeting as described in Article III, Section 11 below.

Your Bylaws can prohibit these alternative meeting venues if you desire.

Section 10. Action by Consent.

Any action required or permitted by law to be taken at a meeting of the Board may be taken without a meeting if a consent in writing, setting forth the action to be taken or so taken, shall be signed by all the Directors. A written communication includes a communication that is transmitted or received by electronic means. Signing includes an electronic signature that is executed or adopted by a Director with the intent to sign.

Discussion: Notice that the Board can act without a meeting only if *all* Directors agree. A majority is not enough and there can be no abstentions. You need to obtain a written consent from each Director that is signed and dated. Consents by email are considered written consents as long as the Director intended to sign it. (For example, if someone else used the Director's account to consent, the Director did not intend to sign.) Your Bylaws can prohibit action by consent if you want to do so.

Article IV: Committees

Section 1. Executive Committee.

The Board of Directors may elect an Executive Committee. The Executive Committee shall have the authority to make on-going decisions between Board meetings and shall have the authority to make financial and budgetary decisions.

Discussion: Many Boards have an Executive Committee that can make decisions between Board meetings. Because these committees can exercise Board authority, the law states that they are supposed to comply with the provisions of Article IV, Section 3 below. This means that the committee should only have Board members on it and is supposed to be elected by the Board by a majority of all Directors in office.

> *Be careful about providing that the actions of the Executive Committee must be approved by the Board. The Executive Committee is then robbed of its function of authorizing actions between Board meetings.*

In practice, most Executive Committees are not elected by the Board. Generally, the Bylaws state that the Executive Committee is composed of the officers of the organization or sometimes the officers plus one or two other Board member elected by the Board. If you want to be sure this complies with the law, the Board can confirm the appointment of the Executive Committee as set out in the Bylaws each time the membership of the committee changes by a vote of a majority of all Directors in office.

Be careful about providing that the actions of the Executive Committee must be approved by the Board. This means that the actions of the Executive Committee are not yet binding on the corporation until the Board meets. Your employees, volunteers, and outside parties cannot rely on them. The Executive Committee is then robbed of its function of authorizing actions between Board meetings.

Section 2. Other Committees.

The Board of Directors may establish such other committees as it deems necessary and desirable. Such committees may exercise the authority of the Board of Directors or may be advisory committees.

Discussion: If the committee the Board sets up does not exercise Board functions (for example, it does fundraising at the Board's direction or it makes recommendations to the Board on personnel matters but does not make the actual decisions), there are no restrictions as to who can be on these committees or how they are selected. If you want to provide for this further—for example, by naming standing committees—you can add these provisions to the Bylaws or enact them as policies, which will be easier to change when your committees change.

Section 3. Composition of Committees Exercising Board Authority.

Any committee that exercises any authority of the Board of Directors shall be composed of two or more Directors, elected by the Board of Directors by a majority vote of the number of Directors prescribed by the Board, or if no number is prescribed, by a majority vote of all Directors in office at that time.

Discussion: This section as written requires that any committee that exercises Board functions (that is, makes Board level decisions) must consist of two or more Directors, should not include anyone else who votes, and must be elected not by majority vote of the Directors at the meeting but by a majority of Directors prescribed or in office at that time. Review the discussion on pages 66 about fixed and variable size Boards. If you do not have a variable Board, you could amend this to read "a majority of the number of Directors fixed by the Bylaws." If you place voting non-Directors on these committees, but this would constitute an example of allowing non-Directors to govern the corporation. These types of provisions need to be in the Articles of Incorporation. See pp. 19-20.

Be careful about providing that the actions of a committee exercising the functions of the Board must be approved by the Board. As with the Executive Committee, your employees, volunteers, and outside parties cannot rely on the committee's decisions until the Board approves them.

Section 4. Quorum and Action.

A quorum at a Committee meeting exercising Board authority shall be a majority of all Committee members in office immediately before the meeting begins. If a quorum is present, action is taken by a majority vote of Directors present.

Discussion: Your Bylaws may regulate your Committee meetings, notices, quorum, and voting to the same extent it can regulate these matter for the Board.

Section 5. Limitations on the Powers of Committees.

No committee may authorize payment of a dividend or any part of the income or profit of the corporation to its directors or officers; may approve dissolution, merger, or the sale, pledge, or transfer of all or substantially all of the corporation's assets; may elect, appoint, or remove directors or fill vacancies on the Board or on any of its committees; nor may adopt, amend, or repeal the Articles, Bylaws, or any resolution by the Board of Directors.

Discussion: The above limitations are set by the statute and cannot be changed. It is useful to include them so that your committees do not inadvertently perform some actions they cannot perform. Your Bylaws can further limit the authority of Board committees to act, if you want to do so.

Article V: Officers

Section 1. Titles.

The officers of this corporation shall be the President, Secretary, and Treasurer.

Discussion: The law says you have to have a President and Secretary, although you can use other terms for these roles and the same person can fill both jobs. The statute does not say exactly what duties these officers shall perform, except that one of them shall be responsible to see that Board minutes are prepared and that one of them shall authenticate the records of the corporation.

Your corporation can have more officers than the two required by law if you want. We highly recommend that you have a Treasurer. Many nonprofits are running into problems with inadequate financial policies. Even small nonprofits need at least two eyes on the finances and an officer, who may be one of those sets of eyes, needs to ensure that this is done. See Chapter 25 for more discussion of this issue of great concern to nonprofits and their regulators.

Oregon law does not state that the officers must be Directors, although in many nonprofits they are. If you want to require that your officers be Directors, you can add a sentence that says *"All officers of this corporation must be members of the Board of Directors."* You should change the title to read "Titles and Qualifications."

Section 2. Election.

The Board of Directors shall elect the officers to serve one year terms. An officer may be reelected without limitation on the number of terms the officer may serve.

Discussion: The officers may be elected by the Board or appointed or designated as provided in the Articles or Bylaws. If you are going to select officers by some method other than Board election, you should get some legal advice. Although the law does not limit the officers' terms, if the officers are required to be Directors, the elected Directors' terms cannot exceed five years. Many nonprofits limit the number of consecutive terms an officer can serve to assure new leadership.

Most nonprofits set one year terms for officers. Otherwise, your Board may run into issues if the officer has a multi-year term and the officer's term on the Board expires before her/his term as an officer expires.

Section 3. Vacancy.

A vacancy in any office shall be filled not later than the first regular meeting of the Board of Directors following the vacancy.

Discussion: You can vary this, but you generally do not want too much time to go by with a vacant office.

Section 4. Other Officers.

The Board of Directors may elect or appoint other officers, agents and employees as it shall deem necessary and desirable. They shall hold their offices for such terms and have such authority and perform such duties as shall be determined by the Board of Directors.

Discussion: The Board has a great deal of authority to appoint other officers. Some corporations may include the Executive Director as an officer so that the Executive Director can sign contracts and forms that require an officer's signature. If you do name your Executive Director as an officer, you need to review some of the provisions above about officers. You may provide that the Executive Director serves as an officer as long as she or he holds the position of Executive Director, rather than requiring the Board to re-elect the Executive Director every year. If you require that your officers be Directors, you will need to modify this unless the Executive Director is a board member. See pages 310-311 and 343 for other challenges with this arrangement.

Some nonprofits make the Executive Director an *ex officio* nonvoting Board member to get around these difficulties. *Ex officio* means that the Director holds a Board position by virtue of an office (in this case, the position of Executive Director). Most Boards do not name the Executive Director as an officer but require that the Executive Director attend Board meetings to keep the Board informed about corporate matters. A Board officer independent of the Executive Director signs contracts and other documents that are important enough to require an officer's signature.

Section 5. President.

The President shall be the chief officer of the corporation and shall act as the Chair of the Board. The President shall have any other powers and duties as may be prescribed by the Board of Directors.

Discussion: You are free to state the powers of the President to suit your needs; however, keep in mind that it is generally better to draft general descriptions rather than specific ones. You can be more specific in Board policies.

Section 6. Secretary.

The Secretary shall have overall responsibility for all recordkeeping. The Secretary shall perform, or cause to be performed, the following duties: (a) official recording of the minutes of all proceedings of the Board of Directors meetings and actions; (b) provision for notice of all meetings of the Board of Directors; (c) authentication of the records of the corporation; and (d) any other duties as may be prescribed by the Board of Directors.

Discussion: The Bylaws or the Board must delegate to one of the officers the responsibility for preparing minutes of the Directors' and members' meetings and for authenticating the records of the corporation. Most Bylaws delegate this authority to its Secretary. The clause above also includes other duties commonly performed by the Secretary. You may want to leave the first sentence in the Bylaws and put the remainder of this in the Board policies, along with any other duties you want to add.

Section 7. Treasurer

The Treasurer shall have the overall responsibility for all corporate funds. The Treasurer shall perform, or cause to be performed, the following duties: (a) maintenance of full and accurate accounts of all financial records of the corporation; (b) deposit of all monies and other valuable effects in the name and to the credit of the corporation in such depositories as may be designated by the Board of Directors; (c) disbursement of all funds when proper to do so; (d) presentation of financial reports as to the financial condition of the corporation to the Board of Directors; and (e) any other duties as may be prescribed by the Board of Directors.

Discussion: The role of Treasurer has become increasingly important. (See p. 342.) As with the duties of other officers, you may want to leave the first sentence in the Bylaws and put the remainder of this in the Board policies, along with any other duties you want to add.

Article VI: Corporate Indemnity

This corporation will indemnify to the fullest extent not prohibited by law any person who is made, or threatened to be made, a party to an action, suit, or other proceeding, by reason of the fact that the person is or was a Director, officer, employee, volunteer, or agent of the corporation or a fiduciary within the meaning of the Employee Retirement Income Security Act of 1974 (or its corresponding future provisions) with respect to any employee benefit plan of the corporation. No amendment to this Article that limits the corporation's obligation to indemnify any person shall have any effect on such obligation for any act or omission that occurs prior to the later of the effective date of the amendment or the date notice of the amendment is given to the person. The corporation shall interpret this indemnification provision to extend to all persons covered by its provisions the most liberal possible indemnification—substantively, procedurally, and otherwise.

Discussion: Indemnification is described in Chapter 17. This indemnification provision allows the corporation to indemnify its Directors and officers to the fullest extent allowed by law. This is the result desired by many Directors; some will not serve without this. You can choose to provide no indemnification or to provide more limited indemnification.

Article VII: Amendments to Bylaws

These Bylaws may be amended or repealed, and new Bylaws adopted, by the Board of Directors by a majority vote of Directors present, if a quorum is present. Prior to the adoption of the amendment, each Director shall be given at least two days notice of the date, time, and place of the meeting at which the proposed amendment is to be considered, and the notice shall state that one of the purposes of the meeting is to consider a proposed amendment to the Bylaws and shall contain a copy of the proposed amendment.

Discussion: In the nonmembership corporation, it is the Board that amends the Bylaws. You can require a greater vote (but not a lesser one) to amend these Bylaws. You can provide a different period for notice to the Board, either longer or shorter. However, your notice does have to state that one of the purposes of the meeting is to consider a proposed amendment to the Bylaws and shall contain a copy or summary of the proposed amendment.

It is possible to set up a nonprofit corporation whose Bylaws can only be amended with the approval of a third person. These Bylaws do not apply to those situations.

DATE ADOPTED: _____

Discussion: It is helpful to include the date your Bylaws are adopted, so that it is easier to track Bylaws and amendments chronologically and so that you can know what your current Bylaws are.

Bylaws for Membership Corporations

This section will assist membership corporations in drafting their Bylaws. Be sure before you conclude that you are a membership corporation that you have reviewed the discussion on pages 25-26 and truly are a membership corporation (whose members vote at least for one member of the Board of Directors) as that term is defined by Oregon law.

In this section, we will examine the "Bylaws of a Membership Corporation" found in the Forms section. This section will first present the language from that sample in italics, then provide information that should be helpful for you in deciding whether this sample fits your situation and, if not, what the permissible modifications are.

If your nonprofit corporation is a homeowner's association, condominium, or timeshare, you have special rules that govern you and sometimes replace the ones in this book. If your special rules don't override the nonprofit corporation rules, you need to follow the nonprofit corporation rules. You should have an attorney draft your Bylaws.

Article I: Purpose

This corporation shall be organized and operated exclusively for charitable, scientific, literary, religious, and educational purposes. Subject to the limitations stated in the Articles of Incorporation, the purposes of this corporation shall be to engage in any lawful activities, none of which are for profit, for which corporations may be organized under Chapter 65 of the Oregon Revised Statutes (or its corresponding future provisions) and Section 501(c)(3) of the Internal Revenue Code (or its corresponding future provisions).

This corporation's primary purpose shall be

Discussion: The reason for writing this section so broadly is to permit your corporation to operate for any legal purpose. Some corporations do not include the first sentence and simply state their current purpose. If you do this, you are restricted to operating only for that purpose. If you later change slightly what you do, you will need to remember to amend your Bylaws. Many groups that adopt restrictive language forget to amend it when they change their purpose and operate illegally because they are then operating outside their purpose.

That said, the statement of your primary purpose is a directive to your Board about how to use your corporation's resources. If the Board is going to substantially change your primary purpose, it will need to amend the Bylaws.

If your organization is not a Public Benefit or Religious Corporation planning to be exempt under §501(c)(3), you will need to amend the first paragraph. At a minimum, you will want to provide:

Subject to the limitations stated in the Articles of Incorporation, the purposes of this corporation shall be to engage in any lawful activities, none of which are for profit, for which corporations may be organized under Chapter 65 of the Oregon Revised Statutes (or its corresponding future provisions).

This corporation's primary purpose shall be

Article II: Members

Section 1. Classes and Voting.

There shall be one class of members of this corporation. Each member shall be entitled to one vote on all matters for which a membership vote is permitted by law, the Articles of Incorporation, or the Bylaws of this corporation.

Discussion: If your corporation is a membership corporation, you may be a simple, one-member-one-vote group, or you may have more complex aspects (such as classes of members, chapters, cumulative voting, or delegates). The provisions about membership organizations in these Bylaws are oriented toward the simple, one-member-one-vote group, although most of it applies to all membership corporations. If your corporation has more complex aspects, you should get legal help to draft your Bylaws.

One of the most common mistakes that membership Bylaws make is to fail to specify *what* members can vote on. By law, if you call yourself a membership corporation, your members must be allowed to vote more than once to elect at least one Director. See the discussion about membership corporations on pages 25-26. However, your corporation can choose whether your members vote on other matters on which members can vote, such as amending the Articles and Bylaws (Chapter 31), selling substantially all of the corporation's assets (Chapter 32), mergers (Chapter 32), dissolutions (Chapter 33), conflict of interest matters (299-303), and, in Mutual Benefit Corporations, certain indemnification issues (pages 371-72).

> *One of the most common mistakes that membership Bylaws make is to fail to specify what members can vote on.*

If you fail to indicate what members can vote on, you create a real problem for your organization when you want to amend your Articles or Bylaws, for example, and are unsure whether you need a favorable vote by the members to do this. The Attorney General at the Oregon Department of Justice that oversees Public Benefit Corporations will probably take the position that you need a membership vote on anything members can vote on, unless you limit this in your Bylaws (or Articles). The sample clause above permits the members to vote on all matters on which members may vote. If you do not want your members voting on all these matters, you need to change the language in the sample clause to clearly reflect what it is that members can vote on.

Remember that your members should **not** be voting on matters pertaining to the management of the corporation, such as hiring, budgets, and policies, unless your Articles authorize this (see pages 19-20).

Section 2. Qualifications.

A person shall become a member of the corporation by _____.

Discussion: You have great flexibility in setting the qualifications of your members. You should consider how much of this you want to put in the Bylaws and how much should be established by Board policies. Any provisions you make for this in the Bylaws can only be changed by amending the Bylaws. If you want to provide that the Board sets the qualifications for membership, you may do so by stating *"A person shall become a member of the corporation by following the policies established by the Board of Directors."*

One thing you cannot do is define your members in such a way that someone is a member without their consent. Page 370 discusses this in more detail.

Section 3. Termination of Membership.

Membership may be terminated by the Board of Directors after giving the member at least 15 days written notice by first class or certified mail of the termination and the reasons for the termination, and an opportunity for the member to be heard by the Board, orally or in writing, not less than five days before the effective date of the termination. The decision of the Board shall be final and shall not be reviewable by any court.

Discussion: Public Benefit and Mutual Benefit Corporations cannot terminate, expel, or suspend members without a fair and reasonable procedure. The procedure set out above is deemed by law to be fair and reasonable. You may change the above procedure and set out your own procedure, but you take the risk that you may have to prove that your procedure is fair and reasonable.

Religious Corporations can expel members without providing any procedure.

Section 4. Annual Meeting.

The annual meeting of the members shall be held on _____ at a place to be determined by the Board of Directors.

Discussion: Oregon law requires that you hold an annual membership meeting. Your Articles or Bylaws are to provide the time. To avoid having to amend the Bylaws in order to change an annual meeting date, many Bylaws provide that *"The annual meeting of the members shall be held on a date [or "a date in March"] set by the Board of Directors."*

Oregon law allows the Board to set the location of the meeting. If you do not include a provision allowing for this, the meeting must be held at the corporate's principal office.

Your members can also hold regular meetings. Regular meetings are those held at a regularly scheduled time and place. Most membership corporations do not hold regular meetings, other than the annual meeting. However, you can provide for this if it is appropriate for you.

Section 5. Special Meetings.

Special meetings of the members shall be held at the call of the Board of Directors, or by the call of the holders of at least five percent of the voting power of the corporation by a demand signed, dated, and delivered to the corporation's Secretary. Such demand by the members shall describe the purpose for the meeting.

Discussion: Special meetings are all meetings that are not annual or regular meetings. Your Bylaws can vary the requirements listed in the sample clause for calling a special meeting. However, the notice of the meeting must list the purpose of the meeting.

Section 6. Notice of Meeting.

Notice of all meetings of the members shall be given to each member at the last address of record, by first class mail at least 7 days before the meeting, or by means other than first class mail at least 30 but not more than 60 days before the meeting. The notice shall include the date, time, place, and purposes of the meeting.

Discussion: You must give notice to your members of all meetings. The notice must be fair and reasonable. The notice described above is deemed by law to be fair and reasonable. In some situations, this is the required notice. Those situations are when members are voting on Directors' conflicts of interest (see pages 299-303); certain indemnification matters (see pages 371-72); amendment of Articles (see Chapter 31); amendment of Bylaws (see Chapter 31); merger (see Chapter 32); sale of assets (see Chapter 32); and dissolution (see Chapter 33). If you choose to change the notice that the law deems fair, you will need to have two notice sections: one with the required notice for the actions described above, and the other for all other actions. You also take the risk that your notice may later be found not to be fair.

The notice is sent to members as of a "record date." This is discussed on page 375. If you want to change how that record date is fixed, you can do so in your Bylaws.

The law that provides for notice was drafted in 1989 before the advent of the Internet and does not provide for electronic notice. It seems quite likely that email is "fair and reasonable" notice as described by the statute. If you take the minimal risk of using email, you are safest if you send your email notice 30 to 60 days before the meeting. You might also consider adopting as a policy the safeguards concerning email discussed on pages 685-86.

Section 7. Quorum and Voting.

Those votes represented at a meeting of members shall constitute a quorum. A majority vote of the members represented and voting is the act of the members, unless these Bylaws or the law provide differently.

Discussion: A *quorum* is the number of votes required to be present at a meeting in order for business to be carried out. The minimum quorum required for a membership meeting is the number of votes present. This means that you will always have a quorum at a membership meeting.

Some groups require a higher quorum, often because they hope this will get more members to the meetings. However, you should think carefully about this before you do so. It is very common among membership groups for the group that requires a higher quorum to be unable to get it. The organization is then unable to elect Directors or engage in other actions requiring a membership vote. If you are having problems getting members to the membership meetings, you may want to look for other solutions that do not cripple your ability to carry on as an organization.

Voting: The majority vote described in the sample clause is the minimum vote you can set, but you can require more than a majority vote if you want. In some situations, the law requires more than a majority vote.

Your corporation can vote by ballot (often called vote by mail) unless your Articles of Bylaws prohibit or limit it. Page 381 discusses how you must conduct a vote by ballot. If you want to provide for voting by ballot, you could consider this provision:

Any action which may be taken at any annual, regular or special meeting of members may be taken without a meeting if the corporation delivers a written ballot to each member entitled to vote on the matter. The written ballot must set forth each proposed action and provide an opportunity to vote for or against each proposed action. Approval by written ballot shall be valid only if the number of votes cast by ballot equals or exceeds any quorum required to be present at a meeting authorizing the action, and the number of approvals equals or exceeds the number of votes that would be required to approve the matter at a meeting at which the total number of votes cast was the same as the number of votes cast by ballot.

All solicitations for votes by ballot shall indicate the number of responses needed to meet the quorum requirements, state the percentage of approvals necessary to approve each matter other than the election of directors, and specify a reasonable time by which a ballot must be received by the corporation in order to be counted.

You can vote by ballot even if you don't include this section. However, the section provides a great deal of important information about what must be done so that the ballot vote is proper. If you don't put this in your Bylaws, be sure that your corporation is set up so that it will properly conduct the vote.

If you want to prohibit voting by ballot, you should add to Section 7:

There shall be no voting by ballot.

Section 8. Proxy Voting.

There shall be no voting by proxy.

Discussion: Voting by proxy means that a member can assign someone else to vote for her/him. If you are going to allow proxy voting, you should become familiar with the rules about proxy voting. These are discussed on page 380. If you don't want to deal with proxy voting by your members, you must prohibit it in your Articles or Bylaws.

Section 9. Action by Consent.

Any action required or permitted by law to be taken at a meeting of the members may be taken without a meeting if a consent in writing, setting forth the action to be taken or so taken, shall be signed by all the members.

Discussion: Notice that the members can act without a meeting only if all the members agree. A majority is not enough. Your Bylaws can prohibit actions without a meeting if you desire.

Article III: Board of Directors

Section 1. Duties.

The affairs of the corporation shall be managed by the Board of Directors.

Discussion: The law requires that your affairs be managed by your Board in a membership corporation. Your Board can delegate some of its authority to committees of the Board if done properly. See pages 336-38. If your corporation allows major decisions to be made by anyone other than the Board or a committee of the Board, you must state this in your Articles of Incorporation. For example, if your members vote on the budget, staff hiring, or policies, you will need to include these rights in the Articles. If you have done this, then the Bylaws in the Forms section will probably not apply to your group. You will need to see an attorney for help in drafting your Bylaws. You should be aware that, if you are applying for tax exemption, this unusual structure may create problems for your application.

Section 2. Number and Qualifications.

The number of Directors may vary between a minimum of three and a maximum of fifteen.

Discussion: If you are a Public Benefit Corporation, you must have at least three Directors. If you are a Mutual Benefit or Religious Corporation, you can have as few as one. There is no legal ceiling on how many Directors you can have.

This section of your Bylaws can specify the exact number of Directors, which is called a *fixed number* (for example, "The number of Directors shall be five."). Alternatively, as above, this section can set a *variable number* of Directors. One reason for a variable number is to allow the Board to expand or contract within the limits you set without going through the procedure to amend the Bylaws. Many organizations like the variable number provision because of the flexibility it gives them.

If you decide on a variable number of Directors, you need to be aware that it is often important to know the specific size of your Board at a particular point in time. For example, this figure is used in calculating a quorum and in calculating how many votes are needed to set up a committee that exercises Board functions. You have two choices about how to set the official size of your Board for these purposes—prescribing it or winging it. Your Board at a meeting can prescribe (set) the specific number of Directors and reflect this in the minutes. For example, the Board may make a decision to have eleven Directors. Later, if it adds or subtracts members, it can reset the number at a meeting and reflect that in the minutes. This is then the figure from which quorum and committee calculations are made. There may be a difference between the prescribed number of Directors and the actual number of Directors. For example, the Board may have decided to have eleven positions and filled them; later, two Directors resigned and were not replaced. Your prescribed size is still eleven, and this is the number (and not nine) that should be used for calculations involving Board size, such as setting a quorum.

The second method you can use to set Board size is to wing it—that is, simply elect Directors without setting a number, as long as you stay within the range stated in the Bylaws. If that is what you do, your Board size is the number of Directors in office immediately before the meeting.

The sample section above doesn't set out any particular qualifications for Directors. All Directors must be individuals, as opposed to corporations or some other legal entity. They can live anywhere in the world. They can be under the age of 18, although there may be some limitations on what they as a minor can do. You can set out any other qualifications that you want. If you do, you should change the heading to read "Number and Qualifications."

One area of some interest is whether you can discriminate in setting the qualifications for your Board. For example, an organization devoted to helping Vietnamese immigrants may want to provide that some or all of its Board consist of people of Vietnamese ancestry. The law is somewhat unclear in this area, but in most cases it appears that you can write in these types of qualifications. You should get legal advice for your own situation.

Section 3. Term and Election.

The term of office for Directors shall be one year. A Director may be reelected without limitation on the number of terms s/he may serve. The Board shall be elected by the majority of the members at the annual meeting of the members.

Discussion: The maximum term of office in Oregon for *elected* Directors is five years. Your Bylaws should not provide that a Director is elected until replaced, without setting a limit on the term, because this could violate the five year rule. A Director can be re-elected without limitation, although you may choose to limit the number of terms a Director may serve. Many Boards do this to assure new leadership.

Many organizations who have longer Board terms want to provide for staggered terms for their Directors, so that the Board always has some experienced members in place. One way to do this is to divide the total number of Directors into groups and elect each group at different times. For example:

Except for the initial adjustments of shorter terms needed in order to create staggered terms, the term of office for Directors shall be two years. The Board shall make provisions to stagger the terms of Directors so that each year the terms of as close as possible to one-half of the Directors shall expire. A Director may be reelected without limitation on the number of terms she or he may serve. The board shall elect its own members, except that a Director shall not vote on that member's own position.

If you have a variable size Board, you can accomplish staggering without this awkward language in your Bylaws. You can do this by setting your Board size the first year at one-half of what you eventually want, and the next year add the other one-half of the Directors.

Your Bylaws may provide that your members elect the Board at some time other than the annual meeting.

The clause above requires that the Directors are elected by majority vote. You may provide for any reasonable method of election that you want.

Some corporations have some or all Directors who are appointed or designated, rather than elected. The five-year term limit rule does not apply to these Directors. Those situations are outside the scope of these Bylaws. If you want to provide for this, you should review page 21 and get legal advice.

Occasionally, an organization will provide that a Director whose term has ended (often the President) will remain on the Board in an *ex officio* capacity. *Ex officio* means "by virtue of one's office," in this case, the office of President. Simply stating that the Board member holds the office in an *ex officio* capacity does not indicate whether the Board member has the right to vote. Organizations go both ways on whether the Director can vote, so it is vital to clarify if the Director is a "voting, *ex officio* Director" or a "non-voting *ex officio* Director."

Section 4. Removal.

Any Director may be removed, with or without cause, at a meeting called for that purpose, by a vote of a majority of the members entitled to vote at an election of Directors.

Discussion: Although it sounds harsh, many corporations opt to permit removal of Directors with or without cause. This means that you do not need to have a reason to remove a Director. If you try to limit removal only to certain circumstances, you run a serious risk that a situation will arise that you did not anticipate that requires removal of a Director and that is not spelled out in your reasons for removal. You are then stuck with a Director you don't want. Alternatively, the members may vote to remove the Director and the Director then has grounds for a lawsuit.

Many groups feel that if the members are willing to vote for removal, it makes no sense to leave that person on the Board. If you do decide to specify reasons for removal, you should get some legal help. These Bylaws are drafted on the assumption that a Director can be removed without the corporation having to prove its reason for removal.

If you do want to provide that your members can only remove Directors for certain reasons (that is, "for cause"), then you must include this in your Articles of Incorporation. Putting it in your Bylaws alone is not enough. If the Articles do not require cause in order to remove Directors, the members can remove with or without cause regardless of what your Bylaws say. If you do decide to specify reasons for removal in your Articles, you should get some legal help.

In order for the members to remove a Director, the number of votes cast for removal must be a sufficient number to elect the Director. The sample provision above requires removal by a majority of members entitled to vote at an election, because under Section 3 above, Directors are elected by a majority vote. If Section 3 had required a higher vote to elect the Board, Section 4 would have to require a higher vote to remove the Board.

A membership corporation may also permit its Board of Directors to remove a Director. You can do this by providing in your Bylaws (or Articles) the reasons for removal. This provision must be in your Bylaws (or Articles) at the time that the Director being removed took office. If it was, then the Board can remove its Director by a vote of the majority of Directors then in office. If your Bylaws (or Articles) do not set out cause for removing a Director, the Board cannot remove the Director.

A Religious Corporation may require different procedures by which the Board or any person can remove (with or without cause) a Director elected by the members. A Religious Corporation can even limit or prohibit the ability of a court to remove Directors.

Section 5. Vacancies.

Vacancies on the Board of Directors and newly created Board positions shall be filled by a majority vote of the Directors then on the Board of Directors.

Discussion: Your Bylaws can permit the Board or your members to fill vacancies. The provision above lets the Board fill it. Many groups choose to do this because they do not want to call a special membership meeting to fill the vacancy.

Notice that the wording above requires the vote of a majority of all Directors in office, not just a majority of those at the meeting, to fill a vacancy. You could word your Bylaws to allow the Board to fill a vacancy with a majority at the meeting; however, if the directors remaining in office are not enough to constitute a quorum, the law requires that they can fill the vacancy only by a majority vote of all the directors remaining in office. To keep it simple, we suggest that you use only one approach, which will work no matter what your situation is.

If you chose to have members fill the vacancy, you could use the following clause:

Vacancies on the Board of Directors and newly created board positions shall be filled by a majority vote of the members at a membership meeting called for that purpose within a reasonable time after the creation of the vacancy or position.

If you wish, your Bylaws can make different provisions than the one above for filling vacancies. For example, your President could appoint Directors to fill vacancies.

Section 6. Quorum and Action.

A quorum at a Board meeting shall be a majority of the number of Directors prescribed by the Board, or if no number is prescribed, a majority of the number in office immediately before the meeting begins. If a quorum is present, action is taken by a majority vote of Directors present. Where the law requires a majority vote of Directors in office to establish committees that exercise Board functions, to amend the Articles of Incorporation, to sell assets not in the regular course of business, to merge, to dissolve, or for other matters, such action is taken by that majority as required by law.

Discussion: A **quorum** is the number of Directors who must be present at a Board meeting in order for it to be held. If fewer Directors than the number set as a quorum show up, the Board cannot do any business and must reschedule the meeting. This is discussed on pages 327-28. A quorum has to be at least one-third of the Directors.

The calculation of the number of Directors needed to make a quorum is complicated by the fact that the Bylaws of some nonprofit corporations provide for a fixed number of Directors and some have a variable number.

If your Bylaws have a *fixed number of Directors*, then you should modify the wording in the sample clause above to state that the quorum is a majority (or some other percentage greater than one-third) of the fixed number of Directors. Be aware that if the actual number of Directors falls below the number fixed by your Bylaws (which can happen when a Director resigns or the term ends and she or he is not replaced or through some other cause), you still use the number fixed by your Bylaws (and not the number of Directors in office) in calculating whether you have a quorum. For example, if your Bylaws state that you have seven Directors and that your quorum is a majority of the Directors, you must have four Directors for a quorum, even if at that point you only have five Directors in office because of vacancies. You could clarify this for future Board by stating in your Bylaws that your quorum was four Directors.

If your Bylaws provide that you have a *variable Board size*, then you must determine how you set the actual number of your Directors before you can figure out your quorum rules. See the discussion above under Article III, Section 2 about deciding the Board number by prescribing it or by winging it. The rather awkward wording in the sample clause above is wording that could be used by any corporation that has a variable size Board. It is important to keep this wording in the Bylaws even if your Board for now has decided whether it will or will not prescribe Directors. This type of decision is rarely passed on to future Boards and the Bylaw provision may alert a future Board to the complexities of this issue.

You can raise the number of Directors required for a quorum to be more than the majority stated above. You can lower it to be as little as one-third of the fixed or prescribed Directors as described above. You cannot set the quorum at less than one-third. Many groups feel that one-third is too few Directors to conduct a meeting. The sample Bylaw above follows the common practice of setting the quorum at a majority of the Board.

Voting. Once a quorum is present, action must be taken by at least a majority vote of the Directors present. You can require more than a majority vote but not less.

There are two traps to avoid here. First, avoid using the phrase "present and voting" when describing the majority needed to take action. The majority must be of the Directors *present,* and not just the Directors *voting.* Consequently, if 11 Directors are present but only 9 vote (because 2 abstain), you need 6 votes, not 5, to decide on an action. It is a good idea to spell this out in your Bylaws, as the sample clause above does.

There are two traps to avoid.
Avoid using the phrase "present and voting"
and avoid replacing the word "majority"
with "50% plus 1."

Avoid replacing the word "majority" with "50% plus 1" as some Bylaws do. These are not the same thing. A majority means any number more than half, including 50.01. 50% plus 1 means one half plus one. So if you have 13 Directors at your meeting, a majority is 7, which is what most people will understand. 50% of 13 = 6½ + 1 = 7½. 7 is less than 7½ and so is not enough to constitute 50% + 1. The Board of 13 Directors at this meeting will need 8 Directors to take action. Some drafters use "50% plus 1" because they want to be clear that if there are an even number of people voting, more than half must vote for the action in order to pass it. However, the phrase "majority" means more than half, so there is no reason to use the misleading "50% plus 1."

There are some types of action (described in the sample clause above) which require the vote of a majority of Directors *in office* in order to be effective. These circumstances are put into the Bylaws so that you are sure to know the proper vote needed in those circumstances.

Section 7. Regular Meetings.

Regular meetings of the Board of Directors shall be held at the time and place to be determined by the Board of Directors. No other notice of the date, time, place, or purpose of these meetings is required, except as otherwise provided in these Bylaws.

Discussion: Regular meetings are those in which the time and place is regularly scheduled by the Board (for example, the first Monday of the month at 7:00 p.m. at the corporation's office). The law does not require additional notice of these meetings. If you change the time or place, this will make the meeting a special meeting, and you must give the notice you require for special meetings.

If you want, your Bylaws can require that you give notice of your regular meetings. The drawback is that, if your Bylaws require you to give notice and you don't, the action taken at the meeting may be invalid. Your Board may choose to give notice of regular meetings without such notice being required in your Bylaws.

Section 8. Special Meetings.

Special meetings of the Board of Directors shall be held at the time and place to be determined by the Board of Directors. Notice of such meetings, describing the date, time, place, and purpose of the meeting, shall be delivered to each Director personally or by telephone or by mail not less than two days prior to the special meeting. Written notice, if mailed postpaid and correctly addressed to the Director at the address shown in the corporate records, is effective when mailed.

Discussion: Special meetings are all meetings that are not regular meetings. If your Bylaws don't provide for a longer or shorter period for notice for special meetings, the law provides that notice is to be not less than two days. There are only certain circumstances in which you are required to state the purpose of special meetings and your Bylaws could require that only in those cases do you need to state the purpose in your special meeting notice. Rather than lengthen the Bylaws with this kind of detail, these sample Bylaws provide that you will always state the purpose of a special meeting. Your meeting will then by limited to the purposes stated. If you want to avoid this result, you will need to check with an attorney to be sure that you can consider the items you want to talk about without giving notice of them.

The presiding officer of the Board, the President, or twenty percent of the Directors then in office may call and give notice of the meeting of the Board. You can make different provisions than this in your Bylaws if you wish.

The law that provides for notice was drafted in 1989 before the advent of the Internet and it is not clear whether the statute allows electronic notice. In spite of this, many organizations use email for notice. If you decide to take the risk that your notice is improper and use email for notice, consult the discussion on pages 685-86 for how to minimize your risk.

Section 9. Meeting by Telecommunication or Computer.

Any regular or special meeting of the Board of Directors may be held by telephone, telecommunications or electronic means, as long as all Directors can hear or read each other's communications during the meeting or all communications during the meeting are immediately transmitted to each participating Director, and each participating Director is able to immediately send messages to all other participating Directors. All participating Directors shall be informed that a meeting is taking place at which official business may be transacted.

Discussion: You can hold a Board meeting by conference call or in a computer conference-type setting as long as everyone can hear or simultaneously communicate each other. The idea is that a meeting is a setting in which dissenters or those with questions about an action have the opportunity to communicate with everyone at once, so that the issue can be hashed out in a group setting.

A "meeting" by email does not meet this requirement, since email communication is not simultaneous and someone is often away from their email and responds later. Similarly, you cannot hold a Board meeting by phone by simply calling each Director individually and polling them. If your email communication or phone calls reveal that all Directors are in agreement, however, you can take action by consent without a meeting as described in Article III, Section 11 below.

Your Bylaws can prohibit these alternative meeting venues if you desire.

Section 10. Action by Consent.

Any action required or permitted by law to be taken at a meeting of the Board may be taken without a meeting if a consent in writing, setting forth the action to be taken or so taken, shall be signed by all the Directors. A written communication includes a communication that is transmitted or received by electronic means. Signing includes an electronic signature that is executed or adopted by a Director with the intent to sign.

Discussion: Notice that the Board can act without a meeting only if all Directors agree. A majority is not enough and there can be no abstentions. You need to obtain a written consent from each Director that is signed and dated. Consents by email are considered written consents as long as the Director intended to sign it. (For example, if someone else used the Director's account to consent, the Director did not intend to sign.) Your Bylaws can prohibit action by consent if you want to do so.

Article IV: Committees

Section 1. Executive Committee.

The Board of Directors may elect an Executive Committee. The Executive Committee shall have the authority to make on-going decisions between Board meetings and shall have the authority to make financial and budgetary decisions.

Discussion: Many Boards have an Executive Committee that can make decisions between Board meetings. Because these committees can exercise Board authority, the law states that they are supposed to comply with the provisions of Article IV, Section 3 below. This means that the committee should only have Board members on it and is supposed to be elected by the Board by a majority of all Directors in office.

Be careful about providing that the actions of the Executive Committee must be approved by the Board. The Executive Committee is then robbed of its function of authorizing actions between Board meetings.

In practice, most Executive Committees are not elected by the Board. Generally, the Bylaws state that the Executive Committee is composed of the officers of the organization or sometimes the officers plus one or two other Board member elected by the Board. If you want to be sure this complies with the law, the Board can confirm the appointment of the Executive Committee as set out in the Bylaws each time the membership of the committee changes by a vote of a majority of all Directors in office.

Be careful about providing that the actions of the Executive Committee must be approved by the Board. This means that the actions of the Executive Committee are not yet binding on the corporation until the Board meets. Your employees, volunteers, and outside parties cannot rely on them. The Executive Committee is then robbed of its function of authorizing actions between Board meetings.

Section 2. Other Committees.

The Board of Directors may establish such other committees as it deems necessary and desirable. Such committees may exercise the authority of the Board of Directors or may be advisory committees.

Discussion: If the committee the Board sets up does not exercise Board functions (for example, it does fundraising at the Board's direction or it makes recommendations to the Board on personnel matters but does not make the actual decisions), there are no restrictions as to who can be on these committees or how they are selected. If you want to provide for this further—for example, by naming standing committees—you can add these provisions to the Bylaws or enact them as policies, which will be easier to change when your committees change.

Section 3. Composition of Committees Exercising Board Functions.

Any committee that exercises any authority of the Board of Directors shall be composed of two or more Directors, elected by the Board of Directors by a majority vote of the number of Directors prescribed by the Board, or if no number is prescribed, by a majority vote of all Directors in office at that time.

Discussion: This section as written requires that any committee that exercises Board functions (that is, makes Board level decisions) must consist of two or more Directors, should not include anyone else who votes, and must be elected not by majority vote of the Directors at the meeting but by a majority of Directors prescribed or in office at that time. Review the discussion on page 59 about fixed and variable size Boards. If you do not have a variable Board, you could amend this to read "a majority of the number of Directors fixed by the Bylaws." If you place voting non-Directors on these committees, but this would constitute an example of allowing non-Directors to govern the corporation. These types of provisions need to be in the Articles of Incorporation. See pp. 19-20.

Be careful about providing that the actions of a committee exercising the functions of the Board must be approved by the Board. As with the Executive Committee, your employees, volunteers, and outside parties cannot rely on the committee's decisions.

Section 4. Quorum and Action.

A quorum at a Committee meeting exercising Board authority shall be a majority of all Committee members in office immediately before the meeting begins. If a quorum is present, action is taken by a majority vote of Directors present.

Discussion: Your Bylaws may regulate your Committee meetings, notices, quorum, and voting to the same extent it can regulate these matter for the Board.

Section 5. Limitations on the Powers of Committees.

No committee may authorize payment of a dividend or any part of the income or profit of the corporation to its Directors or officers; may approve dissolution, merger, or the sale, pledge, or transfer of all or substantially all of the corporation's assets; may elect, appoint, or remove Directors or fill vacancies on the Board or on any of its committees; nor may adopt, amend, or repeal the Articles, Bylaws, or any resolution by the Board of Directors.

Discussion: The above limitations are set by the statute and cannot be changed. It is useful to include them so that your committees do not inadvertently perform some actions they cannot perform. Your Bylaws can further limit the authority of Board committees to act, if you want to do so.

Article V: Officers

Section 1. Titles.

The officers of this corporation shall be the President, Secretary, and Treasurer.

Discussion: The law says you have to have a President and Secretary, although you can use other terms for these roles and the same person can fill both jobs. The statute does not say exactly what duties these officers shall perform, except that one of them shall be responsible to see that Board minutes are prepared and that one of them shall authenticate the records of the corporation.

Your corporation can have more officers than the two required by law if you want. We highly recommend that you have a Treasurer. Many nonprofits are running into problems with inadequate financial policies. Even small nonprofits need at least two eyes on the finances and an officer, who may be one of those sets of eyes, needs to ensure that this is done. See Chapter 25 for more discussion of this issue of great concern to nonprofits and their regulators.

Oregon law does not state that the officers must be Directors, although in many nonprofits they are. If you want to require that your officers be Directors, you can add a sentence that says "*All officers of this corporation must be members of the Board of Directors.*" You should change the title to read "Titles and Qualifications."

Section 2. Election.

The Board of Directors shall elect the officers to serve one year terms. An officer may be reelected without limitation on the number of terms s/he may serve.

Discussion: The officers may be elected by the Board or appointed or designated as provided in the Articles or Bylaws. If you are going to select officers by some method other than Board election, you should get some legal advice. Although the law does not limit the officers' terms, if the officers are required to be Directors, the elected Directors' terms cannot exceed five years. Many nonprofits limit the number of consecutive terms an officer can serve to assure new leadership.

Most nonprofits set one year terms for officers. Otherwise, your Board may run into issues if the officer has a multi-year term and the officer's term on the Board expires before her/his term as an officer.

Section 3. Vacancy.

A vacancy in any office shall be filled not later than the first regular meeting of the Board of Directors following the vacancy.

Discussion: You can vary this, but you generally do not want too much time to go by with a vacant office.

Section 4. Other Officers.

The Board of Directors may elect or appoint other officers, agents and employees as it shall deem necessary and desirable. They shall hold their offices for such terms and have such authority and perform such duties as shall be determined by the Board of Directors.

Discussion: The Board has a great deal of authority to appoint other officers. Some corporations may include the Executive Director as an officer so that the Executive Director can sign contracts and forms that require an officer's signature. If you do name your Executive Director as an officer, you need to review some of the provisions above about officers. You may provide that the Executive Director serves as an officer as long as she or he holds the position of Executive Director, rather than requiring the Board to re-elect the Executive Director every year. If you require that your officers be Directors, you will need to modify this unless the Executive Director is a board member. See pages 310-311 and 343 for difficulties with this arrangement.

Some nonprofits make the Executive Director an *ex officio* nonvoting Board member to get around these difficulties. *Ex officio* means that the Director holds a Board position by virtue of an office (in this case, the position of Executive Director). Most Boards do not name the Executive Director as an officer but require that the Executive Director attend Board meetings to keep the Board informed about corporate matters. A Board officer independent of the Executive Director signs contracts and other documents that are important enough to require an officer's signature.

Section 5. President.

The President shall be the chief officer of the corporation and shall act as the Chair of the Board. The President shall have any other powers and duties as may be prescribed by the Board of Directors.

Discussion: You are free to state the powers of the President to suit your needs; however, keep in mind that it is generally better to draft general descriptions rather than specific ones. You can be more specific in Board policies.

Section 6. Secretary.

The Secretary shall have overall responsibility for all recordkeeping. The Secretary shall perform, or cause to be performed, the following duties: (a) official recording of the minutes of all proceedings of the Board of Directors and members' meetings and actions; (b) provision for notice of all meetings of the Board of Directors and members; (c) authentication of the records of the corporation; (d) maintenance of current and accurate membership lists; and (e) any other duties as may be prescribed by the Board of Directors.

Discussion: The Bylaws or the Board must delegate to one of the officers the responsibility for preparing minutes of the Directors' and members' meetings and for authenticating the records of the corporation. Most Bylaws delegate this authority to its Secretary. The clause above also includes other duties commonly performed by the Secretary. You may want to leave the first sentence in the Bylaws and put the remainder of this in the Board policies, along with any other duties you want to add.

Section 7. Treasurer

The Treasurer shall have the overall responsibility for all corporate funds. The Treasurer shall perform, or cause to be performed, the following duties: (a) maintenance of full and accurate accounts of all financial records of the corporation; (b) deposit of all monies and other valuable effects in the name and to the credit of the corporation in such depositories as may be designated by the Board of Directors; (c) disbursement of all funds when proper to do so; (d) presentation of financial reports as to the financial condition of the corporation to the Board of Directors; and (e) any other duties as may be prescribed by the Board of Directors.

The role of Treasurer has become increasingly important. See Chapter 25. As with the duties of other officers, you may want to leave the first sentence in the Bylaws and put the remainder of this in the Board policies, along with any other duties you want to add.

Article VI: Corporate Indemnity

This corporation will indemnify to the fullest extent not prohibited by law any person who is made, or threatened to be made, a party to an action, suit, or other proceeding, by reason of the fact that the person is or was a Director, officer, employee, volunteer, or agent of the corporation or a fiduciary within the meaning of the Employee Retirement Income Security Act of 1974 (or its corresponding future provisions) with respect to any employee benefit plan of the corporation. No amendment to this Article that limits the corporation's obligation to indemnify any person shall have any effect on such obligation for any act or omission that occurs prior to the later of the effective date of the amendment or the date notice of the amendment is given to the person. The corporation shall interpret this indemnification provision to extend to all persons covered by its provisions the most liberal possible indemnification—substantively, procedurally, and otherwise.

Discussion: Indemnification is described on pp. 360-62. This indemnification provision allows the corporation to indemnify its Directors and officers to the fullest extent allowed by law. This is the result desired by many Directors; some will not serve without this. You can choose to provide no indemnification or to provide more limited indemnification.

Article VII: Amendments to Bylaws

The Board of Directors may vote to amend or repeal these Bylaws or to adopt new ones by a majority vote of Directors present, if a quorum is present. Any amendment to the Bylaws to increase the quorum required for any member action or to add to, change or delete the vote required for any member action must be approved by the members. Prior to the adoption of the amendment, each Director shall be given at least two days notice of the date, time, and place of the meeting at which the proposed amendment is to be considered, and the notice shall state that one of the purposes of the meeting is to consider a proposed amendment to the Bylaws and shall contain a copy of the proposed amendment.

The members may vote to amend or repeal these Bylaws or adopt new ones by a majority vote of the members represented and voting. In amending or repealing a particular Bylaw, the members may provide expressly that the Board may not amend or repeal that Bylaw. Prior to the adoption of the amendment, each member shall be given the notice of meeting required by these Bylaws and the notice shall state that one of the purposes of the meeting is to consider a proposed amendment to the Bylaws and shall contain a copy of the proposed amendment.

Discussion: In a membership corporation in which your members have the power to amend Bylaws, your Bylaws may provide that they can be amended by the Board, by the members, or by both. The provision above is for corporations that want to give both the Board and the members the power to amend the Bylaws.

If you want to give the Board the sole authority to amend Bylaws, you must provide in Article II, Section 1 that members do not have the right to amend Bylaws. You can do this by adding "except that members may not amend or repeal Bylaws or adopt new ones" to the Article II, Section 1 sample provision in this book. You may then use this provision as Article VII to give the Board the sole authority to amend Bylaws:

The Board of Directors have the sole right to amend or repeal these Bylaws and may vote to amend or repeal these Bylaws or to adopt new ones by a majority vote of Directors present, if a quorum is present. Prior to the adoption of the amendment, each Director shall be given at least two days notice of the date, time, and place of the meeting at which the proposed amendment is to be considered, and the notice shall state that one of the purposes of the meeting is to consider a proposed amendment to the Bylaws and shall contain a copy of the proposed amendment.

If you want to give your members the sole authority to amend the Bylaws, you must include a provision to this effect in your Articles of Incorporation or in an amendment to your Articles. Putting it in your Bylaws alone is not sufficient. You should then include this provision as Article VII:

The members have the sole right to amend or repeal these Bylaws and may vote to amend or repeal these Bylaws or adopt new ones by a majority vote of the members represented and voting. Prior to the adoption of the amendment, each member shall be given the notice of meeting required by these Bylaws and the notice shall state that one of the purposes of the meeting is to consider a proposed amendment to the Bylaws and shall contain a copy of the proposed amendment.

We suggest that you consider carefully before you give members the sole power to amend the Bylaws. Bylaws are the guidebook for how to govern the corporation, which is the Board's job. Generally, the Board is best positioned to know when its methods of governance need amendment. Many Board members would hesitate to serve on a Board if they had no say over its governance mechanisms.

You can require a greater vote (but not a lesser one) to amend your Bylaws. You can provide a different period for notice to the Board, either longer or shorter. However, your notice does have to state that one of the purposes of the meeting is to consider a proposed amendment to the Bylaws and shall contain a copy or summary of the proposed amendment.

> *If you want to provide that only the members can amend the Bylaws, you will need to put a provision to that effect in your Articles. Putting it in your Bylaws alone is not enough.*

It is possible to set up a nonprofit corporation whose Bylaws can only be amended with the approval of a third person. You should get legal help to draft this type of provision.

DATE ADOPTED: _____

Discussion: It is helpful to include the date your Bylaws are adopted, so that it is easier to track Bylaws and amendments chronologically and so that you can know what your current Bylaws are.

> *Consult Appendix 1 if you would like information about source material related to this Chapter.*
>
> *If you were using this chapter to draft your Bylaws as part of the process in Chapter 3 of setting up your Oregon nonprofit corporation, you should now return to Chapter 3 and finish that process. Then, if you want your organization to be tax-exempt, you must apply for tax-exempt status. You must apply separately to the federal government and to the state and county. Part II explains how to do this. If you are not interested in obtaining tax exemption, you should go on to Part III.*

PART II

THE TAX-EXEMPT ORGANIZATION

5
FEDERAL TAX-EXEMPT STATUS

THIS CHAPTER COVERS

- Tax Exemption: Do You Want It?
- §501(c)(3): Public Benefit and Religious Organizations
- §501(c)(4): Civic Leagues and Social Welfare Organizations
- Other Exempt Groups
- Affiliated Organizations
- General Information for Organizations Seeking Any Type of Tax Exemption

Your group becomes a nonprofit corporation by meeting the requirements of Oregon law. However, being a nonprofit corporation does not automatically mean that you are exempt from paying all federal, state, regional, and county taxes. In order to avoid paying corporate income taxes and property taxes, you must apply for and receive tax exemption from the federal, state, regional and county governments separately. Not every nonprofit corporation will qualify for these exemptions.

This chapter discusses federal tax exemption; Chapter 11 discusses state, regional and county tax exemptions.

Internal Revenue Code Section 50l(c)(3) of the federal tax code allows an exemption for a variety of groups that work for the public interest. Because this exemption offers the most benefits, it is the exemption that most groups that provide public benefits seek and will be the focus of most of this chapter. When people talk about "being tax-exempt," they are usually referring to exemption under §501(c)(3).

We'll also describe exemptions under §501(c)(4) for social welfare organizations and those available for mutual benefit organizations and political groups. We explain how and why some §501(c)(3) exempt organizations that have activities that don't qualify under §501(c)(3) create affiliated organizations to accomplish all of their goals. At the end of the chapter is some information that may be of interest to all types of tax-exempt groups.

THE OREGON NONPROFIT CORPORATION HANDBOOK

Tax Exemption: Do You Want It?

Being recognized as a nonprofit group is a status that state law confers on your group. The fact that you are nonprofit does not mean that you are automatically exempt from paying taxes. Whether or not your nonprofit is tax-exempt is decided by the federal, state, county, or local taxing agency involved. This chapter discusses federal tax exemption and Chapter 11 discusses the state, county, and local tax exemptions.

The federal Internal Revenue Code taxes individuals, corporations, and other entities on taxable income that they earn. There is a special subsection of the Internal Revenue Code, §501(c), that exempts certain (but not all) nonprofit organizations from paying federal income tax. If your nonprofit is granted an exemption under any of the sections of the Internal Revenue Code that grant tax exemption, you will not have to pay federal income tax (except on unrelated business income). Groups exempt under §501(c)(3) have some additional benefits that most other exempt nonprofits do not have:

- Donors who make donations to §501(c)(3) groups (except to groups that test for public safety) can deduct the donations as a charitable contribution on their tax returns (to the extent allowed by law). This encourages contributions to (c)(3) groups.

- Most foundations are exempt themselves under §501(c)(3) and can only make grants to §501(c)(3) groups or to projects that would qualify as exempt under §501(c)(3). Foundations have to jump through special hoops if the group they give to does not have an exemption. Consequently, most foundations will give only to §501(c)(3) organizations.

- §501(c)(3)s will qualify for Oregon income tax exemption and (c)(3) status is required for some county property tax exemptions.

- §501(c)(3)s may qualify for special bulk mailing rates.

Because of these advantages, §501(c)(3) exemption is the status that many public benefit and religious groups seek. Most groups that want to be recognized as exempt under §501(c)(3) must file an application.

There are some drawbacks to being exempt under §501(c)(3). To apply, you must fill out a fairly involved application and pay a fee. (See pp. 115-16 for the fee.) In addition, your organization will have to file informational returns and may be subject to IRS scrutiny. There are more rules to follow, and occasionally the consequences can be quite drastic if you fail to follow the rules. (See, for example, the discussion about personal Board liabilities in Chapter 17).

For many groups, the benefits outweigh the disadvantages. However, you should examine whether you need tax-exempt status before you go through the process. If you are applying to be exempt because you do not want to pay federal income tax, consider whether you will have a federal income tax obligation. Many nonprofit groups won't pay federal income tax even if they file the corporation tax return, because their income comes from sources (like gifts and grants) that are not taxable, or because they spend all their income on items that are deductible as expenses.

If you are operating for public benefit or are a religious corporation, are you looking to attract funding (such as foundation money or donations that require a charitable deduction) that requires you be exempt under §501(c)(3)? If not, but you want protection from paying income tax, you may want to consider whether you are exempt under §501(c)(4) as a social welfare organization or civic league. (c)(4) organizations are not as closely regulated as §501(c)(3). You do not have to apply for recognition as a (c)(4) although many groups will want to apply so that they know whether the IRS really recognizes their exemption. See p. 143.

If you are nonprofit but not tax-exempt, you should be aware that this creates some interesting accounting issues for you. You may need to get professional help.

§501(c)(3):Public Benefit and Religious Organizations

§501(c)(3) grants an exemption from income taxation for charitable, religious, educational, scientific, and literary groups and for groups testing for public safety or operating to foster national or international amateur sports competitions or to prevent cruelty to animals or children. The advantages to having this status are described above.

This section will discuss:

- Who qualifies for §501(c)(3) exemption,
- Classification of §501(c)(3) groups as private foundations and public charities and what this characterization means,
- Who must file the application,
- When the exemption is effective, and
- What type of ruling you should seek.

Who Qualifies for §501(c)(3) Exemption

In order to qualify as exempt under §50l(c)(3), your group must be able to show these things:

- You are a nonprofit corporation, community chest, fund, foundation or association; and
- Your purposes are exempt; and
- You are both organized and operated exclusively for exempt purposes; and
- No private person or profit corporation is profiting from your group; and
- You group does not do substantial lobbying or engage in any political activity.

Structure

The law requires that your group be a corporation, a community chest, a fund, or a foundation. The statute is an old one and the ways that most groups organize as nonprofit entities has evolved. In practice, the IRS inquires on the application for exemption about whether you are a corporation, an unincorporated association, a trust, or a limited liability company. This book focuses on corporations, although you can use Part II on tax exemption whether you are an unincorporated association or a nonprofit corporation.

If you are a trust, you need legal help. In some very restricted circumstances, the IRS recognizes limited liability companies as exempt. For your limited liability company to be exempt, all of the members of the LLC must be §501(c)(3) organizations. If that is the case, you may not need to apply for recognition that you are exempt unless you plan to seek charitable contributions or foundation funding. You will need legal help if you are a limited liability company that is considering applying for exemption.

Exempt Purposes

50l(c)(3) recognizes these purposes as exempt: charitable, educational, scientific, religious, literary, testing for public safety, fostering national or international amateur sports competitions or prevention of cruelty to animals or children. Health clinics, synagogues, churches, cultural centers, schools, social services, foundations and charities are examples of groups that can qualify under this section.

CHARITABLE

Your group is classified as *charitable* if you provide for the relief of the poor or underprivileged; work to advance science, religion or education; assist in maintaining public works; promote the arts; or promote social welfare by lessening the burdens of government, lessening neighborhood tensions, eliminating discrimination, defending civil rights secured by law, or combatting community deterioration. Your group must benefit a broad class of beneficiaries. A group that expects all of its costs to be paid by the users or beneficiaries of its services will frequently have difficulty obtaining exemption as a charitable organization. To be exempt, charitable groups usually must get some of their finances elsewhere, such as from government subsidies or private donations. Nonprofit hospices, low-income housing organizations, hospitals, land conservancies, and relief organizations are examples.

EDUCATIONAL

The term *educational* refers to teaching individuals to develop their capabilities or instructing the public on subjects useful to the individual or beneficial to the community. Schools, resource centers for racial and ethnic groups, museums, orchestras, and public discussion groups are examples of educational groups. By virtue of a special statute, childcare agencies qualify as educational if substantially all of the care is for the purpose of permitting individuals to be employed, and the services are provided away from the child's home and are available to the general public.

Groups can be educational that advocate for a particular viewpoint. Generally, the IRS accepts a wide range of advocacy, unless your viewpoints are quite extreme and rely on hate tactics rather than education. If your group represents a particular position, your method should present a factual foundation for your viewpoint. The IRS views the following as indications that your method is not educational: viewpoints unsupported by fact that are a significant part of your communications; distorted facts; substantial use of inflammatory and disparaging terms and conclusions based on emotions rather than objectivity; and approaches that are not aimed at developing an understanding on the part of those you communicate with, given their backgrounds.

Groups can be educational that advocate for a particular viewpoint. Generally, the IRS accepts a wide range of advocacy, unless your viewpoints are quite extreme and rely on hate tactics rather than education.

SCIENTIFIC

Organizations with *scientific* purposes are exempt only if they serve a public rather than a private interest. Scientific research is regarded as carried on in the public interest if the results are made available to the public; if the research was conducted for a government agency; or if the research was directed toward benefiting the public. Special rules apply for scientific research funded by for-profit companies. Read IRS Publication 557's section on "Scientific Organizations" if you plan to do scientific research. Organizations that promote motion picture photography and medical services for poor communities have been found exempt.

RELIGIOUS

A *religious* organization is one in which its particular beliefs are truly and sincerely held and in which its practices and rituals are not illegal. Some religious organizations focus on worship, such as churches, synagogues, temples, and mosques. However, the religious category includes other organizations with religious purposes. Exemptions as religious organizations have been given for nonprofits that prepare food products to satisfy religious dietary rules, facilities that bring together young people and religious leaders, and federations of religious groups. If you are a religious organization, you should get and read IRS Publication 1828 "Tax Guide for Churches and Religious Organizations." Because of the constitutional protections for religious groups, the tax laws often contain twists to avoid unconstitutional actions. This publication contains a great deal of information helpful to religious organizations about the special provisions of the law.

LITERARY

The law does not define what a *literary* organization is. Any group that would qualify as a literary organization would probably also qualify as an educational organization.

PUBLIC SAFETY

Organizations that test for *public safety* are nonprofit groups that do consumer testing. An example would be an organization that tests electrical appliances for safety. Unlike all other groups exempt under §501(c)(3), contributors to organizations that test for public safety cannot claim a charitable deduction for their contributions.

AMATEUR SPORTS

If your group fosters national or international *amateur sports* competitions, you may receive tax-exempt status under §501(c)(3) as long as no part of your activities involve the provision of athletic facilities or equipment. However, if your group is a *qualified amateur sports organization*, you can provide facilities and equipment to your members, and your group can be local or regional in nature, rather than national or international. A *qualified amateur sports organization* is any organization organized and operated exclusively to foster national or international amateur sports competition primarily by conducting national or international competition in sports or by developing amateur athletes for national or international sports competitions. Examples are the U.S. Olympic Committee and Little League organizations.

PREVENTION OF CRUELTY

There has been little definition of the term *prevention of cruelty to animals and children*. Types of organizational purposes that would qualify under this section include organizations working against child abuse, humane societies, animal rights groups, and animal sanctuaries.

SPECIAL ISSUES

There are some kinds of groups for which the IRS has developed special guidelines, including low income housing, churches, hospitals, organizations providing legal services, organizations doing research, organizations with programs and activities outside of the United States, and schools. If your organization seems to fit one of these categories, you should get some professional help *before* you file your application.

---

*To determine if you are organized for an exempt purpose,
the IRS will look at your Articles of Incorporation
and your Bylaws. Chapter 3 contains the provisions
that should be inserted in the Articles to meet
the organizational requirements.*

Organized and Operated

In order to qualify for tax exemption under §50l(c)(3), you must be both *organized* and *operated* exclusively for an exempt purpose. In true legal fashion, the word *exclusively* has been interpreted to mean "primarily" or "substantially."

To determine if you are *organized* for an exempt purpose, the IRS will look at your Articles of Incorporation and your Bylaws. These documents must limit your purposes to one or more exempt purposes and cannot contain words allowing you to engage in activities that further a nonexempt purpose, except as an insubstantial part of your activities. Chapter 3 (pp. 33-39) contains the provisions that should be inserted in the Articles to meet the organizational requirements. Be sure that you are prepared to comply with these provisions before you copy them.

You are *operated* for an exempt purpose if in your actual operations you engage primarily in activities which further your exempt purpose. There must be a fairly direct connection between the activity of your group and your exempt purpose. For example, a group that is set up to provide music and cultural enrichment to the public but which in fact spends most of its time and earns most of its money from the sale of food and drinks will probably not be given an exemption. The IRS engages in an ongoing check to be sure this requirement is observed through your annual filing of Form 990.

> *One problem encountered by some groups seeking tax exemption is that the group's main activity is to run a business (provide goods or services for a fee) and the business is similar to a commercial (for-profit) business. The IRS believes that running this kind of business is not an exempt purpose.*

One problem encountered by some groups seeking tax exemption is that the group's main activity is to run a business (provide goods or services for a fee) and the business is similar to a commercial (for-profit) business. The IRS believes that running this kind of business is not an exempt purpose. You need to distinguish your group from a commercial business in order to get an exemption. To do this, it will help if you can show that you engage in other exempt activities besides the business; the business is charitable because it provides goods or services at less than your cost to the needy; or the goods are provided or the service is performed in some way that is different than a commercial business and that furthers your exempt purpose. The fact that you plan to use the money from the business for your other exempt purposes does **not** help you.

> *Example*: A nonprofit bookstore will probably be denied an exemption as long as there is nothing to distinguish it from other bookstores. However, a nonprofit theater group charging for theatrical performances by little known playwrights may get an exemption, if it can show that it chooses plays based on their artistic merit and not on their commercial value.

No Inurement or Insubstantial Private Benefit

The third criterion for exemption is that no insider or other private person or corporation can receive any part of the net earnings of your group. The net earnings are what is left of the gross receipts of the group after reasonable expenses are paid. (People who perform work for the group can be paid a reasonable salary for their work, since this is part of the legitimate expenses of the group.) Upon dissolution, the assets of your group after paying off the debts must be distributed for exempt purposes or to other groups which qualify as exempt under 50l(c)(3). Both of these provisions must be included in your Articles of Incorporation (see pp. 33-39). The area of improper benefit is a great concern of the IRS's and you should get legal help if you have an insider (a founder, Board member, or other person closely associated with you, or their family member or business) that may be benefiting financially from your nonprofit in the form of a salary, compensation, lease payment, or other financial arrangement.

*The law allows most (c)(3) groups
to engage in limited lobbying.*

Lobbying

Your group cannot engage in lobbying as a *substantial* part of your activity. IRS considers these things to be lobbying:

- Engaging in activities designed to influence legislation or the outcome of an initiative or referendum;

- Having a primary purpose which may be attained only by legislation or defeat of legislation and advocating for the attainment of this goal. For example, a group whose main purpose was to work for passage of a constitutional amendment allowing or prohibiting abortion would be considered a "lobbying" group.

The law allows most (c)(3) groups to engage in limited lobbying. Your group may also advocate for social or civic changes or present opinions on controversial issues with the intention of molding public opinion, which is often done in ways that are not lobbying. See Chapter 8 for a more detailed discussion of lobbying. *Note that lobbying has to do with issues and not with candidates or political parties. Those kinds of activities are political activities.*

*Your group cannot participate in any political campaign
on behalf of or in opposition to a candidate for public office.
If you engage in any political activity of this type,
you will not get an exemption.*

Political Activity

Your group cannot participate in any political campaign on behalf of or in opposition to a candidate for public office and the Articles of Incorporation should include a prohibition of political activity. If you engage in *any* political activity of this type, you will not get an exemption. Chapter 8 discusses this in more detail.

Classifications of §501(c)(3) Groups

§501(c)(3) organizations are divided into two broad groupings:

- Private Foundations
- Public Charities

Private Foundations are groups that are usually funded largely by one or a few donors. They generally make grants to other §501(c)(3) organizations, although some run charitable, educational, or other tax-exempt programs.

Public Charities are churches, schools, hospitals, public safety groups, governmental units, or related organizations or are groups that provide tax-exempt programs and that are funded by a number of sources.

Most groups that can do so prefer to qualify as public charities, because there are no taxes to pay (except for the unrelated business income tax), fewer restrictions, and fewer reporting requirements).

Most groups that can do so prefer to qualify as public charities, because there are no taxes to pay (except for the unrelated business income tax), fewer restrictions, and fewer reporting requirements (which means less paperwork and lower legal and accounting fees). In addition, some donors get a greater tax deduction for giving to public charities. Also, funding organizations have fewer restrictions on giving to public charities. Private foundations generally pay more attorney and accountant fees to comply with the heavier government regulation.

Because most groups prefer the public charity status, because the private foundation rules can get very complex, and because most private foundations have funds to obtain professional help, this book will focus mainly on the public charities. We will include some information on private foundations so that you have some idea what to expect if your group is a private foundation. If you know you want to apply as a public charity, you should skip this Private Foundations section and move on to page 101. A good deal of what is covered in this book applies to all §501(c)(3) groups, including private foundations.

Private Foundations

The IRS assumes that every §501(c)(3) is a private foundation, unless it establishes that it is a public charity. Private foundations have been the subject of a lot of abuse in the past. This frequently occurs because a wealthy donor sets a foundation up for tax purposes and then finds ways to use the foundation for his or her own private benefit. To prevent this, Congress has enacted a number of complex regulatory laws which you will see reflected in the discussion that follows.

THE OREGON NONPROFIT CORPORATION HANDBOOK

REPORTING REQUIREMENTS

Private foundations are subject to substantial recordkeeping and reporting requirements. A private foundation must keep records to protect itself against penalties and to protect the various persons who may be part of, or otherwise related to, the foundation against penalties. It must also keep records to establish that transactions it engages in do not involve self-dealing, satisfy minimum distribution rules, do not violate excess business holding laws, do not jeopardize its charitable purposes, and are otherwise acceptable to the IRS. If it makes grants, it must keep records of the grant and, if it makes grants to individuals, it must get advance approval from the IRS of its grant criteria. In addition, a private foundation is required to file Form 990-PF and may be required to file other returns, depending on what it does.

RESTRICTIONS ON OPERATIONS

Congress has enacted a variety of restrictions on the operations of private foundations in an effort to ensure that their assets and income are used for the public benefit and not for the private benefit of those who control the foundation. These restrictions include:

- *Prohibitions against self-dealing.* A private foundation and certain related persons ("disqualified persons") are restricted from dealing with each other in a variety of transactions, such as the sale, exchange, or leasing of property; lending of money or extension of credit; furnishing of goods, services, or facilities; payment of compensation for expenses to a disqualified person; and the use of the foundations assets and income by disqualified persons.

- *Minimum distribution requirements.* A private foundation must distribute a minimum percentage of its noncharitable assets each year.

- *Divestiture of excess business holdings.* The law imposes limits on the combined holdings of a private foundation and disqualified persons.

- *Prohibitions of jeopardizing investments.* A private foundation cannot make investments that jeopardize the carrying out of its exempt purposes. Generally these are investments that are made without exercising ordinary business care and prudence in providing for the long- and short-term financial needs of the foundation.

- *Program limitations.* Private foundations are subject to restrictions on lobbying; election activities; making grants to individuals for travel, study, or similar activities; making grants to organizations that are not public charities; and spending money for noncharitable purposes.

TAXES AND PENALTIES

Private foundations may be subject to a variety of taxes and penalties, including:

- Taxes on unrelated business income.
- Taxes on net investment income.
- Taxes on self-dealing.

- Taxes on failure to distribute income.
- Taxes on excess business holdings.
- Taxes on investments that jeopardize charitable purposes.

Taxes on expenditures in violation of the program limitations rules.

PRIVATE OPERATING FOUNDATION

In the private foundation category, an important subcategory is the private operating foundation. A private operating foundation is a private foundation that, although it lacks general public support, runs its own programs for its educational, charitable, or religious purposes, as opposed to making grants to other organizations for these purposes. A private operating foundation must meet two tests:

1. an *income test*, that requires it to spend a specified minimum of its income directly for its exempt purposes; *and*

2. *either*

    i. an *asset test*, which ensures that the bulk of its assets are devoted directly to exempt activities, *or*

    ii. an *endowment test*, which requires that a substantial part of its investment returns be used for its exempt purposes, *or*

    iii. a *support test*, which requires a broader base of public support for the foundation.

The advantages of being classified as a private operating foundation include more relaxed requirements about what percent return on its investment assets must be distributed each year, a greater ability to attract grants to it, and greater tax deductions for donors who contribute to it. Private operating foundations are sometimes better able to build an endowment fund. In some cases, the private operating foundation does not have to pay the excise tax.

Public Charities

Your organization will be recognized by the IRS as a public charity if you can show you fall in at least one of these categories:

1. A church or a convention or association of churches
2. A school, college, or university
3. A hospital or medical research organization
4. A governmental unit
5. A supporting organization (one that is connected with a group described in #1-4 above or #7-9 below)
6. A public safety organization

7. A development foundation for a state or local government college or university
8. A publicly supported organization (PSO)
9. A fee/activity supported organization (FASO)

The first 6 groups on this list are largely defined in terms of their purposes. The groups referred to as #7, #8, and #9 are defined in terms of where they get their support. (This means that a group might qualify as a church, based on its purpose and might also qualify as a PSO and FASO based on where its support comes from.) Remember that in addition to meeting the terms of the definitions, you must also meet the other requirements set out in the chapter if you want §501(c)(3) status.

Glance at the list above. If none of the first seven seem to describe you, you will probably need to qualify under #8 or #9. Most public charities that are not churches fall in categories #8 or #9.

1. CHURCHES

The IRS and the courts have had some difficulty in defining what is (and what is not) a *church*. Although most of the terminology used by the IRS is drawn from Christian faiths, Jewish, Muslim, Buddhists, Hindu, and other non-Christian religious organizations can qualify as "churches." The IRS makes the determination of what is a church on a case by case basis. It typically looks at whether the organization has:

- a distinct legal existence;
- a recognized creed and form of worship;
- a definite and distinct ecclesiastical government;
- a formal code of doctrine and discipline;
- a distinct religious history;
- a membership not associated with any other church or denomination;
- a complete organization of ordained ministers ministering to their congregations;
- ordained ministers selected after completing prescribed courses of study;
- a literature of its own;
- established places of worship;
- regular congregations;
- regular religious services;
- schools for the religious instruction of its young;
- schools for the preparation of its ministers.

Unfortunately, the IRS criteria for what constitutes a church are drawn heavily from the Judeo-Christian tradition and religions from different traditions have difficulty fitting this structure. If your religion has at its heart a different way of constituting itself, you may need legal help to qualify as a "church" and should get it *before* you submit the application. The IRS will recognize religions outside the Judeo-Christian tradition as a church but you will need to make a special presentation of your history and structure and probably answer numerous questions.

The church category has been the subject of some abuses by individuals and groups who attempt to set themselves up as churches mainly in order to obtain favorable tax benefits. The IRS is aware of this. Although the IRS does not ordinarily try to determine the religious merit of a group, it will reject the application if it finds that the organization is not exclusively organized or operated for religious purposes or that private persons are profiting from the group. Organizations claiming to be churches are scrutinized by the IRS in the application process.

> *Organizations claiming to be churches are scrutinized by the IRS in the application process.*

2. SCHOOLS

In order to qualify for exemption as a *school*, college, or university, your group must be an educational organization that normally maintains a regular faculty and curriculum and normally has a regularly enrolled body of students in attendance at the place where your educational activities are regularly carried on.

If you seek classification as a school, you must demonstrate to the IRS that you follow racially nondiscriminatory policies toward students in admissions, school programs, and educational policies. To establish this, you must, at a minimum, do the following:

- include in your Articles or Bylaws or in a resolution adopted by your Board a statement that the school has and pursues a racially nondiscriminatory policy;

- include a statement of this policy in all your brochures and catalogues dealing with student admissions, programs, and scholarships;

- refer to the policy in all written advertisements;

- publish notice of the policy in a newspaper of general circulation or through one of the broadcast media every year (some schools are exempt from this requirement);

- provide a schedule showing the racial composition of the students, faculty, and staff;

- provide a listing of the racial composition of loan and scholarship recipients; and

- supply the names of your incorporators, founders, Directors, and donors of land or buildings and state whether any of these have as an objective the promotion or maintenance of segregated public or private education.

3. HOSPITALS AND MEDICAL RESEARCH ORGANIZATIONS

A *hospital* is an organization whose principal purpose is to provide medical or hospital care or medical education or medical research for the community's benefit. The organization must provide medical or hospital care to patients on its premises or in its facilities on an in-patient or out-patient basis. A hospital may include a rehabilitation institution, an out-patient clinic, or a mental health or drug treatment center if its principal purpose is the provision of hospital and medical care. It does not include a home for the aged, a home for children, or a convalescent home. The IRS is currently closely scrutinizing hospitals. If you are setting up a medical clinic or other organization that will be classified as a hospital, you really should get legal advice before you file.

> *The IRS is currently closely scrutinizing hospitals. If you are setting up a medical clinic or other organization that will be classified as a hospital, you really should get legal advice before you file.*

A *medical research organization* is one that engages directly in the continued active conduct of medical research in conjunction with a hospital.

4. GOVERNMENT UNIT

This includes any federal, state, county, regional or local government unit.

5. SUPPORTING ORGANIZATIONS

A *supporting* organization is one that benefits one of the types of organizations described on page 100 in #1, 2, 3, 4, 7, 8 or 9 (called the *supported* organization) in carrying out its mission. To qualify as a public charity *supporting* organization, the supporting organization must be operated, supervised or controlled by or in connection with supported organization. For example, a church may consider one of its purposes the care of the sick and elderly. It could set up an old age home as a supporting organization to carry out these purposes. Similarly, a college may set up a publishing company as a supporting organization to do its printing and publishing.

The *supported* organization can be exempt either under §501(c)(3) or under §501(c)(4), §501(c)(5), or §501(c)(6) as long as the (c)(4), (c)(5) or (c)(6) organization meet the requirements of the FASO test (see Chapter 7). For example, a §501(c)(6) chamber of commerce, funded by dues from the area's businesses, could have a (c)(3) *supporting* organization that supports the chamber's downtown business rehabilitation project.

REQUIREMENTS

To get §501(c)(3) public charity status as a supporting organization, your group must meet all of these tests:

> 1) It must be organized and operated exclusively for the benefit of, to perform the functions of, or to carry out the (c)(3) purposes of, one or more of the groups described in #1, 2, 3, 4, 7, 8, or 9 above or of a §501(c)(4), (5), or (6) organization that meets the FASO test; *and*
>
> 2) It must be operated, supervised, or controlled by one or more of those groups; *and*

3) It must not be controlled directly or indirectly by one or more disqualified persons (see pages 153-56 for a description of disqualified persons) other than foundation managers and other than the public charities described in #1, 2, 3, 4, 7, 8 or 9 above; *and*

4) It must itself meet the criteria to be a §501(c)(3) organization.

Because the rules about which organizations can receive funds are complex, some foundations will not make grants to any supporting organization.

If you are setting up a supporting organization, you are most likely to qualify as a supporting organization if:

- you specify in your Articles that your purpose is to benefit a specific public charity that you name;

- your Articles provide that the public charities you support elect a majority of your Board, and

- there are no disqualified persons on your Board.

A complex set of rules does allow you to vary from this model. IRS Publication 557 has much more detailed information on setting up these types of organizations under "§509(a)(3) Organizations." Private foundations are restricted from making grants to certain types of supporting organizations. Because the rules about which organizations can receive funds are complex, some foundations will not make grants to any supporting organization. If you are looking to get foundation grants, you may want to consider whether you might qualify as a public charity under a different classification. You will probably need legal help if you decide to apply for public charity status as a supporting organization.

REASONS FOR SETTING UP SUPPORTING ORGANIZATION

A supported organization may choose to set up a supporting organization for several reasons. PSOs and FASOs (see #8 and 9 below) may get funding for a project that supports their mission but the funding will tip them into the private foundation category. In some circumstances, placing the money in a separate supporting organization may preserve their public charity status. In other cases, the services provided by the supporting organization require the attention of a separate or different kind of Board than the one running the supported organization. Some supported organizations spin off a supporting organization that runs risky programs to avoid having the supported organization's assets subject to claims made against the risky program. Or the supported organization may protect its endowment funds by spinning off a separate supporting organization that manages those funds.

The supporting organization is being used increasingly by PSOs (#8 above) and FASOs (#9 above) that engage in fee supported ventures. It is important to note that your group cannot set up any business it desires as a supporting organization. The supporting organization must meet the §501(c)(3) requirements discussed above—it must have an exempt purpose; it must be organized and operated for that purpose; it cannot provide a private benefit to anyone; and it cannot do substantial lobbying. For example, an organization that helps at-risk youth develop job skills may set up a supporting organization that runs a furniture factory to teach young people skills and that sells the furniture they produce as long as the organization makes its business decisions based on what is most likely to develop job skills rather than on what would make the factory most profitable.

Chapter 9 has more information on nonprofits that conduct a business. If your group sells a product or service, you should read that chapter to determine if you can qualify for exemption with your business and for information on how to separate your business from your other activities in order to get an exemption for your exempt activities if you need to do this.

6. PUBLIC SAFETY ORGANIZATIONS

Organizations that are recognized as exempt under this category commonly engage in testing consumer products to determine if they are safe for use by the general public. The exemption is denied if the IRS feels the testing is being done to further a private interest (e.g., a drug company testing a drug before marketing it). Unlike the other public charities, contributions to a public safety organization are not tax deductible, although the organization is exempt from paying income taxes.

7. DEVELOPMENT FOUNDATION FOR STATE UNIVERSITIES

These are organizations that receive a substantial part of their support from the government or the general public and manage and invest them for the benefit of state or local government colleges and universities.

8. PUBLICLY SUPPORTED ORGANIZATIONS

Groups whose support comes largely from public sources are exempt under this section. The IRS uses a very complicated test to determine whether your group's support comes from what it considers public sources. Chapter 7 describes this test in excruciating (by which we mean extremely boring) detail. Generally, if at least one third of your funding comes or will come from government grants (and not a payment for services), small donations, or small non-governmental grants, you should qualify under this section. "Small" means that each person's donation or each funder's grant is less than 2% of your total funding. If this does not clearly describe you, you should get professional help or wade through Chapter 7.

9. FEE/ACTIVITY SUPPORTED ORGANIZATIONS

If a substantial part of your group's support comes from membership fees and activities related to your group's exempt purpose, you can qualify as a Public Charity under this section. This test is also very complicated and is described in Chapter 7. To meet this test, at least one third of your support must come from membership fees, grants from PSOs, and gross receipts from related business activities. No more than one third of your support can come from the combination of gross investment income and unrelated business income. If you do not clearly meet both of these tests, you are doomed to read Chapter 7 or to get professional help.

Who Must File the Application

All groups wanting to obtain federal tax exemption under §50l(c)(3) must file Form 1023 (the application form) with the Internal Revenue Service, with a few exceptions. Your group does not have to file in order to be exempt, if you are one of the following:

- A church, interchurch organizations of local units of a church, a convention of churches, or integrated auxiliaries of a church, such as a religious school, mission society, or youth group.

- An organization that otherwise meets the criteria for exemption under §501(c)(3), that is not a private foundation (see pages 99-101) and that has low annual gross receipts, normally not more than $5,000 per year. The government defines "normally" to mean that your group has $7,500 or less in gross receipts in your first year; $12,000 or less in your first two years; or, if you have been in operation three or more years, $15,000 or less in gross receipts in the immediately preceding two years plus the current year. "Gross receipts" means the gross amount received by your group from all sources—including contributions; grants; dues; sale of goods, services, or assets, and interest—without deducting for expenses.

- A subordinate organization covered by a group exemption letter (see page 117.)

Although you are not required to do so, if you meet one of these exceptions, you may file Form 1023 if you want to receive the IRS letter recognizing your exempt purposes. Many funders and donors will want to see this letter before they give funds to you.

Effective Date of the Exemption

If you file the Form 1023 within 27 months from the end of the month in which your group was organized and the IRS agrees you are exempt, the IRS will usually recognize you as exempt retroactive to the date you were incorporated. You were incorporated on the date stamped on your Articles that the Secretary of State returned to you after your Articles were filed. If your organization is required by IRS to alter your activities or to make *substantive amendments* to your Articles or Bylaws, your exempt status will begin on the date the changes are made. It is thus very important that you be sure from the start that your Articles and Bylaws will satisfy the IRS.

If Form 1023 is filed after the 27-month period, your exemption will date from the time you filed the Form 1023 unless the IRS grants you an extension back in time that recognizes an earlier retroactive date. The criteria that the IRS uses in granting an extension are discussed on pages 140-41.

If your group has not filed within the first 27 months, you may request §501(c)(4) status for the period between your founding and date of application for §501(c)(3) status. The §501(c)(4) status for this period will protect your corporation from corporate income tax for this period. However, donations during the §501(c)(4) period will not be tax-deductible as charitable contributions.

> *If you file the Form 1023 within 27 months from the end of the month in which your group was organized, the IRS will usually recognize you as exempt retroactive to the date you were incorporated.*

If your organization is a new one and is applying for tax exemption, your tax year may end before you hear from the IRS as to whether you are exempt. You must then determine whether you need to file a tax return and which one to file. You have a choice. You can choose to file a Form 1120 (the one used by nonexempt corporations) and pay taxes, then file for a refund if you get your exemption.

Your other option is to file as though you are tax-exempt. Tax-exempt organizations with gross receipts greater than $50,000 or property worth more than $500,000 file an annual informational return called the Form 990 or the Form 990 EZ. (This is discussed in greater detail in Chapter 12.) If you fall in this category, you would file Form 990 or Form 990 EZ and check the box that says "exemption applied for." However, if you are denied your exemption, you will then owe back taxes, interest, and penalties. Most groups choose the second option in spite of its risks. If you are fairly certain you will qualify or if your tax liability is small, the second option is a relatively safe bet and permits you to avoid going through the procedure of applying for an income tax refund.

Soliciting Contributions Before You Receive Your Exemption Letter

Not surprisingly, many nonprofits want to accept donations before they have received their ruling from the IRS that they are tax-exempt. Your nonprofit can certainly accept contributions but most donors will want to deduct their contribution as a charitable gift on their own tax returns. You must be careful about what you say to donors about the deductibility of their contribution. Even if you feel confident that you will get your exemption, you cannot tell your donors that their contributions are deductible.

> *Even if you feel confident that you will get your exemption, you cannot tell your donors that their contributions are deductible.*

You can tell them that you have applied for the exemption. As described above, if you applied within 27 months of the date you incorporated, your exemption will probably be retroactive to the date of incorporation. If your donor made the contribution to you after you incorporated, he or she can take the deduction if you get your retroactive exemption. But again, because you don't yet know that your exemption will be retroactive, you must be careful that you don't deliver assurances on this point.

Cost of Applying

See pages 115-16 for the fees you must pay to apply for a §501(c)(3) exemption.

§501(c)(4): Civic Leagues and Social Welfare Organizations

If your organization is a public benefit organization but does not need or want to become exempt under §501(c)(3) or does not qualify under that section, you may want to consider applying for exemption under §501(c)(4). Like §501(c)(3) groups, (c)(4) organizations are generally exempt from paying income tax on taxable income. Another advantage of obtaining exemption as a §50l(c)(4) is that (c)(4)s can do extensive lobbying and some political campaigning. The political activity and lobbying rules for §501(c)(4) organizations is discussed in Chapter 8.

The disadvantage of obtaining a §50l(c)(4) exemption instead of a §501(c)(3) is that donations to a §501(c)(4) organization do not qualify as charitable deductions for the donor.

The disadvantage of obtaining a §50l(c)(4) exemption instead of §501(c)(3) exemption is that donations to a §501(c)(4) organization do not qualify as charitable deductions for the donor. Contributions to a §501(c)(3) organization do. Also, private foundations will generally not make grants to a §501(c)(4) organization.

In order to qualify for exemption as a civic league or social welfare organization under §501(c)(4), your group must meet two requirements:

- You must be civic and operated primarily for the promotion of social welfare; *and*
- You must not be organized or operated for profit.

A civic group is one which offers benefits or services which are public, and not private, in nature. In other words, the services must benefit a fairly large segment of the public and not just a few specific individuals. Social welfare is promoted if the organization serves some broad community need. A membership group that limits its services or benefits to its members may have trouble qualifying unless it can show that the general public will benefit from its activities. For example, a homeowners' association that maintains a park open to the public may be exempt.

Private benefit that is more than incidental will disqualify the group from this exemption. Here again, membership groups that offer benefits to its members have faced problems. For example, automobile clubs and dairy farmer cooperatives have been denied exemption because the government felt that their members benefited in a substantial economic way from their membership in the club, even though there were also important public services provided by the groups.

Other Exempt Groups

A wide range of other types of group can apply for exemption from federal income tax, although contributions to these groups are not deductible. (There are minor exceptions for volunteer fire organizations, charitable activities of some lodges, cemetery associations, certain charitable funds, war veterans organizations, and certain organizations that work in conjunction with §501(c)(3) groups.) These other exempt groups and the subsection of Internal Revenue Code §501 under which they qualify are discussed briefly here. You should consult IRS Publication 557 for additional information and get professional help if you need it.

Labor, Agricultural and Horticultural Organizations—(c)(5)

§501(c)(5) exempts several categories of organizations—labor, agricultural and horticultural groups—that seek to better the conditions of people working in those pursuits. A labor organization is an association of workers organized to protect and promote the interests of labor in connection with employment, by bettering the conditions of workers, the improvement of the products of the workers, and the development of a higher degree of efficiency in occupations of the workers. Unions are a common example. Agricultural and horticultural organizations are those that encourage the development of better agricultural or horticultural products and that seek to better the conditions of farmers and others in the industry. Contributions to a (c)(5) organization are not deductible as a charitable donation but are deductible as a business expense if they meet the test for that deduction.

Business Leagues—(c)(6)

Business leagues, chambers of commerce, boards of trade, and real estate boards, among others, are exempt under §501(c)(6). A *business league* is an association of persons having some common business interest, the purpose of which is to pursue the common interest and not to engage in regular business activities. An organization of businesses in the pulp and paper industry is an example. A *chamber of commerce* is usually composed of merchants and businesses of a particular city or town. A *board of trade* is composed of persons engaged in similar lines of business who operate a commodities exchange. A *real estate board* consists of members working to improve the business conditions in the real estate field.

To be exempt under §501(c)(6), your group must be working to improve business conditions in your line of business (for your entire industry or all components of that industry in a geographical area) as opposed to performing services for your members. This means, for example, that you would be exempt if your business league operates to improve standards of communications throughout the computer industry but not if you operate to improve standards of communications for one company within the computer industry or if you operate primarily to offer your members discounts on computer equipment. You are also not exempt if any part of your net earnings privately benefit any individual.

Contributions to organizations exempt under §501(c)(6) are not exempt as charitable contributions but may be deductible as business expenses if they meet the test for that deduction. However, the deduction may be limited if it is used for certain types of lobbying. (See pages 199-200.)

Social Clubs—(c)(7)

Social clubs are clubs that are organized around a common purpose such as pleasure or recreation. Personal contact, a sense of community, and commingling should be a material part of the life of your club. To show that your club has an identity of purpose, membership should be limited consistent with the character of your group. However, you cannot discriminate on the basis of race, color, or religion, except that you can limit your membership to persons of a particular religion in order to further the teachings of that religion (or, in some cases, if you are connected with a fraternity or sorority), as long as you do not exclude people based on race.

Generally, your club may not engage in business, although you may provide meals, refreshments, and services related to your exempt purposes to your members and guests. The rules concerning unrelated business income are somewhat different for social clubs than for most other exempt groups. You should consult an accountant if you are a social club with unrelated business income. Because the club exists to serve its members, your facilities cannot be open to the general public except on an limited basis. No part of the organization's earnings may be used to privately benefit any individual. Examples of social clubs include country clubs, hobby clubs, college fraternities and sororities, and amateur sports clubs.

Fraternal Societies—(c)(8) and (c)(10)

Organizations that operate exclusively under the lodge system are fraternal organizations. Your organization operates under the lodge system if you have a form of organization that comprises local branches chartered by a parent organization and that are largely self-governing. Before applying for your own exemption, you should check your parent organization to see if your organization has been included in a group exemption or if you can be added. (See the discussion below of group exemptions.)

Two types of fraternal organizations are tax-exempt. Under §501(c)(8), a fraternal organization is exempt if it provides life, sickness, accident or other benefits to its members or dependents. Under §501(c)(10), a fraternal organization is exempt if it devotes all of its net earnings exclusively to religious, charitable, scientific, literary, educational and fraternal purposes and if it does not provide life, sickness, accident or other benefits to its members.

Generally, only donations to §501(c)(3) organizations are deductible as charitable contributions. There are a few exceptions to this rule. One exception is that donations to §501(c)(8) and (c)(10) organizations that are used exclusively for religious, charitable, scientific, literary, or educational purposes, or for the prevention of cruelty to animals and children are deductible.

Examples of §501(c)(8) and (c)(10) organizations are the Elks and the Masons. College fraternities and sororities are generally denied exemption under these sections and are classified as social clubs under §501(c)(7).

Veterans Organizations—(c)(19)

An organization of past members of the Armed Forces of the United States is exempt from taxation. §501(c)(19) exempts veterans groups if the post or organization is organized in the United States or one of its possessions; at least 75% of the members are past or present members of the U.S. Armed Forces and at least 97.5% are such members are cadets, or spouses, widows, or widowers of members or cadets; and no part of the earnings benefits any individual. Your organization must be operated exclusively to promote the welfare of the veterans' community. If at least 90% of your membership consists of war veterans, donations to your organization can be deducted as charitable contributions.

Political Organizations—§527

Political organizations that are organized primarily for the purpose of collecting contributions and making expenditures to influence the election or appointment of individuals for federal, state or local public office are exempt from federal income tax, except on their investment income. Examples of such organizations are the Republican and Democratic National Committees, various candidate committees and political action committees (PACs).

Miscellaneous Exempt Groups

A variety of other exempt groups are exempt from federal taxation. We have listed them below, along with the subsection of Internal Revenue Code §501 under which they qualify:

- title holding companies—(c)(2)
- homeowners' associations—(c)(4) and §528
- agricultural organizations—(c)(5)
- garden clubs—(c)(5)
- employee insurance associations—(c)(9)
- local teachers' retirement fund associations—(c)(11)
- certain cooperative organizations—(c)(12)

- cemetery companies—(c)(13)
- credit unions—(c)(14)
- reserve funds for banks—(c)(14)
- small mutual property and casualty companies—(c)(15)
- crop financing corporations—(c)(16)
- supplemental unemployment benefit trusts—(c)(17)
- employee supported pension plans—(c)(18)
- black lung benefit trusts—(c)(21)
- multi-employer benefit trusts—(c)(22)
- religious and apostolic organizations—(d)
- cooperative hospital service organizations—(e)
- cooperative school service organizations—(f)
- farmers' cooperatives—see §521(a)

If your group does not qualify for one of the exemptions we discussed in this chapter and one of these categories above seems to apply to your group, you should contact the Internal Revenue Service for application forms and the appropriate publication that describe which groups qualify. If you still have questions, you should contact an attorney or accountant. You can also call the IRS hotline for exempt organizations at 1.877.829.5500.

Affiliated Organizations

Some exempt organizations find that they want or need to create a second exempt organization that they control. These organizations are called affiliated, connected, or linked organizations. For example, a (c)(3) charity may decide that it wants to create a separate (c)(3) foundation to solicit and invest endowment funds whose income will be returned to the charity for its use. Because it is a separate organization, the foundation's funds are shielded from liability from the charity's creditors. Creating a second organization also allows the foundation to have a Board that can focus on fundraising and that has the connections to engage in fundraising. A Board devoted to the foundation may reassure donors that their endowment funds will be properly managed for their intended purpose. Another example is a (c)(3) school that creates a separate exempt entity to manage the student bookstore. The bookstore needs a Board with a separate set of skills and interests than the school's Board.

An exempt organization may also want to create an affiliated organization because it engages in activities that fit more than one exempt classification. For example, a (c)(6) business league may want to operate a (c)(3) charitable program that collects canned goods and distributes them to the hungry in their community and wants its donors to be able to claim a charitable deduction. A (c)(3) educational organization may want to engage in more lobbying than allowed for (c)(3)s and may create a (c)(4) social welfare organization to handle lobbying. The IRS will not give one organization two different exemption classifications. The route offered by the IRS is for these exempt organizations to create a second, affiliated organization.

> *Some exempt organizations find that they want or need to create a second exempt organization that they control. These organizations are called affiliated, connected, or linked organizations.*

An affiliated organization must be a distinct entity that has its own Board with its own minutes, bank account, records, and employer identification number. It is almost always separately incorporated. Two organizations are affiliated in that one controls the other or has a close connection to the other.

The most common method of control is for one organization to appoint the Board of the other. A second method of control is where a third entity or group controls both organizations. For example, a school bookstore and the school's alumnae association may both be controlled by the school. If a church that is controlled by its members sets up a separate corporation for its low-income housing project whose Board is also elected by the church members, the church and housing project are linked organizations because the church members elect the Boards of both. Some groups do not have a formal mechanism of control but rely on the presence of a majority of the same Directors on each Board to coordinate their activities. Other affiliated organizations may not control each other, but the governance documents for each organization may require that one organization be bound by the decisions of the other on legislative issues.

Most linked organizations will want to have at least one Board member who sits on both Boards and many have several common Directors. Although it is tempting to appoint the same people to each Board, completely overlapping Boards is a poor practice. Each Board needs at least two Directors who do not sit on the other Board. These Directors can then act as disinterested Directors in the event that two of the organizations engage in a transaction that creates a conflict of interest between the corporations. For example, if one of the organizations is exempt under §501(c)(3) and the other is exempt under §501(c)(4), the (c)(3) needs disinterested Board members who are better positioned to maintain clarity about transactions with the (c)(4) organization that may jeopardize the (c)(3)'s exempt status. See pp. 299-303 for a discussion of conflicts of interest.

Linked organizations in which one member is exempt under §501(c)(3) and the other organization is not have some special concerns. (c)(3) organizations are charitable-type organizations that receive special tax benefits. Donors to most (c)(3)s can take a charitable tax deduction, which they cannot do for contributions to most other exempt organizations. Private foundations, who are themselves almost always (c)(3)s, can only make grants to other (c)(3)s (with some exceptions). The IRS wants to be sure that (c)(3) monies and assets stay in the (c)(3) charitable section and monitor linked organizations to ensure that the (c)(3) is not improperly benefiting its connected organization. The key concept is that the non-(c)(3) organization cannot use the (c)(3)'s assets for its own benefit. It must pay at least fair market value for anything of value it receives from the (c)

FEDERAL TAX-EXEMPT STATUS

(3) and cannot receive more than fair market value for anything it gives to the (c)(3). The (c)(3)s assets must be protected.

> *Linked organizations in which one member is exempt under §501(c)(3) and the other organization is not have some special concerns.*

The linked organizations can engage in transactions if they are fair to the (c)(3). If the groups share space or staff, you must allocate the costs fairly between the organizations. You must ensure that the (c)(3) pays no more than its fair share of the expenses. For example, the (c)(3) cannot benefit the affiliated organization by allowing its Executive Director to oversee the (c)(4) without payment from the (c)(4) for this service. Some linked groups share employees under a carefully structured agreement that ensures that the (c)(3) is protected.

The non-(c)(3) can, however, use its assets to benefit the (c)(3). It could, for example, offer free office space or make grants to the (c)(3). The (c)(3) cannot offer free office space to its affiliated non-(c)(3) organization.

Be aware that assets can be intangible. Your mailing list, for example, may have financial value, particularly if it is extensive. If the (c)(3) has developed and managed a mailing list and wants to provide it to the (c)(4) for its use, the (c)(4) will need to pay the (c)(3) the prevailing rate to purchase the list.

Because the IRS scrutinizes such linked organizations carefully, take great care in structuring the Articles and Bylaws, operating structures and financial procedures of such linked organizations. The Alliance for Justice has some excellent publications that discuss these issues. See Appendix 1 under Chapter 8. If you need additional help, you should obtain professional advice from attorneys or accountants familiar with the IRS rules regarding affiliated organizations.

General Information For Organizations Seeking Any Type of Tax Exemption

Cost of Applying

The IRS charges a fee for considering your tax-exempt application. If your annual gross receipts, averaged over the last 4 years, do not exceed $10,000 per year (or, if you are a new organization, and your anticipated average annual gross receipts are not more than $10,000), you must pay $400. If they exceed $10,000 per year, your fee is $850. There is a $3,000 fee for a group exemption letter. The fee must be paid when you submit your application. If you do not pay, IRS will return your application.

The IRS charges for considering your tax-exempt application. If your annual gross receipts, averaged over the last 4 years, do not exceed $10,000 per year, you must pay $400. If they exceed $10,000 per year, your fee is $850.

Annual Returns

We discuss the annual returns that you must file in Chapter 12. Even very small organizations (except churches) must file an annual return. If you fail to file an annual return for three years, you will lose your exemption, unless you are a church or certain church-related entities. There are no other exceptions. Be sure to review Chapter 12.

If you fail to file an annual return for three years, you will lose your exemption, unless you are a church or certain church-related entities.

Public Inspection of Application and Annual Returns

If you receive tax exemption status, you should be aware that both you (see pages 692-93) and the IRS (see below) must make certain of the documents that you file with the IRS available for public inspection.

Applications

The public can inspect tax-exempt applications that have been approved by the IRS, and the supporting documents filed by the tax-exempt group. It can also inspect documents or letters issued by the IRS relating to the approved applications. This means that you can obtain a copy of the applications filed by organizations you know are exempt prior to filing yours. See pages 692-93 for how to obtain copies of the applications of other exempt organizations. The IRS is not required to grant your exemption just because it granted the exemption of a similar organization but your review of another group's application may give you ideas about how to approach the application.

Of course, other people will also be able to look at your application. If your application or supporting documents contain any trade secret, patent, process, style of work, or apparatus that you want to withhold from public inspection, you must request in writing that this information be withheld. The request is filed with the IRS office where you filed the information. Your request must clearly identify (by document, page, paragraph and line) what is to be withheld and why it is to be withheld. The IRS will withhold the information if it decides that its disclosure would adversely affect your organization. The IRS will also not disclose the names and addresses of your contributors unless you are a private foundation or a political action committee (both of which were described earlier in this chapter).

Annual Returns

Annual returns are also subject to public inspection and available on the Internet at *www.guidestar.org*. However, the following information will not be disclosed:

- The names and addresses of contributors to tax-exempts, other than private foundations, will not be disclosed.

- If the amount of a contribution or bequest could reasonably expect to identify the name or address of the contributor, it may be withheld, except that amounts to private foundations can be inspected.

- The names, addresses, and amounts of contributions and bequests of persons who aren't U.S. citizens to a foreign organization will not be disclosed.

Unrelated Business Income

Note that the rules concerning taxation on unrelated business income discussed in Chapter 9 apply to almost all tax-exempt groups. Be sure to read that chapter.

Group Exemption

An organization (called the central organization) that is composed of subordinate organizations (such as chapters, locals, posts, or units) can request a group exemption on behalf of itself and its subordinates. If granted, the IRS will send a determination letter to the central organization that establishes the exempt status of the central and subordinate organizations. Subordinate organizations may be separate corporations, or they may be established by some other organizational scheme. If the central organization has a group exemption letter, the subordinate organizations don't have to apply separately to get their own exemptions.

To get a group exemption, the central organization must get exempt status for itself. At that time or later, the central organization can apply for a group exemption. You do this by letter to the IRS rather than by filling out an IRS form. Before you apply, your subordinate organizations must each have their own EIN, even if they do not have employees. IRS Publication 557 has instructions on the information you nee d to include in your letter to the IRS requesting a group exemption. The IRS fee to apply for group exemption is $3,000, which you will need to send with the letter requesting the exemption.

Time for Processing Applications

When you send in your application, the IRS generally sends an acknowledgment letter within 30 days of its receipt that it received your application. Its time to process applications depends in part on how many applications come in and how many agents are available to handle them. The IRS essentially has two piles—a fast pile and a slow pile. If the agent at the gate reviews your application and concludes that you are clearly exempt or can resolve a minor issue with a quick communication with you, you will generally get your exemption letter in 10 days (very unusual, but possible) to several months, usually two to three months. If the agent feels that there are questions, he or she passes your application on to an examiner. In that case, it will probably be seven to eight months before you get questions from the examiner and a period of time after that (usually a few weeks if there are no further questions) before the examiner makes a decision. It behooves you to do all you can to avoid questions before you send in your application. A legal review by a nonprofit professional is generally helpful.

Consult Appendix 1 if you would like information about source material related to this Chapter. Appendix 1 has references of interest to all readers, not just professionals.

If your group wants to apply for tax-exempt status, the next chapter explains how to fill out the appropriate application.

6 FILLING OUT TAX EXEMPT APPLICATIONS

THIS CHAPTER COVERS

- Filling Out Form 1023
- Filling Out Form 1024
- Questions Back From the IRS

If you have decided that you want to apply for federal tax-exempt status, you do so by filling out an application and sending it to the Internal Revenue Service. Groups applying for §501(c)(3) status fill out Form 1023. Groups applying for §501(c)(4) status and for most other §501(c) exemptions fill out Form 1024.

Filling out these forms correctly requires some understanding as to what information the Internal Revenue Service is looking for. It is very important that you have filled these forms out correctly before you send them to the Internal Revenue Service. This Chapter provides a detailed explanation of how to fill out Form 1023, the more complicated form. We also provide some pointers for those filling out Form 1024.

THE OREGON NONPROFIT CORPORATION HANDBOOK

Filling Out Form 1023

Groups that apply for exemption under §50l(c)(3) fill out IRS Form 1023. Form 1023 and instructions for filling it out can be obtained from the Internal Revenue Office free of charge. Publication 557, *Tax-Exempt Status for Your Organization,* has essential information for successfully completing your application for §50l(c)(3) status. Publication 4042, *Applying for Tax Exempt Status,* provides a good overview of the entire process and includes links to online webinars on specific issues you may confront in preparing your application. Appendix 2 explains how to contact the IRS online to get these publications. You should obtain and read the IRS instructions for Form 1023. Brace yourself for a pretty long and detailed exercise in filling out this application!

If your group has some unusual feature and you know of a similar group that has been ruled exempt or if you just want to look at how someone similar filled out their application before you file yours, you can obtain a copy of the other group's application by contacting that group or the IRS. Pages 116-17 and 692-93 explain how to do this. Let the other group or the IRS know if you want copies of the supporting documents that the other group sent in with its application. You may also request documents and letters issued by the IRS relating to the approved application. This is a particularly good idea if you are obtaining the application because your group is somewhat unusual and the group who qualified is similar to yours. The IRS is not required to grant your exemption just because it granted an exemption to a group similar to yours but this information should be very useful to you in preparing your application. The IRS or the group may charge you a copying fee.

> *The IRS is not a funder and will not send you money, regardless of how wonderful they think your organization is. Your job is not to persuade the IRS that you are fabulous or well-managed but to persuade them that you are exempt.*

In filling out the Form 1023, keep in mind that the IRS receives hundreds of applications a day. Your job is to answer each question completely and concisely. You want to submit a truthful application that an agent can read and understand easily. Avoid technical terms and answer the questions in a way that is comprehensible to a lay person. Do not provide information that the IRS does not request. The IRS is not a funder and will not send you money, regardless of how wonderful they think your organization is. Your job is not to persuade the IRS that you are fabulous or well-managed but to persuade them that you are exempt. Answer all questions with that focus in mind.

There will be a number of places in Form 1023 that ask for explanations. There is no room on the form for explanations. We suggest that you create an "Attachments" document and use the Attachments document as the place to put all the information the IRS asks for that does not fit on the form. You should have a header on each page of the Attachments that includes your organization's name and employer identification number (EIN). Each entry on the Attachments document should indicate what Part and Question number you are answering. You will save space and trees if you simply run one answer after the other (no need for a new page for each new answer).

As you fill out the application, consult the Instructions to the Form 1023. The following discussion (based on Form 1023 revised in June 2006) is intended to supplement the IRS instructions and we will skip lines in which we feel the instructions are adequate. The IRS revises this form from time to time, so the line references in this chapter may not be quite right if you are using a later version. Even if the form has been revised, you should find the concepts in this chapter helpful in filling it out.

Part I – Identification of Applicant

Lines 1-3—Name

Part I of Form 1023 is for identification of your group. Under Line l, put your organization's name exactly as it appears in your Articles of Incorporation. Lines 2 and 3 are self-explanatory.

Line 4—Employer Identification Number

Line 4 asks for the employer identification number. Every exempt organization is required to have an employer identification number (also called an EIN or a taxpayer identification number) whether or not you have employees. If you haven't already gotten an EIN, see p. 47 for how to get one. You must obtain this number *before* you file the Form 1023 but *after* you incorporate (if you are a corporation).

Line 5—Annual Accounting Period

This line calls for the month your annual accounting period ends, written as a double digit. (For example, April is 04.) The annual accounting period your Board chooses should be the one you actually intend to use for maintaining financial records. See page 45 for a discussion of accounting periods (also called your fiscal year). Whatever month is stated here will be considered binding for future tax requirements. If you are granted exempt status, your annual report, the Form 990, must be filed by the 15th day of the 5th month after the close of your annual accounting period. (See Chapter 12 for a discussion of the Form 990 and who must file it.) Your annual accounting period may be changed only through following specific IRS procedures.

Line 6—Primary Contact Person

Fill in Line 3 with the name of someone in your group that the IRS can contact during normal business hours for more information. Be sure this person has a copy of the application, is knowledgeable about it, and can talk to the IRS competently. If this person is not an officer, your organization will need to file Form 2848 (an IRS power of attorney form that you can obtain from the IRS at the address in Appendix 2) to permit the IRS to talk to this person. This person does not have to be an attorney.

Line 7—Authorized Representative

If you have an attorney or accountant or other person that you have authorized *to deal with the IRS for you in connection with this application,* you must provide the IRS with your representative's name and address and submit a completed Form 2848 (see above) with this application. If you are handling this application process yourself, check "No."

Line 8—Paid Consultants

If you have paid or promised to pay anyone, other than an officer, director, trustee, employee or authorized representative (Line 7), to help you set up your organization, raise funds or otherwise advise you, you must provide their name, their firm's name and address, how much you paid and what you paid for.

If you do have a website, the IRS reviewer will look at your website as a first step in understanding your organization's activities, so be sure that the information on the website agrees with what you say in the application and otherwise complies with the rules concerning §501(c)(3) organizations.

Line 9—Website and E-mail

You do not have to have a website. If you don't have one at the time you submit the application, simply say "none." If one is in process and your answer to other questions in this application will refer to it, state that you don't yet have one—it is in process. Do not feel that you have to rush to get a website up so that the IRS can review it.

If you do have a website, the IRS reviewer will look at your website to understand your organization's activities, so be sure that the information on the website agrees with what you say in the application and otherwise complies with the rules concerning §501(c)(3) organizations. You will also want to be sure that the email address you provide will result in IRS messages going to a responsible person who will see that your response to IRS questions is handled carefully by your group.

Line 10—Required to File Returns

Form 990 or 990-EZ is the informational tax form that most §501(c)(3) groups must file every year with the IRS. Some groups are not required to file either of these returns. Check Chapter 12 to see if your group must file this return. If not, explain why you do not have to file the return. For many small groups, the explanation for not filing a return is that the group does not anticipate having gross receipts of more than $50,000 annually and does not have property worth more than $500,000. It is a good idea to add to your explanation that you are aware of your obligation to file the Form 990N each year. See Chapter 12 for why it is critical that you file a Form 990N each year if you don't file a Form 990 or 990-EZ.

Line 11—Incorporation or Formation Date

This asks for the date your nonprofit was incorporated. Put in the date stamped on the Articles of Incorporation that the Secretary of State returned to your organization. If you are not incorporated, fill in the date your Articles of Association or your Constitution was adopted. The IRS wants this in the MM/DD/YYYY format.

Line 12—Foreign Country

If you were formed in a foreign country, you should get legal advice.

Part II—Organizational Structure

You must be a corporation, unincorporated association or charitable trust to be tax-exempt.

Line 1—Corporations

Most groups that use this book are corporations. Groups that are incorporated as nonprofit corporations should check the "yes" box. You must enclose a copy of your Articles of Incorporation and a copy of any amendments or restatements of the Articles. The Oregon Secretary of State does not issue a separate Certification of Filing but they will provide you with a copy of your Articles, amendments and restatements *that includes the stamp from the Corporation Commissioner showing the date filed.* The charge for this is $5 or, for documents filed more recently, you may be able to get a copy from the Corporation Division's website. Look for the Corporation Division's contact information in Appendix 2. The copy that you submit to the IRS must have this information stamped on it.

If you don't have a copy with the date filed stamped on it, you can submit a substitute copy. You have to submit a declaration, signed by an authorized officer, that this is a correct copy. You can do this by writing, either the beginning or the end of both your Articles, amendments, restatements, and Bylaws, the following:

This is to certify that this is a complete and correct copy of the Articles of Incorporation [or the amendment or restatement to the Articles, or Bylaws] of [name of corporation]. It contains all the powers, principles, purposes, functions and other provisions by which this corporation governs itself.

BY:_____

      (NAME)

Officer for [Name of Corporation]

This should be signed by an officer authorized by your Board to sign these papers for your group. The Articles of Incorporation must contain the provisions listed on pages 35-39 pertaining to your purposes and the distribution of your assets on dissolution for 50l(c)(3) corporations or the IRS will return them to you for amendment. Be sure that you keep a copy for your records. These documents will not be returned.

Part III—Required Provisions

In this section, the IRS wants to be sure that you have included in your Articles of Incorporation the provisions concerning your purpose and how you dispose of your assets on dissolution that the IRS requires. If you followed the instructions on pages 35-39 in filling out your Articles, then you can check the boxes in lines 1 and 2.

Line 1—Purposes

If you followed the instructions in this book, your language on purposes is in your Articles of Incorporation, Article 5, paragraph 1. Include the page number (and paragraph number if it is different) on the line provided and check the box. This information is requested again on page 28 of Form 1023.

Line 2—Dissolution Clause

If you followed the instructions in this book, your language on dissolution is in Article 8. Check the box in 2a and include the page and paragraph number (if you have one) on the line provided in 2b. Skip 2c. This information is requested again on page 28 of Form 1023..

Part IV—Narrative Description

This question requests a narrative description of your groups's past, present and future activities. Part IV is the heart of the application. The IRS is interested here in your programmatic activities, not your administrative activities, the functioning or your Board, or your efforts at fund-raising. As you think about your activities, focus completely on those programmatic activities that are about your mission, not the Board's activities that are related to its operations or your administrative and fundraising activities that you do in order to carry out your programming.

Part IV is the heart of the application.

As you answer Part IV, provide the information that the IRS requests and keep your focus on information that explains why you are exempt. Resist the temptation to include information that is not relevant to why you are exempt—for example, how deserving others think you are or how efficient you are.

Example: Runners for Kids is a new nonprofit formed to hold marathons twice a year that will raise money for children with cancer. In filling out Part IV of its IRS application, the group should not describe its programmatic activities as holding marathons. Its programmatic activity is to give money to §501(c)(3) organizations that fight cancer. In Part VIII, Question 4a (the fundraising question), it will explain under "Other" that it holds marathons to raise funds for the organizations's programs.

After thinking about it, Runners for Kids may realize that the marathons are more than fundraisers. Runners for Kids may use the marathons to educate athletes and the public about the problems faced by children with cancer and to encourage them to donate to cancer charities. Runners for Kids may also use the marathon to provide a morale boost for children with cancer (a charitable activity) by bringing them to the marathon to introduce them to elite runners or by having the runners sign cards that the organization will give to the children. If the marathons are more than fundraisers, then Runners for Kids will describe all of these programs in Part IV in a way that shows the marathons are part of its programmatic activities.

Do not assume that the IRS reviewers are familiar with your type of organization or any jargon or abbreviations commonly used by your organization. Do not assume that the reviewer will know whether you are working in a rural area or low income community. Explain your group's activities clearly, as if the reader had no knowledge of any similar groups or activities or of the constraints or needs of communities like yours.

> *Do not assume that the IRS reviewers are familiar with your type of organization or any jargon or abbreviations commonly used by your organization. Explain your group's activities clearly.*

Your first paragraph should be a background paragraph that orients the IRS agent to your organization. We suggest that you begin by stating that your corporation is a new Oregon nonprofit corporation or is an Oregon nonprofit corporation founded in ____[year] that was formed to ____ [here state your purpose]. Be sure that your purpose fits within the type of activities that are exempt.

If you were formed to address an issue or problem that may be novel to the IRS or about which the IRS may need more information to understand why it is exempt, consider putting in couple of sentences that explain why this organization is needed. Be clear and concise—remember, this is not a grant application. You are just trying to orient the reviewer to understand why your purpose is exempt. For example, if research has shown that social conditioning prevents men from obtaining medical help and your organization wants to encourage men to see doctors, give the IRS a sentence or two that gives a description of and summarizes the research on this need. Another example: if your corporation was formed to promote economic development in your distressed rural county, you might provide some statistics showing your unemployment rate, population decline, or similar factors and explain that the state or federal government has classified you as a distressed area. On the other hand, if your organization is a food bank that gives food to the hungry, you don't need to explain this further. Everyone knows that hungry people need to eat.

If your group began as an unincorporated association or as a program of another (c)(3) organization and is now incorporated, describe the unincorporated association or your relationship as a past program. Your description will help the IRS get a sense of where you came from and what you do. If you are a spin-off of another (c)(3), the IRS will likely already be favorably inclined toward your application since it has already approved your activities as exempt. Favorably inclined is good.

After your introductory paragraph or two, your answer should describe the activities that you carry out in ways that allow the IRS to see why they are charitable, educational, scientific, religious, or otherwise exempt. It is probably most helpful in answering this question to group your activities in categories and to describe the categories as programs. For example, an organization devoted to reducing drug addiction among at-risk youth may offer several programs: a counseling program for the young people; workshops for professionals who work with at-risk youth, and referral services for at-risk youth. Detail each activity in separately numbered sections with a caption describing the program (e.g, "Counseling Program," "Workshops," etc.). In each description, be explicit about which of these activities you are already conducting and which are planned for the future. Include the following information:

> *Your answer should describe the activities that you carry out in ways that allow the IRS to see why they are charitable, educational, scientific, religious, or otherwise exempt.*

- The IRS wants you to describe each activity, who conducts it (Board, staff, employees, volunteers, independent contractors, or other organizations that you hire) and when and where it is conducted. You should explain how each activity furthers your exempt purpose. Often this will be obvious—for example, the workshops you present on how to prevent drug addiction are educational and charitable.

- For each activity (past, present, and future), you must allocate the percentage of total time you devote to it. Remember to include volunteer time in your estimate. These are obviously rough estimates, particularly for new organizations. Make your best guess here quickly and move on. Your answer should give the IRS a rough idea of which activities will engage most of your energy and which are more minor programs. For example, your workshops may constitute 40% of your programmatic time and effort. We suggest that you figure your percentages as percentages of your *programmatic* time and effort and leave your administrative time and effort out of these calculations. If you do this, at the end your total programmatic time and effort for the programs you list should add up to 100%.

- You should explain how each activity is funded—for example, through grants, donations, or charges for your services. If you charge for goods or services, explain how you arrive at your charges. If you state that you set your charges based on the costs of the good or service to you, the IRS may determine that you are not providing an exempt service. Your willingness to forego a profit does not make your service charitable in the eyes of the IRS. This is particularly the case if the goods or services you provide are also provided by commercial sources. See the discussion on this in Chapter 9. In order to show that you are charitable even though you are providing commercial products or services at retail or at cost, you should explain why the provision of these goods or services is important to your exempt purposes, how your provision of these goods or services is different from those offered by businesses, and what noncommercial factors inform your decision-making. If you have funding from other sources that allows you to provide your goods or services to charitable recipients at substantially less than your cost, then explain this to the IRS. This is a confused area of law and you should get professional help before you send in the application.

You should carefully review all the activities that you provide and make sure that all those that carry out your exempt purposes are listed.

You should carefully review all the activities that you provide and make sure that all those that carry out your exempt purposes are listed (for example, newsletters, referral services, phone counseling, free or low-cost services, etc.). If part of your group's activities might disqualify you for the exemption, your answer to Question 1 should either point out the insignificance of these activities to your overall activities or should explain what facts exist that prevent these activities from disqualifying you.

> *Example*: A Native American center that provides information and referral services and counseling and that sells at retail price literature on Native American people should stress in their answer to Question 1 the educational, cultural, and any charitable aspects of their work. This group would do this by explaining their information and referral work, describing their newsletter, and elaborating on any classes or educational programs that they have. The same would be done for counseling. This group would minimize its chances of being disqualified as a business for the sale of literature and materials at market rate by presenting its sale of literature on Native Americans as a program that educates Native peoples and the public about Native history and cultures in these ways (if true, of course):
>
> ◊ The group should explain how the particular literature it sells is related to its exempt purpose of educating the non-native public and supporting the survival of cultural traditions within the Native American community.

◊ The Center should point out the unavailability of this information in other places.

◊ The group should note that it makes its decisions about what literature to sell based on how the literature advances its exempt purpose, not on how commercially profitable the literature might be. For example, it might require that literature present the Native American point of view and avoid the romanticism about Native Americans that makes some non-Native publications about Native peoples more marketable.

You may choose to include information related to other questions that the IRS asks in Form 1023 that are better understood as part of the overall explanation of your organization and what it does. You can then answer the other questions by referring the IRS to your answer in Part IV. We'll note some of those places for you as we move through the application.

Part V—Compensation and Financial Arrangements

This section asks for information about the compensation of your Directors, employees, and independent contractors. For all of these categories, compensation includes wages and salary, deferred compensation, retirement benefits, fringe benefits, stipends, and bonuses. The IRS is using this section to determine if your corporation is providing inurement or insubstantial private benefit to insiders—that is, anyone who is in a position to exercise substantial influence over your organization. Remember to enter "none" for any of the individuals that receive no compensation.

If you have relationships with insiders that cause you to answer any of these questions "yes," you will need to assure the IRS that any such transactions are fair to the corporation.

If you have relationships with insiders that cause you to answer any of these questions "yes," you will need to assure the IRS that any such transactions are fair to the corporation. If you adopt the conflicts of interest policy referred to on page 130, be sure to follow that policy for any dealings with insiders and let the IRS know you followed the policy. We recommend that you consult with an attorney if you find that you are answering any of the questions about dealing with an insider with a "yes" before you send in the application.

Line 1a—Board of Directors and Officers

In your response, you must state all compensation that Directors receive from your organization, whether they are paid for their services as directors, employees, independent contractors, or in another capacity. Write "none" if your Directors are unpaid. The figures you use here should match up with your expenses in Part IXA, line 17.

Lines 1b and 1c—Employees and Independent Contractors

Line 1b asks for information on the five highest compensated employees who are or will be receiving compensation of at least $50,000 per year. If you have such employees, you need to provide the information requested. If you have no plans for offering compensation at this level, you can answer these questions with "None."

Line 1b also asks for information about your employees who "will receive" compensation. This can be a more difficult question to answer. If you have made a job offer to an individual who you have hired as an Executive Director to start in three months for at least $50,000 compensation, you will need to disclose the information requested. The wording in the application leaves unclear whether you should provide information in response to this question if you have talked about hiring someone "when you have funds." In other materials, the IRS has indicated that it is not looking for your dreams about what you may do but your more concrete plans for the future. Our sense is that if the Board has not agreed on a specific individual and has not set compensation or a range for compensation, you should answer the question in this section as "None." If you do have more specific plans and include estimated amounts based on those plans, be sure to label them as "estimated."

Line 1c asks for information on independent contractors that will receive more than $50,000 per year. Review Chapter 16 for information on independent contractors. Remember to enter "none" if you do not plan to pay independent contractors at this level. If your plans to hire an independent contractor in the future are vague, you probably don't need to disclose them.

Line 2—Relationships

Read carefully the instructions for definitions of "related," "family relationships" and "business relationships." The relationships defined in the instructions are the only ones you have to disclose. For example, you do not have a family relationship with your stepfather (unless he adopted you and therefore became your legal father) but you do have a family relationship with the spouse of your grandchild. If you have two Directors who have together own a 30% interest in a business, they do not have a business relationship as that term is defined in the instructions.

Line 3—More Compensation Questions

Line 3a refers to the individuals you have listed in any of the three parts of Line 1. Your are required to attach a list showing the name, qualifications, duties, and average hours worked for each one. If your Directors are not paid as Directors, you can list very simple qualifications of one sentence or less. For unpaid Directors, you might list knowledge about the issue your organization is concerned with, an educational or professional achievement, service for another nonprofit, or simply "interested in" and name your issue.

If your Directors are not paid for their service as Directors, compute the hours worked by figuring out how many hours a month/quarter/year each Director will spend in his/her Board/volunteer work for the corporation. You might describe the Director's duties as "the usual Board duties of setting policy and overseeing the management of the corporation and volunteering for the corporation." If your Directors are paid, you will need to supply enough detail so that the IRS can determine that the Director's compensation is reasonable. The Board should set the compensation of paid Directors in accordance with a conflict of interest policy (see below). Your Board should follow this policy in setting compensation for its Directors and you should let the IRS know that this was done.

Line 3b requests information about whether the individuals you identified in any of the three parts of Line 1 are also receiving compensation from another organization, either nonprofit or for-profit, that has "common control" with your nonprofit. If the individuals you've listed in Line 1 are receiving compensation from one or more other organizations, read the instructions for Line 3b carefully to see whether these organizations meet the test for common control. The typical signs of common control involve overlapping Board memberships (where the same people serve as Directors or officers for both organizations) or one organization with the power to select Board members for the other.

Lines 4 and 5—Conflicts of Interest

Although the IRS does not require that you follow the specific practices listed in Questions 4 and 5, we highly recommend that you do. Lines 4b through 4f seek to determine if your approval of compensation for your Directors, officers, highest compensated employees, and independent contractors may run afoul of the IRS excess benefit transactions rules. See pages 700-706 for an explanation of this fascinating subject. Checking "no" on any of the questions on Line 4 is like waving a red flag in front of a bull. Why do it? Of course, if you answer each question with a "yes," you must follow these practices.

Line 5 asks if you adopted a conflicts policy consistent with the IRS Sample Conflict of Interest Policy in Appendix A of its instructions. The IRS sample policy is a confusing policy that does not even satisfy all of the IRS requirements related to excess benefits transactions described in Chapter 30 and it does not cover you for some types of conflicts that are regulated by Oregon law, described in Chapter 14. We have included a sample Conflicts of Interest and Executive Compensation policy in the Forms section that satisfies both IRS and Oregon law. We recommend that you adopt this policy or one like it. This allows you to answer Line 5 as "yes" and, as long as your Board follows the policy, it will be observing the practices listed in Line 4. A "Two for One" deal. Include a copy of the policy in your Attachment showing that your Board adopted it. Adopting the policy is only one step—the Board needs to be familiar with it and follow it carefully. The consequences of failing to do so are described in Chapters 17 and 30.

Lines 6a and b—Non-fixed Compensation Arrangements

These questions are referring to the practice of determining the compensation you will pay as a percentage of the income the individual helps your nonprofit generate. New nonprofits may be tempted to enter into agreements with grant writers or fund raisers who offer to work for a percentage of the funds they help your organization raise. If you have entered into such agreements or plan to, you'll want to read the instructions for these questions carefully and understand that the IRS has concerns about these arrangements. For a discussion about the ethics of this practice, see page 503.

Lines 7a and b, 8, and 9—More Potential Conflicts of Interest

If you have or will be buying or selling goods, services, or assets from or to any of the individuals described in Part V, you will need to review the instructions for Lines 7a and b and provide additional information on how you have ensured or will ensure that these transactions are in the best interest of your nonprofit. Lines 8 and 9 address the conflict of interest issues that may arise if you have or will be entering into leases, loans, contracts or other agreements with the individuals described in Part V.

As you work through these questions, your goal is to provide a clear explanation of how your nonprofit made or will make decisions that are in the best interest of the organization and avoided or will avoid entering into agreements that provide unfair benefit to individuals who may have the ability to influence your decisions. Part of your answer should show that the Board followed its Conflicts of Interest policy (described above) in making its decisions. If you answer any of these questions with a "yes," this is an area that will almost certainly draw the IRS's attention and will probably slow application's processing because of questions back to you. You should really consider seeing an attorney before you submit your application to be sure that you have done all you can to ensure that you are or will properly handle conflicts of interest.

Part VI—Your Members and Others You Benefit

If you answer "Yes" to any question in this section, you may find it simplest to be sure that your narrative statement in Part IV provides the information that the IRS requests in this section and refer the IRS to your narrative statement by saying "See Part IV, Narrative Statement" after any "Yes" answer here.

Line 1—Benefits to Individuals and Organizations

Most nonprofits provide goods, services or funds to individuals or to organizations, so you will probably be answering at least one of these questions "Yes." Rather than repeat what you said in Part IV to explain your answer, refer to Part IV and be sure you have answered this question in Part IV.

Line 2—Limitation of Your Programs

This is a confusing question. The IRS probably means to ask whether your programs limit the provision of your goods, services, or funds to specific individuals or groups not disclosed in Part IV. Many exempt organizations limit their programs to a class of charitable recipients—for example, the homeless—and the IRS does not intend that this kind of limitation requires that you answer this question "Yes." The homeless are a charitable class. (You should have already disclosed that you plan to benefit these people in your narrative statement in Part IV.) The IRS is trying to determine if you limit your programs in some other way that singles out a specific member of a charitable class or that singles out individuals who are not charitable beneficiaries. For example, you are not exempt if you are raising money to help a particular child with cancer or to provide scholarships for the children of the executives of a particular company.

In addition, if you provide benefits to your members *that are not available on the same terms to the general public,* you must answer this question "Yes" and provide a copy of your membership application and a schedule of your membership dues and describe the different membership levels and the benefits your members receive. §501(c)(3) members cannot receive benefits that are worth more than what they contribute in dues. If you offer your members benefits that are available to the public on the same terms, you do not have to answer this question "Yes." For example, many nonprofits offer a newsletter to their members but also supply copies to the public on request or through their website.

> *§501(c)(3) members cannot receive benefits that are worth more than what they contribute in dues.*

The IRS asks this question because it must determine if your organization is *improperly* benefiting individuals. Some programs that benefit specific individuals may be exempt and others are not. See page 97 for a discussion on improper private benefit. You probably need legal advice if you answer this question "yes."

Part VII—History

Line 1—Successor Organizations

The most common successor organization is one that originally began as an unincorporated association and later incorporated as a nonprofit corporation. The corporation continues with the activities of the unincorporated association and receives its property and funds. If this describes your situation, you may think of yourself as one organization but in fact these are two separate legal entities. Your corporation took over (was a successor to) the property and activities of the unincorporated association. You will need to answer this question "yes" and fill out Schedule G.

In contrast, if your nonprofit has been formed to take over the operation of a program that was previously operated through another nonprofit corporation—the situation often referred to as a spin-off—or has been operating under a fiscal sponsorship agreement (described in Chapter 10), you will not be considered a successor organization unless the original nonprofit is transferring more than 25% of its net assets to your nonprofit—a fairly unusual situation.

Line 2—Date Application Is Submitted

Generally, if you file your application within 27 months after the end of the month in which you were incorporated (if you are a nonprofit corporation) or in which you were formed (if you are a charitable trust or unincorporated association), your exemption will retroactive to the date you were incorporated or formed. (See pages 107-08.) You must complete Schedule E if you submit this application after the 27 month period.

Part VIII—Specific Activities

The IRS has special rules about and concerns about certain types of activities. In this Part, the IRS is seeking to determine if and how you conduct these activities.

Line 1—Political Activity

Line 1 asks about political campaign activity. If you answer this question "yes," your application will be denied. See pp. 173-180.

If you answer the question about political activity "yes," your application will be denied.

Line 2—Lobbying

This asks about your attempts to "influence legislation"—that is, lobbying. Read pp. 180-194 for information about this and about the lobbying election referred to in Line 2b. If you can truthfully say so, it is helpful to explain to the IRS that you anticipate that your lobbying will constitute less than 5% of your exempt purposes expenditures (described on page 189). This should reassure the IRS that you plan to operate within the (c)(3) lobbying limits. Because your lobbying should be related to your exempt activities, you should include it among your activities in Part IV.

Line 3—Bingo and Gaming

Because of past abuses, the IRS monitors bingo. Answer these questions thoroughly. If you engage in bingo, it is likely that the IRS will take longer to process your application. In Oregon, the Attorney General's office will not give you a bingo license until you have been in existence at least one year. See pages 487-89 for more about bingo.

Line 4—Fundraising

Most nonprofits conduct some of the fundraising activities listed here. Be sure to attach a description for each type of fundraising you check. You do not have to list individual donors (and you may not want to, since your application is available to the public) but you should explain briefly how you develop donor lists and pursue contacts. If you do not buy mailing lists, most nonprofits can answer that they develop donor lists by getting the names of potential donors from Board members and volunteers and from people who have expressed an interest in their work. Question 4b covers both individual grant writers you may hire and professional and commercial fundraising firms. The latter are heavily regulated and are often abusive. (See pages 504.) If you hire individual grant writers but not professional fundraisers, be sure that you make this clear to the IRS.

Question 4e seeks to determine if you maintain donor-advised funds in which you segregate the donor's funds into a restricted account and allow the donor to make recommendations for how you use these funds over a period of time. The IRS closely scrutinizes donor-advised funds and you don't want to answer this question "yes" unless you really are a donor-advised fund. The key distinction between maintaining a donor-advised fund and the common practice of accepting gifts with donor restrictions is that the donor-advised fund includes a structure through which the donor continues to direct the use of the funds *after* they have been transferred to the nonprofit.

Line 6—Economic Development Organizations

This question is aimed at organizations that seek to assist *businesses* (not unemployed or low income *individuals*) that are located in economically depressed areas. If this described you, read the instructions. If your organization seeks to assist individuals who need help to function in the economy (for example, with job retraining), answer this question "no" and move on.

Line 8—Joint Ventures

If you are part of or plan to enter into a joint venture or partnership with another organization that is not exempt under §501(c)(3), you must answer this question "yes" and describe the arrangement. The rules about these partnerships are quite restrictive and you should get legal advice before you file your application.

Line 9—Childcare Organizations

A childcare organization may be exempt under §501(c)(3) if it qualifies as a school based on its educational program (see Line 19) or if at least 85% of the children in its care have working parents or caregivers (this is the §501(k) exemption). If you qualify under §501(k), answer Question 9a "yes" and continue with this section. Read the instruction for more help. Get legal advice, particularly if you do not meet the 85% threshold.

Line 10—Intellectual Property

Many nonprofits produce reports, instructional materials, artistic products, research results, and similar creative products. These creative products potentially have value and are called intellectual property. If your nonprofit produced the product, the rights to this property will commonly belong to the nonprofit. If that is the case, make clear in your answer to this question that the nonprofit owns all rights to the material. In some carefully structured situations, you may make arrangements that allow the individual who created the product to retain rights to his or her creation. You will need legal advice to do this. You must assure the IRS that the nonprofit has or will receive fair market value for its contribution to the intellectual property. You will probably need legal help to structure any arrangement that does not provide that the nonprofit keeps all intellectual property rights to the creative product that it creates.

Line 11—Contributions

This question asks about certain hot button contributions that the IRS is currently monitoring. The IRS will use the information you supply to determine whether these transactions may be giving donors unreasonable benefits, including facilitating the donors' efforts to claim charitable deductions that are more than the fair market value of their donations.

Line 12 and 14—Foreign Organizations

Questions 12 and 14 ask about your operations in foreign countries. Question 12 is interested in direct programs you operate in other countries and Question 14 wants to know about grants and distributions you make to other governments, to non-governmental organizations (commonly called NGOs), and to other foreign organizations. If you operate direct programs that are clearly exempt outside the United States, you can easily answer Question 12.

You should get legal advice if you answer Question 14a "yes." The IRS has specific rules that prohibit donors from taking charitable deductions for gifts that they give to a (c)(3) organization that are earmarked for a foreign program. The IRS also wants to be sure that any money you give to a foreign grantee is being used for exempt purposes. You will probably want to add language in your Bylaws and to create a Grantmaking Policy to comply with these rules. Unless you are familiar with the rules in this area, you need help.

If you operate in foreign countries, also be sure to read pages 687-92 on the terrorism laws.

Line 13—Distributions to Other Organizations

The IRS wants to ensure that monies you distribute to other organizations are being used for exempt purposes. If you make grants or distributions to other (c)(3)s, the IRS will be unlikely to question your distribution as long as it fits within your exempt purpose. However, if you make distributions to organizations that are not exempt under §501(c)(3), you must follow expenditure responsibility procedures to ensure that the funds are used for (c)(3) purposes. See pages 234-35 for what is required. If you follow those procedures, you should be able to answer both parts of Question 13f with "yes" and to answer Question 13g.

Some (c)(3)s are affiliated with other exempt organizations, most commonly lobbying organizations exempt under §501(c)(4). (See pages 113-115 and 200-202.) Question 13d requires that you disclose these connected organizations. The IRS will, of course, be particularly interested in monies flowing from your (c)(3) to a linked organization. You can make this kind of transfer only if you get goods or services of equal or greater value in return or if you properly document that your linked organization uses the funds to further your (c)(3) exempt purpose. Get professional help to be sure that you handle these transfers properly.

If you make distributions to other organizations, be sure that you included this as part of your programmatic activity in Part IV.

Line 15—Connected Organizations

The IRS asks again (as it did in Question 13d) for any organizations with which you are linked. If you answered 13d by identifying linked organizations, you will answer this question "yes" and refer to 13d. However, many organizations that did not answer Question 13 in the affirmative because they don't make distributions to their linked organizations will also answer Question 15 "yes."

Lines 16-21—Specific Organizations

The IRS lists particular types of organizations here for which it wants additional information. Read the instructions to see if any of these organizations describe you. If so, in some cases you will need to complete an additional schedule. You will probably need legal help.

Line 22—Scholarships

If you provide scholarships or educational loans, you have to fill out Section I of Schedule H. If you are a private foundation that provides scholarships, you can and generally should obtain advance approval of your procedures in awarding scholarships. You do this by filling out Section II on Schedule H. Advance approval ensures that your procedures meet IRS rules. You should get legal advice, particularly if you provide scholarships to employees of a particular employer.

> *Many nonprofits that are not schools provide waivers or reductions of conference fees or other program expenses to low-income individuals or to other nonprofit groups. We recommend that you do not use the word "scholarship" to describe these fee waivers.*

The question about scholarships is geared to uncover payments made to enhance an individual's capacities or talents. Many nonprofits that are not schools provide waivers or reductions of conference fees or other program expenses to low-income individuals or to other nonprofit groups. We recommend that you do not use the word "scholarship" to describe these fee waivers (simply call them "fee waivers") in order to avoid confusion about whether you must file the Schedule H.

Be sure that you described your scholarship program in Part IV.

6 FILLING OUT THE TAX-EXEMPT APPLICATIONS

Part IX—Financial Data

This Part contains the Statement of Revenue and Expense and the Balance Sheet that you must fill out. The IRS wants to get three to five years of financial information. You will supply information for each year you've been in existence. If you have been in existence less than one tax year, complete the statement for that year and provide projections for three future budget years. If you have been in existence less than 5 years and have completed at least one tax year, you should supply the statement for each year in existence plus enough future projected years so that you supply a combined four years of financial information, including both actual revenues and expenses for previous years and budget information for future years. If you have been in existence for five or more years, complete the schedules for the most recent 5 years. You will need to provide a separate statement for one of the tax years, since the IRS schedule only accommodates 4 years. (The IRS expanded to a 5 year requirement after it put out the Form 990.) The instructions explain how to fill out the Statement. Get your bookkeeper or accountant to help you with this part of the Form 1023.

If you have been in existence for less than five years and so must prepare projected budgets, try to project as realistically as possible but don't spend excessive amounts of time on this. Virtually all new groups are estimating and your estimates will very likely be different from your actual results. Chapter 24 on making a budget and Chapter 26 on preparing financial reports should be helpful. Use your organization's method of accounting and your accounting period in preparing projected budgets. If you use a method of accounting other than the cash receipts and disbursements method (see Chapter 26), you must attach a statement explaining the method you use. Be sure to attach itemized lists for those lines that require lists.

The main reason that the revenue portion (Lines 1-13) of Part A is divided into the categories that you see is so that the IRS can use these figures to see if you meet the support tests as a public charity. See pages 99, 101-07. The categories also help the IRS to determine if a substantial part of your purpose is to run a business, if anyone is privately benefiting from your group, if you have unusual grants, etc.

Many groups get or expect to get all of their gross receipts from gifts, grants and contributions (Line 1) or fees from activities directly related to their exempt purpose or from occasional fundraisers (Line 9). If this is your group, you will probably find that these are the only revenue categories that you fill in.

There are several common confusions about the expense portion (Lines 14-24) of the Statement of Revenue and Expenses. Line 15 asks for contributions and similar amounts you pay out to others. As a (c)(3) organization, you should only make contributions to other (c)(3) groups, to groups that use your funds for (c)(3) purposes or to needy individuals. You should have described all this in your narrative statement in Part IV. If you operate programs that benefit others but which do not pay out sums of money, Line 15 will be 0.

Line 16 describes disbursements for members. Most (c)(3)s do not make disbursements to their members. If you do, you will need to show that the dues paid by members equal or exceed the value of what they receive. Your answer here should agree with your answer in Part VI. If you compensate your officers or Directors, Line 17 should correspond with the information you disclosed in Part V, Line 1.

Line 23 should include the rest of your expenses, including any category that didn't meet the definition for the other expense lines. Most of your direct program expenses (other than salaries) should be reflected here. You are required to attach a schedule of expenses you include in Line 23. Group these expenses into the categories you usually use to describe them and make sure that the total of the expenses on your schedule matches your entry on Line 23. Almost all nonprofits will have expenses to include on Line 23.

Part B of Part IX requests your Balance Sheet for your most recently completed tax year. Your "tax" year is your fiscal year. In most cases, the year-end that you enter in this section must match the year-end that you have entered in Part A, the Statement of Revenue and Expenses. If you haven't yet completely a tax year, you can enter your Balance Sheet information at the end of the last month that has been completed and note the date of that month end where it asks for "Year End." If your nonprofit has no funds in a bank account or other assets, and does not have any debts (liabilities), you may either enter zeros or the word "none" on the form or enter a statement that you have no assets, liabilities, or net assets at this time.

After you have completed your budget, re-read the rest of the application with your budget in mind. Make sure that your budget items seem consistent with the programs you described in Part IV, the lobbying you described in Part VIII, and all other information you have provided.

Part X—Public Charity or Private Foundation Status

The IRS uses this part of the form to determine if you are a public charity or a private foundation. Review the discussion on pages 99-107 about this very important distinction. If you are a private foundation, you will answer Lines 1-4. You should get professional help.

If you are a public charity, you should answer Line 1a "no" and skip to Line 5. Use pages 101-07 to pick the category that is appropriate for you in Line 5. To match the IRS categories with the ones on pages 101-02, use this table:

Description	IRS letter on Application	# Used in Chapter 5 (pp. 101-02)
Church	(a)	1
School	(b)	2
Hospital/Medical/ Research Organization	(c)	3
Supporting Organization	(d)	5
Public Safety Organization	(e)	6
Development Foundation	(f)	7
Publicly Supported Organization (PSO)	(g)	8
Fee/Activity Supported Organization (FASO)	(h)	9

Be sure to complete whatever schedules, if any, are required by your choice. Use Chapter 5 to help you with the schedules.

PSOs and FASOs

Many groups can potentially qualify as a Public Charity because they are both a Publicly Supported Organization (PSO) and a Fee/Activity Supported Organization (FASO). The form allows you to permit the IRS to compute your support and place you in one of these categories. If you are applying for an advance ruling and are uncertain about exactly what your future support will be, you are generally safe to check (i) and let the IRS choose for you. If you check (i) and IRS decides you could qualify as both a PSO and FASO, it will usually designate you a PSO. This is generally the preferred designation from your point of view, since the PSO support test is more flexible in many respects than the FASO test. Donors to PSOs can give a higher percentage of their adjusted gross income to PSOs than to FASOs, although this is not an issue for most donors. If you ever spin off another nonprofit and give it funds, that nonprofit can count your funds coming from a PSO as public monies to help it to establish that it is a public charity, unlike money coming from a FASO.

Line 6—Advance or Definitive Ruling

The IRS no longer requires that you go through the Advance Ruling period. Yippee! If you are a newer organization that has been in existence for less than 5 completed tax years, skip question 6. Do not sign page 11.

If you have been in existence longer than 5 completed tax years, you will need to complete Line 6b and sign page 11.

Line 7—Unusual Grants

The "unusual grants" referred to in Line 7 are discussed on page 157.

Part XI—User Fee Information

In this section, you indicate whether you are paying a $400 or $850 user fee. These have increased since Form 1023 was printed. Check any notices that accompany the application in case the IRS raises it again.

Signature Line

Form 1023 must be signed and dated by an officer authorized to sign by the corporation. The signer should review the application carefully. It may also be signed by any person who the corporation authorizes by a power of attorney to sign. Your group must use IRS Form 2848 (Power of Attorney and Declaration of Representative) or Form 8821 (Tax Information Authorization) to grant a power of attorney. The signature attests that the application and accompanying schedules and attachments are true, correct and complete.

Schedules

If you are required to file Schedules, you should get professional help in most cases. The rules concerning specific groups like churches, schools, hospital, supporting organizations, housing, and scholarships are more complex than we can cover in this book. We will discuss Schedule E (used by groups that file this application more than 27 months after they were formed) and Schedule G (on successor organization) as it applies to unincorporated nonprofit associations that have incorporated as nonprofit corporations.

Schedule E—Organizations Formed More Than 27 Months Before Filing

Generally, if you didn't apply for exemption within 27 months after the end of the month in which you were formed, your exemption will be retroactive to the postmark date of your application and not to the date of your formation. There are two exceptions to this rule. One is for groups that are exempt whether or not they apply for exemption. These are the groups described in Lines 1-4.

LINE 5—EXTENSIONS OF TIME

The second exception is for groups that get an extension of time to apply for exemption. Whether the IRS grants an extension depends on whether the IRS contacted you during the 27-month period about your failure to file Form 1023. If it did contact you, you will need to show reasons for your late filing that are specific to your organization, including whether you contacted an attorney, accountant, or the IRS about filing for the exemption; who you contacted and what you were told; how and when you learned about the filing deadline; whether any significant intervening circumstances beyond your control prevented you from filing the Form 1023 after you learned about the filing deadline; and any other information that might establish good cause on your part for not filing in time.

If the IRS did not contact you before the end of the 27-month period, then the IRS will be looking at the following factors to determine whether it should grant you an extension:

- whether you exercised due diligence in finding out the due date of the application and in preparing the application for filing;

- whether you took prompt action to deal with the deadline or to request an extension;

- whether you had the intention of using the extension as a means of evading the deadline;

- whether granting the extension would prejudice the interests of the government;

- whether granting the extension would be consistent with the objectives of the notice requirement and the grace period.

The first three factors are especially important. You need to show you had good reason for not seeking advice from an attorney, accountant, or the IRS about filing requirements (for instance, if you thought you were exempt from filing as an organization that normally receives less than $5,000 per year—see page 107). If you sought advice, you need to explain either that it was wrong (they failed to tell you about the filing deadlines) or why you failed to follow it. Although these criteria seem forbidding, many organizations find that it is worthwhile to file for an extension. Remember that if you fail to qualify for an extension, it does not mean that you can't get an exemption. It just means that your exemption will only be retroactive to the time that you filed your application.

LINES 6 AND 7—ADVANCE RULING

You have to answer 6a as "Yes" to be considered for exemption. However, the IRS no longer issues advance rulings, so you should not fill out Part X, line 6a. You shouldn't have to answer Question 7 either.

LINES 8—§501(C)(4) STATUS

As the question explains, what you are deciding in this question is whether you want to clear the way for the IRS to recognize you as an organization exempt under §501(c)(4) if your §501(c)(3) exemption is not retroactive to the date you were formed. The §501(c)(4) status would cover you from the day you were organized until the date you are recognized as exempt under §501(c)(3) (that is, the day you filed your application). The advantage of getting §501(c)(4) status for that period is that you won't have to pay income tax for that period. However, remember that contributions to your group during that time would not be deductible, as they are for §501(c)(3) groups. Since the alternative to getting §501(c)(4) status at this point would be to have no tax-exempt status, most groups will want to answer Line 8 "yes" and must provide a completed Page 1 of Form 1024. You can find information on how to complete this page at the end of this Chapter.

Schedule G—Successors to Other Organizations

Many nonprofit corporations operated as unincorporated nonprofit associations before they incorporated. Because the law treats the corporation as a separate legal entity, the incorporated nonprofit is a successor to the unincorporated nonprofit association. We are including information about how to fill out this Schedule for those corporations. If you are classified as a successor organization for some other reason, you should get professional help to fill out this schedule.

LINES 1 AND 2—NONPROFIT PREDECESSORS

As a nonprofit corporation that succeeded a nonprofit association, you can answer Line 1a "no" and Line 2a "yes." In an attachment, explain very briefly that your corporation was created by incorporating a nonprofit association whose activities you have continued. If you provided this explanation in Part IV, state "see Part IV" in the section of the Attachment for Schedule G.

Keep in mind in answering Line 2b that your previous nonprofit association was probably itself exempt from taxation even though it never applied for exempt status. If it had gross receipts of less than $5,000 per year or was a church, it may have been exempt under §501(c)(3). (See page 107.) If it was not exempt under (c)(3), it was very likely exempt under §501(c)(4). (See page 109.) If it was not tax-exempt, you will need to explain its tax status. Lines 2c and 2d are self-explanatory.

In Line 2e, you can simply explain that you continued the activities of the nonprofit association but simply changed its organizational form by incorporating or refer to your answer in Part IV, if you covered this there.

LINES 3-5—INFORMATION ABOUT PREDECESSOR

Line 3 is self-explanatory. The EIN is the employer identification number. If you are filling out this schedule because you were an unincorporated association that has now incorporated and your unincorporated association never obtained an EIN, write in "none" for the unincorporated association. If the unincorporated association had an EIN, it may be the same EIN as your nonprofit corporation.

On Line 4, you should list those who had decision-making authority over the association. If the association had no Board but had members who made all the decisions, explain this on your attachment. Since the association was nonprofit, your answer under "Share/Interest" should be "None." If some of the Board members continue to work with you, you will need to explain their relationship in Line 5.

LINE 6—TRANSFER OF ASSETS

If the nonprofit association gave your corporation its assets, answer Line 6a "yes" and explain in your attachment that the nonprofit association gave you its assets. Unless an asset was quite valuable, provide a list that covers very general categories, such as "office supplies worth about $500." Most likely, you do not have an appraisal and you can simply say so. If there was no written agreement of transfer (and there almost never is in cases like this), simply tell the IRS that there was no written agreement in answer to Line 6c.

LINES 7-9—OTHER QUESTIONS

Because Question 7 refers to for-profit predecessors, your answer will be "no." Your answer to Questions 8 and 9 will also be "no" unless you have the dealing described there with individuals listed on Line 4.

Form 1023 Checklist

You must include the Form 1023 Checklist which is printed at the end of the Form 1023 as pages 27 and 28. It is easy to overlook this, particularly if you don't have to fill out any of the Schedules. Review the Checklist carefully and check each box to show that you have included the material required. Be sure to put a check mark by the Schedules (if any) that you filled out. Notice on the second page that you must fill in the location of the Purpose Clause and the Dissolution Clause in your Articles of Incorporation or the amendments to your Articles. Repeat here what you said in Part III, Lines 1 and 2b.

Once you've checked every box, assemble the materials in the order listed in the first item on the Checklist and send them with your check for the user fee on top of the pile (and not stapled to anything) to the IRS at the address at the end of the Checklist. The IRS review process begins by checking to be sure your packet contains all the required information. You benefit from all this fastidiousness because it allows the IRS to process your application more quickly.

Attachments to the 1023

Every attachment (other than IRS forms) should show your organization's name, your employer identification number and an identifiable heading so that the agent reading the application knows what it refers to. Be sure that your application and attachments do not contain anyone's social security number. The Form 1023 becomes a public document and disclosure of a social security number can lead to identity theft.

> *Be sure that your application and attachments do not contain anyone's social security number. The Form 1023 becomes a public document and disclosure of a social security number can lead to identity theft.*

Filling Out Form 1024

Groups that are exempt from taxation under any section other than §501(c)(3) do not have to apply for recognition from exemption. However, most groups can apply if they chose to do so. There are several reasons you may want to apply in order to get a formal letter from the IRS recognizing that you are exempt. One is that you may be somewhat uncertain about whether you qualify. If you fail to pay taxes based on your belief that you are exempt and are later audited and found not to be exempt, your group may find itself owing back taxes, interest, and penalties. Your Directors may want the formal recognition in order to eliminate any chance that they might be personally liable for these sums. Another reason you may choose to apply is that your organization may qualify for certain benefits (for example, the right to cheaper space in public facilities) if it has an IRS letter recognizing its exemption.

In most cases, organizations seeking formal recognition that they are tax-exempt under a section other than §501(c)(3) fill out IRS Form 1024. You should contact the IRS and obtain a copy of Form 1024, the instructions for Form 1024, and Publication 557. (See Appendix 2 for contact information, including the website for obtaining these forms and publication.) Although Form 1024 is different from Form 1023, a number of the questions are the same. We suggest you review the discussion about the Form 1023 above, especially for information about:

- the employer identification number,
- the annual accounting period, and
- the narrative description of what you do.

As you complete the narrative description of what your organization does, remember that one important difference between (c)(3)s and (c)(4)s has to do with lobbying and political campaigning. (c)(3)s can do limited lobbying; a (c)(4) cannot have as its purpose something that can only be accomplished by lobbying (for example, "our purpose is to persuade Congress to repeal the Free Trade Laws) but a (c)(4) has no limits on the amount of lobbying it can do to advance a social welfare/civic league purpose. So, a (c)(4) could have as its purpose "to educate policy makers and the public about the effects of the Free Trade Laws on the U.S. economy and on workers around the world" and could include extensive lobbying among its activities.

(c)(3)s are prohibited from supporting or opposing a candidate or political party. (c)(4)s can engage in some political campaigning, but you must do this on a limited basis, since the promotion of social welfare does not include intervention in political campaigns. The IRS does not have clear guidelines in this area. If you want to do more than incidental campaigning, consider setting up or contributing to a PAC for that part of your work. See pages 200-202, 658-61, and 666-69.

Other groups, such as unions and business leagues, do not have IRS restrictions on their involvement in political campaigns and are typically more involved. See Chapter 29 for other federal and state rules that apply to political involvement for all nonprofit corporations.

There are a few types of exempt groups that do not file any form. Consult Publication 557 to see if you happen to fall in one of these unusual groups.

Appendix 7 gives a line by line description of how to fill out the main body of Form 1024. In addition, each group must fill out a special schedule that pertains to its specific exemption. If you need help with those schedules, you should see an attorney or accountant.

Even if you choose not to apply for recognition of exemption, you are still responsible for filing annual tax returns if you are an exempt organization. See Chapter 12.

Questions Back From the IRS

It is very common for the IRS to respond to your application by sending you a list of questions to answer. Even if the questions seem obvious, you will want to give very serious consideration to your answers since misunderstandings between applicants and the IRS are quite common and can seriously delay approval of your application or even result in denial of tax-exempt status. At this point, you should seriously consider getting professional help.

Consult Appendix 1 if you would like information about source material related to this Chapter.

The next four chapters in Part II cover in greater detail the subjects of PSOs and FASOs, lobbying, unrelated business income, and fiscal sponsorship. Read those if they are pertinent to your organizations. All tax-exempt groups should look at the last two chapters of Part II on state and local tax exemptions and on tax returns for exempt organizations.

7 PUBLICLY SUPPORTED ORGANIZATIONS AND FEE/ACTIVITY SUPPORTED ORGANIZATIONS (PSOs AND FASOs)

THIS CHAPTER COVERS

- Support Requirements for PSOs and FASOs
- How to Calculate the Total Support Base
- Summary of the Formulas
- How to Calculate Your Support from Qualified Sources for the PSO Test
- How to Calculate Your Support from Qualified Sources for the FASO Test
- The Normalcy Period
- Recordkeeping Issues

Welcome to the most boring chapter of this book! In Chapter 5, we discussed the difference between private foundations and public charities, and we listed and described the types of groups that could qualify as public charities. We postponed discussion of two of those groups until this chapter.

The tests described in this chapter are extremely technical. Consequently, you will probably find this chapter confusing (sorry) and boring (double sorry). We've done what we can to make this tedious area of law understandable. Before you plunge in, you should review #8 and #9 on pages 106-07. These sections describe groups that should clearly be PSOs and FASOs without having to get caught up in the details of this chapter.

This chapter will explain the financial support requirements for groups wishing to qualify for or maintain §501(c)(3) public charity status as a Publicly Supported Organization (PSO) or a Fee/Activity Supported Organization (FASO). If you have an accountant, consider having your accountant deal with your public charity classification. Accountants love boring, technical stuff!

You should read this chapter carefully if you are or want to be a §501(c)(3) public charity and:

- You are not a church, school, hospital; medical research organization, development foundation, governmental unit, supporting organization, or public safety organization; and *either*

    ◊ You receive a lot of your support from the government, grants, donations, or membership fees; *or*

    ◊ You receive a lot of your support from receipts from your activities (sale of tickets to events, sale of products or services) or from a business you run.

The information in this section may be necessary both to fill out the application for tax-exempt status and to complete your yearly informational return to the IRS (Form 990).

Support Requirements for PSO's and FASO's

Most of the organizations that are exempt as public charities (e.g., churches, schools, hospitals, etc.) are defined in terms of their purpose. Publicly Supported Organizations (PSOs) and Fee Activity Supported Organizations (FASOs) are defined in terms of where their financial support comes from.

> *The tests described in this chapter are extremely technical. Before you plunge into this chapter, you should review #8 and #9 on pages 106-107. These sections describe groups that should clearly be PSOs and FASOs without having to get caught up in the details of this chapter.*

The support requirements for PSOs differ from those for FASOs. Basically, they are as follows:

PSO – An organization which normally receives a substantial part of its support from a governmental unit or from direct or indirect contributions from the general public.

FASO – An organization which normally receives more than one-third of its support from any combination of:

◊ gifts, grants, contributions or membership fees, and

◊ gross receipts from related business activities;

and normally receives not more than one-third of its support from the sum of:

◊ gross investment income; and

◊ the amount of the unrelated business taxable income less the amount of the unrelated business income tax.

In order to qualify as a public charity under these rules, you need to receive a certain percentage of your total support from "qualified sources." Total support from all sources is the denominator of this fraction, and the income from certain qualified sources is the numerator.

The words in these rules have very specific and sometimes unexpected meanings (for instance, you may be surprised to learn that "normally" means "over five years"). We'll explain the rules that have the most importance for exempt groups, and point out other areas that you should check further if they apply to your group.

In order to qualify as a public charity under these rules, you need to receive a certain percentage of your total support from "qualified sources." The percentage is determined by dividing your total support into the income from qualified sources. Thus, total support from all sources is the denominator of this fraction, and the income from certain qualified sources is the numerator.

First, we'll explain how to calculate your total support base, which will be the denominator of the fraction. Next, we'll talk about how to calculate your support from qualified sources (the numerator) and then the proper tests to apply for PSOs and then for FASOs. At the end of this chapter, there are some worksheets to help you in calculating how you come out on the support test.

Terminology

NUMERATOR = Qualified Support

DENOMINATOR = Total Support Base

In several cases, the rules are too detailed to describe here, and we suggest you see an accountant or attorney if you think those rules affect you.

How to Calculate the Total Support Base

The total support base (denominator) can come from five sources for PSOs, six for FASOs. These sources are:

1. Contributions, grants (excluding unusual grants, discussed on page 157), and membership fees;

2. Gross receipts from related business activities (NOT for PSOs; in most cases, PSOs can have this income, but don't have to count it in either the denominator or numerator);

3. Net income from unrelated business activity, whether or not such activities are carried on regularly as a trade or business;

4. Gross investment income;

5. Tax revenues levied by a government unit for the benefit of an organization and either paid to or expended on behalf of the organization;

6. The value of services or facilities furnished by a government unit to an organization without charge (unless furnished also to the general public without charge).

These six sources are explained below.

1. Contributions, Grants and Membership Fees.

Contributions: A contribution (or gift) occurs when money or property (or the use of property) is given to your group with nothing given by you in return or when what you give in return is worth less than the gift or contribution. In the latter situation, the amount of the contribution is usually the difference between its value and what is given in return. To figure out the value of the contribution, read IRS Publications 526, *Charitable Contributions,* and Publication 561, *Determining the Value of Donated Property,* which you can get free from the IRS. See Appendix 2.

Grants: Grants are made to organizations, often by governmental units and foundations, to make it possible for the group to operate programs which are part of carrying out its exempt purposes. When the government provides the money, it can be difficult to determine whether the government is funding an activity that will benefit the general public (for example, the government grants you money to rehabilitate low-income housing at no cost) or is really contracting for a benefit which the government receives (for example, the government pays an educational organization to train governmental employees in the principles of management and administration). Generally, the government imposes fewer restrictions on grants and is less likely to solicit for grantees. In the case of contracts, the money the organization receives is not a grant but is instead a payment for services. It is either gross receipts from related activities (see #2 below) or income from an unrelated business (see #3 below).

Membership Fee: Groups often have members: people who share a common goal or concern. Sometimes the organization charges a fee to each prospective member as a requirement for joining the group. Payment of a membership fee often entitles the member to certain benefits, such as receipt of a newsletter, the right to attend meetings, and the right to vote. The membership fee is usually used for the general support of the organization.

In some cases, what looks like a membership fee may be something else. If one class of members pays a greater membership fee than another class of members and does not receive any additional benefits, (e.g., individual member, $10; patron, $100), the difference is classified as a gift or contribution rather than a membership fee. Similarly, if the membership fee is really a ticket price to a performance or event or the price of merchandise or services which are sold to the general public, then the fee is not a membership fee but rather income from a related or unrelated business activity.

2. Gross Receipts from Related Business Activities

Receipts from related business activities may come from the following activities:

- Admissions;
- Sales of merchandise;
- Performance of services; or
- Furnishing of facilities.

This category counts gross receipts, not net receipts after expenses are paid. The activity must be related to the charitable, educational or other exempt purpose of the organization. (See Chapter 9 to determine what is related and what is unrelated business activity.)

This support source is usually counted only for the FASO formula, not for the PSO formula. This is an advantage for PSOs because this support is also counted in the numerator for FASOs but *only to a limited extent.* As you read on, you will see that this can make it difficult for a group to pass the required support test. PSOs don't have to count it in either the denominator or the numerator. The exception to this is if substantially all of your organization's support is from gross receipts from related activities and an insignificant amount comes from governmental units and the general public. If this is the case, you cannot qualify as a PSO.

3. Net Income from Unrelated Business Activities

It's important to know the difference between related and unrelated business activity for three reasons. First, if the activity is related, all the gross receipts are counted in the total support base for FASOs in #2 above. If it's unrelated, only the net income is counted (and probably the net loss). Second, net income from unrelated activities is counted in the support base for both FASOs and

PSOs. PSOs will also have to be able to make this determination. Third, both FASOs and PSOs are subject to a tax on some unrelated business income, but not on gross receipts from related activities. Chapter 9 discusses the difference between related and unrelated business activities.

The net income from unrelated business activities is counted as support if the income comes from a trade or business and if the income is not substantially related to your exempt purpose. It does not matter whether the activity is carried on regularly or is sporadic. Note that this is a broader test than the test for determining if you must pay unrelated business income tax. (See Chapter 9). The unrelated business income tax only applies if your activity is regular.

4. Gross Investment Income

This support element includes the gross income from interest, dividends, rents and royalties, unless the income is taxable as unrelated business income. (See Chapter 9 to figure out what is included in this exception.) Examples of these four sources are as follows:

- Interest on savings accounts or investments or interest you charge on loans to individuals or groups;

- Dividends on stock, shares (savings) in credit unions, etc. (In connection with the interest and dividends, you will get a statement from the bank or the credit union at the end of the year showing the total amount credited to your account throughout the year as dividends or interest);

- Royalties (for example, payments to you from sales of a book your group has written);

- Rents from real property and from personal property, leased with real property, to the extent that the rents are not taxable as unrelated business income.

If income from any of these sources comes from activities which further your exempt purpose in any important way, that income would be *gross receipts from related activities* (#2 above) and *not* gross investment income. For instance, if the purpose of the group is to provide facilities or make loans to sick or poor people, rent or interest from such individuals would be gross receipts from related activities.

5. Certain Tax Revenues

Tax Revenues levied by a government unit for the benefit of an organization and either paid to or expended on behalf of the organization must be counted in the total support base.

6. Certain Services and Facilities Furnished by the Government

You must count in your support base the value of services or facilities furnished by a government unit to your organization without charge, unless these services or facilities are furnished also to the general public without charge.

Summary of the Formulas

PSO

Numerator =

Qualified Support

Denominator =

Contributions, grants (excluding unusual grants), membership fees, *plus*

Net Income from unrelated business activities, *plus*

Gross investment income, *plus*

Tax revenues from government, *plus*

Value of free services/facilities from government

FASO

Numerator =

Qualified Support

Denominator =

Contributions, grants (excluding unusual grants), membership fees, *plus*

Gross receipts from related business activities, *plus*

Net Income from unrelated business activities, *plus*

Gross investment income, *plus*

Tax revenues from government, *plus*

Value of free services/facilities from government

The total support received from these sources—all six for FASOs and five (excluding "gross receipts from related business activities") for PSOs—represents the total support base of your group. (Use the worksheet at the end of this chapter to help you calculate your denominator.) This is the denominator for the percentage calculation explained next. The remainder of this chapter describes the different support tests for PSOs and FASOs and explains the "qualified" sources of support which make up the numerator for your calculations.

How to Calculate Your Support from Qualified Sources for the PSO Test

A Publicly Supported Organization is an organization which:

- normally
- receives a substantial part of its support
- from a governmental unity, or
- from direct or indirect contributions from the general public.

Two very specific tests are used to determine whether a PSO is "publicly supported" (as defined by the IRS). One is called the "mechanical test"; the other is the "facts and circumstances" test. If you pass the first, you don't need the second. If you fail the first, you still might pass the second.

Both tests involve a fraction or percentage calculation:

>First you determine your overall support. This is the denominator. (We've already covered this.)

>Second, you determine how much of that total support came from certain qualified specific sources. (We cover this next.)

>Finally, you see what percentage of your total support (denominator) came from qualified sources (numerator).

If support from qualified sources equals $33\frac{1}{3}\%$ of your total support, you have passed the "mechanical test" and are therefore a Publicly Supported Organization.

If not, you and the IRS apply the alternative "facts and circumstances" test: if your percentage of qualified support is at least 10% of total support, and you attract public support, and considering all the facts and circumstances you have the nature of a "publicly supported" organization, you have passed this test.

The Mechanical Test (or One-Third Support Test)

An organization qualifies as a Publicly Supported Organization if it normally receives at least $33\frac{1}{3}\%$ of its total support (the denominator) from qualified sources.

The meaning of *normally* under this test is discussed on page 165.

Qualified sources of support (numerator) are governmental unit support, direct public support, and indirect public support. These are defined and calculated as follows:

Governmental Unit Support

Governmental unit support includes all donations and contributions from governmental units. It also includes grants from governmental units if the grant is made to an organization to provide a service or facility for the direct benefit of the general public. If the grant is to serve the direct and immediate need of the payor, it cannot be included.

Direct Public Support

Contributions, grants and membership fees from individuals, corporations, or trusts, are included. However, there is a limit on how much from each source can be counted. If you have some donations which are large, in comparison with other donations, read this section carefully.

PER PERSON TWO PERCENT LIMITATION

There is a two percent per person limitation on how much direct public support you can include in your numerator. Each contribution, grant or fee amount will be fully included in the numerator only if it is not larger than 2% of the total support base (the denominator). If it is larger than that, then only the amount which represents 2% of total support is counted. This "2% limitation" is a sub-test to which each individual donor is subject. Since these calculations are over the whole normalcy period (usually 5 years, see page 165), you have to know what each donor has given for each year in that period.

> *Example:* Carol donates $120 a year to the local Senior Center, an exempt organization, for the five-year "normalcy" period. During this normalcy period, the Senior Center's total support base was $10,000. Two percent of $10,000 is $200, so $200 is the support limitation per individual donor. Carol has given a total of $600 over the four year period ($120 a year for 5 years). *Only $200 of that $600 can be counted in the numerator for the mechanical test.* However, it will all be counted in the denominator.

DISQUALIFIED PERSON TWO PERCENT LIMITATION

There is a special "lumping" rule where the donor is part of certain disqualified person groups. The five types of disqualified person/groups are:

- Substantial contributors
- Foundation managers.
- 20% owner/entity substantial contributors
- Family members
- 35% disqualified persons/entity owners

For individuals who are not disqualified person, the two percent limitation rule applies only to that individual. Where the donor is a disqualified person, the two percent limitations rule for disqualified persons states that all contributions will be lumped together and treated as one contribution if they are made by a donor and by any entity that is related to that donor in the form of a 20% owner/entity substantial contributor, a family member, or 35% disqualified person/entity owner. The purpose of this lumping rule is to prevent a donor from getting around the 2% rule by giving part of her/his contribution in the donor's name and part through a family member or an organization controlled by the donor.

The starting point for determining if you have contributors who are disqualified persons is to see if you have substantial contributors who contribute to your organization. If so, you then need to examine their business and family relationships to see if you have other disqualified persons as contributors. You also need to examine whether your foundation managers or their families or businesses contributed to your group.

SUBSTANTIAL CONTRIBUTOR

A substantial contributor is any person, trust, corporation, estate, partnership, or association who gives an aggregate amount of more than $5,000 to your group, if that aggregate amount is more than 2% of the total contributions and bequests (gifts made by a will) received throughout your existence up to the close of the taxable year in which the contribution is received. Although the calculation is made based on total contributions at the end of your tax year, a person who is a substantial contributor at that time actually became a substantial contributor on the date that he or she made the contribution that pushed that donor into the substantial contributor category.

Note that the denominator for this 2% calculation is not your total support for five years but is the total of your contributions and bequests throughout your existence up to the close of the taxable year when you got the contribution.

Once a person becomes a substantial contributor, she or he is always a substantial contributor, even though later on as the organization receives more support, her or his contribution may become less than 2% of the total contributions. There is one exception to this rule that allows a substantial contributor to be treated like other donors. To qualify for this exception:

- The donor (and any disqualified persons related to the donor) must go 10 taxable years without making any contributions.

- The donor and any disqualified persons related to the donor must not have been a foundation manager during that 10 year period.

- The aggregate contributions of the donor and any related disqualified persons must be insignificant when compared to the contributions of one other person.

It is these twists in the test that separate substantial contributors from other contributors subject to the Two Percent Limitation discussed on page 153 (and those of us trying to understand this from our sanity).

> *Example:* On July 19, 2010, Claire gave $2,500 to the Rural Assistance Project. On May 17, 2012, she gave an additional $3,000. From its beginning until the close of 2012 (the taxable year that it received Claire's gift), the Rural Assistance Project received

$200,000 in contributions from all sources. 2% of $200,000 = $4,000. Since $5,000 is more than $4,000, $5,000 is the floor that marks substantial contributions and Claire exceeded that limit. Claire is a substantial contributor as of May 17, 2012, as it is on that date that her aggregate contributions of $5,500 met the $5,000 test. Claire will always be a substantial contributor even though the organization receives donations after 2012 that reduce her contribution to less than 2% of its total contributions (unless she eventually qualifies to change this status under the 10 year rule discussed above).

Example: Suppose that Claire contributed as described above but that the Rural Assistance Project received a donation from an unrelated source of $100,000 in November of 2012. At the close of its tax year in 2012, the Rural Assistance Project's contributions now totalled $300,000. 2% of $300,000 = $6,000. Claire with her donations of $5,500 is not a substantial contributor because her donations did not meet the test *as of the end of the year that she donated*.

The consequence of becoming a substantial contributor is that this donor is now a disqualified person. This means that your organization must aggregate the donor's contributions with her or his family and business connections in applying the two percent limitation rules.

> *Once a person becomes a substantial contributor, she or he is always a substantial contributor, even though later on as the organization receives more support, her or his contribution may become less than 2% of the total contributions. There is one exception to this rule.*

The government and other PSOs are not substantial contributors, unless their contributions to your group were given to them by a donor who earmarked them to be given to you.

FOUNDATION MANAGER

This category includes:

- officers and directors of a foundation, or individuals having similar powers or responsibilities; or
- with respect to any act, or failure to act, the employees of the foundation having authority or responsibility with respect to such act or failure to act.

A person will be considered an *officer* if:

- she or he is so designated in the Articles or Bylaws;
- she or he regularly exercises general authority to make administrative or policy decisions on behalf of the organization.

Example: If your group received a contribution from a foundation manager and a contribution from the family members of a foundation manager or a contribution from a foundation manager and from an entity of which the foundation manager owns 35%, these contributions must be combined for purposes of the 2% rules.

There is some ambiguity between the statute and the IRS interpretation on the issue of whether the director or officers of a public charity are "foundation managers." The statute and regulations appear to define this category with reference to private foundations. The IRS seems to interpret foundation managers to include managers of public charities. If the definition makes a difference to your group, you may want to see a lawyer or accountant.

TWENTY PERCENT OWNER/ENTITY SUBSTANTIAL CONTRIBUTOR

This type of "disqualified person" is an owner of more than 20% of:

- the total combined voting power of a corporation which is a substantial contributor;
- the profits interest of a partnership which is a substantial contributor; or
- the beneficial interest of a trust or unincorporated association which is a substantial contributor.

In other words, if one of these entities is a substantial contributor, its owners of more than 20% of the voting power, profits, or beneficial interest also become substantial contributors. Thus, organizations need to inquire into the ownership of entities which are substantial contributors.

FAMILY MEMBERS

Your organization must lump contributions from family members of substantial contributors, foundation managers, and 20% owner/entity substantial contributors with the contributions of those substantial contributors and foundation managers. Family members include the spouse, direct ancestors, lineal descendants, or spouses of a lineal descendant. A brother or sister is not a family member; the spouse of a grandchild is.

35% DISQUALIFIED PERSON/ENTITY OWNER

When a substantial contributor, foundation manager, twenty percent owner/entity, or family member owns 35% of a corporation, partnership, trust or estate, the entity also becomes a disqualified person. This is the reverse of the 20% owner/entity substantial contributor.

There are many special rules in addition to the definitions given here. If you need further information, see an attorney or accountant.

Example of the Mechanical Test:

Raoul is a substantial contributor to the Community Resource Fund because of large donations made in previous years. During the 5-year normalcy period, his donations total $50,000. Raoul owns 60% of Solarheat Company, which also has donated a total of $50,000 to the Resource Fund. The Fund's total support base for the normalcy period is $3,000,000, 2% of which would be $60,000.

Raoul contributed	$50,000
Solarheat contributed	$50,000
TOTAL	**$100,000**
2% limitation	$60,000
Excess over 2% not counted	$40,000

Thus $40,000 will be excluded from the numerator for purposes of the mechanical test. If the disqualified person relationship had not existed between Raoul and Solarheat Company, each contributor could have been fully counted in the numerator.

AMOUNTS EXCLUDED FROM THE TWO PERCENT LIMITATION

The 2% limitation applies only to direct public support, and not to unusual grants (described below), support from governmental units (see page 153), or indirect public support (see below).

UNUSUAL GRANTS EXCLUDED FROM THE TWO PERCENT LIMITATION RULES

Many small groups dream of someday receiving the huge contribution that will end their financial problems. Such a grant could, instead, cause them to lose their public charity status and be classified as a private foundation. Why? Recall that the whole contribution would be counted in the support base (denominator) but in many cases only a small part of it could be included as qualified support (numerator) because of the 2% per person limitation. So, such a gift could throw off a group's financial support percentage so that it failed both the mechanical and the fact and circumstances support tests. This phenomenon is referred to as "tipping." Some private foundations consider this problem when evaluating large grant requests from small organizations.

In some cases, such a grant qualifies for an "unusual grant exclusion" and can be excluded from both the numerator and denominator, thus avoiding the 2% limitation and the distortion of the support test percentages.

To qualify, the grant must come from a disinterested person and:

- Was attracted because of the publicly supported nature of the organization;
- Is unusual or unexpected because of its size or because it is not regularly received (e.g., a bequest in a will);
- Would, because of its size, adversely affect the status of the organization because of its effect on the organization's support percentages.

THE OREGON NONPROFIT CORPORATION HANDBOOK

The IRS has a longer list of facts and circumstances to consider in determining whether a grant qualifies for the exclusion. If you should be so fortunate as to encounter this mythical beast, consult an attorney or accountant immediately and before actually receiving the gift if possible.

Indirect Public Support

The third qualified source of support that goes into the numerator of the PSO calculation is indirect public support. This includes contributions received from another Publicly Supported Organization or any public charity (i.e., nonprivate foundation) that could also qualify as a Publicly Supported Organization. For example, a group classified by the IRS as a church might also meet the IRS criteria for a Publicly Supported Organization. If it did, its contributions to your group would be considered indirect public support and would not be subject to the 2% limitation. Other nongovernmental contributions are direct public support and subject to the 2% limitation rules.

However, if a donor makes a contribution to a government unit or PSO (or a public charity that could qualify as a PSO) and expressly or implicitly earmarks it for your organization, the pass-through gift will be counted as *direct* public support from the original donor and will be subject to the 2% limitation.

Example: The Women's Alliance for Peace is an exempt organization. For the five years 2012 through 2017 (the applicable normalcy period for tax year 2017), it received support as follows:

State of Oregon (a governmental unit)	$20,000
United Fund (a PSO – indirect pub. support)	$45,000
Contributions (direct public support)	$25,000
Women's Cultural Center (a FASO) (direct public support)	$15,000
TOTAL	**$105,000**

33$^{1}/_{3}$% of total = $35,000

To apply the mechanical test, WAP calculates which of those sources listed in total support are qualified sources, and whether they amount to 33⅓% of total support, keeping in mind the 2% per person limitation on direct public support.

State of Oregon (no limit)	$20,000
United Fund (no limit)	$45,000
Contributions (no individual gave more than $2,100 which is 2% of total support)	$ 4,500
Contributions (5 contributions exceeded $2,100, so 5 X $2,100=maximum countable)	$10,500
Women's Cultural Center (max. $2,100)	$ 2,100
TOTAL	**$82,100**

Note that only $2,100 of the Women's Cultural Center's $15,000 contribution was included in the numerator because the Women's Cultural Center is a FASO. If the Women's Cultural Center could also qualify as a PSO, the entire amount of its $15,000 would be counted. Even without counting the FASO money in full, the Women's Alliance for Peace has normally received more than $33^1/_3$% of its support from governmental units and the general public. Therefore, it passes the mechanical test.

PSO:

NUMERATOR =

- ◊ Governmental unit support, *plus*
- ◊ Direct public support, *plus*
- ◊ − below 2% limitation, and
- ◊ − subject to 2% limitation
- ◊ Indirect public support

DENOMINATOR = Same as PSO on page 151

Use the worksheet at the end of this chapter to calculate your numerator as a PSO.

Facts and Circumstances Test

If an organization's qualified support does not equal 33⅓% of its total support, it fails the mechanical test. But if its qualified support equals at least 10% of its total support and it is organized and operated in such a way as to attract public support, then it can turn to the "facts and circumstances" test. "Organized and operated to attract public support" means the organization has a continuous and genuine program for soliciting funds from qualified sources (discussed above), such as governmental units, and direct and indirect public support.

If your organization meets these minimum requirements, the following factors will be considered to determine if your groups has the nature of a publicly supported organization:

- financial support percentages
- support sources
- representative government body
- public facilities, services, programs, policies and participation
- membership relations

Financial Support Percentage

The closer to 33 1/3 % the organization's qualified support is, the less public support it has to demonstrate with the other factors. Of course, the closer it falls to the 10% bottom line, the greater burden it will have with regard to the other factors.

If an organization's qualified support does not equal 33 1/3 % of its total support, it fails the mechanical test. But if its qualified support equals at least 10% of its total support and it is organized and operated in such a way as to attract public support, then it can turn to the "facts and circumstances" test.

Support Sources

Favorable consideration is given to your organization when your existing sources of support come from a number of individuals that are representative of the community you seek to reach, rather than from the members of a single family. Factors to be considered in determining whether the number is representative are:

- the type of organization
- length of time it has existed (has it had time to gather wide support?)
- whether it limits its activities to a particular community or region (so then it only has to show wide support within that region)
- whether it limits its activities to a special field which can be expected to appeal to a limited number of persons (then it only has to show wide support from people within that field).

Representative Governing Body

Here the IRS is looking for a governing body (generally the Board of Directors) which represents the interests of the public, not the personal or private interests of a limited number of donors or officers. They will be satisfied with a Board made up of:

- public officials
- persons selected by public officials
- experts in the field in which the organization is operated
- community leaders representing a broad cross-section of the community
- persons selected by a broadly-based membership according to procedures established in articles or Bylaws

Public Facilities, Services, Programs, Policies and Participation

Favorable factors include:

- providing a service or facility for the general public; for example, museums or libraries;

- regular publication of studies that are widely used by colleges or the public;

- participation in or sponsorship of programs by civic or community leaders or experts in the field;

- maintaining a well-defined ongoing program to accomplish charitable work in the community;

- receiving a significant part of the organization's funds from a public charity or governmental unit to which the organization is held accountable as a condition of the grant or contract.

Membership Relations

The IRS looks for:

- whether solicitation for members is designed to enroll a large number of people in the community or area of special interest;

- whether the individual membership charge is affordable by many persons and not what only a few could afford;

- whether the activities of the organization will be likely to appeal to persons having a broad common interest, such as educational activities, musical activities, etc.

An organization does not have to show favorable facts under every category. In each case, the importance of each factor will be different depending on the nature and purpose of the organization and how long it has existed. The ultimate objective is to find out whether the organization is "publicly supported."

How to Calculate Your Support from Qualified Sources for the FASO Test

A FASO is an organization which normally receives:

- More than ⅓ of its support from any combination of contributions, grants, or membership fees, and gross receipts from related business activities; and
- Not more than ⅓ of its support from the sum of gross investment income; and the amount of the unrelated business taxable income less the amount of the unrelated business income tax.

The meaning of normally is the same as that discussed on page 165.

You must use the cash method of accounting (see page 575) for purposes of calculating your support.

One-Third Support Test

The basic strategy to determine whether more than ⅓ of your support comes from the listed sources is the same as the one for Publicly Supported Organizations (PSOs). Qualified support (numerator) is divided by the total support base (denominator) and has to equal more than ⅓ (mechanical test). The difference is in what support counts as "qualified." Also, there is no facts and circumstances test for FASOs.

> *Qualified support (numerator) is divided by total support base (denominator) and has to equal more than $1/3$.*

Qualified Support

The terms "contributions," "grants," and "membership fees" are defined in the same way as they were for PSOs. However, the contribution, grant, or membership fee is only counted in the numerator if it comes from a "permitted source" (see page 163).

FASOs count their gross receipts from related business activities (defined on page 149) in both the denominator and numerator but there are two limitations on including this figure in the numerator. First, the gross receipts must come from a permitted source (see below). Second, FASOs can only count in the numerator up to $5,000 or 1% of their support in the taxable year (not the normalcy period), whichever is greater, from any one person or governmental bureau. The gross receipts from related activities from public charities listed as #1, 2, 3, 4, 7, and 8 on pages 101-02 are not subject to the 1% limitation and can be included in full in the numerator. The entire amount of the related business income must be included in the denominator.

In this test, "person" includes any individual, trust, estate, partnership, association, company, or corporation. "Government bureau" refers to specialized operating units of the government functioning at the operating, rather than policy-making level. Consult an attorney if you need help in assessing how these terms apply to your group.

The rules discussed on pages 157-58 pertaining to the unusual grant exclusion also apply here and should be considered in figuring qualified support.

PERMITTED SOURCES FOR THE ONE-THIRD SUPPORT TEST NUMERATOR

Permitted sources of support include:

- persons (as defined in the section above) other than disqualified persons
- governmental units
- the public charities that are listed as #1, 2, 3, 4, 7 and 8 on page 100.

If a donor makes a contribution to a FASO by earmarking it for the organization and funneling it though one of the permitted sources, it will be treated as though it were made from the original donor. If that donor is a prohibited source (see next section) it will be excluded from the numerator (i.e., it will not be qualified support).

If a donor makes a contribution to a FASO by earmarking it for the organization and funneling it though one of those permitted sources, it will be treated as though it were made from the original donor.

PROHIBITED SOURCES

Support cannot be included as part of the numerator if it is from any of these prohibited sources:

- Disqualified persons
- Private operating foundations and certain private foundations
- The public charities that are listed as #5, 6, and 9 on pages 101-02.

DISQUALIFIED PERSONS

A disqualified person is:

- a substantial contributor;
- a foundation manager;

- a twenty percent owner/entity substantial contributor;
- a family member; or
- a 35% disqualified person/entity owner.

These terms are defined on pages 153-56.

FASO: SUPPORT TEST

NUMERATOR =

◊ Contributions, grants, membership fees from permitted sources, *plus*

◊ Gross receipts from related business activities from permitted sources

◊ – below 1% limitation, and

◊ – subject to 1% limitation

DENOMINATOR = Same as FASO on page 151.

One-Third Gross Investment Income Test

In your normalcy period (see page 165), no more than $1/3$ of your support in each taxable year can come from the sum of:

- your gross investment income and
- the excess of your unrelated business taxable income over the amount of your unrelated business tax, if your business was acquired or started after June 30, 1975.

Gross investment income is your gross income from interest, dividends, rents, and royalties, to the extent this income is NOT taxable as unrelated business income. See page 150 for a discussion of gross investment income. Note that the One-Third Support Test for FASOs requires a *minimum* of one-third of qualified support, while the One-Third Gross Investment Test states that one-third is the *maximum* investment income permissible.

Use the worksheet at the end of this chapter to calculate your numerator for both the one-third support test and the one-third gross investment income test.

The denominator for this test is the total support described on page 151.

FASO: INVESTMENT INCOME TEST

NUMERATOR =

◊ Gross investment income, *plus*

◊ Unrelated business taxable income less the amount of your unrelated business tax

DENOMINATOR = Same as FASO on page 151.

The Normalcy Period

General Rule

The mechanical test and the facts and circumstances tests for PSOs and the support test/investment income test for FASOs all are defined in terms of what normally occurs. For all these groups, "normally" is the five years ending with the tax year in question. The long time period is used to get a more accurate picture of an organization's usual sources of support. Once an organization meets the test for a given tax year, the test is satisfied for that year and the next year. There are more complicated rules for what happens if an organization fails to meet the test for a particular normalcy period.

"Normally" is the five years ending with the tax year in question.

As an example, the Women's Alliance for Peace (see page 160) has satisfied the test for the years 2017 and 2018. This allows donors to make contributions throughout the year and count on taking their deductions; otherwise, they'd have to wait until the end of the year to see whether the organization they were donating to still qualified. Chaos at the IRS!

The IRS uses the first 5 years of a new organization's receipts to determine if the organization is a public charity. This means that if you didn't qualify the first year of your operations but you do qualify over the 5 year period, you are a public charity. If your organization has been in existence less than 5 tax years, you need to keep track each year to see if you are meeting at least one of the support tests. In figuring out when you came into existence, start with the date you were formed if you are an unincorporated association and the date you were incorporated if you are a corporation. If you operated as an unincorporated association for a period of time and are now a corporation, you can only use the years since incorporation toward the normalcy period.

If you find that you are not meeting the support tests, you should get some professional help as early as possible. There may be some actions you can take that would help you meet the tests. If you don't, the IRS will reclassify your organization as a private foundation at the end of the 5 year period. In some cases, you may owe taxes and penalties and in rarer cases your donors may lose their charitable tax deductions and foundations who gave you grants may be required to pay penalties as well. These are all results you want to avoid.

Recordkeeping Issues

It should be clear from reading the complex set of rules above that detailed recordkeeping about contributions is critical. Your organization needs to know not only who has contributed how much

THE OREGON NONPROFIT CORPORATION HANDBOOK

over the life of the organization, but also a considerable amount of detailed information about the contributing individuals and organizations and their family and business connections. You need to gather from the foundations, organizations, governmental entities, disqualified persons, and individuals who give you money the information you need to calculate your support tests.

Detailed recordkeeping about contributions is critical.

On the following pages are some worksheets you can use to calculate the numerator and denominators for the support tests for PSOs and FASOs.

Consult Appendix 1 if you would like information about source material related to this Chapter.

Now that you've sorted out your nonprofit's status as a PSO or FASO, you'll want to clear your thoughts to tackle the challenge of understanding the IRS rules regarding political activity and lobbying by tax-exempt organizations. Chapter 8 is designed to help you understand these very important restrictions and prohibitions.

PSO
WORKSHEET
NUMERATOR
FOR NORMALCY PERIOD

QUALIFIED SOURCES OF SUPPORT

Governmental unit support (page 153) $_____

Direct Public Support:
    Contributions, grants and membership fees $_____
    below the 2% limitation (page 153)

    Contributions, grants, and membership $_____
    fees subject to the 2% limitation (page 153)
    [Take the number of such items and
    multiply it by 2% of your denominator]

Indirect Public Support: $_____
    Contributions, grants and membership fees
    (page 158)

    Subtract unusual grants (page 157)
        (if included above) $_____

                TOTAL $_____

FASO
WORKSHEET
NUMERATOR
FOR NORMALCY PERIOD

ONE-THIRD SUPPORT TEST

Contributions, grants, and membership fees $_____
from permitted sources (page 162)

Gross receipts from related business $_____
activities from permitted sources not
subject to the 1% limitation (page 162)

Gross receipts from related business $_____
activities from permitted sources
subject to the 1% limitation (page 162)
    [If your total annual support is *$500,000 per year or more:*
      1. Add together the receipts that are each less than 1% of your total support;
      2. Multiply the number of items that are equal to or more than 1% of your total support by the figure equal to 1% of your total support;
      3. Add 1 and 2 together.
    If your total annual support is *less than $500,000 per year*:
      1. Add together the receipts that are each less than $5,000;
      2. Multiply the number of items that are $5,000 or more by $5,000;
      3. Add 1 and 2 together.]

Subtract unusual grants (page 157)
    (if included above) $_____

                TOTAL $_____

FASO
WORKSHEET
NUMERATOR
FOR NORMALCY PERIOD

ONE-THIRD GROSS INVESTMENT INCOME TEST

Gross investment income (page 164) $ _____

Your unrelated business $ _____
taxable income less the amount
of your unrelated business tax

                        TOTAL $ _____

PSO
WORKSHEET
DENOMINATOR
FOR NORMALCY PERIOD

TOTAL SUPPORT BASE

Gifts, grants, contributions, membership fees (page 148) – Exclude "unusual grants" (page 157)	$_____
Net income from unrelated business business activity (page 149)	$_____
Gross investment income (page 150)	$_____
Tax revenues levied by government for your group (page 150)	$_____
Value of free services or facilities furnished by government to your group (page 151)	$_____
TOTAL	$_____

FASO
WORKSHEET
DENOMINATOR
FOR NORMALCY PERIOD

TOTAL SUPPORT BASE

Gifts, grants, contributions, $_____
membership fees (page 148)
  – Exclude "unusual grants" (page 157)

Net income from unrelated business $_____
business activity (page 149)

Gross investment income (page 150) $_____

Tax revenues levied by government $_____
for your group (page 150)

Value of free services or facilities furnished $_____
by government to your group (page 151)

Gross receipts from related business activity $_____
(page 149)

                       TOTAL $_____

POLITICAL ACTIVITY AND LOBBYING BY TAX-EXEMPT ORGANIZATIONS

THIS CHAPTER COVERS

- Who Should Read This Chapter?
- Political Activity and §501(c)(3) Groups
- Lobbying and §501(c)(3) Groups: Two Tests
- Understanding the Lobbying Election
- The Lobbying Election Computations
- Making the Lobbying Election
- Proving Compliance with the Lobbying Rules
- Political Activity and Lobbying by non-§501(c)(3) Exempt Groups
- Affiliated Organizations
- Other Laws Concerning Political Activity and Lobbying

Political activity is defined by the IRS as supporting or opposing the election of a candidate for public office. If you are a §501(c)(3) organization, you can lose your exemption if you are involved in *any* political activity. You can engage in neutral election-related activities. This chapter will explain the IRS rules.

Lobbying refers to efforts to affect legislation. All exempt organizations can lobby, including §501(c)(3)'s. However, there are limits on how much lobbying (c)(3)'s can do. If the limits are exceeded, you will have to pay a tax and, in some cases, will lose your exemption. This chapter will give you the information you need to keep within the limitations imposed by the IRS and help you decide whether you should consider an alternative structure if your activities will go beyond those allowed for §501(c)(3) organizations.

Groups exempt under §501(c)(4), (5), or (6) can engage in more political activity and lobbying, but with some restrictions. This Chapter discusses these restrictions.

If your group engages in political activity or lobbies, you may be subject to other federal and state laws (besides the IRS rules) concerning political campaigns and lobbying that apply to everyone. See Chapter 29.

POLITICAL ACTIVITY AND LOBBYING BY TAX-EXEMPT ORGANIZATIONS   8

Who Should Read This Chapter?

This chapter deals with issues involving organizations exempt under §501(c)(3), (c)(4), (c)(5), or (c)(6) that are involved in political campaigning or lobbying. Most of the regulation—and hence, most of this chapter—focuses on the (c)(3) groups. Other tax-exempt groups can refer to the (c)(3) sections for an understanding of what political activity and lobbying is and then move on.

If you are tax-exempt under §501(c)(3), you may also be able to skim or skip parts of this chapter. If you are exempt under §501(c)(3) and engage in any efforts to support or oppose a candidate for any elective office, you should read the section on political activity. If not, you can skip this section.

If you are exempt under §501(c)(3) and do some lobbying, read page 182 to see if you qualify to make the lobbying election. If so, and if your lobbying activities are very insignificant and you engage in **NO** political activities, you can simply file the lobbying election form, Form 5768.

To determine if your lobbying activities are very insignificant:

- Figure out how much you spend directly on your programs and your salaries for those programs that directly fulfill your exempt purposes. (You cannot count capital expenditures, expenditures that are related to fundraising, or unrelated business income in this.)

- If you are spending less than 5% of that figure for lobbying, you should be able to skip a detailed reading this chapter by making the lobbying election. Read the section on how to make the lobbying election. However, you should skim this chapter to be sure that you are in compliance with the lobbying election and to understand when you are engaging in political or lobbying activities.

Political Activity and §501(c)(3) Groups

Most people would probably consider political activity to be any activity that promotes their political agenda, such as publishing information to persuade others, holding rallies, attending meetings to further these goals, supporting or opposing a ballot measure, or voting. According to the IRS, *political activity* includes any involvement in political campaigns on behalf of or in opposition to *candidates for public office or any political party*. Note that the IRS definition focuses on people (candidates) and not issues and is quite a bit narrower than the common understanding.

Prohibited Activities for (c)(3)s

§501(c)(3) exempt organizations are *prohibited* from participating in or intervening in (including publishing or distributing statements) any political campaign on behalf of or against any candidate for public office or any political party. If you do this, you will not be granted a §501(c)(3) exemption or your existing exemption can be revoked.

---

§501(c)(3) exempt organizations are prohibited from participating in or intervening in (including publishing or distributing statements) any political campaign on behalf of or against any candidate for public office or any political party.

Candidates include people who have filed to run for an elective office, who are considering running, and who are being considered in the media. In Oregon, state judges and some administrative officials like the Attorney General and Secretary of State are elected and are therefore candidates. Oregon allows voters to recall public officials by a referendum procedure and participation by a (c)(3) organization in this process would be prohibited.

If you have a §501(c)(3) exemption and engage in forbidden political activities, the IRS can take several actions against you:

- The IRS may require your group and your managers to pay stiff excise taxes on your political expenditures, *and/or*

- The IRS can get a court order against you barring your political expenditures, *and/or*

- The IRS may revoke your §501(c)(3) exempt status. If this happens, you cannot apply for §501(c)(4) status.

Permissible Activities for (c)(3)s

Individuals who are *appointed* to public office, such as federal judges and Cabinet level positions in the federal government, are not candidates and a (c)(3) can take a position on these positions. (Such action may be lobbying, as described below.)

§501(c)(3) organizations can engage in a variety of election-related activities as long as the exempt organization does not support or oppose a candidate for public office and its activities are nonpartisan. Nonpartisan election-related activities include voter education, voter registration, issue advocacy and candidate education.

Voter Education and Candidate Forums

Education is a permissible activity for (c)(3) organizations. Your (c)(3) can educate the voters with candidate questionnaires, voter guides, candidate debates, and voting records as long as you do so in a nonpartisan manner. Generally, this means that you give all candidates the same opportunities to respond and that you can't focus on specific issues. You may use candidate questionnaires if you send the questionnaires to all the candidates, ask unbiased questions about a broad range of issues, present the candidates' responses in the same manner, and avoid supporting one candidate in any way. You can publish the responses in a voter guide if you do so without editing or favoring one candidate. Your publication cannot comment on the position that you take on the issues. You should include a statement that your organization does not support, oppose or otherwise endorse any candidate for public office.

> *§501(c)(3) organizations can engage in a variety of election-related activities as long as the exempt organization does not support or oppose a candidate for public office and its activities are nonpartisan.*

Your organization can sponsor candidate debates and forums if you do so in a neutral fashion. You must invite all viable candidates, cover a broad range of issues, ask impartial questions, use a neutral moderator, invite an impartial audience, and stick to fair rules in the debate or presentations.

If you want to publish voting records or scorecards, you can do so as long as you do not time them to correspond to an election. Many groups avoid this problem by publishing voting records annually. If you distribute your publication to the *general public*, you must include all the records of all legislators for a geographical area and you must cover a broad range of issues. If you limit your scorecard for distribution to *members*, you must include all legislators in the area and cannot time the scorecard to appear at election time. However, you can focus on issues that your organization is concerned about (rather than cover a broad range of issues) and you can comment on the results.

> *Example*: Banding Together is a (c)(3) multi-racial organization that promotes diversity and rectifying inequities based on race. Banding Together has taken a position on half a dozen legislative bills related to race in the past two years. Shortly before election day, the group produces a legislative scorecard that it distributes to the public showing how the legislators, including several running for office, voted on its bills. Some candidates clearly fared better than others in supporting Banding Together's bills. The scorecard did not cover any other issues. The IRS will probably consider this to be impermissible campaigning.

Candidate Appearances Where Speaking or Participating as a Non-Candidate

You may have occasion to invite a candidate to an event for some reason other than their candidacy. For example, your group may hold an annual dinner as a fundraiser and may invite supporters who are also candidates. You may do this as long as you avoid mentioning the candidacy of your supporters and do not time the dinner to coincide with the elections. You are not required to invite all of the candidates to this event. If your supporter is already in office, you may introduce her or him at the same time you introduce all public officials, but you cannot mention that supporter's candidacy. Candidates cannot bring campaign material to the event or solicit support from those attending.

If the candidate is invited to speak, be sure you have a reason other than her/his candidacy for inviting the candidate to speak and do not mention the candidacy when introducing the speaker or otherwise. For example, you may invite a candidate to speak because the candidate is the mayor and introduce her as the mayor, even though she is in the midst of a contested election, as long as you don't mention the election. When you invite supporters running for office, protect yourself by stating in the invitation that you are a (c)(3) organization and that both the candidate and you need to refrain from mentioning their candidacy at the event in order to protect your (c)(3) status.

Voter Registration

Your organization can engage in voter registration as long as your goal is to encourage people to vote. You must make registration available to everyone and you cannot ask people how they will vote. You must target your location and audience based on nonpartisan criteria. You can, however, focus on disadvantaged or underrepresented groups, even if those groups tend to favor your political party. Your organization can encourage people to vote if you do so in a nonpartisan manner. If you are a private foundation, you are subject to additional requirements if you engage in voter registration activities and should get legal advice.

> *Example*: Rural Oregon educates the public on job-creation issues and lobbies for a jobs bill that will help rural Oregonians. One of the candidates for the legislature from a rural county supports Rural Oregon's job bill. Shortly before the election, Rural Oregon sets up a phone bank to call voters. It tells voters about its position on the bill and asks if the voter agrees. If the voter says yes, Rural Oregon reminds the voter about the election and encourages the voter to mail in her ballot. If the voter does not agree with the bill, Rural Oregon thanks the voter and hangs up. Rural Oregon is engaged in impermissible electioneering when it conducts this get-out-the-vote drive.

Issue Advocacy

Not surprisingly, many groups want to press their cause at election time. You may advocate for your issues during the campaign period as long as you do so in a nonpartisan manner. The issue has to be related to your exempt purpose. You cannot coordinate your advocacy with a candidate or political party and should avoid referring to candidates with code words like "conservative" or "pro-choice" that might associate you with a candidate or party.

> *If your communication contains a reasonably overt indication that your organization supports or opposes a candidate, you have crossed the line.*

The line between commenting on the issues (which you can do) and endorsing or opposing a candidate based on your statements about the issues can be a very thin one. If your comments seem to focus on the candidates rather than the issues or if your communication contains a reasonably overt indication that your organization supports or opposes a candidate, you have crossed the line. The IRS looks at these factors in determining whether a communication is a political campaign intervention:

- Whether the statement identifies a candidate or candidates for public office;
- Whether a statement expresses approval or disapproval of a candidate's positions or actions;
- Whether the statement is delivered close to an election;
- Whether the statement refers to voting or the election;
- Whether the issue addressed is one that has been raised as distinguishing the candidates;
- Whether the communication is part of ongoing communications by your organization or whether it popped up at election time; and
- Whether the communication is related to a non-electoral event, such as a scheduled vote on specific legislation by an officeholder who also happens to be a candidate.

Obviously, what people think is a focus on the candidate over the issues or is a reasonably overt indication of support may differ, so you wander into a gray area when you link issue advocacy with candidates. At a minimum, your advocacy piece should contain a disclaimer that your organization does not support, oppose, or otherwise endorse candidates for public office. You may also want to include a statement that voters should consider more than just one issue in selecting a candidate.

Candidate Education

The law allows your organization to inform candidates about your organization and to educate them about your issues. To avoid electioneering, you should use information that you had before the election, not newly-created publications. You must offer your materials to all candidates.

Individual Endorsements by Organization Leaders

Your corporation's leaders, such as Board members, officers, and your Executive Director, and your employees and volunteers do not give up their right to free speech on political matters because they are associated with your (c)(3) organization. All of these people can support or oppose candidates or political parties in their individual capacity. In making endorsements, individuals can state their organizational affiliation, as long as it is clear that the organization's name is provided only to identify the individual.

> *Example*: The Executive Director of the Chinese Cultural Heritage Society adds his name to others in a full page newspaper ad endorsing a candidate for the U.S. Senate. The ad identifies the Executive Director by name and states that he is the Executive Director of the Society. The ad states, "Titles and affiliations of each individual are provided for identification purposes only." Because the ad was not paid for by the Society and did not appear in a Society publication, and the endorsement by the ED was made in his individual capacity, the ad is not an impermissible political activity by the Society.

In making endorsements, individuals can state their organizational affiliation, as long as it is clear that the organization's name is provided only to identify the individual.

If someone connected with your organization makes partisan comments in your publications or at official functions of the organization, the IRS does consider this to be campaigning.

> *Example*: The minister of a church writes a "My Views" column in the church newsletter, stating that it is her personal opinion that a particular candidate should be elected. For that issue, the minister pays the cost of the portion of the newsletter attributable to her column from her personal funds. In spite of the payment, the newsletter is an official publication of the church and the church has engaged in impermissible campaigning.

The Internet and Political Activity

The growth of the Internet has vastly expanded the ability of advocacy groups to support or oppose candidates. Generally, (c)(3)s using the Internet are subject to the same rules that govern them in their other communications about political campaigns. If you post something on your website that supports or opposes a candidate, the IRS will view this in the same way it views printed material.

In addition to your own postings, the use of links, internet forums, email lists, and email creates some novel issues about how the IRS rules on political activities apply to the web medium. The

IRS reviews the use of the web for political activities on a case by case basis. We discuss some of the issues in this section so that you can think about how you want to approach them.

One issue is whether a (c)(3) can link its website to websites that somewhere make or may later make endorsements for candidates or political parties or are PACs. Since you have control over whether you establish a link to another site, you are responsible for monitoring the link. Because the linked material may change over time, you must monitor it and adjust your links if the link changes to lead to an endorsement of a candidate.

If you conduct nonpartisan voter activities, your (c)(3) should be able to do link to each candidate's website, as long as you treat all candidates equally. This means you must link to the websites of all the candidates and, if a candidate does not have a site, provide information on how to contact the candidate's campaign. It is considerably riskier to link to just one candidate, political party or PAC since this will almost always be an endorsement.

In some cases, an organization will link to the neutral page of a website but the website will contain an endorsement on another page. If you are linking to the website for a reason connected with your mission that is unrelated to the election and your link leads to a webpage that does not refer or link to the endorsement, you are probably okay. You will need to monitor this to ensure that the situation does not change.

> *You should have a policy in place forbidding employees from using your facilities and resources for political activities.*

The Internet offers exciting opportunities for interaction between the producers of a message and the general public. A (c)(3) could produce an internet forum that allows discussion and on-line debate between candidates and voters. If you do this, you should use the candidate forum guidelines described above. Invite all candidates, be sure that you treat them equally in terms of how you place information about them on the web site, make the event available to the general public, and avoid advocating for one candidate.

You may also operate email lists or chat rooms that include discussion about campaigns. You should alert participants that they cannot endorse or oppose candidates on your email list or in your chat room. You should enforce policies that prohibit this by monitoring and deleting messages that violate your policy and by excluding repeat offenders. You need to state that the participants are responsible for the contents of individual posting and not your organization. If your email list has a moderator, be particularly careful to screen partisan messages.

One area of concern for §501(c)(3) organizations is the use by employees of the corporation's email or other web facilities to advocate for or against a candidate. The IRS may attribute the actions of your employees to your organization. You should have a policy in place forbidding employees from using your facilities and resources for political activities. Your employees should be given a copy of the policy. If you have reason to believe that the policy is being violated, you must investigate and take action to protect your organization.

Example: You are a college and your faculty members use college computers in their offices. Many of the faculty belong to email lists related to their discipline. One faculty member circulates a comment on his email list endorsing a Presidential candidate and urging other members of the email list to encourage those they know to vote for the candidate. The IRS would probably view this as an endorsement by the college. Your college needs to notify your faculty and staff that this is not acceptable. Faculty can make these endorsements if done from their home computers and if they make it clear that the endorsement is personal and not being made by their college.

If you are a membership organization, you can disseminate legislative scorecards related to issues of interest to your organization to your members that you cannot make available to the public. See page 175. If you want to put these legislative scorecards on your website, you can only do so if you post them on a page that is accessible only to your members.

Penalties for Engaging in Campaigning

If the IRS discovers that your (c)(3) organization engaged in political activity not allowed by the law, your group may lose your exemption. If the incident seems isolated, the IRS may just issue a warning. The IRS may also impose a tax on your organization and on your Directors, Board members, Executive Director, or other responsible person, if she or he agreed to the expenditures knowing they were for political expenditures.

Lobbying and §501(c)(3) Groups: Two Tests

Most people think of lobbying as contacting a governmental decision-maker to try to influence a decision. To the IRS, *lobbying* means communications that attempt to influence legislation, both by grassroots organizing and by direct lobbying of legislative bodies. Note that the IRS definition is both broader and narrower than the common understanding: broader in that it includes grassroots communications with the public, who are not necessarily decision-makers, and narrower in that it only refers to legislation and does not include decision-makers in administrative agencies and the courts.

> *To the IRS, lobbying means communications that attempt to influence legislation, both by grassroots organizing and by direct lobbying of legislative bodies.*

All organizations exempt under §501(c) are permitted to lobby, but there are some restrictions on how much lobbying a §501(c)(3) organization can do. We will discuss those at some length.

Lobbying Tests

The IRS has two tests to determine whether your §501(c)(3) is doing excessive lobbying—the substantial part test and the lobbying election. The determination of what expenses and activities count as lobbying is not always the same under each test.

The "Substantial Part" Test

The law provides that lobbying cannot be a substantial part of the activities of a §501(c)(3) organization. The problem with this language is the vagueness of two terms.

What constitutes lobbying is not as well-defined under this test as under the lobbying election. More importantly, what constitutes a "substantial part" of a group's activities is very vague. To determine whether lobbying is a substantial part of a group's activities, courts and the IRS have taken a variety of approaches. One approach looks at the quality of the activities directed toward influencing legislation. Who does the work—outsiders or members? What kind of organizational set-up is used? What kind of efforts are used to exert influence—direct contact with legislators, appearances at hearings, volunteered testimony or invited testimony? Do you use public advertisements? Another approach is to look at the amount of money and time an organization spends on lobbying. Cases have found that an organization spending less than 5% of its time and budget on legislative activities is not doing "substantial" lobbying. Some courts balance the public, charitable activity against the non-public, lobbying activity. This test gives greater latitude to a larger organization who does the same lobbying as a smaller one.

Because of the uncertainties of the substantial part test, Congress developed an alternative test, based on a mathematical formula, that most §501(c)(3) groups can choose to use.

The Lobbying Election [the Subsection (h) Election or Expenditure Test]

Because of the uncertainties of the substantial part test, Congress developed an alternative test, based on a mathematical formula, that most §501(c)(3) groups can choose to use. The test allows you to make calculations based on what percentage your lobbying budget is of certain of your expenditures (described later) to determine if your lobbying expenditures are acceptable. Most organizations who are entitled to should choose to use the lobbying election, if the group does any lobbying. Because this test is outlined in subsection (h) of Internal Revenue Code §501, it is often called the subsection (h) election or the (h) election. The IRS sometimes calls it the expenditure test.

WHO CAN MAKE THE LOBBYING ELECTION?

Most §501(c)(3) groups that are not private foundations can choose the lobbying election. These eligible groups include:

- Schools
- Hospitals and medical research organizations
- Development foundations for state universities
- Publicly supported organizations (PSOs)
- Fee/Activity supported organizations (FASOs)
- Supporting organizations

(See pages 99-107 for further discussions of who these groups are.)

WHO CANNOT MAKE THE LOBBYING ELECTION?

Some §501(c)(3) organizations are not permitted to make the lobbying election. These are:

- Private foundations
- Churches and church-related groups
- Governmental units

The substantial part test continues to apply to groups who cannot or do not make the lobbying election.

Understanding the Lobbying Election: What Lobbying Is

The rules governing those who make the lobbying election are fairly complex. We will start by describing what lobbying is for groups who make the lobbying election. We'll then talk about how to make the lobbying calculations to determine if your organization is within the mathematical limits of the lobbying election and finally whether and how to make the lobbying election.

What Is Lobbying

Lobbying means communications that are intended to influence legislation. To understand this, you need to know what *legislation* is and what *influencing legislation* means.

Legislation

Legislation refers to action by a legislative body. Such an action could be the proposal, introduction, enactment, or defeat of a bill or other action before Congress, the state legislature, local governing bodies, or voters (as ballot measures).

Influencing Legislation

Influencing legislation refers to either direct lobbying or grassroots lobbying.

DIRECT LOBBYING

Direct lobbying is an attempt to influence legislation directly, through communications with legislators and their employees, or government officials who participate in the formation of legislation, if the principal purpose of the communication is to influence legislation. The communication counts as direct lobbying only if it refers to specific legislation and reflects your view on the legislation.

> *Legislation includes initiatives,*
> *so attempting to influence the public on ballot measures*
> *is also considered direct lobbying and*
> *not grassroots lobbying.*

Legislation includes initiatives, so attempting to influence the public on ballot measures is also considered direct lobbying and not grassroots lobbying. This is because, in the case of ballot measures, the public is the legislature.

Because of the way the computations for the lobbying election works, you can have more direct lobbying expenses than grassroots lobbying.

> *Example*: The Executive Director of Children's Advocates on behalf of the organization contacts her State Senator and urges her to support the bill protecting those who report child abuse. This is direct lobbying.

GRASSROOTS LOBBYING

Grassroots lobbying (also called indirect lobbying) is an attempt to influence legislation by encouraging the public to contact legislators about a specific piece of legislation. In order to be considered grassroots lobbying, the communication must refer to specific legislation, must reflect your view of the legislation, and must issue a *call to action* by:

- asking the recipient to contact legislators to influence the legislation; *and*
- providing a legislator's or legislative employee's address, phone number, or similar information; *and*
- *either:*

◊ providing a petition, tear-off postcard, or similar material for the recipient to send his or her views to a legislator; or

◊ specifically identifying the stands of legislators who will vote on a piece of legislation or identifying legislators as being on a committee that will vote on the matter (unless it is part of a nonpartisan analysis).

Grassroots lobbying is an attempt to influence legislation by encouraging the public to contact legislators about a specific piece of legislation.

The first three of the above actions are considered to be *direct encouragement* and the last is *indirect encouragement*. This distinction is important for organizations who have members and is discussed on p. 185.

Example: Children's Advocates wants to support a bill in the Oregon legislature that would protect people who report child abuse. The organization sends a letter to the public, describing the legislation, explaining that the organization supports it, and asking them to contact their legislators in support of the bill. This is grassroots lobbying. If Children's Advocates had simply described the legislation and explained why it supported it, without issuing the call to action requesting that the recipients contact their legislators or identifying the stands of the legislators, this would not be grassroots lobbying or any type of lobbying.

Exceptions to the Direct and Grassroots Lobbying Rules

The IRS has developed some exceptions and twists to the direct and grassroots lobbying rules for nonprofits who are communicating with their members and for those using mass media advertisements.

COMMUNICATIONS WITH MEMBERS

If you are a membership organization, you are given more leeway to communicate with your members than with nonmembers. For IRS purposes, members are people who contribute more than a nominal amount of time or money or are certain honorary or lifetime members. Note that this is quite different from the definition of members under Oregon law, which defines a member is someone who votes for the Board. Under the IRS definition, some of your voting members who give only nominally to you may not be members. On the other hand, you may be a nonmembership corporation under Oregon law and yet have members by the IRS definition.

The IRS divides your communications to your membership into three categories—those in which you communicate only with your members, those in which you communicate primarily with your members but include some nonmembers, and those in which you communicate primarily with nonmembers.

COMMUNICATIONS ONLY WITH MEMBERS

Most communications by a (c)(3) organization to the public that include a direct or indirect call to action are grassroots lobbying. (Review the discussion of direct and indirect calls to action on page 183-84 to understand this section.) However, the IRS considers that dedicated members of a nonprofit group that address a legislative issue that is important to the nonprofit's mission are different from the general public. When a nonprofit speaks to its members about issues related to its mission, the nonprofit is not rousing the support of the general public as it does with grassroots lobbying but is speaking to an unusually committed set of individuals who are significantly connected to the organization. It's a bit like the organization is speaking to itself.

> *The IRS considers that dedicated members of a nonprofit group that address a legislative issue that is important to the nonprofit's mission are different from the general public.*

Based on this rationale, the IRS allows nonprofits with committed members some leeway in how it defines lobbying when the issue it addresses is directed only to its members and is of direct interest to its members:

- Your communication is not lobbying if the communication does not *directly* encourage members to engage in direct or grassroots lobbying, even though it includes an *indirect call to action*.

- Your communication is direct lobbying if it directly encourages your members to engage in direct lobbying.

- Your communication is grassroots lobbying if it directly encourages members to engage in grassroots lobbying by contacting nonmembers and encouraging them to lobby.

    Example: Immigrant Access favors an ordinance before the City Council that will fund a program to educate city health employees about special cultural issues that affect the medical care of different immigrant communities. Immigrant Access has members who pay more than nominal dues and vote. Immigrant Access contacts its members to inform them of the ordinance, provides contact information for the City Council members, and identifies the stands of the City Council members on the issue. It does not provide a postcard to send to Council members. This is an *indirect* call for action and is not lobbying. If Immigrant Access provided postcards to mail to the City Council members, this would be direct lobbying and not grassroots lobbying.

If Immigrant Access urged its members to contact nonmembers and have them send in the postcards, this would be grassroots lobbying.

COMMUNICATIONS PRIMARILY WITH MEMBERS

The IRS has a different set of rules if you send communications primarily to members but the materials also reach nonmembers. A communication is designed primarily for members if more than one-half of the recipients are members. As in the case of communications directed only to members, the IRS rules concern materials that are of direct interest to your organization. If you design this type of material primarily for members and if your communication *directly encourages* your readers to engage in direct lobbying, you have engaged in direct lobbying with your members and grassroots lobbying with your nonmember readers.

COMMUNICATIONS PRIMARILY WITH NONMEMBERS

If you distribute your communication primarily to nonmembers, you do not qualify for any special exceptions to the normal lobbying rules. If your communication contains a lobbying message, it is generally grassroots lobbying. In the case of ballot measures, it is direct lobbying. You may want to distribute your message in two mailings, one to members and the other to nonmembers, to take advantage of the special rules for distributions to members.

MASS MEDIA ADVERTISEMENTS

Generally, you must make a call to action in order to engage in grassroots lobbying. However, grassroots lobbying includes some paid mass media advertisements that do not include a call to action. An advertisement on TV, the radio, billboards, or in magazines or newspapers about highly publicized legislation that runs within two weeks before the vote by the legislative body or committee is grassroots lobbying if the ad reflects a view on the legislation and either refers to the legislation or encourages the public to communicate with the legislators. (There are some exceptions to categorizing these ads as grassroots lobbying. If this concerns you, you need legal advice.)

The Internet and Lobbying

The Internet can be an excellent tool for advocacy. Generally, you must follow the rules above when your internet activities constitute lobbying. We'll consider some special issues raised by the internet here. Because these issues are relatively new, many situations do not have definitive answers.

> *The IRS will consider lobbying material posted on your website as grassroots lobbying.*

Websites offer the ability to reach the world. Consequently, the IRS will consider lobbying material posted on your website as grassroots lobbying. If you have pages that can only be accessed by your members, lobbying messages on these pages are direct lobbying. Remember that members are people who contribute more than a nominal amount of time or money. If you post your newsletter on your website and make it accessible to the public, any lobbying messages that would have been direct lobbying when the newsletter went primarily to your members now becomes grassroots lobbying. Similarly, if you post information from third parties that contains a lobbying message, you have probably also engaged in lobbying.

Your website can contain links to legislators and other government officials. If the link is embedded in a lobbying message with a call to action, then it becomes lobbying. If not, the IRS should just treat it as informational.

If you maintain email lists or chat rooms, participants may turn these into lobbying sites and you may have to report the expenses associated with them as part of your lobbying expenditures. If you want to avoid this result, you need to establish and enforce policies to prevent lobbying messages. You should have a clear exempt purpose for the email list or chat room and you should explicitly and repeatedly state that the participants and not your organization are responsible for the postings. If your email list has a moderator, the moderator must carefully screen out lobbying messages. You must exclude repeat offenders who violate your "no lobbying" policy.

What Is Not Lobbying

Legislation does not include actions before administrative agencies or executive officers, unless you are lobbying to persuade the agency or executive to take a position for or against a legislative bill. You may advocate for or against administrative rules and may take positions with respect to cases being heard by an administrative body. None of this is lobbying. Administrative agencies include bodies like school boards, housing authorities, zoning boards and other similar federal, state and local bodies, whether elective or appointive. For example, a meeting to encourage the Oregon Department of Environmental Quality to draft an administrative rule to enhance salmon runs is not lobbying. Similarly, a meeting to persuade the governor to appoint more minorities to high-level positions is not lobbying but a meeting to urge the governor to veto an affirmative action bill is lobbying. Legislation also does not include cases heard by courts, so you can be involved in impact litigation or file *amicus* briefs without lobbying.

> *Legislation does not include actions before administrative agencies, unless you are lobbying to persuade the agency to take a position for or against a legislative bill.*

Lobbying also does not include:

- *Nonpartisan analysis,* which is an independent and objective discussion of a subject. You can advocate for a particular position as long as there is a sufficiently full and fair description of the facts to enable the public to form an independent opinion. The communication must be made available to the public, or a segment of it, or to governmental bodies or employees. You can provide your nonpartisan analysis to legislators. The communication becomes lobbying if it refers to specific legislation, reflects a view on legislation, and *directly encourages* the recipient to contact legislators in favor of or opposed to specific legislation in the manner described on page 184 as *direct encouragement*. Your communication is not lobbying if it refers to specific legislation, reflects a view, and *indirectly encourages* contact with a legislator.

> *Example*: Art for All develops and distributes to the public a 15 page educational piece detailing the importance of art for everyone and describing the dangers of censorship. It refers to specific legislation designed to curtail unpopular artistic expression, explains why this is harmful, and identifies the legislators that are supporting the legislation. It does not directly suggest that the legislators be contacted. This is nonpartisan analysis, since the document does not *directly encourage* the public to contact the legislators.

- *Discussions of broad social, economic, and similar problems* with the public and with legislators, as long as they don't address specific legislation or *directly encourage* the recipients to take action.

- *Requests for technical advice* given to a governmental body in response to a *written* request from the body, and not just one member of it.

- *Self-defense communications,* which are communications with a governmental body regarding legislation which would affect your existence, your powers or duties, your tax-exempt status, or the deductibility of contributions to your group. This exception does not include legislation that affects the funding of your group.

The Lobbying Election Computations

The lobbying election test uses a mathematical formula to determine if your lobbying activities are within acceptable limits. In order to apply the test, you must calculate your *lobbying expenditures* and your *exempt purpose expenditures*.

Lobbying Expenditures

Lobbying expenditures are expenditures for direct and grassroots lobbying and other lobbying-related expenditures. These expenditures include compensation paid for an employee's services attributable to lobbying, all costs of preparing the lobbying communication, and the portion of administrative, overhead, and general expense reasonably attributable to the lobbying effort. You must break these expenses down into direct lobbying and grassroots lobbying expenses.

As you will see below, your organization can do more direct than grassroots lobbying. If a communication is both a direct lobbying and grassroots lobbying communication, the communication is classified as grassroots lobbying, unless you can show it was made primarily for direct lobbying purposes. If you can show this, you can make a reasonable allocation between a direct and grassroots classification. The allocation rules are somewhat complex and you will need to get help with those.

Exempt Purpose Expenditures (EPE)

Exempt purpose expenditures are amounts you spend to accomplish your exempt purposes. They include:

- amounts for exempt purposes;
- amounts to pay employees for services connected with exempt purposes;
- lobbying expenditures (see above);
- amounts for communicating with members;
- amounts for activities not attempting to influence legislation
- reasonable depreciation and amortization of assets to the extent used for one of the above purposes (computed on a straight-line basis); and
- fundraising expenses.

Exempt purpose expenditures do not include:

- expenses connected with unrelated business income
- certain amounts related to property that is transferred;
- amounts for a separate fundraising event of your organization or affiliated organization;
- amounts paid primarily for fundraising to any non-employee or non-affiliated organization;
- capital expenses;
- taxes not imposed in connection with an exempt purpose; and
- amounts for the production of income (whether or not it is an unrelated business activity).

Making the Calculations

There are two limits involved. One is the absolute ceiling limit—if you exceed it, you lose your exempt status. The other is a smaller nontaxable limit—if you exceed it but don't hit the absolute ceiling limit, you are taxed on your excess expenditures. There are two types of calculation you must make with respect to each of these limits—one for direct lobbying and on for grassroots lobbying. Thus, you will be making four calculations.

THE OREGON NONPROFIT CORPORATION HANDBOOK

The amount that you are permitted to spend on lobbying each year is not based on your receipts or income. Your lobbying expenditures limits are based on a percentage of certain of your exempt purpose expenditures (EPE) described above for that taxable year.

- If your EPE is $500,000 a year or less, your total lobbying nontaxable amount is 20% of your EPE.

- If your EPE is between $500,000 and $1,000,000, your total lobbying nontaxable amount is $100,000 plus 15% on the amount above $500,000 up to $1,000,000.

- If your EPE is between $1,000,000 and $1,500,000, your lobbying nontaxable amount is $175,00 plus 10% of the amount over $1,000,000.

- If your EPE is greater than $1,5000,000, your lobbying nontaxable amount is $225,000 plus 5% of your EPE greater than $1,500,000.

The amount that you are permitted to spend on lobbying each year is not based on your receipts or income. Your lobbying expenditures limits are based on your exempt purpose expenditures for any taxable year.

The total lobbying ceiling amount is 150% of the total lobbying nontaxable amount and the grassroots ceiling amount is 150% of the grassroots nontaxable amount. The grassroots nontaxable amount is 25% of the total lobbying nontaxable amount.

You may find it helpful to review the limits above and make a chart of your four calculations. For organizations whose exempt purpose expenditures are $500,000 a year or less, the limits of your lobbying expenditures are:

Total lobbying ceiling amount:	30% of EPE
Total lobbying nontaxable amount:	20% of EPE
Grassroots ceiling amount	7.5% of EPE
Grassroots nontaxable amount:	5% of EPE

Determine your organization's EPE and calculate the four amounts described above.

Special Rules for Affiliated Organizations

There are special rules defining affiliated organizations and providing that the budgets and lobbying expenditures of these groups will be aggregated as though they were one group. This is basically to keep organizations from getting around the limits by splitting up into several groups, or affiliating themselves with separate groups over which they have control and through which they can do some of their lobbying.

Organizations are affiliated if:

- The governing instrument (Articles of Incorporation, Charter, Bylaws, etc.) of one group requires it to be bound by the decisions of the other group on legislative issues; *or*

- The governing board of one group includes people who are designated representatives (or Directors, officers, or executive staff) of the other group, and those people have sufficient voting power to cause or prevent action on legislative issues by the first group.

If you think that your group may come within this definition, you should carefully check the rules governing the aggregation of your lobbying expenditures and plan accordingly. You will probably need professional help.

Consequences of Exceeding Your Lobbying Limits

If you exceed either the total lobbying nontaxable amount or the grassroots nontaxable amount for any year, you will be taxed on the excess expenditures at the rate of 25%. If you exceed both, you will only be taxed on one, whichever is greater. You must file a Form 4720 and pay the taxes.

If you engage in excessive lobbying activities, your group will probably have to pay an excise tax of 5% of your lobbying expenditures, or, in extreme cases, lose your exemption.

If you "normally" (average amount over a four year period) exceed either the total lobbying ceiling amount or the grassroots ceiling amount, you will automatically lose your exempt status. In other words, your total lobbying spending could be within the 30% limit, but if your grassroots spending exceeded the 7.5% limit, you would still lose your exempt status. Conversely, if your grassroots spending was within the limits, but your direct lobbying expenses caused your total spending (counting both areas) to exceed 30%, you would lose your status.

You would not lose your exemption if you exceeded the limits for one year; you have to "normally" exceed them, and "normally" means an average amount over a four year period. If you are in your first, second, or third year since you made the lobbying election, only those years will be used to average your expenditures for the purpose of the normally exceeds test. There are special allocation rules for activities that have both lobbying and nonlobbying purposes.

In addition to losing your exemption, you may also have to pay a tax. In addition, your Directors, Board members, Executive Director, or other responsible person may also have to personally pay a tax, if she or he agreed to the expenditures knowing they were likely to result in revocation of tax-exempt status. You should get professional help if your lobbying activities involve these kinds of complexities.

If you are exempt under §50l(c)(3) and lose your exempt status because of excessive lobbying, you cannot then convert to a §50l(c)(4) exemption. Therefore, it's important to make a good decision about the proper exemption for your group ahead of time. Read this chapter, think about your goals and purposes and how you intend to achieve them, and decide whether you are an educational (charitable, etc.) organization, an action organization or both. If you want to achieve both (c)(3) and (c)(4) goals, you should consider affiliated organizations. See the discussion on pp. 200-02.

Calculating the Lobbying Expenditures and Taxes— An Example

At the end of the year, add up all the lobbying expenditures you've made, including both direct lobbying and grassroots lobbying. This is your total lobbying expenditure. Let's say this was $14,000.

Add up separately the amount you've spent (expenses, salary, etc.) on grassroots lobbying. Let's say the total is $3,000.

To make your calculations with these figures, you also need to know your exempt purpose expenditures (EPE) for the year. Let's say this amount was $50,000.

In this example, then, your EPE was $50,000; your total lobbying expenditures were $14,000, and your grassroots expenditures were $3,000. Have you kept within the ceiling limits so that you don't lose your exempt status? Those limits are 30% of EPE for total lobbying expenses, and 7.5% for grass roots.

In our example, 30% of $50,000 is $15,000, so your total lobbying expenses are within the limits. 7.5% of $50,000 is $3,750, so your grass roots expenses are also within the limits. Your tax exemption is safe.

Do you have to pay any taxes for excess lobbying expenditures? Those limits are 20% of EPE for total lobbying, and 5% for grassroots lobbying. 20% of $50,000 is $10,000, so you have excess total lobbying expenditures of $4,000. 5% of $50,000 is $2,500, so you have excess grassroots expenditures of $500.

Since you exceeded both limits, you will have to pay the tax but only on the larger amount. The tax rate is 25%, so on $4,000 you would have to pay an excise tax of $1,000 on your excess total lobbying expenditures.

POLITICAL ACTIVITY AND LOBBYING BY TAX-EXEMPT ORGANIZATIONS

Making the Lobbying Election

Since the lobbying election is, well, elective, you can choose whether to remain under the old substantial part rules or to elect to come under the lobbying election rules. If you do choose the lobbying election, you need to notify the IRS.

Choosing to Come Under the Lobbying Election

You should consider electing to come under the lobbying election rules in these circumstances:

- If you spend money on lobbying but will stay within the expenditure limits, you can avoid the uncertainties of the substantial parts test.

- If volunteers do most of your lobbying, volunteer time is not counted under the lobbying election rules, but it is considered under the substantial part test.

- If you exceed the nontaxable limits but not the absolute ceiling amounts under the lobbying election, the 25% tax may be cheaper than risking loss of exempt status under the substantial parts test. (See pages 191-92 for information about the tax.)

- If you anticipate greatly exceeding all the limits for one year (for one particularly crucial piece of legislation), the tax cost may be worth it, especially if by not electing, your activities would be considered substantial for that year, resulting in loss of exemption. The lobbying election gives you a four-year-period to average out your expenditures before you lose your exemption. (See page 191.)

- If your lobbying activities will be controversial and attract considerable or intense public attention, you may lose under the substantial part test since the IRS considers the quality, not the quantity, of your lobbying.

- If you're a member of an affiliated group, your expenditures alone may exceed the limits, but when combined with other groups may be less than the limit for the group. (See page 190-91.)

You should probably *not* elect to come under the lobbying election rules in these circumstances:

- If you are a large nonprofit with an EPE of more than $17,000,000 per year and if an insubstantial part of your activity is more than $1,000,000, you can avoid the $1,000,000 cap in the lobbying election.

- If you have significant expenditures that are not EPE, the amount that you can spend on lobbying will be greatly reduced, so you may be able to do more lobbying under the substantial parts test. For example, organizations that purchase land for conservation purposes may have significant expenses that are not EPE.

- If you spend too much on lobbying to qualify as exempt under the lobbying election rules and you have very substantial volunteer time devoted to nonlobbying activities and very little to lobbying and other factors that might let you avoid the substantial parts test, you may refuse the election and try to qualify as exempt under the substantial parts test. This is a very long shot.

How to Make the Election

If you intend to or have engaged in lobbying and wish to come under the lobbying election rules, you need to fill out and send to the IRS Form 5768. It's a very simple one-page form which states the name of the organization and either elects (or revokes a previous election) to come under the lobbying election rules. It has to be postmarked within the taxable year to which it applies. It is effective until you revoke it as described below.

Thus you can, at any time before the end of the taxable year, choose to come under the lobbying election rules for that year. Once you've made the choice, however, it can be revoked only prospectively—you can't revoke for a taxable year after that year has begun. If you have doubts about whether the election is your best choice, you can protect yourself best by making your decision late in the year, when you will have a good idea as to whether it will be to your advantage.

Proving Compliance with the Lobbying Rules

Keep Good Records

Under the Substantial Part Test

If you lobby under the substantial part test, you should keep careful records of the money you spend on lobbying. If you are a public charity (see pages 101-07) with receipts of more than $50,000 per year or assets of more than $500,000, you will need to list your total lobbying expenditures on Form 990's Schedule A and attach a statement giving a detailed description of your lobbying and a schedule of your expenses. If you do not have to make this filing, it is still wise to maintain your records showing lobbying expenses in case you are audited.

You should also maintain a record of your volunteer (unpaid) time, both for lobbying purposes and for other purposes. If you have substantial volunteer time for nonlobbying purposes, this can help you to establish that your lobbying activities are an insubstantial part of what you do.

Under the Lobbying Election

In order to comply with the lobbying election rules, you must keep careful records of the money you've spent. Count both non-personnel *expenses* (like telephone, printing, postage) and *salary* paid to individuals spending their time on lobbying or grassroots organizing. Do *not* count volunteer (unpaid) time. Note that people—paid staff or volunteers—who make out-of-pocket expenditures for lobbying purposes cannot take charitable deductions for that amount. If your staff or volunteer wants to take a charitable deduction, the individual must submit the expense to you for reimbursement. The staff or volunteer can then donate the reimbursement to your corporation and take a charitable deduction. This ensures that the corporation captures all of its expenses related to lobbying when it calculates its lobbying expenses.

You must keep records of the following expenditures separately for direct lobbying and grassroots lobbying:

- direct costs, including payments to other organizations
- allocable portion of amounts paid as compensation for your employees' services
- allocable portion of administrative, overhead, and other general expenditures
- amounts for communications with members
- research
- amounts for direct lobbying or grassroots lobbying of a controlled organization (see the discussion above on affiliated organizations).

In determining some of these figures, you will probably deal with some expenses that contain a lobbying portion and a nonlobbying portion. Common examples are employees who do both lobbying and nonlobbying work, joint usage of space and equipment, and communications that have mixed lobbying and nonlobbying messages and that may go to both members and nonmembers. You need to allocate those expenses between their lobbying and nonlobbying components.

ALLOCATING EMPLOYEE AND OVERHEAD EXPENSES

Organizations that lobby keep employee time sheets in which the employees that do some lobbying keep track of how much of their time is spent on research (in case it later becomes a lobbying expense as described on pages 196-98), direct lobbying, grassroots lobbying, and nonlobbying activity. Overhead expenses are more challenging, since things like lightbulbs can't keep time records. Your group must use a reasonable method to allocate overhead expenses that are not tracked separately for lobbying purposes. One method is to use the percentage of staff time calculated for direct and grassroots lobbying as the percentage to apply to total overhead expenses to compute direct and grassroots overhead.

ALLOCATING EXPENSES ON MIXED MEMBER AND NONMEMBER COMMUNICATIONS

Communications with members and nonmembers can be a more complicated allocation. As we discussed on pages 185-86, many communications sent only to your members are not lobbying if they contain only an indirect call to action and are direct rather than grassroots lobbying if they include a direct call to action. If the communication is direct lobbying, it may contain some material that is not lobbying. For example, your newsletter may contain an article that issues a call to action, a report on your annual conference and an appeal for donations. The IRS requires that you make a reasonable allocation of the costs. You have some leeway to determine what is reasonable. If your newsletter contains three articles of roughly the same length and one contains a lobbying message, you might assign one-third of the cost of producing and distributing the newsletter to lobbying.

The rules get more complicated when you communicate with both members and nonmembers in the same publication. Here you have to juggle several variables. You need to consider who receives the communications (primarily members or nonmembers), what is the content of the communication (entirely lobbying or mixed lobbying and nonlobbying messages) and whether the lobbying message is direct or grassroots lobbying.

Your communication is sent primarily to members if more than half of the recipients are your members. If your communication is addressed primarily to members and has both lobbying and nonlobbying content, you must first determine what part of the costs are lobbying. To do this you use the same rule of reasonableness that you use for communications directly solely to members. Since your communication contains a lobbying message, you have engaged in direct lobbying of your members and grassroots lobbying of the nonmembers who received it. The allocation rules for allocating between the direct and grassroots lobbying in this situation are quite complex and you should get professional help.

If the majority of those receiving your publication are not members, then your communication is addressed primarily to nonmembers. You have engaged in grassroots lobbying unless the subject of your lobbying is a ballot measure, in which case it is direct lobbying. To sort out what part of the costs are lobbying, you must allocate costs attributable to the lobbying message *and* also costs attributable to all parts of the communication that cover the same specific subject as the lobbying message. For example, if the first page of the newsletter that you send primarily to nonmembers describes the problems working parents face getting childcare and the second page discusses a bill that offers tax credits for working parents who use childcare and includes a call to action, you must allocate both pages as grassroots lobbying expenses.

Organizations often include in their newsletter a statement encouraging members to urge their friends to contact legislators about a bill. This is a form of grassroots lobbying. If your communication contains both direct and grassroots lobbying, the IRS will treat it as grassroots lobbying, except to the extent that you can show you made it primarily for direct lobbying purposes. If you can do this, you can make a reasonable allocation between direct and grassroots lobbying. If you are close to the limit on your grassroots lobbying, you should consider whether you want to incur this additional grassroots expense. You may choose instead to leave out the language suggesting that members issue a call to action to their friends.

EXPENSES FOR RESEARCH

Research expenses specifically incurred to support lobbying are a lobbying expense. However, many organizations research and develop policy positions before they engage in lobbying. An organization may later decide to use this material as part of its lobbying efforts. Are these expenses lobbying expenses?

POLITICAL ACTIVITY AND LOBBYING BY TAX-EXEMPT ORGANIZATIONS

Generally, research expenses incurred to develop policy positions are not a lobbying expense if they are used in *direct* lobbying. Research materials may be a lobbying expense if you use certain types of materials—advocacy communications or research materials—in *grassroots* lobbying. Advocacy materials are materials that refer to and reflect a view on specific legislation but don't contain a direct call for action. For example, if your research paper documents the problems that Senate Bill 12 will cause the homeless population, it is not advocacy material. If your research paper concludes that Senate Bill 12 would hurt the homeless population and your organization should oppose it, this would be advocacy material.

> *Generally, research expenses incurred to develop policy positions are not a lobbying expense if they are used in **direct** lobbying. Research materials may be a lobbying expense in **grassroots** lobbying.*

Even if your research document is advocacy material, you may still avoid classifying it as a grassroots lobbying expense if either of the following is true:

- You paid the expenses for the research more than six months before its use in grassroots lobbying. You are home free.

- The primary purpose in preparing the research material was not for use in lobbying. One way to show that your primary purpose was not lobbying is to show that you made a substantial nonlobbying distribution of the research communications (that is, one that did not include a call to action). If the materials were *partisan* research, you will need to show that your nonlobbying distribution was at least as great as your lobbying distribution of the materials. The nonlobbying distribution must be made before or at the same time as the lobbying distribution. If you can show that the primary purpose of preparing the material was not lobbying, you don't have to include the research costs in your grassroots lobbying expenditures, but you do have to include all expenses of transforming and distributing the advocacy research into grassroots lobbying materials.

    Example: Indigenous Peoples Thriving produced a research paper documenting the success of cultural empowerment programs for young Native Americans in urban communities. Three months later, IPT wants to use the research material as part of a grassroots call to action to urge the state legislature to support funding for more empowerment programs.

    IPT distributes its original research study without a call to action to its normal list of policy-makers, schools, churches, and tribal members, totalling 1,000 people. IPT later distributes the material as part of a call to action to 800 voters in the districts whose representatives it is targeting for contact. The research costs should not be lobbying expenditures because IPT made a substantial nonlobbying distribution of the study before its lobbying distribution. The costs of preparing and sending the materials to the 800 voters are grassroots lobbying expenditures.

Educate and Monitor

Whether you make the lobbying election or fall under the substantial part test, you should:

- Inform any staff involved in the activity of the rules and record keeping requirements; and
- Monitor your systems, especially for the first two years. Check on how records are being kept, how lobbying expenditures are being tabulated, how decisions are being made about whether a particular activity is lobbying activity, etc.

Political Activity and Lobbying by Non-(c)(3) Exempt Groups

Tax-exempt organizations other than §501(c)(3) organizations want to support or oppose candidates for public office and political parties and take positions on legislation as part of realizing their exempt mission. The most common organizations are §501(c)(4) social welfare organizations, (c)(5) labor unions, and (c)(6) business leagues and chambers of commerce. These organizations are not subject to the same constraints on their political activities and lobbying as are groups exempt under §501(c)(3) but the IRS does have some restrictions on these groups.

§501(c)(4) Organizations

§501(c)(4) groups can participate in some activity for or against candidates for public office or political parties, as long as campaigning is not a primary activity. Campaigning is forbidden to (c)(3) groups. The limits of political campaigning by (c)(4)s are currently being tested. See the discussion below.

Lobbying is not an exempt purpose for §501(c)(4) groups but (c)(4)s can do extensive lobbying. If you are exempt under §501(c)(4), you cannot have lobbying or passing legislation as your primary *purpose* but you can lobby as your primary *activity* to realize your (c)(4) purpose. So, for example, your (c)(4) organization could have as its primary purpose to support recycling and then as its primary activity engage extensively in lobbying for laws requiring returnable bottles. You should be aware that if you do any lobbying, you are not eligible to receive most federal funds. See pages 672-73. In some rare cases, your members may not be able to deduct a portion of their dues attributable to your lobbying. See the discussion on this point below.

POLITICAL ACTIVITY AND LOBBYING BY TAX-EXEMPT ORGANIZATIONS

§501(c)(5) and (6) Organizations

The IRS recognizes that (c)(5) labor unions and (c)(6) business leagues will engage in political activity and lobbying as part of their missions to promote the interests of workers and business. The limits of political activity by (c)(5)s and (c)(6)s, as well as (c)(4)s, are uncertain. The IRS addresses the lobbying by unions and business leagues by not allowing members whose dues contribute to lobbying to write off that portion of their dues as a business expense as described below.

Limits on Political Activity by Non-(c)(3) Groups

The *Citizens United* case, discussed in Chapter 29, now allows corporations to receive unlimited contributions and make unlimited expenditures on political campaigns. Many donors contribute through political action committees (PACs) but PAC rules require that the identity of larger donors be disclosed. Some large donors are contributing to tax-exempt organizations, primarily (c)(4) and (c)(6) groups, who use the funds to support or oppose a candidate. These organization do not have to disclose their donors. To address the new interest in campaigning by these non-(c)(3) groups, the IRS is currently working to clarify how much campaigning a (c)(4), (5), and (6) corporation can do.

Deductibility of Dues Used for Lobbying

Tax-exempt organizations frequently are supported by dues. In many cases, the members can write off these dues as a reasonable and necessary business expense. However, there are some special rules that disallow part or all of these deductions when the organization engages in certain lobbying or political expenditures described below. The disallowance rules apply to social welfare organizations exempt under §501(c)(4) that are not veterans organizations; unions exempt under §501(c)(5), and groups exempt under §501(c)(6). If you are not exempt from taxation under one of these subsections, you can skip this section.

For most nonprofits, your best option is to notify your dues-payers about what portion of their dues are allocable to lobbying and political expenditures.

If you are subject to the disallowance rules, your members cannot deduct that portion of their dues that is attributable to amounts that your group expended on lobbying the federal or state legislature (but not the local level) and some federal executives. Amounts paid for political campaigning are also not deductible.

If your nonprofit makes these kinds of federal or state expenditures, you must either:

- Send a notice to each of your members specifying what portion of dues are allocable to the lobbying or political expenditures, or

- Pay a lobbying tax (if you elect this option, you must also pay a state proxy tax).

For most nonprofits, your best option is to notify your dues-payers about what portion of their dues are allocable to lobbying and political expenditures. You should do this at the time you assess the dues. You also have to report your political campaigning and lobbying expenses and the portion of dues allocable to them to the IRS.

There are a few exceptions to the disallowance rules. If you are a §501(c)(4), (5) or (6) that is covered by the rules, you do not have to comply with the rules if you fall within one of the following exceptions:

- You do not have to follow the disallowance rules if you receive substantially all of your dues from members who do not deduct their dues as a business expense.

- All (c)(4), (c)(5) and (c)(6) groups are excepted from the rules if you receive more than 90% of all your annual dues from §501(c)(3)s or any other exempt organization to whom these rules do not apply (described in the paragraph above) or from state or local governments.

- (c)(4) and (c)(5) groups that receive more than 90% of your dues from members who pay annual dues of $151 (in 2012) or less are also excepted from the rules. This amount is adjusted for inflation so you may need to update the amount to determine if you must follow the disallowance rules.

- Your in-house lobbying expenditures are less than $2,000.

The reporting requirement exceptions are broad enough to eliminate almost all exempt groups except §501(c)(6) business leagues and some (c)(4)s and (c)(5)s.

The rules are complicated and lobbying here is not defined the way this chapter defines lobbying for other purposes. For example, lobbying here includes lobbying some federal executives but does not include lobbying local legislative bodies. If your group is not clearly eliminated from compliance, you may need to get legal help to understand how these rules apply to you.

Affiliated Organizations

Many groups have both a (c)(3) purpose and another purpose that requires significant lobbying or campaigning. The IRS will not grant two exemptions to one organization. In order to realize both objectives, these groups can form separate affiliated corporations. The corporations are affiliated if there is a method of common control or a close connection between the corporations. Affiliated organizations in which one organization is a (c)(3) are scrutinized carefully by the IRS. We describe these arrangements in more detail in Chapter 5 and you need to review that material if you are considering affiliated organizations.

(c)(3)s often create linked organizations because the (c)(3) wants to find a way to carry out more lobbying than the (c)(3) can do or to engage in campaign activities that are forbidden to (c)(3)s. The (c)(3) can do this if it carefully follows the affiliated structure arrangement on pages 113-15 and ensures that (c)(3) monies and resources are not benefiting the other organizations. To accomplish this, the (c)(3) corporation limits its purpose and activities to those which would qualify for §501(c)(3) status. A second corporation includes action work as a purpose and can conduct extensive lobbying and some political activity under a (c)(4) classification.

> *(c)(3)s often create linked organizations because the (c)(3) wants to find a way to carry out more lobbying than the (c)(3) can do or to engage in campaign activities that are forbidden to (c)(3)s.*

If the (c)(4) organization wants to run or raise money for federal election campaigns, it may also form a §527 political action committee (PAC). If the organization wants to run or raise money for state election campaigns or ballot measures, it may form a political committee under Oregon law. Because the (c)(3)s have restrictions on political activity, in most cases the (c)(3) should have no direct link with the PAC. The PAC should be controlled and funded through the affiliated (c)(4) organization. The rare exceptions are that (c)(3)s can be connected to Oregon PACs that are restricted to being issue-related PACs and PACs whose sole purpose is to influence appointments (not elections) to political office. See pp. 669-70.

Linking your (c)(3) website to the website of a (c)(4) that endorses candidates has some challenges, since (c)(3)s cannot engage in any electioneering. Some organizations want to maintain one website, usually to save expenses, and others may have separate websites. If the (c)(4) does not endorse candidates, the (c)(3) probably has no issues whether it maintains a single website or links with the website of its affiliated (c)(4). At worst, the (c)(3) expenses associated with the website or linkage might constitute a lobbying expense, if the (c)(4) lobbies, but the (c)(3) expense will probably be very insubstantial. Since the (c)(3) can engage in some lobbying, this should generally not be a problem.

> *Linking your (c)(3) website to the website of a (c)(4) that endorses candidates has some challenges, since (c)(3)s cannot engage in any electioneering.*

When the (c)(4) or a connected PAC engages in electioneering, the (c)(3) has a more serious issue, since it can do no campaigning. The (c)(3) is in a better position if the organizations have separate websites. The IRS needs to determine whether the (c)(4) website seems to attribute its endorsement of a candidate to the (c)(3). Some factors that the IRS considers are the context of the link by the (c)(3), whether the link advances the exempt purpose of the (c)(3), and whether the link goes directly to a page that contains the candidate endorsement. Your (c)(3) link to the (c)(4) site is best protected if your reference on the page that makes the link shows why the link advances your exempt purpose and if the link takes the user to a page that does not contain the endorsement.

If your (c)(3) and (c)(4) share a website and your (c)(4) makes candidate endorsements, you need to do all you can to maintain visual and content separation between the two organizations. Be sure that all of your (c)(4) pages look different from the (c)(3) pages and do not link to the (c)(3), other than by backing to the (c)(4)'s main page and linking from there. Users should be able to easily tell when they are on the (c)(4) page. Do not let the (c)(3)'s banner or logo appear on your (c)(4) pages. The (c)(4), of course, must pay for its share (or more) of the proportional costs of the website.

Other Laws Concerning Political Activity and Lobbying

This Chapter discussed laws about political activity and lobbying that apply to organizations exempt from federal income taxation. There are a number of other federal and state laws and government funder requirements that pertain to electioneering and lobbying that cover non-exempt as well as tax-exempt organizations. In many cases, those laws define lobbying much more broadly than the IRS rules in this chapter and include efforts to influence administrative agencies as well as legislative bodies. We've covered those in Chapter 29. It is very important that you become familiar with those laws as well as the ones in this chapter.

Consult Appendix 1 if you would like information about source material related to this Chapter. Appendix 1 has references of interest to all readers, not just professionals.

BUSINESS ACTIVITIES BY TAX-EXEMPT ORGANIZATIONS

THIS CHAPTER COVERS

- Running a Business as a Nonprofit
- Unrelated Business Income
- Examples of Unrelated Business Income
- Exceptions to Unrelated Business Income Rules
- The Unrelated Business Income Tax
- Protecting Your Tax-Exempt Status
- Joint Ventures

Nationally, over 70% of the income that nonprofits receive each year is generated through fees for services or goods the organizations provide. Nonprofit organizations continue to develop new and innovative strategies to generate income, including setting up business ventures, social enterprise activities, or joint ventures with other nonprofits or with for-profits. If your nonprofit will generate income through charging fees for its mission-focused activities or operating a business venture, your success will depend upon developing a sound business plan and making sure you build the skills and infrastructure needed to make it work.

Tax-exempt organizations, unlike for-profits and nonprofits that are not tax-exempt, do not have to pay income tax on their taxable income. However, the IRS does classify some income as "unrelated business income" and tax it, even though you are tax-exempt. If your unrelated business income activities are too substantial, you can lose or be denied your tax-exempt status. The IRS also scrutinizes joint ventures with for-profits.

This chapter will help you develop a business plan and avoid the pitfalls connected with the unrelated business income classification and with joint ventures. You can find more information on specific types of income generating activities you may be considering in Chapter 22.

Running a Business as a Nonprofit

Although it may seem paradoxical, many nonprofits operate a business. Art museums charge admission to view exhibits and sell reproductions of artwork they exhibit. An animal shelter may charge a fee to adopt a pet. A social club may operate a golf course and a dining room that both charge fees. A community center may charge for a fundraising dinner to raise money for a new roof. The nonprofit National College of Amateur Athletics charges companies who advertise at March Madness and other sports games. At one time, New York University operated a macaroni factory to support its school. In some cases, these nonprofits charge fees for activities that are related to their missions. In other cases, nonprofits operate businesses that have no particular connection with their programs other than as a way to raise funds to support the programs that are central to their mission.

If some nonprofits operate a business, what distinguishes the nonprofit from a for-profit business? The key distinction is that the nonprofit doesn't have shareholders or owners, as does a for-profit business. In the for-profit business world, the owners (in a corporation, the shareholders are the owners) share the profit that the business makes. A nonprofit corporation cannot distribute its profits (it has no owners) but must keep them to use for its nonprofit mission. Lawyers know this as "the nondistributional constraint."

The nondistributional constraint has important implications for your efforts to operate a business. For-profit businesses typically raise capital by attracting investors who provide funds for the business in return for a share of the profits. In the case of corporations, the profits are paid as dividends. Nonprofit corporations cannot raise funds to start and expand a business in this way. Nonprofits must find start-up and expansion money for businesses it runs through the kind of sources described in Chapter 22—usually, donations, grants, and fees for services.

While the inability to pay a return on investments restricts a nonprofit in significant ways, tax-exempt organizations (remember that not all nonprofits are tax-exempt) that operate a business have one advantage over their for-profit counterparts. Tax-exempt organizations don't have to pay income tax on their taxable income. There is an important exception to this rule—the income is taxable if it is classified as unrelated business income. This exception is explored in detail later in this chapter.

In many other respects, a nonprofit that charges fees for goods and services related to its mission or operates a business unrelated to its mission deals with the same constraints as any for-profit business. This means that the nonprofit must consider what its objectives are for the business, how it will get funding to capitalize its business, what kind of legal structure the business should have and how it will be connected to the nonprofit, what the business will provide, how to market the business, what employees to hire, and how it will track the finances of the business. To do this, the nonprofit will want to develop a business plan for its enterprise.

BUSINESS ACTIVITIES BY TAX-EXEMPT ORGANIZATIONS

Creating a Business Plan

Whether your business activities will be directly related to your exempt purpose or be unrelated to your mission, you will need to develop a clear business plan in order to ensure their success. Start your business planning effort by describing the overall purpose of your business venture clearly. Why are you considering a strategy that will involve selling something to someone?

If your business will involve charging fees for services or products that directly help advance your mission, you will probably answer this question by stating that the fees or sales income you generate will cover part or all of the cost of delivering the service or product and make it possible to achieve your mission. In most cases you'll have to be prepared to combine some contributed income with the income your generate through fees/sales in order to cover the full cost of these mission related services.

Start your business planning effort by describing the overall purpose of your business venture clearly.

If the business you are considering will involve selling goods or services that don't directly accomplish your mission, you motivation may be partially or fully to generate a net profit that can be used to fund your mission focused activities. So you'll want to be certain that you create a plan that will actually result in generating profit.

In either case, you'll need a clear business plan. Start by describing the service or product that you will be offering for sale. Move on to identify the target audience for your product—who will actually want to obtain it. Look at your service/product through the eyes of the potential consumer to identify the factors that will most influence their decision to choose your product/service rather than another that they perceive as similar. Once you are clear about the market for your services, you can identify the strategies that will be most effective to reach and mobilize your market to purchase your services/goods.

All of the steps above are typical of for-profit business planning. An additional element of market analysis will be essential if you are considering providing services or goods to individuals who lack financial resources to purchase the items they need at the going rate. For example, if your nonprofit intends to provide quality child care to individuals who cannot afford the cost of quality child care, your business plan will have to differentiate the role of consumer (the family using the child care) from the role of purchaser (the state agency or other third party payer who will pay for the service for eligible individuals). Business planning in this situation will be more complex because you will have to do market analysis and develop marketing strategies to accommodate the different needs and priorities of the consumer and the purchaser.

Once you are clear about your market and the strategies you will use to reach it, you will be able to flesh out your business model, projecting both income and expenses. You'll need to create a 3 to 5 year financial projection to test various assumptions about the volume of sales you will have and the costs you will incur for all components of your business, including marketing and managing as well as delivering the service or producing the product. To develop your financial model you'll have to test a variety of options for pricing, marketing strategy, service delivery, and management functions to learn which approach appears to produce the best financial results.

A key part of developing your plan will be figuring out what skills and systems you will need to have in place in order to be successful. Will you need to add managers with business and marketing expertise? Invest in new technology and improve your website? Improve or expand your facilities?

You will also need to think carefully about how your Board of Directors will provide effective oversight for your business venture. Will your Board have the time, energy, and expertise needed to guide the business venture while still fulfilling all of its critical roles for your charitable functions?

While there are many examples of successful business ventures operated by nonprofit organizations, there are many more nonprofit efforts to develop business ventures that have failed. Of course, this is true for the creation of for-profit businesses as well. Experts estimate that approximately 90% of small business start-ups fail. Why? The two most common reasons for business failure are lack of management expertise and lack of sufficient capital. Both are challenging problems for nonprofits considering business ventures.

To address these challenges you will want to be sure that your business planning effort includes a realistic projection of the start-up costs and expertise that will be required for successful development and operation of your business venture. Consider seeking help from the small business development center at your local community college or from others in your community who have experience developing and managing small businesses.

One of the questions your advisor will almost certainly ask is whether your nonprofit will have to pay unrelated business income tax on the profits from your business venture. Check out the discussion below in this chapter to build your understanding of this somewhat complex question. Remember that even if the income from the business venture you choose will be considered taxable unrelated business income by the IRS, you will only be required to pay tax on it if you generate a profit and like all businesses, you will get to keep much more of the profit than you will pay in taxes.

Unrelated Business Income

As we noted earlier, your nonprofit, if it is tax-exempt, does not have to pay taxes on the taxable income generated by your business. If your nonprofit is not tax-exempt, you will pay taxes like a for-profit and the unrelated business income discussion in this chapter does not apply to you.

If your tax-exempt nonprofit will be generating income through business activities, you need to know whether the IRS will consider the resulting income to be unrelated business income. If so, you may be required to file an additional tax return, the Form 990-T and to pay corporate tax on the profit generated through your unrelated business activity. On the other hand, if the activity for which you charge fees is sufficiently related to your exempt purpose, the IRS will characterize

BUSINESS ACTIVITIES BY TAX-EXEMPT ORGANIZATIONS

it as "related "and you will not have to file the 990 T or pay tax on the "profit" that arises when they income from fees exceeds the costs of services or products for which the fees are charged.

> *In cases where an organization generates too much unrelated business income or expends too many of its resources on its unrelated business activities, the IRS can refuse to recognize the organization as exempt or can revoke its exemption.*

In cases where an organization generates too much unrelated business income or expends too many of its resources on its unrelated business activities, the IRS can refuse to recognize the organization as exempt or can revoke its exemption. These rules apply to all exempt organizations, not just those exempt under §501(c) (3). Consequently, understanding the IRS concept of unrelated business income is important for organizations exempt under any section of §501(c). You can view an easy to understand IRS video on this subject at *http://www.stayexempt.irs.gov/virtualworkshop/UnrelatedBusinessIncome/ubitest.aspx* .This chapter covers the subject in more detail.

Unrelated business income (UBI) is defined as income derived from the *regular* conduct of a *trade or business* that is *not substantially related* to the organization's exempt purpose.

> *All three parts of the unrelated business income test must be met before you have to classify your income as unrelated business income.*

This definition breaks down into three requirements which, if *all* are met, mean that you have unrelated business income:

1. You conduct a trade or business; *and*

2. You do so regularly, *and*

3. Your trade or business is not substantially related to your exempt purpose.

Trade or Business

A trade or business includes any activity carried on for the production of income from the performance of services or the sale of goods. This description has been broadly defined and includes activities like the production of an affinity credit card, the sale of mailing lists, advertising income, and fundraisers at which donors get something of value (e.g., dinner) for their contributions. Most types of income producing activities will be a trade or business. A trade or business includes a multi-million dollar book company that publishes and distributes religious books and a fundrais-

207

ing dinner held by a community center to raise money for a new roof. Activities that encourage people to donate, rather than to give money in exchange for something of value, are not income producing and therefore are not a trade or business—for example, a campaign requesting contributions.

Regularly Carried On

Your trade or business is not subject to unrelated business income tax unless it is regularly carried on. In determining whether your trade activity is regularly carried on, the IRS will generally compare the way you conduct your activity to the way a commercial business carries on similar activities. The IRS will look at the frequency and continuity with which the activities are conducted and the manner in which they are pursued.

If the activity is the kind normally conducted by commercial businesses on a year-round basis and you conduct the activity for a few weeks, then this would not be construed to be regularly carried on. For example, if you sponsor an arts and crafts sale once a year for a week in December, you are not regularly carrying on the business of selling arts and crafts. However, the conduct of a year-round business one day a week would constitute the regular conduct of business. An example would be if you sold books year round and were open only on Saturdays. If your activities are the type that commercially are only conducted seasonally (e.g., the sale of Christmas wreaths), then you are regularly conducting business if you engage in that activity during a significant portion of the season.

If the activity is the kind that is normally carried on intermittently by commercial organizations (for example, the publication of advertising at a play), the IRS will compare the manner that you conduct the activity with the way that commercial groups conduct the activity. If you conduct the activity without the competitive and promotional efforts typical of commercial endeavors, the activity will not be considered to be regularly carried on. Similarly, where you engage in the incidental sale of goods (for example, refreshments sold at a workshop), this activity is not treated as a regular business.

Substantially Related to Exempt Purpose

It is a common misunderstanding to think that a business activity designed solely to raise money for your exempt activities is substantially related to your exempt purpose and is therefore not an unrelated trade or business simply because the funds will be used for exempt purposes. This misunderstanding comes from confusing what is *essential* with what is *substantially related*. Having money is usually essential to carrying on exempt activities. But the method of raising that money is not necessarily substantially related to the exempt purposes of the group. Consequently, the need for funds to realize your mission does not constitute an exempt purpose or make fund-generating business activity exempt from unrelated business income tax.

For an activity to be substantially related there must be a substantial causal relationship between the activity and the accomplishing of the exempt purpose. The causal relationship must be an important contribution to the achievement of those purposes. This test basically requires a comparison between the group's program for accomplishing its mission or purposes, and the purpose of the income producing activity in question.

Example: A charitable organization that seeks to improve the lives of the poor in a village in Nigeria and to support Nigerian culture may sell artwork produced by poor artists in the village. The proceeds from the sales are substantially related to the charity's exempt purposes (to help low income Nigerians and to support Nigerian culture) and are not unrelated business income. However, an Oregon soccer club that regularly sells Nigerian artwork to raise proceeds for its soccer programs does generate UBI.

It is a common misunderstanding to think that a business activity designed solely to raise money for its exempt activities is substantially related to its exempt purpose, and is therefore not an unrelated trade or business.

Mixed Activities

In determining whether your fee-generating activities contribute importantly to the accomplishment of your exempt purpose, the IRS considers the size and extent of your activities in relation to the purpose they are supposed to serve. If your activities relate in part to your exempt purpose but are performed on a larger scale than necessary, the income attributable to that portion of the activities in excess of your exempt needs is unrelated income. Similarly, if you have unrelated income mixed in with related income, you must separate that out and count it as unrelated.

Example: A museum has a theater auditorium which is used for showing educational films in connection with its program of public education in the arts and sciences. The theater is an important part of museum activities and is operated continuously during the hours the museum is open to the public. Income from admissions would be considered income from related activity and not be considered to be unrelated business income. However, if the organization were to operate the theater as an ordinary motion picture theater showing commercially made films for public entertainment during the evening hours when the museum was closed, income from that operation would be from an unrelated business income activity.

Advertising

The IRS scrutinizes income from the sale of advertising by exempt organizations. The IRS is concerned with sale of commercial advertising space in tax-exempt publications, with corporate "sponsorships" of nonprofit events, and with income associated with nonprofits using their websites to provide links to for-profit business websites.

SALE OF ADVERTISING

Many organizations publish newsletters or periodicals that contain advertisements. In most cases, the IRS will consider the, advertising income to be unrelated business income. In some rare cases, ad money can be considered related business income. This occurs where the ads themselves further an exempt purpose. For example, an AIDS related periodical that published only ads related to the latest medical advances in combatting AIDS with the intention of educating its readers might be exempt. However, an exempt medical organization that publishes medical ads for the purpose of generating additional revenue has unrelated business income.

Recall also that even if the advertising is unrelated to your exempt purpose, the sale of advertising must be regularly carried on in order to be treated as unrelated business income. If you sell ads only in your annual fundraising concert program and you are involved for a fairly short time in putting together the ads, the income is probably not unrelated business income.

If your ad income is unrelated business income, the IRS has developed special rules for calculating how you are taxed on this income. IRS Publication 598, *Tax on Unrelated Business Income of Exempt Organizations* explains how these rules work.

CORPORATE SPONSORSHIPS

Businesses frequently sponsor nonprofit events or organizations in exchange for an acknowledgment by the exempt organization of the business's sponsorship. The IRS may classify the money you receive from the business as a contribution that you acknowledge by naming the sponsor or as advertising income that you receive in return for publicizing the sponsor. Your organization would prefer that the money be characterized as a contribution, since contributions are not taxable. The IRS has developed a series of rules spelling out what you must do to justify treating corporate "sponsorships" as contributions rather than as taxable advertising.

> *The IRS has developed a series of rules spelling out what you must do to justify treating corporate "sponsorships" as contributions rather than as taxable advertising.*

If the sponsor gets no substantial benefit from the event (other than an incidental acknowledgment of the sponsorship), the payment is a donation and is not unrelated business income. You are allowed to promote your sponsor in limited but important ways:

- You can display the sponsor's logos and slogans as long as there are no comparative or qualitative descriptions.
- You can list the sponsor's locations and phone number and offer a value-neutral description of the sponsor and the sponsor's brand names, trade names, and listings.
- You may list your sponsors on your website and you can provide a link to the sponsors' websites.

BUSINESS ACTIVITIES BY TAX-EXEMPT ORGANIZATIONS

The sponsor can condition its payment on the occurrence of the event; that is, if it does not occur, the sponsor does not have to pay. The sponsor can also distribute its product at the event, as long as it does not engage in the conduct described below that constitutes advertising. If these rules are followed, the sponsor's payment is an acknowledgment and is not unrelated business income.

Messages that contain any of the following elements are advertisements and generate unrelated business income:

- qualitative or comparative language ("We have the best shoes in town.");
- price information, value, or savings ("10% off on Fridays.");
- an endorsement ("Our nonprofit believes these shoes are the best.");
- an inducement to acquire the sponsor's product ("Shop with Big Corp and get a free watch.").

If the amount of the sponsor's payment is contingent on factors like the number of people attending the event or ratings on television or the radio, then the income is advertising.

If the sponsor receives a substantial return benefit, part or all of the sponsorship payment becomes unrelated business income. Such benefits include advertisements, exclusive provider arrangements, goods, facilities, services, privileges, and the right to use an intangible asset (for example, your mailing list). If the value of these benefits is more than 2% of the sponsor's payment, then the entire fair market value of these benefits is a substantial benefit. Only the portion of the sponsorship payment that exceeds the value of these benefits is a qualified sponsorship payment and thus treated as contributed income rather than unrelated business income.

- *Example:* A music shop agrees to act as a corporate sponsor for a concert series produced by a nonprofit symphony. The symphony acknowledges the sponsorship and includes a link to the music company's internet address. This is an acknowledgement and the money the symphony receives for the series is not unrelated business income.

- *Example*: a car club exempt under §501(c) (7) plans an auto show. A local car dealer well-known to the members for its excellent selection of cars sponsors the show. The club acknowledges the sponsorship in its show program, giving the name and telephone number of the club with the statement, "Thanks to the best dealer in town." This is not an acknowledgement because of the comparative statement ("best dealer in town"). The IRS will treat the sponsorship payment as unrelated business income.

You should consult a lawyer if you have corporate sponsorship of events of a significant size.

PAYMENTS FOR WEBSITE LINKS

If you receive payments to link your website to another nonprofit or for-profit organization, that payment may constitute advertisement income unless you make the linkage to accomplish part of your exempt purpose. The IRS may also treat your income as a corporate sponsorship acknowledgment or a royalty. You need professional advice on this.

Examples of Unrelated Business Income

You might generate related business income by providing services or goods which are directly related to achieving your exempt purpose. The income from these related activities is not considered unrelated business income so you will not be required to file Form 990T to report it or be subject to Unrelated Business Income Tax, even if the income generated exceeds the actual cost of providing the goods or services. The best way to understand whether the income that various activities generate is *related or unrelated* business income is through examples.

Services

Many nonprofits sell services that are related to their exempt purpose.

> *Example:* An organization operating to combat racial discrimination presents an annual conference with workshops for organizations, governmental entities, and businesses interested in addressing racism. The fees received for the conference are related to the organization's exempt purpose. These fees are not unrelated business income.

Sales of Goods

Where the Exempt Activity Itself Produces the Product

Sometimes an exempt activity produces a product. If that product is sold in its original state, the income produced is not from an unrelated business. But if the product is exploited beyond what is necessary to prepare it for sale, then the income would probably be from an unrelated business.

> *Example:* An exempt vocational education program maintains a dairy herd to provide students with educational experiences related to dairy herd management. The sale of milk and cream produced by the herd would not be income from an unrelated business because milk is an inevitable by-product of maintaining a dairy herd. But if the organization used the milk and cream in the further manufacture of cheese, ice cream, etc., the sale of those products would be from an unrelated business, unless the manufacturing activities themselves contribute importantly to the accomplishment of the exempt purposes of the organization

Other Sales of Goods

Example: An art museum's gift shop sales of watches and souvenirs are unrelated business income, because the primary purpose of the items is ornamental or utilitarian. However, the sales of reproductions of artwork and books about artists are not unrelated business income because they are chiefly educational and enhance visitor awareness of art and culture.

Example: An exempt organization publishes an educational magazine which furthers its educational purposes. It also sells commercial advertising space in the magazine. The advertising income is derived from an unrelated business activity. In contrast, selling subscriptions to the magazine generates income which is related to the organization's exempt educational purposes.

Example: An exempt organization which trains children in the performing arts (singing, dancing, acting) presents performances by students and receives income from the sale of tickets to the performances. The students' participation in the performances is an essential part of their training. Since the income is produced from activities which contribute importantly to the accomplishment of the organization's exempt purpose, it is not income from an unrelated trade or business. If the performance included a program that contained advertising, the advertising income would not be unrelated business income because it did not result from conduct regularly carried on

Example: A Cherokee community center that works to preserve Cherokee culture rents out its auditorium on a regular basis to a Cherokee dance group in order to promote Cherokee culture. The rentals received are related to the group's exempt purpose.

Exceptions to the Unrelated Business Income Rules

There are a number of exceptions to the rules defining unrelated business income. The more significant ones are listed below. In each of these cases Congress has excluded the income from what otherwise would be unrelated trade or business from taxation:

- A trade or business where substantially all the work in running the business is done by volunteers—for example, an exempt organization that operates a retail store run by volunteers.

- A trade or business which consists of selling merchandise which has been donated to the organization—for example, a thrift shop operated by an exempt organization with donated clothes, books, furniture, etc., which are sold to the public.

- A trade or business which is operated primarily for the convenience of the organization's members, students, patients, officers or employees—for example, a college laundry operated by the college for laundering dormitory linens and students' clothing.

- Bingo, if operated in states in which only nonprofit organizations may operate such gaming activities. Oregon is such a state.

- Distribution of low cost articles and member lists. This exception applies to §501(c)(3) organizations (except public safety groups) and a few other exempt organizations to which contributions are deductible. Your organization can distribute low-cost articles as part of certain solicitation campaigns and you can rent or sell your mailing list.

- Certain conventions and trade shows, by §501(c)(3), (c)(4), (c)(5), and (c)(6) Groups.

In addition, income from the following is specifically excluded from unrelated business income:

- dividends
- interest
- some rental income (unless it is from rental of debt-financed property) and
- royalties (in most cases)

There are also exceptions to the above exclusions for debt-financed property and income from controlled corporations and various other special rules. Court cases have allowed mailing list sales and affinity card income to avoid classification as unrelated business income. These rules are complicated. If you think they may apply to you, read the free IRS Publication 598 Tax on Unrelated Business Income of Exempt Organizations *http://www.irs.gov/pub/irs-pdf/p598.pdf* or talk to a professional for more information.

The Unrelated Business Income Tax

Who is Subject to the Unrelated Business Income Tax (UBIT)?

The unrelated business income tax is imposed on almost all tax-exempt organizations, except for state colleges and universities, certain charitable trusts, certain title-holding companies, and certain government corporations. Groups that are covered by the unrelated business income tax include those exempt under §501(c)(3), (c)(4), (c)(5), (c)(6), (c)(7), and (c)(19). The unrelated business income tax is imposed in a somewhat different way than is described in this chapter on social clubs [§501(c)(7)], veterans organization [§501(c)(19)], and a few other specialized categories of exempt organizations. If your organization is one of these specialized groups, you should see an accountant or an attorney for advice specific to you if you generate taxable income.

How to Calculate and Pay the Unrelated Business Income Tax

If you have determined that some part of your organization's activities fall within the IRS definition of unrelated business income, you may have to file an additional annual return with the IRS, Form 990T. Organizations with gross annual unrelated business income of $1,000 or more must file the 990T. However, the IRS assesses the unrelated business income tax only if the net income from unrelated business activities is greater than $1,000. So, you may file the form but not owe a tax. For example, if you have paid staff operating a gift shop, you would file the Form 990T if you grossed business income of $1,000. You would then compute net unrelated business income by subtracting all the expenses of operating the shop from the income the shop brings in. You are only taxed on the net income from unrelated business activity. If your expenses exceed your income, you won't owe a tax.

For organizations generating significant amounts of unrelated business income revenue, good recordkeeping is essential for costs incurred for both the exempt and the unrelated business income activity.

In computing the expenses which can be attributed to the unrelated business income activity, you are permitted to consider both direct and indirect costs. Direct costs such as salaries and commissions, long distance phone calls, and expenses incurred to buy needed materials paid in connection with the unrelated activity are clearly deductible. Indirect costs may include a proration of the organization's total cost for rent, phone service, utilities, etc.

For organizations generating significant amounts of unrelated business income revenue, good recordkeeping is essential for costs incurred for both the exempt and the unrelated business income activity. You will have to be able to prove to the IRS that your allocation of shared costs has a reasonable basis. It's important to record all the costs of unrelated business income activity because these costs will reduce the unrelated business income net income, and consequently reduce the tax you must pay. IRS Publication 598 "*Tax on Unrelated Business Income of Exempt Organizations*" is essential reading, preferably before you begin your unrelated business income activity, and definitely before you file either your Form 990 or your 990T. The Unrelated Business Income Tax Return (990T) is due the 15th day of the 5th month after the close of the fiscal year (November 15th for June 30th fiscal year organizations; May 15th for December 31st calendar year organizations), the same deadline as for the Form 990. The filing of the 990T is required in *addition* to the filing of the 990, not as a substitute.

If you must pay unrelated business income tax, you must make estimated tax payments in the same manner as for-profit corporations. Contact the IRS or your accountant for the proper forms and time deadlines for your group.

Protecting Your Tax-Exempt Status

When Does Unrelated Business Income Threaten Your Tax Exemption?

If your organization engages in too much unrelated business activity, the IRS can deny your exemption or revoke your exempt status. The question of how much unrelated business income activity an exempt organization can conduct without threatening its tax-exempt status is difficult to answer. The IRS considers that an organization whose unrelated business activities are "more than an insubstantial part" of the organization's activities is not exempt.

In determining when your unrelated business activities would be considered substantial, you should consider

- what percentage of your income is attributable to unrelated business income,
- how much of your organization's time is spent on your UBI activities,
- whether and how much your UBI activities have influenced the composition of your Board,
- how much volunteer energy goes into your organization's exempt mission that may not show up on your books, and
- how your UBI activities affect the public perception of your organization.

The IRS seems to consider factors other than the percentage of income that an exempt organization realizes from its unrelated business. For example, occasionally groups that make 50% of their income from unrelated business activities have been granted an exemption. Although the regulations are uncertain, this doesn't have to close off the possibility of participating in successful business ventures. It just requires careful planning and good professional advice.

Forming a New Corporation

If your group's unrelated business activity appears to be substantial or clearly heading toward substantial, you may want to consider protecting your tax-exempt status through the formation of a separate corporation to conduct unrelated business income activity. In this approach, the new corporation can be either nonprofit or for-profit. If it is nonprofit, you will want its Articles of Incorporation to specify the right of your existing corporation's (the parent) Board to appoint a controlling interest of the new corporation's Board. If the new corporation is a profit entity, you will want the existing nonprofit (parent) corporation to own a controlling interest in the shares of the profit corporation.

Whether profit or nonprofit, the new corporation is designed to conduct the unrelated business activity and generate profits which will be given to the tax-exempt parent corporation. You will need good legal and accounting advice to set up the new corporation and minimize its tax liabilities. Your accountant or attorney can help you evaluate the benefit of choosing a nonprofit or profit structure for the new corporation. Remember that the new corporation can purchase goods or services from the parent exempt organization at fair market value. This may permit transfer of significant amounts of the new corporation's income to the parent while creating deductible expenses for the new corporation, reducing the new corporation's net income and corporate income tax liability.

> *If your group's unrelated business activity appears to be substantial or clearly heading toward substantial, you may want to consider protecting your tax-exempt status through the formation of a separate corporation to conduct unrelated business income activity.*

If the new corporation is a profit entity, it can pay dividends to the parent nonprofit corporation out of after tax profits. The dividends are not considered unrelated business income to the exempt organization and therefore they are not taxable. If the new corporation is a nonprofit corporation, it can make contributions to the exempt corporation. These contributions are also not considered unrelated business income to the exempt corporation. Structuring the arrangement as a partnership by the exempt organization does not offer the same benefits as these corporate alternatives. Income from partnerships is unrelated business income to the exempt organization.

These alternative structures are necessary and desirable only for exempt organizations with substantial unrelated business income activity. If your group is testing a small profit-making idea, it's probably best to wait until it succeeds before investing in the legal work necessary to set up a new corporation to conduct the activity. However, you should obtain experienced legal and tax advice before beginning even a small business venture type activity.

Joint Ventures

In recent years, exempt organizations have increasingly entered into joint ventures with businesses. A joint venture is one in which your tax-exempt organization and another business or nonprofit enter into a verbal or written agreement to carry out an income-producing venture together and to share the profits of that venture. For example, your affordable housing nonprofit may enter into a joint venture with a for-profit developer to jointly develop an affordable housing project.

A joint venture is one in which your tax-exempt organization and another business or nonprofit enter into a verbal or written agreement to carry out an income-producing venture together and to share the profits of that venture.

If your organization is exempt under §501(c)(3) and your joint venture partner is not, this is an area of great interest to the IRS. The IRS is concerned that the business partner may be taking advantage of its partner's exempt status to realize private benefit and that the exempt organization may be diverted from carrying out its exempt purposes. The IRS rules are complex and you need legal advice if your (c)(3) organization plans to enter into a joint venture with a non-exempt organization. In order to ensure that your Board is aware of the pitfalls in this area, you may want to consider adopting a Board policy that requires the corporation to get legal advice before entering into a joint venture arrangement with non-(c)(3) partners. For a simple version of this policy, see the Joint Venture Policy in the Forms section.

Consult Appendix 1 if you would like information about source material related to this Chapter.

10 FISCAL SPONSORSHIP

THIS CHAPTER COVERS

- Proper Uses of Fiscal Sponsorships
- Fiscal Sponsorship Alternatives
- Misuses of Fiscal Sponsorships
- Issues in the Fiscal Sponsor Relationship
- How to Structure a Fiscal Sponsorship

There are occasionally situations in which a group that doesn't have §501(c)(3) recognition from the Internal Revenue Service, needs the assistance of a group that has received its §501(c)(3) recognition of exemption. This commonly occurs when a group is told by a donor or funder that it would like to give the group money but that it will only give to a group that has §501(c)(3) status. The group may not be planning to apply for its own §501(c)(3) status or it may be willing to apply for (c)(3) status but needs or wants to get the money before it will get its notice of exemption from the Internal Revenue Service. In many cases, the group will look for a §501(c)(3) group that will "sponsor" it by letting the new group use the existing §501(c)(3) tax exemption number and by receiving the money in its name and then passing the money on to the nonexempt group.

This relationship is often referred to as a fiscal sponsorship and it can be done if it is carefully structured. Many of the groups that enter into this relationship are unaware that there are serious implications for the sponsor, the project, donors to the project, and foundations that make grants to the project if the relationship is not properly set up. If you are considering entering into this type of relationship or are already in such a relationship, either as the sponsor or as the project, or if your group is thinking about giving money to such a project, you should read this chapter. You will need a basic understanding of Chapter 5 to follow some of the material in this Chapter.

A note on terminology:

In the past, fiscal sponsor relationships have been referred to as "pass throughs" or "umbrella" relationships and the sponsoring organization was called the "fiscal agent." These terms are misleading and can result in serious problems with the IRS.

Currently, the relationship is generally called a "fiscal sponsorship" and the sponsoring organization is the "fiscal sponsor" or "sponsor." We use these terms in this book. The sponsored group is the "project."

Proper Uses of Fiscal Sponsorships

A fiscal sponsorship, as we are using the term, is a relationship between a sponsoring organization that is exempt under §501(c)(3) and an independently-run project which may or may not be incorporated and that is not tax-exempt under §501(c)(3). In this relationship, the sponsor has determined that the project operates for (c)(3) purposes and is in compliance with (c)(3) rules. The sponsor agrees to fund the project by collecting grants, donations, and other revenues intended for the project and distributing them to the project under a carefully structured relationship that ensures that the funds are used for (c)(3) purposes.

Most of the legal rules discussed in this chapter assume that the mission of the sponsor is advanced by its sponsorship of the project.

A good fiscal sponsor relationship can have many positive advantages for all the parties and for the community. The most successful sponsor relationships are generally those in which the project complements the mission of the sponsor. For example, the sponsor may provide education about AIDS and support to people with AIDS and the project may provide financial assistance for those who are HIV positive and who have used up their resources. Most of the legal rules discussed in this chapter assume that the mission of the sponsor is advanced by its sponsorship of the project. We believe that these are the only types of fiscal sponsorship that an exempt organization should consider. So, for example, if your (c)(3) arts organization is approached by a project that wants to provide care for the pets of homeless people, this sponsorship would not be a good fit for your organization.

Fiscal sponsorship may allow a new organization to get off the ground and can give birth to a worthwhile project or service that would otherwise not exist. If the service provided by the project is a needed one, sponsorship can enhance the sponsor's reputation and relationships in the community as well.

Fiscal sponsorship relationships can be properly set up in a variety of situations. We describe four of the most common below. In all cases, the project has not been recognized as tax-exempt. In all of these situations, you must set your relationship up very carefully, so don't try these at home until you have read this entire chapter.

Fiscal sponsorship relationships can be properly set up in a variety of situations. You must set your relationship up very carefully.

New and Small Projects

A sponsor may support a project, often new or small in scope, that would itself qualify to be tax-exempt but it hasn't received an exemption letter. This is the most common use of fiscal sponsorships. The project may be in the process of applying for its own exemption or it may have decided that it doesn't want to get its own exemption but prefers to focus its energies on the project and not on setting up or administering a nonprofit. The project needs sponsorship because there are donors or foundations that want to give it money but who will only give to a §501(c)(3) organizations. *In a carefully constructed arrangement*, this can be done. For example, a drug prevention program has begun its work and has an interested funder but has not yet received its own tax exemption.

Projects of Limited Duration

Most nonprofits are established to last indefinitely but some nonprofits have a specific goal and will cease operations after achieving it. If this type of nonprofit wants to forego the work and expense of setting up a new nonprofit and obtaining tax-exempt status for it, a fiscal sponsorship could be a solution. An example would be a group organized to raise support for and build a memorial to a hometown service member killed in action.

Ongoing Project with a Major Donor/Funder

Occasionally, a project may be ongoing and have one or a few primary funders whose support is substantial. If the project were to obtain its own §501(c)(3) exemption, it would not qualify as a public charity because its funding does not meet the criteria described in Chapter 7. Instead, it would be classified as a private foundation with more regulation by the IRS and with lower charitable contribution limits that may discourage contributions by wealthier donors. A fiscal sponsor with a broader support base may be able to handle the project without jeopardizing its own public charity classification. If the donors are willing to relinquish some of the control over the project to a fiscal sponsor, a fiscal sponsorship could work. For example, several wealthy private donors who want to entirely fund a program to offer music opportunities to low income young people may look for a fiscal sponsor.

Assistance to Qualified Individuals

A donor may be interested in giving money to a particular individual but cannot take a charitable deduction if she or he does this. If that individual is within a category of individuals to whom an existing §501(c)(3) organizations can make grants (for example, the poor, artists, or students), *in a carefully constructed arrangement* the donor can give the money to a sponsor who makes grants to that type of individual.

The sponsor cannot accept monies to be passed to specific recipients, but it can pre-qualify the specific individuals that the donor is interested in, as long as any person meeting the criteria could apply for and have the same chance of receiving funds as that individual. The sponsor has to have objective criteria for providing assistance to individuals that would meet the requirements of §501(c)(3). For example, friends of a child with leukemia want to establish a fund to help with her medical expenses. These types of arrangements require legal help to arrange.

The sponsor cannot accept monies to be passed to specific recipients, but it can pre-qualify the specific individuals. These types of arrangements require legal help to arrange.

Fiscal Sponsorship Alternatives

There are a number of situations that are sometimes called fiscal sponsorships but are not. We describe two of the most common here. If one of these will work for you, you may want to consider it instead of a fiscal sponsorship.

Programs of the Sponsor

A new project contemplating a fiscal sponsorship arrangement in order to carry out its program ideas might consider whether the project can be run by and be part of the organization it is considering as a sponsor. If the potential sponsor took over the project, it would become one of the sponsor's program. The project would need to fit within the sponsor's mission, the sponsor would maintain control of the project and the ultimate use of the funds, and the project should be the type of activity that the sponsor described as one of its activities to the IRS on its own §501(c)(3) application.

The advantage for the project is that it does not have to set up a new corporation or deal with a fiscal sponsorship agreement. The individuals who seek to run the project would be volunteers or employees of the potential sponsor. The disadvantage is that the founders of the project would not be in control of the project, although it may have a board of advisors that makes recommendations to the sponsor. However, the potential sponsor controls the project, is responsible for any liabilities, and owns any property of the project.

Administrative Assistance for Another §501(c)(3) Organization

In a some cases, the project that has itself been recognized as exempt under §501(c)(3) wants a sponsor to handle its bookkeeping or other administrative matters in order to provide credibility and assurance of experienced management to funders. These arrangements are sometimes called fiscal sponsorships but are actually a contract between the two organizations for fiscal management or other services, not really fiscal sponsor services as we are using the term. The "sponsor" doesn't take on the obligations of oversight that a fiscal sponsor assumes when it is the only (c)(3) entity involved (described below). The sponsor doesn't account for the funds it handles as its own income and expenses in its financial statements, although the funds do show up on the sponsor's balance sheet. Among other issues, sponsors contemplating these types of contractual arrangements do need to consider whether providing bookkeeping or other services is related to the sponsor's mission and whether income received by the sponsor is unrelated business income. See Chapter 9.

Misuses of Fiscal Sponsorships

Fiscal sponsorship relationships are misused in a variety of circumstances.

> *The IRS treats the pass-through arrangement as a gift directly from the donor to the new nonexempt group. The donor cannot take a deduction for the donation.*

Pass-Through Donations and Grants

A donor cannot take a charitable deduction for a contribution to an organization that is not recognized as exempt and most foundations cannot give money to an organization that is not recognized as exempt unless the foundation follows certain accountability procedures. Frequently, an organization that has not been recognized as exempt (often a new organization) has an interested donor and will ask a §501(c)(3) group to act as an umbrella or a pass-through organization. The donor or funder writes the check to the (c)(3), which has agreed to and does pass the money through to the new group without exercising any control over the money or requiring the specific accountability mandated by the IRS rules. The IRS treats the pass-through arrangement as a gift or grant directly from the donor or funder to the new nonexempt group. This is an improper use of a fiscal sponsorship. The donor cannot legally take a deduction for the donation, the funder may have jeopardized its own (c)(3) status, and the (c)(3) umbrella may have made an improper grant.

Conduit for Gifts or Grants to Individuals

IRS rules forbid donors from making tax deductible contributions to specifically named individuals. Fiscal sponsorships are sometimes used by a donor who gives money to an exempt organizations with instructions to pass it on to a specific individual who is not properly qualified to receive the money. The donor then takes a tax deduction. Since the donor could not get a tax deduction had she or he given this money directly to the individual, this type of fiscal sponsorship is a misuse of the fiscal sponsorship arrangement. The donor cannot take a deduction for the donation and the (c)(3) has violated IRS rules that require certain procedures before making gifts to individuals.

Conduit to Nonexempt Organizations

Occasionally an organization that would not qualify for exemption under §501(c)(3) asks a §501(c)(3) organization to act as its sponsor. Funders and donors who could not give to the non-§501(c)(3) organization then give to the (c)(3) organization. The (c)(3) organization is supposed to pass the money through to the nonexempt organization. This is a misuse of the fiscal sponsorship arrangement. The donors cannot legally take a deduction and the (c)(3) has jeopardized its own exemption by giving money to a group that does not meet the (c)(3) criteria.

Avoidance of the Public Support Test

The IRS classifies all §501(c)(3) organizations as either private foundations or public charities. Private foundations generally are groups that get much of their income from one person or family or another private foundation. There are significant constraints and legal and accounting rules that private foundations must meet. Most groups prefer to avoid this classification if possible. (See pages 99-101 for a more detailed discussion of private foundations.)

The private foundation classification is commonly avoided by showing that an organization receives support from a variety of public sources. Chapter 7 discusses the tests that establish this in considerable detail. Sometimes a private donor wants to give a small organization a large sum of money that will tip the organization out of the publicly supported category and into the private foundation category. Occasionally the donor will donate that money to another §501(c)(3) organization (in this book, we call this a PSO—see Chapter 7). If the PSO is large enough, the donation does not tip it into the private foundation category. The donor **requires** that the PSO pass the money on to the smaller organization. PSOs do not tip public charities into the private foundation category. Because the PSO and not the donor is giving the money to the ultimate recipient, the recipient does not appear to be tipped into the private foundation category. However, the IRS will characterize this gift as having been made by the original donor to the intended recipient organization, since the original donor has controlled its direction. The IRS will classify the smaller organization as a private foundation.

Avoidance of the Lobbying Excise Tax by Private Foundations

Private foundations are restricted from using money to lobby and must pay excise taxes when they do. In order to avoid this tax, some foundations will attempt to give the money to a §501(c)(3) group that is not a private foundation and which can do limited lobbying without paying a tax. When the gift is to be disbursed for lobbying purposes, the fiscal sponsorship arrangement does not prevent the IRS from characterizing this as lobbying by the private foundation.

Consequences of the Misuse of Fiscal Sponsorships

All the parties involved in the misuse of a fiscal sponsorship may face consequences. The sponsor may lose its own tax exemption for its involvement in activities that are improper for (c)(3) organizations. The project may be classified as a private foundation based on the reclassification of the source of funds by a large private donor. If the donor is a private foundation, it may have to pay a penalty tax. If the donor is a private individual looking for a charitable tax deduction, the donor can lose the tax deduction.

The organizations and the officers and Directors face some additional potential liabilities. The IRS may impose excise taxes or other penalties on the officers and Directors of the exempt organization for misuse of funds. Donors who have lost an expected tax deduction may have sufficient losses to consider legal action against the organization and its officers and Directors. The future Directors of the sponsor may bring suit against the former officers and Directors whose negligent conduct caused the organization's loss of tax-exempt status. Bottom line: you want to do fiscal sponsorships right!

Issues in the Fiscal Sponsor Relationship

Four different participants may have an involvement in the fiscal sponsor relationship: the sponsor, the project, the donor, and the grantor. All of these parties have an interest in ensuring that the relationship is properly established. A number of issues come up in the fiscal sponsor relationship that will impact each of the participants differently. Before you set about structuring your sponsorship agreement, you need clarity about how you want to handle these issues.

Characterizing the Use of Project Funds

The parties have two choices about how to characterize the relationship in which the sponsor will handle funds raised for the project: the funds can be solicited as unrestricted or restricted funds.

Unrestricted Funds

If the parties agree that the sponsor has complete discretion over the use of any funds raised for the project, the funds are unrestricted. The parties will be aware that the sponsor plans to fund the project with the funds, but all contributors and funders understand when they provide the funds that the sponsor has the right to use the funds in any manner that it wants. Most sponsors will not be willing to antagonize potential funding sources and community relations by exercising their power to use the funds for other purposes without a good reason, but the sponsor has this right under this arrangement.

The parties have two choices about how to characterize the relationship in which the sponsor will handle funds raised for the project: the funds can be solicited as unrestricted or restricted funds

---

When funds are taken in as unrestricted funds, the funds are being held by the organization in a manner that is akin to Board-designated funds. An accountant would not classify the funds as restricted, since the Board has the right to change how the funds are used. Nonetheless, the Board may want its financial statements that show these funds set aside for the project. One consequence of this arrangement is that, if the project fails, the Board can use the funds in any manner that it wants.

From the sponsor's point of view, this is generally the simplest and preferred manner of handling funds and this probably is the most common form of sponsorship relationship. Occasionally, contributors, as well as many projects, may want more assurance that the funds contributed for the project will go to the project or, at least, for activities similar to those envisioned by the project.

Restricted Fund

The alternative is for the sponsor to collect funds that can only be used for the project. In order to avoid classification as a pass-through relationship, the sponsor must pre-approve the project **before** the funds are received and retain some control over the use of the funds. Because the funds have been solicited for a particular purpose, the sponsor will hold the funds in a restricted account. The power to exercise control to refuse to give the funds to the project is sometimes called a variance power.

One central issue in the sponsorship arrangement concerns the circumstances under which the sponsor may refuse to give the restricted funds to the project. In order to define the situations that could trigger the sponsor to vary from using the restricted funds for the project, the parties need to consider several potential factors:

- what the parties need to do to ensure that the relationship is not treated by the IRS as a pass-through relationship
- what commitments the sponsor made to the grantor;

- what representations the sponsor or donor made to individual contributors in soliciting funds;
- under what circumstances the sponsor itself may want to refuse to fund the project; and
- what happens to the funds if the parties terminate their relationship before the funds are distributed.

AVOIDING THE IRS PASS-THROUGH DESIGNATION

In order to avoid the IRS classification as a pass-through transaction, the sponsor needs to exercise the right to control the funds. One control the IRS requires is that the funds will be used in compliance with the rules for organizations exempt under §501(c)(3). The IRS relies on the (c)(3) sponsor to ensure this. At a minimum, the sponsor must exercise the expenditure responsibility described on pages 234-35. This means that if the project acts in any way to jeopardize the sponsors (c)(3) status, the sponsor must have the right to stop payments to the project and to recoup any monies that were not properly used. All grantors and contributors must be aware that the sponsor has the right to exercise this power.

COMMITMENTS MADE TO THE GRANTOR

The foundation or governmental entity that makes a grant to the sponsor to be used for the project acts on the basis of a grant application and grant agreement that sets out the terms of the relationship. Although the funder anticipates that the funds will be used for the project, the monies are actually given to the sponsor. In almost all cases, the sponsor will sign a grant agreement with the funder which commonly includes agreements to spend the funds in certain ways and anticipates designated outcomes. In these circumstances, the sponsor will want the power to terminate its relationship with the project if the project is failing to comply with the grant terms.

REPRESENTATIONS TO INDIVIDUAL DONORS OR THE PUBLIC

Many projects raise money from individual and sometimes corporate contributions. In the course of raising money, the project persuades the public to donate based on claims about what it will do. Because the contributions actually go to the sponsor to hold in a restricted fund, the sponsor must hold the money for the purposes for which it was solicited. Consequently, the sponsor needs to be sure that the project is correctly representing what it will do and that it in fact does it. To do this, the sponsor should review and approve all solicitations by the project before the project approaches donors or the public. The sponsor also needs to have the right to refuse to disperse funds from its restricted account to the project if the project is not using the funds as promised. The sponsor will want to be sure that the solicitation and any other descriptions about the project make clear to the public and contributors the sponsor's right to exercise these controls.

SPONSOR'S DECISION TO DISCONTINUE FUNDING THE PROJECT

The sponsor needs to consider whether circumstances might arise, in addition to those described above, that would cause the sponsor to terminate the sponsorship. One such circumstance might be if the project was operating in such a way that might negatively affect the sponsor's reputation in the community—for example, if the project director was being disrespectful to clients or community members important to the sponsor.

TERMINATION OF THE RELATIONSHIP

If the sponsor becomes concerned with how the project is operating, it is generally in everyone's best interest for the sponsor and project to talk and attempt to resolve the difficulty. If after that the sponsor determines that it must exercise its control over the funds to refuse to continue its funding of the project, the sponsor then needs to decide how to handle any funds that remain in its restricted account. In some cases, the sponsor may also need to attempt to recoup misspent monies from the project and add those funds to the restricted account.

In determining how to handle the restricted funds upon the termination of the project, the sponsor should first consult the funding agreements for any provisions requiring that foundation or government monies be returned. If the grant agreement requires a return, then of course the sponsor must return the funds that have not been spent.

The sponsor's next step is to consider what to do with the remainder of its funds. Because it collected funds as restricted funds, it has to spend the funds for the purpose for which they were collected. For example, if your nonprofit educates the public about children with cancer and the project you sponsored raised money to grant wishes for young cancer patients, you will need to spend monies restricted to the project to grant children's wishes. You may do this by establishing your own program or by finding another (c)(3) that can honor the terms of your restriction.

If the sponsor determines that it can comply with the terms of the restriction, it may want to consider having conversations with its funders and donors before it continues. The sponsor will want to do what it can to maintain good relationships with the funding community. The sponsor may want to explain to the grantor or donor why it is redirecting the funds and its plan for the use of the monies. Some grantors who did not retain a right in their grant agreement may want the funds returned to them and, though the sponsor is not obligated to do this, it may want to consider it as long as the grantor is a governmental entity or exempt under §501(c)(3).

If the sponsor is considering whether to return funds to an individual donor, both the sponsor and donor may want to get professional advice. The sponsor will need to be sure that the restriction supports a return to the donor, since normally a (c)(3) sponsor can't give money to individuals except those who are its charitable beneficiaries. The donor will want to consider the tax impact on the donor of accepting the return of a failed gift which it has already deducted.

If the sponsor is not in a position to spend the funds in accordance with the restriction without giving them to the project, it needs to consider what it will do in those circumstances. It may need to get the approval of the Department of Justice or a court to keep or dispose of the funds.

Control

As described above, the sponsor must exercise control in certain important areas in order to protect its §501(c)(3) status and the commitments it made to funders and donors. At a minimum, the sponsor should collect all pertinent financial information and records; it should approve all financial expenditures, hiring and firing, and all significant decisions in running the project; and it should have the power to terminate the relationship if the project engages in any activity that jeopardizes the sponsor's tax-exempt status or funder or donor commitments. To the extent that the sponsor maintains control, it may also find itself taking on responsibility for the liabilities of the project.

> *Control is a central issue for both the sponsor and project. In order to protect its §501(c)(3) status, the sponsor must exercise some control over any money that it gives to the project.*

The project typically wants to exercise as much control as possible over policy and administration. It can set policy about the project, subject to the sponsor's right to veto its decisions if these decisions threaten the sponsor's tax-exempt status. It may want to hire employees and run the day-to-day activities of the project. In some cases the project may want the sponsor to provide bookkeeping, hire employees, and handle other administrative matters.

Internal Accounting of the Project Funds

How the funds are recorded in your books depends on the how you decided to characterize your arrangement as described above. If you are treating the funds as unrestricted, you will record the funds in your operating budget. If you accepted the funds as restricted, the funds will be kept in and classified as a restricted fund. Because the project has not been recognized as exempt, the sponsor under either classification has the right to exercise some control over the funds received for the project. The accounting implication of this is that the revenue and expenses of the project will be reported on the sponsoring organization's books.

Be sure to avoid the use of terms like pass-through or acting as an agent. These terms have specific meanings to the accounting profession as well as the IRS. If the sponsor has an independent audit and presents the relationship to its auditor as a pass-through or an agency relationship, the auditor will not include the amounts received and expended as revenues and expenses. Instead, only the balance of funds remaining at year end will show up on the sponsor's audited financial statements—and it will be classified as a liability. This will mean that the independent audit does not support the donor's claim to have made a contribution to the organization. The proper treatment of a fiscal sponsorship project involving a sponsored project which is does not have §501(c)(3) status will be reflected in the audit in both revenues and expenses. Thus the audit report will agree with the Form 990 and the tax returns filed by the donors.

An important implication of showing the project's figures as revenues and expenses on the sponsor's books is that if the sums are large, this may distort the sponsor's true financial picture and may create problems with the sponsor's own funders or donors. Sponsors need to consider this before they agree to become sponsors.

Ownership of Property

In many cases, the project will generate or acquire property. It may generate property by producing a work of art, a book, or some other marketable item. It may acquire property, such as office furniture. The sponsor and project need to decide who will own this property upon the termination of the sponsorship. The decision may be influenced, in part, on how the parties structure their relationship, as described above.

Payments to the Sponsor

The parties need to decide what fee, if any, will be paid to the sponsor for its administrative services. The amount of the fee will vary depending on the sponsor and what is involved. In order to exercise the control needed to protect its own tax-exempt status, the sponsor will need to provide, at a minimum, some bookkeeping services and some supervision of the project. It needs to decide how much time and energy the fiscal sponsorship will take. Factors it may want to examine are whether the project has employees; what the sources of the project's income are; how much control the sponsor is exercising; and how much bookkeeping and compliance reporting on the sponsor's part is required.

Many sponsors charge for their services. Often they charge a percentage of the funds that they handle for the project. If you are considering a percentage charge, both parties need to be sure that this will not violate the terms of any grants that are being given to the project. In some fiscal sponsorship relationships, the sponsor takes a hefty percentage of the funds that it is handling. Although there are no hard and fast rules about usual percentages, projects can expect to pay up to about 15% for the service. Percentages over 30% are probably excessive. 15-30% is somewhat negotiable.

In addition to a fee for acting as a sponsor, some sponsors charge for other costs. Many grants permit adding overhead costs on top of the amount granted for the program. Some institutions add the cost of employee fringe benefit to their sponsorship fee. If you want to work with one of these large institutions, explore whether this add-on method would be acceptable to your funder. You will also want to have an explicit agreement about what costs the institution covers as part of its fee.

If the sponsor's charges for its services are more than just a reimbursement for expenses, its fee in excess of the expense reimbursement may be classified as unrelated business income (see Chapter 9). If so, the sponsor may need to file the Form 990-T and to pay the UBIT tax.

Liabilities

Typically, the sponsor will prefer not to assume the liabilities of the project, but the law may impose liabilities, depending on how much control the sponsor exercises over the project. The sponsor needs to identify the aspects of the project's operations that may create the greatest exposure to risk. It may be helpful for the sponsor and the project to review the description of common risks and insurance and other strategies to address them on pages 566-68. The parties should plan for this and discuss insurance and the payment of insurance premiums.

Public Relations

To some extent, the project will be perceived as associated with the sponsor. Each party needs to evaluate the reputation of the other to determine whether this association will help or hurt it with funders and with the community it serves. Many sponsors require that any publicity by the project must identify the sponsorship and the sponsor and that the sponsor pre-approve any publicity materials.

Protecting the Sponsor's Funding Sources

Sponsor organizations recognize that many foundations are unwilling to make multiple grants to the same organization during a specific time period. A funder that funds a grant to the sponsor that is solicited by the project may then refuse to award other grants to the sponsor for its own work. Most sponsors will want to protect their own funding sources. Typically, sponsors prioritize submission of proposals on behalf of the sponsor's core activities and limit the funders to which projects may apply. The sponsor may require that the project have the sponsor's explicit permission to seek contributions or grants which will be handled through the sponsorship relationship.

Special Issues for the Sponsor

If you are planning to act as sponsor for a project, there are two additional issues you must consider.

Mission and Purpose

The proposed project must fit within your own mission statement and purposes. You should review your Articles of Incorporation, your Bylaws, and any Board resolutions on the subject to see what your mission statement or purposes are. If the mission of the project does not fit within your own mission, you need to decide whether you are the most appropriate sponsor for this project. If you decide to sponsor the project even though it does not fit within your current mission or purposes, you may need to amend your purposes and mission statement so that your governance documents authorize this type of activity.

Activities Disclosed to IRS

When you applied for tax exemption, you submitted an application to the IRS that listed the activities in which you planned to engage. It was on the basis of those activities that the IRS granted you an exemption. The IRS rules provide that if you substantially change those activities, you must notify them.

You need to find your Form 1023 application for tax-exempt status and review what you told the IRS you would be doing. This is found in Part IV of the applications filed in or after October 2004 and Part II of most applications filed before that. If you cannot locate your application, contact the IRS to see if it can supply a copy. If the activities of the project fit the activities in your narrative description to the IRS, you do not need to do anything further. However, if the activities are substantially different from those you described to the IRS, the funds you are giving to the project are substantial, and your sponsorship is going to extend for a period of time, you may need to notify the IRS that you have substantially changed your activities.

> *Example*: Neighborhood Health Clinic, a §501(c)(3) organization that provides health services to those who cannot afford them, has been approached by an environmental group that wants to advocate for the clean-up of a toxic site in the neighborhood. The group wants the Clinic to act as its sponsor. The Clinic needs to review its IRS application, because it is very likely that this kind of project was not disclosed to the IRS.

You can notify the IRS in your Form 990 (see Chapter 12) that includes a brief paragraph explaining what your new activities are. The IRS can inquire if it wants to know more.

How to Structure a Fiscal Sponsorship Agreement

After you have made your decisions about the issues described above, you are ready to structure your fiscal sponsorship agreement. To avoid the improper pass-through arrangement, both parties need to recognize is that there are actually two relationships taking place, and each relationship must follow proper procedures. The donor or funder is making a contribution or grant to the sponsor. This grant may be unrestricted or it may be restricted, as described above. In either case, it must follow the rules discussed below about funding. The second relationship occurs when the sponsor becomes a funder by passing the money to the project, either by re-granting it or by hiring the project as an independent contractor. In any fiscal sponsorship arrangement, the parties should have a contract setting out the terms of their agreement.

Both parties need to recognize is that there are actually two relationships taking place, and each must follow proper procedures.

Phase 1: Handling the Initial Contribution or Grant

Earlier in this chapter we described two arrangements that the sponsor and project might make with reference to how the sponsor classifies project funds—the sponsor could make no binding commitment about how it spends the funds or it could receive the funds as a restricted gift to be used for the project. The choice you make is central to how you structure your fiscal sponsorship agreement.

Unrestricted Funds

Where there is no binding commitment to the funders to use the funds for the project, your agreement will reflect that the sponsor retains the right, without approval from any funding source, the project, or anyone else, to redirect the use of the funds away from the project. The sponsor may use the funds for its own purposes or give them to another beneficiary capable of fulfilling the purpose of the project. The sponsor should take the funds with an internal but not legally binding commitment to use the funds for the project as long as this does not threaten the sponsor's exempt status. All donors and funders need to be aware of the Board's right to change the use of the funds.

Restricted Funds

The sponsor and project can agree that the sponsor will restrict the funds for the project's use but this is a tricky arrangement about which there is some legal and accounting uncertainty. You should get legal and accounting advice if you are considering this option. We describe the broad contours of the relationship so that you can see what it entails.

If the sponsor and project agree that the Board will restrict the funds for the project's use, the sponsor needs to pre-approve the project as a project of the sponsor's **before** it receives money for it. Pre-approval means that the sponsor must gather information about the project—what it plans to do, how it fits within the corporation's mission, whether it meets the (c)(3) requirement, and how it plans to fund it—much like the Board or staff would do before adding any new program. It is particularly important that a sponsor considering a restricted funds arrangement be sure that the project advances the sponsor's mission. In most cases, this pre-approval of a new program should be done by the Board. If the Board wants to delegate this task to the Executive Director, it should get legal advice. Upon pre-approval, the Board can collect funds. It is now collecting funds under an agreement that they are restricted for a particular purpose and, like any restricted fund, must be spent for that purpose.

However, unlike a restricted fund (which accountants call a designated fund) used by the sponsor for its own internal programs, the sponsor will have notified the funders and donors of additional conditions on the restricted fund. At a minimum, these restrictions will include the right of the sponsor to terminate funding the project if the project does anything that jeopardizes the sponsor's (c)(3) status. If the sponsor has signed grant agreements with a funder aimed at funding the project, the sponsor will need the ability to terminate funding the project if the project fails to comply with the terms of that grant agreement. The sponsor may also need to terminate supporting the project if the project is misleading the public about the sponsorship relationship or what the project is doing or is in other ways negatively affecting the sponsor. The sponsor should have the right to control the investment of the project's funds and the timing of their distribution.

If the project fails or the Board terminates its relationship with the project because it operated in ways that violated the rules regulating (c)(3)s or funder requirements or donor commitments, the sponsor will need to establish its own program that satisfies the restriction or it can make a grant to another (c)(3) that satisfies the restriction.

All donors and funders must be aware of the limitations of the restricted fund to which they contribute—while the fund is restricted to the use of the project, if the project fails or operates outside the (c)(3) and funder rules or donor commitments, the Board can make an alternate distribution. Some grantors may require that unspent funds be returned to them, which you must do if you accept the grant with those terms. If an individual donor puts such a restriction on his/her gift, the donor should talk with a tax adviser to determine if the restriction means that the gift is not deductible until the funds are spent.

Phase 2: Funding the Project

Once the sponsor has received the funds for the project, it can fund the project in two ways. The most common mechanism is to distribute the funds to the project as a grant. Because the project doesn't have (c)(3) status, the sponsor must follow special expenditure responsibility rules to ensure that the grant is used for (c)(3) purposes. Another option is to hire the project as an independent contractor to carry out the project. In some cases, this option can work but it does have the challenges and limitations described below.

Expenditure Responsibility for the Grant to the Project

As the funder of the second grant (the re-granting arrangement), the (c)(3) sponsor is making a grant to a non-(c)(3) organization. To do this, the sponsor must exercise *expenditure responsibility* by engaging in these steps to correctly complete this type of funding process:

- The project is pre-approved by the sponsor after receiving a written request from the project and before funds are solicited from donors. The pre-approval should be made only if the project fits within and advances the sponsor's mission in its Articles or Bylaws and within the activities for which it received its tax-exemption, all as described above. The sponsor also needs to be sure that the project does not operate in any ways that would prevent if from being tax-exempt—for example, by engaging in political activities or improperly benefiting insiders.

- The sponsor and project must comply with the expenditure responsibility rules by signing a *written grant agreement* setting forth the terms and conditions of the grant from the sponsor to the project, the use of the money by the project, the control by the sponsor, the ability of the sponsor to terminate the grant and demand return of the funds if they are misused, and reporting requirements to the sponsor about the use of the money. This grant agreement needs to be carefully written and may be part of a fiscal sponsorship agreement. Except for very small projects, you should have an attorney with some experience in this area prepare this agreement.

- The sponsor or the project solicits the funds for the specific grant to the project. The funding sources are made aware of the sponsor's control in writing.

- As the sponsor receives funds for the project, the sponsor takes the funds in as contributions or grants income to the sponsor and then disburses the funds as a grant payment to the project, subject to the terms of the grant agreement.

- The project makes periodic written reports to the sponsor, showing its actual expenditures of the funds and its progress toward accomplishing the purposes of the grant.

The project can control the use of the funds after they are re-granted to the project, as long as they are used within the parameters of the grant.

Any property that is acquired in connection with the project is generally owned by the project, although the parties have some room to negotiate about this.

The responsibility for the liabilities of the project is somewhat uncertain. The parties will generally agree that the project is liable, but this is not necessarily binding on third persons who are owed money. The ultimate resolution of liability questions may rest on the amount of control the sponsor retains and on the circumstances giving rise to the liability.

Independent Contractor

In the independent contractor model, the project is really the sponsor's project. However, the founders of the project are not working on the project as volunteers or employees of the sponsor subject to the sponsor's control over how they carry out the details of the project. Rather, the sponsor contracts the project out to the founders of the project who can control the details of how the project is run.

The independent contractor arrangement means that the sponsor and not the project makes the major decisions about what the project does and how it does it. Of course, in a fiscal sponsorship situation, the sponsor will be heavily influenced by the creators of the project in making these decisions. When the sponsor jobs the project out to the founders of the project, it will need to walk a fine line between creating a true independent contractor relationship in which the sponsor has little influence in how the project is carried out but still allow the sponsor the ability to ensure that the founders are carrying out the project in compliance with (c)(3) and grantor rules. To create this relationship, the parties must become familiar with the requirements for establishing independent contractor status (see Chapter 20) and understand how to mesh this with the IRS rules. You will need legal help with this arrangement.

If the parties successfully create an independent contractor relationship, the monies from donors and foundations will belong to the sponsor, as will any property acquired or created by the project. The funders need to be aware of the nature of this relationship. Generally, the independent contractor is responsible for the project's liabilities, but, depending on the factual situation that gives rise to the claim, the sponsor may also be liable.

Drafting an Agreement

Once you have determined the central structure of your agreement, you are ready to draft your agreement. The type of agreement you use will vary depending on whether you are re-granting funds to the project or hiring the project founders as independent contractors.

Fiscal Sponsorship Agreement

If you are re-granting funds to the project, your agreement should consider the following provisions:

- a description of the sponsor's services, including a provision that describes whether the funds are restricted or not (see above), the sponsor's right to control the funds, fund management by the sponsor, and sponsor's compensation;

- a description of the project's rights and obligations; including property rights to property acquired by the project, a commitment to use funds for the purposes stated in the grant agreement from sponsor, any restrictions on grant-seeking by the project, requirements that project provide a budget for sponsor's approval, any requirements concerning project's publicity and use of the sponsor's name, and a requirement that project inform donors about the funding relationship the parties have established;

- reporting requirements so that the parties are informed about what each other are doing;

- a limitation on the project from using any of the sponsor's grant for a political campaign, lobbying, or for improper private benefit or inurement;

- an acknowledgement that the sponsor is not the project's agent;

- an agreement that the project is liable for its actions and a clause indemnifying the sponsor from damages arising from actions of the project; and

- a provision describing the circumstances under which the agreement can be terminated and what happens to the remaining funds on termination, including the right of the sponsor to recover misspent funds from the project.

The agreement should, of course, include any other provisions important to the parties.

Independent Contractor Agreement

Your independent contractor agreement will include many of the elements above but will need to be drafted with the requirements of Chapter 20 in mind. As we noted above, you will need legal help with this agreement.

FISCAL SPONSORSHIP 10

Consult Appendix 1 if you would like information about source material related to this Chapter. Appendix 1 has references of interest to all readers, not just professionals.

11 STATE AND LOCAL TAX EXEMPTIONS

THIS CHAPTER COVERS

- State Income Tax Exemption
- Tri-Met and Lane Transit District Taxes
- County Business Tax Exemption
- County Property Tax Exemption
- Local Business License Fees

State and local laws impose a variety of taxes on groups doing business, having employees, and owning property in Oregon, including state income tax, regional taxes, county business taxes, and county real and personal property taxes. The law grants exemption from these taxes for many nonprofit groups. Although you may have federal income tax exemption, this does not mean you are automatically exempt from all state and local taxes.

This chapter will help you understand if your group is exempt from state and local taxes.

State Income Tax Exemption

Who is Covered by the Exemption?

All organizations that are exempt from taxation under any subsection of §501(c), as well as many other sections of the federal law, certain insurance companies, and public utility districts, are exempt from income taxation under Oregon law.

In addition to §501(c) groups, Oregon also exempts from state income taxation nonprofit corporations organized and operated primarily to furnish permanent residential, recreational, and social facilities primarily for the elderly. In order to qualify, you must:

- Receive not less than 95% of your operating gross income (excluding investment income) solely from payments for your services and facilities, paid on or behalf of the elderly who use your facilities, and

- Not permit your earnings to benefit a stockholder or any individual, and

- Provide in your Articles or other governing instrument that all your assets (after paying your lawful debts) be distributed on dissolution to tax-exempt religious, charitable, scientific, literary, or educational corporations.

How to Apply for the Exemption

Most groups do not need to apply to the state for an exemption. Your IRS exemption letter is sufficient. There are a few exceptions for homes for the elderly, some health maintenance organizations, some insurance companies, and people's utility districts.

Other Forms You Must File

If your group has taxable unrelated business income under the federal law (see Chapter 9), you must also pay state income tax on this. Use the Oregon Department of Revenue's Form 20 and attach to it a copy of your federal Form 990-T. If your group is a charitable organization, you may be required to file an annual state form, the CT-12. (See pp. 261-62.)

Homeowner's associations may elect to be treated as tax-exempt for purposes of its exempt function income. You should contact the Department of Revenue for what to file to claim this exemption.

Tri-Met and Lane Transit District Taxes

All employers who pay wages in the tri-county Portland area (Tri-Met district) and in the Eugene-Springfield (Lane Transit District) must pay an excise tax, unless they are exempt. Among the exempt employers are all organizations, except hospitals, that are exempt from taxation under §501(c)(3). If you are going to claim this exemption, you need to contact the Oregon Department of Revenue at 503.945.8100 for instructions.

County Business Tax Exemption

Some counties have county business taxes, assessed on the income on entities doing business in their county. You should check with your county to see if there is such a tax and if your group is exempt. Multnomah County, for example, has a business tax but exempts from it §501(c) groups and many nonprofit old age homes. These groups do have to pay taxes on unrelated business income (see Chapter 9).

County Property Tax Exemption

Each county assesses taxes on the real property (land and buildings) and the personal property (including computers, vehicles, and other equipment) used by businesses, in that county. The law exempts certain nonprofit groups from paying these taxes.

> *Having a §501(c) exemption, even a §501(c)(3) exemption,*
> *does not automatically mean you will get*
> *the county property tax exemption.*

Having a §501(c) exemption, even a §501(c)(3) exemption, does not automatically mean you will get the county property tax exemption. On the other hand, some groups are eligible for the exemption that may not be exempt under any provision of the federal law. Because of the property tax limitations passed by the voters, many counties that in the past were lenient about exemptions for nonprofits now take a much harder line about granting the exemption. The tax courts are often more lenient than the county assessors' offices in granting exemptions for charities. If your group does not clearly qualify, you may want to get legal help before you file your application.

STATE AND LOCAL TAX EXEMPTIONS

Whether to Apply for the Exemption

The county property taxes are used to pay for purely local services. These include things such as local roads, fire services, schools, libraries, and sheriff departments. Some of these are services that your group will use. The effect of your group's obtaining an exemption from the property tax is that either fewer funds are available for county services or that other property owners (many of whom are not wealthy people) must pay more. This may cause resentment among your neighbors, particularly if your group is in a small or poor county. Consequently, your group may want to first decide whether to apply for the property tax exemption.

What Groups Are Covered by the Exemption

A variety of types of nonprofit group can qualify for a property tax exemption.

Literary, Charitable, Scientific Groups, Art Museums, Voluntary Fire Departments

Property is exempt if it is owned by a literary, charitable, or scientific corporation; art museum, or voluntary fire department and is used primarily for the corporation's literary, charitable, or scientific work. Although the meaning of "scientific" has not been much discussed, the meaning of "literary" and the meaning of "charitable" has been. "Literary" has been interpreted to refer to written materials, including plays, which means that nonprofit theatres may be exempt.

Generally, an organization is "charitable" if it meets three criteria:

- the organization must have charity as its direct object; and
- the organization must be performing in a manner that furthers its charitable object; and
- there must be an element of a gift or giving in the organization's work.

An organizations that sell goods or services may be able to establish an element of giving by showing that it gives its goods or services to those who cannot afford them for a reduced fee or no fee. You may also be able to show an element of giving if you can show that, because of contributions, the efforts of volunteers, or other assistance, you are able to provide the goods or services at a lower price than you would otherwise have to charge. An organization cannot be denied an exemption solely because its primary source of funding is from one or more governmental entities.

Example: Rural Education Services offers classes to residents in rural Oregon to help them address the challenges of rural living. RES charges for the classes. RES receives 75% of its funding from government grants, foundation money, and private donations and relies on dozens of volunteers who donate hundreds of hours a year. Because of these contributions of money and labor, RES can show that it charges significantly less for its classes than it otherwise would be required to do. This should constitute the element of gift-giving necessary to meet the test. RES will further its argument if it offers and documents that it does not charge residents who are unable to pay for classes.

The law also exempts as charitable the property of a rehabilitation facility or any retail outlet connected with it. A rehabilitation facility is one licensed by the state or one that provides individuals with physical, mental, or emotional disabilities with occupational rehabilitation activities, even if the individual is paid.

Three specific types of retail thrift stores are exempt:

- Retail thrift stores which deal only in donated goods and which either give the goods to the needy or use the money received from the sale of the goods to provide food, shelter, clothing, or health or dental care to the needy; and

- Retail thrift stores that deal regularly in inventory, at least one-half of which is donated or consigned; whose store workers are all volunteers, and whose inventory is given or sales proceeds of it are used to support the needy as described above.

- Retail stores owned by a nonprofit corporation that deals exclusively in donated inventory and whose proceeds are used to support and whose proceeds support certain nonprofit housing programs for low-income individuals.

The property for which the exemption is sought must be *reasonably necessary* to accomplish the literary, charitable, or scientific purposes of the corporation. This is sometimes a very hazy criterion. For example, a literary society that uses its property as space for free poetry readings and discussion groups is entitled to an exemption but other property that it owns on which it operates a retail bookstore may not be exempt (although bookstores are sometimes granted an exemption, so it is worth applying for the exemption). If your corporation buys land on which it plans to erect buildings for its exempt purposes, the exemption will not be granted while the land is vacant but will be granted once the buildings are under construction.

Religious Groups

Religious organizations are entitled to exemption from property tax. The exemption extends to property used for administration, education, and literary, charitable, entertainment and recreational purposes.

Some Schools and Educational Organizations

Schools, academies, and student housing owned by charitable or religious corporations are exempt from property taxes. A day care center that has a significant educational component and that is certified by the state of Oregon to provide educational day care can qualify as a school. If a day care center serves a significant enough number of low-income people and charges them rates that are less than its costs to provide the service, the county may grant it an exemption as a charitable corporation.

Other types of educational organizations that are not schools are not exempt from property taxes unless they qualify under another exemption.

Fraternal Organizations

Fraternal organizations, other than college fraternities or sororities, can also claim property tax exemption. These are nonprofit groups which are not solely social clubs that have a ritualistic form of work, a representative form of government, and regularly engage in charitable activities. The organization's income cannot be distributed to its members, directors, or officers, and any salaries paid must be reasonable and fixed and approved by the members, directors, or other governing body of the corporation. Examples of fraternal organizations are the Masons, the Grange, the Knights of Columbus, and the American Legion.

Other Groups

There are also exemptions available for specialized purposes for which nonprofit organizations may qualify. These include property used for public parks or public recreation, housing assistance for the elderly, student housing, low income housing, senior centers and cemeteries. You should consult an attorney if your group is involved in any of these projects.

How to Apply for the Exemption

The state property tax exemption for both real and personal property is administered through the counties. Most organizations claiming an exemption obtain it by filing a form listing the property for which you are claiming your exemption with the county assessor. The form or forms you need can be obtained from the county assessor's office. Be careful that you describe the nature and purpose of your organization in such a way that it reflects the exempt purposes of your organization.

For example, a day care center that offers a preschool program might describe itself as a preschool. A day care center or other group that wishes to qualify as a school should stress on its application and in its conferences with the county those parts of its program designed to stimulate learning, the qualifications of its staff in terms of academic background or prior experience in teaching, the availability of educational materials, degrees granted, etc.

Once the application is submitted, the county will probably send an inspector out to visit the property and talk to you about your group. Be sure to give the inspector all the information you have that is favorable to your group obtaining an exemption. Be prepared to give him or her copies of written statements you may have about your group, copies of advertising that you have done, statements you have prepared for funding sources, etc. The exemption is not automatic, and you might want to consult with an attorney before sending in your application or before the inspector's visit to get an idea of what you can present to the county to enhance your chances of getting an exemption.

The state and county tax year runs from July 1 through June 30. The application must be filed on or before April 1 to get the exemption for the upcoming assessment year. If you file a late claim for exemption, you can get an exemption for that year if you pay a late filing fee. If the county denies the exemption, your group may appeal to the state Department of Revenue. Your group should probably hire an attorney for the appeal. If you obtain an exemption and your use of the property changes, you must file a new application for the new use. If your use of the property changes to a use that is not exempt, you must notify the county assessor within 30 days.

Leases and Lease Options

Building/Land

If you meet the qualifications for property tax exemption and you lease space, you should negotiate with the owner of your building to get a rental reduction. The owner can then qualify for a partial tax exemption on your space. Your lease or lease option agreement must specifically state that your rental amount reflects the savings below market rent that your organization receives from the tax exemption, so be sure to put this clause in your lease.

If you are leasing or have an option to lease on your space and want to obtain an exemption, you must request the form for this purpose from the county where your space is leased.

The exemption applies to the tax year beginning July 1 of the year for which the claim is filed. Your application must be filed on or before April 1 unless the lease or lease-option agreement was entered into after March 1 and before July 1. In that case you must file your application within 30 days after the agreement is entered into if the exemption is claimed for that year or pay a late fee. The exemption continues as long as use of the property remains unchanged and during the period of the lease or lease-option agreement. If your agreement terminates before July 1, the exemption expires on January 1 of the same calendar year. If your use changes you must file a new application.

Personal Property

Leases for personal property (such as telephone equipment, copiers, etc.) are not covered by your organization's general property tax exemption. If your lease for personal property requires your organization to pay the property taxes, you will need to obtain an exemption for the specific property. The process for seeking this exemption is the same as described above.

Local Business License Fees

Many local jurisdictions create requirements that businesses obtain licenses. These business license fees are primarily a revenue-generating mechanism. Most jurisdictions will exempt charitable nonprofits from business license requirements. Check with your local government to determine whether your nonprofit is required to obtain a license and how to request an exemption from fees.

STATE AND LOCAL TAX EXEMPTIONS

Consult Appendix 1 if you would like information about source material related to this Chapter.

Even if your nonprofit becomes exempt from all of these state, regional, and county taxes, as well as exempt under Section 501(c)(3) of the Internal Revenue Code, you may still need to file informational returns with the various taxing authorities. Chapter 12 offers guidance about which returns you'll need to file, where to file them, and most importantly, when to file them. Even when no tax is due, there are some penalties for failure to file and filing late. Check out Chapter 12.

12

TAX RETURNS FOR TAX-EXEMPT ORGANIZATIONS

THIS CHAPTER COVERS

- Filing Federal Returns
- Filing State Returns
- Filling Out the Inventory and Personal Property Assessment

Just because you are a tax-exempt organization and don't pay income taxes does not mean that you don't have to file annual reports with the IRS. If you are tax-exempt under §501(c), you MUST file one version of the Form 990. If you fail to do so for three years, you will lose your exemption. You may also be required to file state and local returns. This chapter will give you basic information about filing the following:

- Federal informational tax returns (Form 990 or Form 990 EZ and Form 990 Schedule A);
- Federal informational form (Form 990N);
- State tax return (CT-12) that applies to most §501(c)(3) tax-exempt groups; and
- The county's personal property tax statement.

This chapter does not cover, but you should be aware of, the following:

- If your group is a trust, you may have additional annual forms to file.
- If your group is a private foundation that has at least $5,000 of assets at any time during the tax year, you will file Form 990-PF, rather than Form 990. You may also have additional forms to file.
- If your group had unrelated business gross income of $1,000 or more, you must file Form 990-T, and state Form 20. See Chapter 9. There are special rules for churches and certain governmental groups.

Tax-exempt organizations with employees also must file a variety of payroll tax returns. Those requirements are discussed in Chapter 27. Additional information about specific tax forms for exempt and non-exempt organizations is in Appendix 2.

Filing Federal Returns

Nonprofit corporations that have received federal tax-exempt status under §501(c)(3) and other §501(c) subsections file Form 990, 990 EZ, or 990N. These are informational returns rather than a tax returns. The purpose of Form 990 or 990 EZ is to document for the IRS and the public that the purposes and activities of the group still merit tax-exempt status. Although there is no tax to pay with Form 990 or 990 EZ, the IRS has a stiff daily penalty if the return is filed late. The purpose of the Form 990N, filed by smaller organization, is to allow the IRS to keep its records up to date and eliminate exempt organizations which have ceased operating.

Although there is no tax to pay with Form 990 or 990 EZ, the IRS has a stiff daily penalty if the return is filed late.

Who Must File Form 990, Form 990 EZ and Form 990N

All groups that qualify for tax exemption under §501 (c) of the IRS code must file Form 990, Form 990 EZ, or Form 990N unless they are one of the groups which are specifically exempted.

Very small organizations, those which normally have annual gross receipts that are less than $50,000, are required to file Form 990N. This is a one page informational form that is only available online. Essentially, it reassures the IRS that you are still in existence. If you do not file the Form 990 or 990 EZ and you fail to file the Form 990N for three years, you will lose your tax exemption. If you are a small organization that is not required to file the Form 990 or Form 990 EZ, be sure that someone is responsible for filing the Form 990N.

If you are a larger organization that must file the Form 990 or 990 EZ, you must file one of those forms and not the 990N. If you are near the end of the three year period and have not filed the required Form 990 or 990 EZ, filing the Form 990N will not save your exemption.

Organizations with annual gross receipts greater than $50,000 but less than $200,000 and total assets at the end of the year of less than $500,000, must file Form 990 EZ. Organizations with annual gross receipts of $200,000 or more, as well as those with lower gross receipts but total assets of $500,000 or more, must file Form 990.

THE OREGON NONPROFIT CORPORATION HANDBOOK

Your group may be specifically exempted from filing the 990N, 990 EZ or 990 if you are:

- a subordinate of a parent organization and your organization's financial activities are included on the parent organization's group return. If the parent organization fails to include your organization on its group return, you must file the appropriate 990 form—see below to determine if that will be the 990N, 990-EZ or 990.

- a church, interchurch organizations, convention or association of churches, or certain church auxiliary, certain schools below college level that are affiliated with a religious order

- a governmental entity meeting certain requirements

- a political organizations meeting specific requirements.

If you believe that your group qualifies for one of these exemptions, be sure to review the detailed requirements on the IRS website. Start by reviewing the exemptions from filing the Form 990N at *http://www.irs.gov/charities/article/0,,id=169250,00.html*.

Details about which organizations are required to file which form are available for larger organizations as part of the instructions for filing the Form 990 at *http://www.irs.gov/pub/irs-pdf/i990.pdf*.

You must file the Form 990, Form 990 EZ or Form 990N if you claim to be exempt even if you never applied for exemption, unless you are a church or convention of churches. This applies to organizations who are exempt under §501(c)(3) but did not apply for recognition because you have less than $5,000 per year in gross receipts (see p. 107) or are exempt under §501(c)(4), (c)(5), or other subsections of §501(c) and chose not to apply for recognition of exemption (see p. 143).

Revocation of Tax-Exempt Status for Failure to File Returns

If you fail to file a Form 990, 990 EZ or 990N for three years, the IRS will automatically revoke your tax-exempt status. The IRS will send a notice of revocation to the last address they have for your group and will remove your group's name from Publication 78, its list of tax-exempt organizations. The IRS does revoke the exemption for organizations that were small enough to only be required to file the 990N as well as for larger organizations required to file the 990 or 990EZ.

If you fail to file a Form 990, 990 EZ or 990N for three years, the IRS will automatically revoke your tax-exempt status.

Unfortunately you may not be aware that your tax-exempt status has been revoked for the same reason that you didn't file the 990N. You may have failed to keep the IRS informed about how to reach your organization and the IRS notices may simply not be reaching you. If you are concerned that this may have happened to your organization, you can check to see if you are still listed in Publication 78 at *http://www.irs.gov/app/pub-78/*.

If your exempt status has been revoked for failure to file the 990N, you can apply to have your tax-exempt status reinstated by following the process outline on the IRS website at *http://www.irs.gov/charities/article/0,,id=240101,00.html*. You will have to pay a fee to request reinstatement. If the IRS determines that you meet the requirement for reinstatement, it will issue a new determination letter and once again list your nonprofit in the Publication 78, the list of tax-exempt organizations. Usually your new determination letter will list the date of your exemption as the date at which you submitted the request for reinstatement. You may request retroactive reinstatement to request that your reinstatement be retroactive to the date of your revocation.

> *You may not be aware that your tax-exempt status has been revoked.*

What Is Schedule 990A and Who Must File It?

Schedule 990A is an addition to Form 990 or 990 EZ and is intended to give more information about the corporation. It must be filed by all organizations described in §501(c)(3) of the IRS code, except private foundations filing Form 990-PF. Schedule 990A must be attached to Form 990 or 990 EZ. It calls for, among other things, a list of people who provided large contributions to the corporation.

When and Where to File Form 990 or 990 EZ and Schedule 990A

Forms 990, 990 EZ and Schedule 990A must be filed on or before the 15th day of the fifth month following the close of your accounting period. Groups which use a calendar year accounting period must file by May 15th each year. Groups with a fiscal year ending June 30th would be required to file by November 15th; and year end September 30th would require filing by February 15th. The instructions to Forms 990, 990 EZ and Schedule 990A indicate where to file them. (See Appendix 2 for the address for Oregon filers.) If you know you will not be able to file the 990 by its due date, request an extension of time by completing Form 2758. The request for extension must be filed on or before the due date of the return or it will not be granted.

How to Deal with 990, 990 EZ and Schedule 990A Late Filing Penalties

Because the penalty for late filing of the Form 990, 990 EZ or Schedule 990A is assessed for each day the return is late, failure to file on time can pose a major threat to your organization. If you have filed late and received a penalty notice you may be able to get the penalty waived. Follow these steps:

1. Respond to the penalty notice immediately. Ignoring it will escalate the problem, eventually leading to the possibility of the IRS seizing funds from the corporation's bank account.

2. Don't pay the penalty without at least one request for waiver or abatement of penalties. If you respond to the notice with a request for waiver/abatement the IRS must respond to your request before taking any action to seize the funds.

3. To request a waiver you must identify the name and ID number of the corporation and explain that you "request a waiver or abatement of the penalty for late filing of Form 990 or 990 EZ and Schedule A, if required, for the year ending_____." You must give a reason for the lateness and state the hardship the penalty would impose on your organization.

4. Don't assume your request for waiver or abatement has been denied because you get another penalty notice. The IRS will eventually respond to the request stating either that the penalty is waived or denying the request. If it is denied, request that the denial be reconsidered. Be sure to respond to each penalty notice with a copy of your request for waiver until you get a response to the request.

5. If you have not received a response to your request for a waiver or abatement of penalty within six weeks of submitting it, you are entitled to call your local IRS office and request help. Explain your situation and the IRS representative will see that you receive a response to your request.

What Is the Accounting Period for Form 990, 990 EZ and Schedule 990A?

In filing Form 990, 990 EZ and Schedule 990A, you use the accounting period that you established for your corporation when you filed your application for tax-exempt status when you answered the questions "what month is the end of your fiscal year". The 12 month period ending in the month you identified is referred to as your fiscal year. Exempt organizations may choose the calendar year (January through December) or any other fiscal year—either the calendar year or a fiscal year. The IRS letter of determination of tax-exempt status will also state your fiscal year end. The IRS creates a specific Form 990, 990-EZ and Schedule 990 A for each calendar year. Use the date of the first month in your fiscal year to determine which year's form you should file. For example, if your fiscal year is 7/1/12 to 6/30/13, file Form 990, 990 EZ or Schedule 990A on the form labeled Form 990 or 990 EZ-2012.

How to Change Your Fiscal Year

Changing your fiscal year requires attention to specific IRS requirements. First, determine what fiscal year you would like to adopt. Then calculate when the Form 990 or Form 990 EZ will be due for that new fiscal year end. To change your fiscal year, start by being sure you file the 990 or 990 EZ for your most recent "old" fiscal year on time. Then, submit your Form 990 or 990 EZ (along with Schedule A) by the due date for your new fiscal year and write "change of accounting period" across the top of the form. In order to meet this requirement, you will need to create a "short" accounting year which begins with the first month of your original fiscal year and concludes with the last month of your new fiscal year. Your 990 or 990 EZ return will report on this short year.

For example, an organization with a current year end of June 30, that wants to change to a September 30 year end will first file its return for the year that ended June 30th on time (by November 15). Next the organization will create a "short" year, running from July 1st through September 30th. The organization must then file a 990 or 990 EZ for the short year ended September 30th on or before the 15th day of the 5th month after September 30 (which is February 15), and will write "change in accounting period" across the top of the form.

If your organization has already changed its fiscal year within the past 10 years, you must also submit Form 1128 to the short period return.

What Are the Acceptable Accounting Methods for the 990, 990EZ and Schedule 990A?

An accounting method is a set of rules under which:

- you determine when and how to record income and expenses in your books; and
- you determine how to prepare the financial statements necessary for your accounting period.

Each nonprofit corporation must choose an accounting method since the annual report must be computed on the basis of a *fixed* accounting period and in accordance with a *fixed* set of rules which determine the time and manner of reporting income and deductions. No particular method of accounting is prescribed by the IRS for nonprofit corporations. Each nonprofit corporation is allowed to choose the accounting method that is best suited to its needs as long as that method clearly reflects its activity. The corporation must be consistent from year to year. Thus, once an accounting method is chosen by the nonprofit corporation, it is often necessary to receive written consent from the IRS to change to another accounting method. The methods of accounting considered "generally acceptable" by the accounting profession are discussed in Chapter 26 You should read that chapter before deciding which methods your nonprofit will use.

The following four methods are generally permissible:

1. Cash method

2. Accrual method

3. Special methods—such as those for installment sales (deferred-payment methods and long-term contracts are not discussed in this book—an accountant should be consulted before using these)

4. Any other method that clearly reflects income including combinations of the three preceding methods.

Any combination of accounting methods will be permitted by the IRS as long as the records clearly reflect income and are applied consistently. There are many specialized tax rules which apply to various accounting methods. Each nonprofit corporation should consult an accountant or similar person if there is no one in the group who is thoroughly familiar with all of the rules and regulations which apply to the various accounting methods. See Chapter 26 for a more detailed discussion of accounting methods.

How Do You Change Your Method of Accounting?

On filing your first tax return with the IRS, your nonprofit corporation may choose any appropriate accounting method without the consent of the IRS Commissioner. Thereafter, any change in the accounting method requires the consent of the IRS Commissioner before making the change. Also, if within a particular accounting method, you decide to change the way you treat any material item, you must also receive prior consent from the IRS Commissioner. Some examples of changes requiring consent are:

- a change from the cash to the accrual method or vice versa;
- a change in the method used in the valuation of inventories;
- a change in the method of computing some forms of depreciation.

To secure the consent of the IRS Commissioner for a change in accounting method or practices, you must file IRS Form 3115 within the first 180 days of the tax year in which the change is to become effective. The IRS provides an exception to this rule for organizations that have chosen to follow Generally Accepted Accounting Principles (GAAP) as expressed by the Financial Accounting Standards Board (FASB). When FASB announces changes to GAAP for nonprofits, your nonprofit may adopt the new methods without seeking consent from the IRS. You can learn more about FASB and GAAP in Chapter 26.

Public Inspection of Your 990, 990 EZ and Schedule 990A

Forms 990 and 990 EZ and Schedule 990A must be made available for public inspection. The lists of contributors on both Form 990 and Schedule A may be excluded from public inspection. This is discussed on page 631. Many nonprofits find it easiest to meet the requirements for public inspection by posting their 990/990EZ, and 990A on their website or being certain that it is correctly posted on the *www.guidestar.org* website which has been given 990 info by the IRS. If you decide to use the website posting approach, be sure to remove the lists of donors which you are not required to disclose.

TAX RETURNS FOR TAX-EXEMPT ORGANIZATIONS 12

Many fundraisers and individual donors now routinely check out nonprofit organizations on Guidestar (*wwwlguidestar.org*). Your organization has an opportunity to provide a compelling description of your activities on the 990. Nonprofits can no longer dismiss the 990 as something of interest only to accountants. Be sure that you compare your description of your work on the 990 to what you regularly tell donors and funders about your organization.

Forms 990 and 990 EZ and Schedule 990A must be made available for public inspection.

How to Complete the 990, 990EZ, and Schedule 990A

Because the 990, 990 EZ and Schedule 990A forms are revised frequently, this book does not offer line by line instructions. Instead, we will define many of the terms most likely to frustrate 990 or 990 EZ filers and explain the key rules for tax-exempt organizations which questions on the 990 or 990 EZ and Schedule 990A are designed to address.

First, some general tips:

- Be sure you are using the correct form. Each year the IRS should mail you Form 990 or 990 EZ and Schedule 990A. If you do not receive the forms, you may print them from the IRS web site, *www.irs.ustreas.gov,* or call to request them 1.800.829.1040. Be sure to download or to request the instructions as well as the forms.

- Answer every question. If the answer is zero, enter "0" or "none." If the question doesn't apply, enter "N/A" for not applicable. Failure to supply answers to all the questions can be construed by the IRS as failure to file the return on time and result in a late filing penalty.

- Use your actual accounting records to complete the answers. Don't estimate answers or supply budget figures. If your organization maintains a general ledger, the numbers on the 990 or 990 EZ should agree with the year-end general ledger balances. If your organization has an annual audit, use the audit report numbers. If you simply keep a cash receipts and cash disbursements journal, use the year-end totals from these journals.

- Be sure to look at the 990 or 990 EZ filed for the previous year. The opening balances you enter for the current year must agree with the closing balances for the previous year as reported on that year's 990 or 990EZ.

- Use whole numbers. The form will be easier to read and you will be more likely to spot mistakes.

- Keep a copy of every 990 or 990 EZ and Schedule 990A that had been filed with the IRS in your organization's files.

- The instructions to the 990 or 990 EZ and Schedule 990A include line by line definitions of terms. This guide does not reiterate these definitions. Don't assume that you know the IRS's definition of terms without reading the instructions. Some terms have very specific meanings to the IRS.

Form 990 asks for two different types of financial information:

- revenues and expenses; and
- balance sheet accounts (assets, liabilities and net assets)

Net Assets

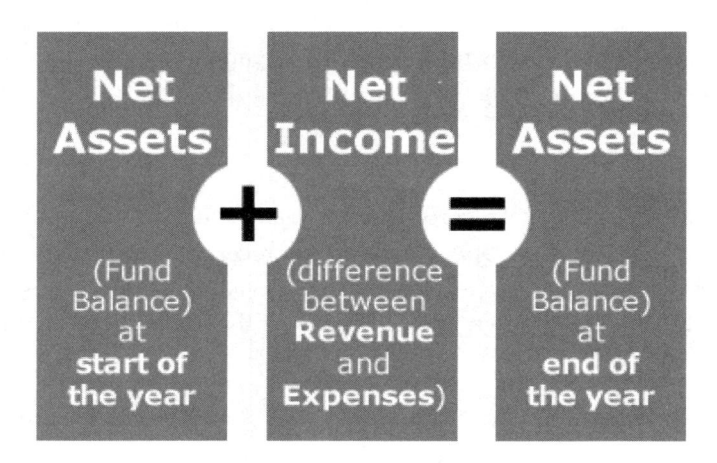

Net Assets (Fund Balance) at start of the year + Net Income (difference between Revenue and Expenses) = Net Assets (Fund Balance) at end of the year

If you are unclear about these two different types of information, read Chapter 26. If you are still unclear, get help from an accountant.

The most common problem non-accountants have with the Form 990 is making the two types of information described above connect. For Form 990 to be completed successfully the equation above must be true:

This equation proves the books are in balance. If you cannot make it work with the numbers in your books, get help from an accountant.

Form 990 Part VI Governance Questions

The Form 990 (but not the Form 990EZ) asks questions about your governance. Review the 990 Instructions to be sure you understand the exact meaning of the terms officer, Director, trustee, and key employee. These terms will also be central to completing a separate section focusing on compensation which we will discuss below.

The governance questions are part of an IRS effort to identify organizations that are paying insufficient attention to best practices for Board oversight. The questions ask about whether your Board has adopted policies to deal with conflicts of interest, protections for whistleblowers, records retention and destruction, entering into joint ventures with other entities, and other governance matters. None of these policies are required under the Internal Revenue Code but many nonprofits have adopted them, both to ensure proper operation of their organization and because they understand that the media and donors frequently read this section of their 990 now that it is so readily available online. See the Forms section for a sample Board and Committee Minutes Policy, Joint Ventures Policy, and Whistleblowers Policy, all policies or procedures the Form 990 asks about. These are basic versions of the Form 990 policies. You should consider whether your organization wants more detailed policies. The conflicts of interest policy is discussed on page 301 and the transparency and records retention and destruction policies are discussed on pages 347 and 349. The Forms section contains these policies as well.

If your organization considers adopting some or all of these policies, you'll want to think clearly about whether you will have the time and resources needed to actually follow the policy. The 990 questions ask about the steps you have implemented to follow these policies and you don't want to be in the position of having adopted policies which you don't follow.

> *None of these policies are required under the Internal Revenue Code but many nonprofits have adopted them, both to ensure proper operation of their organization and because they understand that the media and donors frequently read this section of their 990.*

One final note on the governance questions. Form 990 asks whether you have provided a copy of your Form 990 to all Board members prior to filing it with the IRS. This is actually a very good idea. Your Board members should be familiar with the information you are sharing with the IRS which will be posted online very quickly. Board members may be able to spot opportunities to describe your work more clearly. Form 990 also asks you to describe the process that Board members used to review your 990. If you run into a time crunch around getting the 990 filed with the IRS on time, it is acceptable to have Board members conduct their most detailed review after the form has been filed. See the Form 990 Review Policy in the Forms section for a sample policy on this.

Most Common 990 Mistakes and Problems

Recent studies show that many nonprofits have difficulty completing the 990 or 990EZ accurately. The IRS is working to improve the instructions. The order of questions on the form changes slightly each year, so we will focus here on some of the most troublesome areas. You may file the 990, 990 EZ and Schedule A electronically. Very large nonprofits—nonprofits with total assets over $100 million and meet certain other requirements—must already file electronically. Whether you use paper or the electronic option, you will still need to keep a copy of all returns you file.

Questions about Directors, Officers, Trustees, Key Employees and Independent Contractors

Form 990 asks a series of questions about compensation paid to and relationships with and among Directors, officers, trustees, and key employees. The underlying purpose of the questions is to identify anyone in a position to substantially influence your nonprofit's decisions who receives compensation that is unreasonable in relation to benefit that he or she provides to the organization—in other words, a person who is taking advantage of his/her position for private gain.

In order to answer this series of questions, you will need to identify each person who meets the definition of Director, officer, trustee, and/or key employee for your nonprofit. One area of particular confusion surrounds the treatment of your top managers—the Executive Director and Fiscal Director. In almost all cases, your Executive Director will be considered an officer for the purposes of the 990 questions. If your Fiscal Director has substantial authority for making or influencing fiscal decisions independently, they may also be considered an officer.

Completing these questions also requires a clear understanding of the IRS definitions of various types of compensation and of related entities. At first glance the questions may seem daunting, especially when they inquire about relationships which may exist among your officers and directors and their families. Once you read the instructions more carefully, it becomes clear that the more complex type of relationship tracking will not be necessary for most community-based nonprofits that don't provide compensation that is high enough to trigger the more complex reporting requirements.

The details of the reporting requirements in this area lies outside the scope of this book. If your organization employs staff through multiple related entities or engages in substantial financial transactions with Board members, you made need to seek professional assistance with the 990.

Functional Accounting

The expenses portion of a Form 990 is set up for a functional presentation of expenses. In other words, you must separate expenses associated with management and fundraising from those associated with program or services activity. This concept is discussed on pages 530-536 and again in Chapter 26. If your organization has gross receipts above $100,000, you are required to present the expense information on a functional basis. If you haven't maintained your records on a functional basis you will have to estimate. Start by analyzing salary and related personnel costs (the salary of a development director is a fundraising cost, the salary of a bookkeeper is a management cost, etc.) Once you've broken the personnel costs down correctly, you can use percentages based on personnel cost to allocate remaining costs.

Reporting Fundraising Expenses

Form 990 requires reporting the cost of raising funds in two distinct ways. First, if your nonprofit has held fundraising events (dinners, auctions, etc.), you will report the gross proceeds from the events (everything you took in), and the direct costs you incurred for the event in Part I, the income section on the first page of the 990.

TAX RETURNS FOR TAX-EXEMPT ORGANIZATIONS 12

For example, if your nonprofit held a fundraising dinner at a hotel, you will report the total you received for through selling tickets for the dinner as fundraising event income, and you will report the amount you paid the hotel for the dinner, plus any costs for decorations, door prizes, signage, etc. as fundraising event expenses in Part I of the 990. The line for these expenses is directly below the fundraising event income in the revenue section. You will subtract the event expenses from the event income to report the net income from the event.

These same rules will apply if you conduct bingo or raffles. You will list the gross handle from Bingo or the gross sales of raffle tickets as income and then show the cost of the bingo or raffle prizes as expense. Once you subtract the event expenses from the event income, you will have your net income from bingo or the raffle.

This reporting of event income and expenses is separate from reporting the cost of your general fundraising activity. You will report the cost of staff time, direct mail appeals, fund raising brochures, and other costs associated with you efforts to generate contributions in the Expense section of the 990. The 990 requires that you report your expenses on both a line-item and functional basis. Chapter 24 on pages 530-36 provides more discussion of the concept of functional expenses. For 990 purposes, you will need to divide each line item expense (like salaries, supplies, postage) into three categories—reporting the portion of that line item expense which was used for fundraising, program, and management purposes.

Even if you don't employ a staff member with a title like "fundraiser" or "development director," you probably have some staff time spent to raise funds. Fundraising is defined as making unsolicited requests for contributions. So, if you have a staff member who is creating direct mail appeals or meeting with donors to ask for contributions, some portion of the Salary expense should be put in the Fundraising column. Of course, if you hire a professional fund raising firm or consultant, the entire amount of their fee will go into the Fundraising expense column.

As discussed in Chapter 26, GAAP accounting has very specific rules (SOP 98-2) regarding the allocation of costs when an activity or publication has a dual purpose, working both to carry forward your mission and to solicit contributions. The IRS now also requires compliance with these rules. The primary concept is that unless an activity which is carried out for both program purposes and fundraising purposes meets three specific tests, the entire cost of the activity should be considered fundraising expense. If the activity meets the three tests, you are permitted to allocate the cost between fundraising and program expenses. If you are using your newsletter or other publications or events for both program and fundraising purposes, be sure to read the 990 directions carefully in this area.

Among the most common mistakes made in completing Form 990 is the incorrect reporting of borrowing and repaying funds.

257

Loans

Among the most common mistakes made in completing Form 990 is the incorrect reporting of borrowing and repaying funds. The proceeds of a loan (borrowed money) are not revenue and should not be listed as income. The repayment of the principal of a loan is not an expense; payment of interest is an expense. Loans received and payments made on loans will not be included in revenue and expense totals (nor in the gross receipts test). Instead, the amount of money still owed—the loan balance payable on the last day of the fiscal year—appears on the Balance Sheet as a Liability. Oregon nonprofits cannot make loans to officers or Directors except in very limited circumstances. (See page 303.)

Unrelated Business Activities

Another common misunderstanding involves the definition of activities unrelated to the organization's exempt purpose. See Chapter 9 for an extensive discussion of unrelated business activity. Most tax-exempt organizations do not have unrelated business income. Instead, in most organizations, any revenue generated by charging fees or selling products is considered related activity income because the services or products are an essential part of the organization's exempt purpose activity. However, the fact that your organization needs the income generated by an activity to continue in existence does not make the income into related business income. This is an area of concern to the IRS. So, if your organization charges fees or sells products, be sure to review Chapter 9.

The IRS is interested in the sources of income of tax-exempt groups and is probing for possible under-reporting of unrelated business activity income. Consequently, Form 990 now requires a detailed analysis of different types of revenue. The goal of this part of the form is to classify all the revenue as either related to the exempt purpose; specifically excluded from the definition of unrelated business income by an IRS code section; or unrelated business income. Since most organizations do not have unrelated business income, if you think yours does this may be a signal to get help from an accountant.

Another source of great confusion is the distinction between political activity and lobbying.

Political Activity and Lobbying

Another source of great confusion is the distinction between *political activity* and *lobbying*. Organizations exempt under §501(c)(3) may not engage in any political activity but may engage in limited lobbying. Political activity is defined as activity in support of or in opposition to the election of candidates (see pp. 173-80). It includes contributions (cash or in kind) to candidates, political parties, or political action committees and actual or implied endorsements. Lobbying is not candidate-related. Instead lobbying is activity intended to influence legislative outcomes. The IRS defines two types of lobbying: grassroots and direct, and requires organizations exempt under §501(c)(3) to maintain records of the costs of both types. For a complete discussion of this, see Chapter 8.

TAX RETURNS FOR TAX-EXEMPT ORGANIZATIONS

In completing Form 990 or 990 EZ, answering "yes" to questions relating to political activity will be a definite red flag if you are a §501(c)(3) organization. The 990 and 990 EZ ask whether your organization has made the Lobbying Election by filing Form 5768. See pp. 180-81 for a discussion of the benefits of making the Lobbying Election.

Private and Non-private Foundation Status

Perhaps the most mystifying of all parts of the 990 is found on Schedule 990A in questions relating to private or non-private foundation status and disqualified persons. The key to understanding these questions is being very clear about whether your organization is or is not a private foundation. If it is, it should be filing Form 990PF, not Forms 990 and 990A. (The questions on 990A are designed to help you verify that your organization is not a private foundation, i.e., that you are a public charity. See pages 99-107 for a general description of private foundations and public charities. Remember that "non-private foundation" means "public charity.")

The issue is first addressed in the application for tax-exempt status (Form 1023) in questions that ask organizations that claim not to be private foundations to identify which exception to being a private foundation they meet. (See pages 101-07 for an explanation of what each exception requires.) Review your copy of the Form 1023 which your organization submitted to the IRS to see which exception you claimed. If you can't find a copy of it, look at the IRS determination letter which granted your organization tax-exempt status. Your determination letter assigned you an advance ruling or a definitive ruling on your status as "not a private foundation." Compare the code section referenced to the list given on the 990A list of exceptions to private foundation status. When you find the match to the code section referenced in your advance or definitive ruling you'll know which exception the IRS thinks that your group meets. You should check the box identifying this exception on the 990A and proceed to answer the questions.

The key to understanding these questions is being very clear about whether your organization is or is not a private foundation.

Most social service, art, and education organizations (other than schools) will be covered under code sections 509 (a)(1) or 509 (a)(2), having established themselves as either a Publicly Supported Organization (PSO) or a Fee/Activity Supported Organization (FASO). (Chapter 7 provides a detailed discussion of concerns related to each category.) The 990 Schedule A requires different information for each of these two types of public charities. Answer only the questions which pertain to your type of public charity.

The 990 Schedule A instructions explain the calculations required of each type of public charity. It's helpful to understand the purpose of these questions. They are designed to identify major contributions to your organization in order to see whether or not these major contributions can be included as public support for the purpose of deciding whether your organization is a private foundation. Organizations which receive substantially all their funding from United Ways, public charities, and numerous small donors have very little likelihood of running afoul of the public support test.

Organizations primarily funded by a limited number of major donors (individuals, private foundations, or businesses) may have difficulty establishing public support. Such organizations should seek professional advice regarding alternative methods available to establish public charity status.

Related Organizations

Schedule A now requires disclosure of certain relationships between §501(c)(3) and other types of §501(c) organizations such as §501(c)(4)s or §501(c)(6)s. Elements which may comprise a relationship include purposeful common Directorships (your Bylaws require that a portion of your Directors also serve as Directors of the other organization), shared facilities, shared staff, regular coupling of the organizations through joint publications, etc. The IRS does not consider incidental overlaps in membership or Directors to comprise a relationship.

The point of the relationship disclosure question is to identify situations in which contributions to the §501(c)(3) organization may, in fact, be benefiting a non-§501(c)(3) group. §501(c)(3) organizations that work closely with a §501(c)(4) related organization should seek professional advice to be certain that they are maintaining adequate records, including financial records and corporate minutes, to document that tax-deductible contributions to the §501(c)(3) corporation are not, in fact, supporting activities not permissible for (c)(3) organizations through financial arrangements with the (c)(4) organization. See pp. 113-15 and 200-02. You may also find useful information on this challenging subject at the Alliance for Justice website at *www.allianceforjustice.org*.

Social Security Numbers

Studies are disclosing that about 20% of the filed Form 990s contain social security numbers—donors, clients, employees, volunteers, tax preparers, and others. The Form 990 never asks for this information. Often it is included as part of an attachment. The IRS cannot redact this information—it all becomes public and can be obtained on *www.guidestar.org* or through the IRS or the filing organizations. Be sure that your Form 990s do not contain social security numbers. This is an invitation to identity theft and you may be liable for damages for making it public.

Be sure that your Form 990s do not contain social security numbers. This is an invitation to identity theft and you may be liable for damages for making it public.

Signatures

An officer of the corporation must sign and date the completed Form 990 or 990 EZ. This person must be the President, Vice-President, Treasurer, Assistant Treasurer, chief accounting officer, or other corporate officer (such as tax officer) authorized by the Board of Directors to sign. Your officer should review the Form 990 for accuracy before signing it.

If the Form 990 return is prepared by someone outside of the corporation who is paid to prepare the return, the paid preparer must also sign the return. If the return is prepared by a regular full-time employee of the corporation, that employee's signature is not required. If the 990 or 990EZ return is prepared by a volunteer or group member paid for this task, they must sign the return in addition to the officer. In many organizations, the Board also wants to get the Form 990 for review before it is filed.

Filing State Returns

Public Benefit Corporations that were required to register with the Attorney General (see page 47) and that file Form 990 or 990EZ must file the Oregon Form CT-12 with the Charitable Trust Division of the Oregon Department of Justice. If your group has gross receipts not more than $25,000 and assets not more than $50,000, you should file Form CT-12E instead of Form CT-12. You do not have to pay a fee if you file Form CT-12E. If your organizations is incorporated in another state but has registered as a charity doing business in Oregon, file Form CT-12 F.

Who Must File Form CT-12 and When Is It Due?

All organizations registered with the Charitable Activities Section of the Oregon Department of Justice are required to file Form CT-12 unless they meet specific exceptions. Check page 47 to see if your nonprofit is required to register.

Form CT-12 must be filed by the officers of any group described above. Form CT-12 is due no later than the 15th day of the 5th month following the close of the calendar year or tax year of the corporation. This is the same as the 990 filing deadline. You may request a 90 day extension of the deadline to file the CT-12. If necessary, you may request an additional 90 day extension, for a maximum extension of 180 days.

You may submit your request for extension online through the Department of Justice website. If you submit your extension request by mail be sure that your request reaches the Department of Justice by the due date for your return. Enclose a copy of the federal extension form with a request for extension and submit it to the Department of Justice before the due date of the return. The extension of time to file the CT-12 is not automatic. The Department of Justice has the right to make its own decision without regard to that of the IRS. They do not provide a formal notice that your extension has been approved. You can assume it has been approved unless you hear from them.

Form CT-12 is a public record and is maintained by the Office of the Attorney General of the State of Oregon. You may reach the Attorney General's charitable office at 503.229.5725 or obtain information from their website at *www.doj. state.or.us*.

Filling Out Form CT-12

Form CT-12 has two sections: Section I: General Information and Section II: Fee Calculation. The form will be relatively easy to complete if you have already prepared your Form 990 or 990EZ. You are required to attach a copy of your 990 or 990EZ and you will want to be sure that your answers on the CT-12 are consistent with the information you have submitted to the IRS. Note that you are not required to submit a copy of Schedule B which includes details about your donors. Your CT-12 will be treated as a public record by the Department of Justice, subject to public inspection, so be sure you do not inadvertently include Form B.

If your organization has filed the 990N rather than the 990 or 990EZ, attach a copy to your CT-12. The Department of Justice has the authority to require certain organizations that do not file Form 990 or Form 990 EZ with the IRS to prepare the IRS forms and submit them with the CT-12, even though the returns are not filed with the IRS. In the unlikely event that these provisions apply to your group, you will be contacted by the Department of Justice and they will let you know what information in addition to the 990N is required.

Fortunately, the Department of Justice has adopted the same definitions of terms that the IRS uses for the Form 990. This is especially helpful in completing Section II of the CT-12 which you will use to calculate the fees your organization must pay to the Department of Justice based upon your total Revenues and in some cases on your total Net Assets or Fund Balances.

Filling Out the Inventory and Personal Property Assessment

If your group has received an exemption from the property tax, you will probably still have to fill out a Statement of Assessable Personal and Affixed Real Property or, if you own nonexempt land or buildings, a combined return of real (land or buildings) and personal property. Check with your county to see what is required. Get assistance from the county assessor's office if you need help filling these forms out. If you don't file timely statements, you will be assessed a penalty.

If your group has already obtained an exemption from the county and still has to fill out the Statement, be sure to send a letter to the County when you send in this Statement explaining you are exempt and enclose a copy of the letter from the County giving you your exemption. Keep a copy of the letter you sent to the County.

Consult Appendix 1 if you would like information about source material related to this Chapter.

PART III

SUCCESSFUL FUNCTIONING: BOARD OF DIRECTORS

13 WHAT THE BOARD DOES

THIS CHAPTER COVERS

- Establishing the Corporation's Purpose
- Determining Your Management Type
- Direct-Management Corporations
- Delegated-Management Corporations

Your Board of Directors has an incredibly important job to do—it makes sure that your organization achieves its mission. While the way your Board handles that job will change as your organization grows and adds professional staff to take on management responsibilities, the Board will continue to hold ultimate responsibility for obtaining and using resources wisely, operating lawfully, and accomplishing your goals.

This Chapter will discuss *what* the Board does to manage your nonprofit corporation. Chapter 14 discusses *how* your Board carries out its responsibility to manage the corporation. Once you understand what it is your Board does and how to do it, Chapter 15 helps your Board understand how it finds, selects, trains, and, if necessary, removes the people on the Board. Chapter 16 describes how the Board manages itself. Chapter 17 covers when Board members may be personally liable for their actions and how the Board can protect itself.

Part III is intended to serve as a "Board manual" that you can use to recruit and orient new Directors and to educate your current Directors about what their duties are and how they should carry them out.

If you would like to obtain reprints of the five chapters in Part III to give to your Directors, please visit the website of co-author Cindy Cumfer at *www.cumfer.net* or co-author Kay Sohl at *www.kaysohlconsulting.net* for information.

Your Board is charged by law with the ultimate responsibility for managing the affairs of your nonprofit corporation. (Your Articles of Incorporation can assign some or all of these duties to another person or entity but this is very rare and should only be done with professional help and after careful consideration of the risks and liabilities involved.) Corporate management can involve tasks as lofty as defining the purpose (mission) for the corporation and as detailed as ensuring good financial controls.

The Board in every corporation is responsible for approving the big picture for the corporation—that is, what the corporation's purpose is and, hopefully, a long-range map for how it plans to realize this purpose.

The Board then needs to figure out the most practical way to implement its vision and plan. How the Board does this in a particular organization depends on the type of corporate management that the Board adopts. We distinguish between two major types of nonprofit corporate management—direct management and delegated management corporations. Many corporations operate with a variation of one of these models. The type of management that the Board chooses will depend in significant part on the size and complexity of the corporation.

Your Board is charged by law with the ultimate responsibility for managing the affairs of your nonprofit corporation. How the Board does this in a particular organization depends on the type of corporate management that the Board adopts.

Many consultants talk about Boards as the governing authority for nonprofit corporations, and they are. Governance refers to the highest level decision-making, direction-setting, and oversight, which is part of managing the corporation that the Board is charged by law to do. Applying this concept to this Chapter, Boards that chose direct management are Boards that carry out both the responsibility for high-level governance and the direct responsibility for administration of the corporation as part of their management of the corporation. In contrast, Boards that have chosen delegated management generally will focus most of their work on high-level governance functions, one of which is to oversee the work of those to whom they have delegated administration to be certain that they are carrying out their responsibilities appropriately. These Boards who have chosen delegated management do much less or no administration of the corporation.

Another note on terminology: those who serve on the Board are called Directors or Board members. Be careful not to confuse the Board's Directors with the Executive Director (sometimes also called "Director"). The Executive Director's role is discussed later in this Chapter.

Establishing the Corporation's Purpose

The Board's most fundamental responsibility in a new corporation is to articulate the purpose of the corporation. The purpose is the corporation's answer to why it exists and should be stated in the Bylaws. The Board is charged by law with devoting the resources and energies of the corporation to this purpose.

> *Example*: Many cities contain large populations of Native American people living separately from their traditional nations who encounter a number of problems because of this separation and because of discrimination. When a group of urban Native Americans found the Native American Resource Center, they establish its mission: "to bring Native Americans into a community that offers them support and resources."

Ideally, the Board then considers what the organization will do in the next five years or so to move toward realizing its purpose and strategizes about how it will do this. Boards may engage in this planning in collaboration with members or an Executive Director but ultimately should approve the plan. In practice, many newer Boards begin by jumping right into the more concrete details like raising money and getting programs started.

As time passes, the Board should review the corporate purpose to be sure that the corporation continues to follow its purpose. If the corporation has added programs or moved away from its purpose, the Board will need to determine whether to correct the drift or amend its purpose. If the Board did not make a strategic plan at the beginning, many Board find it helpful to do so after the organization is more established. Boards who did make a strategic plan should be reviewing progress toward the plan and need to make corrections, as needed, to the plan.

Determining Your Management Type

The Board works toward advancing the corporate purpose and plan, if one was made, by managing the corporation's activities so that the purpose is realized. The role that Board members play in implementing its plan for the corporation is very different in direct management and delegated management corporations. Your Board members should start by being clear about which type of corporate management is in place in order to understand their job in carrying out the corporate purpose and plan.

In some corporations—generally smaller ones without employees—the Board sets the direction for the corporation *and* handles the implementation of its direction in the day-to-day activities of the corporation. In this book, we call these corporations *direct management corporations*. In some of these corporations, the Directors do absolutely everything. In others, Directors and other volunteers carry out the activities the corporation but the Board retains the authority over the administration of the corporation. Occasionally, the Board of a *direct management corporation* hires an employee or a few employees for specific jobs but retains its authority to administer the organization. All lines of authority flow directly to the Board.

> *The critical distinction between a direct management and a delegated management corporation has to do with whether the Board has delegated its administration of the corporation to someone other than the Board as a whole.*

Organizations that grow in size and complexity will reach a point where the Board cannot possibly directly manage all of the corporate activities in a responsible way. In some cases, Boards in smaller corporations with adequate resources choose not to be directly involved in the administration of the corporation. In these corporations, the Board delegates some or all of the administration of the corporation to an administrator, usually an Executive Director. The Board then provides the direction for the corporation and oversees its management. The Executive Director is occasionally a volunteer but in most cases is paid. We call these *delegated management corporations*.

The critical distinction between a direct management and a delegated management corporation has to do with whether the Board has delegated its administration of the corporation to someone other than the Board as a whole. In a direct management corporation, none of the Board members, volunteers, or employees function as a chief management official overseeing the administration of the corporation. Instead, each Board member, volunteer, or employee may carry out a specific task or tasks, such as running a program or fundraising. Some of these individual volunteers and employees may report to an particular Board member or another volunteer but the Board as a whole makes the administrative decisions that individual Board members and others carry out. Any activity that has not been assigned remains the responsibility of the Board to perform.

In a delegated management corporation, the Board delegates the management of the corporation to an Executive Director, though the Board may keep some aspects of administration for the Board to handle. Typically, the Board considers that any administrative matter that the Board does not retain has been delegated to the Executive Director. Except to the extent that the Board has retained responsibility for management, the lines of authority for carrying out the work of the corporation run through the Executive Director. The Executive Director, or someone designated by the Executive Director, makes the administrative decisions for those matters delegated to him or her. The Executive Director than reports to the Board about the corporate operations and the Board oversees the Executive Director's performance.

Direct Management Corporations

To run a direct management corporation responsibly, the Board needs to function as a good Executive Director would function in a delegated management corporation. This includes understanding and carrying out management duties, keeping records, and addressing several issues that are often problems for direct management corporations. The Board also needs to do the visioning and long-range planning that all Boards do.

Most direct management corporations rely on some division of labor. Often individual Directors or committees of the Board will take on one or more tasks or activities associated with the programs the organization runs, with the administration of the corporation, and with fundraising.

Management Tasks

The Board needs to take a broad view of corporate management. The Board should be sure that all the tasks necessary to properly run the corporation are considered. In most nonprofits, the primary tasks are ensuring that the organization has:

- adequate funding;
- good financial controls and accurate financial information
- program management;
- volunteer management (see Chapter 21);
- outreach to clients and the community;
- systems to ensure compliance with law and agreements, and
- general administration.

After the Board determines what tasks are necessary, the Board sees that people who are competent to perform the activities are charged with carrying them out. These people in a direct management corporation are usually Board members or volunteers and occasionally may be an employee hired for a specific job or role.

> *To run a direct management corporation responsibly, the Board needs to function as a good Executive Director would function in a delegated management corporation.*

Your Board needs a mechanism to ensure that the lines of authority are clear about which decisions the Board makes and which decisions can be made by individuals charged with carrying out specific tasks or activities. The Board needs to provide for oversight—usually by reporting at regular Board meetings and by the presentation of financial information—to ensure that those tasked with jobs are carrying them out properly. The Board will want to maintain good lines of communication to ensure that all of the parts speak to each other.

As your Board assigns duties and tasks, it should keep in mind some special areas of concern and some expectations of nonprofit Boards:

- All Boards need to ensure that the organization has adequate funding. In many organizations, the Board will help to ensure this by participating in raising funds itself. See p. 275 for more discussion of this.

- The Board should take particular care with its assignment of duties related to maintaining good financial controls. This is particularly challenging in smaller nonprofits in which Board members lack understanding of the most important controls. Financial controls relate to managing funds flowing in from donors and other sources and flowing out through payment of bills, and protecting the corporation's assets, including cash and property and equipment. Chapter 25 discusses key financial controls and includes a reference to a sample set of financial policies and procedures to ensure that small organizations have adequate controls. This includes having two people overseeing the financial controls. The Board must also ensure that the organization has accurate and complete financial information available to the Board as a foundation for sound Board decisions.

- Many Boards in both direct management (and delegated management) corporations take on the responsibility to act as ambassadors for the organization by spreading the word about what you do to the larger community. This job is described on page 275.

- Like the larger nonprofits, your Board has the duty to investigate any suspicious activity or circumstances that comes to its attention. See pp. 284-85.

- Your Board cannot make illegal distributions as described on page 282.

- Because Directors in small as well as larger nonprofits are check-signers, your Board should review the rules on signing checks on pages 282-83.

- If you are exempt under §501(c)(3), your Board needs to ensure that you do not take positions for or against or support in any way a candidate for public office or a political party. Your Board also needs to be aware of the rules on lobbying and ensure that your corporation follows them. See Chapter 8.

Recordkeeping

Your Board needs to ensure that you are keeping proper records. You should have a copy of your filed Articles of Incorporation and any amendments or restatements, your Bylaws and your Board policies. See page 292 for how to get copies of the Articles if you can't find them. You also need to retain important financial and management information. See pages 677-680 for basic records and the length of time you should retain them. Your Board should keep good minutes of its meetings and Board committees that exercise Board authority should also keep minutes. See pp. 330-332.

Protecting the Corporate Status

At the most fundamental level, the Board needs to protect the corporate status. To do this, your Board has to operate the corporation as a separate entity from your Directors and members. This means that you must be sure to file the annual report with the Corporation Division each year or the state will dissolve your corporation. The Board must establish and maintain a separate corporate bank account and cannot allow the corporation's funds to be mixed with those of any individual or other organization. The corporation must have its own business records. The Board must meet as often as needed to run the corporation and needs to keep minutes of its meetings.

Independent Contractors

Your Directors should be alert to the common tendency in smaller nonprofits to misclassify people providing paid services to you as independent contractors and not employees. Your agreement with the service provider that the service provider is an independent contractor is virtually irrelevant. The various government agencies (the IRS, Oregon Department of Revenue, the Worker Compensation Department, State Unemployment, Bureau of Labor, etc.) involved in this classification all have somewhat different standards for what makes a person an independent contractor or an employee. In some cases, your worker may be an employee under some laws and an independent contractor under others. A misclassification can create serious financial liabilities for your organization and your Directors personally. If you are treating people you are paying for services as independent contractors, be sure to read Chapter 20 to be sure that you classify workers correctly.

Founders

Many direct management organizations are founded by one person or a small group of people who are very passionate about a cause and started the nonprofit to advance their ideas. This type of passion, commitment, and energy is very important in the nonprofit world and these small organizations often perform important services in the community. Some of these organizations have grown to have a major impact in our society. Very often the founders sit on the Board and are often financial donors as well.

If your organization's Board has a founder or founders as members, the Board will want to appreciate them but does need to be aware that each Board member needs to act responsibly as described in this chapter. Your Board cannot defer to your founders if that means you are not fulfilling your own duties. If you do, you may jeopardize the corporation and may even find yourself personally liable if there are financial repercussions. See pp. 353-56.

If the founder, members of the founder's family or businesses in which the founder has an interest may benefit financially from a transaction with the corporation, you will at least need to follow Oregon conflicts of interest rules. See pp. 299-303. If you are exempt under §501(c)(3) or (c)(4), you will need to follow the IRS rules on excess benefit transactions. See pp. 700-706. Your Board needs to adopt a Conflicts of Interest policy to ensure that it follows the proper steps. See p. 301 for a discussion about these policies. The Forms section includes a sample Conflicts of Interest and Executive Compensation policy that organizations exempt under §501(c)(3) and (4) may want to consider.

> *Your Board cannot defer to your founders if that means you are not fulfilling your own duties.*

Members

If your corporation has members, especially voting members, the Board needs to be attentive to managing its relations with its members. See Chapter 18.

Delegated Management Corporations

In the delegated management nonprofit, the Board has generally delegated most or all of its administrative responsibility and authority to the Executive Director or someone with another title that oversees the administration of the corporation. Because the Board is delegating its power, it needs to consider several issues to ensure that its delegation is and remains responsible:

- Decide when to delegate;
- Be clear about what is delegated and what is retained;
- Describe the limitations on what is delegated;
- Decide who will be responsible to carry out the delegation and ensure that s/he is competent; and
- *Oversee* what is delegated.

To the extent that the Board decides not to delegate its responsibilities, it must follow same requirements as a direct management corporation with regard to the responsibilities it does not delegate.

When to Delegate

At a minimum, your Board needs to delegate the management of your organization when it no longer has the capacity or time to properly manage the corporation. In smaller organizations, this may occur because the Board is unable to attract volunteers to the Board who can handle essentials tasks (like managing the finances or programs) or because Board members no longer want to do this. Often, a successful organization has become more complex and the Board is not competent to deal with its more sophisticated operations or complex funding streams or accounting rules. In many cases, the corporation has obtained funding that makes hiring a part- or full-time Executive Director feasible.

> *In the delegated management nonprofit, the Board has generally delegated most or all of its administrative responsibility and authority to the Executive Director*

If your Board is in the position of needing to obtain an Executive Director but unable to afford one, you might look for a qualified volunteer who will fill the role while you seek funding. If you are unable to find one, you will need to consider scaling back what you do to something that the Board can manage. The Board should not continue to run a nonprofit that it cannot properly manage. This is not fair to your donors, to the public, or to yourselves, and you may be putting yourself in jeopardy of personal liability for your actions. See Chapter 17.

Terms of the Delegation

Generally, when a Board delegates the management of the corporation to an Executive Director, all management powers except those retained by the Board are delegated. This allows the Executive Director to manage with clarity about what his/her powers are and without constantly being micromanaged by the Board. The Board should always retain the right to change the terms of the delegation if it chooses.

Almost all Boards will retain the power to provide the vision for the corporation and to develop a strategic plan and long-term goals for the organization. Many will do so with the assistance of the Executive Director. Generally, the issues of delegation revolve around the delegation of the power to manage the implementation of the goals through the corporation's day to day activities.

The Board needs to decide how much of its administrative power and responsibility it wants to delegate. Some Boards delegate all of their administrative responsibilities to an Executive Director. Others retain some management responsibilities—often the power to approve the budget, the right to authorize expenditures for unbudgeted items over a certain limit, or the right to approve the hiring of some or all employees. Some funders, especially government funders in community action agencies and Head Start programs, may require that the Board perform some of these jobs.

> *The Board will want to look at its resources and needs to make its decision about how much power to delegate.*

The Board will want to look at its resources and needs to make its decision about how much power to delegate. If the Board wants to delegate virtually all of its management responsibilities and has sufficient funds to hire an Executive Director qualified to handle those responsibilities, the Board will probably choose that route. In many cases, the Board is not ready to give up all of its administrative duties, cannot afford to hire someone who can handle complete management, or prefers to hire a particular person who is strong in some program or management areas but not others. In these cases, the Board's decision needs to ensure that the essential management functions not delegated will be carried out responsibly by the Board.

Another fairly common expectation in the nonprofit world is that Directors, particularly of public benefit nonprofits, will act as informal ambassadors for the organization. Many nonprofits encourage their Directors to spread the word about the organization in other personal, professional, and nonprofit settings in which the Director moves. Both fundraising and community relations are management powers and responsibilities that the Board could (and often does) delegate to the Executive Director, so Boards that obligate their members to perform some of these duties have decided not to delegate all of these responsibilities. Of course, close coordination between the Executive Director and the Board will be essential to be sure that all of the efforts result in consistent messages to the community.

Whether the Board keeps or delegates an important management power, it needs to ensure that whoever (whether Board or Executive Director) is carrying it out has the resources and skills to do so. In some cases, the Board may decide not to delegate a power that it can better perform itself. For example, if the organization does not have the resources to allow the Executive Director to hire a finance director and the Board has a Treasurer with a strong finance background, the Board may choose to retain the final decision on financial matters like the budget and to give the Treasurer more detailed financial management responsibilities. If the Executive Director is experienced in dealing with personnel and the Directors are not, the Board may find it fruitful to let the Executive Director do the hiring and use its time for other matters.

> *The terms of the delegation should also include some understanding about how your Board and the Executive Director and staff interact.*

The terms of the delegation should also include some understanding about how your Board and the Executive Director and staff interact. If individual Board members routinely approach staff other than the Executive Director with questions, requests for information, or concerns, this can undercut the authority of the Executive Director to manage the staff's time and job performance expectations and be confusing to the staff about who their supervisor is. If a staff member takes a complaint or request to the Board, this also undercuts the Executive Director and the staff member's immediate supervisor. Some Boards respond to this by directing that all contact between staff and Board take place through the Board President and Executive Director. Others are more flexible, allowing Board members to communicate directly with staff about matters in which they share an organizational interest—for example, the Board Treasurer may work directly with the chief financial officer. Each organization needs to find the arrangement that works best for it but it is helpful to be clear about what the arrangement is for staff/Board communication.

There are two responsibilities that many Boards, especially in Public Benefit nonprofits, generally do not entirely delegate and expect that its Directors will perform—fundraising and community relations.

Fundraising by the Board

All Boards need to be certain that the organization is adequately funded. Although some Boards may delegate this responsibility and exercise oversight to make sure that the corporation is funded, many nonprofits expect their Directors to be strong financial contributors to help with funding. Directors, especially those in public benefit nonprofits, are also often expected to participate in helping the organization obtain contributions from individuals, corporations, foundations, and government. In part, this is because many donors expect to see Board involvement before they will give and some nonprofits populate their Boards with individuals that have connections to major donors. If your nonprofit expects your Board to raise funds, you will want to make this clear when you invite people to consider joining your Board. Your Board should decide what is expected in your organization.

Community Relations and the Board

Most nonprofits are concerned with the profile that they have in the community. Nonprofits commonly turn to the community for support in the form of contributions and volunteers, access to foundation and government grants, spreading the word to potential clients of the nonprofit's services, encouraging business support, potential Board members, advocating for an issue of importance to the nonprofit and its clients, and many other areas.

Some nonprofits may delegate the responsibility for community relations to the Executive Director, but many recognize that community members look to the Board as well as the administrative side for cues about the nonprofit and its work. These nonprofits often expect their Directors to spread the good word about the nonprofit to other groups, communities, and individuals with whom each Director has a connection. This may be as simple as informally talking to friends, may involve making presentations to groups like the local Rotary Club about the nonprofit, or may require the Directors to contact or testify before governmental bodies that are considering legislation that might impact those that the nonprofit serves.

Limitations on the Delegation

The Board needs to think about any limitations it wants to impose on the responsibilities it does delegate. Such limitations may be related to values, management, or financial matters. Of course, the more limitations that the Board places on the Executive Director, the more it restricts the Executive Director's choices about management and ability to manage flexibly. At some point, the Board needs to decide how fundamental its restrictions are to the organization's mission and whether the Board or Executive Director is best positioned to make those choices.

The Board may require the Executive Director to follow certain values in carrying out her/his duties. For example, the Board may emphasize local hiring and purchasing, environmentally-friendly practices, child and family friendly policies, or paying a living wage, particularly if these values are connected to the organization's mission. The Board needs to be sure that its values are communicated to the Executive Director, either through Board policies (see pp. 345-50) or otherwise.

Your Board may want to impose limitations on the management of the corporation's programs or personnel. Most Boards will want to approve the establishment of major new programs. Some corporations require that special care be taken to foster an inclusive and culturally diverse workplace. Other Boards may want to retain the right to approve some or all of the hiring.

Most Boards will want to consider some limitations on financial matters. Many Boards will expect to approve the annual budget and many will require Board approval of unbudgeted items over a certain amount. Virtually all Boards will require management to provide complete, accurate financial reports for Board review. Some will require specified safety or other reserves in the budget and adopt a policy of always budgeting for income to exceed expenses in order to build those reserves.

The Board should consider whether the corporation faces serious special risks that the Board needs to ensure are covered.

The Board should consider whether the corporation faces serious special risks that the Board needs to ensure are covered. Most corporations that face special risks do so because they deal with vulnerable populations, engage in dangerous activities, or take controversial positions. Examples of organizations that deal with vulnerable populations are child care center, church nurseries, nonprofit assisted living and nursing care facilities, and mental health centers. Mountain rescue groups and organizations like Habitat for Humanity engage in dangerous activities. Numerous advocacy groups take controversial positions, as do, at times, neighborhood associations.

The Board needs to know that its chief management official has taken action to identify and minimize the risks and to protect the organization in the event that there are problems. The Board does not need to tell its Executive Director how to do this (and in all likelihood the Executive Director is better positioned than the Board to know how to handle the risks) but the Board should know and document that the Executive Director has taken reasonable steps to handle the risks.

Choosing an Executive Director

Most nonprofit Boards that delegate management authority do so to an Executive Director (ED). Other organizations call their chief management official the Chief of Operations, or COO. Some organizations delegate to a Chief Executive Officer, or CEO, particularly if the individual is well-known in his/her field. In some schools, the principal is the chief management official and in many churches, the senior minister or occasionally a church administrator serves this role. You can, of course, use whatever title you want. You should be aware that the title may make a difference if you have to justify your compensation practices to the IRS. CEO's, for example, generally receive higher compensation than EDs, but are also expected to have the background and reputation to justify the title of CEO. For convenience, in this book we typically refer to the chief management official by the title Executive Director.

The most important consideration in choosing an Executive Director is to ensure that you hire an individual who has the skills and background to handle the powers you are delegating. If the Executive Director does not have the necessary skill set, you need to provide the resources needed so that he or she can get the necessary training or can hire others who can do so. You have the right (and at a certain point in organizational growth, the duty) to delegate management responsibilities but only if you can reasonably expect the person to whom you delegate these duties to handle them.

Smaller nonprofits hiring their first Executive Director often hire an individual known to the organization. Frequently the person is a founder, sits on the Board and/or has a passion for the mission of the organization. The Board has a history with the person and believes that s/he can best lead the organization. Occasionally larger nonprofits face this issue as well.

> *The most important consideration in choosing an Executive Director is to ensure that you hire an individual who has the skills and background to handle the powers you are delegating.*

Founders and Board members can make excellent Executive Directors but the Board needs to consider several issues. The most important is whether the hiring is in the organization's best interests. The individual's passion and history with the organization may be assets, but the Board should consider whether there are other candidates whose skills would be more beneficial to your organization. Your nonprofit does not exist to reward its founders but to use its resources to realize its mission.

A second consideration is whether the individual can perform the management responsibilities of an Executive Director. If the individual does not have the background and skills, the Board needs to reconsider hiring the person or needs to find other mechanisms to ensure that the necessary management skills are available.

> *Example.* The Board for the Environmental School, an elementary school with an experimental curriculum, hires a principal to manage the school. The principal was a founder of the school and is excellent with the curriculum, students, and parents. However, he has no management background and struggles with the management of the finances and personnel. The Board needs to find a qualified volunteer to handle the finances and personnel or provide funds so that the principal can get the training he lacks or can hire an operations manager who is qualified to pick up the slack. If it cannot do these things, the Board should not delegate these roles.

Chapters 19 and 23 to 28 are useful to Executive Directors who want assistance with managing personnel and finances.

THE OREGON NONPROFIT CORPORATION HANDBOOK

In addition to necessary skills, Boards who hire and compensate a founder or Board member need to consider whether the hiring is a conflict of interest or violates any IRS rules on excess benefits transactions. If the individual is a Director or officer, you will at least need to follow Oregon conflicts of interest rules. See pp. 299-303. If you are exempt under §501(c)(3) or (c)(4), you will need to follow the IRS rules on excess benefit transactions if the individual is a founder, Director, officer or other insider. See pp. 700-06. Your Board needs to adopt a Conflict of Interest policy to ensure that it follows the proper steps. See p. 301.

Oversight

If the Board has acted reasonably in hiring an Executive Director and in any other hiring that it does, it is entitled to rely on the reports from those it hires or those that its Executive Director hires. Even so, the Board needs to exercise oversight over the duties that it delegates.

The Board needs to exercise oversight over the duties that it delegates.

Management Oversight

Your Board needs to monitor the success of your programs in meeting your mission and oversee issues related to employees and volunteers and general administrative matters. The Board does this in part through the reports of the Executive Director and possibly staff at Board meetings. Where most or all of the management responsibility was delegated to an Executive Director, one major assessment tool for most Boards is the evaluation of the performance of the Executive Director. See pages 424-25 for how to do this.

PERSONNEL POLICIES

The most common source of lawsuits against the corporation and Directors personally is an unhappy employee—often a terminated Executive Director or an employee claiming harassment, discrimination or other mistreatment. Good up-to-date personnel policies and an employee handbook (see Chapter 19) that encourages good employment practices may prevent harassment, discrimination and mistreatment from occurring and shows that management took its responsibilities seriously. The Board does not have to produce or even approve the personnel manual, but it should look to the Executive Director to report that the manual exists, was created by or reviewed by an employment attorney, and is being updated as recommended by the attorney.

If your organization relies heavily on volunteers, the Board should receive some information from the Executive Director about volunteer recruitment, training and performance.

RECORDS RETENTION

Corporations may need to provide documentation of their activities to a variety of sources—internal users, clients, funders, regulators, the public, the press, members, and litigants are some of the more likely groups interested in your records. To comply with various laws and the possibility of litigation, you need a schedule that ensures that you keep some records for a minimum period of time. You also have to comply with a variety of privacy statutes that require that you maintain the confidentiality of some of the information that you have. One very challenging area in developing a policy has to do with the retention of electronic records, including emails. See 677-682.

Larger Boards generally rely on the Executive Director to ensure that the corporation retains the records it needs. The Board will want to ensure that the Executive Director has a written policy on record retention that will protect the corporation. In addition, Form 990, the annual informational return for larger tax-exempt corporations (see Chapter 12), asks filers if they have record retention policies. If your corporation is a Form 990 filer, a written records retention policy will allow the corporation to answer the Form 990 question in the affirmative. See the Forms section for a sample Records Retention and Destruction policy.

Financial Oversight

Most cases in which nonprofit corporations make the headlines in a negative way relate to financial issues—often fraud, embezzlement or allegations of excessive executive compensation. Nonprofit Boards are increasingly being pushed to maintain greater financial oversight. Your Directors should be familiar with the financial condition of the corporation and they should get regular and timely financial reports. If the Board does not approve the budget, it should review it and have an understanding of its basic features. The Board needs to assure itself that the organization has the resources to support its operations and meet its obligations. The Board of a larger corporation should have and be familiar with a multi-year financial plan which may have been developed by an Executive Director or chief financial officer or possibly by the Board.

> *Nonprofit Boards are increasingly being pushed to maintain greater financial oversight.*

The Board's involvement in other areas of the organization's finances depends on what level of financial expertise the corporation has on the administrative side. If your delegated management corporation has hired a qualified chief financial officer, the Board will generally rely on the CFO to ensure that the corporation's assets are protected and good internal controls are in place. If your corporation does not have the resources to hire a CFO and is relying on personnel with bookkeeping backgrounds to track your funds, the Board should ensure that the corporation has good internal controls in place. The Board also needs to consider the corporation's major risks and know that the corporation has protected its assets through insurance and by bonding those who handle funds. See pp. 566-68 for more information on this.

In some organizations, particular events trigger Board concerns. If the organization has significant investments, receives restricted funds, or has an endowment, the Board will generally want to have a clear process for ensuring that these issues are handled properly or in overseeing management performance related to them. The Board also must be concerned if the organization distributes its nonprofit funds for purposes that are not nonprofit, such as excessive compensation to insiders. As organizations grow and become more complex, many Board choose to have an annual independent audit performed by a CPA. Chapter 28 provides more information about the value and cost of having an independent audit or review. See pages 642-44.

INVESTMENTS

Boards of nonprofits with significant investments will want to be sure that the money is invested in accordance with a responsible investment policy. See pages 497-98. If the expertise to develop the policy is on the administrative side, the staff may draft the policy but is should be discussed, understood, and approved by the Board. Additionally, Boards of organizations with substantial investments must be sure that their investment policies are being properly implemented.

RESTRICTED FUNDS

The term "restricted funds" describes funds a nonprofit has accepted with donor restrictions on how or when the funds may be used. These funds will remain restricted until the donor's restrictions have been fulfilled. Your Board needs to ensure that it does not spend restricted funds for improper purposes. The Board must use donor restricted funds according to the donor's instructions. If the donor is still living, the nonprofit may ask the donor to authorize a change in restrictions in writing. If the donor is no longer living, the nonprofit will need to ask the Attorney General to approve a change if it is not possible to fulfill the donor's restriction.

In addition to donor restricted funds, some Boards decide to set aside funds for specific purposes. Boards often refer to these as restricted funds but accountants describe these funds as Board designated funds. Boards can change their minds about Board designated funds and decide to make them available for general purposes or for other specific purposes. This is very different from the situation with donor restricted funds. The financial statements that the Board receives should list donor restricted funds and Board designated funds separately, so that the Board can be sure that the funds are being used properly.

Your Board needs to ensure that it does not spend restricted funds for improper purposes.

Of course, getting money is wonderful, but the corporation does need to consider whether to accept restricted contributions. In a few cases, the donor may be someone whose image is at odds with the corporate mission, which can cause problems with public perception and other donors. More commonly, if the gift is going to require more administrative time and expense over the long term than the value of the gift, the corporation may need to talk to the donor about easing restrictions or, in the worst case, turn it down. The corporation also needs to document the restrictions, so that the donor, the donor's heirs, future Boards and your financial people are aware of how the money can be spent. If the corporation receives restricted funds, it is important that the Board or the Executive Director have a gift acceptance policy detailing when the corporation will accept restricted funds and how to document the acceptance. In most organizations, the Board will want to approve the policy. Be sure that your organization keeps these written restrictions in a permanent file that future Boards or the Executive Director can locate. Chapter 26 provides more information about recording and reporting on receiving and using restricted funds. See pp. 586-88.

ENDOWMENTS

An endowment is typically a type of restricted fund in which the income is usually available to be used for the operating budget but the principal is retained to generate investment income to support future activities. In some cases, the endowment contains a restriction that requires the income to be used for a specific purpose. Accountants generally describe gifts in which the donor requires retention of principal as *permanently restricted*. Oregon law regulates how your corporation manages endowments which contain funds from outside donors. The Board's role is to ensure that endowment income is invested responsibly and is spent in accordance with whatever promises were made to the donor and in compliance with the laws on endowment spending. Your Board should get legal advice about how to manage its endowments responsibly.

AUDITS

The primary purpose of the independent audit is to let the Board know whether the information in the organization's financial statements presents fairly the actual financial condition and results of the organization. This is extremely important since Boards rely on the financial reports the staff produce to make multiple significant decisions.

> *The Board and not the Executive Director should select the auditor and sign the audit engagement agreement to clarify that it is the Board for whom the auditor works.*

In some cases, outside sources like funders require that nonprofits have independent audits. In others, the nonprofit elects to be audited. Oregon law does not require nonprofits to be audited. Many accountants will recommend an audit to nonprofits with gross receipts above $1 million or to those below that level that have funding from government, other complex funding streams, or other special issues.

If you are audited, your Board should be involved. The Board and not the Executive Director should select the auditor and sign the audit engagement agreement to clarify that it is the Board for whom the auditor works. The Board (generally through its Treasurer, Finance Committee, or Audit Committee) should also be involved in overseeing the audit process. The audit contract should require that the auditor disclose to the Board all critical accounting policies and practices used by the corporation that were discussed with management; all alternative treatments of financial information, ramifications of its use, and the treatment preferred by the auditor, and all other material communications between the auditor and management, such as the management letter or schedule of unadjusted differences. The contract should provide that the auditor provide copies of the audit report and management letter directly to the Board and that a member or members of the Board be present at the audit exit conference. All of these provisions are contained in the auditor's engagement letter and are considered part of the professional standards for CPA's who provide audit services. Chapter 28 provides more in-depth discussion of audits. See pp. 642-650.

EXECUTIVE COMPENSATION

Both the state of Oregon and the IRS are concerned that nonprofits do not overpay their Executive Directors, key employees and other insiders. (We know, we know, this should be your problem!) If you are a Public Benefit Corporation under Oregon law (see p. 27) or are exempt under §501(c)(3) as a public charity or under §501(c)(4) (see Chapter 5), your Board will need to exercise special care in approving compensation of the Executive Director and other key employees. The IRS regulations are discussed on pages 700-706 and the Board or at least the Board's Finance Committee or Compensation Committee should be familiar with the rules.

ILLEGAL DISTRIBUTIONS

The major characteristic that distinguishes a nonprofit corporation from a profit organization is that the nonprofit corporation cannot pay a dividend or any part of its income or profit to its members, officers, Directors, or anyone else (other than reasonable payment for goods received or services performed in furtherance of the corporation's purposes). If the nonprofit corporation does make this kind of payment, it is called an *illegal distribution*. Your Directors cannot vote for these distributions.

> *Example*: In a rare occurrence which caused some staffers to believe they were living in the Twilight Zone, Coalition for Community Progress, a nonprofit public benefit corporation, found itself with a substantial surplus at the end of its fiscal year. The Board had worked very hard and decided to reward itself by holding its annual meeting at an exclusive resort in Hawaii and to pay all expenses of the Board members to attend the meeting and enjoy a week in the sun. This is an illegal distribution to its Directors.

In certain limited cases, Oregon law allows your corporation to make distributions to a member, if that member is a Religious or Public Benefit Corporation or a foreign nonprofit corporation which, if incorporated in Oregon, would qualify as a Religious or Public Benefit Corporation. Mutual Benefit corporations cannot make distributions while the corporation is operating to members but can distribute any property after payment of your debts to members on dissolution. However, if your corporation is or plans to become tax-exempt under §501(c)(3), you must limit yourself (in your Articles) by agreeing not to make any distributions to anyone, including members, and by agreeing that assets on dissolution after payment of liabilities go to another §501(c)(3) or the government.

CHECK SIGNING BY DIRECTORS/OFFICERS

In many nonprofits, at least one of the Board members is a check signer. In choosing which Board members will sign checks, remember that the check signer cannot sign checks to him or herself. The check signer should not be the person who reconciles the bank statement for the corporation.

When the Director or officer is presented a check, the check signer should review several items before signing the check—*authorization, amount, name, date,* and *reasonableness*. Feel free to copy this list and give it to your check signers.

- The check should be accompanied by an original invoice initialed by the person authorized to approve payments or by a note to pay from that person. The Director or officer should compare the check to the invoice or note authorizing payment to ensure that the *authorizing* initials or note is there.

- The signer should compare the *amount* on the check with the amount on the invoice or note to be sure the figures match.

- Compare the *name* on the invoice or note with the name on the check. Be sure that the names match exactly. Embezzlers will sometimes set up an account in a name very close to that of your vendor—for example, your vendor may be Printer Inc. and the embezzler's account may be Printer LLC—then have you sign a check to Printer LLC.

- Check the *date* on the invoice or the note against the date of signing the check. If the difference is more than 60 days, get written approval from the person authorized to approve payments before signing the check. This is to mitigate the risk that the organization is paying the same expense twice.

- The signer should consider whether the expense seems *reasonable*. The signer is not expected to check line-item authorizations but should question a check that seems unreasonably large or for a purpose that the signer knows is not related to anything the corporation does. For example, a check for $20,000 to pay a printer when you know the organization does very little printing should prompt a question. Payment to a pension fund when the corporation does not pay pension benefits would be suspicious.

- The signer should *never* sign a blank check.

When the Director or officer is presented a check, the check signer should review several items before signing the check.

Check signers should be familiar with the information in Chapter 25 in order to fully understand the risks they expose their organization to by signing unauthorized or blank checks.

COMMITTEES

Most Boards will establish one or more committees to provide financial oversight. The most common is a Finance Committee. The Finance Committee is typically chaired by the Treasurer. Ideally, at least one member of the Finance Committee will be very knowledgeable in nonprofit financial matters. Directors who are accountants or have managed finances for their own businesses or other nonprofits are excellent for this role. The Finance Committee acts as the Board's arm to oversee the corporation's finances. At a minimum, the Finance Committee will develop or review the budget and make a recommendation to the Board on the approval of the budget, if the Board approves the budget. The Finance Committee will review the financial statements and raise questions or concerns about the financial statements with the Executive Director or chief financial officer. At

Board meetings, the Finance Committee will often explain the financial statements to other Board members and raise any concerns that it has to the Board. Chapter 28 explores the questions the Finance Committee should ask as they review the financial reports.

The Finance Committee may monitor other financial matters as well—such as overseeing investments, audits, executive compensation, gift acceptance or endowments. In organizations where these other financial activities are significant and the Board has enough knowledgeable personnel to sit on separate committees, the corporation may have a separate Investment Committee, Audit Committee, Executive Compensation Committee, Gift Acceptance Committee, Endowment Committee, or any other committee the Board feels it needs.

Program Oversight

The Board should be informed about how the organization is meeting its mission. Although corporations may have different means of measuring success, your Board should ensure that the corporation's resources are devoted to its mission and should have some method to ascertain whether the resources are being used efficiently.

The most likely means by which the Board will uncover fraud, embezzlement, or mismanagement of funds is not through an audit but from tips.

Suspicious Circumstances

The most likely means by which the Board will uncover fraud, embezzlement, or mismanagement of funds is not through an audit but by tips from staff, volunteers, or program participants. People reporting perceived wrongdoing are referred to as whistleblowers. Whistleblowers may also alert the Board to other problems in the organization—for example, a hostile work environment, discrimination, or other poor employment or volunteer practices. Your Board should seriously consider developing a good whistleblower policy or ensuring that your Executive Director has one in place to encourage employees and volunteers to report suspicious circumstances.

Your Board members must report to your Board any suspicious circumstances that come to their attention. The Board needs to investigate any concerns that are reported to it to see if the concerns are founded.

> *Example*: A reliable staff member of a nonprofit corporation tells a Director that the bookkeeper is siphoning money from the savings account. The Director has a duty to inform the rest of the Board and the Board must investigate.

In investigating the concern, the Board will need to consider privacy rights of the parties involved and should document the investigation and resolution in writing. If the allegations are serious, the Board should get legal advice before proceeding. The Board will also need to consider with the attorney any legal whistleblower protections that might apply in the case of employees who report concerns. Failure to follow the whistleblower laws may deter other employees from reporting mismanagement or fraud and can result in costly and embarrassing litigation against your nonprofit. At the same time, the corporation will need to be alert to and respond properly to an employee who is using the whistleblower procedure improperly. An attorney's advice before action is taken is critical.

Members

If your corporation has voting members, the Board needs to be attentive to the governance requirements related to running a membership corporation. The Board should ensure that the proper notice is given to the members of their annual meeting or any special meeting, that a quorum is present at any membership meeting, and that voting is handled properly and recorded in membership minutes. The Board should report the results of membership voting at a Board meeting and confirm the vote in its minutes.

The Board may choose to delegate to the staff or volunteers other tasks related to members, such as handling responses to requests to inspect records by members, collecting dues and communicating with members about the organization's programs. Your Board will need to assess how important it is to your organization for the Board to maintain more direct contact with its members.

Special Concerns of Smaller Delegated Management Corporations

In smaller delegated management organizations in which the corporation does not have the funds for a chief financial officer, your Directors will want to be sure that your organization is meeting all of its obligations on time, including payroll tax deposits. You'll want to pay particular attention to recording donor restrictions correctly. One important step to avoid financial trouble is to be sure that your annual budget uses conservative income projections and realistic expense projections. You should budget for income to exceed expenses so that you have a cushion in case income falls short or unplanned expenses have to be covered.

The Board in nonprofits without solid financial expertise on staff will need to be more attentive to the financial statements. Smaller nonprofits without fully skilled chief financial officers often get into trouble through weak internal controls, improper handling of restricted funds, late payment of taxes, and the misclassification of people being paid for services as independent contractors. Chapter 24 provides basic budget practices and tools to help establish or improve your budget practices.

Internal Controls

Nonprofits in Oregon and elsewhere have suffered numerous losses in recent years from fraud and embezzlement because of poor internal controls. In other cases, organizations lose funding, face government challenges or pay for costly remedial services because of accounting errors. Internal controls are financial practices that are designed to ensure that funds that come into and flow out of your organization are handled properly. Good internal controls require that all funds received are deposited into the corporation's bank account with no exceptions and all disbursements, except for a controlled petty cash fund, are paid out of the bank account.

In most cases of fraud, the perpetrator was someone who had been with the organization for several years and was trusted by the organization. Often the perpetrator is described as "the most trusted person in the organization." And, of course, anyone can make a mistake and good financial controls can also protect a person from being falsely accused of theft. Good controls seek to ensure that every step of the financial process is checked by someone other than the person performing the function. At its most basic level, you want to segregate duties so that the person who authorizes a transaction is not be the person who signs the check for the transaction and the check-signer is not the person who reconciles the bank statement. Two people should count cash for which no receipt can be issued.

Chapter 25 describes internal controls in more detail and we have Financial Controls Policies for Small Nonprofit Organizations in the Forms section that covers the basic controls most small nonprofits need. The Financial Management Checklist provided at the end of Chapter 23 will help you ensure that you have addressed all of the major components of sound financial management.

If your nonprofit cannot afford to hire a knowledgeable financial officer, your Board or your Executive Director must be trained, locate a knowledgeable volunteer, or find some way to ensure that you have good internal controls.

Temporary Borrowing of Restricted Funds

As described earlier in this Chapter, restricted funds are funds given to the organization by an outside donor to be used only for a specific purpose or in a specified time period. Your Board must use restricted funds in accordance with the restrictions.

> *Example*: The Children's Assistance Project has received a substantial bequest that is restricted to use for teen programs. The Board experiences a funding problem with its pre-school program and wants to divert some of the bequest to the pre-school program, which it deems to be more important than the teen program. It may not.

Many Boards use restricted funds for a purpose outside the restriction with the idea that the Board is borrowing the funds and will repay them when a projected grant is received or other monies come in. The Board does not feel that this is a misuse of the funds since the Board is not intending to permanently divert the funds. However, the Board has a responsibility to manage the restricted funds reasonably. In almost all cases, the "loan" of the funds is a very risky loan. Usually it is done because the organization is already experiencing a cash flow problem. Unless the organization has collateral that can guarantee repayment of the loan (possibly with interest) and the liquidity or a line of credit to repay the funds when they are needed for their restricted purpose, the Board has no right to jeopardize the restricted funds by using them as a loan. Get legal help for this.

The issue of using funds that the Board previously set up as Board designated funds is significantly different. If the Board, rather than an outside donor, sets funds aside for a specific purpose, the funds are described as being Board designated. If the Board has a designated fund for a purpose and no outside donor has contributed to it, the Board (even a future Board) can authorize temporary use of the Board designated fund for another purpose. It may be clearer for the Board to decide to remove the Board designation and treat the funds as available for operations with the understanding that if the nonprofit's finances improve, the Board may once again designate funds for a specific purpose.

See the discussion above in this chapter and in Chapter 26 for other issues related to restricted funds.

Payment of Taxes

Your Board should be sure that all taxes are being paid on time. This includes payroll, unemployment, and unrelated business income taxes. Be sure to provide worker compensation coverage on workers where it is required. You do not have to personally write the check for the taxes withheld but you should get a financial report or a bookkeeper's statement that shows it is being done. Chapter 27 provides more detail on payroll tax requirements.

> *Your Board should be sure that all taxes are being paid on time.*

Example: Your corporation is experiencing cash flow problems and your bookkeeper has paid the staff salaries but has not deposited the federal and state withholding taxes for several months. The Board is aware of the situation but is anticipating a large grant. The grant does not come through. Your Board has not exercised reasonable care when it failed to pay these taxes, even if to do so means that you must lay off personnel. The IRS may find the Directors personally liable to pay the taxes, interest and penalties. See page 356.

Independent Contractors

We discussed the tendency of direct management corporations to misclassify workers as independent contractors on page 271, but smaller delegated management corporations are prone to do this as well. If your organization has independent contractors and your Executive Director does not have much management experience, be sure the Executive Director is aware of the issues and consequences surrounding the correct classification of independent contractors. Be sure to review Chapter 20 to be certain that you are making potentially expensive errors in this area.

Consult Appendix 1 if you would like information about source material related to this Chapter. Appendix 1 has references of interest to all readers, not just professionals.

This Chapter has described what your duties are as a Director—to manage the corporation. The next Chapter describes how you do this.

14 HOW THE BOARD MANAGES THE CORPORATION

THIS CHAPTER COVERS

- Setting Up a Management Structure
- Getting Informed
- Participating in Decisions
- Following Standards of Conduct

Chapter 13 describes *what* it is your Board does—it manages the corporation—and describes the two types of corporate management. The broad rules regulating how the Board manages the corporation are the same regardless of which management style the Board uses, but there are important variations in applying these rules depending on the type of corporate management the Board chooses. This chapter addresses *how* your Directors carry out their duties to manage the corporation.

Many Directors in Oregon nonprofit corporations are unaware that by agreeing to serve on the Board of Directors they take on certain legal duties, responsibilities, and liabilities. This ignorance may be due in part to the fact that most Directors in Oregon serve on nonprofit Boards without being paid. Perhaps because the Board is volunteering its time and expertise, Directors may not expect that they will take on legal responsibilities and liabilities by agreeing to serve.

> *Many Directors in Oregon nonprofit corporations are unaware that by agreeing to serve on the Board of Directors they take on certain legal duties and responsibilities.*

It may be easier to understand why duties and responsibilities are forced on a volunteer Director if we look at the nonprofit corporation from the state's point of view. When the state gives an organization the status of "nonprofit corporation," the organization gets certain benefits. It can hold itself out to the public as nonprofit. Its nonprofit status may be a necessary step in order to obtain tax-exemption. It may be able to engage in certain types of activities, for example, bingo, denied to other groups.

Because the organization has no owners, there is no particular individual or group to whom the state can look to be responsible for the actions of the corporation. Unlike a sole proprietorship or a partnership, a corporation is really just a legal fiction. However, someone has to be responsible for it. By law, that group is the Board of Directors. In some cases, the corporation may change this (see pages 19-20) but generally the law looks to the Board to be responsible for directing the corporation.

As members of the Board of an Oregon nonprofit corporation, your Directors have the obligation to be attentive to its management of the affairs of the corporation. This means that, in making decisions, your Directors must:

- set up a management structure;
- be informed about what is going on;
- participate in the decision-making ; *and*
- follow certain standards of conduct.

Setting Up a Management Structure

The kind of management structure your Board established varies depending on whether you are a direct management or delegated management corporation.

Direct Management Corporations

Boards that are directly managing their corporations commonly do so using one of three structures. Some Boards perform all of the corporate tasks described in Chapter 13 themselves or with volunteers who work with the Board as a whole. In other Boards, individual Directors divide up the tasks and volunteers may work with each Director to carry out that Director's tasks. A Board using a third structure sets up committees, usually with a Board member on each committee, and the committees are charged with carrying out some of the responsibilities of the Board.

Your corporation may set up a different management scheme as long as the Board ensures that it covers all the necessary tasks, that competent people are handling each task, that there is clarity about who does what, and that the Board oversees what is done. Regardless of the management structure your Board uses, the Board should be making all the major decisions about how the corporation is run. The Board should reflect its decisions in the minutes. These decisions are actually policies, since the Board intends them to operate into the future. These policies help clarify for everyone what their role is and what issues need to go to the Board for a decision. Chapter 16 covers these Board policies in more detail and explains the importance of keeping a copy of the decisions in a separate Board Policy Manual.

Delegated Management Corporations

The Board in a delegated management corporation has already established the core of its management structure by delegating some or much of its authority to manage the corporation to the Executive Director. The management issues for these Boards center around determining what management authority the Board delegated and what authority it retained. To the extent that the Board retained some of its management authority, its management issues are similar to Boards using direct management authority. The Board will need to establish mechanisms to provide for its own management responsibilities. Usually much of the retained management is done by a Board committee, such as a Finance Committee or Personnel Committee, with the committee reporting to the Board and going to the Board for major decisions.

> *Governance policies, especially in delegated management nonprofits, are one of the most important and most overlooked areas of Board policy-making.*

To the extent that the Board has delegated authority, the Board needs to determine what it has delegated, what limitations it places on its delegation, how to ensure that its Executive Director and staff are competent, and how it oversees the management it delegated. We covered these issues in Chapter 13.

The Board should seriously consider adopting governance policies that reflect how the Board handles its direct and delegated management structures. Governance policies, especially in delegated management nonprofits, are a very important mechanism for establishing clear guidelines for how the Board handles the delegation of its authority. This is one of the most important and most overlooked areas of Board policy-making. We discuss the types of policies your Board should consider in detail in Chapter 16.

Getting Informed

In order to govern your corporation, whether your Board uses direct management or delegated management, your Directors need to be attentive to the affairs of the corporation—that is, they need to be informed, participate in decision-making, and follow certain standards of conduct. In order to be informed, your Directors should understand the governance rules of your nonprofit corporation and should obtain whatever information they need to manage it properly.

Information about Your Corporation's Governance

In order to understand your nonprofit's governance rules, each Board member should have a copy of and read your Articles of Incorporation and any amendments or restatements to the Articles, your current Bylaws and your current Board policies. The Board should give all this material to each new Board members. If you haven't done so, now is a good time.

Your Articles of Incorporation and amendments and restatements to the Articles are the documents you filed with the Secretary of State's Corporation Division to set up the corporation or to make amendments to your original Articles. Your corporation should have a complete copy of these documents on file. Be sure that any copies of the Articles of Incorporation and amendments that you have are actually copies of documents that were filed with the state, and not drafts of documents that were never filed. If you cannot find your Articles or are uncertain if you have a copy of the filed documents or of all the amendments to the Articles, you can obtain a complete packet of these documents from the Secretary of State for a small fee. Go to their website or call them for information about how to get a packet. (See Appendix 2 for contact information.)

> *In order to understand your nonprofit's governance rules, each Board member should have a copy of and read your Articles of Incorporation and any amendments or restatements to the Articles, your current Bylaws and your current Board policies.*

Each Board member should read the governance documents. As your Board reviews the documents, it is important to know that the documents have a hierarchy. The Articles with any amendments and restatements have precedence over all the other documents, and your Bylaws have precedence over Board policies. This means that if there is any contradiction between the three types of documents, the Articles trump the others and the Bylaws trump the policies. If a Director finds a discrepancy, he or she should point it out to the rest of the Board for proper correction.

HOW THE BOARD MANAGES THE CORPORATION 14

The first thing your Directors should look for is the corporate purpose. The Articles and/or Bylaws should describe the corporate purpose. The Board is limited to using the corporate assets for these purposes and no others. If the Board finds that the corporate has changed its purpose over time without amending its Articles and/or Bylaws, it needs to change the purpose or amend your Articles or Bylaws. See Chapter 31 for more information on how to do this.

The corporate documents (generally the Bylaws) should give you all the information you need to understand how your Board is chosen and how it holds legitimate meetings and makes proper decisions.

Remember that a purpose statement in the Bylaws cannot change the purpose stated in the Articles, since the Articles trump the Bylaws. If your Articles or the amendments or restatements to your Articles include a purpose that no longer reflects what you do or want to do, you will need to amend the Articles to state the correct purpose or to delete the purpose altogether and state the purpose only in your Bylaws. The latter option is usually better. The Articles do not need to state your purpose (except for the general language required by the IRS for §501(c)(3) organizations as described on pages 35-39) and, if they do, it is easy for future Boards to overlook the Articles and thus operate incorrectly. The Bylaws are generally the best location for the purpose clause.

After understanding the corporate purpose, your Directors should review the documents for information on how the Board operates. In most organizations, this information is found in the Bylaws, supplemented by Board policies. However, in some organizations, especially those incorporated before 1989 (when the statues changed), the Articles, amendments or restatements may contain some instructions about how the corporation operates, often in relation to the number of Board members or how the Board is selected. Be sure that the corporation is following the requirements of its highest ranking document. If not, the Director should bring that to the Board's attention.

The corporate documents (generally the Bylaws) should give you all the information you need to understand how your Board is chosen and how it holds legitimate meetings and makes proper decisions. The governance documents should describe how many Directors the organization has (a range is permissible as long as the minimum number meets Oregon law as described on pp. 27-29), how the Board is chosen, the term of office for Directors, notice for regular and special meetings, and quorum and voting requirements at meetings. If your corporation has voting members, the documents should describe the classes of membership and how many votes each member has, what members can vote for, when the annual meeting is, what the quorum is for a meeting, and what notice is given for annual and special membership meetings.

If your corporation is not operating according to its corporate documents, it will probably need legal help. Common examples of problems include:

- Bylaws that contain a provision that conflicts with the Articles (for example, the Articles states that the Board has 5 members and the Bylaws say the Board has 9-15 members);

- the Articles say that the corporation is a membership corporation (which means that members elect at least one of the Directors, as described on pp. 25-26), but the Bylaws provide that the Board elects all the Directors;

- Articles and/or Bylaws with outdated corporate purposes; and

- Bylaws that contain a conflicts of interest policy that is different from a Board conflicts policy.

It is not uncommon for Directors to fail to read the corporation's governance documents or, if they do read them, to forget what the Articles and Bylaws say as time goes on. We recommend that one of the jobs of the Board officers, on being elected, should be to review the corporation's governance documents. Since the officers are generally more directly involved in Board affairs, this safeguard should help the Board stay in compliance with its Articles and Bylaws.

In addition to reading your governance documents, your Directors need to understand what governance model your organization uses. Are you a direct management or delegated management nonprofit? What is your management structure? A few organizations have Board policies that describe their governance model, but most nonprofits have either agreed verbally on a model or, more likely, have an implicit model that has evolved over time but not been discussed. As a Director, you need to know what implicit or explicit model you are using. See Chapter 13 for a description of governance models.

After reading your governance documents and understanding what type of management (direct or delegated) your Board uses, your Directors can use the information in this chapter to understand what their job as Directors is. To carry out their direct or delegated management responsibilities, your Directors need to attend to their job by getting the information they need, participating in meetings and decision-making and observing certain standards of care and loyalty in their actions as Directors.

Information about Your Corporation's Operations

Your Directors can get information about the operations of the corporation itself from a variety of sources. The type of information your Directors needs will depend in part on whether this is a direct management or delegated management corporation and on the variation of these models your Board has chosen, as described above.

Regardless of whether your corporation uses direct management or delegated management, many Boards rely on several common mechanisms for obtaining information necessary to govern in their management structure:

> 1. *Board Packets*. Most Board provide an agenda and Board packet prior to the meeting to Board members for their review. The Board packet may contain Board committee reports, Executive Director and/or staff reports, financial statements and other information necessary for Board discussions and decisions. In direct management organizations, the packet is generally assembled and distributed by the Board President or Secretary. In delegated management organizations, the

Executive Director or staff member may assemble and distribute the packet, often in consultation with the Board President. If the organization does not use a Board packet, management and financial information needs to be available at the Board meeting.

> *Many of the high-profile cases of nonprofits that get into trouble concern mismanagement of finances or improper spending. It is particularly important that the Board in any nonprofit corporation get regular financial information and review it.*

2. *Management Reports at Board Meetings.* If your organization is a direct management corporation, the Board will want to have its Directors or volunteers who are actively managing the corporation attend and report at Board meetings, so that it is kept up-to-date on what is going on in the corporation.

In organizations with an Executive Director, the Board generally expects the Executive Director to attend Board meetings to report on the condition of the organization and to answer any questions the Board has. Boards hire Executive Directors to manage the corporation, and most Board rely strongly on their Executive Director for management information. The best Boards are often those in which the Board and Executive Director work collaboratively to realize the corporation's mission. The Board is entitled to rely on its Executive Director, unless the Board has reasons for concern, in which case the Board needs to explore and resolve the issue.

Many of the high-profile cases of nonprofits that get into trouble concern mismanagement of finances or improper spending. It is particularly important that the Board in any nonprofit corporation get regular financial information and review it. In very small direct management corporations, this may consist of the Treasurer (or whoever oversees the finances) bringing the bank statements to the Board for review. In most other nonprofits, the staff person who oversees the finances should generate financial statements for Board review. See Chapter 28 for information on how to read financial statements and how to understand your corporation's financial health.

3. *Board Committees.* Both direct management and delegated management organizations will probably have Board committees. These committees often generate or obtain information that is useful to the Board. See pp. 336-40 for a discussion of Board committees. The committee should either provide a written report or report at a Board meeting to pass on what it learns and is doing to other Board members.

4. *Board Policies and Board Policy Manuals.* Boards are increasingly turning to a more developed set of Board policies that clarify for the Board and future Board members whether their corporation is a direct management or delegated management corporation, how the Board and management relate to each other, how the Board oversees what it delegates, and how the Board manages itself so that it acts attentively in carrying out its duties. Written policies keep Board members on track to attentively manage their particular corporation and transmit that institutional memory to future Boards. A Board Policy Manual gathers all the policies in one place and organizes them so that they are more readable. See pages 345-50 for more on Board policies and Board Policy Manuals.

Participation

Ensuring that your Directors have the information to make good decisions is the first step toward fulfilling their Board responsibility to be attentive to the nonprofit. The second step is that your Directors must participate in Board operations. This means that they must show up for meetings and be involved in the decision-making process.

> *As a general rule, we suggest that the Board consider whether a Board member who is missing more than 30% of the Board meetings should be replaced.*

There is no specific rule for how many meetings a Director must attend. If a Director never shows up, the Director is clearly not meeting his/her Board responsibilities. Some Directors simply lend their name to the corporation by allowing themselves to be named as a Board member but remain uninvolved. This does not preclude that Director from being held liable for the decisions of the Board. In fact, it may be a factor in suggesting that that Director did neglect her/his duty.

Example: Bob, a wealthy businessman, agreed to serve on the Board of Watchdogs Inc., a (c)(3) organization that monitored government spending and reported on corruption. Bob did not attend Board meetings. Watchdogs Inc. operated improperly by distributing most of its funds to political action committees, a violation of its mission and (c)(3) rules which resulted in heavy penalties by the IRS. Subsequent Board members sued the former Board, including Bob, for failing to exercise their duty of due care. If the former Board did fail to exercise due care, Bob will probably be personally liable for the judgment.

Of course, most Directors will miss some Board meetings and there may be occasions where a Director needs to miss a number of meetings. Each Board will need to decide at what point a Director's non-attendance interferes with the Board's work and that Director's ability to serve well.

HOW THE BOARD MANAGES THE CORPORATION 14

As a general rule, we suggest that the Board consider whether a Board member who is missing more than 30% of the Board meetings should be replaced.

> *Communication by email is not a meeting.*
> *Because email is not a proper meeting venue,*
> *your Board cannot meet or vote by email.*

The purpose of becoming informed and of participation is to ensure that your Directors make reasonable and legally valid decisions about the corporation. Your Board can make decisions in two ways—at a meeting or by 100% consent. A meeting is a venue in which all of the participants can communicate simultaneously with each other. This allows those who have questions or who disagree with a proposed decision to thrash it out. The meeting may take place with all the Directors in the same room, by teleconference, or by a computer chat-room type setting in which all the Directors can communicate simultaneously. Communication by email is not a meeting. Simultaneous communication does not always occur, since you don't know that everyone is sitting at their computers at the same time and servers are sometimes slow to deliver emails.

A decision made at a meeting is only valid if it is made at a properly called meeting following a legally-recognized process. The Directors need to ensure that they follow the correct procedures to make decisions at a meeting. Reading and following the corporate documents as described above is one part of this. The Board also needs to know that the corporate documents comply with the law on meeting notice, quorums and the proper vote needed to pass an action. The Board can do this by having the Articles, Bylaws and policies reviewed by a knowledgeable attorney or by reviewing the information in Chapters 4 and 16. Because email is not a proper meeting venue, your Board cannot meet or vote by email.

Your Board can also make decisions by consent without a meeting, as long as 100% of all Directors agree in writing and the Board properly documents the action. Boards can make decisions by consent by email if 100% of all the Board members agree and the Board properly documents the decision. See Chapter 16 for a longer discussion of Board meetings, including a discussion of voting by email and decisions by consent without a meeting.

Standards of Conduct

In making decisions, your Directors must follow certain standards of conduct. Directors must act in good faith and in a manner he/she reasonably believe to be in the best interests of the organization. As your Board makes decisions and manages the affairs of the corporation, the Directors must observe three standards. Your Directors must follow the corporate mission, act with due care, and be loyal to the corporation.

Duty of Follow the Corporate Purpose

Your Articles and Bylaws should describe the corporation's purpose and the public, funders, regulators and your clients may rely on this. As a Director, you must be faithful to the corporate mission. Your decisions should be made to advance that corporate mission. If you want to fund programs or engage in actions that do not advance the corporate purposes, you need to change the purposes before you act. See Chapter 31.

Duty to Act with Due Care

Your Board has an obligation to act with due care in managing the corporation's affairs. Due care is the care an ordinarily prudent person in a like position would exercise in similar circumstances. This is the "common sense test." The law holds the Director responsible for running the organization much as a Director of a profit corporation is responsible for its operation. Your Board should be exercising the same care in running a nonprofit corporation that you would exercise in running your own business.

> *Your Board should be exercising the same care in running a nonprofit corporation that you would exercise in running your own business.*

If you have Directors with special skills or expertise, those Directors cannot ignore their skills in their decision-making. For example, if you have a Director who is an accountant and that Director notices something wrong in the financial statements, he or she is required to inform the Board. The Director does not have to act as the Board's accountant but s/he cannot leave her/his special expertise at the office when attending Board meetings.

Your Board must make reasonable decisions. The law gives your Directors a wide scope for what is reasonable. You don't have to make perfect decisions, just reasonable ones.

> *Example*: Your Board received a grant to build a million dollar Youth Center, but the site under discussion for the facility was yours only by virtue of a short-term lease. The Acquisitions Committee recommended a contractor who had the qualifications for the job. Some Directors wanted to choose a different contractor. After some discussion, the Board decided to build on the property with the short-term lease and went with the original choice for contractor. The organization subsequently had to pay cost overruns on the building and then lost its lease on the property.
>
> The choice to build a million dollar facility on property on which you had only a short term lease was not an exercise of due care at the time it was made. This decision just doesn't make sense. However, in connection with the selection of the contractor and the cost overruns, the Board did not breach its duty of due care. The decision about whether the selection of that contractor was reasonable is based on what the

Board knew or should have known at the time of hire and is not based on what hindsight shows.

If you are on the Board of a homeowners association, most of what is said in this chapter will also apply to you, but you should be aware that the Boards of homeowners associations have specific requirements imposed on them by special statutes in addition to those listed here. You will need to get legal help for more information.

Duty to Be Loyal to the Corporation

In addition to your Board's duty to act reasonably in managing your corporation, your Directors also have a duty to be loyal to your corporation. The duty to be loyal to the corporation means that you must place the corporation's interests above your own in any transaction in which the two may come into conflict. If a Director is involved on both sides of a transaction, she or he has torn loyalties.

> *The duty to be "loyal" to the corporation means that you must place the corporation's interests above your own in any transaction in which the two may come into conflict.*

In lay terms, you might apply "the smell test". If you or another Director are in a situation that "smells" funny, the duty of loyalty may be involved. The most common circumstance in which this occurs is a conflict of interest.

Conflicts of Interest

In some situations, your Board may find that one or more of your Directors or officers have a direct or an indirect financial interest in transactions with the corporation on whose Board you sit. A *direct* conflict of interest occurs when a Director himself or herself is a party to a transaction with the corporation and stands to benefit financially from it.

> *Example*: Your Bylaws specify that the Executive Director, an employee, is also to serve as a Board member. The Board is deciding whether to raise the Executive Director's salary. That Executive Director, as both a Board member and staff, has a conflict of interest, since she has a direct material interest in this decision.

> *Example*: Your Board is about to buy computer equipment. One of the Directors is the sole proprietor of a company that sells computers. The Board wants to buy from your Director. The Director has a direct material interest in this transaction and so have a conflict of interest.

An *indirect* conflict of interest is present when the Board enters into a financial transaction with a business in which one of its Directors or a close family member is a general partner or has a material interest. The Director benefits financially but it is indirect because s/he benefits as part of a business or family connection to the transaction. An indirect conflict of interest is also present if the Director is on the Board of or an officer of another profit or nonprofit corporation and the transaction is significant enough that it should be considered by the Board of the other corporation. Your Director has torn loyalties—which nonprofit should he or she be advocating for?

> *Example*: Your nonprofit corporation is about to buy a building. One of your Directors is a major partner in a commercial real estate firm. One of the other Directors suggests that your real estate partner handle the sale for which your firm will receive a commission. Regardless of the fact that another Board member suggested the arrangement, your Director has an indirect material interest in this transaction and so has a conflict of interest.

> *Example*: Animal Rights, Inc., an Oregon nonprofit corporation, does lobbying for animal protection. Animal Rights has established an educational arm, Center for Animal Education. Center for Animal Education has some common Directors with Animal Rights, Inc. and some independent Directors. The two organizations are having a disagreement on how to split the proceeds from a very successful fundraiser. The Directors who sit on both Boards have an indirect conflict of interest.

In an ideal world, perhaps, a Board would not engage in any transactions in which its members had a conflict of interest, and it is best if you can avoid conflicts. However, conflicts of interest are quite common in the nonprofit world, particularly among small and mid-size nonprofit corporations. In many cases, the Board is well-served by engaging in the conflict after following the proper procedure. For example, it is not uncommon for a Board member to offer the corporation a greatly discounted price on a product or service the corporation needs because that Board member is committed to and wants to support the nonprofit's work.

> *The fact that a Director has a conflict of interest with the corporation does not necessarily mean that the transaction cannot occur.*

Proper Handling of Conflicts of Interest

Directors are very vulnerable to personal liability if they benefit from a transaction that breached their duty of loyalty to the corporation. The fact that a Director has a conflict of interest with the corporation does not necessarily mean that the transaction cannot occur. Generally, the Board is best advised to avoid approving transactions where a conflict is present. However, there may be occasions when the Board wants to engage in the transaction even with the conflict and the law allows this if proper procedures to protect the corporation are followed.

If your Board does want to proceed with a transaction in which a Board member has a conflict, you need to first determine whether you need to comply with both the Oregon conflicts rules and the IRS regulations. All Oregon nonprofit corporations need to comply with the Oregon rules described below. In addition, §501(c)(3) and (c)(4) tax-exempt organizations must also comply with IRS regulations related to conflicts of interest as well. Because so many corporations are exempt under §501(c)(3) or (c)(4), we start with the IRS rules.

TAX-EXEMPT ORGANIZATIONS

If your organization is a §501(c)(3) private foundation (described on pp. 99-101), your conflict of interest is probably an act of self-dealing and you cannot engage in it. You should get legal help.

If your corporation is exempt as a public charity under §501(c)(3) or is exempt under §501(c)(4), you are subject to much more restrictive regulation about how to handle transactions between your corporation and your officers, Directors, their family members and businesses, as well as other insiders. You need to follow both Oregon law as set out below and the IRS rules. The IRS rules are found on pages 700-06. We have included a Conflicts of Interest and Executive Compensation policy in the Forms section. This policy was designed to integrate Oregon and IRS conflicts rules and applies the more restrictive IRS procedures to handle conflicts. Form 990 (see p. 255) inquires about whether your tax-exempt corporation has a conflicts policy and monitors it and our policy provides for such monitoring.

If your corporation is exempt under subsections of §501 other than (c)(3) and (c)(4), there are no specific IRS rules about conflicts of interest that apply to you. Like all Oregon nonprofit corporations, you need to follow the rules described below.

ALL OREGON NONPROFIT CORPORATIONS

If your Board is faced with a conflicts situation, you should first check your own Articles, Bylaws, and Board policies. If your corporation has established rules for conflicts of interest, you must follow those rules, even if they are stricter than the rules below. However, your rules cannot be more lenient than the rules set out below. If they are, you need to follow the rules in this chapter.

Your Board can always engage in a transaction that involves a conflict of interest if the transaction is fair to the organization at the time it is entered into or approved. This rule applies to all types of nonprofit corporations and applies whether or not the vote of the Director with the conflict is counted. However, it is extremely important that the corporation document carefully its proof that the transaction is fair to the corporation.

It can be quite risky to rely on proving that a transaction was fair to the corporation, particularly if there was any dissent on the Board. The law provides another and better method for approving conflicts. This method involves a favorable vote by Directors who are not involved in the conflict. The rules for voting vary depending on what type of nonprofit corporation is voting. Even if you rely on the voting method to resolve your conflicts, it is still a good idea to document that the transaction is fair to your organization.

PUBLIC BENEFIT AND RELIGIOUS CORPORATIONS

Public Benefit and Religious Corporations can approve a transaction in which a Director has a conflict of interest by a vote of the Board or committee of the Board if the material facts and Director's interest are known. To be approved, the transaction must receive a majority vote by those on the Board or committee who have no interest in the transaction. *Note that this is a majority of everyone on the Board or committee and not a majority of those who are present at the meeting.* Also, that majority must be more than one Director.

Although the law does not forbid the Director with the conflict from participating in the discussion and the vote, the corporation's best policy would be to exclude the Director with the conflict from voting and from at least some of the discussion so that the corporation could arrive at a truly independent assessment that the transaction was fair to the corporation.

> *Example*: Your nonprofit corporation is a public benefit corporation that is not exempt under §501(c). You want to purchase a computer system from a company completely owned by one of your Directors. This is a direct conflict of interest. You may make the purchase as long as a majority of your Board in office, knowing about the conflict, and without counting the vote of the interested Director, vote to purchase. The Board would best protect itself if it documented facts showing this transaction was fair to the corporation (for example, with a couple of written price quotes from competitors).

MUTUAL BENEFIT CORPORATIONS

The rules for Mutual Benefit Corporations are not as strict as those for Public Benefits because the law relies on the members who have a stake in the success of the corporation to ensure that transactions are fair or at least acceptable to the members. Mutual Benefit Corporations can approve a conflict of interest transaction in advance by the Board or a committee if the material facts and director's interest are known, or it may be approved in advance or ratified after the fact by the members if the material facts and director's interest are known. If the Board is voting on the transaction, the transaction must receive a majority vote by those on the Board or committee who have no interest in the transaction. Note that this is a majority of everyone on the Board or committee and not a majority of those who are present at the meeting. Also, that majority must be more than one Director.

Although the law does not forbid the Director with the conflict from participating in the discussion and the vote, the corporation's best policy would be to exclude the Director with the conflict from voting and from at least some of the discussion so that the corporation could arrive at a truly independent assessment that the transaction was fair to the corporation.

If the *members* of a Mutual Benefit Corporation are voting on a conflict of interest transaction, the approval is effective if it receives a majority of the votes entitled to be counted. In that case, all votes, even those controlled by a Director with a conflict, are entitled to be counted. See page 389 for more discussion of this.

A quorum for this vote is a majority of the members, whether or not present, that can vote on this transaction. If your Bylaws state that a quorum is the members present at a meeting, note that the quorum for the conflict vote is a higher number since it requires a majority of the voting members, whether or not present.

APPROVAL BY OUTSIDE SOURCES

Public Benefit Corporations and Religious Corporations have one additional route to obtain approval of a conflict of interest transaction. The transaction can also be approved by the Attorney General or a judge. In practice, this almost never happens.

You will also need to check your funders' regulations. Some funders, particularly federal government funders, may have prohibitions or additional restrictions on and requirements for how to handle a conflict of interest.

No Loans to Directors and Officers

If you are a *Public Benefit* or a *Religious Corporation,* your Directors and officers cannot borrow money from the corporation, except for very special circumstances involving recruitment of a Director or officer. Your corporation also cannot guarantee the loan of a Director.

> *Example*: One of your Directors has asked your public benefit corporation to co-sign on a loan so that the Director can buy a house. This is a direct conflict of interest.

A *Mutual Benefit* corporation may not lend money to a Director of the corporation unless the particular loan is approved:

- by a majority of the votes of members entitled to vote, excluding the votes of members under the control of the benefited Director; or

- the corporation's Board of Directors determines that the loan benefits the corporation and either approves the transaction or a general plan authorizing it.

Other Breaches of the Duty of Loyalty

There are a variety of other circumstances in which a Director may be in a situation of torn loyalties. The Director cannot chose his or her own interest or desires over the corporation's interest.

> *Example*: You are on the Board of a social service agency. Your Board decided to terminate your chief financial officer, over your objection. You plan to meet with the CFO to explain why you feel the termination is unfair and to urge her to consider legal action against the corporation. You will be breaching your duty of loyalty to the corporation by engaging in this action.

> *Example.* You are on the Board of a nonprofit homeowners association that is incorporated. You also sell cable television services on a commission basis. The Association has decided to market cable television services to its members and has compiled a list of members in order to begin its marketing campaign. You use that list to solicit subscribers for your company before the Association does. You have breached your duty of loyalty by putting your interests ahead of the corporation's interests.

Example: You are on the Board of Directors of a nonprofit church that is planning to build a hospice for the terminally ill. You have been personally involved in securing verbal funding commitments for your church. Shortly before the funders sign the loan documents, you break away and start your own nonprofit for the purpose of building and operating a hospice. You use your contacts with the funders to persuade them to renege on their verbal commitment to the church and to fund the new nonprofit's hospice. You have probably breached your duty of loyalty to the church by usurping this corporate opportunity.

Protecting Your Directors

If your Directors are informed about your corporation and its affairs, participate in its management and follow the corporate mission and act reasonably and loyally to the corporation, they have satisfied the requirements expected of Directors in Oregon nonprofit corporations. This is their best protection. However, situations can arise in which Directors are called to account for how they served. The law and your corporation can provide protections for your Directors and we cover this in Chapter 17.

Consult Appendix 1 if you would like information about source material related to this Chapter. Appendix 1 has references of interest to all readers, not just professionals.

In addition to attentively managing your nonprofit, your Board also needs to attend to how the Board sustains itself. The next chapter describes how the Board recruits, trains, and supports the Directors who make up the Board.

15 WHO SITS ON THE BOARD

THIS CHAPTER COVERS

- Recruiting and Retaining the Directors Your Organization Needs
- Diversity
- Staff as Directors
- Board Orientation
- Clarifying Board Expectations
- Key Board Transitions
- Replacing Directors and Officers

To manage the corporation well, the Board itself needs to function well. To function well, Boards need to be concerned with who is on the Board and how the Board operates.

Chapter 13 described what the Board does to meet its responsibility to manage the corporation and Chapter 14 explained how the Board carries out its duty to manage the corporation. In this chapter, we will talk about who should sit on your Board. Many organizations start with the "who" first and then try to mold their Directors into a workable Board. We think it is useful for your nonprofit to understand what it is that Directors do before you recruit for Directors. Part of your decision to invite a prospective Director to join your Board needs to be whether that person can perform the job of a Director. Once you have found the right people for your Board, Chapter 16 will discuss how your Board manages itself.

Recruiting and Retaining the Directors Your Organization Needs

Your Board will want to develop a process for recruiting new Directors and for supporting their involvement on the Board. Start with an honest assessment of how you've gone about finding new Directors in the past. Have you used the "warm body" method—i.e. "Are they breathing? Will they serve? Let's take them!"

Not surprisingly, there is a better way. Start with a discussion of the types of experiences, skills, and contacts your Board needs. Consider the strengths and contributions of current Directors but keep in mind that they won't serve forever (hopefully). Once you're clear about the types of qualities and experiences you're seeking, develop a list of prospects. Your best Board prospects will be people who already have some connection to your organization—volunteers, individuals active in your organization, or professionals in related fields.

> *Start with an honest assessment of how you've gone about finding new Directors in the past. Have you used the "warm body" method—i.e. "Are they breathing? Will they serve? Let's take them!"*

If you cannot find all the qualities you need from among this group of individuals already connected to your organization, work through connections to people associated with your group. Friends and colleagues of Directors may not be aware of your organization, but their respect for a Director may translate into willingness to learn about your nonprofit. You can also ask funders, donors, and Directors of similar organizations for suggestions and for personal introductions to promising candidates. Remember, for most organizations, capturing the "big fish"—the prestigious or wealthy community member—won't really help your Board if the person will lend only their name. You need Directors who can become involved, participate in decisions, and carry your message into the community.

Once you've identified good prospective Directors, have a current Director meet individually with them. Focus the conversation at this pre-invitation meeting on both the individual you are recruiting and the work of your Board. Be sure you take time to find out about the prospect's interests, time commitments, and other Board experiences. Be honest about your organization and its strengths and weaknesses. And be clear about the expectations you have of Directors. If your organization expects all Directors to help with fundraising or to make a personal contribution, let the prospective Director know. If you sense that the prospect is interested and would be a good addition to your Board, you'll want to let them know if your organization is facing some difficult choices or financial problems.

WHO SITS ON THE BOARD 15

Your Bylaws will guide the length of Directors' terms of office. Many nonprofits find it helpful to bring on new Directors in groups rather than as isolated individuals throughout the year. The group approach allows you to focus attention on orienting the new Directors and taking time to build relationships between the newcomers and the continuing Directors. You may want to consider using a buddy system in which each new Director is paired with a continuing member. Buddy systems work best when the continuing Directors are clear about their roles. In some Boards, this may include meeting the new Director buddy for coffee before the first few Board meetings or offering rides home from meetings. The goal is to provide an informal opportunity for the new Director to explore the issues and practices which puzzle them outside the context of a formal Board meeting. The buddy approach also yields useful information for placing the new Director on committees or with special projects based on their interests and enthusiasms.

> *Your best Board prospects will be people who already have some connection to your organization—volunteers, individuals active in your organization, or professionals in related fields.*

You'll want to be sure your Board leadership finds at least one specific responsibility for each new Director within the first three months of their Board service. Just assigning new Directors to committees may not achieve this goal. The new Director needs to feel that something important to the organization hinges on their effort. Even something as short-term as making a phone call or representing the organization at a meeting can help the new Director feel certain the she or he has a real role in the organization.

It seems to be human nature to take more interest in things we plan for ourselves than those already put in place by others. You can build interest and commitment in new Directors by scheduling your annual Board planning retreat shortly after the new Directors join your group. Planning retreats typically include the type of background briefing and analysis which is most useful to new members, and a well structured retreat will involve the new members in setting the Board's agenda for the year.

You may also want to structure a check-in with new Directors somewhere in the first three to six months of their Board service. The check-in should be an individual conversation with a continuing Director designed to determine the extent to which the new Director feels satisfied with their work on the Board. The check-in can provide useful insights into difficulties with the Board's structure, use of time, or openness to new members.

Beyond the issues of building involvement of new Directors, your Board may face great challenges in leadership development. One good leader isn't really enough. You'll want to be developing new leaders continually through your committee system or through special projects. Leaders are willing to look at issues in the context of the whole, willing and able to help Directors bring their best contribution to Board work, and able to set priorities for the use of Director time.

Some Board consultants tell new Board chairs that their first job as chair is to identify and cultivate their replacement. Your Board may want to develop ongoing strategies to be certain that new leaders will be available to replace current leaders. Some Boards work with the formal or informal expectation that the individual serving as vice chairperson will become chair the following year.

But many Boards are finding this approach no longer works consistently. Many good Directors find their lives so full of work, family, and community demands that they are hesitant to make commitments beyond one year. In fact, a growing number of Boards are finding members unwilling to commit to a full year of holding an office or leading a committee. If your Board is experiencing this time pressure or commitment pressure problem, you'll want to explore ways to fulfill Board responsibilities through short term, project oriented commitments.

The increasing time pressures which many Directors are experiencing heighten the importance of individual attention to the quality of each Director's experience on the Board. You may want your Executive Director or Board chair to plan an individual conversation with each continuing Director as well as each new Director at some point in each year. The conversation should provide opportunities to learn more effective ways to utilize the individual Director's time and skills.

You can build interest and commitment in new Directors by scheduling your annual Board planning retreat shortly after the new Directors join your group.

In practice, providing support for Board involvement is one of the most important responsibilities within a nonprofit organization. Some Boards meet this need through assigning explicit responsibility for Board support and development to an individual Board leader or a Board committee. Other organizations assign primary responsibility for Board support to the staff. In many organizations, the responsibility is shared, with staff providing dependable information (Board packets, briefing papers, etc.) and Board leadership providing recognition and personal appreciation.

Diversity

The most successful Boards include Directors who reflect the perspectives of multiple parts of the communities they serve. Involving Board members from diverse cultural, educational, economic, age groups, and religious backgrounds helps ensure that Board discussions and decisions reflect differing experiences and norms. Board members can play key roles in connecting your nonprofit to potential staff, volunteers, donors, and program participants from varied backgrounds.

Boards that have very little diversity among their current Board members face some significant challenges in recruiting new Board members who more fully reflect the diversity of their communities. Most of us tend to know other people like ourselves so our suggestions for potential Board members may turn out to be more of the same. This frequently leads to Boards attempting to recruit only very well known leaders from underrepresented groups. And just like the error of recruiting the "big fish" wealthy individual to the Board, recruiting an individual who already has multiple civic commitments and relatively little interest in your mission is usually a mistake.

> *The most successful Boards include Directors who reflect the perspectives of multiple parts of the communities they serve.*

No one enjoys being invited into a group as a token. It rarely works to invite someone to join your Board solely because they are a woman or because they are under 30 years old. Boards are successful in increasing the diversity of their Board members by focusing first on identifying the types of skills and relationships the Board needs and then talking with a network of individuals who care about your issue and your organization to get suggestions of individuals who fit the profile of your Board needs, including your need for individuals from diverse backgrounds.

Many Boards find that it is particularly important to have new Board members who have very different backgrounds from current Board members join the Board with others who also will be expanding the diversity of the Board. And as with all other new Board members, you'll want to pay particular attention to understanding the skills and interests of the new members in order to involve them quickly in satisfying roles.

> *Before your Board expends the effort that will be required to recruit members from diverse backgrounds, you'll want to be sure that you are prepared to actually benefit from their contributions.*

One final note on working towards your goal of building a Board that truly benefits from the diversity of its members. Research has shown repeatedly that most of us have difficulty absorbing or even hearing information that is very different from what we expect to hear. Unfortunately, this phenomenon plays out frequently in Boards that work to recruit members from different cultures or economic backgrounds and then can't seem to "hear" what the new Board members say when they raise concerns about priorities or organizational practices. Before your Board expends the effort that will be required to recruit members from diverse backgrounds, you'll want to be sure that you are prepared to actually benefit from their contributions. The Nonprofit Association of Oregon (*www.nonprofitoregon.org*) and other community resources offer trainings and other resources to help Boards prepare to succeed in becoming more fully reflective of the communities they serve.

Staff as Directors

One frequently asked question is whether staff members can also sit on the Board of Directors. The answer is that they can, with the possible exception of private foundations. (See pages 99-101 for a discussion of private foundations.) Oregon law contains no prohibition against this. However, the presence of staff on the Board can raise a number of problems—internal problems with conflicts of interest, IRS concerns about excess benefits, wage and hour issues, and unfavorable responses from funders.

Staff members who sit on the Board will find themselves in situations in which the staff member will have a conflict of interest. Whenever the Board votes on the salary or on other conditions of employment for that staff member, the Board must observe the rules for conflicts covered on pages 299-303. The Board must be very careful to document that the compensation paid to that staff member is reasonable. State law requires this. In addition, your Board member who is paid as staff may lose the protection from personal liability offered to volunteer Directors under federal and state law. (See page 359.)

> *The presence of staff on the Board can raise a number of problems: internal problems with conflicts of interest, IRS concerns about excess benefits, wage and hour issues, and unfavorable responses from funders.*

If the organization is exempt as a public charity under §501(c)(3) or under §501(c)(4), the IRS will view your employment of a Board member as an excess benefits transaction. This is an area of great concern to the IRS. If you fail to follow the excess benefit rules, you risk having both the staff member who is a Director and the Directors and managers who approved the staff member's salary and benefits be personally subjected to severe taxes. See pages 700-706 for more information about this important topic.

The wage and hour laws contain some restrictions on voluntary overtime by hourly (non-exempt) employees. (See page 395.) The drafters of the law were concerned that employers could put unfair pressure on workers to work extra hours without pay. Consequently, the law restricts the right of employers to avoid paying workers for what either party characterizes as volunteer work. This part of the law applies to those workers who are labelled as non-exempt. Generally these are non-managerial hourly employees and the prohibition covers work that they perform that covers the same function for which they are also paid. In most instances, Board service will be completely distinct from a non-exempt employee's paid duties and will not fall under the wage and hour restraint. However, if that employee does end up performing tasks for the Board that are similar to those he or she perform as an employee, you need to take notice. For example, if a staff member who is an Administrative Assistant paid to perform word processing duties sits on the Board and takes on word processing tasks for the Board, such as reformatting the Board manual, you may have problems. If your nonprofit would like non-exempt employees to serve on the Board, you may want to review the specifics of your situation with your attorney.

Board members who are also managerial employees of the organization do not have wage and hour issues. They may not want to consider time spent at Board meetings or on Board activities as work time. Instead, they are volunteering their time as Board members. Treating their Board service as unpaid allows them the protection against liability offered to volunteer Board members.

Many funders also frown on the practice of having staff members sit on the Board and may refuse to fund you if a substantial portion of your Directors are also paid staff.

Board Orientation

Once you have located individuals to serve on your Board and they have consented, you are well advised to offer a Board orientation so that your new Board members understand what their role as a Board member is in your organization.

One avenue that many corporations use to educate their Board is to provide a Board orientation manual that is given to each new Director. The manual may contain:

- a copy of the Articles of Incorporation and any amendments;
- the current Bylaws;
- the Board's policy manual (see p. 350) or a copy of all the Board's policies;
- a brief background on the corporation, its mission, its programs and activities, and on the Board's culture;
- the current year budget;
- the most recent financial statements;
- the most recent independent audit;
- a summary of the duties of the Board;
- a listing of the Board's committees and who currently serves on them;
- a flowchart showing the organization's structure;
- a phone list of the names and address of all the Directors and any individuals (e.g., the Executive Director, the Controller) the Board may need to reach.

Many organizations also give their Directors a copy of Part III in this book or variations of Part III to help them understand their duties. Please visit the website of co-author Cindy Cumfer at *www.cumfer.net* or co-author Kay Sohl at *www.kaysohlconsulting.net* for more information.

As described above, some Boards continue the orientation by assigning new Directors a mentor or buddy, someone who has served on the Board for awhile, to answer any questions and to check in with the new Director from time to time to see how they are doing. Diverse Boards find it very helpful to provide mentoring and social opportunities to allow Board members from differing backgrounds to get to know each other and to understand Board expectations, informal processes, and culture.

Clarifying Board Expectations

We've talked about some of the key distinctions between Boards that decide to provide direct management and those that choose to use delegated management. Within each of these frameworks, Boards adopt different approaches to working together effectively. Many Boards find that their decision about using direct management or delegated management shifts over time as they obtain more resources and undertake more complex program, management, and fund raising responsibilities. And even when Boards decide to stick with either direct or delegated management, the ways they work together and the expectations of Board members may shift as the needs of the organization and the time availability of Board members changes.

In order to deal effectively with all of these changes, your Board may need to set aside time periodically—at least every two years—to focus attention on how Directors perceive the Board's role, and identify the structures and decision making processes which will help them work together effectively to fulfill their responsibilities. Because most Boards find that regular Board meetings are filled with ongoing business, special Board planning retreats may be needed to focus on the Board's roles and responsibilities. Your Board may want to consider asking a professional facilitator to help you plan and conduct your Board planning retreat to be sure all Directors are encouraged to participate actively.

> *In order to deal effectively with all of these changes, your Board may need to set aside time periodically—at least every two years—to focus attention on how Directors perceive the Board's role, and identify the structures and decision making processes which will help them work together effectively to fulfill their responsibilities.*

While Oregon law and your Bylaws provide the basic framework for both the Board and corporate officers, each Board must choose its own way of conducting business. Directors need to reach agreement about the extent to which they will rely on committee work or address all items in committee reports for further discussion by the whole Board.

You'll also want to make explicit your Board's expectations of individual Directors. Are all Directors expected to serve on a committee, to help raise funds, or to contribute financially? Boards may change their expectations of Directors over time. Whatever your current expectations, you'll want to be sure that they are communicated clearly to prospective Directors. Remember, not all Boards are alike. Prospects for your Board may assume its expectations are the same as those of other Boards on which they have served unless you give them specific information about your Board's expectations.

You will also need to clarify your expectations about the type of leadership your Board chair and committee chairs will provide. Do you want your leaders to see their roles as primarily facilitation, seeing that all are heard and consensus is reached? Or do you expect leaders to exert control, and take special responsibility for setting directions? Like all the choices we've described, your Board's answers to these questions may change over time. Most importantly, a variety of approaches can work, as long as all Directors understand the expectations and you are careful to match expectations to your organization's values and stage of development.

Key Board Transitions

The role of the Board in start-up nonprofits is usually quite different than that of the Board of a well established nonprofits. Community-based organizations that start out through the grassroots efforts of individuals with concerns about a local need are quite different from those that are set up to assume responsibilities that were previously held by government or large nonprofit institutions. Nonprofits that began as community-based organizations and begin to grow and smaller nonprofits that are "spun off" of larger nonprofits or by the government face some key transitions as they find themselves changing.

Board Transitions for Community-Based Nonprofits

Many community based groups operate for months or years with no paid staff. Directors use the direct management approach, dividing up responsibilities for the program, management, and fundraising activities, as well as assuming the Board governance responsibilities discussed earlier in this chapter.

During this all volunteer or almost all volunteer period, Directors often have little awareness of the distinction between their governance role as Directors and the management roles they have assumed. In fact, time may be spent at Board meetings working out the details of volunteer projects rather than focusing on strategic planning, financial management, or other Board oversight roles. Expectations of individual Directors may include a mixture of Board legal responsibilities and volunteer duties, like answering the phone or taking tickets at events.

A key transition for these groups occurs when the Board decides that the organization can be much more effective if it hires paid staff. This decision may reflect plans for more activity than can be sustained by Board members and other volunteers, need for greater skills, or simply a sense of exhaustion by Board members trying to keep the organization together while working and caring for their families. In many groups, the decision to have paid staff is prompted by one of the founders deciding that she or he would rather work for the organization than in their current job.

The transition from being a direct management Board to delegating management to paid staff or specific individual volunteers is challenging. While the Board may initially perceive the change as reducing their responsibilities, in fact, the Board has traded direct management responsibilities for some new responsibilities. First, there is the commitment to pay for work done and to comply with employment law and payroll tax regulations. Next, there is the need to make responsible choices about the selection of staff, provide ongoing supervision, and evaluate the executive Director. Exercising due care in the selection and supervision of the Executive Director may be particularly challenging when the first staff are individuals who were part of the founding volunteer group. Directors may be uncomfortable shifting from being peers to being supervisors.

> *The transition from being a direct management Board to delegating management to paid staff or specific individual volunteers is challenging.*

The person accepting the first paid position in an all-volunteer organization confronts challenges as well. Will the Board members and other volunteers slip away—reassuring themselves that now paid staff is available to do all the tasks formerly performed by volunteers? Will very active volunteers resent the fact that one person is being paid for work that others are doing for free?

One of the great challenges for these Boards is to let go of some of the day to day decision making to allow the staff the flexibility they need to do their jobs effectively. Without paid staff, Directors have probably made every decision—from major choices about priorities for the year to selection of stationary and organization of the filing system. Now Board energy must be focused on direction setting and oversight, and responsibility for management shifted to staff.

Many nonprofits are committed to remaining community based after the start-up period. The term "community based" generally describes a Board composed of individuals with direct knowledge of the issues the nonprofit addresses. For example, in most cases, a third or more of the Directors of community development corporations, which develop and manage affordable housing in low income communities, reside in the low income community they serve. Or, a battered women's program may decide that more than half of its Board should be composed of individuals who have experienced domestic violence or worked closely with victims.

Community based Boards face particular challenges around differences in experience, education, and access to resources. Typically, as the organization develops and expands the range of its activities, new Directors are recruited who have particular professional skills or experiences—accountants, attorneys, human resource managers, etc. These Directors can make important contributions, not only to the Board's understanding of increasingly complex issues, but also in connecting the organization to the larger community.

However, if some Directors have little formal education or professional expertise or discretionary income, they may feel intimidated by those Directors who do. Yet, these community members have great expertise about the experiences, values, and needs of their community. These Boards will need to work actively to be sure the expertise of all Directors is brought to bear on the issues the Board confronts.

Community based Boards frequently struggle with differing Board expectations and preferences for Board style and meeting format. For some members, the Board provides an important opportunity for networking and socializing, and an informal, relaxed approach to Board meetings is preferred. For others, particularly those with intense business and family commitments, a more focused, brief, and business-like format for Board meetings is preferred.

Board Transitions for Institutional Spin-off Nonprofits

Not all nonprofits are created through the grassroots process described above. Some nonprofits begin life as spin-offs from larger nonprofits or are created by government or by coalitions of government and civic groups to meet specific community needs.

Nonprofits which are formed in response to institutional decisions like these almost always utilize Board delegated management and begin life with paid staff. The process which leads to the creation of these nonprofits usually includes obtaining start-up funding which will support at least one paid position.

Board members are recruited as part of the start-up process. In many cases, few of the Directors know each other before being asked to serve. Some may know a great deal about the subject area the organization will address but very little about nonprofit corporations or the role of Boards. For these groups, the start-up process will require a great deal of attention to building Board relationships and understanding of the issues the organization will address.

One of the great challenges for these organization is building Board ownership. Directors frequently report they feel like spectators—listening to the interesting ideas presented by the planners for the organization and its initial staff, but not really prepared to provide leadership.

Typically, the institutionally based Board is composed of individuals with professional expertise and social, economic, and political contacts which can benefit the organization. Directors may be motivated to serve by factors outside the organization's work—general community service, opportunity for business or political contacts, community recognition, etc.

Ironically, institutionally based Boards often struggle to achieve the diversity of members which characterizes community based Boards. Many of the institutionally based nonprofits are designed to address the needs of specific populations or communities. Directors recognize that the perspective of members of the target community is really important for priority setting and evaluation of the work of the organization. So, institutionally based Boards actively recruit Directors who can reflect the diversity of income, culture and values of the communities they serve.

The typical Director for these nonprofits is an extremely busy business or community leader with extensive business and family responsibilities. These Directors perceive their time as very valuable and expect staff to manage the affairs of the corporation and to provide concise briefings to the Board on all key decision items. The mix of these Directors and Directors who reflect the community the organization serves can create challenges. Finding a meeting format and communication style that meets the needs of all Directors will require open discussion among Board members and willingness to try new strategies to engage the full Board.

Replacing Directors and Officers

Every nonprofit corporation needs to plan for transitions in the Board of Directors. Your Board will change when terms of office expire, when the Board expands to take on new Directors, when a Director dies, resigns, or otherwise vacates an office, or when your Board removes a Director. You should, as much as possible, anticipate and plan for these occurrences. Although most Directors of nonprofit corporations are elected, some are appointed or designated (see page 21). The manner in which a Director took office will affect how she or he is replaced.

You should consult your Articles of Incorporation and Bylaws to see if your corporation has addressed these issues. If your Articles or Bylaws have these provisions, check them against the rules below to be sure your Articles and Bylaws are legal. If your Articles and Bylaws do not address the election of Directors and officers, the filling of vacancies, and the removal of Directors and officers, you should amend your Bylaws to include these provisions. It is very important that the corporation be clear about how these matters are handled.

Expiration of Terms of Office of Directors

Your Bylaws (or possibly your Articles) should contain provisions for replacing Directors whose terms have expired. Your terms for *elected* Directors cannot exceed five years although the Director may be re-elected for an indefinite number of terms. *Designated* and *appointed* Directors can serve for terms of any length. Many groups provide for staggered expiration dates so that the Board has continuity in its membership.

Resignation of Directors

A Director may resign at any time by delivering written notice to the Board of Directors, its presiding officer, or to the President or Secretary. The resignation is effective when the notice is effective as described on pages 685-86 unless the notice specifies a later effective date. Once it is delivered, the notice of resignation cannot be revoked unless the Board of Directors permits it to be revoked.

Removal of Directors

The decision to remove a Director is not an easy one. Your Board should consider whether removal is the best option for dealing with a problem involving a Board member. Removal of a Director may damage your organization's reputation, alienate funders, participants, or volunteers, or create distress for the Board members who remain. Your Board may want to discuss working with a facilitator or consultant to see if there are other strategies that can be used to resolve the problem without taking on the risks associated with removal of a Director.

> *Your Board will want to consider whether removal is the best option for dealing with a problem involving a Board member.*

If after exploring alternative strategies to resolve the underlying problems your Board concludes that removal of a Director is necessary, your Board should exercise great care to identify and follow the correct procedure for removal. To determine what your procedure is for removal, you need to look at whether your Articles or Bylaws provide for removal with or without cause or require that there be cause for removal; whether you are removing an elected, designated, or appointed Director; and whether you are a nonmembership or membership corporation.

Removal with or without cause means that your Board does not have to establish a reason for removing its Directors. This may seem harsh to some, but from the point of view of the corporation it is generally the preferred method. Correctly describing what constitutes cause in your Articles or Bylaws can be tricky and organizations often find out too late that they did not cover all the bases they would like to have covered. Proving cause can also be very difficult. An unhappy ex-Director may take you to court and require that you prove cause in exactly the way it was written in your Articles or Bylaws (quite possibly by a Board 15 years ago). To avoid this kind of fight, you may prefer to permit removal without requiring yourself to prove cause. As you will see below, if your Articles or Bylaws provide for removal of a Director with or without cause, you must have a large vote for removal. For most corporations, this provision should be enough to protect its Directors from casual removal by the Board.

> *Removal with or without cause may seem harsh to some, but from the point of view of the corporation it is generally the preferred method.*

If your corporation is a Religious Corporation, your Articles or Bylaws may use *any* procedure to remove a Director, and you are only bound by the rules in this section if your Articles and Bylaws do not set out a different procedure.

Removal of Directors Elected by Directors

A Director elected by your Board may be removed with or without cause, unless your Articles or Bylaws provide that your Directors can only be removed for cause. If removal is with or without cause, it requires a vote of *two-thirds* of the Directors *then in office*.

If, at the beginning of a Director's term on the Board, the Articles or Bylaws provide that the Director may be removed for reasons specified in the Articles or Bylaws, the Board may remove the Director only for such reasons. A vote of the majority of Directors *then in office* is required.

If your corporation is a religious corporation (see p. 28-29), you can disregard the rules in this section if you do so in one of your governance documents. Your Articles and Bylaws can provide the vote and procedures by which the Board or any person may remove a Director, with or without cause, who was elected by the Board.

If removal of a Director by the Board is with or without cause, it requires a vote of two-thirds of the Directors then in office.

Removal of Directors Elected by Members

If your Director was elected by the members, s/he must be removed by the members. Taking a vote of the members on removal of a Director is likely to be extremely stressful for your organization. Your Board will want to have gotten help resolving the underlying problem with the Board member and using the process for removal by the members only in situations for which there appears to be no other remedy.

If your membership corporation has decided on removal, in most cases your members do not have to have a reason (cause) to remove a Director. A Director may be removed by the members with or without cause unless the Articles of Incorporation provide that a Director may only be removed for cause. Note that a requirement that your members must have cause to remove your Directors in your Bylaws is not enough; it must be in your Articles. Whether or not you need cause, your Director may be removed only if the number of votes cast to remove her or him would be sufficient to elect the Director at a meeting to elect Directors. If your organization is a complex membership organization (see Chapter 18), consult pages 383-84 for rules on removal of your Directors. A Director elected by your Board to fill the vacancy of a Director elected by the members may be removed by members but not the Board.

If your corporation is a Religious Corporation (see pp. 28-29), you can disregard the rules in this section if you do so in one of your governance documents. Your Articles or Bylaws can provide the vote and procedures by which the Board or any person may remove a Director, with or without cause, who was elected by the members.

Removal of Designated or Appointed Directors

A designated Director may be removed by an amendment to the Articles or Bylaws deleting or changing the designation. An appointed Director may be removed with or without cause by the person appointing the Director. The person removing the Director must give written notice of the removal to the Director and either the presiding officer of the Board or the corporation's President or Secretary. The removal is effective when the notice is effective, as described on pages 685-86, unless the notice specifies a later effective date.

Automatic Removal of Directors for Nonattendance at Meetings

Some Bylaws provide that a Director is automatically removed from the Board if the Director misses a certain number of meetings. You should consider carefully such a provision. Many groups who have the provision fail to monitor it and Directors who missed too many meetings continue to sit on the Board and vote. This creates an issue, since their votes may not be valid.

Automatic removals also create problems if your Bylaws have a provision that allows you to remove Directors with or without cause. A provision for automatic removal undercuts the rationale that the Board can remove someone without cause. These clauses also conflict with the rules described above governing how designated and appointed Directors are removed.

There are better solutions to the problem of Directors who miss meetings. A Board officer should talk informally to the Director to determine what the issue is. Many Directors will simply resign. If not, and the Board decides it doesn't want the Director to continue, it can remove the Director or speak to the person who appointed the Director.

Vacancy on the Board

If a vacancy occurs on the Board of Directors (including a vacancy that results from an increase in the number of Directors), it may be filled in one of several ways:

- Your members entitled to vote for Directors, if any, may fill the vacancy;
- Your Board of Directors may fill the vacancy; *or*
- If the Directors remaining in office constitute fewer than a quorum of the Board, they may fill the vacancy by a majority vote of all the Directors remaining in office.

There are two exceptions:

- If a vacant office was held by an *appointed* Director, only the person who appointed the Director may fill the vacancy, unless your Articles and Bylaws provide otherwise.
- If the vacant office was held by a *designated* Director, the vacancy must be filled as provided in the Articles or Bylaws. If the Articles or Bylaws do not provide for how to fill the vacancy, the vacancy may *not* be filled by the Board.

Your Articles or Bylaws may provide some other way to fill vacancies.

Resignation and Removal of Officers

An officer may resign at any time by delivering notice to the corporation. The resignation is effective as described on pages 685-86, unless the notice specifies a later effective date. If the resignation specifies a later effective date and the corporation accepts that date, your Board or any other person authorized by the Articles or Bylaws may fill the pending vacancy before the effective date if the Board or such other authorized person provides that the successor does not take office until the effective date. Once it is delivered, a notice of resignation cannot be revoked unless revocation is permitted by the Board.

Your Board or any other person authorized to do so by the Articles or Bylaws may remove any officer at any time with or without cause.

Conclusion

Your Board can provide the deep community roots necessary for your organization to grow strong and serve the community effectively. Just as allowing roots to dry out or be severed will eventually damage the tree, allowing Board interest to wither and Board connections to be severed will weaken your organization. Time devoted to Board cultivation, support, and evaluation can build the strong roots your organization needs to achieve its mission an sustain its efforts.

Consult Appendix 1 if you would like information about source material related to this Chapter.

Now that you've found the right people for your Board, the next chapter helps your Board think about how your Board can structure its operations so that it makes the best use of the time and talents of its Directors.

16 HOW THE BOARD MANAGES ITSELF

THIS CHAPTER COVERS

- Board Meetings and Decision-Making
- Board Committees
- Board Officers
- Board Policies
- Evaluating the Effectiveness of Your Board
- Perpetuating Institutional Memory

Chapter 15 explored strategies boards use to find and train good Board members. Once the Board has recruited great people, it then needs to figure out the best ways to function as a Board.

To manage the corporation well, the Board itself needs to function well. To function well, Board members will need to reach clear agreements about how to:

- make and document valid decisions;
- use committee and other structures to work effectively and make the best use of every Board member's time and expertise;
- develop and adopt clear governance and management policies;
- evaluate its performance; and
- pass on its wisdom to future Boards.

This chapter first presents the legal requirements for holding Board meetings, taking board action, and recording Board decisions. But simply meeting legal requirements does not guarantee that your Board will be effective. The chapter also provides practical strategies to help your Board to organize meetings, make good use of committees, and work together to provide effective leadership and oversight for your nonprofit.

Board Meetings and Decision-Making

The primary site of Board decision-making is the Board meeting. Because Boards make most of their decisions at meetings, it is vital that Boards ensure that their meetings and the decision-making process at meetings are legal. Boards need to carefully follow the rules for calling a Board meeting, for running a valid meeting and for proper voting. The time that most Boards have for meetings is limited, so it is also important that Boards get the most out of their meeting time.

Why Have Meetings?

Many of us don't like meetings, so why have them? The answer may seem obvious, but it is worth reflecting on. A nonprofit corporation is a legal entity. It is run by people, almost always in the plural. The people who run it need a mechanism for making decisions. One possible model would be a dictatorship model, in which one person makes all the decisions. However, the model required by law is a more democratic model, in which a group of people, commonly a Board of Directors, makes decisions, with each person on the Board having one vote.

> *The democratic model envisions that the Board makes its decisions in a setting in which each member has a chance to be heard, if there is any dissent on an issue.*

The democratic model envisions that the Board makes its decisions in a setting in which each member is aware of the meeting, understands the issues the Board is dealing with, and has a chance to be heard if there is any dissent on or questions about an issue. This requires that meetings take place in an environment in which each Director can simultaneously communicate with and respond to each other. Only if there were no dissent and no questions would a meeting be unnecessary.

The rules discussed below are what the law generally requires for Board meetings. However, it is possible that your Articles of Incorporation or your Bylaws provide for different practices. If so, you should follow your Articles or Bylaws if the provisions are legal. In order to determine if your provisions are legal, compare your Bylaws with and read the sections that apply to you in Chapter 4.

In some cases, your Board can make decisions without a meeting. In these situations, 100% of the Board members must be in agreement on the action and so there is no need for discussion or a meeting. We'll discuss the requirements for taking action without a meeting, including requirements for using email, after we've covered the legal framework for holding meetings and key strategies to be sure meetings work well.

HOW THE BOARD MANAGES ITSELF 16

Types of Meetings

Regular Meetings

Oregon recognizes several types of Board meetings: *regular, special,* and *emergency.* A regular meeting is one in which the date, time, and place is fixed by the Articles or Bylaws or one that is regularly scheduled by the Board. For example, a regular meeting would be a meeting set on the first Monday of every month at 7:00 p.m. Your Board is not required to have regular meetings. As a matter of convenience, most Boards will schedule regular meetings, because this makes planning easier for the Directors and because the requirements about notice are easier.

The Board can hold regular meetings without giving notice of the meeting, unless your Articles or Bylaw require differently.

The Board can hold regular meetings without giving notice of the meeting, unless your Articles or Bylaw require differently. In some special circumstances, the law requires notice—for example, when the Board is voting on amendments to the Articles or Bylaws (Chapter 31), on mergers (Chapter 32), and on dissolution (Chapter 33).

Special Meetings

Special Board meetings are all Board meetings that are not regular or emergency meetings. Special meetings must be preceded by at least two days notice to each Director of the date, time, and place of the meeting. In some cases, the notice must include the purpose of the meeting. Your Articles or Bylaws may change these requirements, so check them.

Emergency Meetings

Oregon law also makes provision for emergency meetings. An emergency exists if a quorum of your corporation's Directors cannot readily be assembled because of some present or imminent catastrophic event (like an earthquake or a zombie attack). In the case of an emergency, your Board or the corporation has the power to modify lines of succession to accommodate the incapacity of any Director, officer, employee, or agent. Unless you have emergency Bylaws that provide otherwise, one or more of your officers present at the meeting of the Board shall be deemed to be Directors for the purposes of the meeting in order of the officers' ranks as necessary to achieve a quorum. Of course, if your officers are already Directors, this provision does not apply to you.

In the case of an emergency meeting, you are only required to give notice to those Directors whom it is practical to reach. You may give notice in any practical manner, including telephone calls, publication in a newspaper, radio announcements, or other public manner.

Annual Meetings

Oregon law does not require that nonprofit corporations hold annual Board meetings. Most Oregon nonprofit Boards do not hold specially-designated annual meetings, although they will generally have a particular meeting at which Board members are elected. In some organizations, the Bylaws require a specially-designated annual meeting that often requires special notice. This is usually the meeting at which the Board elects new Board members.

Oregon law does not require that nonprofit corporations hold annual Board meetings.

While Oregon law does not require nonprofit corporations to hold a specially-designated annual meeting for their Boards, it does require membership corporations to hold an annual meeting for their members (not their Boards) so that the members can elect their Boards. See p. 377.

Before the Meeting

Calling a Meeting

In most corporations, the Board agrees on a regular meeting schedule. If there is a need for a special meeting, the President calls the meeting. Oregon law allows the presiding officer of your Board, your President or 20% of your Directors then in office to call and give notice of a Board meeting. Your Articles or Bylaws may provide for a different means for calling a meeting.

In order to hold a valid meeting, you must give your Directors proper notice.

Frequency

Your Board is required to meet as often as necessary in order to run your corporation. In practice, this varies widely depending on the size and complexity of what you do and on whether your Board has an active Executive Committee that allows the Board to meet less frequently. You are not required to have any particular number of Board meetings. Some smaller groups with very little in the way of ongoing activity may have Boards that meet only three or four times a year. Some larger organizations whose Board members have many other commitments also meet several times a year but have Executive Committees that meet monthly. Most groups have monthly Board meetings. It is hard to imagine a group in which the Board would meet less than once a year.

Notice

In order to hold a valid Board meeting, you must give your Directors proper notice. If you fail to do this, the actions you agree upon at a meeting may not be valid. Pages 63 and 80-81 describe the rules for regular meetings and pages 63-64 and 81 describe the rules for special meetings. The rules are the same for membership and nonmembership corporations. More detailed rules about notice are on pages 685-86. In some situations noted throughout this book, you must give notice of the purpose of the meeting.

Waiver of Notice

Your Director can at any time give up (waive) his/her right to any notice of meeting. If your Director is not present at the meeting, the waiver must be in writing, must be signed by the Director entitled to the notice, must specify the meeting for which notice is waived, and must be filed with the minutes or corporate records. See the "Waiver of Notice of Meeting of the Board of Directors" in the Forms section. If your Director attends the meeting, she or he waives notice of it, unless at the beginning of the meeting, or promptly upon arrival, s/he objects to holding the meeting or transacting business and after that doesn't vote for or agree to any action taken at the meeting.

At the Meeting

Who Attends Board Meetings

Each member of your Board of Directors must attend Board meetings on a regular enough basis to be able to effectively govern the corporation. As we discussed in Chapter 13, when a person agrees to serve on a Board, he or she has agreed to take on the responsibilities of governance of the corporation. All Directors must be allowed to attend Board meetings, except as they are excluded for conflicts of interest.

> *Each member of your Board of Directors must attend Board meetings on a regular enough basis to be able to effectively govern the corporation.*

Generally, the law does not require Board meetings to be open to the public or to members of the corporation. Occasionally a government funder may require or encourage open meetings in community based organizations. If there is no legal or funder requirement, your Board can decide if anyone other than Board members can attend the Board meetings. In corporations with an Executive Director, your Board is going to want the Executive Director there to keep you up-to-date on the affairs of the corporation, participate in the discussion of key issues, and understand fully the decisions of the Board. Your Board can choose to exclude the Executive Director (unless the Executive Director is also a Board member) if you wish, but you will want think very carefully before doing this because it will generally make it much more difficult for your Board to get the management information you need and to work together effectively. Your Board should go into executive session without the Executive Director in order to discuss your Executive Director's performance and/or compensation.

If your Articles or Bylaws state that the Board meetings are open, then you must hold open meetings. Although the practice of holding open meetings is often admirable, we caution organizations about including these provisions in your Articles or Bylaws. While most Bylaws will spell out exceptions to their open meeting requirements, the exceptions are often too narrow and preclude flexibility in an unexpected situation where confidentiality is important. Types of discussions that require confidentiality include employee issues; medical issues of a Board member, a staff person or a client; situations in which litigation is a possibility; difficulties with a problematic member; meetings with an attorney; donor confidentiality, and a discussion of funding sources not known to competitors. Boards occasionally find themselves involved with issues where the Directors need to have a private or confidential discussion and are stopped from doing so by an open meeting provision in their Bylaws.

> *Most Oregon nonprofit corporations are not subject to the Open Meeting Law. However, if your organization exercises sufficient governmental functions, the Open Meeting Law may apply to you.*

If your Board does want to hold open meetings, it can establish this as a Board policy, not a Bylaw provision. This allows the Board to create an exception when it needs to, without going through the formal amendment process required to amend a Bylaw. Alternatively, if the Board is committed to keeping the provision in the Bylaws, be sure to draft the clause broadly enough that the Board can hold executive sessions if an unexpected situation arises. In most cases you will want to avoid requiring compliance with Oregon's Open Meeting Law, which is discussed below. Avoiding this requirement will allow your board to define for itself the degree to which its meets will be open and to establish its own criteria for making exceptions to the general policy of open meetings.

In a few cases, there is some question about whether the Board meetings of Oregon nonprofit corporations are subject to Oregon's Open Meeting Law (also called Public Meeting Laws). The Open Meeting Law requires that all meetings of governing bodies of a *public body* shall be open to the public, with certain exceptions. The law also requires that certain public notice be given and that minutes be kept and made available to the public. Most Oregon nonprofit corporations are not subject to the Open Meeting Law. However, if your organization exercises sufficient governmental functions, the Open Meeting Law may apply to you. See pages 29-31 for a further discussion on this. You should get legal advice if you think that the Open Meeting Law might apply to your nonprofit.

The Location of the Meeting

Board meetings must be held in a venue in which all Board members can communicate with each other simultaneously. Most meetings are held in one location with everyone coming together in person. Unless your Articles or Bylaws prohibit it, you can also hold meetings by telephone conference, by Skype or similar technology, or in a computer chat room-type setting in which everyone can communicate simultaneously. If you meet by teleconference or computer, your Chair should begin the meeting by informing everyone that a meeting is taking place in which official business may be transacted and that Directors participated are considered to be present in person at the meeting.

Conducting the Meeting

QUORUM

Whether you are meeting in person, by teleconference, or by computer, the law requires that a certain number of your Directors be present at a meeting in order for you to conduct business and make decisions. The minimum necessary number is called a quorum. This requirement guards against the corporation taking action based on the desires of a very few Directors at a poorly-attended meeting.

Oregon law allows you to set your own quorum in your Articles or Bylaws but requires that the quorum be at least one-third of the number of Directors. If you fail to set a quorum in your Articles or Bylaws, the law sets the quorum for you as the *majority* (not the possible minimum of one-third) of the number of Directors.

> *The law requires that a certain number of your Directors be present at a meeting in order for you to make decisions. The minimum necessary number is called a quorum.*

In order to calculate your quorum, you first need to determine if your corporation has a fixed or variable number of Directors. Consult your Bylaws to see whether the Bylaws state a flat number for the number of Directors (for example, "this corporation will have 8 Directors") or if the Bylaws allow you to have a number of Directors within a certain range (for example, 3 - 15 Directors). Quorums are easy to calculate in Boards with a fixed number of Directors. Use the number of Directors stated in your Bylaws to calculate the quorum, even if there are vacancies on the Board.

If you have a variable size Board (e.g., between 3 and 15 Directors), the quorum calculation is more complicated because the Bylaws do not state how many Directors you are supposed to have. Corporations with variable-size Boards can set the number of Directors in one of two ways. Most Boards simply add and subtract Directors as they wish within the range set in the Bylaws without the Board setting a particular number as the number of Directors the Board will have (the willy nilly or winging it method). For these Boards, the minimum quorum is computed using the number of Directors in office immediately before the meeting begins.

Some Boards do make a decision to "prescribe" a particular number of Directors within the range allowed. For example, a Board with a range of 3 - 15 Directors might make a decision that "prescribes" the number of Directors to be 11. For these Boards, the quorum is calculated using the number of 11 Directors, even if there are only 9 Directors in office at the time of the meeting because of vacancies. Because this latter method is likely to be misleading to most Boards when they make a quorum count, we recommend that your Board consider very carefully whether prescribing the number of Directors on a variable range Board is a good idea. The willy nilly method is more intuitive for most people.

In order to calculate your quorum, you first need to determine if your corporation has a fixed or variable number of Directors.

NO ACTION WITHOUT A QUORUM

There is a common misconception that your Board can take action without a quorum if no one calls for a quorum count or challenges the absence of a quorum. This is not true. Those present can have discussions, if they want, but the only decision that the Board can make without a quorum is to adjourn the meeting for another time. Any other decisions that the Board purports to make are not valid. The Board may ratify such decisions at a future meeting called with proper notice at which a quorum is present, but the decision is not valid until it is ratified at the future meeting.

COUNTING PROXIES TOWARD THE QUORUM

Another common misconception is that your Board can create a quorum if an absent member has provided a proxy so that the meeting can be held. Proxy voting occurs when someone with the right to vote cannot attend a meeting and wants to give someone else the authority to attend and to vote in their place. A proxy is not a present member whose mind can be changed by the discussion. There is no provision in Oregon law that a proxy can apply toward the quorum count.

DOING BUSINESS LEGALLY

Once you have a meeting with a quorum, you can do business. Check your Articles, Bylaws, and Board resolutions to see if there is anything governing how you conduct your meetings.

If your Articles and Bylaws do not specify how to run your meetings, you have a great deal of flexibility about how you conduct your meetings. Generally, the President of the Board presides at Board meetings but your Board can choose another chair as long as the Bylaws do not provide otherwise. In most larger nonprofits, the agenda was compiled by the President or an Executive Committee and sent to the Directors before the meeting. Smaller groups may create an agenda at the meeting. Many groups begin by creating, modifying, and approving the agenda for the meeting. Agendas commonly include correcting and approving the Board minutes of the last meeting (which have been circulated prior to the meeting so that the Board has had an opportunity to read them), making announcements, hearing committee reports, passing consent items, and handling old and new business.

Unless your Articles or Bylaws provide for a decision-making process, your Board has quite a bit of discretion about the process you use to decide issues. You are not bound to make motions and

HOW THE BOARD MANAGES ITSELF

second them but can certainly use that procedure if you prefer. The important thing is to be sure that, no matter what procedure you use, your Directors understand exactly what they are voting on and the decision needs to be clearly stated in the minutes. It is a good idea for the Secretary to read the action being voted on before the vote to be sure that everyone understands what is on the table.

The law requires a majority vote of the number of Directors at the meeting in order to take action, unless your Articles or Bylaws require a greater vote. *Note that this is not a majority of Directors voting, but a majority of Directors present.* There are some types of actions that require a greater vote than a majority vote—for example, to remove a Director from office in a nonmembership corporation, to amend your Articles, to merge, to dissolve, etc. See pages 317-18, 713-14, 739, and 749 for a discussion of these types of actions. If you are a Director that objects to an act of the Board, you must promptly enter the objection. You should check to be sure that the minutes accurately reflect your name and the nature of your objection.

> *The important thing is to be sure that, no matter what procedure you use, your Directors understand exactly what they are voting on and the decision needs to be clearly stated in the minutes.*

If your Board is finding that its meeting process is unsatisfactory or ineffective, review the discussion below on holding effective meetings for some tips that may help.

ROBERT'S RULES OF ORDER

Some Bylaws require that you follow *Robert's Rules of Order*. If your Bylaws require this, you must familiarize yourself with *Robert's Rules* and follow them or amend your Bylaws to eliminate this requirement. There are some real problems with using *Robert's Rules*. There are many editions and many publishers of *Robert's Rules*. You'll need to specify which one you are using. Most editions are several hundred pages long. If the Bylaws specify using them, then you must follow *Robert's Rules* and will probably need a parliamentarian who is familiar with *Robert's Rules* to interpret them for you. *Robert's Rules* can be useful for large membership organizations with many people who want to be heard in sometimes contentious settings but can be burdensome and intimidating in smaller nonprofit Board meetings where most people are only familiar with a few of the practices.

> *We suggest that nonprofit Boards whose Bylaws require Robert's Rules consider removing this as a requirement for your corporation.*

We suggest that nonprofit Boards whose Bylaws require *Robert's Rules* consider removing this as a requirement for your corporation. If you really want to use them, have the Board adopt a policy that recognizes them as the mode by which you will try to conduct your meetings, so that you have flexibility about using them.

VOTING BY PROXY

Occasionally, a Director who cannot attend a meeting seeks to vote by proxy—that is, to allow someone else to attend the meeting and vote for them. Although members of a nonprofit can vote by proxy at a membership meeting (see page 380), there is no provision in Oregon law that permits a Director to vote by proxy at a Board meeting. It is probable that an Oregon court would not uphold this type of voting in a Board meeting. If the court allowed proxy voting, this would mean that dissenters at the meeting would not have the ability to influence the Director who gave the proxy.

There is no provision in Oregon law that permits a Director to vote outside of a meeting by proxy, ballot, telephone poll, or email.

VOTING BY BALLOT, TELEPHONE POLL OR EMAIL

Oregon law does not authorize the Board of Directors to vote outside of a meeting other than by using the consent procedure discussed below. This means that you cannot mail or email ballots to vote, conduct a telephone poll by calling each Director individually, or vote by email, and then assume that a majority vote allows you to act. This method does not give dissenters a chance to influence the majority in a setting in which everyone can communicate simultaneously. However, if you conduct a telephone poll or email vote and *all* of the Directors are in agreement, you can use the consent procedure described below to make a valid decision.

EXECUTIVE SESSIONS

An executive session is a session of the Board that is closed to all except Board members and those the Board invites into the session. Boards commonly hold executive sessions to consider confidential or sensitive matters, such as legal matters in which the Board wants to protect the attorney-client privilege or is not ready to make public for other reasons, deliberations that involve discussing someone's medical condition, discussions about donors or funders that may be confidential, and personnel matters. It is not always possible to predict what might be confidential or sensitive, so most Boards want to keep open the possibility to go into executive session if the Board feels the need arises.

Minutes

Your Secretary or some other officer designated by the corporation needs to keep, or be sure that someone else is keeping, records (called minutes) of your meetings. At a minimum, your minutes should reflect:

- the date, time and place of the meeting;
- the notice given, if any is required;
- what Directors (and what others) were present and whether this constituted a quorum;

HOW THE BOARD MANAGES ITSELF 16

- if your Bylaws require that absent Directors be excused (a practice we do not recommend, see p. __), an indication of whether such Directors were excused;
- what items were submitted for a vote; and
- who voted for, against, or abstained.

> *The minutes should be very clear about what decision was made.*

The minutes should be very clear about what decision was made. It is up to you as to how much of the discussion about issues you want to record; if the issue is likely to come up again, sometimes a record is helpful. There are some exceptions where you do need to record more than decisions. If the Board deals with a conflict of interest, the minutes should record all the information to show that the Board correctly followed your conflicts policy. If someone brought a suspicious circumstance (pp. 284-85) to the Board's attention, the minutes should describe the circumstance, how it was handled by the Board, and why the Board reached the decision that it did.

Some major agenda items generally come up once a year. It is particularly important that these be reflected in the minutes if they apply to your corporation. Included are:

- adoption of the budget,
- election of the Board and officers,
- assignment of committee chairs and appointments,
- evaluation of the Executive Director,
- audit oversight,
- board self-evaluation, and
- review of the Form 990.

> *The minutes should also include references to any item that the Board should be doing to fulfill its legal obligation to oversee the corporation.*

There are some items that do not come up at every meeting but that should be considered as needed by the Board and reflected in the minutes. These include:

- opening/closing bank accounts,
- approval of check signers,
- Approval for borrowing, obtaining a line of credit, obtaining a corporate credit card
- approving executive compensation of insiders (see pp. 700-706),
- proper handling of conflicts of interest (see pp. 200-303), and

331

- new member orientation.

The minutes should also include references to any item that the Board should be doing to fulfill its legal obligation to oversee the corporation—e.g., budgets and financial reports, personnel matters, and assessments of risk. Be sure to attach copies of the financial statements and any other materials used at the meeting to the minutes or save the Board packets that contain these materials with the minutes. If you have all this data on an electronic file, be sure that the files are archived in a way that is accessible to those in the future who look for it.

There is no specific law stating how minutes are validated as being accurate. Some corporations review the minutes of the previous meeting and approve them at the current meeting. Others have the Secretary or President sign the minutes. You should consider having the Board develop a policy to handle this so that there is some way to authenticate minutes. As a practical matter, the whole Board needs to read the minutes to be certain that they accurately reflect the decision made at the meeting. Without review and approval by the whole Board, you may find the same issues returning for discussion repeatedly because some Directors do not agree that the decision recorded in the minutes was the decision really made. If you are exempt under §501(c)(3) or (c)(4) and the Board decides to engage in a transaction between the corporation and an insider, the Board needs to review the minutes of this transaction. See pp. 200-02.

The minutes should be kept with the corporate records. A skeleton outline of "Minutes of Meeting of the Board of Directors" is included in the Forms section.

If the Board goes into executive session (see p. 330), the Board should keep minutes of the session. Your Board will need to provide for some mechanism to ensure that these minutes remain confidential.

As you work out your Board's approach to meetings, pay special attention to the distinction between items which require Board decisions, items for which Board input is sought, and items which are really just information you want to share with the Board.

Holding Effective Meetings

Boards do much of their work in meetings, so it's very important for your Board to find effective ways of conducting meetings. It's probably worth discussing your meeting format and style regularly because the membership of your Board will change over time and many of the choices in Board meeting style really come down to individual preferences. The very act of discussing how the Board will conduct its meetings tends to re-energize Boards. Most people are more committed to processes they feel they helped to design.

The box on page 334 lists some common agreements for Board meeting format. You may want to use this list as the starting point for a discussion of your meetings. Ask members which of the items on the list they would like to see incorporated into your meeting process and which they may find particularly unappealing. Then ask for other suggestions. Be sure you write down the outcomes of this discussion and agree upon a trial period for your new approach to meetings. At the end of three or six months, take a few minutes to discuss how the new approach to meetings is working and decide whether you will continue it or try other ways.

As you work out your Board's approach to meetings, pay special attention to the distinction between items which require Board decisions, items for which Board input is sought, and items which are really just information you want to share with the Board. While information can be shared in writing and input can be collected through individual conversations or written feedback, decisions can be made effectively only in meetings. So, you'll want to be sure that your format for Board meetings emphasizes using meeting time for decision items, with second priority given to input discussions. This will help avoid having your corporation's Board described as "the body that saves minutes but wastes hours."

You can avoid some of the most common and destructive Board meeting problems by making sure your Board meetings follow these guidelines:

Start and End on Time

Directors notice when meetings actually get going. If your Board forms the habit of starting well after the announced starting time, you'll find Directors come later and later.

Without an agreed upon ending time, Board meetings tend to go on well past the point of good concentration. Besides, meetings which lack ending times place considerable power in the hands (or bottoms) of people who can stay the longest, thus excluding those with family or work responsibilities from participating in important decisions.

Encourage your chairperson to plan your meeting agenda so that the really important issues come up relatively early in the meeting.

Make Clear Decisions and Make Decisions Clear

If your Board discusses the same issues again and again, you may be having difficulty with the clarity of your decisions. Good minutes can help, but the problem may go deeper. Be sure that each decision is made in response to a specific, clear proposal for action. Even if your Board chooses not to use parliamentary procedure with formal motions and seconds, you will still need to work with specific proposals and to be sure they are correctly recorded in your minutes.

CHECKLIST FOR EFFECTIVE MEETINGS

1. Each participant receives adequate *notice* of the *date*, *time*, *place*, and *purpose* of each meeting.

2. The closing time for each meeting is agreed to at the beginning and changed only with consent from the group.

3. The agenda for the meeting is announced at the beginning and changed only with the consent of the group.

4. A *timed agenda* (which sets limits on the time spent on each item) is used if there is difficulty covering all the topics within the overall meeting time limit.

5. Information items, input/feedback items, and decision items are clearly defined.
    ◊ Information items are brief and relevant
    ◊ Items presented for input/feedback are clearly differentiated from those on which the Board will be asked to make a decision at the meeting. Input/feedback is only sought if it will actually be used by those who will make the decision
    ◊ Decision items are discussed at a time when most group members are present

6. The limits of the group's decision making authority are known by all. Decision items are considered in light of the presence or absence of final authority within the group.

7. Committee reports recommend action with clearly stated proposals.

8. Financial information is presented with written copies for everyone.

9. The President, Chairperson or Facilitator:
    ◊ Keeps the discussion on one topic at a time
    ◊ Helps all members be heard
    ◊ Recaps points of the discussion
    ◊ Restates proposals clearly
    ◊ Announces the decisions made on proposals
    ◊ Refers issues to committees for more detailed work when necessary

10. Minutes or notes are maintained as described on pages 288-289.

11. All items which are referred to committees and deferred to future meetings are clearly stated in the notes and reviewed at subsequent meetings.

Provide Enough Time to Resolve Important Issues

If you find the ends of your meetings filled with conflict and frustrations, take a good look at what has taken up the time earlier on in the meetings. Many Boards find that they inadvertently delay getting to important but difficult issues by spending a great deal of time on minor matters. Encourage your chairperson to plan your meeting agenda so that the really important issues come up relatively early in the meeting. Ask your chair to help members keep focused on the need to keep moving.

Make Good Use of Committee Work—Avoid Having the Full Board Re-do It

If the whole Board discusses all the issues which committees have discussed, not only will the meetings be long, but the committees will grow discouraged. What is the point of committee members meeting outside the Board and working through issues if the Board revisits each issue in detail at its meeting? Committees can help prevent this detailed rehash by preparing recommendations which clearly urge the Board to adopt a specific course of action and present a summary of the reasons for the recommendation.

Make Meetings Productive and Enjoyable

Many Boards find that Directors have two sets of needs around Board meetings. They want to feel their time is used well—that they are making a real contribution, and that it really does matter whether they are present at the meeting or not. They also want the Board meeting to provide opportunities to get to know other Directors and to feel connected to one another and the work of the organization. If some of your Directors still aren't sure of other Director's names or roles in the community, you probably aren't meeting these connection needs.

Decisions Without a Meeting

Although most Board decisions will be made at a meeting, it is possible for the Board to reach a decision without a meeting if all of the Board members agree. Board members cannot reach a decision without a meeting based on a majority vote. 100% of the Directors must agree.

Actions by Consent

If *everyone* on the Board is in agreement about an action, there is no reason to require a meeting. In that case, action can be taken without a meeting if *all* of the Directors sign a written consent or consents describing the action taken. There can be no opposition or abstention. The action is effective when the last Director signs the consent unless the consent specifies an earlier or later effective date. Consequently, your Directors should date as well as sign the consent.

You can also obtain the consents by email. The email asking for consent should clearly state the action that is being proposed and should inform the Board that the action will become a decision of the Board if all of the Directors agree. If the Director replies to an email sent to the Director with the intent of giving consent to a proposed action, the Director has signed the consent. The email signature is treated like a handwritten signature. The corporation should print a copy of the proposed action and each consent and file them with the Board minutes.

---

*Action can be taken without a meeting if **all** of the Directors sign a written consent or consents describing the action taken.*

Note that to act by consent without a meeting *all* the Directors must agree; a majority is not enough, and no one can abstain. A sample "Consent to Corporate Action Without a Meeting by the Board of Directors" is included in the Forms section. You must file these consents with your corporate records. The best place is generally with the corporate minutes.

Voting by Ballot, Telephone Poll, or Email

As noted earlier in this Chapter, Oregon law does not authorize the Board of Directors to vote outside of a meeting other than by using the consent procedure discussed above. The Board cannot act on the basis of a majority vote that is taken by mail-in ballot, telephone poll, or email.

Board Committees

In addition to making valid decisions, your Board needs to consider how it structures itself to make the best use of its time and talents. Many Directors are very busy people who will not tolerate sitting on a Board that they feel wastes their time. Most Boards find that they can operate most efficiently by using committees to handle specific governance, management, or other tasks and by assigning special governance responsibilities to their officers, so that someone is tasked with handling governance jobs. Almost all Boards will function best if they have policies that document what the Board does and how it does it.

Committees that Exercise Board Authority

Here's a question you may not have considered. Regardless of whether your organization is a direct management or delegated management nonprofit, when your Board sets up a Board committee, you need to ask yourself an important question—will the committee have the authority to make Board-level decisions? For example, many Executive Committees have the power to act in place of the Board between Board meetings. This means that the Executive Committee can make Board-level decisions. On the other hand, many committees carry out Board tasks or make recommendations to the Board but do not actually exercise Board powers. For example, many Development Committees explore fundraising opportunities but do not make decisions about what the Board's general fundraising approach will be.

HOW THE BOARD MANAGES ITSELF   16

Because committees that actually exercise Board powers are in effect acting as the Board, Oregon law has some very specific (and somewhat ambiguous) rules about how these committees are set up and who can be on them. The creation by the Board of committees *that exercise the authority of the Board* and the Directors who are going to serve on them must be approved by the *greater* of:

- a majority of all the Directors in office at that time; *or*
- the number of Directors required by your Articles or Bylaws to take action in voting matters.

Example: Your corporation has nine Directors but only seven show up for the meeting at which committees are formed. Your Bylaws require a majority vote of the Directors present at a meeting with a quorum in order to take action. (At this meeting 4 of the 7 would be enough.) In your group, the majority of all Directors *in office at that time* (5 of 9 Directors) would be a *greater* number of Directors. That number is needed to set up a committee that can exercise Board functions and to name Directors to the committee.

> *Because committees that actually exercise Board powers are in effect acting as the Board, Oregon law has some very specific (and somewhat ambiguous) rules about how these committees are set up and who can be on them.*

Committees that exercise Board-level responsibilities must be composed of at least two Board members. Although the statue is ambiguous, it is likely that only Board members can serve as voting members of these committees. This means that your Executive Director (if not a Board Member) and others interested people cannot be voting members of these committees, although they can certainly sit in on meetings if the committee desires or the Board as a whole requires it.

If you intend for a committee to exercise Board-level authority, be careful about how you draft the language charging the committees. If you give the committee Board authority but then require approval of the committee's action at a Board meeting, the committee does not have Board-level authority and your corporation cannot act based on the committee's action until the Board has ratified it. Generally, this kind of language will defeat the purpose of giving the committee Board authority. If you do not require Board approval of the committee's actions, you can and should require that the committee reports to the Board any actions that it takes.

Actions Board Committees Cannot Take

Generally, each committee of your Board may exercise the authority of your Board of Directors to the extent specified by the Board or given in the Articles or Bylaws. However, a committee of the Board may *not* :

- Authorize the payment of a dividend or any part of the income or profit of a corporation to its members, Directors or officers (except as payment for value of property received or services performed or payment of benefits in furtherance of the corporation's purposes);

- Approve or recommend to members that the corporation dissolve, merge, or sell, pledge or transfer all or substantially all of the corporation's assets;

- Elect, appoint or remove Directors or fill vacancies on the Board or on any of its committees; or

- Adopt, amend or repeal the Articles or Bylaws.

Meetings, Notices, and Minutes of Committees Exercising Board Authority

The provisions concerning meetings, actions taken without meetings, notice, waiver of notice, quorum, voting requirements, and minutes of the Board described above in this chapter apply to committees exercising Board authority and their members as well. The IRS Form 990 (p. 254) inquires about whether your committees exercising Board authority keeps minutes. The Forms section includes a Board and Committee Minutes Policy that requires this. Consider adopting this policy if it will help your Board and Committees to keep all the minutes you need.

Board Committees that Don't Exercise Board Authority

Many Boards, especially in mid-sized and large nonprofits, work extensively through committees that don't exercise Board authority. These committees of the Board do not make policy-level decisions but prepare recommendations to the Board or carry out tasks to implement Board decisions and policies. Even Boards for smaller nonprofits often use some committees to carry out their work.

Although these committees do not exercise board authority, they may be very important to your organization and you should give some thought to the committees to make them as valuable as possible.

For example, a Bylaws Subcommittee may meet to make recommendations to the Board about the amendment of the Bylaws. A Fundraising Committee may carry out the Board decision to hold an annual dinner. These committees do not exercise any Board powers. The Board may select members for these committees and the committees may be run as the Board sees fit. The Board may choose to invite some individuals who are not Board members to serve on these committees along with Board members.

HOW THE BOARD MANAGES ITSELF 16

Boards in direct management nonprofits (see Chapter 13) may use committees to handle different aspects of the administration of the nonprofit. For example, one Board committee may focus on running the programs, another on handling finances, another on fundraising, and another on marketing.

In delegated management organizations, Board often form committees to provide more in-depth oversight over the corporation than is possible at Board meetings and to carry out tasks the Board has retained for itself. The Board should give some thought to what committees it needs to establish to ensure that the committee structure reflects the best use of the Board's needs, time, and talent. In deciding on committees, the Board will want to consider what its oversight encompasses in its particular organization. This will depend in large part on what the Board has delegated and what it has kept for itself and what kind of Board support the Board can expect from the staff.

Although these committees do not exercise board authority, they may be very important to your organization and you should give some thought to the committees to make them as valuable as possible. Important committees may be both standing (permanent) committees and temporary (*ad hoc*) committees. For example, you may have a standing Finance Committee that works with your chief financial officer to ensure timely and accurate financial reports to the board and that flags problems for the Board. You'll want to recruit committee members who are knowledgeable about finances to sit on such a committee. You may also have an *ad hoc* Capital Campaign Committee if you are engaged in a major fundraising effort to remodel your building. You will probably place members on this committee who have connections to major donors, experience with fundraising, or a background in construction.

> *Most board members will find working on either a task focused work group or a standing committee more satisfying if they establish very clear goals and time lines and celebrate achieving their goals.*

All Boards will need to provide some oversight over the financial affairs of the corporation and the Board will want its members with the greatest financial expertise on these committees. Most Boards of larger nonprofits have a Finance Committee. Very large or complex nonprofits may also have an Audit Committee, Investment Committee, and Executive Compensation Committee. In nonprofits in which the Board retains the right to approve hiring, some Boards have a Personnel Committee. If the Board has retained the responsibility to do some fundraising, the Board may want a Fund Development Committee.

Today many boards are finding that busy Board members prefer to work in task focused *ad hoc* committees or as task forces. These task focused committees/task forces are given a very specific charge by the board with a clearly defined beginning and end date for their efforts. Unlike standing committees that meet regularly to deal with whatever issues emerge in their area, the short term task group uses a project management approach to lay out their plans for accomplishing their tasks. Task force members like knowing exactly what the board has asked them to do and having a defined end point for their work together, including having a chance to celebrate completing a task rather than making an ongoing open-ended commitment.

Standing committees, like Finance or Fund Development, can provide members with some of the same satisfaction by obtaining a clear charge for the committee's work from the board, developing a clear work plan to accomplish their charge over a defined time period, and focusing on deliverables—specific accomplishments like recommending the annual budget for the next year, selecting the auditor, or recommending revisions to the Bylaws. Most board members will find working on either a task focused work group or a standing committee more satisfying if they establish very clear goals and time lines and celebrate achieving their goals.

Separate Advisory Boards and Committees

The committees discussed above function as part of the structure for the Board to do its work and almost always include some Board members. In fact, most Boards require that the chair of a standing committee or a short-term task focused committee be a Board member, while other committee members may not be members of the Board. This structure is quite different from that of Advisory Boards or Committees created in connection with some nonprofits and many governmental entities. These advisory bodies typically have an identity in the community that is somewhat separate from that of the nonprofit or governmental entity they advise.

Some nonprofits are required to work with specified types of advisory committees as a condition of receiving funding. The funder imposing the requirement may also require that the Board obtain approval from the advisory committee for specific actions. For example, Head Start grantees are required to form a Parent Policy Council, a committee composed of parents with children participating in the program. The governing Board of the nonprofit receiving the Head Start funding must consult the Parent Policy Council before approving the budget for the program or selecting the Program Director.

In other cases, nonprofit Boards themselves want to create advisory committees that include individuals with specific expertise or connections to specific parts of the community. Unfortunately, it is common for such advisory committees to become somewhat confused about their role and authority within the organization. Boards working with this type of separate advisory committee should prepare a clear statement of the purpose of the advisory committee which states explicitly that its role is advisory rather than decision-making.

Board Member Responsibilities for Board Committee Work

Each Director has an obligation to keep abreast of what the committees are doing. This is commonly accomplished by committee reports, either in writing or verbally, to the Board. Your Board cannot ignore problems which come up in connection with the committees but must deal with them.

16 HOW THE BOARD MANAGES ITSELF

Board Officers

Oregon law requires that your nonprofit corporation have at least two officers: a President and a Secretary (unless you are a Religious Corporation Sole as described on p. 33). You can call these officers by different names and one person can hold more than one office. You do not have to assign the duties to the officers as we have assigned them below, but you do need to ensure that these duties are being carried out by someone.

There is no requirement in the law that your corporate officers be on your Board of Directors although in practice many, if not most, corporations elect their officers from their Board. You may put such a restriction in your Articles or Bylaws if you want.

Although the law has few requirements, your Board needs to consider how it can best use its officers to responsibly manage the corporation. Because of the importance of being responsible about your finances, this means that most nonprofits will have a third officer, a Treasurer. In some cases, your officers' duties will vary, depending on whether you are a direct management or delegated management nonprofit. See Chapter 13 for a description of that distinction.

Your Board needs to consider how it can best use its officers to responsibly manage the corporation.

President

Generally, your President is responsible for overseeing the operations of the Board. The President is commonly the Chair of the Board. The President sets, or with an Executive Committee and/or in consultation with the Executive Director, sets the agenda for Board meetings. The Board generally has the right to add to or modify the agenda. The President ensures that the Board meets as frequently as needed to perform its job. In many organizations, the President has the right to sit on every Board Committee and often to appoint or nominate committee members.

Your President should be able to work with others to set an agenda and should have the skills to chair a meeting. The President will be dealing with the other officers, committee chairs, and, in delegated management corporations, with your Executive Director. Your President needs to be someone who can see the big picture, deal well with people, and manage details. The President also needs to understand the culture of the Board and the organization and be able to operate within that culture.

Some larger nonprofits choose to have the Chief Executive Officer/Executive Director serve as the President of the corporation and have the top volunteer leadership position be titled Chairperson of the Board. In this structure, the Chairperson of the Board will fulfill the roles we've described above for the President. Most small to mid-sized nonprofits find this structure confusing and prefer to have the President position be reserved for the top volunteer leaders. Occasionally, nonprofits will appoint the CEO/Executive Director to serve as both President and Chair Person of the Board.

THE OREGON NONPROFIT CORPORATION HANDBOOK

This is usually ill advised since it concentrates virtually all of the organization's leadership authority in a single person.

Secretary

Oregon law requires that your corporation keeps certain records and that an officer have the authority to authenticate records in cases where an outside party might require that. In most corporations, this job is assigned to the Secretary. The Secretary is usually responsible for keeping the Board records, including:

- seeing that minutes are taken at all Board, committee, and members' meetings,
- if members vote by ballot, ensuring that the ballots are counted and reporting the results to the board
- ensuring that Board policies are copied from the minutes into a policy folder or Board Policy Manual,
- providing proper notice of meetings, and
- certifying records for the corporation.

In direct management corporations, the Secretary will also need to keep or ensure that someone keeps all of the corporate records. See pp. 270-71 for a description of what those records are.

In delegated management corporation, the Board has usually delegated the responsibility for keeping the corporate records to the staff. The Secretary needs to ensure that the records related to Board activity are kept. In larger nonprofits, a staff person may handle these functions as well but the Secretary needs to monitor to ensure that the tasks are being performed.

Your Secretary needs to be someone who is detail-oriented and able to grasp the rules that apply to the Secretary's job. S/he needs to be able to work without supervision to ensure that the Board always gives proper notice and that minutes are complete and correct. The Secretary will need to follow through when the Board enacts a policy to be sure that the Board Policy Manual stays complete and up-to-date.

In some larger nonprofits, the corporate office of Secretary is filled by a paid professional staff person. This person is accountable for maintaining corporate records and responding to legal requests for information. The Board then elects a Secretary of the Board who performs the review of the minutes and other functions described above. For most small and mid-sized nonprofits, this approach is not particularly helpful due to confusion about the two roles.

Treasurer

The Treasurer handles the oversight of the books and finances. In direct management corporations, the Board must establish the financial controls policies and other financial polices of the corporation and carry them out. Most Boards will want to turn to their Treasurer to recommend policies. Remember, though, that at least two people will be needed to carry out good financial policies. See page 270.

In delegated management corporations, the management of finances has almost always been delegated to staff but the Board needs to oversee this delegation of authority. Typically, Boards rely on their Treasurers, often as Chair of the Finance Committee, to ensure that this is done and to keep the Board updated on any financial issues that arise.

Your Treasurer should be knowledgeable about financial matters and have the ability to explain financial matters in language the rest of the Board can understand. Ideally, your Board will have a Treasurer who has some accounting background or experience as a chief financial officer or controller. Many nonprofits, especially smaller ones, have difficulty finding Board members with this level of training or experience, so try to get a Board member with as much of a financial background as possible. Your Treasurer should also be committed to the vision of the organization and meet the other requirements you expect of your Directors. If you cannot find someone who meets your requirements that has a financial background, you might consider naming your best qualified Director to be the Treasurer and seeking a volunteer with a stronger financial background who would serve as an advisor to your Treasurer.

> *Your Treasurer should be knowledgeable about financial matters and have the ability to explain financial matters in language the rest of the Board can understand.*

While some larger nonprofits choose to have the Chief Financial Officer, an employee, serve as Treasurer of the corporation, this approach is generally confusing in small and mid-sized organizations.

Executive Director as Officer

Some nonprofit corporations choose to have the Executive Director named as an officer. This is often done as a convenience to the organizations so that the Executive Director can sign documents which require an officer's signature, like bank account cards and contracts. Some organizations name the Executive Director as an officer because they believe that the Executive Director must be an officer in order to come to Board meetings. This is incorrect. The Board can have anyone they want at a Board meeting and will almost always expect the Executive Director to attend.

There are some drawbacks to the practice of making the Executive Director an officer. One is that it is often important that a Board officer that is not the Executive Director sign the types of documents that require an officer's signature as a way of exercising Board oversight over important corporate actions. Another disadvantage is that there are occasions where you have to report your officers that are compensated. This may occur because a funder requests the information or because a government regulator, such as the Oregon Department of Justice or the IRS, requests it. It is not illegal to have a compensated officer but, depending on the circumstances, you may not look good. If you are about to apply for exemption under §501(c)(3), you will need to report this and it might slow up your exemption process. See Chapter 6. For these reasons, you may choose not to name your Executive Director as an officer.

One additional source of potential confusion lies in the position that the IRS has taken with regard to treating Executive Directors as "officers" of the corporation for the purpose of the Form 990. In most cases, Executive Directors do fulfill the functions what the IRS attributes to officers and must be included in lists of "officers" on the 990. This does not make your Executive Director an officer of your corporation for purposes of state law. This means, for example, that if your bank requires an officer's signature on a document, your Executive Director whom your Board has not named as an officer cannot sign the document, regardless of how the IRS characterizes her/him.

Other Officers

Your group can appoint additional officers besides those above, and these officers may perform other functions or may share the functions described above.

Standard of Conduct for Officers

Each of your officers must act in good faith, with the care an ordinarily careful person in a like position would exercise under similar circumstances and in a manner your officer reasonably believes to be in the best interest of the corporation. Your conflicts of interest policy should cover officers as well as Directors. See page 301.

Training the Next Officers

The jobs of the President, Secretary, and Treasurer each have a learning curve. Each job has specific requirements, and how the officer performs the job in your particular organization will require special knowledge. For example, the Secretary may need to know what notice is required for a special Board meeting and where to find the list of names and addresses for Board members in order to give notice.

Your Board should consider how it might ease the transition as new people step into their roles as officers.

Your Board should consider how it might ease the transition as new people step into their roles as officers. There are a number of practices that might help this transition. In some organizations, the former President remains on the Board after his/her term ends, often in a non-voting, ex officio position, to mentor the new President. Some Boards have a President-Elect or a Vice President, an officer who is next in line for the Presidency, who has the opportunity to learn the job before becoming President. Other Boards consider that the Secretary serves this role. If this is the case, you need to consider that the skills needed to be a good Secretary are not necessarily the skills you need in a good President and consider whether the same individual can fill both roles.

Most organizations do not provide for a Secretary-Elect or a Treasurer-Elect but you should provide for the retiring officer to give some training to and be available for questions by the incoming officer. All incoming officers should review the Articles, Bylaws, and Board policies for information about their jobs.

Resignations

Although in practice, most officers and Board members resign by verbally informing the organization, officers should submit their resignations in writing. An email is generally fine. The officer position should be filled as soon as possible, and a written resignation allows the organization to know with certainty that the position is vacant.

Board Policies

Boards make important decisions about the management of the corporation and management of the Board itself and often learn a great deal in the process. Board policies capture that wisdom and act as a guidebook for the Board so that it does not have to make the same decisions again and again for ongoing issues. Board polices are a guidebook for staff and volunteers who are bound to follow Board rules on management. Board policies also function as a mechanism for perpetuating the institutional memory of the Board. The specific Board policies you should have depends on whether you are a direct management or delegated management nonprofit. See Chapter 13 to determine which type of management you have.

> *Board polices are a guidebook for staff and volunteers who are bound to follow Board rules on management. Board policies also function as a mechanism for perpetuating the institutional memory of the Board.*

There has been a great deal of discussion in the nonprofit world about Board policies, particularly since the for-profit corporate Board oversight scandals in the early 2000s. Regulators, commentators, and consultants have pressed nonprofits to adopt some of the policies that for-profit corporations are required to have to lessen the chance of corporate malfeasance. Nonprofits can find all kinds of extensive lists of "policies every nonprofit should have" and "best practices for nonprofits." The IRS revised its Form 990 (see pp. 254-55) in 2008 to ask exempt organizations whether they have certain governance policies and procedures. The policies and procedures the IRS inquires about largely grew out of the larger nonprofit-sector discussion about policies.

One problem with these lists of policies and practices is that they mostly reflect issues in the for-profit world and often do not represent the policies nonprofits need the most. The major defect in nonprofit policies tend to be around two issues: clarifying governance and financial controls. With the exception of conflicts of interest policies, neither of these two needs is significantly addressed by the commentators responding to the for-profit corporate scandals.

In addition, the policies and best practices lists usually urged on Boards do not distinguish between direct management and delegated management nonprofits. In many cases, the Board of a delegated management corporation is not the proper body to adopt a policy that is, for larger organizations, more appropriately an administrative policy established by the Executive Director rather than a Board policy. For example, while the Board of a direct management nonprofit is the proper body to be concerned about record retention and destruction, the Boards of most delegated management nonprofits would expect their Executive Director and staff to be much more knowledgeable about records issues. The Executive Director would establish administrative policies on this issue, although the Board may want to adopt a policy requiring the Executive Director to develop administrative policies on record retention and destruction, as described below.

> *The policies and best practices lists usually urged on Boards do not distinguish between direct management and delegated management nonprofits.*

The policies we propose below are primarily Board governance policies, including financial controls policies for smaller nonprofits. We incorporate some of the major policies discussed by nonprofit regulators and commentators because so many funders have been persuaded by commentators and consultants to consider these policies to be important to well-run nonprofits. See the discussion about Form 990 governance policies on pages 254-55. You can check co-author Cindy Cumfer's website at *www.cumfer.net* for updates on policies and for information about particular policies that may be helpful to you in drafting and adopting policies. While many sample policies are available, it is very important for your organization to customize the policies we provide and other samples you obtain to meet the needs and capacities of your organization

Board Policies for Direct Management Corporations

As described in Chapter 13, the Board in a direct management corporation is managing all of the affairs of the corporation as well as managing itself. These organizations tend to be small organizations that operate using volunteers. Board policies for direct management corporations should include provisions for corporate governance and administration and Board management.

Organizational Mission and Plan

Even small corporations should have a statement of the corporate purpose or mission, the corporate values, and the major goals for the next few years.

Administration of the Corporation

These policies should describe how the direct management corporation is handling its management of the day-to-day activities. One format is to describe:

- what programs the corporation operates and who the program manager is or what committee is responsible for the program;

- how the Board handles administrative matters, which may include volunteer recruitment and training, dealing with mail and calls, filing the paperwork required by regulators, etc.;

- financial management, which should include financial controls, budgeting, asset protection, a whistleblower policy to encourage the disclosure of suspicious circumstances, and any other financial matters the Board may need to address; and

- records management, including transparency, privacy, retention, and destruction of records. See the sample Transparency Policy (for tax-exempt organizations) and Records Retention and Destruction Policy in the Forms section.

The Board may want to name a manager or committee for each activity. The manager will often be a Board member but may be a volunteer or occasionally an employee. The manager may be responsible for particular tasks but the Board will make all significant decisions. The policies reflect these decisions.

Board Operations Policies

Board operations policies supplement provisions in the Bylaws about how the Board itself functions. These policies provide a job description for Directors; standards of performance for Directors, including a conflicts of interest policy; the roles of officers, policies about Board meetings, and descriptions and charges for committees.

Board Policies for Delegated Management Corporations

Boards in delegated management corporations delegate the administration of the corporation to an Executive Director or to an individual with another title or occasionally to co-Executive Directors. As described in Chapter 13, the Board may set values and parameters for the Executive Director to follow and may retain authority over certain management decisions. All other management powers not reserved to the Board are exercised by the Executive Director. Board governance policies are particularly important in these more complex organizations and should cover the issues listed below.

Organizational Mission and Plan

Delegated management organizations need a clear statement of their mission, values, strategic plan, and goals, since this is roadmap for the Executive Director to know how to use the organization's resources.

Board-Executive Director Relationship

The Board needs to ensure that the Board and Executive Director have a clear understanding of the relationship between the Board and the Executive Director. The policies should delegate the responsibilities for corporate management to the Executive Director, subject to any limitations in the policies. It is particularly important that the Board clarify how communication between Board and staff occurs. Can any Board member contact any staff member for information? Can any staff member speak directly to a Board member without going through the Executive Director? Does the Board want to limit communications to those between the President of the Board and the Executive Director? Can the Treasurer talk directly to the Chief Financial Officer or Controller? Most Boards will want to address these questions.

> *It is particularly important that the Board clarify how communication between Board and staff occurs.*

Executive Director's Responsibilities

The Board policies should clarify the responsibilities of the Executive Director. Having delegated the management responsibilities to the Executive Director, the Board will want to set out any limitations on the exercise of this authority by the Executive Director. Most nonprofits will want to consider restrictions in at least four areas.

VALUES

One important area of Board work is to articulate corporate values, particularly those related to the organization's mission. The Board will want to ensure that the Executive Director applies these values to the decisions s/he makes and the administrative policies that s/he or other staff create. Some values may relate to your organization's culture—for example, you may value transparency and ethical behavior (hopefully you do!). Other values may be more specific to your mission—an environmental organization may require that the Executive Director follow good environmental practices in running the organization; and an organization dedicated to helping families may want the Executive Director to maintain family-friendly employment policies and workplace environment. Of course, these types of restraints may come at a financial cost, so your Board will need to give the Executive Director some guidance on how to balance values and cost.

FINANCIAL MANAGEMENT

In the arena of financial management, the Board will want to establish some guidelines for budgeting and authorization of major expenditures. In most cases, the Board will retain the final authority to approve the annual budget plan but delegate authority to manage the expenditure of funds to the Executive Director, including the authority to approve expenditures that differ somewhat from the budget plan, generally expressed as authority to approve variances under a specified threshold. Note that the role of the budget in the nonprofit is quite different from that in a governmental entity in which managers cannot generally authorize expenditures that exceed the adopted budget. In nonprofits, Board approval of the annual budget provides authorization to move forward with the plan represented in the budget. The Board will want to charge the Executive Director to ensure that appropriate financial controls are in place and assets and investments are protected. The Board may require additional constraints if the organization has restricted funds or engages in joint ventures.

PERSONNEL MANAGEMENT

The Board will want to consider any limitations it wants to place on the Executive Director's management of personnel. Most Boards in organizations with employees will want to consider whether to require that the Executive Director develop a personnel manual and have it reviewed periodically by an employment lawyer. Depending on the sophistication of your staff, your Board may want to enact other directives related to independent contractors and volunteer retention.

A whistleblower policy has become one of the more commonly mentioned best practices and is one of the best mechanisms the organization can have to detect fraud or embezzlement. This policy can be enacted as an administrative policy, but if the Board wants a component that allows for review by or an appeal to the Board, then the Board will need to enact it. Since unfortunately the largest losses through fraud occur through improper actions of top managers, most Boards will want to establish whistleblower policies which include a process for reporting concerns to the Board through specified procedures. A sample Whistleblower Policy is in the Forms section.

PROGRAM MANAGEMENT

Most Boards turn over program management to the Executive Director but will retain the right to approve new programs. Some Boards set performance expectations with respect to the organization's programs and evaluate the Executive Director on the basis of how well the Executive Director meets the performance targets.

RECORDS MANAGEMENT

Larger nonprofits may want to leave all records policies to be managed by the Executive Director. However, federal law does prohibit certain types of record destruction when there is an investigation underway. For example, if your corporation falsifies or destroys records in response to an IRS audit of your Form 990, you have committed a crime. Your Board rather than your Executive Director may want to enact a policy requiring the Executive Director to develop a procedures for records retention and destruction as a way of showing the seriousness with which it takes this issue. See the Records Retention and Destruction Policy in the Forms section for a sample. Some Boards of delegated management nonprofits may want to enact transparency policies, also as a way to show the Board takes transparency seriously. In other organizations, this policy may be a management policy. See the Transparency Policy in the Forms section that covers transparency for records that tax-exempt organizations must disclose.

Board Operations

As with direct management corporations, Board operations' policies supplement provisions in the Bylaws about how the Board functions. These policies provide a job description and standards of performance for Directors, including a conflicts of interest policy; the roles of officers; policies about Board meetings, and descriptions and charges for committees.

Board Policy Manuals

Your organization needs to maintain a copy of its policies in one place—generally a board policy manual—so that they are accessible. Simply adopting them and recording them as part of the Board minutes does not ensure that individuals in the future will know about them and be able to find them. You also need to be sure that future Board members, staff and volunteers (as necessary) get a copy of the policies that pertain to them and familiarize themselves with your policies. Some Boards have their Secretary keep copies of all Board policies in a loose leaf binder. Other Boards create a more readable manual generally in electronic form that organizes the policies in a booklet format.

> *Your organization needs to maintain a copy of its policies in one place—generally a board policy manual—so that they are accessible.*

Evaluating the Effectiveness of Your Board

Because Board roles and priorities change over time and because the composition of a Board changes regularly, evaluation of the effectiveness of your Board needs to be based on both your understanding of the legal responsibilities of the Board and on the specific roles your Board has decided to play within the organization. Your evaluation should focus on the needs of your organization, not comparison with other organizations and other Boards.

Hopefully, you will use a Board meeting style which encourages Directors to provide feedback on how the Board is working throughout the year. Directors should feel free to express both pride in accomplishment and frustration with process. Most importantly, Directors should be encouraged to ask questions and be honest about areas of confusion or reservation.

Beyond striving for a supportive, open atmosphere on the Board, you may also want to set aside time at Board retreats for explicit evaluation of how the Board is doing. Focus evaluation discussions on Director agreements about Board roles and activities and recognition of what has worked well—as well as acknowledgment of difficulties. Use the evaluation as an opportunity to reach new agreements about Board roles and develop more realistic plans about Director commitments and activities.

HOW THE BOARD MANAGES ITSELF 16

Perpetuating Institutional Memory

Most Boards tend to be composed of members who leave after a few years. This means that these Boards are going to be constantly re-inventing themselves unless they find a way to pass on what past Boards and Board members have learned. This mechanism of perpetuating institutional memory may occur in several ways:

- orientation sessions for new Board members (see pp. 311-12);
- periodic Board trainings that update Boards on their responsibilities;
- staggering Board terms of office so that the Board is never composed entirely of new members (see p. 60);
- having a retiring President remain on the Board as an ex-officio, nonvoting Board member; and/or
- capturing governance wisdom in board policies.

We suggest you assess how your Board ensures that it does pass on what it learns. Some organizations may have a long-time Executive Director or accountant who acts as the institutional memory for the Board. This is very useful, but the Board should have some mechanisms of its own in place that don't rely on individuals outside of the Board who can die or leave. Board policies and trainings are often the best bet.

Consult Appendix 1 if you would like information about source material related to this Chapter.

In the next Chapter, we cover the important topic of how your Board and officers can protect themselves from personal liability for their actions.

17 PROTECTION OF THE BOARD

THIS CHAPTER COVERS

- Personal Liability of Your Directors and Officers
- Protection of Your Directors and Officers

Generally, lawsuits brought against a nonprofit are filed against the corporation itself and not its Directors or officers. There are some circumstances in which a lawsuit may be filed against the Directors or officers personally. Although the possibility of being sued is small, most Directors want as much protection as possible from suits. We discuss these important topics in this Chapter.

Personal Liability of Your Directors and Officers

Personal liability refers to the circumstance in which you as a Director or officer may be required to pay out of your own pocket a judgment that arose from your actions as a Director or officer. One of the major reasons most organizations incorporate is to protect the Directors and officers who run the organization from being personally liable for actions that they perform on behalf of the organization.

To a large extent, incorporation accomplishes this. Most lawsuits against nonprofit corporations can only reach money, property, and other assets the corporation owns, and not those owned by individual Directors and officers. However, there is a myth in some parts of the nonprofit world that Directors and officers are never personally liable for their actions. This is false. There are circumstances where you as Director (and occasionally as officer) may be found to be personally liable.

> *There is a myth in some parts of the nonprofit world that Directors and officers are never personally liable for their actions. This is false.*

When You Are Personally Liable

You as a Director or officer face the risk of personal liability if you:

- Fail to act with due care in governing the corporation or in otherwise acting for the corporation;
- Engage in a conflict of interest or other act of disloyalty to the corporation; or
- Agree to be personally liable.

Failure to Act With Due Care or Breach of Duty of Loyalty

You can be personally liable as a Director if you negligently fail to carry out your duties and responsibilities to act with due care and to be loyal to the corporation. Those duties were described on pages 297-304.

> *Example*: The Board of the Jackson Childcare Center, a nonprofit corporation directly managed by the Board, has not established any policy to investigate potential employees who will work with the children. The Board hired a man with an Oregon record of several child abuse convictions. The employee abuses a child at the Center.

353

If the Board is found to have been negligent in failing to have proper hiring procedures, the Directors may be personally liable to the child for the damages caused by this employee.

If the Board delegates management of the corporation to an Executive Director that it reasonably believed was competent to manage a childcare center, the Board does need to be aware that the agency is serving a vulnerable population. The Board would want to include as part of the delegation a requirement that the Executive Director ensure that responsible policies were in place to protect the children. The Board should monitor to ensure that the Executive Director did establish such policies and procedures. If the Board does this, it should not be liable if the procedures its competent Executive Director put into place were defective. (Even so, the Board might still be personally sued and have costs of defense as discussed below, so keep reading!)

The most common source of lawsuits against Directors personally are brought by unhappy employees. The employee may be an Executive Director who was terminated by the Board and claims that the Board intentionally breached an employment agreement with the Executive Director or illegally discriminated against him or her. In other cases, employees may claim that the Board was aware of but failed to address harassment or discrimination against the employee.

In addition, various statutes impose personal liability on Directors who do not exercise due care to ensure that the corporation meets its obligations to the government. Your Directors can be personally liable for:

- the corporation's failure to pay federal and state payroll and other taxes (pp. 614-15);
- failure to maintain workers' compensation insurance (p. 615);
- violating the political activity restrictions if you are exempt under §501(c)(3) (pp. 173-80);
- improper classification of independent contractors (Chapter 20);
- engaging in excess benefits transactions (pp. 700-706); and
- entering into certain contracts with professional fundraisers that are prohibited by the state of Oregon (pp. 504-05).

Example: Your corporation has a §501(c)(3) exemption and the Board allowed impermissible political activity. The IRS can hold Directors personally liable for taxes, interest, and penalties in some cases where the political activity rules are violated. If your actions caused the organization to lose its tax-exempt status, the future Board of the organization may sue you for damages caused by the loss.

Directors of private foundations can be personally liable for agreeing to a variety of transactions that violate private foundation rules.

Agreement to Be Liable for the Corporation's Debt

You may become personally liable for the liabilities of the corporation if you agreed to be personally liable. This commonly happens in one of two circumstances. You may have knowingly agreed to personal liability. This often occurs if the corporation is attempting to obtain a large loan (often to purchase property) and the lender is only willing to grant the loan if Directors co-sign individually for the loan. As a co-signer, you will be personally liable if the corporation fails to meet its obligation.

You may also agree to be personally liable without realizing it. This occurs if you sign a document that imposes liability (for example, a lease, promissory note, or contract) that you think you are signing on behalf of the corporation but the document does not indicate that you are signing as an agent for the corporation and you fail to indicate in the document that you are signing as an agent. If you are signing as an agent for the corporation, be sure that your signature is followed by the words "Agent [or President or Secretary] of _____ Corporation."

Who Can Sue You

There are several parties that might bring a lawsuit against you as a Director or officer of a nonprofit corporation.

Your Nonprofit Corporation

The remainder of the Board of Directors of your nonprofit corporation or a future Board of Directors may sue you for your actions in your capacity as a Director if they feel you have breached a duty to the corporation which caused the corporation injury. For example, if a future Board feels you failed to properly invest the funds of the corporation, it may sue you for lost principal or income.

Employees, Members, and Others Associated with the Corporation

> *The most common source of lawsuits against individual Directors are claims by former or unhappy employees, often an Executive Director who was fired by the Board.*

As noted earlier, the most common source of lawsuits against individual Directors are claims by former or unhappy employees, often an Executive Director who was fired by the Board. These claims may take the form of discrimination suits or unlawful termination cases. Members may also sue if they believe you have mismanaged the corporation or improperly terminated their membership. An injured volunteer may sue if she or he believes the Board actions in some way contributed to that volunteer's injury.

The Government

Several government agencies are particularly concerned with laws that impact nonprofit corporations. In Oregon, the state Attorney General's office is charged with overseeing Public Benefit Corporations. If the Attorney General's office believes there has been fraud, mismanagement, or other wrongdoing, it can investigate and proceed against the corporation and its Board and officers. Often an Attorney General investigation is initiated by a complaint by an unhappy member, Director, or other person connected with the nonprofit.

Although it occurs less frequently, other state agencies could impose personal liability on your Board or officers. The Oregon Department of Revenue could proceed against the Board and officers personally for failing to withhold state taxes. Oregon law provides that the Board can be personally liable if an organization fails to provide worker compensation for its workers (p. 615). The Worker Compensation Department might choose to enforce this.

The Internal Revenue Service may also, on occasion, proceed against Directors, officers, and even the check signers personally. This can happen if the organization fails to perform mandatory payroll withholding or recklessly classifies a worker as an independent contractor rather than an employee. (See Chapter 20). The IRS may also impose personal liability on Directors and officers who are responsible for violations of the political activities rules (see Chapter 8), unrelated business income tax laws (see Chapter 9), or excess benefits transaction rules (see pages 700-706).

Outsiders

Individuals not connected with the corporation may be injured by someone connected with your nonprofit. If the individual alleges that the Board failed to act reasonably (that is, acted negligently) or violated its duty of loyalty, you may find yourself individually named in the suit.

> *Example*: Your all-volunteer nonprofit drives children on field trips. Your direct management Board has no policy in place to be sure that the drivers are licensed. An unlicensed volunteer driving children as part of your program runs a red light and the children in the van are injured. The parents sue the Board individually for negligence in failing to have policies in place to ascertain that your drivers were licensed and competent.

Which Boards Are Most Vulnerable to Being Sued

Boards of certain corporations are more vulnerable to being sued. Consider whether your organization has or deals with any of the following:

- employees
- children, the elderly, the disabled, clients with mental or emotional conditions, or other vulnerable populations
- food, drink (e.g., sold by your group or available at special events), drugs, or medicines

- alcohol (e.g., at holiday parties, fundraisers)
- activities that can cause injuries (e.g., driving, construction, mountain climbing, rescue operations, dealing with violent people, medical care, sports)
- activities that may create opposition (environmental activities, neighborhood issues, political causes, unpopular publications, etc.)

The above activities are associated with a more significant risk of lawsuit. You need to pay particular attention to the protections that your corporation has in place for your Board and officers if your corporation has any of these risk factors.

Protection of Your Directors and Officers

As the discussion above indicated, there is some risk that Directors and officers can be personally liable for their actions as Directors or officers. Fortunately, there are a number of actions the nonprofit and its Directors can take to cover or minimize this risk.

There is some risk that Directors and officers can be personally liable for their actions as Directors or officers. Fortunately, there are a number of actions the nonprofit and its Directors can take to cover or minimize this risk

Educate Your Board

Some corporations provide training for new Directors and officers to ensure that these individuals understand what their service as an officer or Director entails and how to carry out their duties. See pages 310-11.

Maintain Proof of Correct Behavior

There is often a big difference between what actually happened and what you can later prove happened. It is important to maintain written records that verify events you may later need to prove.

- Keep accurate minutes of Board meetings. You need to keep records (called minutes) of your meetings. Pages 330-32 explain what should be in your minutes in order to protect the Board.

- Make or confirm resignations as Director and other important matters in writing if these matters do not appear in your minutes. Keep a copy for your own records.

- Keep your records for the period of time for which proof may be required. See page 677-80.

Reliance on Reports

The law does not expect you to know everything about running a corporation. You as a Director can rely on information, opinions, reports, and statements from reliable officers and employees, reliable Board committees as to matters within its jurisdiction, reliable religious authorities (in the case of Religious Corporations) and outside experts such as attorneys and public accountants.

> *Example*: The Board is considering hiring an independent contractor on a half-time basis to write grants for the corporation. The Board has obtained a written opinion from its accountant that this person is properly classified as an independent contractor. The Board can rely on this opinion. If the IRS later classifies this individual as an employee, the Board would not be personally liable for the tax owed (although the corporation would be and may have a claim against its accountant).

> *Example*: Your Board has delegated the management of the corporation to your Executive Director. The Board acted reasonably in hiring someone who could handle the responsibilities. The Board is entitled to rely on the reports of the Executive Director about the condition of the corporation.

However, if you have information suggesting reports are unreliable, you must investigate.

Proper Handling of Conflicts of Interest

Directors are very vulnerable to personal liability if they benefit from a transaction that breached their duty of loyalty to the corporation. The fact that a Director has a conflict of interest with the corporation does not necessarily mean that the transaction cannot occur. Generally, the Board is best advised to avoid approving transactions where a conflict is present. However, there may be occasions when the Board wants to engage in the transaction even with the conflict. The proper way to handle conflicts is described on pages 299-303 and 700-706.

Create an Advisory Board

If your Board has members who want to lend their name to the corporation but who do not intend to exercise the duties of a Director, consider creating an Advisory Board, clearly designated as such, for these people. The Advisory Board cannot make decisions for the corporation, but it can, if it chooses, make recommendations to your Board. Because the Advisory Board does not have any power to govern the corporation, its members would have no personal liability for corporate actions.

Limited Liability of Directors and Officers

Federal Law

Federal law extends some special protection from liability to volunteers, including volunteer Directors, of many nonprofit organizations. See pages 461-62.

State Law

Oregon law offers some special protection from liability to "Qualified Directors." You are a qualified Director *if you serve without pay* and:

- if your organization is or could be tax-exempt under any section of §501 of the Internal Revenue Code;
- if your organization has as its primary purpose religion, charity, providing goods or services at no charge to the general public, education, scientific activity, or medical or hospital activities at reduced costs; *or*
- if your organization is a trade and business organization, a condominium, a planned community, or a homeowners association.

In most cases, unpaid officers of these organizations are also entitled to the protections offered to qualified Directors. If you have more specific questions about whether you are covered, you should see an attorney.

You are not a qualified Director if you receive any payment for your services (other than reimbursement for expenses). Payment is not necessarily in the form of cash but can include anything of value. Examples of such payment might be reduced tuition for your child, free admissions to events; or discounted merchandise. You may be paid for your services in some other capacity for the organization without losing this protection. If this is the case, the corporate records should be clear that this is what the payment is for.

In the absence of special protection, your Directors are liable for their negligence (that is, their failure to act with reasonable care) as well as gross negligence (that is, extreme negligence), reckless misconduct, and intentional misconduct. Qualified Directors are not liable to *anyone* for their negligence but only for gross negligence, recklessness, and intentional acts. This makes it considerably harder for anyone to get a judgment against you.

> *Example*: You are an unpaid member of the Board of a §501(c)(3) community center. You and the other Directors negligently failed to institute proper policies to ensure that the pool had a lifeguard on duty at all times and a child drowned. You are personally sued by the child's parents, who allege gross negligence. The jury finds that you were negligent but not grossly negligent. Because you are a qualified Director, there will be no judgment against you.

The protection offered to qualified Directors is helpful but does not end your concerns about personal liability. Most suits brought against Directors personally are by ex-employees for intentional wrongful termination or discrimination and do not involve a claim of negligence, so you continue to be at risk for those. In addition, while the law protects you from your ordinary negligence, you are still responsible for your gross negligence. Although this is much harder to prove, you may still face lawsuits alleging this. At the very least in those cases, you will incur legal costs to get out of the lawsuit.

All Directors and Uncompensated Officers

Your Articles of Incorporation may contain provisions limiting liability for all your Directors, whether qualified or not, and for uncompensated officers. These provisions may provide that the Director has no personal liability *to the corporation or its members* for monetary damages for conduct as a Director. Many potential Directors want to see this provision in the Articles before they will agree to serve. Provisions that provide this protection are found on pages 39-40.

There are some actions for which your Articles cannot eliminate liability. These are listed on pages 39-40. Your Articles also do not eliminate liability for actions by parties *outside the corporation* (although remember that the law provides some protection for qualified Directors in these types of situations).

Your Articles of Incorporation may contain provisions limiting liability for all your Directors to the corporation or its members. Many potential Directors want to see this provision in the Articles before they will agree to serve.

Reimbursement by the Corporation When You Are Sued

If you are an officer or Director who does get sued or threatened with a lawsuit in your personal capacity arising out of your actions as a Director or officer, you may potentially incur two kinds of expense. One expense is a judgment against you if you lose a lawsuit or settle a claim. The other expense is legal fees and costs you incur whether you win or lose a lawsuit. It is not uncommon for the cost of defending a lawsuit to be $20,000 to $80,000 which you will owe whether you win or lose. You may then want to look to the corporation to reimburse you for your expenses and any amounts you had to pay to the other party.

"Indemnification" means the corporation will pay for an attorney to defend its Director or officer who is threatened with a lawsuit and will repay its Director or officer for any judgment and expenses that the Director or officer must pay as a result of being sued because of being a Director or officer.

PROTECTION OF THE BOARD 17

Example: A former staff member sues the corporation for discrimination and names all the Directors personally in the lawsuit. If the corporation has indemnified its Directors, it may be required to pay their legal fees to defend against the suit as well as any judgment the court awards the staff member against them.

> *"Indemnification" means the corporation will pay for an attorney to defend its Director or officer who is threatened with a lawsuit and will repay its Director or officer for any judgment and expenses that the Director or officer must pay as a result of being sued.*

The law provides that there are some circumstances in which a nonprofit corporation *must* indemnify its Directors and officers, some circumstances in which it *may* indemnify its Directors and officers, and some circumstances in which it *cannot* indemnify its Directors and officers.

When the Corporation Must Indemnify Its Directors and Officers

Your corporation *must* indemnify its Director or officer when the Director or officer wins the lawsuit (unless the Articles provide otherwise).

When the Corporation Can Indemnify Its Directors and Officers

Your corporation *can* indemnify its Director or officer when:

- the conduct of the Director or officer was in good faith;
- the Director or officer reasonably believed his or her conduct was not opposed to corporation's best interest; or
- in criminal proceedings, the Director or officer had no reasonable cause to believe his or her conduct was unlawful.

When the Corporation Cannot Indemnify Its Directors or Officers

The corporation *cannot* indemnify its Director or officer when:

- the corporation sued the Director or officer and won; or
- the Director or officer improperly received personal benefits.

Many corporations, to attract Directors, agree in their Articles or Bylaws to indemnify their Directors and officers to the maximum extent permitted by law. Check your Articles or Bylaws for a provision similar to this:

> "This corporation will indemnify to the fullest extent not prohibited by law any person who is made, or threatened to be made, a party to an action, suit, or other proceeding, by reason of the fact that the person is or was a Director, officer, employee, volunteer, or agent of the corporation or a fiduciary within the meaning of the Employee Retirement Income Security Act of 1974 (or its corresponding future provisions) with respect to any employee benefit plan of the corporation. No amendment to this Article that limits the corporation's obligation to indemnify any person shall have any effect on such obligation for any act or omission that occurs prior to the later of the effective date of the amendment or the date notice of the amendment is given to the person. The corporation shall interpret this indemnification provision to extend to all persons covered by its provisions the most liberal possible indemnification—substantively, procedurally, and otherwise."

Many corporations, to attract Directors, agree in their Articles or Bylaws to indemnify their Directors and officers to the maximum extent permitted by law.

There are a number of very detailed laws about indemnification. You need to see an attorney if you are concerned about this.

Insurance

Indemnification is only good if the corporation has assets or insurance that will cover your expenses when indemnification is needed. You can't get money from a bankrupt and uninsured corporation. Consequently, unless your corporation is very financially secure, you may want to look into insurance coverage to cover your Directors and officers in the event you are threatened with a lawsuit.

Directors and Officers Insurance

Directors and Officers insurance (D & O insurance) is a policy the corporation buys to protect its officers and Directors from the types of liability we have been describing in this chapter. Ideally, every nonprofit would have this insurance. The problem is that not everyone can afford it. You should look for an insurance agent who has dealt with nonprofits. Don't be discouraged by someone else's story about how expensive the coverage is. Each nonprofit is rated differently, depending on what the insurance company feels your risk is. Check it out.

Your Directors and Officers insurance should advance defense costs during the course of the lawsuit, not just reimburse them after it is over. It should cover actions brought by employees, committee members, volunteers, and the organization itself. You should look for broad coverage for employment-related claims.

> *Directors and Officers insurance (D & O insurance)*
> *is a policy the corporation buys to protect its officers*
> *and Directors from the types of liability we*
> *have been describing in this chapter.*

Errors and Omissions Insurance

This is similar to Officers and Directors insurance but may cover some of your employees as well as your officers and Directors.

Personal Insurance Coverage

If you have checked out Officers and Directors insurance and found you can't get it or you don't have enough to make you feel comfortable, your Directors can check their own insurance policies. Occasionally, a homeowner's or renter's policy will cover your Board services or you may be able to add this coverage for yourself at little or no charge. A more common source of coverage is in the umbrella policies many people purchase to supplement their other insurance. Insurers for these policies more often are willing to cover your service on nonprofit Boards, sometimes for free and sometimes for an additional premium. Talk to your insurance agent. The major limitation to these policies is that they cover bodily injuries and property damage. Many lawsuits initiated against Directors and officers are for other types of claims (such as employee claims or poor financial decisions) so your homeowners or umbrella insurance would not cover you for those suits.

Other Types of Insurance

Your corporation should have other types of insurance to protect itself in the event of a problem or lawsuit. These types of insurance coverage are discussed on page 566-68. However, be aware that having these other coverages does not protect your Board from its own errors. The insurance described above is what is needed for this occurrence.

Final Note

This chapter has pointed out the major areas that a Director may be personally liable for her or his actions on behalf of the corporation. It is important to plan for this possibility. However, before you panic too much, remember that the vast majority of Directors are never sued personally. You will decrease considerably the chances that you will be sued by exercising the care described in this chapter and will protect yourself if you are sued in most cases by following the recommendations above to protect the Board.

Consult Appendix 1 if you would like information about source material related to this Chapter.

There are many people besides the Board that are needed to operate a successful nonprofit organization. The next Part discusses members, employees, independent contractors, and volunteers. You should read any chapter that applies to you.

PART IV

SUCCESSFUL FUNCTIONING: PEOPLE

18 MEMBERS AND MEMBERSHIP CORPORATIONS

THIS CHAPTER COVERS

- Admission of Members
- Rights, Obligations, and Liabilities of Members
- Notice of Meetings
- Meetings of Members
- Voting by Members
- Election of the Board
- Inspection of Your Records by Members
- Resignation and Termination of Members
- Special Rights of Members in Mutual Benefit Corporations
- Change from Membership to Nonmembership Corporation

The law defines a "member" as someone who votes for one or more of your Directors more than once. This means that if your members do not vote, they are not members for legal purposes. As we discussed in Chapter 2, the legal definition of a member is quite a bit different from the common understanding of member in the nonprofit world. Most people understand a member to be someone who supports the goals of an organization and is associated with it in a special way, often by paying dues or providing volunteer services.

Because members (as the law defines that term) have the special right to vote, membership corporations are subject to quite a bit of regulation. If you don't have voting members, you don't want to be subject to the rules of this chapter. In order to clarify your situation for legal purposes, you should review the discussion on pages 25-26 about this and consider talking to an attorney. This chapter assumes you have read pages 25-26 and have determined you are a membership corporation as the law defines that term.

As you read this chapter, keep in mind that your own Articles of Incorporation or Bylaws may have provisions for how your membership corporation is regulated. If those provisions comply with the law, you must follow them.

Organizations choose to be membership corporations for a variety of reasons. At one time, most Oregon nonprofit corporations were membership corporations in which members elected the Board and participated in other corporate decisions. In the last 60 years, this picture has changed. Most Public Benefit and many Religious Corporations are not membership corporations. Many who have members do not have voting members but have members who pay dues and may get a newsletter or email alerts.

However, some Public Benefit Corporations do have voting members. In many cases, these organizations see membership as a vibrant form of democracy that ensures those who are invested in the organization have control of the corporation or a voice in its governance. Some Religious organizations have voting members as a reflection of denominational beliefs about the location of church authority in the congregation. Most Mutual Benefit Corporations are formed to benefit its members and are membership corporations whose members do vote.

In 1989, the Oregon statute was amended to define a member of a nonprofit corporation as someone who has the right to vote for at least one Director more than once. Consequently, those Oregon nonprofit corporations that have only nonvoting members should file or have filed Articles of Incorporation with the state as a nonmembership corporation.

> *In 1989, the Oregon statute was amended to define a member of a nonprofit corporation as someone who has the right to vote for at least one Director more than once.*

As a membership corporation, your corporation has some special responsibilities. Because members can elect at least one Director who then participates in governing the corporation, your corporation needs to have clear rules about who voting members are, what voting rights they have and what their obligations are, what notice they get of meetings in which they can vote, how and when those meetings occur, how voting and Board elections are handled, what records members can access so that they can vote responsibly, and how to remove members. Members in Mutual Benefit Corporations have some rights that are different from those in Religious and Public Benefit Corporations. This chapter covers these issues.

We will also discuss how a corporation that starts out as a membership corporation can change to a nonmembership corporation. Particularly problematic is a membership corporation that changes over time into a corporation that no longer has members but the last members do not amend the corporate documents that describe the corporation as a membership corporation. Often the Board begins electing its own Directors, creating some serious problems. We will describe your options for handling this situation.

Admission of Members

Criteria for Admission

Since your members elect at least one Director who makes corporate decisions, it is very important that you have no ambiguity about who your voting members are. Your corporation needs to spell out your criteria for admitting members and must keep an alphabetical list of the names, addresses, and membership dates of all your members. Many corporations put the criteria for membership in their Bylaws and a few in their Articles. The problem with putting criteria in these corporate documents is that these documents require that a process be followed to amend them. Most corporations would be better served by putting a provision in their Bylaws that a person becomes a member by following the policies established by the Board. The Board should then enact a policy that describes the criteria and procedure for admission of members.

> *Since your members elect at least one Director who makes corporate decisions, it is very important that you have no ambiguity about who your voting members are.*

Generally, your corporation can set any criteria that you want for admitting members. If your criteria discriminate against members based on race, religion, national origin, gender, handicap, or sexual orientation, they may be illegal if your activities involve the members and cause you to be classified as a public accommodation. If you do have discriminatory criteria of these types, you will need to get legal advice.

> *Example*: The Gentlemen's Professional Association is a membership civic association of established businessmen in a mid-sized town who invite younger men to join. The Association offers educational programs on how to advance in business, networking, and individual mentor relationships to its younger members. Women are excluded. Even though this is a private association, it is probably violating anti-discrimination laws.

Your corporation can admit members without charging dues or can permit the Board to set a fee unless your Articles or Bylaws provide differently. The Articles, Bylaws, or a policy or action adopted by the Board can set membership dues and assessments. Generally, the amount of dues is best set by Board action rather than set in your Articles or Bylaws, so that it can be changed without having to amend your Articles or Bylaws.

Consent of Members

The law requires that your members consent to be members. This is not a problem in most groups. However, some groups define membership in a very broad way so as to encompass people who have not consented.

> *Example*: The Park Neighborhood Association, an Oregon nonprofit corporation, defines its members as all residents and business owners within the geographical boundaries of the Park Neighborhood. This definition describes as members people who have not consented to be members and conflicts with the law.

There are significant problems with having members who do not consent. One is that membership corporations are required to keep a list of the names, addresses, and dates of membership of its members, which would not be possible for a group with undetermined members. Another is that the group must give all its members notice of meetings (see pp. 373-74) which is extremely difficult with an undetermined membership. Finally, the nonprofit corporation must allow members access to certain of its books and records (see pp. 384-87) which may be awkward when you cannot know with certainty who your members are.

The law requires that your members consent to be members. There are significant problems with having members who do not consent.

There are several possible solutions to this dilemma:

- You may choose not to incorporate. The rules in this chapter only apply to non-profit membership *corporations*, not to unincorporated groups. However, being unincorporated has other disadvantages. (See pp. 12-13.)

- You may decide to incorporate in another state. Oregon law is considerably more regulatory than that of other states. However, many groups find this idea awkward.

- You may reword your membership requirement to add an additional step in order to be a member. For example, you may state as follows:

    Anyone that lives in or works in Park Neighborhood is eligible to be a member of this corporation. The law requires that all members must consent to become a member. Anyone that lives or works in Park Neighborhood can consent and become a member by signing a Statement of Membership with this corporation and supplying this corporation with their name and address.

- Your corporation would have everyone who expressed an interest in your corporation and who met your other criteria sign a Statement of Membership that stated they consented to membership and that listed the date and their names and addresses, so that you could keep proper records. These would be your voting members.

Rights, Obligations, and Liabilities of Members

Classes of Members

Membership corporations can be very simple or quite complex. The most common type of membership corporation is the corporation that has one class of members with each person having one vote. Many corporations have at least two classes of members—one class that votes and the other class of members that is nonvoting. Other corporations, usually Mutual Benefit Corporations, such as yacht clubs, homeowners associations, and country clubs, have different classes of members with different voting or other rights and/or different privileges. There are many examples of large national organizations that have state chapters, including a chapter in Oregon, and local chapters throughout the state. In these corporations, the members may have voting rights at the chapter level and the right to elect delegates to the state or national meetings.

Your Articles or Bylaws must provide for the rights and obligations of your classes of members. If your Articles and Bylaws are silent about classes of members, then the law assumes each member has the same rights. If this is not your situation, you should consider getting legal help to be sure that you have considered all of the implications of creating different classes of voting members. This is particularly true if you are a Mutual Benefit Corporation, since you will need to consider, among other issues, how to distribute your property on dissolution, as discussed below.

One of the most common mistakes in membership corporations is the failure of the corporation's Bylaws (or Articles) to state what voting rights its members have.

Members' Rights and Obligations

One of the most common mistakes in membership corporations is the failure of the corporation's Bylaws (or Articles) to state what voting rights its members have. Your Bylaws (or Articles) should spell out whether your members vote only for the Board or whether they vote in connection with other matters. In addition to voting for the Board, your corporation can permit them to vote on issues of major interest to the corporation—that is, amendments to Articles and Bylaws, a sale of substantially all of the corporate assets, merger, dissolution, removal of Directors, conflicts of interest, and, in Mutual Benefit Corporations, some matters connected with authorizing indemnification. If you fail to set out the voting rights of your members, the law will probably consider that all members have all of the rights set out above.

There are restrictions on the rights you can give members. Members do not have the right to make management decisions—that is the Board's job. This means that members do not approve the budget, approve the hiring or dismissal of employees, or vote on the mission statement. If you want your members to have the power to do these things or to manage other affairs of the corporation, you need to provide for this in your Articles or by an amendment to your Articles. Putting these powers in your Bylaws is not sufficient.

> *There are restrictions on the rights you can give members. Members do not have the right to make management decisions—that is the Board's job.*

Giving members the powers and responsibilities to make management decisions will probably mean that the members will be treated like they are members of the Board of Directors for the purposes of these decisions. This means that they could become personally liable if they are sued personally for one of these management decisions. The most common source of lawsuits against Board members individually is unhappy employees, usually an Executive Director who feels that he or she was wrongfully terminated or an employee that believes he or she was discriminated against. If your members made the decision that the employee complains about, your members may be sued. Your members should consider whether they want the responsibility for these powers before they take them on. While the Board may protect itself from paying a judgment or attorneys fees that comes out of a lawsuit against Board members personally by purchasing Directors and Officers insurance (see p. 568), it is not clear that D&O insurance will cover members who make a Board decision. In addition, your Board will want to consider whether it can manage the corporation when some management powers are taken out of its hands.

> *Giving members the powers and responsibilities to make management decisions will probably mean that the members will be treated like they are members of the Board of Directors for the purposes of these decisions.*

Liability of Members

Except as noted above, your members are protected from personal liability for the acts, debts, liabilities, or obligations of the corporation. However, if there are unpaid dues, assessments, or fees for which the member is liable to the corporation, the creditors of the corporation, if they are unable to collect their judgment against the corporation, can, in a proper proceeding, require the member to pay to them the amount that the member owes to the corporation for her or his unpaid dues, assessments, or fees. Although your members are not liable to the corporation by virtue of their membership, they may of course incur liability for some other reason. For example, a member of a church is not liable for the church debts outside of the amount of unpaid pledges or dues, but the church and the member may be liable if she or he abuses a child while volunteering in the church nursery.

Membership Dues

One important contribution of members is the revenue generated by the payment of dues. The payment of dues as a fundraising strategy is discussed on pages 483-85.

Notice of Meetings

Members tend to be a larger and more dispersed group than Directors and consequently the provisions for giving notice of membership meetings are more complicated. Actions your members agree upon at a meeting may not be valid if you did not give proper notice. Since one of these actions is the election of Directors and in other cases like dissolution the members' vote is also important, it is vital that your notice be given correctly.

Who Gets Notice?

The first issue about notice is who must get it. You are required to give notice to members entitled to vote at any meeting. Since the corporation may be adding new members all the time (and losing some), you need to know what date you are using for purposes of membership notice. This date is called the "record date" to determine who gets notice. Page 375 describes how to determine your record date. You then mail the notice to everyone who is entitled to notice of the meeting as of that date.

Contents of Notice

Your notice should state the place, date, and time of the meeting. Unless your Bylaws (or Articles) provide differently, you are not required to state that the purpose of an *annual* or a *regular* meeting is to elect the Board of Directors. However, you may choose to do this to keep up good communication with your members.

In most other situations in which members may be voting, you are required to let them know what the issues are. Notice of an *annual* meeting must include a description of any matter or matters which must be approved by the members in connection with removal of Directors, conflicts of interest, determination and authorization of indemnification and certain indemnification expenses, amendments to the Articles, amendments to the Bylaws, adoption of a plan of merger, sale of corporate assets other than in the regular course of business, and dissolution of the corporation.

In the case of *special* meetings, your notice should always include a description of the purpose or purposes for which that meeting is called.

How Notice Is Given

Your notice must be given in a fair and reasonable manner and must comply with any provisions in your Bylaws. The law provides a definition of what it will consider to be fair and reasonable but this does not preclude the possibility that other methods of notice might also be fair and reasonable. It does, however, give you assurance that if you follow what the statute says is fair that you have satisfied this criteria.

According to the statute, your notice is fair and reasonable if it tells your members of the place, date, and time of the meeting at least seven days before the meeting or, if the notice is mailed by other than first class registered mail, at least thirty and no more than sixty days before the meeting. The law setting out this notice was drafted in 1989 before the advent of the internet and does not provide for electronic notice. We don't know yet how the courts might treat email and, since it is not first class mail, whether it must be given in the 30-60 day period. You are probably safest if you send emails during that period.

Some corporations find that it is impracticable to follow the notice the law deems fair. This may happen if the corporation has a large number of members and does not send out a regular newsletter. You should consider getting some legal help to develop fair and reasonable notice that varies from that described above.

In some situations, the notice described above defined by the law as fair is the *required* notice. Those situations are when members are voting on Directors' conflicts of interest (see pp. 301-03); certain indemnification matters (see pp. 360-62); amendment of Articles (see Chapter 31); amendment of Bylaws (see Chapter 31); merger (see Chapter 32); sale of assets (see Chapter 32); and dissolution (see Chapter 33). The most likely circumstances where the notice is not required is when your members vote for the election or removal of Directors.

Notice of Adjournment of Meetings

If an annual, regular, or special meeting of members is adjourned to a different date, time, or place, notice does not need to be given of the new meeting if it is announced at the original meeting before adjournment, unless your Bylaws require new notice. If a new record date (see below) for the adjourned meeting is or must be fixed, then notice of the adjourned meeting must be given to those who are members as of the new record date.

Waiver of Notice

A member may at any time decide that he or she does not need or want the notice to which they are entitled. The member's action in declining notice is called a waiver. The waiver must be in writing, be signed by the member entitled to notice and be delivered to the corporation for inclusion in the corporate records. See the sample "Waiver of Notice of Meeting of Members" in the Forms section.

Record Date

In a number of circumstances, your membership corporation needs to fix a "record date." Although this has a musical flavor, the record date is the date used by your corporation to determine which members are entitled to notice of a members' meeting, which members may demand a special meeting, which members may vote, and which members may take other lawful actions.

The record dates for each of the events requiring a record date will probably not be the same date. For example, you'll want to set a record date to send out notice of the members' meeting on a date that is days or weeks before the meeting, so that the notice can reach members before the meeting date. You may want to set the record date for voting as the day of the meeting. That way, you can exclude a member from voting who received notice of the meeting but fell out of membership by the time of the meeting for failure to pay their dues. New members who joined after the notice went out but before the meeting can still come and vote. You are just not legally required to give them notice of the meeting.

Your Bylaws may make provisions for how your record dates are set. If the Bylaws do not fix a record date, your Board may fix the dates (and how could your Board miss a chance to do something this exciting?). If neither your Bylaws nor your Board have addressed this issue (which is the case for most organizations), the record dates are set as follows:

- To determine the members entitled to *notice* of a members' meeting, the record date is the day before the day on which the first notice is mailed (or otherwise transmitted to the members) as described above; or, if notice is waived, the day preceding the day on which the meeting is held.

- To determine the members entitled to *demand* a special meeting, the record date is the date the first member signed the demand for the meeting.

- To determine the members entitled to *take action without a meeting*, the record date is the date the first member signs the consent to take action without a meeting.

- To determine the members entitled to *vote* at a members' meeting, the record date is the date of the meeting.

- To determine the members entitled to *exercise any other legal rights*, the record date will be the date on which the Board adopts the resolution that is involved or the 60th day prior to the date of any other action, whichever is later.

In no case can your record date be more than 70 days before the meeting or action requiring the determination of members. If these days are acceptable to your Board, you don't need to set a record date.

The members entitled to notice of or to vote at a membership meeting can decide to adjourn the meeting, unless the Board fixes a new record date. The Board must fix a new record date if the meeting is adjourned to a date more than 120 days after the date fixed for the original meeting.

Meetings of Members

As we discussed in the section about meetings of the Board of Directors, the law assumes a democratic model for Board meetings in nonprofit corporations. This model is also used for membership meetings. This means that the decision-makers vote and that a majority vote usually prevails. Your Bylaws and Articles can regulate this to some degree but, in the absence of such regulation on your part, this is the model you must use.

Unlike the Board model, in membership corporations decisions can be made without everyone being able to communicate simultaneously to persuade each other. The law allows members to vote by ballot—that is, vote without a meeting, usually by mail—if the corporation chooses. In order to give members a chance to persuade each other, the law permits members access to the membership list (and certain other records) so that members can be informed and can communicate their viewpoints with other members before they vote. Pages 384-87 discuss your members' rights to inspect and copy records.

The law allows members to vote by ballot—that is, vote without a meeting, usually by mail— if the corporation chooses.

Who Attends the Membership Meetings

All voting members can attend the membership meetings. Oregon law is not clear as to whether nonvoting members have a right to attend membership meetings but they probably do not. There is no requirement that anyone else be allowed into the meetings, except that the President and any other officers designated by the Board or President shall attend the annual meeting and report on the activities and financial condition of the corporation. Your Articles or Bylaws may state that the meetings are open in which case those documents must be followed.

There is some question about whether membership meetings of nonprofit corporations are subject to Oregon's Open Meeting Laws. The Open Meeting Law requires that all meetings of governing bodies of a *public body* shall be open to the public with certain exceptions. The law also requires that certain public notice be given and that minutes be kept and made available to the public. The issue for nonprofits is "Are nonprofits 'public bodies?'" A second issue for membership corporations is whether membership meetings are meetings of a "governing body." The answer in most cases to both questions is "no." However, if your nonprofit exercises sufficient governmental functions, the Open Meeting Law may apply to you. You will need to get legal advice or check the Resources section on *www.cumfer.net* for more information about this.

Types of Members' Meetings

There are three types of meeting: annual, regular, and special. The annual meeting is actually a type of regular meeting that is held once a year. A regular meeting is one that is regularly scheduled as to time and place. Special meetings are all meetings that are not regular meetings.

Annual Meeting

Oregon law requires that you hold an annual meeting of your members. Your Bylaws (or Articles) are to provide the time for the meeting. The annual meeting is held at your principal office unless your Bylaws fix another location. At the annual meeting, the President, or another officer designated by the Board or the President, must report on the activities and financial condition of your corporation. You also elect your Directors unless your Articles or Bylaws provide for some other time for election. Your members can act on any other matters that may be raised consistent with the notice requirements described on page 374. Many nonprofits use their annual meeting as an opportunity to encourage members to socialize or to offer educational presentations or workshops about the work that the nonprofit is doing. These meetings can be an excellent occasion to promote your programs, to deepen member loyalty, and to encourage financial support from the members.

> *Oregon law requires that you hold an annual meeting of your members.*

Regular Meetings

Your membership corporation can but is not required to hold regular membership meetings. The regular meetings are held at the corporation's principal office unless your Bylaws state another location. At regular meetings, the members consider matters that are raised in the meeting's notice, consistent with the notice requirements given below.

Special Meetings

Your Board of Directors or those authorized to do so by the Articles or Bylaws can call a special meeting of the members of a corporation. The holders of at least five percent of the voting power of the corporation can also call a special meeting. They do this by signing, dating, and delivering to the Corporate Secretary one or more written demands for the meeting, describing its purposes. The record date (see page 375) for members entitled to demand a special meeting is the date the first member signs the demand. These meetings are to be held at your principal office, unless your Bylaws make a different provision. However, if the corporation fails to send out notice for a special meeting that was called by five percent of the members holding voting power within thirty days after the date the written demand was delivered to the corporation's Secretary, the person signing the demand may set the time and place of the meeting and give the required notice. Only matters within the purpose set out in the meeting notice may be conducted at a special meeting of members.

Conduct of Meeting

You have great flexibility in conducting your meetings. You do need to check your Articles, Bylaws, and Board resolutions to see if they govern how to conduct meetings. For example, some Bylaws require that you follow *Roberts Rules of Order*. If your Bylaws requires this, you must familiarize yourself with *Roberts Rules* and follow them or amend your Bylaws to eliminate this requirement. See page 329 for a discussion of *Robert Rules*.

> *One often overlooked responsibility by membership corporations is keeping records of the members' meeting. This is especially important if voting takes place.*

The first item of business at the membership meeting is generally to ensure that a quorum is present. The quorum is the number of votes that must be present in order to hold the meeting. See pages 379-80. In some membership meetings, people tend to come and go. In addition to having a quorum at the beginning of the meeting, you may need to have a quorum count whenever a vote is taken. If there is any doubt that a quorum is present, an officer should recount the number of votes present and ensure a quorum before the vote. If the quorum in your corporation is defined as the number of votes present, you don't need to do quorum counts.

Typically the next item of business in a membership meeting is to hear reports from the President and Treasurer about the condition of the corporation. The reports may be followed by discussions about matters on which members vote—usually the election of Directors—and the vote itself. See pages 380-83 for more on voting. If there is no other business, the meeting is adjourned.

Minutes

One often overlooked responsibility by membership corporations is keeping minutes—that is, records of the members' meeting. This is especially important if voting takes place. The Board needs to ensure that someone does this—often the Secretary. The minutes should reflect the date, time, and place of the meeting and the notice given (with a copy of the notice). They should indicate the count of voting members attending and the presence of a quorum. If members have differing voting rights, the minutes should be broken down to reflect attendance by category. The minutes should reflect what matters were voted on and the outcome of the vote, with the decision clearly stated and with a vote count. If proxies were submitted, the minutes should have the proxy or a copy. It is up to you as to how much of the discussion about issues you want to record; if the issue is likely to come up again, sometimes a record is helpful. A skeletal outline of "Minutes of Meeting of the Members" can be found in the Forms section.

Action Without Meeting

If all your members agree about an action, there is no reason to require a meeting. An action required or permitted to be taken at a members' meeting may be taken without a meeting if *all* your members entitled to vote sign a written consent describing the action taken and it is delivered to the corporation for inclusion in the minutes or filing with the corporate records. Notice that a majority vote is not enough; all voting members must consent. The action is effective when the last member signs the consent unless the consent specifies an earlier or later effective date. See the "Consent to Corporate Action Without a Meeting by the Members" in the Forms section for a sample. Your Bylaws (or Articles) may prohibit actions without a meeting.

Delegates

A delegate is a person elected or appointed to vote in a representative assembly for the election of Directors or on other matters. Larger organizations, usually those with geographical chapters and a regional or national central organization, are most likely to utilize delegates. The delegates represent the members at regional or national meetings so that the meetings can be conducted without having huge numbers of people there. Your corporation may provide in your Articles or Bylaws for delegates who have some or all of the authority of members. If you do this, your Articles or Bylaws should describe the characteristics, qualifications, rights, limitations, and obligations of delegates, including their selection and removal. Your Articles or Bylaws should establish how notice is to be provided for meetings of the delegates and should provide for carrying on corporate activity during and between meetings of delegates.

Voting by Members

Voting by your members is a critically important part of properly running your corporation. The members' votes determine who is on your Board. Since the Board is the group that directs your corporation, it is essential that you conduct your voting procedures in such a way that you leave no doubt as to who the properly elected Director are.

Voting by your members is a critically important part of properly running your corporation.

Quorum Requirements

In order to make binding decisions at a meeting, you must have a quorum. A quorum is the number of votes that need to be cast in order for the action taken to be valid. If your Articles or Bylaws do not set a quorum for membership meetings, the law sets the quorum to be those votes represented at the meeting—in other words, those who show up make a quorum. This very liberal provision means that you will always have a quorum and don't have to do quorum counts.

Some corporations in their Articles or Bylaws do require more than this legal minimum. Often a quorum is set at a percentage of the total votes. If you have a provision requiring a quorum of more than the legal minimum of those who show up, you should seriously think about amending it. Many membership corporations get into difficulty when they do not have a quorum at their annual meeting. The group is supposed to adjourn and schedule another meeting but many organizations don't do that. Often, the group votes on the Board without a quorum and continues to operate. Occasionally, the Board will begin to elect its own Directors without amending its Articles and Bylaws to reflect that it is no longer a membership group. In both cases, the corporation is no longer operating legally. It is possible that all decisions made by the improperly elected Directors are invalid. This could be avoided by using the legal minimum (that is, those who show up) for your quorum requirement.

One of the reasons that many corporations are tempted to require a higher quorum is that the group wants to maintain the commitment of its members to the organization. This is a laudable goal but potentially crippling the organization in order to encourage involvement is like shooting yourself in the foot in order to run faster. We encourage you to pursue membership loyalty by other means. You might consider combining the annual meeting with an event that is more attractive to your members. You might also consider providing services to your members that will increase their sense of identification with the organization. Rather than requiring a higher quorum, you might also consider voting by written ballot (i.e., voting by mail), described below, to increase involvement.

> *If you have a provision requiring a quorum of more than the legal minimum of those who show up, you should seriously think about amending it.*

Voting Requirements at Meetings

If a quorum is present, a majority vote of those represented and voting at a membership meeting is sufficient to act unless your Bylaws (or Articles) require a *higher* number.

Voting by Proxy

Proxy voting means that the member gives someone else the right to vote or to otherwise act for the member. Your members may vote by proxy. You must allow this unless your Bylaws or Articles forbid it. In order to authorize a proxy, the member must sign a form and deliver it to the Secretary (or other officer or agent authorized to tabulate votes). See the "Proxy Vote" in the Forms section for a sample. The appointment of a proxy is valid for eleven months unless a different period is stated in the form. The member can revoke the appointment of a proxy. If the member who appoints a proxy dies or becomes incapacitated, the corporation can continue to accept the proxy's authority until the Secretary (or other officer or agent authorized to tabulate votes) receives notice of the death or incapacity of the member.

The person who appointed the proxy can revoke it by attending any meeting and voting in person or signing and delivering to the Secretary (or other officer or agent authorized to tabulate proxy votes) either a statement that the appointment of the proxy is revoked or a form appointing a new proxy.

Voting By Written Ballot (Vote by Mail)

Unless your Articles or Bylaws prohibit or limit voting by ballot, any action that can be taken at any meeting of members can be taken without a meeting if your corporation delivers a written ballot to every member entitled to vote on the matter. Some nonprofits prefer voting by ballot, especially those with large memberships who are committed to the goals of the organization but don't have the time to attend a membership meeting. The ballot must list each proposed action and provide an opportunity to vote for or against each item. Approval by written ballot is valid only when the number of votes cast by ballot equals or exceeds any quorum required to be present at a meeting authorizing the action. The number of approvals must equal or exceed the number of votes that would be required to approve the matter at a meeting if all those voting by ballot had voted at the meeting. Voting by written ballot doesn't have to be done by mail. In some homeowners associations, for example, it may not be. In most cases, though, voting is done by mail and is referred to as voting by mail.

If your corporation does vote by ballot, pay close attention to the unusual requirements listed above.

When your corporation provides the written ballots to your voters, you have to provide the voter with certain information in your cover letter or on the ballot. You must indicate the number of responses needed to meet the quorum requirements, state the percentage of approvals necessary to approve each matter other than election of Directors, and specify a reasonable time by which a ballot must be received by the corporation in order to be counted. The Forms section includes samples of balloting for the election of Directors and for other actions. See the "Ballot for Election of Directors" and "Ballot for Proposed Action" in the Forms section. A written ballot may not be revoked.

If your corporation does vote by ballot, pay close attention to the unusual requirements listed above. As we noted earlier, you must be very careful that your voting is properly done so that there is no doubt about what the result of your elections is.

Voting and Vote Splitting

Each member is entitled to one vote on each matter voted on by the members unless your Bylaws or Articles make other provisions. If the membership of record is in the names of two or more people and only one votes, that vote is counted as the vote of all of them. If more than one of them votes, the vote is divided on a pro rata basis unless your Bylaws or Articles provide differently. Your Articles or Bylaws may provide for classes of members in which members of some classes have more votes than those of other classes.

The law allows nonprofit organizations to choose a procedure called cumulative voting. Cumulative voting refers to a type of voting in which a member may multiply the number of votes that that member is entitled to cast by the number of Directors for whom the member is entitled to vote and to cast the entire product for a single candidate or distribute the product among two or more candidates. For example, if each member has one vote on each of 8 Board seats up for election, a member under cumulative voting could cast all 8 votes for one position or 5 for one position and 3 for another. Cumulative voting is sometimes used by business corporations so that members who are in a minority may have some representation on the Board. In order for a corporation to use cumulative voting, the Articles or Bylaws must provide for it. Very few nonprofits employ this procedure and you should get legal help if you decide to draft a provision like this.

Corporation's Acceptance of Votes

If the name signed on a vote, consent, waiver of notice, or proxy appointment corresponds to the name of a member, your corporation, if acting in good faith, is entitled to accept it and give it effect as the act of the member. You are not required to do any additional checking or confirmation.

In some cases, a nonprofit has voters who are not individual people. If the name on a vote, consent, waiver of notice, or proxy does not correspond to the record name of a member, your corporation, if acting in good faith, is still allowed to accept it and give it effect as the act of the member if:

- The member is an entity (such as another corporation) and the name signed purports to be that of an officer or agent of the entity;

- The name signed purports to be that of an attorney of the member and, if the corporation requests, evidence acceptable to the corporation of the signer's authority to sign for the member has been presented;

- Two or more people hold the membership and the name signed purports to be the name of at least one of the co-holders and the person signing appears to be acting on behalf of all the co-holders;

- If the corporation is a Mutual Benefit Corporation and the name signed purports to be that of an administrator, executor, guardian or conservator representing the member and, if the corporation requests, evidence of the fiduciary status acceptable to the corporation has been presented; or

- If the corporation is a Mutual Benefit Corporation and the name signed purports to be that of a receiver or trustee in bankruptcy of the member, and, if the corporation requests, evidence satisfactory of this status acceptable to the corporation has been presented.

Your Board may reject a vote, consent, waiver of notice, or proxy appointment if the Secretary (or other officer or agent authorized to tabulate votes) acting in good faith, has reasonable basis for doubt about the validity of the signature or about the signer's authority to sign for the member. The corporation and its officer or agent who acts in good faith and follows the above standards is not liable in damages to the member for the consequences of the acceptance or rejection. Corporate action based on the acceptance or rejection of the vote is valid unless a court determines otherwise.

Election and Removal of the Board

Election of Directors

In nonprofits with one class of members, the members elect the Directors at the annual meeting of the members. Your corporation may provide in your Articles or Bylaws for the election of Directors by delegates, on the basis of chapter or other organizational unit, by region or other geographical unit, by preferential voting, or by any other reasonable method.

Vacancy on the Board

A vacancy that occurs in the case of an elected Director or a vacancy that results from an increase in the number of Directors is often filled by a vote of the Directors rather than the members. This occurs because calling special membership meetings to fill vacancies is often expensive and time-consuming. The Articles or Bylaws may make different provisions for filling these vacancies, including allowing the members to fill them. If the vacant office was held by a Director elected by a class, chapter, or other organizational unit, or by region or other geographic grouping, only members of that unit or grouping are entitled to vote to fill the vacancy (if it is filled by the members).

Removal of Directors

One of the most difficult issues for nonprofits to handle is removal of Board members. Sometimes removal becomes an issue because a Director is not doing her or his job or is doing it in a way that the organization sees as destructive or at least not in the corporation's best interests. The issue of removal of a Director in membership organizations can be particularly volatile. In membership corporations, Directors elected by the members must generally be removed by the members. Often the Director has at least some members in his or her corner and sometimes the issue of removing the Director is disguising a larger unhappiness of some groups with the organization.

The issue of removal of a Director in membership organizations can be particularly volatile.

Because of the potential for explosiveness in these situations, the Board should move carefully in taking action. Your Board may want to consider whether a mediation would help the parties resolve the tension without removing a Director. If you do decide to proceed with removal, be very sure that you are following the legal rules. Because you are going to need your members to vote for removal (unless as discussed below), you will need to consider how you will explain the situation to your members. If you can afford it, you should get some legal advice.

Grounds for Removal

Members may remove a Director elected by them with or without cause, unless the Articles of Incorporation state that Directors can only be removed for cause. Having this provision in your Bylaws is not sufficient; it must be in the Articles.

Vote Required for Removal

If all your members elected the Director whose removal is sought, the Director can be removed if the number of votes to remove the Director would be sufficient to elect the Director.

If your Director is elected by a particular class, chapter, or other organizational unit or by region or other geographic grouping, only the members of that unit or grouping entitled to vote may participate in the vote to remove the Director. That Director may not be removed if the number of votes against removal equals or exceeds the number of votes of that unit or grouping sufficient to elect the Director. Similarly, if you use cumulative voting, your Director may not be removed if the number of votes against removal equals or exceeds the number of votes sufficient to elect a Director.

If your corporation is a religious corporation, you do not have to follow the rules about removal if your Articles and Bylaws do not require that you do. Your Articles or Bylaws can state the vote and procedures by which the Board or any person may remove, with or without cause, a Director that is elected by the members (or the Board).

The law is unclear but it is possible that the Board may remove a Director if the Articles or Bylaws at the beginning of the Director's term allow for removal for reasons set out in the document. A majority of Directors in office must vote for the removal.

Inspection of Your Records by Members

Your members have special rights to access your records so that they can oversee the activities of the corporation and so that they have an opportunity to influence other members in matters requiring a vote. Your members are entitled to inspect and copy certain of your records described below if the member gives you notice at least five business days in advance. These records are divided into two categories: those which the member is entitled to inspect without having a reason and those for which you can require a proper reason.

Your members are not entitled to review all your records but you may choose to allow members to see records not on this list. If you do so, you need to be careful that you are not disclosing records that violate privacy rights or concerns. For example, you should get legal advice before you open up personnel records, medical and mental health records, records related to pending litigation, records with Social Security numbers, client records, and financial records that might contain bank account numbers or other information that could lead to identity theft.

> *Your members are entitled to inspect and copy certain of your records described below if the member gives you notice at least five business days in advance.*

Records Subject to Inspection Without a Reason by the Members

In order for members to monitor the affairs of the corporation, members have access to certain records related to the corporation's governance and financial picture. In the case of the records in this section, your members do not have to give any reason for inspection but you may charge a reasonable amount for copying to cover the costs of your labor and materials.

- Articles of Incorporation, Restatements of Articles, and amendments

- Bylaws and amendments

- Resolutions adopted by the Board related to the characteristics, qualifications, rights, limitations and obligations of members

- Minutes of all meetings of members and records of all actions approved by members for the past three years

- Written communications required by law (e.g., notices of meetings) and those regarding general membership matters made to members within the past three years

- List of the names and business or home addresses of your current Directors and officers

- Most recent annual report delivered to Secretary of State

- Financial statements, if any, for last three years at least

- Last three years of accountants reports, if annual financial statements are prepared by a public accountant.

Inspections That Require a Proper Purpose

Members get access to additional corporate records if they can show a proper purpose to examine them. In the case of the records listed below, you must allow your member to inspect and copy these records if the member's demand is made in good faith and for a proper purpose, the member describes the purpose and the records she or he wants to inspect, and the records are directly connected to this purpose. You may charge a reasonable fee to cover the cost of your labor and materials for copying these records.

Your members always have the right to inspect the membership list with the names, addresses, and membership dates for the purpose of communicating with other members concerning membership meetings.

- You must allow inspection of all minutes of meetings of your members and Board, all records of actions approved without a meeting by your members and Board, and records of all actions taken by committees of the Board making Board level decisions that you did not have to provide for inspection above.

- You must allow inspection of your accounting records.

- You must allow inspection of your *membership list* of the names and addresses and membership dates of all members in alphabetical order by class (if you have classes of members) showing the number of votes of each member as long as the member's purpose is related to their interest as a member. Without the consent of the Board, membership lists cannot be used to solicit money or property unless the money or property will be used only to solicit the votes of members in an election to be held by the corporation. Membership lists cannot be used for any commercial purpose and they cannot be sold or purchased by anyone.

- Your members always have the right to inspect the membership list with the names, addresses, and membership dates for the purpose of communicating with other members concerning membership meetings, beginning two business days after notice of the meeting is given for which the list was prepared and continuing through the meeting. The member is also entitled to copy the list at a reasonable time, during the period it is available for inspection.

What Is a Proper Purpose?

A critical question for many groups is "What is a proper purpose?" This phrase is not defined but a proper purpose would be the desire to contact other members in order to influence their votes on issues before the members. An improper purpose would be to obtain the list in order to use it for commercial solicitation. Another improper purpose would probably exist where a person joined a group in order to obtain a list of the members in order to harass them because of their membership in the group.

> *Example*: A developer joins an environmental membership organization in order to discover the names of its members so that he can embarrass them in their communities. This would almost certainly be an improper purpose.

Restrictions on Members' Rights to Inspect and Copy

Your Articles or Bylaws may restrict or abolish the rights of your members to inspect and copy corporate records in these circumstances:

- If you are a *Religious Corporation*, your Articles or Bylaws may restrict or abolish the right of a member to inspect or copy any record referred to above.

- If you are a *Public Benefit Corporation* organized primarily for political or social action (such as political or social advocacy, education, litigation or a combination of these purposes), your *Articles* may limit or abolish the right of your members (and their agent or attorney) to obtain information as to the identity of contributors to the corporation and to inspect or copy the membership list. *Notice that this must be in your Articles; a provision in your Bylaws is not sufficient.* If you limit access to the membership list, you must provide a reasonable means to mail communications to the members through the corporation at the expense of the member making the request.

Resignation and Termination of Members

Resignation

Your members may resign at any time. Resignation does not relieve the member from any obligations the member may have to the corporation that were incurred prior to the resignation.

Expulsion, Suspension, or Termination

Many membership corporations operate as democracy at its rawest and it is not uncommon for these corporations to attract a wide variety of personalities among its members. Some of these members may be disruptive or dishonest or engage in conduct that the corporation believes is harmful to it or the corporation may have other reasons for wanting to expel, suspend, or terminate a member.

You may expel, suspend, or terminate your members for any reason unless your Bylaws (or Articles) provide differently. It is generally a good idea to permit your corporation to expel members for any reason rather than to try to list reasons for termination. If you try to list reasons, you will almost always miss something and then may find your corporation stuck with a member who causes serious problems. If you are concerned that the organization treat its members fairly, you may want to try to ensure this by requiring more than a majority vote in order to terminate a member rather than requiring that good cause be shown in order to expel a member.

> *Example*: Parents Preschool Helpers, a membership corporation, has Bylaws that require each parent to work at least 5 hours a month with the children at the community preschool. Its Bylaws also provide that members shall not be expelled unless the member "engages in conduct harmful to the preschool." The preschool has just learned that one of the member/parents was convicted of child abuse fifteen years ago. The member has not currently engaged in conduct harmful to the preschool. The Helpers may have difficulty expelling this member under its current Bylaws.

You may expel, suspend, or terminate your members for any reason unless your Bylaws (or Articles) provide differently.

However, Public Benefit and Mutual Benefit Corporations may not expel or suspend members or terminate or suspend memberships in the corporation unless this is done through a *procedure* which is fair and reasonable and is carried out in good faith. Your procedure is considered fair and reasonable when it provides at least 15 days' prior written notice of the expulsion, suspension or termination and the reasons for the action. You must also offer an opportunity for the member to be heard, orally or in writing, at least five days before the effective date of the expulsion, suspension, or termination by a person authorized to decide that the action not take place. A procedure may also pass muster if it is fair and reasonable, taking into consideration all of the relevant facts and circumstances. Notice that these provisions require a certain *procedure* but do not require that you have *cause* to suspend, expel, or terminate members.

Any written notice given by mail must be given by first class or certified mail sent to the last address of the member shown on the corporation's records. If a member wants to challenge an expulsion, suspension or termination, or claims that defective notice was given, that member must file a proceeding within one year after the effective date of the action.

A member who has been expelled or suspended, or whose membership has been suspended or terminated, may be liable to your corporation for dues, assessments or fees incurred prior to the expulsion, suspension, or termination.

Special Rights of Members in Mutual Benefit Corporations

Voting on Conflicts of Interest

Public Benefit and Religious Corporations operate for public purposes—either to benefit the public generally or to benefit a charitable class of the public.

A Mutual Benefit Corporation generally operates for the benefit of the corporation's members and not for the benefit of the public or a charitable class of people. Its Board of Directors is usually chosen by its voting members. Board members may find that they have conflicts of interest since they are running a corporation that operates in part for their own interests. As long as the Board's actions don't target specific Directors or their businesses, the Board's decisions are probably not conflicts, but there are occasions where there are conflicts or questions of conflicts.

This means that conflicts of interest rules need to operate differently for Mutual Benefit Corporations, and they do. Where the Board is voting on a conflict of interest, the law is similar to that for Public Benefit and Religious Corporations. However, Mutual Benefit Corporations can also approve a conflict of interest involving a Board member by a vote of the members. In that situation, all voting members can vote, including the Board member, and all the votes will be counted. See pp. 299-303 for a discussion of all the conflicts rules.

> *Example*: A Board member of a business league formed to promote antique retailers owns the only antique shop in a small coastal town. The Board member wants the league is to sponsor an antique awareness day in the town where the Board member's shop is located by distributing flyers and running an ad in the local paper. Other Directors are concerned that this is not the best use of the organization's resources. This is probably a conflict. The Board should follow the conflicts rules. Alternatively, the Board could avoid a conflict if it wanted to run an antique awareness campaign that covered the locales in which all its members had shops.

One of the most important distinctions between members in Public Benefit, Religious, and Mutual Benefit Corporations is what happens to the assets of the corporation on dissolution.

Right to Assets on Dissolution

One of the most important distinctions between members in Public Benefit, Religious, and Mutual Benefit Corporations is what happens to the assets of the corporation on dissolution. By state law, Public Benefit Corporations must distribute their assets on dissolution to an organization organized for a public or charitable purpose, to a religious corporation, to a §501(c)(3) organization, or to the government. If the Public Benefit Corporation is exempt under §501(c)(3), the IRS rules will require that it give its assets to another (c)(3) or the government. Oregon law does not require a particular distribution of assets on dissolution of a Religious Corporation, but since most are (c)(3)s, they will have to make the IRS distribution.

Traditionally, Mutual Benefit Corporations distributed their assets to their members, though some may make other distributions. This means that a Mutual Benefit Corporation with assets needs to take great care to ensure that its membership rolls are current and that its classifications of members reflects who shares in the assets and how. Typically, the members who get the assets are those who are members at the time of dissolution. Occasionally, this can amount to quite a windfall for those lucky individuals. If your Mutual Benefit corporation wants to distribute its assets to its members but does not necessarily want to distribute all its assets to those members who happen to be members at the time of dissolution, you will probably need legal assistance to plan for your distribution.

Change from Membership to Nonmembership Corporation

It is not uncommon for corporations that begin life as a membership corporation to find that the interest of its members flags over time. Members gradually leave and the corporation does not attract new members. Occasionally, membership corporations decide to change to nonmembership corporations for other reasons.

Making Changes When You Have Members

If your membership corporation wants to change to a nonmembership corporation, you will need to amend your Articles to change your corporation to a nonmembership corporation and will need to amend your Bylaws to take out any provisions related to membership, to reflect how your Board will now be elected, and to make any other appropriate changes. Your first step is to figure out who has the right to amend your Articles and Bylaws.

To determine who amends your Articles and Bylaws, check your Articles and Bylaws to see what rights to vote the members have. One of these documents (usually the Bylaws) should have a provision describing the members' rights to vote. The provision should include a description of what members can vote on. At a minimum, members of course must vote for at least one Director. The Articles or Bylaws may also specifically authorize members to vote on amendments to the Articles or Bylaws. If your Bylaws copied the provision on membership voting in this book, members are authorized to vote on all issues allowed by the law, which includes voting for amendments to the Articles and Bylaws.

MEMBERS AND MEMBERSHIP CORPORATIONS 18

Many corporations fail to include in their Articles or Bylaws a statement about what their members' voting rights are. In that situation, members are generally considered to have all the voting rights that Oregon law gives them, including the right to vote on amendments to the Articles and Bylaws. However, if your Articles or Bylaws contain specific provisions for how they are to be amended and the provisions do not state that members vote for the amendment, it is likely (thought subject to some doubt) that you can follow the provision in the document and do not need a vote by the members. If you think that the issue may be contested, you should get legal advice before proceeding. Follow the steps in Chapter 31 to amend your Articles and Bylaws.

If your membership corporation has Articles and Bylaws that require a membership vote for amendment and you have no members, you have a serious problem.

Making Changes When You Have No Members

Unfortunately, some corporations fail to amend their Articles and Bylaws while they still have members. If your membership corporation has Articles and Bylaws that require a membership vote for amendment and you have no members, you have a serious problem. If the members do not elect all of the Directors and there are enough remaining Directors to govern the corporation, the corporation can continue to do business but the Board may not be able to amend the Articles or Bylaws. If the members elect all or almost all the Directors, the Board cannot function legally because no one has the authority to elect Directors. Many corporation discover this problem years after the membership has died out and find that their Board has operated the corporation without being properly elected for year. This means that all the decisions that the Board made and all of the activities undertaken by the corporation under Board supervision were not authorized.

So what do you do? You should get an attorney to assist you, particularly if there are unhappy ex-members, dissent on the Board, or significant transactions during the period you did not have a validly functioning Board. You and your attorney have several options:

- If at all possible, you should try to reconstitute a list of the last members and hold a valid membership meeting or to vote by ballot (see p. 381) to elect the current Board and to amend the Articles and Bylaws to change to a nonmembership corporation. At its next meeting, the Board should ratify all actions taken by the corporation during the interim period.

- If you cannot determine who the last members were, cannot locate them or cannot get a quorum to attend a meeting or to vote by ballot:

    ◊ You can allow the corporation to be administratively dissolved and start over;

    ◊ You can petition the court for relief; or

◊ You can "repair" the problem as best you can and move on. This means that the Board will amend the Articles and Bylaws, ratify its election and all actions taken by the corporation in the interim period, and function after that in accordance with the amended Articles and Bylaws. This is not a perfect solution because it could be challenged in the future but often the most practical one.

Consult Appendix 1 if you would like information about source material related to this Chapter.

19 EMPLOYEES

THIS CHAPTER COVERS

- Wage and Hour Laws
- Discrimination and Harassment Issues
- Unionization
- Personnel Policies and Employee Handbooks
- Excessive Compensation
- Evaluating the Executive Director
- Independent Contractors and Volunteers as Employees

Many nonprofit organizations have employees and are faced with the challenges of employee/employer relationships. To function well as an employer, you need to be educated about the various employment-related laws governing those relationships. Prominent among these laws are those pertaining to compensation, discrimination, harassment, unionization, and collective bargaining. In addition to being familiar with the laws that affect employers, you should develop and adhere to good personnel practices. Being fair, consistent and clear about how you deal with your employees is key to good employee relations.

The subject of employment law is too complex to be covered adequately in one chapter. As a result this chapter informs you about some special issues faced by nonprofits as employers and directs you to other resources for Oregon employers. This chapter also assists you in developing personnel policies. You may also want to consult Chapter 27, which covers how to handle payroll issues for employees and discusses fringe benefits for employees.

In almost all situations, nonprofit organizations are governed by the same employment laws and regulations as profit businesses. Nonprofit employers should not hesitate to call the Oregon Bureau of Labor and Industries (BOLI) with questions or for employment related information. The BOLI Technical Assistance for Employers telephone is 503.731.4200, and its website (*http://www.boli.state.or.us/*) contains a wealth of information and guidance. Oregon is fortunate to have a state agency such as BOLI which offers useful workshops and publications for employers. The Board and staff of all nonprofits should make a concerted effort to be well informed about employment laws.

Wage and Hour Laws

Who Is Subject to the Laws

Both the federal government and the state of Oregon have laws that set some standards for how employers must treat employees with respect to wages, hours and working conditions. The U.S. Department of Labor, Wage and Hour Division (DOL) is responsible for enforcement of federal wage and hour laws. In Oregon, the Bureau of Labor and Industries is responsible for enforcement of state wage and hour laws.

Virtually all nonprofits with employees are covered by state law and many are covered by federal law. While the minimum wage amount and certain requirements regarding working conditions (like mandatory breaks) vary between the state and federal rules, there are many regulations imposed by both. When a particular issue is governed by both federal and state law (e.g., the minimum wage rate), the law most favorable to the employee governs.

Federal Law Coverage

The federal law applies to all organizations that fall into one of these categories:

- the organization has employees engaged in commerce and has a gross volume of sales or business equal to or greater than $500,000 per year, or

- the organization is a hospital, a nursing home, a residential institution for the aged or mentally ill, or a school.

Except for the specific organizations listed above, smaller nonprofits with receipts of less than $500,000 are not covered by the federal law. Some nonprofits with receipts over that amount may also fall outside the coverage because you are not engaged in commerce or because your receipts, if they are contributions, may not be categorized as coming from a "business." You will need to get legal advice to make the determination about whether you are covered by the federal law if you have receipts greater than $500,000.

State Law Coverage

Oregon wage and hour law covers every employer with at least one employee. If you have only volunteers, you are probably not covered by Oregon's wage and hour laws but you should review the discussion on pages 453-56 to be sure that your volunteers really are volunteers and not employees.

Exempt and Nonexempt Employees

Both Oregon and federal law use a classification scheme that divides employees into exempt and nonexempt categories. To understand how wage and hour laws apply to your organization, you must first determine which employees will be considered "exempt" from the law and which are "nonexempt." All employees are classified as exempt or nonexempt.

Exempt employees generally are in executive, high-level administrative, professional, or certain high-level technology positions and regularly exercise independent judgment and discretion. These employees are paid on a salary basis and are not subject to minimum wage and overtime requirements.

Nonexempt employees are subject to minimum wage and overtime requirements. Nonexempt employees generally are paid on an hourly basis. Whether they are paid on an hourly basis or whether compensation is described as a weekly or monthly salary, nonexempt employees must be paid time and one-half for all hours worked in excess of 40 hours per work week.

In general all positions are nonexempt except those that meet specific exemption requirements. The main exemptions are for high-level administrative, executives, professional and computer positions (sometimes referred to as "white collar" exemptions). Both the state and federal agencies have publications defining each type of exemption. Job title has little bearing on the determination of exemption; rather, the key factors generally are:

- the nature of the duties performed; and how often the employee performs these duties in an average work week;

- whether the employee regularly exercises independent discretion and judgment; and whether the employee is paid on a salary basis and the amount of that salary.

Overtime and Volunteer Time

Wage and hour laws restrict the right of nonexempt employees to work in a volunteer capacity for their employer. The laws were written with for-profit employers in mind and lawmakers feared that employers could pressure employees to work some hours without pay. Unfortunately, the same laws apply to nonprofits. You may need professional help to figure out if these laws apply to you in your specific situation.

Both state and federal rules require that any nonexempt employee permitted to work more than forty hours in a seven-day work week must be compensated for all hours worked in excess of forty at time-and-a-half the employee's regular pay rate. Personnel policies stating "we do not pay overtime" do not excuse an employer from this obligation. Even when the employee chooses to work the extra hours and states that she or he does not want overtime (or any payment), the employer is bound to pay at the time-and-a-half-rate. Consequently, the only way an employer can avoid overtime pay for nonexempt employees is through controlling the hours they are permitted to work and limiting the work time to forty hours within a work week.

Because employees of nonprofits often are deeply committed to the cause the organization is addressing, many nonprofits have difficulty limiting the hours worked by nonexempt employees. It is important to understand that even extra hours worked voluntarily can result in wage or overtime claims.

What can an employer do to prevent nonexempt employees from working extra or volunteer hours? First, the employer should provide the employee with a written statement regarding the number of hours to be worked and the procedure required to obtain authorization for overtime. Next, supervisors should counsel or discipline employees who work beyond their authorized hours. All hours worked must be paid even if the employee has been directed not to work the hours. Ultimately, and unfortunately, the employer's control over the hours worked by employees rests in the employer's ability to discipline or terminate any employee who continues to work beyond the established work hours. This approach may be distasteful but the consequences of permitting extra work hours are quite serious, including liability for unpaid overtime for up to three years, penalties, and attorney fees.

"Comp"Time

"Comp"(short for compensatory) time systems are set up to allow employees who are required to work hours beyond their normal work week to take time *off* with pay at some future time. It is important to understand however, that comp time is not permitted for private sector employees, including nonprofits, in Oregon.

> *The only permissible comp time system for nonexempt employees is one which requires the employee to use up the comp hours within the same work week they are acquired.*

The only permissible type of comp time system for nonexempt employees is one which requires the employee to use up the comp hours within the same work week they are acquired. For example, if nonexempt employee Mary worked ten hours on Monday instead of her normal eight, she may be allowed to work two hours less than normal at some point within the same work week. If her hours are not reduced within the remaining work week, resulting in her working 42 hours during the week, she must be paid time-and-a-half for the hours worked beyond forty.

Most employment law specialists discourage using any form of comp time for exempt employees as well. The recording and exchanging of extra hours worked for extra paid time off endanger an exempt employee's exempt status, thus triggering overtime and other requirements for nonexempt employees. Instead, employment law advisors encourage employers to reach an understanding with exempt employees that their jobs require them to fulfill the responsibilities assigned to their position and that their compensation is based on satisfactory fulfillment of their responsibilities, not on hours worked. Under this approach, a supervisor may encourage an exempt employee to take an afternoon off (without reduction in pay) after a period of peak effort. However, an employer is not advised to keep records of "extra" hours and employers should not create any expectation of an hour off for an extra hour worked.

If your organization uses a formal approach to comp time for exempt employees, you should discuss it with an employment law attorney to determine whether your nonprofit may be exposed to substantial risks under applicable wage and hours laws.

Attendance at Trainings, Conferences and Staff Meetings

Both state and federal rules require that nonexempt employees be paid for all hours worked. Consequently, any activity that the employer requires the employee to attend must be considered part of the employee's hours of work. Staff meetings, training events, Board meetings and conferences are part of the employee's hours of work if the employee is required either explicitly or implicitly to attend. Stating that attendance at staff meetings or training events is voluntary does not prevent such activities from being hours of work if the employer attaches explicit or implicit negative consequences to failure to attend or attaches explicit or implicit positive consequences to attendance.

Out of town conferences pose special problems. You must pay employees for travel that is a principal part of that employee's work duties. For example, you must pay your employees for the time it takes to travel to a one day assignment in another city more than 30 miles from your employee's fixed work station, regardless of the day of the week. In addition, you must compensate your employees for any work that is required to be performed while traveling, even if such work occurs outside the employee's normal work day. If the out of town conference will keep the employee away overnight, then you must pay the employee for all time spent driving (if the employee drives) or for all travel time that occurs during business hours (if the employee is a passenger).

Employers concerned with controlling wage and overtime costs should develop systems and policies to clarify which meetings or other events are required and for which staff, and which employees will have authority to require attendance.

Enforcement of Wage and Hour Laws—the Real Whammy

Employees who believe they have not received the wages or other compensation they are owed may file complaints with BOLI or DOL or the employee can file a private lawsuit. An agency or a court can compel the employer to pay any unpaid back wages, additional penalties and, in some cases, the attorney fees incurred by the employee in recovering unpaid compensation.

If an agency investigation reveals that other employees also are owed unpaid compensation, the agency may require the employer to repay those employees as well, even though they have not filed claims. Consequently, the stakes can be quite high for employers failing to follow wage and hour rules.

Employers also should remember that there are Oregon laws regulating payroll deductions and final paychecks. A violation of these laws also can result in money damages, civil penalties and attorney fees against the employer.

Discrimination and Harassment Issues

Nonprofit employees are governed by a variety of state and federal laws designed to prevent illegal discrimination and harassment in employment. These complex laws and regulations lie outside the scope of this book. However, every nonprofit employer should become familiar with at least basic employment discrimination laws. Not only is illegal employment discrimination and harassment morally unacceptable, violation of civil rights laws and regulations can result in costly litigation and penalties.

> *If the investigation also reveals other employees with similar amounts owing, they must be paid as well even though they have not filed claims.*

Classes protected by federal or state law include race, national origin, religion, gender, gender identity, sexual orientation, age, marital status, and disability. Some cities protect additional classes. In addition, the law protects employees in a variety of other circumstances—such as those who testify at Employment Division hearings, file lawsuits, and donate bone marrow. This list of protected classes is not meant to be exhaustive and in any case, the list changes with time.

An employer's basic obligations are:

- to have practices and policies preventing discrimination or harassment on the basis of any of the protected classes,

- to have a clear reporting procedure for anyone observing or experiencing illegal discrimination or harassment,

- to promptly investigate any such reports,

- to immediately stop any correct the consequences of illegal discrimination and harassment, and

- to prevent retaliation against anyone involved in the reporting of illegal discrimination or harassment.

The Oregon Bureau of labor and Industries provides a more complete list of protected classes on its website and is a good resource for employers.

Unionization

Workers in nonprofit organizations are increasingly turning to unions to represent them in bargaining with their employers. Like discrimination law, labor law is complicated and outside the scope of this book. We do discuss what you as an employer can say and do about a union so that you can avoid mistakes before you have the chance to consult your attorney.

Employees can organize a union in one of three ways. The most common route is through a certification election conducted by the National Labor Relations Board. A second route is by the employer's voluntary recognition of a union without an election. You should be aware that you may be violating the law by entering into an agreement to recognize a union that does not have the support of the majority of the workers in the bargaining unit, so get legal advice even if you are agreeable to accepting a union. In rare cases, the government may order a union. This only occurs if the employer engages in serious illegal behavior.

If any of your workers have begun a campaign to unionize, you need to educate your supervisors about what they can and cannot do. Generally, your supervisors can oppose unionization openly, can tell your employees that you oppose the union, can tell your employees that the law allows them to vote against unionization, can explain your benefits to your employees and compare them to benefits in unionized companies, and can campaign against the union. However, you and your supervisors cannot make threatening statements (for example, if the union wins your nonprofit will cut back on positions), ask questions about the unionization campaign, make promises to generate opposition to the union, or engage in spying or creating the impression of surveillance of union activities.

As soon as you become aware of a union campaign, you should consult a labor attorney. Various laws regulate what you can and cannot do and carry penalties that apply even if you violate a law without knowledge of it.

Personnel Policies and Employee Handbooks

Most people associated with nonprofit corporations (whether Directors or staff) share a strong commitment to working together to provide needed community services. It is sometimes uncomfortable for both staff and Directors to acknowledge that an employee/employer relationship exists between staff and the nonprofit corporation. This is particularly true in small or new organizations where both Board and staff may perceive the work as service to a cause rather than as traditional employment. Nonetheless, the nonprofit Board or Executive Director, if the Board has delegated this duty, must make decisions about how it treats its employees. When the nonprofit wants these decisions to be applicable as a general rule it enacts them as policies, generally referred to as personnel policies. Many organizations print the part of their personnel policies that relate to the conditions of employment of the employees in a booklet form often called an employee handbook that they distribute to some or all employees. Larger organizations may produce two handbooks—one for managers and one for nonexempt employees.

The law does not specifically require that you have personnel policies or an employee handbook. But there are many reasons to adopt personnel policies and to put appropriate policies into a handbook. Certain policies—such as a clear harassment complaint procedure or an "at-will" employment policy—provide the employer with valuable legal protections. Moreover, having a clear statement of consistent policies is a good management practice. Most employees function better if they know what is expected from them and what is expected from others. Employees of nonprofit corporations benefit from the same clarity with respect to their relationship with the nonprofit organization as they would in any other employment situation.

Clear and explicit personnel policies that are put in an employee handbook helps to reduce intra-organizational conflicts. The development of those policies that are put in an employee handbook can be a useful process for both the Board or Executive Director and staff because the process often assists in the goal of striking a balance between the needs and desires of employees and the responsibilities and capabilities of the nonprofit organization and results in protecting the interests of both the employee and the corporation.

A clear and explicit employee handbook helps to reduce intra-organizational conflicts.

Developing Personnel Policies

Your Board decides whether it retains the responsibility to develop or approve personnel policies or whether it delegates this job to the Executive Director. If the Board retains the responsibility, there are several procedures Boards of Directors use to prepare, adopt, and/or administer personnel policies. The Board may direct its Personnel Committee to draft personnel policies for approval by the full Board. Or the Board may hire a professional consultant to draft policies for Board approval. The Board also may direct the Executive Director or other staff to prepare personnel policies or direct the Personnel Committee to work with the Executive Director and other staff to prepare the first draft of policies. The Board then approves the final version and in some corporations administers the policies.

Directors should realize that adopting personnel policies which contain provisions which cannot or will not be followed (such as granting four weeks paid vacation when funds will not be available to cover this benefit) can lead to serious difficulties.

Boards of larger nonprofits are more likely to believe that the Executive Director and staff are better qualified to adopt and administer personnel policies. These Boards do need to know that reasonable policies are adopted. Your Board may have a simple policy that requires the Executive Director, in consultation with an employment attorney, to adopt personnel policies that comply with the law and to submit the policies to an employment attorney for an annual review (or whatever frequency the attorney suggests). The Board then needs to follow up periodically, often at the Executive Director's evaluation, to ensure that this is being done. Alternatively, the Board may want to make the basic decisions about how to approach personnel policies outlined below and then assign the development of the policies to the Executive Director.

Your Board decides whether it retains the responsibility to develop or approve personnel policies or whether it delegates this job to the Executive Director.

Regardless of whether or not the Board delegates the development of personnel policies, if someone brings violations of the personnel policies to the Board's attention, the Board needs to follow up to be sure that the policies are adequate and are being followed.

Your Approach to Personnel Policies

Before an employer (the Board or Executive Director) begins to make decisions about specific policies, the employer needs to make some basic decisions about three key issues. One issue is whether you want to be legally bound by your personnel policies. In Oregon, the courts treat your personnel policies as a contract between you and your employees, unless you clearly state that this is not the case. If the policies are a contract, then an employee who feels that you have violated a policy can sue you for damages or to enforce the policy. If your policies make it clear that they are not a contract and that your internal decisions about the policies are final, then your employees generally cannot successfully sue you for a violation of the policies. For that reason, legal counsel representing the employer routinely advise that a handbook given to employees clearly state it is not a contract and can be altered unilaterally by the employer. A disclaimer that your handbook is not a contract does not, however, limit the responsibility of your corporation to comply with employment related state and federal laws (e.g., discrimination, wage and hour requirements, treatment of injured workers and employment benefits).

The second issue you must decide is whether you want to retain the right to fire your employees without having to prove a justification for the termination. This is called "employment at-will" and, again, is routinely recommended by legal counsel representing the employer. Aside from reducing the chances of costly wrongful termination litigation, the "at-will" policy is preferred by many employers because it gives them greater flexibility to manage their personnel. On the other hand, employment at-will can create some unhappiness among your employees and may not be consistent with your organization's goals about how you want to treat employees. It is important to remember however, that even if you adopt an at-will policy, most at-will employers do not terminate an employee without a reason because of the fact that such decisions are more likely to be challenged legally.

> *The thread running through all of these issues is the extent to which you make legal commitments to your employees versus the flexibility you keep to make decisions as the employer.*

The third area you need to consider is what kinds of other specific commitments you plan to make in your personnel policies. Virtually all policies make specific commitments about vacation time and sick leave. However, there are numerous other items about which you need to decide whether you want to bind yourself to specific commitments or whether you want to be more flexible. For example, you may want to preface discussion of benefits with a statement such as the following: "as long as the corporation's Board, in its sole discretion, determines the corporation's budget can sustain it, the corporation will provide…." You may want to state that you generally promote from within or you may want to maintain flexibility by stating that you look first at employees within your nonprofit but maintain the right to promote as you choose. The thread running through all of these issues is the extent to which you make legal commitments to your employees versus the flexibility you keep to make decisions as the employer.

As you fashion your approach to your relationship with your employees, you might consider three models:

> **Employer Flexibility Model**. In the first model, you retain maximum flexibility and make no commitments other than to specific benefits. This is the model advised by attorney advisors seeking to protect the nonprofit. In this model, you do not refer to personnel policies in the handbook given to employees, because the word "policies" suggests a commitment. Instead, you have an "Employee Handbook." The handbook makes clear that it is not a contract with the employees and that the employer's decisions about all personnel matters are final. The handbook also makes clear that employment is at-will.
>
> Because the employer can fire employees at any time, for any reason, the handbook does not include specific statements about actions that might lead to termination, because to do so may imply that other actions would not lead to termination. The handbook avoids the use of "probationary employees" and "permanent employees," because these categories suggest that permanent employees have more job security. The handbook also does not generally provide for progressive discipline and a grievance procedure, though with an attorney's help, such provisions can be drafted while maintaining employer flexibility.

Employee Protective Model. The second model is a contract that is very protective of the employees. In this model, the personnel policies given to the employees are called "Personnel Policies." They are a contract with the employees, providing employees with a firmer base to file a lawsuit for a violation of policy. These policies make specific commitments about a variety of personnel issues. They protect the employees by limiting the circumstances under which an employee can be disciplined or terminated and provide for progressive discipline. These policies also provide a grievance procedure for employees who are unhappy with a personnel action.

Because employment law is complex, and lawsuits arising from employment relationships are potentially costly, your nonprofit should strongly consider having its employment policies reviewed by an attorney with specialized knowledge in employment law.

Mixed Models. A variety of "mixes" of the above two models are possible. Any set of policies that tries to "mix" the first and second models must be carefully drafted because creating a "mix" typically is more complicated.

Regardless of the approach you take, you should consider consulting with an employment lawyer. Drafting clear personnel policies that reflect your intentions requires legal input. You can reduce your organization's legal expenses by considering the following issues before consulting with an attorney. Decide what approach you want to take among those described above and consider what specific policies will be appropriate for your organization.

What to Include in Your Personnel Policies

We won't attempt to include a detailed discussion of all policies that employers may want to consider when drafting and implementing personnel policies. The list that follows is intended to raise questions, provide information, and encourage you to select the policies and approaches most compatible with the financial resources and philosophy of your group.

The following is a list of common policies an employer should consider as topics for personnel policies: We discuss these in more detail below.

- Philosophy
- Nondiscrimination and anti-harassment policies
- Obeying all laws
- Conditions of employment
- Employment categories
- Compensation

- Benefits
- Job reclassification
- Employee evaluation
- Disciplinary action
- Termination
- Appeals Process for Discipline and Termination
- Amendments to policies

This list is only an example of possible topics. You may want to consider consulting with a human resources specialist or employment lawyer for consideration of additional topics of particular relevance to your workplace.

The Philosophy and Purpose of your Organization

This section serves as an introduction to your personnel policies, particularly those that you may include in your handbook. A short statement of the philosophy and purpose of your organization establishes a context for the document. Being explicit about your mission and values establishes your general expectations in terms of attitude and approach to clients and the community.

NONCONTRACTUAL NATURE OF THE EMPLOYEE HANDBOOK

If you want language making it clear that your handbook is not to be construed as making a contract with your employees, that should be included here in capital letters or bold type so that the language is not easily overlooked. If you choose to deny that your handbook or policies is a contract, be sure that other language in the document does not contradict this. For example, statements like "the employer *shall* provide the following grievance procedure," suggests a contractual commitment.

ORGANIZATIONAL CHART

It's a good idea to include a chart illustrating the lines of authority within the organization. A typical chart is shown here. The one in your personnel policies should reflect the way things really are managed in your organization, not some idealized version.

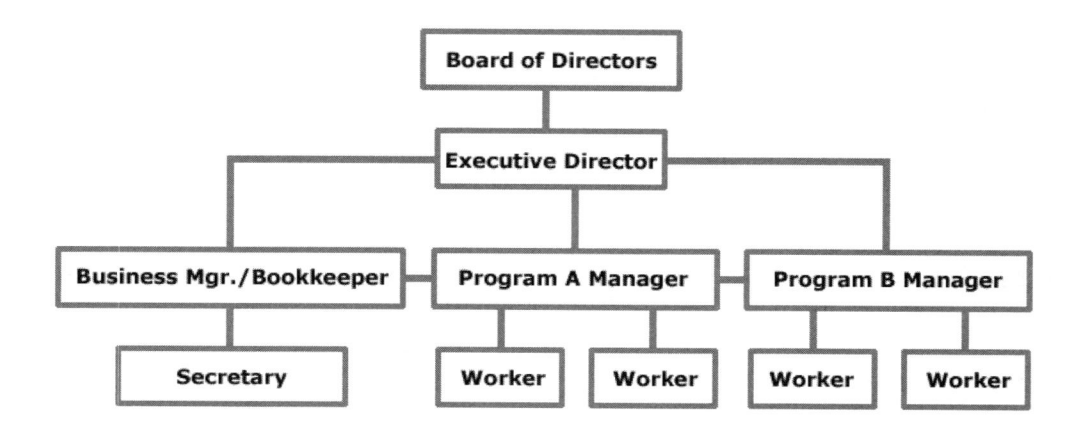

Nondiscrimination and Harassment Policies

NONDISCRIMINATION

Many groups want to make a statement indicating that the organization does not permit illegal discrimination or harassment on any basis protected by federal, state, or local law. It is a good idea to include such a statement. Many organizations go on to state they are committed to affirmative action. The phrase "affirmative action" is generally understood to mean giving preferential treatment to certain minority classes. But preferential treatment based on race, sex, sexual orientation, or many other classes not job-related is illegal. In recent years, courts have become increasingly skeptical of affirmative action. Unless it is very, very carefully done, an affirmative action policy puts the organization at serious legal risk. If the nonprofit is committed to following an affirmative action policy, any such policy needs to be carefully reviewed by an attorney.

SEXUAL HARASSMENT AND OTHER FORMS OF HARASSMENT

Harassment, when based on any protected class and is severe or pervasive, is considered to be a form of discrimination. As such, it is against the both federal and state law. Most nonprofit employers are committed to maintaining a workplace environment that is free from harassment. Your policies and employee handbook can assist in this effort by spelling out what is acceptable and unacceptable conduct.

> *Court cases have underlined the importance of having a sexual harassment policy and other anti-harassment policies in place.*

Recent court cases have underlined the importance of having an anti-harassment policy, together with a clear complaint procedure and a promise of nonretaliation against people who report harassment or assist in an anti-harassment investigation. Having such a policy is no longer optional.

Your harassment policy should describe harassment in terms that your employees can understand and that correspond with the legal definitions. The policy should also clearly outline a procedure that the employee can follow to complain about harassment. The procedure should provide that the complaint must be prompt and in writing to two or three people in upper management and on the Board. There must also be some alternative for the employee if the person the employee would normally complain to is the alleged harasser. The policy should state that complaints will be investigated and that if harassment is found, you will take prompt corrective action. In addition, the policy must clearly prohibit retaliation against employees who make harassment complaints in good faith.

Obeying All Laws

In a recent case, an Oregon court held an employer liable for an employee's illegal conduct, on grounds that the employer had never clearly stated that employees were required to follow laws. Okay, we might think it's obvious that employees should obey the law but it's not quite that simple. For example, sometimes employees are given instructions by a supervisor to do something illegal and you need to let your employees know that they should not follow these orders. Employee handbooks are a good place to put that policy.

A single sentence is sufficient: that employees are required to follow all federal, state, and local laws, and any employee who believes himself or herself to have received instructions otherwise must immediately inform the members of the Board in writing.

Conditions of Employment

AT-WILL EMPLOYMENT

Employers choosing an at-will employment approach should include a clear statement that all employees are at-will. The statement should explain that this means the employee can terminate the employment relationship for any reason at any time and the employer can terminate the employment relationship for any legal reason at any time.

ATTENDANCE

- How are attendance records kept?
- How does an employee call in sick or late?
- If substitutes are required, state clearly the process for obtaining a substitute. Who calls the substitute?

Attendance is a major cause of failure of the employment relationship. Since the advent of the state and federal Family Medical Leave Acts, attendance is also a major cause of employer liability. If the employer is covered by the state or federal family medical leave acts, be sure your attendance tracking procedures carefully track which absences or tardies are protected leave and which are not.

THE WORK DAY

- Define the minimum work day for each job classification (How many hours per day? How many days per week? When is "starting time" and "quitting time"?)

- Define the work week for purposes of overtime (typically 12:00 a.m. Monday through 11:59 p.m. Sunday).

- Specify when and how lunch breaks and rest breaks are to be taken. Oregon law requires that employees working shifts of six hours or more be given a lunch break of at least one-half hour of uninterrupted time. If that period is completely uninterrupted, you do not have to pay for it. Also, for each period of two to four hours worked, employees must be given a ten minute paid break during which they are completely relieved of all duty. The rules are slightly different for minors.

- Specify when and if staff meetings will be held. Who is required to attend?

- Describe the procedure to get authorization for overtime.

- Inform employees if you will be expecting them to work long hours or to be available outside normal work hours.

STANDARDS OF PERSONAL BEHAVIOR

- List any standards that you require such as dress codes.
- Include here who can make statements as an official spokesperson of the organization.

NO EXPECTATION OF PRIVACY

The advent of computers and email has created new opportunities for an employee to mix business and his/her private life. Organizations may be sued for invasion of privacy if they have no policy on the topic of privacy. Specifically, you should inform employees that all material and communication sent by, received by, or stored in the organization's communications tools, even personal email and voice mail messages, may be viewed or listened to by the Executive Director, by the Board of Directors, by any member of management, by anyone designated by management, or by law enforcement at any time without further notice. You need to tell employees that anything any employee brings onto the organization's property or into the organization's buildings or vehicles are subject to search by the organization without notice. Employees need to know that they have no expectation of privacy in any item or communication on employer property.

Employees need to know that they have no expectation of privacy in any item or communication on employer property.

This not an appealing policy, and there is rarely a reason an organization needs to follow through on such searches. But reserving the right to do them is critical to the organization's ability to conduct investigations, or even to cope with situations in which, for example, an employee simply fails to show up for work and another employee must pick up that employee's workload. Organizations exempt under §501(c)(3) may need to check employee emails and other communications to ensure that employees are not engaging in supporting or opposing candidates using the organization's computers or other resources that can result in your organization losing its tax exempt status. See pages 179-80.

DRUG AND ALCOHOL USE

Many employers are developing drug and alcohol policies. These policies are useful to avoid and defend against negligent hiring and retention claims. You are certainly permitted to prohibit illegal drug use on the job. In dealing with prescription drugs, your policy will need to accommodate employees who need these drugs. If you want to conduct drug searches or drug tests, your policies should be drafted by a knowledgeable attorney. If your drug or alcohol policy refers to "under the influence," you should define that term. Otherwise, you may be challenged by employees who claim that some drug or alcohol use does not constitute "under the influence." One option would be to define "under the influence" as "any detectable level."

Be aware that many contracts for government funding will require that your policies meet the requirements of the federal Drug Free Workplace Act. If you accept funding that requires compliance, be sure your personnel policies contain all required provisions.

CONFIDENTIALITY

If your organization does work in which confidentiality is important, you should indicate this to your employees and explicitly describe your policy regarding confidentiality. If your approach is to require cause for discipline and termination, you should state the consequences of violating this policy.

OUTSIDE EMPLOYMENT

You should make a clear policy on whether an employee can have outside employment.

- Must the employee inform your organization of outside employment?
- Can outside employment be restricted if it appears to be detrimental to or in conflict with your policies?

POLITICAL OR LOBBYING ACTIVITIES

The organization's 503(c)3 status is endangered if employees of the organization engage in political or excessive lobbying activities on work time, using workplace equipment, or in their capacity as employees for the organization. It is important to have a policy informing the employees of this. The IRS has some sample policies available which are helpful in drawing the line between what political activities employees can engage in on behalf of the employer (very little) and what employees can do on their own time (a great deal). See Chapter 8 for more discussion on this topic.

CONFLICT OF INTEREST

- Can the corporation purchase or rent goods, space or services from employees, including the Executive Director?
- Can employees receive gifts, money or gratuities from persons receiving benefits from the program? From funding sources? From contractors?

Again, this is an area of interest to the IRS and to some funders, particularly federal funders. See the Conflicts of Interest and Executive Compensation Policy in the Forms section for a policy that includes key employees under its conflicts provision. If you have federal funders with additional restrictions on gifts to employees, you check with your funder or get professional help to draft a proper policy.

Employment Categories

EXEMPT AND NONEXEMPT EMPLOYEES

You should briefly outline exempt versus or non-exempt job positions. See page 395 for a discussion about these categories and their significance. You may want to indicate that exempt employees may find that additional hours of service are necessary and that it's the organization's expectation that exempt employees will work sufficient hours to accomplish the duties of the position and will not receive overtime pay. Be sure to define the impact of exempt or nonexempt employee status on the availability of specific benefits.

TRIAL PERIOD

Your approach toward at-will employment will in part determine whether you have a trial period and what its meaning is. If you are an at-will employer, you can fire anyone, any time, for any legal reason, so a trial period is meaningless for purposes of job security. Some at-will employers will have an introductory period for purposes of determining when employees become eligible for benefits.

> *Your approach toward at-will employment will in part determine whether you have a trial period and what its meaning is.*

If you are not an at-will employer, then you will want to consider in more detail issues about a trial period. Here are some decisions you will need to make:

- Is there a trial period?
- How long is it for each job classification?
- Do employees who are transferred within the organization or promoted within the organization have a new trial period?
- How is termination to be handled within the trial period? (Many employers allow for termination during the trial period without cause. This avoids time consuming steps to document cause when it is clear the relationship just isn't working out. If your organization wants to be able to do this be sure the personnel policies say explicitly that "during the trial period an employee may be terminated without cause.")
- Who can terminate an employee during the trial period? How is notice of termination given in this case?
- Do vacation time, sick time and other benefits accrue during the trial period? Can they be used during the trial period?
- Are benefits given at all during the trial period?

EMPLOYEE CLASSIFICATIONS

Your approach toward termination will also govern how you handle the classification of employees. If you are an at-will employer, you may want to refer to your employees as regular full-time, regular part-time, temporary full-time, and temporary part-time employees. The use of the word "regular" rather than "permanent" avoids the implication that the job is somehow protected.

If your employees do have protection from termination without cause, then possible employment classifications might be permanent full-time, permanent part-time, temporary full-time employees, and temporary part-time. These classifications could be further defined by whether there was a predetermined terminal point of employment and how many hours per week will be worked.

Regardless of the approach you take, you should define clearly which benefits can be received with each classification at what rates.

Compensation

SALARY RANGE

You will need to familiarize yourself with the minimum wage laws to be sure your salaries comply with them. You may also want to consult compensation studies that report wages and benefits paid by other nonprofits or businesses with similar positions. If you are exempt under §501(c)(3), you should also consult the IRS rules on excess benefit transactions discussed on pages 700-706. Some issues to consider as you develop your policies about salaries include:

- How will salary ranges be determined?
- Are they to be comparable to similar positions in other nonprofits?
- Are they determined primarily by budgetary considerations?
- Explain how employees will be notified of the salary range currently in effect.

SALARY INCREASES

- What are the criteria for raises?
- How does this fit with availability of funds?
- Are salary raises automatic or based on performance?
- If salary raises are automatic, are merit increases in salary available?
- Explain that due to the uncertainty of the organization's financial situation into the future, discretion in making salary changes is retained by management regardless of any other provision.

PAYROLL PROCEDURES

- Describe the basis (hours, days, weeks, months) on which payroll is calculated.
- How often do employees get paid? (Employees must be paid at least every 35 days, unless you have a written agreement with your employee before work begins to pay in a different manner.)

- What if payday is on a weekend or a holiday?
- Can employees take a draw on their salary?
- What is the procedure for draws? (advanced draws on compensation are generally not recommended)
- Who will maintain the time sheets?
- Who will sign and approve them?
- Inform your employees that IRS Form W-4 and U.S. Department of Justice I-9 will be filed by the employee on the first day of employment. Your manual may also inform your employees that on or before January 31st of each year, each employee will receive a statement showing total earnings and the amount of tax, by type, withheld.
- List all the deductions which will be made from the employee's salary. Which are voluntary (i.e., those to which the employee must consent)? Which are involuntary? (Health care and insurance benefits may require voluntary deductions, for example.)

Benefits

PAID HOLIDAYS

The employee handbook or personnel policies should list the regular paid holidays such as Christmas, New Year's Day, Memorial Day, July 4th, Labor Day, and Thanksgiving, as well as any other paid holidays specific to the organization, such as Washington's Birthday, Martin Luther King's Birthday, or President's Day. A policy for days such as the Friday after Thanksgiving or Christmas Eve can be included. If an employee is on vacation during a paid holiday, it is usually added to the accrued vacation days. Your policy should explain your position on this.

VACATION

You are not required by law to provide any vacation time for your employees. But most employers recognize that they need to provide this to keep employees for any length of time and to keep up morale. If you do elect to provide vacation time, you should decide what happens to accrued but unused vacation time on termination. If there is no clear employer policy, the law will assume all accrued but unused vacation time is paid out at the time of termination, and your employee may be able to enforce her or his right to this under the wage and hours laws. Your policies and handbook should clarify these issues:

- Do employees receive vacation time? Paid or unpaid?
- How does it accrue for each employment classification?
- Is there a minimum period of employment before vacation can be taken?
- Is there a limit on the amount per year?
- How is it to be scheduled? Is advance notice required? Usually vacation time is taken at a time which is mutually agreeable to all the parties concerned so as not to disrupt the efficient operations of the organization. Final say on vacation leaves must remain with management, though.

- Who approves vacation leaves? In writing?
- Is there any limitation on the amount of vacation time which may be accrued? Use it or lose it policies force the employee to take the accrued vacation time within a specified time period or lose the benefit. Some organizations offer to cash out unused vacation time once a maximum amount is accrued.
- Will you pay out any accrued but unused vacation time upon termination of employment?

SICK LEAVE

There is no legal requirement that you provide any sick leave, other than the unpaid leave required for employees with long-term or serious health conditions under the disability acts (see page 414) and unpaid family leave (below) required under federal and state family leave acts. If you do want to provide for short-term sick leave in addition to that required under those laws, you might consider the following issues:

- Do employees receive sick leave beyond their legal entitlement? Paid or unpaid?
- How does sick leave accrue for each job classification?
- Is there a limit per month? Per year?
- Can accumulated sick leave be added to vacation leave?
- Will employees be paid for sick days accrued but not taken by end of year?
- You should define what is considered sick leave (apart from employee illness). Illness in the immediate family? Who is the immediate family?
- It is a good idea to conform your definition to that of the family leave laws, for ease of administration and consistency. Do mental health days to relieve stress qualify for sick leave?
- Will you cash out unused sick leave at termination? Most employers do not, but you should be clear about your policy.

FAMILY LEAVE

State and federal law contain some requirements about family leave. Not all employers are required to follow these statutes.

OREGON LAW

Under Oregon law, you must provide family leave if you have 25 or more employees for 20 or more weeks in the year in which the leave is taken or in the preceding year. Your employee has to have worked at least 180 days to be eligible. For most types of leave, the employee also has to have worked at least 25 hours per week to be eligible.

You must give family leave for an eligible employee to care for an infant or newly adopted child or newly placed foster child, to care for a family member with a serious health condition, to care for the employee's own serious health condition that keeps that employee from performing at least one essential function of the job, and to care for the employee's child who does not have a serious health condition but requires home care. "Family member" includes parents, children, spouses, same-sex domestic partners, and parents-in-law.

Generally, you must give your eligible employee at least 12 weeks of leave every year in the circumstances listed above, with an additional 12 weeks for women who cannot perform their regular duties because of an illness, injury, or medical condition related to pregnancy or childbirth. Employees may be eligible for more leave under some circumstances. You do not have to pay for the leave. However, your employees are entitled to use any accrued paid vacation and may be entitled to use paid sick leave if it is consistent with your sick leave policy. Employees who are taking leave to care for a newborn or newly adopted child are also entitled to use any accrued leave, including sick leave. When an employee's leave is over, you must reinstate that employee to his or her former position, even if it is currently filled. If the position was eliminated, you must return the employee to an available, equivalent position.

FEDERAL LAW

Under federal law, you must provide family leave if you have 50 or more employees for each working day during 20 or more calendar weeks in the current or preceding calendar year. You must give leave to any employee who has been employed at least 12 months and for at least 1,250 hours during the 12 months preceding the start of the leave.

Generally, you must give your eligible employees at least 12 weeks of leave every year in the circumstances similar to those covered by the Oregon statute, except that federal law does not require leave for a sick child who is home but not seriously ill.

Federal law also does not provide leave for the serious illness of a same-sex domestic partner or parent-in-law. You do not have to pay for the leave. Federal family leave and Oregon family leave run concurrently when an employee is eligible under both laws.

The scope of coverage is generally similar to that provided by Oregon law, with a few exceptions. Employees covered by the federal law who are taking leave to care for seriously ill family members are entitled to use any paid accrued leave. Under the federal law, the employer must generally continue the employee's coverage under any group health care plan, a benefit Oregon law does not require. There are other minor differences between the two laws. Because the Oregon and federal leave laws can sometimes overlap in complicated ways, it is important that you understand what each law requires and consult an attorney when you have questions.

WORKER COMPENSATION

Employers are required by law to provide employees with Worker's Compensation insurance. You should take care that any policy you state concerning this does not promise your employee more than the law provides, unless that is your intention. Many employers also want to provide an explicit description of the return to work rules required under the worker compensation law, so that the injured employee and those dealing with her or him follow the correct procedure. Many workers' compensation carriers, such as SAIF, will provide you with a return-to-work policy upon request, and recommend its implementation.

JURY DUTY

You must permit your employee to leave work to serve jury duty. You are not required to pay for jury duty service, except for exempt employees. Even where not required by law, employees are often granted leaves with pay when they are required to report for jury duty. Will the employee be paid regular earnings less the per diem compensation received for jury duty? Must the employee present a jury summons before the leave is granted? Should the employee report to work during periods when excused from appearing for jury duty? If any pay is extended to employees on jury duty, do you want to limit the amount of time? Consider the circumstances of an extended jury trial—can the organization sustain the financial burden of payments to an employee who is gone for weeks or even months?

MILITARY LEAVE

You must give leave for members of a Reserve Unit of the U.S. Armed Forces when they are required to report for duty and for other military service. You do not have to give the leave with pay. If you do grant the leave with pay, will the employee be paid full salary or full salary less the per diem compensation received for duty?

DISABILITY LEAVE

Both state and federal laws require that an employer provide reasonable accommodation for employees with disabilities as long as that accommodation does not create an undue hardship for the employer. Such accommodation may include a leave of absence to receive treatment for disability. Because disability laws require employers to deal with each request for accommodation on a case-by-case basis, you may want to keep any policies fairly general.

OTHER COMMON OPTIONAL LEAVES

Many employers do want to clarify policies about other leaves. You need to decide which leaves will be granted with pay and which without pay. In deciding this, you will need to consider the effect on your budget and operations of having employees gone for extended periods of time. You will also need to decide how long the employee must have been working to receive a leave, the length of the leave granted, and who has the final authority to grant leaves or to extend leaves. You should also coordinate this leave with your other leave policies.

Finally, you need to consider what arrangements you will make when the employee returns to work. Your policies should address whether any type of doctor's letter is required and whether you will guarantee the employee reinstatement.

EMERGENCY LEAVE

In what situations will emergency leave be granted? Who will decide if it should be with pay or without pay? How many days will be granted? Death in the immediate family of an employee is usually considered an emergency. You should state clearly other such emergency situations where leaves could be granted with pay. Under unusual circumstances, can leave with pay be granted on an individual basis? By whom?

BEREAVEMENT LEAVE

Many employers provide for bereavement leave to cover bereavement situations not otherwise covered by family leave. If you do so, the questions detailed in the Emergency Leave section must be answered.

EDUCATIONAL LEAVE

Some employers grant educational leave for their employees, particularly if the education improves the employee's job skills. If you elect to provide this, your policy should clearly state the circumstances in which leave applies, who has the authority to approve the leave, whether the leave is with or without pay, and whether the employee has to present any documentation to substantiate the leave.

TIME BANK CONCEPT

Some employers are moving away from the separate vacation and sick leave policies to a time bank concept. Under this approach, each employee accrues a defined number of paid leave hours for each pay period. The employee is free to use these paid leave hours for vacation, personal illness, the illness of a family member or friend, mental health days, or whatever they choose. These policies must be carefully drafted to ensure that they comply with all of the mandatory leave rules. Be sure you have stated clearly your policy with regard to paying out accrued but unused leave amounts upon termination.

Fringe benefits and retirement benefits planning is an area of complex regulation. Professional assistance from an attorney/ accountant or retirement and fringe benefits planner is essential.

OTHER BENEFITS

List all other benefits available to employees:

- Health Care and Dental Insurance
- Dependent Care Assistance Plans
- Tax Sheltered Annuity (a type of retirement plan)
- Other Retirement Plan (State whether or not you have a retirement plan. They are not mandatory, but if you have one, it must meet certain requirements.)

The policy and handbook should state whether benefits are transferable when an employee transfers or is promoted within the organization.

Fringe benefits and retirement benefits planning is an area of complex regulation. Some nonprofits now offer flexible benefit plans which permit employees to choose from an array of benefits such as health insurance, dependent health insurance, dependent care assistance plans, medical reimbursement plans, etc. In order to maintain the tax-free status of such a flexible fringe benefit approach, the organization must have a written §125 flexible benefits plan which meets IRS requirements.

Tax-exempt groups may establish a special type of retirement plan known as a Tax Sheltered Annuity (403(b) plans) or they may offer certain types of retirement plans also available in for profit organizations. Fringe benefits and retirement benefits planning is an area of complex regulation. Professional assistance from an attorney, accountant, or retirement and fringe benefits planner is essential. It is easy to make serious errors in this area. Many fringe benefits carriers provide excellent assistance for low fees or for free. Be sure that any plan documents have been reviewed by an attorney who has expertise in the appropriate legal specialties. Penalties for failure to comply with fringe benefit and retirement plan regulations can be extremely costly.

REIMBURSEMENTS

- Which expenses can be reimbursed (telephone calls, parking fees, field trip expenses, conference and meeting fees)?

- Is advance approval necessary? By whom?

- How are reimbursements paid to employees?

- If travel expenses are reimbursable, what is the rate per mile?

- If a chauffeur's license (beyond the expense of an individual driver's license) or food handler's card is required in the line of duty, will this expense be reimbursed?

- For travel expenses, do mileage records need to be kept on specific forms?

Job Reclassification

Because of budgeting uncertainties, many nonprofits need the flexibility to reclassify jobs. If you are an at-will employer, you have this flexibility. If you are not, you will need to address the adjustments needed when you reclassify a job. If the reclassification results in an upgrade, what is the employee's new salary level? If the reclassification results in a lower salary grade, does the employee take a pay cut?

Employee Evaluation

Employee evaluation is a complicated topic that is the subject of many books. For purposes of your policies, you should consider stating the frequency, content, methods, procedures, and goals and objectives of staff evaluations. Be sure to indicate who will perform the evaluation and what will be done with the evaluation when completed. Make provision for employees to disagree with evaluations of their performance. Indicate different evaluation procedures for different job classifications, if any. Be careful if you are an at-will employer not to include language that implies that employees have any job security resulting from the evaluation process.

Disciplinary Action

At-will employers will often not have a disciplinary action section, since the employer can discipline at any time for any reason. In order to maintain consistency and to protect against future discrimination claims, some at-will employers develop a separate supervisor's manual, not included in the handbook, which includes disciplinary procedures so that the organization can enforce an organization-wide policy of discipline without making commitments to the employees subject to discipline.

If your corporation is not an at-will employer, the disciplinary policy is important because it establishes the procedures by which you handle employee problems and also provides some protection against discrimination claims by showing you use a uniform nondiscriminatory discipline procedure for everyone.

Disciplinary action might be one or more of the following:

- A verbal warning or discussion
- A written reprimand (placed in the personnel record)
- Suspension (with or without pay)
- Dismissal

> *At-will employers will often not have a disciplinary action section, since the employer can discipline at any time for any reason.*

Each of these actions is independent of one another and need not follow in the order of the sequence listed above. The following might be grounds for disciplinary action:

- Misconduct
- Inefficiency
- Incompetence
- Insubordination
- Dishonesty
- Disloyalty
- Willful violation of established corporate policy
- Any other conduct that the company deems to be detrimental to its interest.

The personnel policies should state when and how written notice is to be given to the employee against whom disciplinary action is being considered.

- How are allegations to be made?
- How are they substantiated? By whom?

- For suspension without pay, clearly state the grounds for the suspension and how long the suspension shall last. Also indicate how the employee is notified of the suspension, the date of the suspension and its cause.

For dismissal, the typical policy by employers who require cause for dismissal is to provide that dismissal will be for just cause. It is important to list the causes and to be sure that your list both covers all circumstances for which you will want to dismiss and provides one clause that is general enough to justify dismissal in those cases that fall outside the list but for which dismissal is needed. Causes for dismissal or suspension might include:

- Failure to perform the job adequately
- Drinking on the job
- Taking illegal drugs on the job
- Arriving for work under the influence of alcohol or drugs
- Habitual absence or tardiness
- Unauthorized release of information
- Stealing
- Repeated instances of conducting personal business on office time
- Failure to maintain businesslike relationships with others
- Disobedience or insubordination
- Any other circumstance in which the company deems dismissal to be in its interest.

If you find yourself considering dismissal of an employee, be sure to read the section below on Dismissal before you act.

Termination of Employment

At-will employers will generally not have this section, except possibly to address questions about benefits. Other employers may want to consider these issues:

LAYOFF

You need to retain the flexibility to reduce your work force if funding changes or other actions require it. Your policy should state the circumstances that could result in layoff, provide for notice, and describe the system which will be used to determine order of lay-off and recall.

VOLUNTARY TERMINATION

- How much notice is necessary?
- Should it be written notice? To whom?
- Who can approve an early termination date if it serves the interest of the employee or the nonprofit?

RETIREMENT

You should be aware that imposing a mandatory age for retirement is illegal in most cases as age discrimination. You can impose age limitations if the limitation is a bona fide occupational qualification, but these are rare. You should get legal advice if you are considering mandatory retirement.

INVOLUNTARY TERMINATION

- How much written notice is required before the effective date of termination? (Usually ten days to two weeks.)
- Is a termination interview required?
- If the reasons for dismissal are serious, can the employee be suspended without pay until the effective dismissal date?
- If necessary, can pay be provided to personnel in lieu of proper notice by the organization?

Appeals Procedures for Discipline and Termination

If you are not an at-will employer, your appeals procedure should describe the mechanism for appeal, including how the employee accesses the system, what the time limit is for appeal, who the employee contacts, what evidence the employee must submit, who makes the decision and in what time frame, whether there is a further level of appeal, and how the employee is notified.

GRIEVANCE PROCEDURE

A grievance procedure cannot be a replacement for your Harassment and Discrimination complaint procedure. This should be made very clear at the beginning of each policy. The purpose of the grievance procedure is quite expansive, covering a wide variety of employee concerns, often encouraging employees to take a first step of talking with each other. The purpose of the harassment and discrimination policy is to put upper management or the Board on immediate notice of any possible incidents of harassment and discrimination, so that the employer can immediately swing into action with an investigation and prompt intervention. A harassment and discrimination policy which requires an employee to first talk over his or her harassment with the alleged harasser would almost certainly be found to be inadequate by a court.

The term grievance means a complaint dispute or employee expressed feeling of dissatisfaction with working conditions or working relationships. At-will employers who decide to use a grievance procedure need to be careful that the grievance procedure is written in such a way that it does not implicitly suggest that an employee cannot be disciplined while using it.

It is important to establish a channel for grievances, a time limit for appeals and a clear statement of final authority. The usual steps for a grievance procedure are to specify that:

- First, the aggrieved parties must talk to each other (with or without a facilitator).
- Second, there is discussion between them and the Executive Director or chairperson of the Board of Directors.

- Third, a hearing is conducted before the personnel committee of the Board of Directors or a committee established by the Executive Director.

Personnel policies usually state that employees may file a grievance without fear of recrimination, although at-will employers may not want to include this commitment.

In addition, your organization should consider these questions:

- Must all grievances be in writing to be considered?
- Who should receive grievances?
- How much time is allowed to attempt to resolve the grievance at each step?
- How involved does the Board want to be in a personnel matter?
- Who has the final authority in resolving grievances?

Creating an Employee Handbook

Most employers want to gather the personnel policies that relate to the conditions of employment for their employees into an employee handbook for distribution to the employees. Larger employers may distribute two handbooks—one to management employees and the other to nonexempt employees. These handbooks contain most, but not all, of the employer's personnel policies.

Personnel Policies Outside the Handbook

Not all personnel policies are relevant to the handbook that you give employees. Those that are not relevant should be retained with the corporation's policies but not included in the handbook given to employees. Two common policies are hiring policies and policies on confidential records.

HIRING AND RECRUITING POLICIES

Employment lawyers do not generally advise include hiring policies in the employment handbook. Many Boards actively participate in the creation of the organization's hiring policies, which may then be kept in a separate place.

The Board may want to work with the Executive Director in considering:

- whether jobs must be posted internally first;
- how applicants are screened and interviewed; and
- who makes the hiring decisions.

PERSONNEL AND MEDICAL RECORDS FOR EACH EMPLOYEE

A personnel record should be maintained for each employee. The record should contain:

- A completed application (including address, phone and education)
- Letter of agreement for employment

- Date of employment
- Form W-4 and I-9 (proof of citizenship or permission to work)
- Payroll records
- Any evaluations
- Record of accrued vacation and sick leave (but no medical information)
- Job description
- Record of any training certificates required for employment

The personnel policies should state who (what position) maintains the personnel records. The personnel records of the employee must be made available to the employee, who must be given a copy if it is requested. The personnel policies should include a statement as to whether the records are open to anyone else.

> *The personnel records of the employee must be made available to the employee, who must be given a copy if it is requested.*

By law, you must keep any medical records concerning your employees separate from the employees' personnel file, with extremely restricted access. Only need-to-know management may have access to employees' locked medical records. It is critical that your system maintain confidentiality of the medical records.

POLICIES RELATED TO EXEMPT EMPLOYEES

Your corporation will want to have some policies related to the compensation and conditions of employment for your managers and other employees exempt from the wage and hour laws. Most corporations prefer to keep these policies out of their nonexempt employee handbooks.

Amendments to Personnel Policies and Employee Handbooks

Your policies and handbook need to have a provision that reserves your right to change them. The policies and handbook should state who has the authority to amend them. Many employers add a specific provision alerting employees that no one else has the authority to amend the policies or to make any promises about employment that are not contained within the policies. The reason for doing this is to prevent a claim by an employee that a promise about employment was made verbally to her or him by a supervisor.

Many employers add a specific provision alerting employees that no one else has the authority to amend the policies or to make any promises about employment that are not contained within the policies. The policies should indicate whether employees must be given notice of the changes in order for the changes to be effective. Whether or not your policies require you to notify the employees, it is a good practice to do so and to have the employees sign to indicate they have received a copy of the new policies. Some corporations give the changes to the staff with their paychecks and require a sign-off at that time.

Many employers add a specific provision alerting employees that no one else has the authority to amend the policies or to make any promises about employment that are not contained within the policies.

Distribution of the Employee Handbook

You need to decide whether to give a copy of your personnel policies that pertain to the employee's conditions to some or all of your employees. Most organizations that decide to do so print the policies in the form of an employee handbook, although you can of course call the document by another name. The advantages of distributing your policies is that your employees are clearly informed about what their benefits are and what your expectations are concerning the employment relationship. The handbook prevents employee confusion and incorrect expectations about your policies that may arise from gossip or mistaken information from other employees. If your employees have access to your policies, the law often charges them with knowledge of the policies whether or not they actually read them.

There are some disadvantages to distributing policies. Some organizations do not want non-managerial employees to know what benefits managerial employees enjoy. These groups may choose to have separate sets of policies for managerial and non-managerial employees or may choose not to distribute this information in their handbook. Occasionally, your organization may be constrained by your employees' knowledge of your policies. If your employee was aware of a policy and relied on it, you may be legally bound to follow it, a result that may not have occurred had the employee not been familiar with your policies. Each of these problems can, however, be avoided through careful drafting with the guidance of an employment attorney.

If you do decide to distribute an employee handbook, be sure to have each employee sign to acknowledge that he or she received a copy and to keep these acknowledgments in your employee files. Acknowledgments should include statements indicating the employee's understanding the at-will standard (if you use it), harassment policies, the obligation to obey all laws, and any other appropriate disclaimers. If you do decide to distribute an employee handbook, you will need to design workable procedures for being sure that all employees have access to the most recent version of the document. The date of issuance or most recent update should appear prominently in the document. Many employers now place the most recent version of the handbook on a share drive of their computer system and include reference to the employee's responsibility to check for recent updates in the acknowledgement of receiving the copy provided at the time of employment.

Administering Personnel Policies and the Employee Handbook

Most Boards of Directors delegate responsibility for day-to-day administration of personnel policies and the handbook to the Executive Director and other key supervisory staff. However, if the Board has not delegated its authority to administer policies to the Executive Director, ongoing involvement by the Personnel Committee of the Board is essential if your policies are to have the full support of the Board. How the Personnel Committee functions will vary depending on the approach to personnel policies or your employee handbook your organization has chosen. If your corporation is an at-will employer and has avoided making specific commitments in your employee handbook, the job of your Personnel Committee may be limited to reviewing and revising the policies as needed.

If your Board has chosen a model that makes specific commitments and provides for a grievance mechanism, the Personnel Committee is typically needed to fulfill policy making and appeal functions including:

- resolution of grievances;
- final interpretations of personnel policies. and
- preparation of annual revisions and updates of personnel policies.

Dismissal or Termination of Employees

The most common cause of lawsuits against nonprofit corporations are suits by unhappy employees, usually those who have been dismissed. If you are in the position of considering dismissal or termination of an employee, plan carefully for the dismissal termination. Do not dismiss an employee in the heat of the moment. Keep in mind some of the warning signs that suggest you might be particularly vulnerable to a lawsuit:

- Your employee is a member of a protected class (based on race, ethnicity, religion, gender, age, sexual orientation, disability, etc.).
- Your corporation has a verbal or written agreement about the employment with the employee.
- Your corporation has personnel policies or an employee handbook promising "just cause termination," or failing to provide for "at-will" employment.
- There has been no previous history of discipline leading to termination.
- Your employee has difficulty accepting criticism and therefore possibly more prone to litigate.
- Your corporation has strong governmental connections.

It is always a very good idea to discuss dismissal or termination with an employment lawyer before you dismiss or terminate the employee but you really should do so if you have any of the warning signs above.

Excessive Compensation

If you are exempt from taxation under §501(c)(3) as a public charity or under §501(c) (4), you are subject to IRS regulations aimed at ensuring that you do not pay too much to certain of your high-level employees. This includes employees like your Executive Director, your chief financial officer, your chief operating officer, and others. The IRS will assume that you are paying too much unless you follow certain steps before you agree to a compensation package. This is an area of great concern to the IRS. We urge you to read pages 700-706.

Evaluating the Executive Director

While most personnel policies provide a supervisory structure within the staff, the Board itself must provide a structure for supervision and evaluation of the Executive Director. Typically, the Personnel Committee or Executive Committee of the Board conducts an annual evaluation of the Executive Director. Ongoing consultation and feedback can be provided through regular meetings between the Board Chair and the Executive Director.

Unfortunately many Boards ignore their responsibility to provide a meaningful evaluation for the Executive Director until there is substantial dissatisfaction with the individual's performance. It is not surprising that many executives perceive such evaluations to be unfair and unreasonable in light of the Board's earlier tacit approval of their work. In contrast, most Executive Directors deeply appreciate regular, well-planned performance reviews both as structures for important feedback and as opportunities to reflect on personal goals and strategies for professional development within their position.

Meaningful Executive Director evaluations require clarity on both the process the Board will use and the content or focus of the review. We'll start with process issues first. Your Board will want to provide a clear charge to the committee asked to take the lead on the Executive Director evaluation, including offering guidance about whether the evaluation process should include input from the full Board or selected Board members, from some portion of the staff, and/or key community stakeholders. The Board must also be clear with the committee regarding the extent of their authority. Does the committee have full authority to complete the evaluation and place a record of it in the executive's personnel file? Or is the committee being asked to formulate a recommended evaluation which must be approved by the full Board or some sub-committee before being deemed final?

Once the evaluation committee is clear about the scope of its charge, it can lay out and share with the executive a clear description of the steps that will be utilized and the timeline for completing them. Evaluations are stressful for most of us, so letting executive know the plan and timing is an important stress reduction strategy.

The question of whether your Board should seek input from multiple sources or rely primarily on the perceptions of the evaluation committee members is complex. The value of multiple viewpoints may be offset by concerns about creating a perception that the executive is "in trouble" or that the Board has doubts about his/her performance.

Regardless of whether you will ask evaluation committee members to seek input from multiple parties or rely primarily on their own observations, you will want to be sure that the committee is clear about the legal issues which surround the evaluation of the executive. You may want to consult resource materials from the Nonprofit Risk Management Center or your Board liability insurance provider, or seek local legal advice. Key issues include confidentiality, fairness, and objectivity.

Which brings us to discussion of the content of the evaluation. If your Board has required that the job description for the Executive Director position is regularly updated, and if you have been asking your executive to describe their goals and priorities for each year, you will be well prepared to focus the evaluation on your mutually agreed upon expectations for the position. Unfortunately, in many nonprofits, the expectations of the executive grow and shift as the organization becomes more complex but the job description is never formally revised; the Board fails behind in conducting regular evaluations of the executive director; and the executive never finds the time to articulate specific goals for the year. If this is your situation, one of the first steps of the evaluation process will be clarifying the current expectations of the position. And your evaluation may have to acknowledge that while there are areas where you see opportunity for improved performance, there has not been clarity about the expectations previously.

Many executive directors tell us that they find their Board's evaluation of limited value because Board members are too concerned with being nice and too overwhelmed by the sense that the job is actually impossible to do. An evaluation that offers only unspecific praise for doing a fabulous job has two key weaknesses. First, it's not actually a source of support for an executive unless it calls out the specific areas of excellent work and also helps the executive identify areas of personal and organizational challenge. Like any other employee, the Executive Director benefits more from careful attention and dialogue than from high marks without careful, honest thought. Equally important, providing an overly generalized "great job" evaluation can set the stage for resentment and legal conflict when serious problems are identified in subsequent evaluations, especially if the behaviors giving rise to those problems were present during the period for which the praise-only evaluation was given.

Independent Contractors and Volunteers as Employees

In two situations, you may have people providing services who you have not classified as employees but who should be.

Independent Contractors

It is tempting for an employer to try to avoid the complexities of the wage and hour laws, as well as other employment laws, by simply calling its workers independent contractors. This is a very common mistake. State and federal regulations strictly limit who can be considered an independent contractor, and misclassifying a worker can be extremely costly for an employer. The IRS and the state of Oregon are currently scrutinizing these classifications.

It can be costly for a nonprofit's Board of Directors too. Businesses do not withhold payroll taxes from amounts paid to independent contractors. Should federal or state tax agencies decide the worker was really an employee all along, Directors can be held individually liable for unpaid payroll taxes.

The definition of who is an independent contractor varies depending on the purpose of the classification. The fact that you and your service provider agree that the service provider is an independent contractor generally makes NO difference in how the government classifies the person. If you use independent contractors regularly in your business, you should review Chapter 20. If you remain uncertain, consult with an accountant or an attorney to make sure the classification fits.

Volunteers Who Are Paid

If you have volunteers who receive something of value in exchange for their volunteer services, you may be converting them into employees, at least for some purposes. See pages 453-56 for a discussion of this issue.

Consult Appendix 1 if you would like information about source material related to this Chapter.

As noted above, many nonprofits incorrectly designate their service providers as independent contractors with serious consequences for your organization. The next chapter discusses this very important issue in depth.

20 INDEPENDENT CONTRACTORS

THIS CHAPTER COVERS

- Who is an Independent Contractor?
- Federal Income Tax and Social Security Issues
- State Income Tax Issues
- Worker's Compensation Issues
- State Unemployment Issues
- Federal and State Wage and Hour Laws
- The Importance of Complying With the Laws
- Danger Signals
- Protections for Your Nonprofit Organization

One of the most common mistakes made by nonprofits is to classify incorrectly people who are providing services for them as independent contractors, rather than as employees. A mistake in this area can be very costly and can result in liability for taxes, interest, penalties, unemployment claims, worker's compensation claims, wage and hour claims, and other employment related issues. The fact that you and the person who is providing the services have agreed that your relationship is that of an independent contractor does not necessarily protect the organization. The IRS has announced that independent contractor classifications are an area of interest for the agency and that it will be focusing on these classifications. If you currently have or are contemplating hiring independent contractors, you should be familiar with the topics covered in this chapter.

Who Is an Independent Contractor?

Many nonprofit groups designate someone who is performing services for them (referred to as a "service provider" in this chapter) as an independent contractor, rather than as an employee. This designation often is made because the group does not want to pay employer taxes and fringe benefits and complete paperwork associated with having an employee. Nonprofits often are unaware that the agreement of the nonprofit and the service provider to call that person an independent contractor is not binding on state and federal agencies and courts and can have little or nothing to do with how that person is legally classified.

If you are trying to determine whether your service provider is an independent contractor, you may find that your question is answered with another. (Don't you love this?) The answer is often "For what purposes?" You need to determine if you are trying to figure out the status for purposes of personal injury law, federal taxation law, state income tax law, worker compensation law, state unemployment law, labor law, pension law, federal civil rights law, state civil rights law, health and safety laws, wage and hour law, agency law, copyright law, or other laws. There is no single definition of independent contractor, although most definitions have some common features.

> *Nonprofits often are unaware that the agreement of the nonprofit and the service provider to call that person an independent contractor is not binding on state and federal agencies and courts and can have little or nothing to do with how that person is legally classified.*

Because these tests do not use the same guidelines, this means a service provider may be an employee for some purposes and an independent contractor for others. Although the many tests used in this area have different wrinkles, at the heart of virtually all of them is this: how much control does or could the nonprofit exercise over the manner and means by which the service provider does his or her job?

This is a complicated area of the law and much of it is a gray area, so you should not expect to become an expert. Instead, this chapter describes the general rules, some specific factors to look for, and some danger signals that should alert you to seek an expert opinion. We focus on the areas of federal tax law, state tax law, workers' compensation, state unemployment tax, and wage and hour laws because these are the areas most likely to be of interest to nonprofits. If you have questions about whether your service provider is an independent contractor for purposes of other laws (such as personal injury law, labor law, pension law, civil rights law, health and safety law, agency law, or copyright law, or whether you are liable for the actions of your service provider), you should get the advice of a lawyer or an accountant.

INDEPENDENT CONTRACTORS 20

You should be aware that it is fairly common that a nonprofit will establish a genuine independent contractor relationship with a service provider that over time slips into an employer/employee relationship. If you have independent contractor relationships that extend over time, you should review them periodically to ensure that you are still correctly classifying the relationship.

Federal Income Tax and Social Security Issues

The federal tax law requires that you withhold a portion of the salary you pay to your employees for income and social security taxes. Employers must also match the amount withheld for social security with their own funds. You do not have to withhold income or social security tax or pay a share of the social security tax of independent contractors.

The IRS 20-Factor Test seeks to determine if the nonprofit exercises sufficient control over the service provider for the service provider to be classified as an employee.

The key question is: who does the IRS consider to be your employee? For purposes of IRS withholding (income tax), FICA withholding (Social Security and Medicare), and FUTA (federal unemployment tax), the government focuses on the extent of control that your nonprofit exercises over the service provider. The IRS looks at behavioral and financial controls and at the type of relationship you have. As a guideline to the particular items the government considers, check out the Federal 20-Factor Test. The test can be found on pp. 430-31.

The IRS 20-Factor Test seeks to determine if the nonprofit exercises sufficient control over the service provider for the service provider to be classified as an employee. The IRS looks at these features:

Behavior—whether the nonprofit has the right to control what the service provider does and how s/he does it. The IRS believes that if the services provided are key to your mission, it is likely that the corporation will want to control the service provider. Consequently, a childcare center that wants to label its childcare workers as independent contractors is probably misclassifying them, while it generally can label as an independent contractor a bookkeeper who operates her own business as a bookkeeper.

Financial—whether the business aspects of the relationship are controlled by the nonprofit, such as how the service provider is paid, whether expenses are reimbursed, who provides the tools or supplies.

THE OREGON NONPROFIT CORPORATION HANDBOOK

Federal 20-Factor Test

1. **Instructions**: Is the person required to comply with instructions about when, where, and how the work is to be done? If a person is required to comply with instructions as to when and how to perform the work, that person is generally considered an employee.

2. **Training**: Is the person provided training? Did the individual receive training by another experienced employee working with him or her? Training typically points to employee status, since it indicates that the employer wants the services to be performed in a particular manner and is exerting considerable control.

3. **Integration**: Are the services for the operations of the company? The more integrated the individual's task is, the more likely the company has control—making the individual an employee.

4. **Service Rendered Personally**: Are the services provided personally by the individual? If the service must be rendered by a particular individual, then the employer likely has control, meaning the service provider is likely an employee.

5. **Hiring, Supervising and Paying Assistants**: Does the company hire, supervise or pay assistants to help the person? If the company controls these activities, employee status is indicated.

6. **Continuing Relationship**: Is there a continuing relationship between the person and the company? An ongoing relationship with an individual in a company tends to indicate the existence of an employer/employee relationship.

7. **Set Hours of Work**: Does the company set the work schedule? If the company can set specific hours when the individual must be "on the job," the individual is most likely an employee.

8. **Full Time Required**: Does the person devote his or her full work time to the company? If the company requires an individual to devote full time to the business, that individual will be considered an employee.

9. **Location of Work**: Is the work performed at the company's place of business or at specific places designated by the company? Control is the key word. Control over the place of work—on company premises or a site determined by the company—indicates an employer/employee relationship.

10. **Order or Sequence of Work:** Does the company direct the sequence of the work performed? If the employer can set the sequence in which services are to be performed, then control is being exercised—and the individual providing services is an employee.

11. **Oral or Written Reports**: Are reports regularly given to the company? If oral or written reports are required by the company, then control and employer/employee relationship is indicated.

12. **Payment by Hour, Week, or Month**: Is the person paid hourly, weekly, or monthly (as opposed to "by the job")? An independent contractor is normally paid by the job or on a commission basis, rather than on a schedule or by a guaranteed amount.

13. **Payment of Business or Traveling Expense**: Does the company reimburse the person for business or travel expenses? The fact that the "employer" will pay for an individual's work related expenses is indicative of control—and employee status.

14. **Tools and Materials**: Does the company supply materials or tools to the person? Providing tools and materials to an individual suggests that a company is also exercising control, which again means that the individual is an employee.

15. **Significant Investment**: Does the person have equipment or facilities to perform services? If an individual has significant personal investment in facilities or equipment, that person is likely to be an independent contractor.

16. **Profit or Loss Potential**: Is there an exposure to loss, or the potential of profit for the individual? A person who is in a position to realize a profit or suffer a loss as a result of the service provided is more than likely an independent contractor.

17. **Working for More than One Firm**: Does the person work exclusively for the company? If an individual works for more than one company at the same time, the person is normally an independent contractor.

18. **Making Service Available to the General Public**: Does the individual in question make his or her services available to the public at large? Advertising to the general public the availability to perform a particular service normally indicates an independent contractor.

19. **Right to Discharge**: Can the worker be dismissed for reasons other than nonperformance of contract specifications? The right to discharge an individual is clearly an act of control and is indicative of an employer/employee relationship.

20. **Right to Terminate**: Can the person terminate his relationship with the company without liability for failure to complete the job? Employees can usually terminate the relationship with the employer at any time without incurring any liability. An independent contractor normally has obligations to complete specific jobs or a legal obligation to satisfactorily perform a particular service.

Relationship--whether the parties have a written agreement, whether the relationship is continuous, and whether the service provided is a key aspect of the nonprofit's work.

Because there are so many factors, the tests are very vague.

Example: Your new organization is treating its Executive Director as an independent contractor and is not withholding from payments to him for federal tax purposes. Your Executive Director works about 25 hours per week at your offices. He is paid $2,500 per month. He supervises two of your part-time employees and five of your volunteers. Your organization provides all of the equipment and supplies he uses. The Executive Director reports to the Board, which has the right to control the Executive Director by law. In all likelihood, the Executive Director is an "employee," for federal withholding purposes.

Example: Your organization decides to hire a consultant to work with your Executive Director to develop a new program. She has her own consulting business with about 20 clients and provides her own supplies. She agrees to meet with the Executive Director over a two month period and will charge you a flat fee of $2,000 for her services. She has signed a written contract with you for consulting services. In all likelihood, this consultant is an independent contractor for federal withholding purposes.

State Income Tax Issues

All Oregon employers must withhold part of their employees' pay for state income tax purposes; such withholdings are not required for independent contractors. The state of Oregon has a state statute to determine if a service provider is an independent contractor for several purposes, including withholding for state income tax. The primary focus of the Oregon statute is whether the service provider is free from direction and control over the means and manner of providing the services and whether there is other evidence that he or she really acts as an independent business. It is easier to meet the test if your service provider files federal and state tax returns as a business or files a business Schedule C or farm Schedule F on his or her individual tax returns.

The state definition of independent contractor, which applies to income tax withholding, defines an independent contractor as someone performing services that meets *all four* of these tests:

1. Your service provider must be free from your direction and control over the means and manner in which he or she provides the services, subject only to your right to specify the desired results.

2. If the services for which you contract require a license, your service provider must be licensed.

3. Your service provider must be responsible for obtaining all business registrations or licenses required by law to conduct his or her business.

4. Your service provider must be customarily engaged in an independently established business. This criteria is met if your service provider filed the Schedule F or Schedule C as part of his/her federal income tax return above and you can move on to criteria 3 below. If your provider does not file either of these Schedules, he or she can meet this test by meeting any 3 of the following requirements:

    a. Your service provider does not rely solely on one person or one entity to obtain customers or your provider performs all services in the provider's own name or business name and collects payment for the labor or services directly from the customer.

    b. Your service provider assumes the risk of loss related to his or her services as shown by factors that include:
    ◊ fixed-price contracts,
    ◊ responsibility to correct defective work,
    ◊ warranty for services
    ◊ purchase of performance bonds or insurance covering the work, or
    ◊ other indicia.

    c. Your service provider provides services to two or more different persons during one year or routinely engages in business advertising, solicitation or other marketing efforts reasonably calculated to obtain work.

    d. Your service provider makes a significant investment in the business, such as for tools, equipment, rent, or specialized training.

    e. Your service provider has the authority to hire and fire employees to perform the services.

If your service provider meets all four parts of these tests, then he or she is an independent contractor for purposes of Oregon state income tax withholding.

Example: Sing Out, a nonprofit organization that encourages young women to get involved in music, engages a marketing consultant to design a brochure and develop an outreach program for the organization. The consultant formerly worked for Sing Out but left two years ago to care for her aging father. She hasn't filed a Schedule C or F. She worked for Sing Out on another project as a consultant after she left but is too busy with her father to look for other business. She works from her own house. Sing Out signs a consulting agreement in which it agrees that the consultant directs and controls her work and that she will do all the work herself. She warrants her services under the contract and collects her payments. She has obtained all the licenses she needs.

THE OREGON NONPROFIT CORPORATION HANDBOOK

In all likelihood, the consultant will be treated as an employee for state withholding purposes. She passes #1,3, and 4 of the test but has not filed a Schedule C or F nor does she meet at least 3 of the 5 requirements of #2. She fails to meet the third, fourth, and fifth requirements of #2. She could meet the test by marketing more broadly or investing in business tools.

State Unemployment Issues

For purposes of the state unemployment tax, an employee is any person employed for pay under a verbal or written agreement to hire that person. A person who volunteers services to a religious or charitable entity without expecting adequate payment for the services is not an employee. By law, employers are required to provide for unemployment benefits coverage for their employees. Nonprofits may choose between two options for primary unemployment coverage. These options are discussed on page 620. Regardless of which option your organization chooses, you will be required to provide coverage for everyone who performs services for your organization for pay, unless that person:

- Is an independent contractor as defined by Oregon law; *or*
- Is free from the control or direction over the performance of such services, under an actual contract; *and* is customarily engaged in an independently established business of the same nature as that involved in the contract with you.

If your relationship with your service provider satisfies either one of these tests, the service provider is an independent contractor. The first test is a little more certain, so you should start there to see if the service provider meets the criteria. The test is found above on pages 432-34.

If your service provider does not satisfy the criteria for the independent contractor test, your provider needs to qualify under the second test. Note that if the service provider has an independently-established business but contracts with you for a different type of service, she or he will not meet the test.

Example: You hire someone who operates a bookkeeping service with lots of nonprofit clients to write grants for you. You may need to provide unemployment coverage on this person, because the activities for which you are hiring him are not his normal business of bookkeeping.

Example: Music for All produces an annual music festival for the public each year. MFA hires a conductor and about 80 orchestra musicians to play at the concert. MFA has the right to and does direct their activities. MFA has individual contracts with the Director and each musician as independent contractors. MFA has misclassified these artists and needs to pay unemployment insurance for them.

There are numerous exceptions in which an employer does not have to provide unemployment coverage even though a service provider is an employee. Generally, the exceptions most likely to be of interest to nonprofits include certain job training programs, AmeriCorps participants, rehabilitation centers for the disabled, and certain services by students. Nonprofits that engage musicians, performers, crew members, contestants, and the like to put on symphonies, operas, plays, rodeo, festivals, and similar events do not have to pay an unemployment tax if they offer only gratuities, prizes, scholarships, or reimbursement of expenses to the people they use.

An employer does not have to provide unemployment coverage if its total payroll during any calendar quarter is less than $1,000 or if the employer does not employ one or more individuals in each of 18 separate weeks during a calendar year. You should check with your accountant or attorney if you have questions about these or other applicable exceptions.

Workers' Compensation Issues

Your Service Providers

Oregon employers are required to provide workers' compensation insurance for all workers covered by the statute. An employer under the workers' compensation statutes is anyone who agrees to pay a remuneration for and secures the right to direct and control the services of any other person. A worker is a person who engages to furnish services for a remuneration, subject to the direction and control of an employer. This means that if your organization pays someone and you have the *right* to direct and control their services (whether you do so or not), you must comply with the workers' compensation laws.

The Test for "Worker"

The issue for employers is whether a person is a "worker"; that is, whether the employer has the right to direct and control that person. The courts generally look at the following four factors:

1. *The employer's right to, or exercise of, control.* If the employer exercises control over the methods of how the job is performed, this suggests the relationship is worker-employer. If your only control is over the results, this suggests an independent contractor relationship.

2. *The method of payment.* If the service provider is paid by the hour, week, month, or other time unit, this suggests an worker-employer relationship. If the service provider is paid a fixed sum for a fixed job, this is more typical of an independent contractor.

3. *Furnishing of equipment.* If the employer furnishes the equipment, supplies, or means of carrying out the job, your relationship is likely worker-employer. In an independent contractor arrangement, the contractor would furnish these items.

4. *Right to fire.* If you have right to fire the service provider, this suggests a worker-employer relationship. Where the parties have an independent contractor relationship, an employer generally can only terminate the job if the project is not being performed as agreed.

Example: You have contracted with an individual to assist in putting together a major fundraiser. She will be working in your office with your staff using your supplies. She will be working about 20 hours a week for 3 months and will be paid $1,000 per month. You can fire her if you want. Although you have the right to direct her work, you leave most things up to her to handle as a matter of practice. You must pay for her workers compensation coverage because she probably is not an independent contractor under the Oregon statutory definition based on your *right* to control her work.

If the above test is inconclusive, the courts typically apply what is called "the relative nature of the work" test. This test applies various factors to see how integral the services that your service provider supplies are to the employer's business. The courts look at two sets of factors:

- the character of the provider's services (the skill level, the degree of provider's independence, and extent to which the provider can carry the burden of an accident); and

- the relationship of your service provider's business to your business (the extent to which the provider's work is an essential and regular part of your work and whether provider is hired on temporary or continuing basis).

Example: Your agency provides counseling services to low income clients. You hire 4 counselors as independent contractors. Each counselor works 20 hours a week for your organization while also maintaining his or her own half-time private practice. While working for your organization, the counselor sees your clients at your location. The counselors determine how the sessions are run but are supervised by your agency. The counselors are paid $20 per session but they provide their own licenses and pay their own professional fees. You can fire the counselor if you wish. It is very probable that these counselors would be employees under the "relative nature of the work" test because they are working on a continuous basis doing work to carry out your operations in the same manner as your employees would do it.

Exceptions to the "Worker" Test

Employers must provide workers' compensation insurance for all of its workers unless the service provider falls within certain exceptions. These exceptions generally fall into these categories:

- certain construction and landscape contractors;
- casual labor (as specifically defined);

- volunteers performing services primarily for board, lodging, meals, nominal reimbursement, or vouchers for meals, lodging, or expenses for a religious, charitable, or relief organization;
- certain amateur athletes;
- persons performing foster parent and adult foster care duties pursuant to certain statutes;
- volunteers under the ACTION program;
- volunteer ski patrols who receive no cash wages and who perform ski patrol or certain ski area activities;
- referees and assistant referees for recreational soccer matches who are hired on a match-to-match basis;
- volunteer municipal personnel (unless they are covered under the municipality's workers' compensation insurance).

If any of these exceptions might apply to your organization, talk to an attorney or accountant.

Workers for Those With Whom You Subcontract

If an employer awards a contract for labor that is a normal and customary part of its business and the employer is responsible for providing workers' compensation coverage to the individual or entity that has the contract, *the employer* must also provide workers' compensation coverage for all workers under the contract, unless the person who is awarded the contract provides coverage before work begins. Because of the difficulty of knowing whether you have to provide coverage for the person you are contracting with and the possibility that you may be required to provide coverage for all of his or her subcontractors, be sure you get professional advice if you are subcontracting.

> *Example*: Your nonprofit runs several homeless shelters and contracts out the management of one of the shelters. The contract provides that the shelter manager is to pay all taxes and workers' compensation coverage for his employees. You maintain substantial control over how the shelter is run. The individual with whom you contract hires several people to run the shelter but fails to provide workers' compensation coverage for the workers. You are probably liable to provide worker compensation coverage for the individual running the shelter because of the amount of control you exercised. Therefore you are also liable for worker compensation claims filed by the manager's injured workers. Your contract with the manager does not change this result as far as the workers are concerned.

Federal and State Wage and Hour Laws

Federal and state law requires most employers to pay a minimum wage and overtime wages and to comply with other wage and hour requirements, as we discussed in Chapter 19. If your "independent contractor" is deemed to be an employee for purposes of these laws, you will be in violation of federal or state laws if you fail to comply with the wage and hour requirements. Remember that wage and hour laws (but not discrimination claims) apply only to your non-exempt employees and not to management. Review pages 394-397 to determine whether federal and state wage and hour laws apply to your corporation.

Federal Law

Federal courts determine whether a service provider is an independent contractor or an employee by looking at the economic realities of the relationship. The economic realities test seeks to determine how much the service provider is economically dependent on you. The test is vague and includes factors such as:

- your right to control the manner in which the work is done;
- the dependence of the service provider's opportunity for profit or loss on his or her managerial skills;
- the service provider's investment in equipment or material required for the job;
- whether the service requires special skills; the longevity of the working relationship; and
- whether the service is an integral part of your mission.

State Law

The state statute does not define "employee" for purposes of describing who is protected by the wage and hour laws and who is an independent contractor. The law does say an employer is anyone who employs another person (duh). "Employ" means "to suffer or permit to work," a very broad definition. "Employ" does not include voluntary services performed for a religious, charitable, educational, public service, or similar nonprofit organization for free or without expectation of adequate compensation. The courts have interpreted the definition of "employ" expansively.

> *Example*: If you pay solicitors to go door to door to collect money for your cause, assign them neighborhoods, give them a script and train them on their pitch, you have probably exercised enough control that you have employed them. However, if the solicitors are volunteers or receive some compensation but work for you because they agree with your cause and they don't expect their pay to be adequate compensation for their services, you have probably not employed them under state law if you

are a public benefit or religious nonprofit. Remember, though, that although you may be safe under state law, federal law may be different.

A separate statute covers other types of wage claims, such as discrimination claims and piece-work wages. It also sets out rules about regular paydays and procedures for recovering unpaid wages. That statute does define "employee," but the definition does not apply to who is covered by wage and hour laws. As you can see, this is a confusing area. Get professional help if you are not observing the wage and hour law in connection with someone who you "suffer or permit to work" for you.

The Importance of Complying with the Laws

It is very important for employers to comply with the laws described above. An employer that incorrectly classifies someone as an independent contractor but who is later determined to be an employee may be liable for:

- Back taxes, interest and penalties (even if you had an agreement with your service provider that she or he would pay her or his own taxes);

- Payment of an injured service provider's medical bills, lost wages, and other damages in workers' compensation cases;

- Payment of unemployment benefits to a service provider who is laid off or terminated;

- Payment of unpaid wages, overtime, vacation time, penalties and attorney fees to a service provider with a wage and hour claim; and

- Personal liability on the part of Directors for the above expenses from their own pockets.

Danger Signals

In practice there are some especially telling warning signs to be aware of in a relationship with an independent contractor, including:

- Telling the independent contractor how to perform the job or otherwise directing his or her activities;

- Training the independent contractor;

- Scheduling particular hours of work for the independent contractor;

- Supplying the independent contractor with a substantial portion of the supplies and materials for the job;

- Giving the independent contractor a job title that would normally be associated with one of your employees, such as "Executive Director" or "Program Manager";

- Allowing the independent contractor to use business cards identifying him/her with your nonprofit;

- Paying the independent contractor by the hour, week, or month (as opposed to "by the job");

- Retaining the ability to fire the independent contractor for reasons other than non-performance of the contract specifications;

- The independent contractor does not have other customers or doesn't work for anyone else;

- The independent contractor does not have his or her own office (or separate office within his or her home) with a business phone number;

- The independent contractor does not maintain the licenses and insurance common to his or her profession or business;

- The independent contractor can terminate his or her relationship with you without being liable to your organization.

Protections for Your Nonprofit Organization

If you have read this chapter and are feeling a little unsure, we have made our point that the laws about independent contractors are confusing and ambiguous. In many cases, you are left in a gray area. This doesn't mean that you have to assume all of your service providers are employees and begin withholding and paying workers' compensation and unemployment premiums on everyone. You *should* treat as an employee anyone who clearly is an employee. We suggest these strategies for your other service providers:

- If you have service providers in the gray area, consult with an accountant or an attorney.

- Ask the IRS for a non-binding opinion.

- Assess and limit how much exposure your organization has if individuals are incorrectly classified.

- If you are going to continue to classify your service provider as an independent contractor, be sure the factors you can reasonably control point that way and insist on a written contract.

> *This doesn't mean that you have to assume all of your service providers are employees and begin withholding and paying workers' compensation and unemployment premiums on everyone.*

Expert Opinion in Writing

A significant protection in classifying service providers is to get an opinion from an accountant or attorney about the proper classification of any service provider for whom there is a possibility that your service provider may be other than an independent contractor. If you have an accountant, we generally recommend going to your accountant first, since your accountant will need to make this classification for accounting purposes anyway. A professional opinion can alert you to any problems you may have. This opinion will not protect your organization from being liable as described above if your attorney or accountant is wrong but your organization may be able to pursue a claim against the attorney or accountant for bad advice. This opinion will almost always protect Directors individually from personal liability.

Ask the IRS—Form SS-8

You can ask the IRS how they will classify your service provider. You do this by filing Form SS-8, which is available from the IRS. The IRS has also developed a computer program called SS-8 Determiner for this purpose. The drawback to requesting IRS classification is that your request may trigger an audit. Remember that the IRS opinion is issued in reference to federal withholding. Do not assume that the opinion answers the independent contractor question for all the other state and federal activities covered in this chapter, because the tests are different.

Assessing and Limiting Your Exposure

If you have service providers in the gray area, you might give some thought to how much and what kinds of exposure you have and how much risk you are willing to take. The amount of the withholding tax claim for taxes, penalties, and interest against your organization is related to the amount you paid the service provider. If you are paying large sums to a service provider, then your exposure for unpaid taxes is larger; conversely, if the amounts are small, you might be willing to risk paying the unpaid taxes, interest, and penalties. If the worker has other employment or operates her or his own business with other clients, your risk of an unemployment claim is less. If not, you may want to find out how much unemployment coverage would cost. It is usually relatively inexpensive.

The most serious potential exposure for many nonprofits is a workers' compensation claim. The amount of these claims is not related to how much you paid the service provider. You can owe tens of thousands of dollars on a claim made by a service provider who was injured on the first day of the job. Unlike tax withholding claims, the amount of the workers' compensation claim may be very disproportionate to what you save by not paying the workers' compensation premium. Although you can generally assess how safe the service provider's work environment is, a workers' compensation claim can be generated when your service provider's back goes out while picking up a pencil.

> *The most serious potential exposure for many nonprofits is a workers' compensation claim. The amount of these claims is not related to how much you paid the service provider.*

After assessing your organization's potential exposure, you may want to take some steps to limit your risk short of reclassifying the service provider as an employee.

- Provide workers' compensation coverage;
- Provide unemployment coverage;
- Require your service provider to submit proof to you that she or he is making her/his estimated tax payments to the federal and state governments.

There is, however, some risk in paying workers' compensation premiums and unemployment taxes and still classifying your service provider as an independent contractor. Your service provider or a government agency may later try to use this as evidence for other classifications that you acknowledged that your service provider was an employee. Your best strategy here is to include in your written independent contractor agreement (discussed below) a provision stating that these payments are not evidence of an employee relationship and include a release of claims clause. Your Board or Executive Director will want to carefully assess your policy and decisions in this area.

Independent Contractor Agreement

If you have decided that a service provider should be classified as an independent contractor, be sure that the factors that you can reasonably control agree with your classification. Here are some items you may be able to arrange to support your classification:

- Restrict as much as possible the amount of control you have over the job;
- Pay by the job and not by time spent;

- Do not allow the service provider to use your space or equipment;
- Do not give the service provider a title suggesting a job link with your organization;
- Require your service provider to have or get his or her own business cards and business phone listing.

You should also have a written agreement with your independent contractors, showing that you do not have the right to control their work and listing as many of the factors as are applicable to establish an independent contractor status. This agreement is not binding for purposes of establishing independent contractor status, but it is evidence of your intent. You should get legal help in drafting such a contract because each one is individual.

Consult Appendix 1 if you would like information about source material related to this Chapter.

21 VOLUNTEERS

THIS CHAPTER COVERS

- Recruiting, Screening, and Placing Volunteers in Your Organization
- Orienting, Training, Supervising, and Evaluating Volunteers
- Recognizing and Rewarding Volunteers
- Volunteers Who Are Really Employees
- Volunteers and Liability
- When Your Volunteers Face Personal Liability
- When Your Organization Is Liable for the Actions of Your Volunteers
- When Your Volunteer Is Injured
- Protection for Your Volunteers and Your Organization

Volunteers are the lifeblood of many nonprofit organizations. Volunteers deliver key services and provide incredibly valuable behind-the-scenes support in every community. For many Oregonians, volunteer experiences are life changing. Positive experiences of volunteering for your organization can motivate volunteers to become financial donors and active community spokespersons for your organization.

Perhaps because volunteer services appear to be free, many nonprofits do not put much thought into the recruitment, training, or supervision of volunteers. Your success in working with volunteers will affect the public perception of your nonprofit and the quality of the work you do. Working effectively with volunteers requires careful planning, consistent attention, and dedication of organizational resources. This chapter identifies the basic elements of an effective program.

This chapter also addresses the challenging realities of potential legal liabilities for both volunteers and the organizations they serve. Many volunteers are unaware that they may face personal liability for their actions as volunteers. Your nonprofit corporation can in some cases be required to pay for damages caused by your volunteers. Volunteers also face the risk that they may themselves be injured while serving as volunteers. This chapter will discuss how you and your volunteers can protect yourselves from these occurrences.

VOLUNTEERS 21

Volunteers can be a great resource for nonprofit organizations. But they are not free. Finding and keeping effective volunteers for your organization will require the investment of time and energy, either by paid staff or by other volunteers. We probably all know of organizations in which volunteers have made enormous contributions—organizations which literally could not do their work without volunteers. You probably also know of organizations in which volunteers come and go, never making much impact despite their commitment to the cause and willingness to work. What makes the difference?

Recruiting, Screening, and Placing Volunteers in Your Organization

Recruiting Volunteers

Before you put out the call for volunteers, you'll want to think very carefully about the types of tasks you want them to do and the level of responsibility you will allow them to take. You don't need to work out every detail of each job but you do need to make basic decisions about the type of tasks which you think are appropriate and the types of people you are looking for to do those tasks.

> *Before you put out the call for volunteers, you'll want to think very carefully about the types of tasks you'll want them to do and the level of responsibility you'll allow them to take.*

Start by thinking about all your motivations for recruiting volunteers and the organizational needs you are hoping they will meet. Get clear about the basics:

- Are you really just looking to get specific jobs done without having to pay an employee or are you hoping to expand your organization's identity through volunteer involvement?

- Do you have staff or dependable volunteers available to orient, train, and supervise the volunteers you recruit or do you really need folks who can work well with very little supervision or support?

- Do you need volunteers for one-time, minimal skill activities like putting donated food on shelves or are you looking for individuals who will commit to an ongoing role which requires more knowledge of your organization?

- Are you looking for people willing to learn a set of skills which your organization has mastered or are you looking for people to contribute their own professional skills, like legal and accounting work, with no particular training from you?

- Is building diversity among your volunteers important to your organization? Do volunteers need who speak languages other than English and have a basic understanding of specific cultures?

- Are the jobs dangerous? Do they require special skills? Does the job demand special characteristics for its performance?

Unfortunately, nonprofits often start their efforts to recruit volunteers by thinking about ways to publicize volunteer opportunities rather than by clarifying exactly what the opportunities are. Once you've agreed upon the answers to the questions above and gotten clear about the types of people you want as volunteers, you can begin working on strategies to find the "right" people.

Of course, you'll want to use an approach to finding volunteers which seems likely to connect you to the types of people you want to find. There are several common approaches to finding volunteers:

- Ask people already working, volunteering, or participating in your organization to ask people they know. This approach is particularly valuable when you are looking for specific skills and qualities.

- Put notices on your website and in your newsletter or other publications, describing the types of volunteer opportunities you offer.

- Post your volunteer opportunities on CNRG (*www.cnrg-portland.org*) or Craig's list (*http:portland.craigslist.org*).

- Announce volunteer opportunities at all your gatherings and events.

- Contact SOLV (*www.solv.org*), a statewide agency; Hands-on-Portland (*www.handsonportland.org*), or other volunteer coordination services and talk with them about how they can help you recruit volunteers.

- Contact colleges and high schools in your area to see if they have community service programs for their students. Many schools now have a community service graduation requirement.

- If you have work which would be appropriate, contact senior centers and other social service programs to see if their clients may be able to perform the services.

- If you are looking for professional services, contact the appropriate professional association in your community—i.e. the Oregon Bar Association or the Oregon Society of CPAs.

Whether you'll be talking with people face to face or using written recruitment announcements, you'll want to be sure you present your volunteer opportunity in the ways most likely to motivate the people you are seeking to follow up on your request. Start by thinking about the possible motivations your desired volunteers might have. If you already have volunteers, ask them what drew them to your group and what makes them stay.

> *If you already have volunteers, ask them what drew them to your group, and what makes them stay.*

Remember, folks will decide to volunteer with very different motivations. Some common motivations for volunteering include:

- Commitment to your cause or to the people you serve
- General desire to serve the community
- Interest in developing new skills
- Resume building
- Forming social relationships
- Forming business relationships

Of course, your staff and volunteers can think of many more motivations. Once you've considered what may motivate folks to volunteer for your organization, craft your invitation carefully. You want to communicate to individuals that they will find what they are looking for if they volunteer for your group.

Whatever approach you decide to use, be sure you have a person ready to respond quickly when people inquire about the volunteer opportunities you have announced. If you will use a written application for potential volunteers, keep it short and simple and be sure it's ready before you announce the opportunity. Plan your volunteer screening strategy before you make your announcements as well, so that you are totally ready to deal with responses.

Screening Volunteers

Once you are clear about the types of tasks you will be asking volunteers to perform, you can decide what types of information you will need to learn about the individuals who offer to help you. Then, you'll need to decide how you will obtain the information.

You probably will not need much information about volunteers who will only perform short-term tasks under the supervision of an individual already known to your organization and will not have direct contact with your program participants. At a minimum, you'll want to make a record of their name, address, and phone number so that you can contact them again to ask for their help, send them a thank you note, or potentially, to ask for a contribution.

As the level of responsibility required increases and the amount of direct supervision your organization provides decreases, you will want to learn more about the potential volunteers. You'll have to decide how to obtain this information. You may want to ask all potential volunteers to fill out a written application form. Increasingly, individuals interested in volunteering prefer to complete initial inquiries online. There are a number of free or low cost tools that can be used to add this feature to your website.

Before collecting lots of info about people expressing an initial interest, you may want to schedule group meetings to explain the volunteer opportunities. This allows people to screen themselves out before spending time completing applications.

Some organizations prefer to use individual interviews before asking for extensive written information. This approach will probably be necessary for recruiting professionals to provide their services.

Screening volunteers is not that different from screening potential employees.

Whichever method of collecting information you choose, you'll want to have agreements about the minimum requirements your organization will set for each type of volunteer work. Some basic questions might be:

- Will we accept volunteers with a criminal record or with mental health issues?
- Will we do a criminal records check? Will we require evidence that the individual has experience performing functions similar to those included in our volunteer job?
- Will we require and check references?
- Does the volunteer's performance in the job expose us to liability? (See page 403.) If so, what screening is reasonable to ensure that the volunteer is appropriate for the job?
- Are we required to conduct particular screening procedures to exclude individuals with particular histories by law, regulation, or funding agreement?

In the final analysis, screening volunteers is not that different from screening potential employees. If you have Directors or volunteers who work in personnel management or human resources, ask for their help.

Placing Volunteers in the Right Spot in Your Organization

Once you've decided to accept an individual as a volunteer for your organization, you will need to assign that person to specific responsibilities. You'll need a clear system within your organization to determine who ultimately decides which volunteers are given which assignments.

VOLUNTEERS 21

The process of placing volunteers within your organization involves matching sets of needs—your organization's need for help and the individual volunteers' needs for satisfaction in their volunteer work. You'll need a systematic way to look at both sets of needs and a perceptive person to bring the two together.

Some organizations create a common pool of pre-screened volunteers and encourage project managers or volunteer team leaders to come "shop" through the list of volunteers and contact those they are interested in directly. Other organizations feel that this may appear chaotic to the volunteer, resulting in several different phone calls from the same organization. These organizations put one person in charge of placement. That person makes the best matches they can, clears them with the person who will be supervising the volunteer, and makes the contact with the volunteer.

If you decide to use the first, more autonomous approach, be sure you create a system for letting others in the organization know that a volunteer has been "taken" so your group is not annoying the volunteer with multiple calls.

The process of placing volunteers within your organization involves matching sets of needs — your organization's need for help and the individual volunteers' needs for satisfaction in their volunteer work.

The placement function is completed after the volunteer is given a detailed explanation of what will be expected and both the volunteer and their supervisor have agreed to give it a try. You'll want to be sure your system provides opportunities for both volunteers and their supervisors to let the person doing placement know how well the matches are working out.

Orienting, Training, Supervising and Evaluating Volunteers

Orienting Volunteers

Many organizations provide a general orientation for all volunteers in addition to any specific training required for the volunteer to do a particular volunteer job. Your orientation can be done through written materials or group meetings. It can also be included as part of the training that the supervisor for a particular volunteer project provides to volunteers.

The orientation should provide basic information about your organization, your mission, your size, and your programs. It should also present any important philosophical basis for your work, including your values and guiding principles. Your orientation should include explanations of any organizational policies which you expect volunteers to follow, such as confidentiality and respect for all cultures. Finally, the orientation should include procedures you have established for volunteers to follow.

Training

The amount of training your volunteers will need will vary greatly depending on the type of activities they will perform. The paid or volunteer supervisor for each volunteer position should consider carefully the information and skills the volunteer will need. The supervisor should also plan to upgrade skills for volunteers who have been with you for a period of time as needed. You will also need to establish safety procedures and provide ongoing training to keep all volunteers up-to-date on them.

> *The paid or volunteer supervisor for each volunteer position should consider carefully the information and skills the volunteer will need.*

Here are some questions which may help your volunteer supervisors develop effective training for different types of volunteers:

- What is the minimum level of information the volunteer will need to do what you are asking them to do? You'll want to be sure you provide this information both in writing and verbally.

- How available will the supervisor be while the volunteer learns the job? If the supervisor will be readily available, more things can be learned by doing than if the volunteer will need to work fairly independently from the beginning.

- How much background does the particular individual you will be training have? If they have worked in similar positions or have substantial professional training in a related area, you will want to concentrate primarily on what's different in your organization.

- How does this volunteer learn best? You'll have to ask the volunteer to find out. Some people strongly prefer reading to listening; others cannot read or hate to read and get more from verbal instructions. Still others really will have to try it before they can focus on what they will need to learn. If you can't ask volunteers individually about their learning styles, try to design your training to use some of each method.

- What do current volunteers believe was the most important information they needed when they began their volunteer positions? This may prove the most useful information.

- Have you developed written rules and procedures to be followed by the volunteers? The rules and procedures should be designed to minimize the possibility of problems and injuries.

Supervising Volunteers

Volumes have been written on this topic. Probably the most important piece we can emphasize here is be sure you have clear supervision for all volunteers. Later in this chapter, we'll discuss your organization's potential liability for the actions of your volunteers and for injuries your volunteers may sustain while volunteering for you. Adequate supervision is an essential protection against these potential liabilities.

Be sure you have clear supervision for all volunteers.

Some nonprofits struggle with the concept of supervising volunteers because they associate the term "supervision" with oppressive bosses hounding workers, criticizing their efforts, and threatening them with dismissal. Obviously, these techniques will not work with volunteers.

You will want the individuals who supervise your volunteers to see their roles primarily as facilitators—people whose job it is to make sure that the volunteers are able to do their best work and make the greatest contribution to the organization. The supervisor needs to check in with the volunteers to be sure they have the information and tools they need to do the job. And of course, the supervisor will want to provide positive feedback to let the volunteers know how well they are doing and that the organization appreciates their efforts.

You should also be sure to provide the support that volunteers need to carry out their jobs in the form of staff time, materials, and access to expertise when it is needed.

Evaluating Volunteers

Like supervision, the word "evaluation" has a negative sound to some individuals who have worked in situations in which evaluations were only performed as justification for termination or used as opportunities to unload criticism.

Volunteer evaluations are an important opportunity for your organization to learn from your volunteers. Volunteer evaluations should be done individually, in a confidential setting. The volunteer should be encouraged to reflect on the parts of their volunteer work which they most enjoy and those which they find most frustrating or least satisfying. The supervisor should also provide specific feedback on the areas of the volunteer's performance which are especially well done and valued by the organization. If there are areas in which the volunteer's performance has not been adequate, the supervisor should share the concern and ask the volunteer what help is needed to support improvement.

The information shared in the evaluation can help the organization learn about volunteer needs and satisfactions. The supervisor will want to consider which of the needs the volunteer has identified can be met with reasonable investment of time and resources. If some of the volunteer's needs cannot be met, the supervisor should acknowledge this.

Volunteer evaluations are an important opportunity for your organization to learn from your volunteers.

If you determine that the supervisor cannot provide the volunteer with the level or type of supervision which the person would need to do the job adequately, you will want to offer the volunteer a different assignment within your organization. Occasionally, a nonprofit will conclude that a specific volunteer just does not fit in their organization. Be sure you have clear procedures for terminating such a volunteer's involvement with your organization. Of course, you want the individual to remain supportive of your organization even after their volunteer experience is over, so take care to be supportive of the individual while being clear that you no longer can offer an appropriate volunteer opportunity for them.

Recognizing and Rewarding Volunteers

Many newer nonprofits consider some of the traditional methods of recognizing and rewarding volunteers to be corny and old-fashioned. They believe that pins and plaques honoring years of service will have little meaning to younger volunteers. Yet recognition and rewards are important elements in retaining valued volunteers.

Your organization may want to talk with organizations which involve volunteers similar to yours. Determine what approaches they are taking in recognizing and rewarding volunteers. You may also want to convene a volunteer committee to discuss the types of recognition and rewards they would find meaningful.

Here are a few of the ideas we've seen used lately:

- Send individual notes from the Executive Director or Chair of the Board to recognize a specific contribution by a volunteer—a call handled really well, a mailing completed quickly, a newsletter article written, etc.

- Publish thank you's to specific volunteers for their contributions on your website or in your newsletter.

- Set up a volunteer bulletin board with photos of all your volunteers and their names and roles within the organization.

- Put together an annual "volunteer book"—a publication with pictures and write-ups on key volunteers with an attractive cover—suitable for coffee table display.

- For special achievements, create customized framed certificates which recognize specific contributions and include photos or drawings of the organization's clients or work.

- Plan a fun social occasion with Board, staff, and volunteers with enough structure to assure that volunteers are introduced and commended for their work.

- Be sure volunteers are mentioned by name in newsletter articles and reports to the Board whenever possible. Share copies of these items with the volunteers.

- Consider writing letters of commendation to the volunteer's employer or church or civic group to let others know about the person's contribution to your organization. Be sure your volunteer is comfortable with this before you try it.

- Create a special place in your facility—a wall, a garden, a room—which incorporates volunteers' names into the decor.

The key to successful recognition and reward is finding a way to say thank you which conveys that your group values the individual and their specific contribution. Try a variety of approaches and let your volunteers' reactions guide you in deciding which ones to continue.

Volunteers Who Are Really Employees

Most people think of a volunteer as someone who provides their services for free. However, there are limited situations in which the person you think of as a "volunteer" may in fact be classified as an "employee" for purposes of the wage and hour laws or other employment laws. This classification can have serious repercussions for your organization. You may find that you owe back wages and penalties or you may find that you are liable for a worker compensation or unemployment claim.

Federal and State Wage and Hours Laws

The federal wage and hour laws are the most worrisome. Review page 394 to determine if your organization is covered by the federal wage and hour laws. If your organization is covered, you need to think about how you use your volunteers to be sure that the law does not classify them as employees. If your volunteers engaged in non-commercial activities, do not expect to receive material benefits from your organization, work part-time or on a temporary basis and perform services that are traditionally considered volunteer, you do not need to be concerned with this issue. However, you should be concerned if your volunteers fall in any of the following categories:

- Your volunteers work for you as a nonexempt employee and "volunteer" extra hours above their paid work week doing work that is similar to what they do as employees. See page 395 for a discussion on this.

- Your volunteers work in a commercial type of enterprise (such as a publishing firm, restaurant, parking lot, mail order business, etc.)

- Your volunteers expect some form of compensation for their services. The compensation does not have to be in the form of money but may be anything of value. Your organization may trigger an expectation of compensation by providing your volunteers with a small payment, free or discounted access to services that you charge others to receive, room, board, meals, passes to events or activities carried on by the organization, books, or other items of value.

- Your volunteers provide services that produce income or commercial advantage for you even though the volunteers get job skills or are rehabilitated as a result of the employment.

> *There are limited situations in which the person you think of as a "volunteer" may in fact be classified as an "employee" for purposes of the wage and hour laws or other employment laws.*

If you have volunteers whose service fits in any of these categories, then you should get legal advice, because this area of the federal law is unclear.

> *Example:* The Good News Church grosses more than $500,000 per year and operates a printing company to publish religious books and also does some nonreligious commercial printing. It mails its books around the country. It maintains a rehabilitation program that uses former alcoholics and drug addicts as volunteers to do the printing and provides them with meals and free copies of the religious books. Because of the commercial nature of this enterprise and because there is some payment (meals and books), the Church may be required to pay minimum wage and overtime to its volunteers. The result might be the same even if its volunteers did not receive free meals and books, because of the commercial nature of the operations.

Even if you are exempt from the provisions of the federal law, you may have to comply with Oregon wage and hour laws. Oregon law is more lenient. It excludes from its definition of "employ" those volunteer or donated services performed for no compensation or without an expectation of compensation as adequate consideration for services. This exclusion applies to religious, charitable, educational, public service or similar nonprofit organizations for community service,

VOLUNTEERS 21

religious or humanitarian reasons. For these non-profits, Oregon law clarifies that these volunteers are not employees even if they receive room and board or small payments. If your nonprofit does not fit within the types described in the exclusion (for example, a social club), your volunteers may be employees.

Under both federal and state law, if any of your volunteers work for your nonprofit as full-time employees, you also need to exercise care. If the volunteer wants to work more than 40 hours per week at her or his job and call the extra work volunteer service, you cannot permit this and must pay her or him for the time. However, if the volunteer works 40 hours per week at a regular job for your organization and then wants to volunteer to perform a service that is very different from that regular job and is one that is traditionally filled by volunteers, you can permit this.

Another circumstance that some nonprofits face is the use of trainees who are earning stipends that are less than minimum wage. In some cases, these are acceptable but in many cases these will be considered sub-minimum wage jobs. You should get legal advice to be sure that your situation is in compliance with wage and hour laws.

State Unemployment and Worker Compensation

In addition to considering wage and hour laws, you also need to keep in mind your responsibility for unemployment taxes and worker compensation coverage if you provide your volunteers with something of value in exchange for their work. Compensation might be in the form of a small per diem payment, free passes to events or programs, or free meals or goods of some kind. If you do this, you need to figure out if the compensation is significant enough to trigger either the unemployment tax or worker compensation coverage. If it is, you need to determine if your volunteers are employees under the unemployment tax test or workers for purposes of worker compensation or if, alternatively, you can classify them as independent contractors. Your volunteers might also fall under some category that excludes them from coverage.

Keep in mind your responsibility for unemployment taxes and worker compensation coverage if you provide your volunteers with something of value in exchange for their work.

Under the state unemployment statutes, volunteers who receive benefits of enough value to fall under the statute will be treated as employees if they meet the tests for an employee. In one Oregon case, volunteers at a nonprofit ski foundation that organized ski races and trainings each received a free ski pass worth $910, enough to trigger the unemployment insurance tax at that time. The court found that the nonprofit had to pay the tax. The nonprofit went to the legislature and got a special exemption from the tax for ski patrols, but a nonprofit that provide a pass for, say, an athletic facility or a season pass to the opera might find itself paying the tax.

State worker compensation laws often categorize volunteers who receive compensation as workers. Compensation may not be wages but may be something else of value. You need to review the

THE OREGON NONPROFIT CORPORATION HANDBOOK

discussion at page 435 to determine if your payment triggers the worker compensation rules, in which case you must obtain worker compensation coverage for them.

Example: The Regional Arts Center holds a three day art fair every year. Volunteers work the month before to prepare the site and exhibits and receive a per diem allowance. This is likely sufficient compensation to trigger worker compensation responsibilities to its volunteers who are functioning as workers.

Volunteers and Liability

Because volunteers provide services for free and often out of the goodness of their hearts, there is a tendency in the nonprofit world to treat volunteer services as "extras" rather than as services for which the organization is responsible. It may be helpful to think of your volunteers as employees as you assess the circumstances in which your use of volunteers may give rise to lawsuits.

> *Because volunteers provide services for free and often out of the goodness of their hearts, there is a tendency in the nonprofit world to treat volunteer services as "extras" rather than as services for which the organization is responsible.*

The use of volunteers raises questions about liability in three contexts:

- When are your volunteers personally liable to those they injure?
- When is your nonprofit organization liable for the volunteer's negligence?
- When is your nonprofit organization liable to your volunteer for injuries suffered by the volunteer while volunteering?

Assessing the Risk of Harm by Volunteers

As you balance how much of your resources to devote to volunteer recruitment, screening, training and supervision, one consideration should be to assess how much risk there is that your volunteer may cause harm. To do this, you need to examine whether there are elements to your program that present a significant degree of likelihood of injury to others or may give rise to lawsuits. Consider whether your volunteers are involved in programs, activities, or fundraisers that deal with or include the following:

- children, the elderly, clients with physical or mental disabilities or limitations, or other vulnerable populations
- food, drink (e.g., sold by your group or available at special events), drugs, or medicine

- alcohol (e.g., at holiday parties, fundraisers)
- driving
- dangerous or risky activities that can cause injuries (e.g., construction; mountain climbing; rescue operations; dealing with violent people; medical care; sports)
- controversial activities that may create opposition (environmental activities, neighborhood issues, advocacy, unpopular publications, etc.)

As you balance how much of your resources to devote to volunteer recruitment, screening, training and supervision, one consideration should be to assess the degree of risk that your volunteer may cause harm.

If your program, activities, or fundraisers contain these or other elements of risk, you and your volunteers are more vulnerable to lawsuit than the average nonprofit. You should look particularly carefully at how you are handling your volunteers.

When Your Volunteers Face Personal Liability

Serving as a volunteer can carry risks for the volunteer. In 1994 in Oregon, two volunteers found themselves on the losing end of a serious lawsuit which resulted in a judgment against them personally for about $3 million.

Volunteers will be personally liable for their own negligence in the same circumstances in which any individual is liable for negligence. An individual generally is liable for negligence if that individual breaches a duty of care to another and that carelessness causes injury to the other person. The volunteer for your organization may be somewhat more likely to encounter a situation in which negligence is an issue because the work of your organization may create a duty of care.

> *Example:* An individual stops to watch children at a youth center playing ball and sees that the players are playing too roughly. Shortly after that, one of the players gets hurt as a result of the rough play. The bystander is generally held not to be liable, since she had no duty to care for the children. However, if a volunteer at the youth center was assigned the job of supervising the play and failed to stop the inappropriate play, that volunteer is negligent, since the volunteer did have a duty to care for the children.

It seems harsh to many people that volunteers, who are often performing a service for free out of the goodness of their hearts, are held liable and may have to pay damages for their actions.

However, it is helpful to think about the issue from the other side—the injured party. Suppose you were the parent who left your 5 year old child at the youth center because you understood the play was supervised. Your child was left brain-damaged because she was slammed to the ground by an older child who was playing too rough. The volunteer who was supposed to supervise the play saw that the play was too rough but failed to stop it because he was chatting with his friends. As you face hundreds of thousands of dollars of medical bills and a lifetime of care for your child, do you really feel that the volunteer should not be held financially responsible for his actions because he was not getting paid?

> *Volunteers will be personally liable for their own negligence in the same circumstances in which any individual is liable for negligence.*

Regardless of which position you take on this issue, seeing the problem from both sides highlights the importance to the nonprofit of treating the work its volunteers do seriously.

When Your Organization is Liable for the Actions of Your Volunteers

Your nonprofit corporation is liable for your volunteer's negligence in two situations. One is when your organization's negligence put the volunteer in a position to cause injury. You are also liable for your volunteer's negligence, even if your organization was not negligent, if your volunteer was acting in the course and scope of her or his duties and was acting at least in part to further your mission. Note that both of these situations require that you or your volunteer has to be negligent before you are liable. Generally, if neither your organization nor your volunteer is negligent, you should not be liable.

When Your Nonprofit Is Negligent

Your nonprofit is liable for your volunteer's negligence if your negligence placed your volunteer in a position to cause harm. You may be negligent in failing to exercise reasonable care in selecting, training, or supervising the volunteer.

> *Example:* Your church has initiated nursery care for children while the parents are attending services. The nursery is staffed by volunteers. At the early service, the nursery is staffed by only one volunteer who abuses a child. The volunteer has a criminal record for child abuse. The church failed to run any background check and

was unaware of the record. Your church, if found negligent for failing to run the check, will be liable to the child for damages. (The volunteer is also liable.)

Example: Your crisis line posts notices around town inviting troubled and suicidal individuals to call for help. You provide no significant training for your volunteer phone staff. A volunteer mishandles a call from a suicidal teenager. The teenager kills herself and her parents are suing your agency. Your failure to train your volunteers may be found by a jury to be negligent and, if so, you will be liable for damages. (The volunteer may or may not also be liable, depending on the facts.)

Example: Your organization provides and installs weatherization on homes for low income people. One of your volunteer trainees improperly installs a window which falls onto a child and injures him. The trainee's supervisor, your employee, was supposed to check the work but forgot to do so. The supervisor's negligence makes your organization liable. (The volunteer may or may not also be liable, depending on the facts.)

Example: Your agency provides services for low-income pregnant women, including providing volunteers who drive them to and from medical appointments. You screen your volunteers to be sure they have valid drivers' licenses, a good driving record, and insurance. You provide them with training. You also monitor and follow up on any complaints about your drivers. One of your drivers gets angry at another driver and deliberately rams that driver's car, injuring your client who is in the car. The volunteer driver is liable but, on these facts, your agency is not. The volunteer was not acting to further your mission.

When Your Nonprofit Is Not Negligent but Liable

It is a surprise to some nonprofits to learn that they may be liable for the actions of their volunteers even if the nonprofit did everything it reasonably could to prevent injury or damage. If you have the right to control your volunteer's activities, your volunteer will probably be treated as a "gratuitous employee" and subject to the same tests as an employee. As an employer, you are liable for your volunteer's negligence under the legal doctrine of *respondeat superior* when the volunteer's activities giving rise to the claim are within the scope of the volunteer's "employment"—that is, their duties. The volunteer's activities fall within the scope of the volunteer's employment when the conduct is of the kind the volunteer has been solicited to perform; it occurs substantially within the authorized limits of time and space of the volunteer's tasks; and the volunteer's conduct is motivated at least in part by the purpose to serve your organization. You cannot escape liability simply by telling your volunteers to act carefully.

The reason that you are liable for the actions of your volunteers in these circumstances is that your volunteers, like your employees, are considered to be acting for your nonprofit. Since they are, their actions are your actions. In most cases, you are not liable for all of the actions of your volunteers but only where the volunteers are negligent. This means you are generally not liable if your volunteer was not negligent and also not liable if your volunteer acted intentionally rather than negligently.

Example: Your Boy Guides group has carefully screened, trained, and supervised its volunteers. A volunteer supervises a game of touch football among the boys, which is allowed by your rules. Your volunteer negligently fails to notice that the field is full of potholes and a boy is injured. The volunteer is personally liable for his negligence and your organization is also liable under the doctrine of *respondeat superior* for the volunteer's negligence.

It is a surprise to some nonprofits to learn that they may be liable for the actions of their volunteers even if the nonprofit did everything it reasonably could to prevent injury or damage.

Example: Your daycare center investigates your childcare volunteer, who has a clean background, and you have controls to ensure that two adults are present with the children. The volunteer later molests a child whose family is visiting the program and who he encounters in the bathroom. The volunteer is liable, but your agency is probably not. You were not negligent in your hiring and controls and you are probably not liable under the doctrine of *respondeat superior* since your volunteer's conduct was intentional and not motivated by a purpose to serve your agency.

When Your Volunteer Is Injured

Occasionally, your volunteer is injured while performing her or his volunteer tasks. This could happen in any nonprofit. For example, your volunteer may slip and fall in your offices. A volunteer may hurt her or his back while lifting a table.

You are liable for injuries caused to your volunteer if your negligence substantially contributed to the volunteer's injury. Remember that if the injuries were negligently caused by one of your other volunteers or employees acting within the scope of their duties, this is considered to be your nonprofit's negligence.

Example: One of your volunteers is driving your nonprofit's car with faulty brakes which your program Director negligently failed to have repaired and is hurt when the brakes fail and he hits another car. Your organization is liable to the volunteer. (Note that your nonprofit will, by the doctrine of *respondeat superior*, be liable to others hurt in the collision as well. Your program Director will be personally liable to the volunteer and the others hurt because of the program manager's negligence.

However, the volunteer will not be liable to the others who are hurt because the volunteer was not negligent.)

You are liable for injuries caused to your volunteer if your negligence substantially contributed to the volunteer's injury.

Assessing the Risk of Harm to Volunteers

You should assess the nature of the work that your volunteers do to see how much risk you have that the volunteer may be injured. This is a somewhat different assessment than the one to determine how much risk there is that your volunteer may injure someone else. Consider whether your volunteers engage in the following activities as part of their volunteer tasks:

- lifting
- construction
- driving
- sports
- dealing with potentially dangerous populations (criminals, people with mental illnesses, abusers, aggressive animals, drug addicts or alcoholics, etc.)
- dealing with natural disasters
- dangerous rescue work

Protection for Your Volunteers and Your Organization

There are several methods of protection for volunteers and for your organizations. Federal law and, in very limited circumstances, state law offers some protection. Your nonprofit and your volunteers can also act to prevent or minimize problems concerning the liability of your volunteers and of your organization by using both preventive strategies and damage control.

Federal and State Law Protections

The federal Volunteer Protection Act provides considerable protection to volunteers of certain nonprofit organizations. Your organization falls under this law if you are exempt under §501(c)(3) or are organized and conducted for public benefit and operate primarily for charitable, civic, educational, religious, welfare, or health purposes, and do not engage in hate crimes. If your or-

THE OREGON NONPROFIT CORPORATION HANDBOOK

ganization so qualifies, your volunteers are those who provide services without an expectation of pay and who do not receive anything of value from your corporation worth more than $500 per year for their services. This prevents a volunteer from losing coverage because he or she receives small gratuities, such as free admission to an organization's theatre productions. In addition, volunteers can be reimbursed for their out-of-pocket expenses. If required by law, the volunteer must be licensed or certified by the appropriate agency to be protected from liability.

Volunteers acting within the scope of their responsibilities are not liable for their negligence except to your corporation. This means that those outside your corporation cannot recover their damages from your volunteer. Your nonprofit can recover from the volunteer if the volunteer's negligence causes damage to you. Your volunteers are liable to all those they injure for gross negligence, reckless misconduct, and conscious, flagrant indifference to the rights or safety of anyone harmed by their actions.

There are a number of exceptions to the law's protection. The federal statute does not apply if your volunteer caused harm by a motor vehicle, craft, or vessel for which the volunteer must be licensed. It also does not apply if your volunteer is under the influence of alcohol or drugs at the time of the misconduct. This protection does not apply if the volunteer's misconduct constitutes a violent crime or a hate crime under federal law, involves a sexual offense under state law for which the volunteer is convicted, or is a violation of a federal or state civil rights law. The law also imposes restrictions on the type of damages for which your volunteers can be sued.

Although those outside your corporation can't recover for their injuries if your volunteer is negligent, they can still sue. The injured person may pursue a lawsuit by claiming that the volunteer was grossly negligent. Although the volunteer may win the suit, he or she will spend a considerable sum of money on legal fees and costs defending the case. Consequently, many organizations and volunteers want insurance (discussed below) even with the more favorable federal law.

In some rare cases, Oregon law protects volunteers from liability. For example, some volunteers who are transporting the elderly and disabled and some volunteers who are assisting in hazardous waste cleanup are immune from suit.

Preventive Actions

In addition to legal protections, you can act in a preventive way to head off problems. This means following the actions outlined earlier in this chapter to be sure that you are care- fully selecting, training, and supervising your volunteers. This will permit you to avoid most problems that can occur.

Damage Control

The second strategy is *damage control*: to minimize the consequences of problems that do occur. You and your volunteers can take some actions to minimize the impact if your volunteer is involved in causing an injury or damage. There are three sources to look to for help: recordkeeping, releases and insurance.

Recordkeeping

There is a big difference between what happened and proving what happened. One of the purposes of good recordkeeping is to provide a way to prove what happened. You should keep records of your volunteers and of the duties they perform. Good records would permit your organization at a later date to know who did what, when, where, and how. Your records should also document the procedures you followed in recruiting, selecting, training, and supervising your volunteers. Good records can also provide you with other information to document that you act reasonably.

> *Example:* Volunteers at the Helping House are given a route slip when they deliver meals to the elderly. The route slip tracks when, where, and to whom the volunteer does deliveries as well as provide a space for the volunteer to note any special food requests that those receiving food make and why, so that the organization can avoid sending the wrong food to those who may be allergic or have medical conditions that restrict their diet.

You and your volunteers can take some actions to minimize the impact if your volunteer is involved in causing an injury or damage.

Of course, the amount of recordkeeping you can realistically do will be governed by factors such as your budget and staffing. However, it is important not to treat recordkeeping as an extra but to recognize that it can be an important protection for your organization and volunteers.

Releases

Your organization can get written releases from the people you serve or deal with in which those people agree not to sue you or your agents, employees, and volunteers in the event that an injury occurs. Releases are often ignored by the courts, particularly if the release is signed by someone who may not be completely competent or in a position to act freely (such as some elderly people or those who fear they won't get benefits if they don't sign). Still, there are circumstances when they are enforced. Releases are discussed in more detail on page 686.

Insurance

The most practical protection your volunteer and your organization can have is insurance. Insurance is useful for two reasons. One is that it covers any judgment against the insured party up to the policy limits. The second, and often most important reason, is that the insurance company pays the insured party's legal expenses. Most nonprofits win suits when they are sued, but the costs of defense often fall between $20,000-80,000. You and your volunteers can look to several sources to see if you have or can get insurance:

VOLUNTEERS' PERSONAL INSURANCE POLICIES

Volunteers should check their personal insurance policies listed below to see if they have coverage. This coverage may be found in several policies. You should be aware that if the volunteer's personal policy covers the volunteer, this coverage will not protect the nonprofit organization because the volunteer but not the nonprofit is the insured party under these coverages.

> *The most practical protection your volunteer and your organization can have is insurance.*

HOMEOWNERS OR RENTERS INSURANCE

Your volunteer's homeowners or renter insurance may cover claims against the volunteer based on personal injury or property damage. This coverage usually applies even if the injuries occurred away from home and often applies to volunteer activities. Even if it is included, most policies do exclude intentional harm caused by the insured. This would eliminate most child abuse claims from coverage. Some policies also exclude claims from commercial child care, which may exclude coverage of the nonprofit providing childcare if it is done for a fee. Your volunteers should talk to their insurance agents to see what their policy covers.

AUTOMOBILE INSURANCE

Volunteers will often have personal car insurance policies which would normally cover them while driving in connection with their volunteer work.

UMBRELLA POLICIES

Some volunteers will have umbrella policies that expand the coverage available on homeowners and renters policies. Some of these umbrella policies also will cover volunteer work. If they don't, your volunteers can sometimes buy that coverage. As with homeowners or renters insurance, umbrella policies generally cover only personal injuries and property damage and so may not provide the coverage your volunteers need.

Some nonprofits want to reimburse their volunteers who have to buy volunteer coverage. If you are going to reimburse your volunteer to buy coverage, you should talk to an attorney first to be sure you set this up correctly. Your nonprofit may have restrictions on providing private benefit for individuals. Providing umbrella coverage could violate that rule if you are not careful, since you are paying for coverage that not only protects your volunteer for liabilities incurred as a volunteer but also for liability elsewhere in their lives.

ORGANIZATIONAL INSURANCE POLICIES

Organizational policies are ones your nonprofit purchases to protect itself. In most cases, you would purchase the policy to cover your volunteers as well. These policies protect you by covering any judgments (up to the limit of the policy) against your organization and the insurance company pays your attorney fees and costs incurred in connection with claims. If the policy also names the volunteer as an insured party, the insurance company would similarly protect the volunteer.

GENERAL LIABILITY POLICY

You should check your organization's general liability policy (see page 567 for a discussion of this policy) to see if it covers volunteers as well as your nonprofit. Some policies cover only your employees. The word "volunteer" should appear under the list of insureds or as an endorsement, usually called "Additional Insureds—Volunteers." If you don't have this coverage, you can usually add it quite cheaply, sometimes for free. Be aware that these policies are limited in what they cover and often exclude risks such as child abuse and car accidents. Another disadvantage is that when the volunteers are included, they share the policy limits with the organization. For example, if the volunteer and the organization are each held liable for $700,000, a million dollar policy would come up short.

VOLUNTEER LIABILITY POLICY

Your organization can purchase a volunteer liability policy. The sole purpose of this policy is to protect volunteers who are sued. The cost of this policy is often very cheap. In the case mentioned in the introduction to this chapter, the nonprofit organization had purchased this insurance for its volunteers and it was the insurance company that covered the $3 million judgment that had been entered against the volunteers.

If you buy insurance to protect your volunteers, there are a few pointers to keep in mind. If you provide trainings to your volunteers or have operating policies or safety procedures for your volunteers, this may reduce the cost of your insurance policies covering volunteers. Give your agent a copy of your written materials. Be sure that any volunteer liability policy you purchase defines "volunteer" broadly, especially if the volunteer gets any compensation or perks from volunteering. It pays to shop around and get an agent who is familiar with nonprofit insurance policies.

Protection for Your Nonprofit Organization and Your Volunteer When Your Volunteer Is Injured

Somewhat different damage control strategies need to be considered in connection with the situation in which the volunteer is injured while acting as your volunteer.

Releases

You could consider getting a release from your volunteers in which each volunteer agrees not to sue you if she or he is injured while volunteering. However, there are obvious problems with this in terms of your ability to attract volunteers.

Worker Compensation

In addition to the insurance described above, you may want to consider purchasing worker compensation coverage for your volunteers. In Oregon, you are not required to purchase this coverage for volunteers, but it is available. You may particularly want to consider this if you have volunteers who engage in risky activities as described above. There are advantages to the volunteer and possibly advantages to you in having worker compensation coverage. The advantage to the volunteer is that the coverage applies whether or not the volunteer can show your organization's negligence caused her or his injury and may be more extensive than the other coverage you have available.

> *Example:* Your volunteer injures his back while lifting a box in your soup kitchen. If you did not have worker compensation coverage and if your general liability policy did not cover this injury, your volunteer would be have to pay his bills through his own insurance, if any. He would not have grounds to recover from your organization because you were not negligent. Even if your liability insurance covered the volunteer, it would generally only pay for his medical bills but would not pay for any permanent or temporary disability. However, worker compensation would pay the medical bills, lost work, and an award for permanent disability, if any, without regard to whether your organization was negligent.

There are two advantages to your organization. One is that your volunteers will be happier if they are covered for injuries while they are volunteering. The second potential advantage to you is that the volunteer may be prevented from suing you in those situations where you were negligent. Since you could potentially lose a lot of money in that type of lawsuit, most nonprofits would prefer not to take that risk. Instead, the volunteer may have to take the coverage offered by the worker compensation system and cannot also sue you. This is the rule where employers provide worker compensation coverage for their employees. However, the law is not quite clear as to whether this would be the result where a nonprofit voluntarily elects to cover its volunteers.

You may want to consider purchasing worker compensation coverage for your volunteers.

There is one disadvantage to covering your volunteers under your worker compensation policy. Injuries to your volunteers could affect your premium ratings and raise your rates. You can discuss this with your insurance agent. You may decide that it is more advantageous for you to cover your volunteers under an accident policy.

Because the law is ambiguous about whether your nonprofit would get protection from lawsuits if you elect to cover your volunteers under the worker compensation system, you may want to have them sign releases agreeing not to sue you in exchange for providing the worker compensation coverage. Although the courts could strike this type of release down, its chances of being upheld are better than average. A sample "Complete Release and Hold Harmless Agreement by Volunteers" is included in the Forms section. Have your attorney review and modify this if necessary before you rely on it.

If you are thinking about providing worker compensation coverage for your volunteers and asking them to sign a release, you may want to consider talking it over with them and getting their input. If the volunteers don't understand what they are signing and what the advantages to them are, this may create some antagonism between your organization and your volunteers.

One Final Protection—Good Communication

Despite your best efforts, accidents do happen. No nonprofit wants to see its clients, volunteers, or community members injured or damaged in any way. And certainly, none of us wants to end up devoting time, energy, and money to dealing with lawsuits which arise from injuries and damages.

As anyone of us who has been injured in an accident knows, good communication really matters. When the other party is courteous and concerned about our welfare, we are less likely to feel angry and determined to punish them for their actions. Your nonprofit will want to provide guidance to all of its employees and volunteers about how to behave when accidents occur or other potentially damaging situations unfold. Your training should include strategies to communicate concern without making statements that can potentially damage the organization if legal action does ensue. You'll also want to establish clear procedures for staff and volunteers to document what has happened and communicate immediately with the appropriate person within your organization.

Your nonprofit will want to develop a crisis management plan to deal with the most unfortunate and damaging situations, including automobile accidents, fires, and, unfortunately, abuse of vulnerable program participants. Your plan should identify who will be the public spokesperson for your nonprofit and should be sure that person is prepared to deal with the media, investigators, staff, volunteers, participants, donors, and the community.

Many liability insurance providers offer risk management guides and trainings for the nonprofit clients. You can check out the excellent resources for crisis management provided by the Nonprofit Risk Management Center, at *http://www.nonprofitrisk.org/*.

Consult Appendix 1 if you would like information about source material related to this Chapter.

PART V

Successful Functioning: Money, Records, and Rules

22. FUNDING: OBTAINING RESOURCES FOR YOUR ORGANIZATION

THIS CHAPTER COVERS

- How nonprofits are funded
- Foundation grants
- Corporate and business support
- Individual contributions—the most sustainable source of support
- Fundraising events
- Membership fees
- Civic and religious organizations
- Bingo, raffles, and gaming
- Government grants and contracts
- Program service fees
- Product sales
- Social enterprise and business ventures
- Investment income
- In-kind contributions
- Using the internet and social media to raise funds
- Ethical and Legal Issues in Fundraising
- Final tips

Whether your nonprofit is brand new or has been in business for a number of years, you will need to obtain funding and find other resources in order to carry out your mission. For many nonprofits, finding resources poses a substantial challenge.

In this chapter we'll take a look at many of the ways nonprofit organizations obtain funds and other resources, and provide tools to help you evaluate which approaches are best suited to the strengths of your organization. Increasingly, nonprofits are finding they must use multiple strategies to obtain all the resources they need. Think of the options described in this chapter as a menu, and plan to prepare a multi-course meal

Nonprofits obtain resources in three distinct ways:

- Contributions—including gifts from individuals, businesses, and foundations
- Program fees and product sales either related to or unrelated to their missions
- Government contracts, awards and agreements

How Are Nonprofits Funded?

Over 70% of the dollars that support charitable organizations in the United States are obtained through fees or sales of services and products that are directly related to the organization's mission. Contributions comprise the remaining 30%. Of course, there are very significant differences in these ratios among different types of nonprofit organizations. Health care, child care, and recreation organizations often receive nearly all their funding through charging fees for the services they were created to provide. Here is Oregon, most performing arts organizations receive 50 to 60% of their support through ticket sales. In contrast, food pantries and homeless shelters may be supported entirely by contributions, or may combine contributions from individuals, businesses, and foundations, with support from governmental entities that purchase specific services for specific eligible populations.

A variety of factors will influence what turns out to be the best way to fund your nonprofit. Start by understanding how organizations with purposes similar to yours are supported. You can check out their sources of support online by reviewing their Form 990, annual report to the IRS at the National Center for Charitable Statistics website http://nccsdataweb.urban.org/PubApps/search.php or by talking with leaders of similar organizations.

Next think through your strengths and limitations in relation to generating each type of support. Many organizations get started with a core group of volunteers contributing their time and holding small scale fund raising events to generate small amounts of cash. Once they've demonstrated both that their service is needed and that their approach works, they may be able to able to obtain start-up funding from foundations, churches and civic groups, and in some cases, local government. Unfortunately, building a solid base of financial support often becomes more difficult after the start-up period. The more your nonprofit does, the more support it will need. And once your projects or programs are no longer new, some funders will no longer be interested in providing support.

So it is essential to start from the beginning to figure out strategies that will ensure your ability to keep doing the things that matter most and expand and innovate as needs and opportunities emerge. For many nonprofits, this will mean developing a base of individual donors and/or figuring out ways to receive payment (earned income) for some or all of the services and products that you develop as part of your core mission.

As you start thinking through your approach to obtaining contributions, it's helpful to understand how charitable giving in the United States actually works. Overwhelmingly, most contributions that tax-exempt organizations receive are from individuals—both living and dead. If you check the latest statistics at *www.givingusa.org*, the national organization that tracks charitable giving throughout the country, you'll realize that while the percentage of contributions from foundations and corporations shift a little bit from year to year, living individuals always account for at least 75% of charitable contributions and individuals continue their support from beyond the grave through bequests that generally comprise another 8 to 10%.

So why do so many newer nonprofits focus on foundation grants—in part because even small foundation grants are larger than the gifts that a first-time individual donor may be willing to make to a new nonprofit. And for some new nonprofits, the process of submitting written proposals for foundation support seems less intimidating than actually asking a friend or neighbor for a contribution. In reality, it's not an either or choice. Successful nonprofits build relationships with both individuals and foundations, and eventually with corporate giving programs as well, in order to provide the strongest base of support for their work.

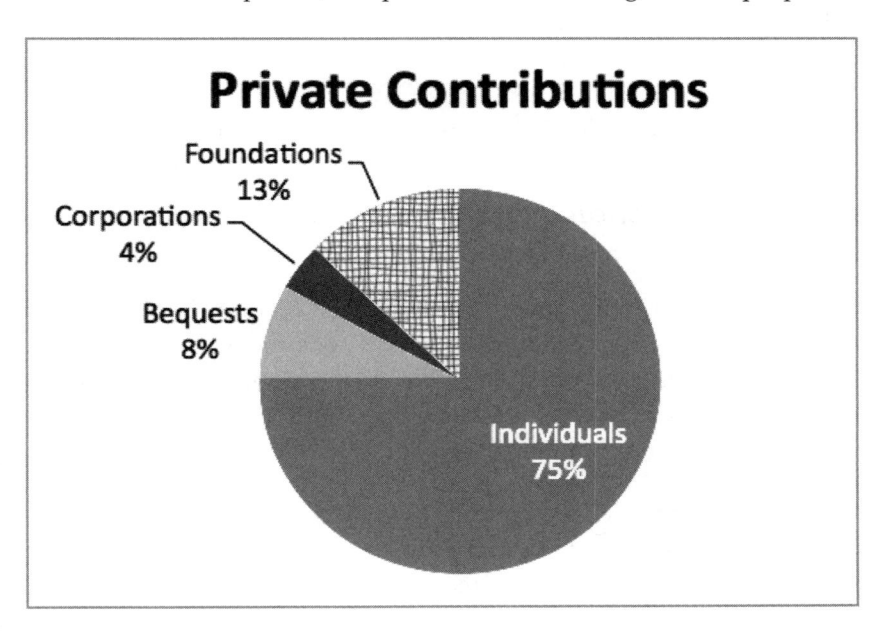

We'll discuss the realities of foundation grant seeking first. But as you think through your foundation strategies, keep the reality of charitable giving clearly in mind. Unless your nonprofit will be supported entirely by earned income or governmental sources (as only a relatively small portion of nonprofits are), you will eventually need to focus on the individual giving strategies, the earned income strategies, and the governmental strategies covered below.

Foundation Grants

Foundations, sometimes described as "a body of money completely surrounded by people who want some," are tax-exempt entities which make contributions, characterized as grants, to nonprofit organizations. Almost all foundations require that their grants be given only to organizations which have obtained tax exemption under §501(c)(3). A few foundations are willing to make special grants to other nonprofits. These grants to non- §501(c)(3) organizations require the foundation to take additional steps and precautions to be certain that all funds are expended for §501(c)(3) type purposes.

Foundations may use either a formal or informal process to determine which organizations they will fund. Foundations choosing the more formal approach are open to receiving written proposals from nonprofit organizations, and considering requests from both nonprofits they already know, and others with which they have had no previous contact. Those choosing the more informal approach make grants primarily to organizations of particular interest to the foundation's Directors, frequently making decisions primarily on the basis of personal knowledge and relationship. While these informal approach foundations may also require the organizations they fund to prepare a written statement describing the proposed use of the funds, they are generally not open to considering unsolicited requests.

Many foundations prefer that proposals focus on a new project or expansion of an existing service, rather than continuation of your organization's basic activities.

Most foundations which do accept unsolicited requests have fairly specific guidelines about the types of activities they will fund. While some foundations are open to providing general operating support, most prefer requests which identify specific activities or needs for which funding is sought. Many foundations prefer that proposals focus on a new project or expansion of an existing service, rather than continuation of your organization's basic activities.

Oregon nonprofits seek support from a variety of foundations—including some with an exclusive Oregon focus, others with regional interests, and some which fund throughout the nation. Most foundations receive many more requests than they are able to fund. Asking for funding provides no assurance of obtaining funding. New nonprofits, or those that have not previously obtained foundation support, face particular challenges to obtain their first grants. Regional and national foundations often look for evidence of support of the organization by local foundations. Oregon foundations look, in turn, for evidence of support by other Oregon foundations. So the question becomes who will give your organization its first opportunity.

If you are new to the world of foundation grants, you will want to devote your initial energy to learning about foundations that are most likely to be interested in funding your nonprofit. The Oregon Foundation *Databook* by Craig McPherson (*www.foundationdatabook.com*) may be particularly helpful. The Databook is available in both print and electronic formats and facilitates searching for foundations by the types and sizes of grants they make.

You will also want to check the resources at your local or regional library. Many libraries have access to several internet based grants research tools as well as the directory published by the Council on Foundations. If your local library does not have the resources you need, ask them to help you connect with the nearest library with a foundation resource center.

You may also find it helpful to attend seminars or workshops which deal with foundation funding. The Nonprofit Association of Oregon (NAO) *http://www.nonprofitoregon.org/* offers workshops regularly. You can also access GrantStation, a weekly national grants newsletter, simply by joining NAO.

Many foundations provide a specific form or format which applicants must use to be considered. Many of the smaller foundations prefer a two page letter which contains a basic description of your organization and the project for which you are seeking funding. Foundations making larger grants often use a multi-step process in which the initial request is very brief, and more extensive information is required of organizations and proposals of particular interest to the foundation. You can learn of the specific requirements of each foundation by going to the foundation's website or by requesting their guidelines for funding and any application forms.

Foundation Funding Preferences

In our experience, there are several factors which have the greatest influence on a nonprofit organization's success in obtaining foundation support. They are:

The Strength of the Organization

Foundations prefer to support organizations which they perceive as well-managed, stable, and effective. While some foundations prefer larger, older nonprofits, others are particularly interested in newer, community based organizations. In either case, foundations want to feel confident that the organization is capable of carrying out the project for which funding is sought.

The Clarity, Logic, and Importance of the Project for Which Funding Is Sought

Most foundations want to fund proposals which are well thought out and clearly explained. Many are particularly sensitive to the relationship between the amount of money sought and the scope of the issues the organization proposes to address. Discussing the need to end world hunger and then requesting $1,500 to print brochures about a free food program suggests that the organization has not thought clearly about the specific problem or issue it seeks to address.

Small organizations with big dreams face particular problems. If your organization is small or new, you will probably have greater success with proposals to do one or two small things well than with a global description of every need and every idea you have developed.

Larger organizations may confront the reverse problems. Proposals for very small amounts or limited projects may cause foundations to wonder why the organization does not meet this small cost with its own funds.

Funding Priorities

Many foundations have either permanent or periodically determined funding priorities and will not consider proposals outside these priorities unless foundation Directors or staff have a very strong personal relationship with the organization requesting funding.

Personal Relationships

Foundations are besieged by unsolicited requests. The total requests received by almost every foundation are vastly greater than the amount of funds the foundation has available for grants. Foundation decisions are made by people—the Directors and to a lesser degree, the staff. "People give to people" is a truism of fundraising. People pay special attention to suggestions made by people they know.

So you will be wise to determine whether any of the people your organization knows—your Directors, staff, volunteers, supporters, etc.—know any of the people in decision making roles for the foundations. The foundation reference books and websites noted earlier include names of the officers of each foundation. You can also review copies of foundations' Form 990 or 990PF by entering the name of the foundation into the National Center for Charitable Statistics website (*http://nccsdataweb.urban.org/PubApps/search.php*). Foundations are required to identify their Board members or Trustees on these forms.

If someone you know does have a relationship with a foundation decision-maker, ask them to introduce your organization's spokesperson to the foundation. If no one you know knows any of the foundation people you'd like to get to know, check with other nonprofit organizations you work with to see if they have relationships with specific foundations, and ask them to introduce you. Or, look for workshops and conferences with representatives of foundations speaking on panels and introduce yourself and your organization.

Organization and Persistence in Your Efforts

Do your research carefully. Submit only appropriate, well-presented applications. Systematically try again. Ask for help thinking about your project from foundation staff. Avoid putting foundation staff people on the spot by asking why their foundation did not fund your proposal. Instead, explain what your organization is trying to accomplish and ask for suggestions on how to communicate your ideas to other foundations as well as their own. Never complain about not being funded. Be positive about the progress your organization is making and appreciative of the time the foundation staff person has made available for you. Most foundation staff people are particularly wary of organizations asking "well what would you fund?" because it suggests that the organization does not have its own clear direction and is only looking for money.

Final Note: Remember, foundation funding comprises less than 10% of all charitable contributions made in the United States. It is unlikely that foundation funding will be an ongoing, primary source of general operating support for your organization. It is more likely that foundation funding will allow an established organization to launch a new project, expand a current service, or build specific organizational capacities.

Corporate and Other Business Giving

Some corporations and businesses have established separate foundations which make grants in ways very similar to the foundations described above. Typically, these corporate foundations have guidelines for funding, standard application forms, and staff charged with specific responsibility for charitable giving. Some of these corporate foundations are listed in the foundation directories described earlier in this chapter. In fact about the only difference between these corporate foundations and other foundations is that they are frequently influenced by the corporation's managers, and in some cases, by line level employees. Check their websites to learn what role corporate employees play in the decision making. Then check with your Board and supporters to see if you have any potential relationships with employees who could advocate for your proposal.

In addition to these corporate foundations, many businesses have active charitable giving programs and will consider requests for both money and goods and services (which we discuss later in this chapter under In-Kind Contributions) from nonprofit organizations. As with foundations, businesses will always require that an applicant for a charitable gift have proof of §501(c)(3) status. In some cases, a business may offer to sponsor an event you put on in exchange for being listed as a sponsor. The contribution that the business makes may be considered a donation rather than taxable advertising income to your organization if you follow the corporate sponsorship rules on pp. 210-12.

> *Many businesses have active charitable giving programs and will consider requests for both money and goods and services .*

Some businesses do make non-charitable contributions to organizations exempt under other (c) sections like 501(c)(4) or (c)(6). These contributions are considered marketing expenses are thus tax deductible by the business as operating expenses rather than as charitable contributions. The key issue for the business is whether associating itself with your organization will have a positive impact on customers, potential customers, or regulators with which the business seeks a positive relationship.

In many businesses, the managers making decisions about charitable contributions operate separately from the managers making decisions about "marketing" contributions. If you do not have a contact in the marketing department, ask the charitable giving staff to help you think through whether your organization or project may have potential value for marketing purposes strategy for the business, and ask for their help in contacting the appropriate person.

Business Giving Contrasts with Foundation Giving

In our experience, there are some significant differences between seeking and obtaining funding from businesses and dealing with foundations. Among them are:

- Businesses place even more emphasis on relationships. In fact, many businesses give only to organizations recommended by managers or owners of the business.

- Most businesses want very short proposals. They are generally inclined to either like a concept or not like it. Details will not persuade them.

- Businesses may want to play it safe by funding well known and well respected charitable organizations unless they have personal knowledge of the people involved in a less known organization.

- It may help to point out the connections which exist between people interested in your organization's work and the business employers or customers or political groups with which the business would like to cultivate a strong relationship.

- Some businesses are more open to the concept of general operating support than foundations. If they are persuaded that your organization is meeting an important need and doing a good job, they may be less inclined to want to control exactly how you use their gift.

- Some businesses are willing to make repeat grants. Be sure you keep them involved and knowledgeable about what your group is accomplishing, and give them public credit for their support in meaningful ways and they may well want to stick with a winner and fund your organization repeatedly.

Remember, corporate and business giving generally accounts for less than 5 to 8% of all charitable giving in the United States. So, unless your organizations develops particularly strong relationships with major decision makers, business giving will probably not be your best source of funding.

Individual Contributions

Obtaining charitable gifts from individuals is the subject of countless books, workshops, and college courses. So, we will not attempt to provide a comprehensive discussion of the myriad approaches nonprofits use to obtain individual contributions. But in order to develop your overall funding strategy, there are several key facts about individual giving which you will need to know.

Gifts from individuals (living and dead) comprise more than 85% of all charitable giving in the United States. Individuals tend to give repeatedly to the same organization and generally give because they believe in the organization's work. Most individuals do not attach specific restrictions to their gifts. Taken together, this means that gifts from individuals may be among the most dependable, repeatable, and unrestricted sources of money your organization can find.

However, obtaining gifts from individuals typically takes considerable effort, and sometimes considerable financial investment. Most organizations find that relatively few donors send money without any prompting or request to do so. If fact, many believe that one of the reasons why religious organizations receive nearly half of all charitable contributions is because they ask—often and repeatedly.

> *Gifts from individuals may be among the most dependable, repeatable, and unrestricted sources of money your organization can find.*

If your organization is new, and does not involve wealthy individuals or folks with access to wealthy individuals, you'll probably be interested in what's called grassroots fundraising.

Studies show that poorer people actually give a higher percentage of their incomes in charitable gifts than do upper-middle class or wealthy individuals. Working with a grassroots fundraising strategy will mean you have to obtain smaller gifts from more people than an organization which has access to wealthy individuals who can be cultivated to become major donors.

But whether your organization is approaching people of modest means or people with substantial wealth, you will want to start from the understanding that most people give to people—i.e. make gifts when they feel a sense of relationship with individuals involved in specific charitable organizations.

Almost all of us are constantly besieged by mail and email solicitations and sometimes phone calls from charitable organizations which are undoubtedly doing very worthwhile work. But we can't give to everything. So most of us target our giving to situations in which someone we know asks us to give, or an organization gives us such a strong sense of affinity to our values and priorities that we feel that we know the people involved with it.

As you plan your various strategies for seeking gifts from individuals, you'll want to build on your strengths and minimize your weaknesses. Here are some basic steps to formulate your strategy:

- Start with the people who know the most about what your group does—its Board, volunteers, program participants, and their immediate families. After you have obtained gifts from this closest group, ask them to help you identify individuals who they know and think would be interested.

- Make your fundraising as personal as possible. If you send letters, have Directors or volunteers sign them by hand, and write personal notes if they know the person who will receive the letter. Try phone calls if your supporters are comfortable with this approach. Use face-to-face meetings with individuals who you believe may be able to make larger contributions. Be sure the person who has the best relationship with the prospective donor makes the introduction and indicates that she or he has given to your organization.

- Lay out your plan for asking individuals for a whole year. Avoid "nickel and diming" donors—i.e. coming back again and again for small amounts rather than being direct about the whole amount you are asking the person to give. You can still offer your donors the opportunity to make monthly or quarterly payments if they prefer, but most people get fed up with repeated small requests.

- Discuss the level of investment in fundraising that makes sense for your organization. If you will be asking a fairly large number of people for fairly small contributions, you probably will want to make the request look interesting but not lavish. On the other hand, if you are asking relatively few people for relatively large amounts, be prepared to do something special

---

Whether your organization is approaching people of modest means or people with substantial wealth, you will want to start from the understanding that most people give to people—i.e. make gifts when they feel a sense of relationship with individuals involved in specific charitable organizations.

Repeat Giving

Repeat giving is essential. Successful individual giving programs work hard to maintain relationships with each donor and consistently ask for repeat gifts. Research shows that each time an individual makes a charitable gift, they become more committed to the issue and to the organization. Many repeat givers increase the size of their contributions over time.

To understand how your nonprofit can build a core of repeat givers, think about your own charitable giving. Chances are good that the organizations you continue to support have thanked you promptly for each gift and stayed in touch—letting you know what has been accomplished with support from donors like you.

Key Numbers

There are three key numbers you'll want to pay attention to as you work to grow your support from individual donors:

- The number of donors
- The average size of gifts
- The percentage of donors who give a second, third or fourth time

Tracking these key numbers will help you evaluate the success of each of your efforts to connect with individual donors and guide your strategies to make the most productive use of your time and money to strengthen your base of individual donor support.

Do People Need to Get Something in Return for Giving $ to Your Nonprofit?

Before you jump into the next section of this chapter dealing with Fundraising Events, you'll want to have an honest conversation with Board members and volunteers about a big question that involves some potentially uncomfortable issues.

Many people are very uncomfortable with the idea of asking friends, neighbors, or others to make contributions. Still others are uncomfortable with the idea of asking strangers for gifts. Still more are just uncomfortable asking for "hand-outs".

In many nonprofits, this discomfort about asking for gifts leads to more and more time consuming and costly approaches to raising money—from selling candy bars to planning elaborate dinners with entertainment. Unfortunately, some of these strategies end up not only taking time and money that could be better used, they may also result in the people making the "gifts" not really understanding the good work your nonprofit is doing.

It may be helpful to ask members of your group to pause and reflect on their own experiences in being asked for donations and making the decision to give a gift rather than buy a product or attend an event. It turns out that most of us make our decisions about giving based on feeling a positive connection with the person asking for the gift, feeling confident that the money will be used well, and feeling comfortable with the values that guide the organization asking for the gift.

That's why the most successful nonprofits focus on providing a simple, clear message about the work they are doing and why they are doing it and building relationships with potential donors. No chicken-dinner or candy bar may be required.

Donor Acknowledgement

You will want to set up procedures to be sure that your nonprofit acknowledges every gift it receives promptly. Donors who want to claim a charitable tax deduction on their tax returns will need a written acknowledgement on your letterhead in order for any single gift over $250 to be deductible. Most nonprofits find it simpler and more effective to provide a written acknowledgment for every gift, whether it is over $250 or smaller.

If your donor includes both a contribution and a payment for something of value received by the donor, different rules apply. This commonly happens when a donor pays for tickets to gala fundraising dinners or special fundraising concerts. In these situations, the donor is receiving something of value (the dinner or the entertainment) and is also making a contribution in the form of paying more than the fair market value for what they will receive. The IRS requires charities to provide a written disclosure statement to donors who receive goods or services in exchange for a single payment of $75 or more.

We cover these rules in more detail on pages 694-98. You can keep up with IRS requirements for gift acknowledgement and disclosures at the IRS website. (See Appendix 2.)

> *Donors who want to claim a charitable tax deduction on their tax returns will need a written acknowledgement on your letterhead in order for any single gift over $250 to be deductible.*

Gift Acceptance Policy

While new nonprofits often feel that they should accept any contribution that they are offered, there may be certain types of gifts that your organization will need to decline. In order to be ready to make wise choices and maintain good relationships with potential donors, your Board should adopt a Gift Acceptance Policy which outlines the type of gifts you will and won't accept and the process you will use to determine whether a proposed gift should be accepted or declined. A good Gift Acceptance Policy will help you avoid accepting gifts that have questionable value, will be costly to manage, will conflict with your values, or will involve unreasonable restrictions. See p. 280.

Fundraising Events

Again, volumes have been written on fundraising events, and numerous workshops are available. Here are three major issues you will want to think about as you consider whether and how your organization should do fundraising events.

Determining the Purpose of the Event

First, you will want to be very clear about the purpose of any event you decide to do. Is your primary intention to raise money, or are you considering the event because it will help your organization become more visible, help you identify potential donors or volunteers, or provide a good team building opportunity for volunteers? If any of these are your primary purpose for the event, you may want to clearly describe the proposed event as a "special event" rather than a fundraising event, even if there will be some money raised through it. You'll want everyone to understand the primary purpose so that you can make the numerous decisions associated with any event based on your intended goals.

Projecting the Income and Expenses for the Event

If fundraising is the primary purpose of the event you are considering, be sure you project both the gross receipts and the expenses you anticipate incurring for the event. Working with specific projections for income from the different components of the event (corporate sponsorships, tickets, food sales, etc.) will help you focus your efforts and avoid spending too much time on a component which will not yield much. You'll also want to work with detailed projections of each cost item. These expense projections provide guidance for the volunteers and staff working on the event, and are essential for projecting what the net income will be.

Once you've done your detailed event income and expense projections, you'll be able to compare different event concepts. Increasingly, Boards and volunteers tell us that they prefer making one big effort around an event to the endless demands of multiple small events. Be sure to check this concept out with your group—they may prefer the multiple small ones.

Considering the True Cost of the Event

While you may not keep detailed staff time records, it is important to have paid staff keep some record of the time they spend making fundraising events happen. Frequently, all staff become involved as an event approaches, disrupting other work and wearing folks out. If this is true in your organization, you'll need to think about the concept of "opportunity costs." This refers to the funds you didn't raise through grant writing or providing services because your staff were tied up working on a fundraising event.

Is It Worth It?

Once you're clear about the true cost of fundraising events, you'll probably want to know "Is it worth it?" Well-organized and interesting fundraising events raise your visibility, put you in touch with potential new supporters, and can create great team spirit for Directors and volunteers. Many types of events produce increasing net amounts as they are repeated from year to year. In the first year, everything takes longer, and you make mistakes. As the event develops, you should be able to increase the net. So it may be worth making a tremendous effort with a new event even if it doesn't generate a huge amount in the first year, if you can see that it has potential for increased net income in future years.

One final thought on events. Be alert for opportunities to have church or social organizations produce events for you. This can produce money and visibility for your group with very little effort on your part. If you are approached by a civic group proposing to do an event (auction, fair, etc.) with you as the beneficiary, explore the concept carefully. Be sure you are confident the group can follow through and do a quality event. And be sure they are not counting on your staff, volunteers, and supporters to carry major roles. In fact, you may want to draft a brief and friendly letter of understanding to be sure you have a true meeting of the minds.

Membership Fees

Many nonprofits generate income by charging fees for membership. As explained earlier in this book, the term "membership" has a very specific legal meaning for nonprofits in Oregon. If your organization is not technically a membership corporation, you may want to find a different term to describe individuals who support your work but do not have the legal rights of members in a membership corporation or take some precautions to avoid confusion about this issue. See pp. 25-26.

A further distinction exists between the concept of membership as a form of being a "financial supporter," and the concept of membership as being an "exchange" method for individuals to purchase certain goods or services from the nonprofit. The typical financial support type membership offers the purchaser little of financial value in exchange for their membership fee. Such supporter-members may receive a newsletter or an opportunity to attend special social gatherings but do not receive very large discounts on the organization's admission fees or very substantial "thank you" gifts for their donation. Established individual donor solicitation efforts find these supporter memberships a very helpful tool both for introducing new donors to the organization and for building donor commitment, particularly by moving donors through a graduated series of membership levels. Even very small organizations may find memberships an attractive way to ask individuals for relatively small contributions which are renewed each year.

Other organizations use the exchange concept of "membership" to offer forms of volume purchase discounts. Examples would include a membership to a museum or zoo which offers unlimited free or reduced-price admission to members, or a membership in a literary society which allows the member to choose five free books with a value which almost equals or exceeds the membership fee. The exchange concept memberships have much in common with the program service fees and product sales described later in this section. Careful planning is required to design packages of membership benefits which are both appealing to potential purchasers and financially helpful to your organization. If too many discounts, free admissions, etc. are offered in the membership package, your organization may find the cost of producing the goods and services offered consumes a great portion of the membership fee income generated. If you are exempt or plan to apply for exemption under §501(c)(3), the IRS may deny or revoke your exemption if your members receive more in value than they pay in dues.

In planning your fundraising strategy, you'll need to be very clear about the type of support you are seeking. If you will be approaching individuals who are likely to contribute to your organization simply because they care about your work, you may not want to reduce the net value of their contribution by offering them a lot of exchange-type rewards. Simply the pleasure of knowing they have helped your group and been thanked for their support may be the best motivation for their gift. If so, giving other rewards or incentives simply wastes your organization's resources.

On the other hand, if your organization produces events, services, or goods which are highly attractive, even to people who would not otherwise be strongly motivated to contribute, creating membership packages which offer "deals" on volume purchases may be an effective marketing strategy. And since these exchange membership purchasers will experience your organization's work repeatedly, they may become promising contributor prospects. In other words, you may be able to motivate some of your exchange type members to become true contributors based on their appreciation for the work you do.

If you are considering developing a membership campaign, take a look at the membership programs of a variety of similar and somewhat different organizations. Not only will you get good ideas about ways to approach memberships, you may also be able to offer prospective members to your group a format for membership which is familiar to them. Be sure you think through the full cost of each approach to membership, and consider the long term benefits as well. Building a significant membership will help your organization's credibility and facilitate getting the word out on issues of concern to you. The concept of membership helps supporters feel connected to your organization, and the stronger their connection, the greater the likelihood of repeat and increased giving.

Civic and Religious Organizations as Funders

Many nonprofits find that religious and civic groups (like Rotary, Altrusa, Kiwanas, etc.) in their communities are willing to provide financial support. While contributions from individual churches, synagogues, or civic organizations are generally relatively small, the large number of religious organizations and civic groups in many communities can make this a more substantial source of funds. Working with civic organizations and faith communities can also provide great opportunities for more individuals to get to know about your work.

Civic Organizations

Start exploring this source by obtaining or developing a list of civic organizations in your community. The Chamber of Commerce often maintains lists of civic organizations and their current officers.

> *Many nonprofits find that religious and civic groups (like Rotary, Altrusa, Kiwanas, etc.) in their communities are willing to provide financial support.*

Next, you will need to determine which of the civic organizations makes charitable contributions and what process they use to do so. Ask your Directors, volunteers, staff, and other friends whether they or their friends belong to any of the civic groups. You may also want to ask about fraternal organizations, like the Moose or the Elks. Ask your supporters to make the initial contact with the group to which they belong. Once they have learned how the organization goes about making contribution decisions, staff and other Directors can help them prepare the request.

Typically, civic groups have regular meetings and invite outside speakers to present programs. Most do not want the program to have an explicit fundraising purpose. Instead, their members are seeking information and understanding about community needs and resources. You'll need to develop a brief presentation about the work that your organization does. Slides or videos may be helpful.

Different groups use different approaches to the issue of allowing speakers to ask the group for money. Some groups allow a group member to propose "passing the hat"—i.e. asking those in attendance to each contribute to the speaker's cause right at the time of the presentation. Others would be offended by this idea. Most have some time during the year when contributions from the group's treasury to community organizations are considered. For these, your presentation will be background information. You'll need an advocate who is a member of the group to promote the idea of supporting your organization. Some groups will accept written proposals for consideration.

To be effective with civic groups, you will need to learn both their process for handling requests for funds and the types of issues which appeal to their members. For example, some groups like to provide funding for vans or other equipment so that their name can be prominently displayed on the item. Others have special interests, like children or certain health issues. You'll want to focus your presentation and requests on the things the group is interested in supporting.

One of the great benefits of working with civic organizations is their willingness to be repeat supporters. Your group will want to develop an ongoing relationship with civic groups which fund your activities, inviting leaders to special events and sending them newsletters and pieces of good news about your progress.

Religious Organizations

Religious organizations often have multiple approaches to supporting nonprofit groups. The major denominations typically have national—and sometimes regional—funding programs which operate with written applications, funding guidelines, and other formal tools. In addition to these formal funding arms, individual local congregations develop their own process for considering requests for support. Some congregations have a social concerns or missions committee which brings recommendations to the church budget process about support for local organizations. Others will consider requests made to the synagogue or church Board or rabbi or pastor throughout the year. Still others will allow nonprofit leaders to speak from the pulpit during services and take up special collections for organizations they believe are doing particularly important work.

Start exploring the potential for religious organization support by asking your Board, staff, and volunteers about any affiliations they may have with local religious organizations. Ask those who are affiliated to learn the process for their church or religious group. Generally, if the person affiliated with the religious organization will make the initial contact, others from your group can make presentations, etc. Your contact will need to find out the preferences of their organization. Be sure they explore the potential for general operating support before proposing restricted funding for narrowly defined purposes. Many religious organizations are open to general operating support requests because they want to see your organization achieve its mission, and are prepared to trust that your Board knows where the money is most needed.

Even religious groups which have no contributions process and would not consider taking up a special collection may have various youth and adult groups which would enjoy a presentation about your organization. This may prove to be an important avenue for building visibility.

The regional and national religious organization funding arms make some substantial grants to nonprofit organizations. For most of these groups, you will need to have made some connection with a local congregation and obtain letters of support from church or synagogue leaders. Sometimes individual members of local congregations are not aware of the granting process their denomination uses on the regional or national level.

Consider scheduling appointments with local pastors, rabbis, or religious leaders and seeking their advice about funding. Ask them about opportunities for national or regional funding. Once you've identified the potential sources, obtain their guidelines and determine if your organization will qualify. Many of the national and regional religious funders do not require that the applicant organizations have a primarily religious purpose. However, most will want to see some connection between your organization and their local congregations.

Bingo, Raffles, and Other Gaming

Although the many exceptions in Oregon seem to overshadow the rule, gambling (also called gaming) is illegal in Oregon. Generally, participation in gambling is a crime. One exception to this rule allows certain nonprofit organizations to carry on limited types of gambling—specifically, bingo, raffles, and Monte Carlo events. To determine whether your organization can engage in any of these activities, you must first figure out whether you are the type of nonprofit that can engage in gaming. If so, you need to know whether the activity you want to carry on is legal and if the Attorney General requires that you get a license from the state.

The Attorney General's office permits any nonprofit, tax-exempt organization to engage in the permissible gaming activities. Your organization has to be organized primarily for purposes other than to engage in gaming. You have to have a valid organizational structure and exercise independent control over your budget and activities. If you are required to get a bingo or raffle license, you must have been exempt from federal income taxation (see Chapter 5) for at least one year preceding your application. When you apply for a license, you will need to produce your exemption letter. If you do not have an exemption letter because you are exempt under a section of the law that does not require you to apply for an exemption, you must produce a written opinion from a lawyer or accountant that you qualify for federal tax exemption. Contact the Attorney General's office for more information.

Your nonprofit can only conduct certain forms of bingo, raffles, and Monte Carlo events. pull tabs cards are illegal.

Exceptions to Licensing

In most cases, you must get a license from the Attorney General's office to conduct bingo, raffles, or Monte Carlo. However, if you are exempt from federal income tax and engage in very limited amount of gaming, you may avoid the license requirement. This is the case even if you have been exempt for less than a year. You are not required to contact the Attorney General's office but you should maintain proof that you are exempt in case the Attorney General's office contacts you. The following activities are exempt from licensing:

> *If you are exempt from federal income tax and engage in very limited amount of gaming, you may avoid the license requirement.*

- Door prize drawings, which are drawings conducted at your regular meetings where you sell the ticket and conduct the drawing at the same meeting and where the total value of prizes does not exceed $500 per calendar year;

- Bingo and Monte Carlo where the total amount of sales revenue (called "handle") is no more than $2,000 per event and no more than $5,000 per calendar year;

- Raffles with a total handle of no more than $10,000 per calendar year. *Example:* handicapped veterans, Inc., a §501(c)(19) veterans group, wants to raise money by including a raffle at its annual conference. It plans to sell $1,500 worth of tickets. It may engage in this gaming and does not need a license. If it decided to sell over $10,000 worth of tickets during this calendar year, it would need to get a license from the Attorney General's office.

All individuals involved in the operation of bingo, raffles, and Monte Carlo events must be your employees or volunteers, with some exceptions. If you are planning to use independent contractors in connection with these events, contact the Attorney General's office to be sure that you comply with their rules. If you conduct Monte Carlo events, you should call the Attorney General's office for the rules. Some of these apply to you even though you do not have to be licensed.

Getting A License

If your activities do not meet the exceptions for licensing, you need to contact the Attorney General's office to get a license. The Attorney General issues a set of rules that applies to gaming licenses and you need to be familiar with those. The address and phone number for the Attorney General/Oregon Department of Justice is found in Appendix 2.

FUNDING: OBTAINING RESOURCES FOR YOUR ORGANIZATION 22

Note for §501(c)(3) Tax-Exempt Groups

Although Oregon law allows all tax-exempt groups, including §501(c)(3) groups, to run bingo and raffle games, the federal tax-exempt rules distinguish between bingo and raffle proceeds. Bingo proceeds are treated as related business income. Raffle proceeds are treated as unrelated business income, unless the raffle falls within some exception that allows it to be treated as related business—e.g., it is done by volunteers; it does not qualify as "regularly carried on", etc. This means that you may have to pay tax on your raffle proceeds. In extreme cases, it also could mean that you lose your tax-exempt status if your raffle proceeds are too large. See Chapter 9.

Is Bingo the Best Strategy for Your Nonprofit?

Beyond being sure you meet the legal requirements to conduct bingo, there are some practical issues you'll need to consider. Before you invest in setting up a bingo operation you'll want to check out some key issues that will impact whether you actually will be able to raise a significant amount of income through bingo, including:

- **Competition:** How many charitable bingo games are being conducted in your area? You can check the public records of the Department of Justice to find out how many licenses have been issued and the history of organizations that may have started and then abandoned bingo. The typical bingo player is not actually interested in which charity is operating the game. They are motivated by location, prize money, and for most, wanting to be with a large crowd. Find out if there are already highly successful games in your area. It may be very difficult to lure regular players away from them. Getting a big crowd is essential for success in bingo.

- **Initial Investment:** Today's successful bingo operation involves comfortable facilities with lots of expensive electronics. You'll want to develop a complete business plan which estimates how much it will cost you to equip, market, and staff your game and what it will be realistic to expect to gross and net from the operation over the first year.

- **Shared Spaces and Equipment:** In some communities, a business has obtained a large space and invested in bingo equipment which it then leases to charities that obtain a bingo license. In some cases, a charity that is has hit the maximum income allowable from bingo under Oregon rules looks for other charities to take on operation for a portion of each week. If you are considering using one of these shared spaces, evaluate the proposed agreement very carefully. Remember that the goal of the business operator is to maximize the business income and the goal of the charity offering use of its facilities will be keep the most profitable days and times for its own use.

- **Management and Oversight:** Skilled management is essential, not only to meet the requirements of Oregon regulations but to actually make a profit from bingo. How will you select and evaluate your bingo managers? Your Board or staff will have to devote some portion of their time to reviewing the bingo operation to be sure that it complies with state rules and is actually generating profits for your organization.

Government Grants and Contracts for Services

In general, government at almost every level is in cutback mode. Federal, state, and local decision-makers are struggling to find ways to spend less not more. Still, many government programs do provide grants to nonprofits. More significantly, many governmental entities find that contracting with nonprofit organizations to deliver specific services is a way to spend less than operating the services themselves. So if your organization delivers social, health, or targeted recreation or environmental services, you may find government contracting a good potential source of funds.

Government Grants

Government grants differ from government contracts primarily in the degree of discretion the nonprofit organization exercises in designing the project. While to some extent the terms "grant" and "contract" have begun to be used interchangeably, it is still possible to say that grants, particularly federal grants, describe a general area of interest and require the organization submitting a proposal to come up with their own plan.

In general, it is very difficult for an organization which does not have a track record of receiving government grants to get the first one. Of course there are exceptions. You may want to attend workshops specifically focused on federal grant opportunities and consider working with a consultant who has been successful in obtaining federal grants for organizations similar to your own.

The State of Oregon still offers some grants. To track down these opportunities, you will need to identify programs and departments within State government which address your areas of interest. Start by asking other organizations doing work with similar populations about their experience with government grants. Then contact the funding sources they identify and request an informational interview so that you can get an overview of funding opportunities. You don't need to find a nonprofit which does exactly the same thing you plan to do, only one which works in related areas.

One final reality check. Government grants and contracts can be important components in your funding strategy. But be realistic in your expectations. There is intense competition for government funding. Organizations which currently work with government grants and contracts are facing cutbacks and are working very hard to sustain their funding. Cracking into the world of government funding will be very challenging and may take several years. You should also be aware that the government often places restrictions (such as prohibitions against lobbying) on some recipients of government grants. (See pages 672-73 for a discussion of some of these restrictions.) In almost all cases, governmental funding will require compliance with myriad accounting and management requirements. Be sure you have reviewed all the requirements before signing a grant agreement or contract and get help from someone experienced in meeting the same requirements.

Government Contracts

Most governmental contracts require that the nonprofit contractor provide specific types of services for specific types of clients. For example, residential care facilities for youth in trouble with the law typically are under contract to a state or county government to provide housing and support services for a specified number of young people at a specified rate per day.

Ask other organizations with program services similar to yours whether they have any government contracts. Find out which governmental entity and which department funds them. If you know them well, ask to see a copy of their contracts so that you can understand more specifically what they are being paid to do. Contact the government staff responsible for these contracts and ask how your organization may be considered to become a contractor.

If you do not know other nonprofits with government contracts, try approaching your elected officials—city council, county commission, representatives in the state legislature, etc. Ask for an appointment. Ask the elected officials to help you identify specific programs and the persons to contact to get more information.

> *You'll want to weigh the pros and cons of government contracts as a potential source of revenue. On the pro side, many contracts continue for years. But contracts may impose limitations on the way you serve the clients and on which individuals you may help.*

Many counties and some cities have "purchasing" offices which handle all the legal requirements for the government to enter into a contract for the purchase of services. Check online for information about the general requirements to do business with their government and to add your organization to their email mail list of interested parties who receive notice of all contract opportunities.

Most governments take specific steps to assure that their decisions about contracts are fair to all parties. Be sure you ask about any Request for Qualifications (RFQ) process which may be required. Such RFQ processes are used to establish a list of organizations qualified to do business with a particular governmental entity. Only organizations which have been "qualified" to do business may submit applications through a Request for Proposals (RFP) process.

Although there is a lot of emphasis on fair processes and sometimes a lot of formal scoring of proposals, it is unlikely that a completely unknown organization will ever be selected to be given a contract. If yours is a new group or hasn't been involved in government contracting, you will need to establish relationships with the government staff who work in the appropriate programs and with other nonprofit providers. Frequently, nonprofit providers contracting with a specific governmental program have meetings to discuss issues of mutual concern. Ask if you may attend these meetings even without having a contract. They can provide good insights into the nature of the program and some of the challenges of working with government.

You may need help to prepare your first proposals for government contracts. Special vocabulary is used and sometimes special formats for information are important. Look for a consultant or volunteer who is familiar with this particular government program or similar ones.

Purchase of service agreements may contain restrictions and specific requirements for record keeping and independent audits. Be sure you understand what is required and how much it will cost you to comply.

Organizations already working with government contracts will need to be alert for changes in the contracting approach impacting many local governments. Read the actual contracts carefully to be sure you understand whether you are permitted to keep any profit generated by providing all the required services at costs which are lower than the amount you receive through the contract. Hopefully you are entitled to keep such profits, because virtually all contracts for service require that you provide the service even it costs you more that the contract provides. Since you will be liable for any excess cost, it seems only fair that you will also be entitled to retain the profit when you are able to provide the services, and do a good job, at a lower cost. Unfortunately, many governments currently propose "lose-lose" contracts in which the nonprofit must return any surplus and bear any losses.

You'll want to weigh the pros and cons of government contracts as a potential source of revenue. On the pro side, many contracts continue for years and provide substantial revenues to serve individuals and families with great needs. But contracts may impose limitations on the way you serve the clients and on which individuals you may help. Additionally, contracts require careful bookkeeping, extra reporting, special audits, sometimes lengthy applications, and maintenance of relationships with funder staff. Finally, the government often places other types of restrictions (such as prohibitions against lobbying) on some recipients of government contracts. (See pages 672-73 for a discussion of some of these restrictions.)

Program Service Fees

The term *program service fees* is used to describe the income generated by charging for the services which the nonprofit provides as a primary part of achieving its mission. For example, child care centers charge for child care, counseling agencies charge for counseling, theater companies charge admissions, etc. Program service fees may be paid directly by the person receiving your service or may be paid by a third party—i.e. an insurance company or a government contract to provide specific services for specific types of individuals, or in some cases, specified individuals. Many nonprofits set program service fees on a sliding fee scale basis, varying the amount charged for particular services by the income levels of the individuals receiving the services.

Program service fee income has become an increasingly large portion of all revenue generated by nonprofits. Some would say that nonprofits can exercise the greatest degree of control over their own efforts by developing significant program fee income. While foundations, governments, and to a lesser degree, individuals may be impacted by changing perceptions of what nonprofit work is important, income from program fees depends upon the nonprofit correctly identifying the services individuals need, delivering the services in ways preferred by the participants, and pricing the services appropriately. While none of these components of generating program fee income is easy, the nonprofit is in control of how they are accomplished, and not subject to the "whims" of funders.

> *Program service fee income has become an increasingly large portion of all revenue generated by nonprofits.*

Simply stated, fee generation requires business planning skills. The decisions described below are similar to ones made by small businesses. You can get help working through these choices by talking with other nonprofits delivering similar services. If you have small business owners on your Board or among your volunteers, they may have exactly the skills needed to help you plan your fee generating activity.

To successfully generate program fee income for your nonprofit you will need to consider the following issues:

- **Need for specific services.** Correctly identify specific services which are needed in your community.

- **Market:** while there are always a large number of needs in any community, a market exists for a service only when there is a customer who is willing to pay for it or a third party who is willing to purchase the service for service recipients who are not able to pay for it themselves.

- **Subsidies and Third Party Payers:** are there government programs or insurance payments available to pay for the services you will offer. These sources could allow individuals who need your service to obtain it even though they cannot pay the full cost. Most subsidy or insurance programs will impose requirements that will make providing the service more costly to your nonprofit so be sure you understand the full costs and limits of working with them.

- **Cost:** Determine how much it will cost you to deliver the service at varying levels of volume. It will be helpful to project the cost per unit of service you will deliver (i.e. cost per day of residential care, cost per hour of counseling, cost per theatrical production, etc.) Use the tools provided in Chapter 24 to determine the full cost, including the fair share of costs like rent and phone and management. Be sure to include the cost of marketing your services to both customers who will pay for them directly and, if you will be working with subsidy programs, the costs of establishing relationships with and meeting the requirements of various subsidy providers.

- **Price:** What others are charging for similar services? What is the price that customers with the ability to pay for services will consider fair? At what price level will potential customers be likely to choose a cheaper alternative? Remember the key distinction between price and cost. Cost is what you will have to spend to produce, market, and manage the service. Price is what you will charge the customer for the service.

- **Credit:** Determine your policy about extending credit. Will you require that participants pay fees before they receive the service, or immediately after? If you decide to extend credit by allowing participants to delay payment, you will need to establish an accounts receivable system which includes billing the participants, keeping track of their payments, and making needed efforts to collect unpaid amounts.

- **Using Contributions to Partially Fund the Cost of Services Provided for Fees:** If participants can't pay the full cost of the service, and there are no outside parties to pay or the outside parties also will not pay the full cost of the service, your organization will need to decide whether you will use other income (probably contributed income) to subsidize the cost of delivering the service. This may be a good choice if the service is very close to the heart of your mission, and you have enough other funding to cover the rest of the cost. Charging something for the service will allow you to stretch the other funds you have to provide more services or improve the quality of the current level of services.

Sales of Products Related to Your Mission

Product sale income is generated by selling products related to your mission. For example, a sexual assault prevention program develops a booklet to be used in high schools to promote discussion of date rape, or a chamber orchestra produces CDs of its most popular concerts. These sales differ from the fundraising event strategy of selling candy bars or Christmas trees in several key ways. Typically, the mission-related products are sold throughout the year, not just during limited fundraising drives. Secondly, the sale of the product furthers the mission of your organization directly, not simply by providing funds.

You will need to do careful planning to succeed in generating income through product sales. While many ideas sound promising, the process of developing products, obtaining financing, producing or obtaining the product in a cost effective way, and dealing with inventory, marketing, and distribution will require substantial business skills. Strongly consider developing a written business plan which carefully explores your organization's management and financial strengths and weaknesses; the market for your product; competitive products; costs of production, storage, and distribution; marketing strategies; pricing; and projected net income.

FUNDING: OBTAINING RESOURCES FOR YOUR ORGANIZATION 22

Nonprofits are often more familiar with the concept of "need" than the concept of "market." While many individuals or organizations may "need" the product you are considering, your potential "market" for the product includes only those who that need it, prioritize it as important, have resources to purchase the product, can readily learn about your product, will believe your product is superior to other alternatives, and will be able to obtain the product. Many nonprofits have worked very hard to develop booklets and videos which contain needed information only to find that a market does not exist for their product.

> *Many nonprofits have worked very hard to develop booklets and videos which contain needed information only to find that a market does not exist for their product.*

Product sale income may be an excellent potential source of funds for your organization. But be sure you get the help you need to develop a business plan for the product you are considering before you make a substantial investment of time and money in its development.

Internet Sales of Goods and Services

Today, an effective website is essential to market virtually all goods or services. An enormous portion of potential customers or program participants search the web as the first step in finding what they need. You may need to get help with search engine maximization to be sure your organization's website shows up when potential customers search for what they want.

You'll also need to put in place some protections for both your nonprofit and customer from potential identity theft and fraud during their web purchases.

Exempt organizations will also want to review page 211 to learn about how payment for web links may create a risk that the payment will be treated as advertising and considered Unrelated Business Income by the IRS.

Social Enterprise and Business Ventures

Increasingly nonprofits are exploring the concept of "social enterprise." This term has varied meanings, each promoted by a cadre of consultants and trainers. It is most commonly used to describe the concept of nonprofits identifying programs which may be fully or substantially supported through the generation of income through sale of goods or services.

You may be familiar with nonprofits already using this strategy. For example, a nonprofit working to help individuals recover from alcohol or drug addiction creates a janitorial service. The nonprofit obtains contracts to clean businesses and then has program participants at various stages of recovery operate the janitorial service. Program participants who have very little job experience and are new to recovery fill the most basic jobs, while individuals who have proven their ability and stability, move up to become supervisors, bookkeepers, account managers, etc. The fees charged for the janitorial services provide funds to pay the program participants for their work and may generate enough income to pay the program staff who work with the participants to help them overcome barriers to being good employees.

The key concept here is that in carrying out the business activity, the nonprofit is also achieving its mission by helping participants obtain work experience and prepare for employment once they have completed the program. A similar concept is at work in a much publicized program with a national ice cream franchise that has allowed a nonprofit working with street youth to set up an ice cream shop to employ the young participants.

You will find great resource materials about this concept at *www.redf.org*, including a study of over 100 similar projects. While many board members would like to imagine that the business ventures created in this way will be so successful that they will create profits that can be used to underwrite other portions of the nonprofit's activities, this is generally not the case. Successful social enterprise ventures are able to pay the full cost of operating the business venture, including not only wages for participants and for staff to work with them but also a fair share of agency overhead costs.

What does it take to be successful with a social enterprise strategy? Like small businesses, social enterprises require excellent management and sufficient start-up capital to establish the business on a scale which can be sustained. All of the issues discussed in the sections on program fees and product sales come into play in social enterprise. They also require great clarity of purpose and making some difficult choices about priorities.

Your nonprofit will need to be very clear about the relative importance of maximizing income generation and profit and giving the clients with difficult problems a chance to be employed. Like private employers, nonprofit social enterprise ventures quickly learn that skilled dependable employees lead to better customer relations and higher profits. But, the mission of many nonprofits is to serve and help individuals with very low skills and multiple barriers to being dependable employees. Managing a social enterprise business which has the dual mission of sound business operation and helping very needy clients master employment skills is extremely challenging. You will need to identify staff and advisers with multiple skill sets and clear commitment to your organization and its clients.

Can Social Enterprise or Providing Goods and Services Threaten Our Tax-exempt Status?

Tax-exempt organizations will need to be very clear about how the IRS views the sale of goods and services. Chapter 9 describes the key concepts of Related and Unrelated Business Income and explains how the IRS determines whether exempt organization must pay corporate income tax on their net income from unrelated business income activities.

FUNDING: OBTAINING RESOURCES FOR YOUR ORGANIZATION 22

Investment Income

Obviously, the key to generating investment income is having funds available to invest. If your organization struggles month to month to have the cash it needs for payroll and basic expenses, investment income will not be a factor in your funding strategy. But if you have excess funds or have generated specific support for an endowment or reserve fund, your nonprofit has the opportunity to use those funds to generate additional funds.

You will need to analyze your operating cash needs in order to determine how much cash you will need to set aside as operating reserve. This cash should be invested in ways that ensures that it is available for operating needs without penalties or delays. Whether you will be investing cash reserves or endowment funds, your Board will need to adopt a sound investment policy to guide all decisions relating to the placement and oversight of excess cash.

Components of an Investment Policy

Investment policies generally have three major components: risk, return, and social responsibility screening.

Risk

In the risk section, your Board will determine the level of risk your organization is willing to take in its investments. A very conservative policy would be a no risk policy. This would require that all funds be placed in federally insured bank deposits or Treasury bills. A less conservative policy would set limits on what portion of the funds invested must be maintained in federally insured accounts, and what portion may be placed in investment opportunities with other levels of risk.

Return

Your policy on risk is highly related to your policy on return. As a general rule, return potential (what you can earn on specific investments) increases as the risk factor increases. In other words, very safe investments tend to yield lower rates of return. Of course, very risky investments may yield no return at all or they may yield significantly higher earnings than playing it safe. Your investment policy should reflect your Board's view on an acceptable level of risk and expected levels of return.

Social Responsibility

Finally, your Board will want to discuss whether your organization should limit its investments based on the level of social responsibility practiced by the corporations whose stocks you purchase. Many environmental organizations refuse to invest in corporations with particularly bad environmental policies. Some organizations working for peace refuse to invest in corporations which manufacture weapons. Still more organizations working in low income communities refuse to invest in corporations that fail to pay a living wage.

Who Makes Investment Decisions?

Your Board must also determine how investment decisions will be made. Organizations with relatively large amounts to invest (over $1 million) may want to talk with trust departments of banks or other institutional investment managers about investment management services. These firms employ highly skilled investment analysts and are extremely careful to follow the investment policy guidelines established by their clients. Their fees are generally set as a percentage of your investment portfolio—i.e. not related to charges for individual stock trades or other specific activities.

Organizations with relatively small amounts of excess cash (under $50,000) may decide that simply directing staff to find the highest yielding federally insured certificate of deposit is the simplest and safest way to manage their funds.

Organizations in the middle, with too little money to be of interest to the institutional investment managers and too much money for Directors to feel comfortable with a very basic, federally insured only policy, have some difficult choices. Some Directors will suggest engaging an investment adviser or stock broker. While these individuals will be interested in managing your funds, their fees will often be based on trades executed. Your Board will need to establish a committee of individuals highly knowledgeable about investments to monitor the performance of such an investment adviser. Committee members should be individuals who track the stock market and investment opportunities regularly and are committed to spending enough time reviewing the reports you receive from the your investment adviser to be able to determine that the adviser is following your policies and generating an appropriate level of return.

Some organizations decide that a Board committee can function as the investment manager for the organization. Taking this approach requires very careful screening of the individuals asked to serve on the committee, and additional monitoring by others not on the committee. Your Directors have a duty to protect the assets of the corporation, so they must be sufficiently knowledgeable about current investment opportunities to determine whether your funds are being managed properly. If your Board feels it does not have this expertise, then they will need to either rely upon a reputable professional investment manager or choose a very low risk strategy such as federally insured certificates of deposit.

If your nonprofit has an endowment fund to manage, you may want to explore working with the Oregon Community Foundation, a §501(c)(3) organization that manages over $1 billion in assets. Your organization can transfer your endowment to the Oregon Community Foundation with the stipulation that earnings on the endowment are to be awarded as grants to your organization. OCF uses its professional expertise, and the power of having substantial amounts of money to invest, to be certain that your funds are invested safely and profitably.

In-Kind Contributions

No discussion of resource generation would be complete without considering in-kind contributions. In-kind is a term used to describe the provision of free or reduced priced goods and services by a donor to a nonprofit organization. For example, you may find a printer willing to do some or all of your printing for free. You may find an attorney willing to review contracts at no charge or a graphic artist who gives a 50% discount to nonprofit clients. In each instance, your organization is able to reduce a cost you would otherwise have to raise funds to meet.

You'll want to build awareness of the potential for in-kind contributions into every part of your fundraising program. Individuals, businesses, foundations, and government all may make in-kind contributions. Your challenge is to determine whether a cash or in-kind gift from a particular supporter has greater value for your organization. Once you're clear about which you would prefer, you can begin by asking for what you want, and then be prepared to propose the other as an alternative if the donor declines to provide your first choice.

> *You'll want to build awareness of the potential*
> *for in-kind contributions into every part*
> *of your fundraising program.*

Like all fundraising activity, working on in-kind contributions requires cost-benefit analysis. Asking for in-kind gifts is most frequently done in person or on the phone. This means that it is relatively time consuming. You'll want to be sure that the dollars you save by getting the items contributed in-kind are worth the direct cost (letting paid staff solicit the gifts) or the opportunity cost (using volunteer time for in-kind solicitation instead of other activity). In-kind gifts can be enormously important. For example, several youth groups have received special fall-cushioning playground surfaces as an in-kind contribution from a local company. The groups would have had to pay thousands of dollars to obtain alternate playground surfacing. On the other hand, one local group devoted over 16 hours to phone calls to generate food contributions for a volunteer event at which the total food cost would not have exceeded $150 even if the group had purchased every item.

If you will be working with in-kind contributions be sure you check the In-kind Contributions record keeping information on page 592. You will need to acknowledge donor's in-kind contributions. In-kind contributions can raise some sticky tax deductibility questions, particularly for businesses. Be careful to avoid giving tax advice to your donors. Many organizations use phrases like this in their acknowledgments of items received in kind: "XYZ Child Care is a nonprofit organization which is tax-exempt under §501(c)(3). Your contributions qualifies as a charitable deduction to the fullest extent allowed by law." If donors press for more information about the deductibility of their gifts, encourage them to consult their own tax advisor.

One final word on in-kind contributions. Beware of white elephants. Sometimes donors want to contribute equipment or supplies which really have no value to your organization. The equipment may be outdated, need expensive repairs, or simply not be compatible with your systems. You'll need to think carefully about your response to these offers. If you believe that the donor has real potential for more valuable gifts in the future, you may want to accept the gift and then dispose of it to another organization, or potentially to recycling. If you do not anticipate any continuing relationship with the donor, you may choose to decline and perhaps suggest another organization for the donor to contact. If you do decide to accept the unusable gift, be sure you do not promise to use it. Instead, say you appreciate the gift, will check out how it can be used in your program, and will be pleased to pass it on to another group if it does not work out with your systems.

Using the Internet and Social Media to Raise Funds

Solicitations Across State Line

Many nonprofits are now using the internet to solicit contributions by including a "Donate Now" feature on their websites, by emailing solicitations for contributions to current and prospective donors, and by emailing invitations to fundraisers. If you use a website, your appeal for funds will always cross state lines. About 1,200 states and localities regulate charitable solicitations that occur within their jurisdiction with a multitude of different restrictions, often by requiring registration and sometimes a bond or other requirements. There are no clear guidelines as to when your use of the internet is considered a solicitation in another state. Most states are not treating a Donate Now button as solicitation that requires registration, although a few do. It is unclear how a court would rule on this issue but it is likely that courts will require more contact with the state than an internet appeal before a state can subject you to its jurisdiction.

States are more likely to consider you to be soliciting in their jurisdiction if your organization:

- targets residents of a specific state or area within a state,
- receives repeated or substantial sums of money from a jurisdiction, or
- sends solicitations to specific email addresses, including those you collect from those that hit your Donate Now button.

Some states will weigh these as factors they consider in determining whether you are soliciting. You may need to register with regulators in these states and follow their rules.

If you are engaged in charitable solicitations, the Attorney Generals of most states (including Oregon) have developed a single form that you can use for registration in the cooperating states. You can find this form and information about all the states at *www.multistatefiling.org*. If you do use this form, you may need to pay a registration fee in some jurisdictions and many will have annual reporting requirements that also include a fee. If you registered with the Department of Justice in Oregon when you incorporated (see Chapter 3), this covers your registration for charitable solicitation in Oregon. The legal rules pertaining to charitable solicitation on the web are uncertain and confusing. You need professional help if you solicit or do business over the Internet.

Other Social Media Issues

Other forms of fundraising using social media are raising novel issues for regulators in addition to the issue of soliciting funds across state lines. Individuals, nonprofits, and businesses are using twitter, Facebook, and other social networking platforms to solicit donations from users that users can target to a particular charity. In many cases, the user may receive a service or something in return. These arrangement raise a variety of questions, including whether the organization receiving the donations is aware of and has consented to the use of its name in the arrangement, whether organizations are receiving gifts that the donors believe are restricted for a particular purpose, and whether donor are making a deductible gift if they receive something in return. Regulators are still sorting this out.

If your organization is involved in social media solicitation or is the recipient of funds from an arrangement like this, you need to consider whether you are soliciting across state lines, as described above. You may have other legal issues you are not aware of. A nonprofit (and others) that engages in soliciting for other nonprofits must have the written consent of the nonprofits whose names it uses. The Oregon Department of Justice may consider a nonprofit that allows another nonprofit or for-profit to solicit funds or to sell products for its benefit (for example, in an online mall) to be engaging a professional or commercial fundraising arrangement. A nonprofit that does this must follow the rules described on p. 504. In some cases, the Board may be personally liable for its failure to follow the DOJ rules. If you are considering involvement in a social media solicitation or sale of goods or services for the benefit of a nonprofit, you should contact the DOJ (see Appendix 2) or get some legal advice.

Email Promotions

You also need to be aware of the federal C-SPAM law. This law applies to commercial advertisements and to promotions that are unsolicited. If you send an email to your members notifying them of a membership meeting, this is not commercial and is not covered by the C-SPAM law. However, if you email the public invitations to your upcoming silent auction, you are probably sending a commercial and unsolicited email. You can still send the email but you need to follow certain rules:

- Send from an active email address, one from which the recipient can reach you if he or she hits "Reply."

- Identify yourself in the "From" section and include your post office address in the body of the message.

- Use the word "Advertisement" in the subject line.

- Give the recipient a way to opt out of your list and remove those who opt out within 10 days.

If you are soliciting and accepting donations on your website or through email, you will need to keep up with this evolving issue. Check with your attorney or accountant, watch the Oregon Attorney General's website, and check the website at *www.cumfer.net* for updates.

Ethical and Legal Issues in Fundraising

There are many ways that Directors, staff, and volunteers can raise money from individuals without help from fundraising professionals. However, as your organization expands the amount it hopes to raise from individuals, you may want to explore getting help from experts. There are several useful ways nonprofits do this, and several ways which are not considered ethical.

Ethical Fundraising

Ethical ways to obtain fundraising help include:

Consulting

A fundraising consultant can help you figure out which approaches are most likely to work for your organization at its current stage of development. She or he may also help you research prospective donors, draft specific appeals, train volunteers to do fundraising, and provide a variety of other useful advice. However, your Board, volunteers, and staff will be responsible for implementing the consultant's advice, so you will need to be very realistic and honest with the consultant about the amount of time and energy you have available.

Staff Fundraiser

Many nonprofits employ staff with specialized responsibility for fundraising. In fact, larger organizations will frequently have multiple positions for all the different types of fundraising. Typically, a fundraiser on staff will be responsible for implementation as well as development of your fundraising strategy. If you are considering a staff position, you'll need to be very clear about the types of fundraising you want the staff person to do. The skills required for most individual fundraisers are quite different than those of a grant writer. And success in fundraising for a large, well established nonprofit does not always predict skill in raising money for a small organization or one with little experience working with donors.

Contract with a Fundraising Organization

Some professional fundraising firms will provide help both developing and implementing specific fundraising activities. Ethical firms charge on an hourly or per project basis, and do not set fees as a percentage of the amount raised. If you are considering such a contract, request that the firm give you a complete list of all their clients, not just selected references. Determine which of their clients have had situations most similar to your own size, experience with individual donors, type of activities, etc. Be sure to find out not only what the fundraising firm did, but what the organization's Board, staff, and volunteers did to facilitate the fundraising activity.

Consider whether your organization can provide the back-up which the firm needs to succeed. When in doubt, contact the Oregon Department of Justice Charitable Activities Section to learn if any complaints have been filed about this firm. Also contact the Better Business Bureau, and other nonprofits in your field.

Oregon regulates contracts you make with certain commercial and professional fundraising firms and the law can hold your Board members personally liable if you enter into an illegal contract. See the discussion below.

Workshops and Trainings:

The Nonprofit Association of Oregon (*www.nonprofitoregon.org*) and Financial Stewardship Resources (*www.financialsteward.org*), both (c)(3) organizations, maintain a calendar of training events throughout the state. Check your local community to find your regional association of fund development professionals.

Unethical Fundraising

Several fundraising practices are either unethical or questionable:

Grantwriting with the Fee Determined as a Percentage of Grant Funds Received

Not only is this considered unethical by professional fundraisers, it is specifically prohibited by most grant making organizations. Grant funds are to be used for the purposes described in your proposal, not for costs of preparation of requests. In addition, this basis of payment may encourage the grant writer to pursue strategies based solely on their likelihood of being funded rather than on their merit or appropriateness for your organization.

Fundraising Events or Individual Donor Solicitations in Which the Fundraiser is Paid a Percentage of What is Raised

Again, fundraising professionals consider this in general to be an unethical approach. However, some professionals are comfortable with a contract which provides a basic fee to the fundraiser with a bonus if net proceeds exceed certain levels.

If you are not certain whether a fundraising practice is ethical or right for your group, you may want to talk with the staff of the Oregon Department of Justice Charitable Activities Section, with leaders of other similar nonprofits, or with representatives of the National Society of Fundraising Executives.

Fundraising Companies which Keep Most (above 60%) of the Money for their "Costs" but Use Your Nonprofit's Name and Tax-exempt Status:

You may be contacted by an individual or a for-profit or mutual benefit nonprofit business offering to do fundraising for you. If the fundraiser solicits funds by selling goods or services on a regular basis, it is called a commercial fundraising firm. If it manages or solicits funds other than by selling goods or services, it is called a professional fundraising firm. The business will often use telemarketing to solicit ticket sales or contributions, telling the purchaser that they are supporting your organization's work.

But many of these businesses actually keep 80 to 95% of what is raised, sending your organization the remaining small percentage. You will need to decide whether you are comfortable knowing that donors think they have given a dollar to you, but you have only received 10 cents. In addition, the firm may use the mailing list they develop with your help from your campaign in other of its solicitations.

In some cases, these arrangements are illegal. The law restricts your Officers and Directors from entering into certain agreements with professional and commercial fundraising firms and holds them personally liable when they do. See the discussion below.

Cautions When Working with Professional Fundraising Firms

If you decide to work with a professional fundraising firm, the firm must give you a written financial plan that includes a good faith estimate of total revenues and expenses for each solicitation campaign. Often one goal of your campaign is to develop a donor list. If you are targeting individual donors, the written financial plan provided by the fundraiser must specify whether the campaign is directed toward acquiring new donors, renewing prior donors or a combination of both.

The law puts some responsibilities on your officers and Directors to act responsibly in engaging professional fundraisers.

The law puts some responsibilities on your officers and Directors to act responsibly in engaging professional fundraisers. Your officers and Directors breach their duty if they enter into an agreement with a professional fundraising firm and if the period of the agreement is more than 2 years unless your corporation has obtained written proposals from at least 2 other professional fundraising firms. Your officers and Directors also breach their duty if one of the purposes of the solicitation campaign is to acquire a donor base for your future solicitations and you do not keep the exclusive rights to the ownership and use of the list. You can give the professional fundraising firm a security interest in the list. The law assumes that one of your purposes is to develop a donor list unless your agreement with the fundraising firm explicitly denies this.

Commercial Fundraising Firms

If you are using a commercial fundraising firm, you should be aware of some of the limits the law imposes on your contracts with that firm. If the firm is going to identify your nonprofit as part of its solicitation campaign, it must designate the amount that will be paid to you. The amount can be specified in terms of an amount per unit of goods or services purchased, it can be a specified percentage of the gross funds solicited, or it can be a good faith estimate of the gross funds solicited. Your nonprofit must receive at least 90% of that good faith estimate, excluding any expenses your nonprofit has to pay for the solicitation campaign.

The descriptions given above for professional and commercial fundraisers are somewhat generalized. Because of the personal liability that may be imposed on your officers or Directors, you may want to get legal advice before contracting with these types of fundraiser.

Rules on Solicitation for Non-(c)(3) Exempt Groups

Generally, if you are tax-exempt under any section other than §501(c)(3) and you engage in fundraising solicitations, your solicitations (both written and verbal) may need to contain a conspicuous and easily recognizable statement that contributions or gifts to your organization are not deductible as charitable contributions for federal income tax purposes. This requirement applies if you normally have gross receipts of more than $100,000 per year and the solicitation was made in writing or by television, radio, or telephone. You are exempt from the rules if your solicitations are by letter or phone call and you contact no more than ten people per year this way. These rules apply to billings for dues as well as requests for contributions, donations, or support.

The IRS has some detailed rules about how you satisfy the disclosure requirements in the various media. If these rules seem to apply to you and your media is print media, you can satisfy them by stating: "Contributions or gifts to [Name of Your Organization] are not tax deductible as charitable contributions for federal income tax purposes." The statement must appear in the same or larger print size as the primary message. It must be on the same page or in close proximity to the request for funds. If you have a returnable card or tear-off section, the statement must appear on the message side that the contributor sends in with the contribution. The statement should be the first sentence of a paragraph or its own paragraph.

If you solicit on your website, the user must see the statement without following a link. It must also appear before the user hits a button to make the contribution.

> *Example:* Preserve Our Farms, a corporation exempt under §501(c)(4), has gross receipts of more than $100,000 per year. Each year it mails a letter billing its 500 members for their dues. The bill needs to contain the statement that contributions

and gifts to preserve Our Farms are not deductible as charitable contributions in print size at least as large as that in the rest of the letter in the first paragraph or in its own paragraph.

If you are soliciting through some other media, you should get professional advice to be sure you comply with these rules.

If you are tax-exempt under any section other than §501(c)(3), and you engage in fundraising solicitations, your solicitations (both written and verbal) may need to contain a conspicuous and easily recognizable statement that contributions or gifts to your organization are not deductible as charitable contributions for federal income tax purposes.

Final Tips

Consider all the funding strategies described in this chapter to be like a giant menu. You'll want to order from several sections. Most nonprofits need multiple types of funding for long-term survival and growth. You will need both short term and longer term plans for generating resources. While obtaining the funds you need to operate this year is obviously your first priority, you'll also want to think ahead to opportunities for future years and make choices about current funding activities which can lead you to your future goals.

Consult Appendix 1 if you would like information about source material related to this Chapter. Appendix 1 has references of interest to all readers, not just professionals.

As you bring in funds, you need systems and procedures for handling them. Chapter 23 describes these.

23 UNDERSTANDING FINANCIAL MANAGEMENT

THIS CHAPTER COVERS

- Signs of Good Financial Management
- The Big Picture
- Timing for the Financial Management Cycle
- Financial Management Checkup

Good financial management is a goal of almost every nonprofit corporation. Your Directors, staff, and volunteers want to have confidence that the resources you have worked so hard to obtain are being used effectively. And donors want assurances that their funds are being used for the purposes they intended.

THE OREGON NONPROFIT CORPORATION HANDBOOK

Signs of Good Financial Management

What does "good financial management" mean in a nonprofit? How will you know when you have it? Here are four key signs:

Achieving Your Mission

The most important sign of good financial management is that your organization is actually doing what it was formed to do. This means you are obtaining the resources you need to do your work and using those resources effectively. In this and subsequent chapters, we'll talk about the systems and strategies you'll need to be sure your organization stays on track financially.

The most important sign of good financial management is that your organization is actually doing what it was formed to do.

Solvency—Staying in the Black

To be sure that your organization stays around to keep fulfilling its mission, you'll need to build a positive net worth. This means your assets—the things of value which your nonprofit owns, should be greater than your liabilities—the amounts you owe to others. We'll talk about the planning and monitoring steps you'll need to take to avoid "red ink."

Liquidity—Having the Cash You Need When You Need It

You'll want your nonprofit to have the cash it needs to meet its obligations to employees, taxing authorities, and creditors on time. Without careful planning, even a nonprofit that has a positive net worth—i.e. is solvent—can find it doesn't have the cash it needs when it needs it. We'll talk about techniques to project your cash needs, and be certain you can meet them.

Documenting the Compliance with Restrictions

Nonprofits face considerably greater scrutiny than most businesses. Nonprofits regularly accept funding from governmental agencies, foundations, and individual donors with strings attached—specific restrictions on how you can and cannot use the money. We'll talk about the controls, recordkeeping, and reporting needed to be sure you are staying straight with restrictions and able to prove your compliance whenever asked.

UNDERSTANDING FINANCIAL MANAGEMENT 23

So how can you be sure your nonprofit is managing its finances in ways which will lead to these results? A good starting point is understanding that nonprofit financial management involves a recurring cycle of five basic functions. We'll tackle the details of each of the five in the chapters which follow. But first, let's start with the Big Picture.

The Big Picture

The financial management cycle includes five key elements:

- Planning
- Execution
- Recording
- Reporting
- Monitoring

Let's look at these five elements in the financial management cycle one by one.

Planning

Every nonprofit needs to develop a plan for how it will obtain and use resources. The first tool you'll need is an annual budget. The annual budget is your plan for where you will get resources and how you will spend them over your fiscal year. Your Board will need to adopt the annual budget to provide authorization for staff (or volunteers if there are no staff) to expend the corporation's funds.

Your fiscal year is the twelve month period you selected to use to keep track of your financial activity. You may have chosen the calendar year as your fiscal year, meaning that you will plan and keep track of finances using the 12 month period from January to December. Nonprofits are free to choose fiscal years other than the calendar year. Many choose fiscal years that match those of their largest sources of funds. Common fiscal years include July 1 through June 30 (used by many state and local governments) and October 1 through September 30 (used by the federal government).

Whatever fiscal year your organization has chosen, your annual budget should provide a complete picture of all the sources of income you will have and all the costs you will incur. See Chapter 24 for help setting up your annual budget and dealing with the specific budgets required for some grant funding.

Execution

Once the plan is made, you're ready to act. Financially speaking, this means do the things you planned to do. Rent the office, hire the staff, buy the supplies—actually spend money on the costs that were authorized in the budget. It also means raising funds, charging fees, and doing whatever else your plan calls for to generate income. Chapter 22 describes fundraising in more detail.

You'll need systems and procedures to handle receipt and disbursement of funds, authorize purchases, keep track of employee time, and perform all the other financial activities encompassed in your budget plan. Chapter 25 will help you set up the systems you need for execution, and evaluate whether the ones you already have in place are protecting your corporation from errors and dishonesty.

Recording

Keeping good records of all financial activity is the heart of any good financial management system. In the recording phase of the financial management cycle, your organization will need to use standard accounting practices to track all financial activity. Chapter 26 will explain the choices you'll need to make about methods of accounting and both simple and more complex ways to handle your accounting needs. Chapter 27 will cover the more specialized topic of handling payrolls, taxes, and benefits.

Reporting

While in the early days of an organization it may be possible to just take a look at the accounting records and get a good idea of how things are going, once your organization is in full operation, you'll need financial reports in order to understand what has happened and what impact it has had on your organization's financial position.

Chapter 26 explains the standard reporting formats for nonprofit organizations and suggest some other specific reports your organization may want to develop for the Board, management, or funders.

Monitoring

It really won't matter how great your recording and reporting is—if no one ever reads and understands your financial reports, you'll be making decisions without the information you need. In the fifth stage of the financial management cycle, the Board, the staff, and in some cases outside parties review the financial reports, compare them to the budget plan, and determine whether changes in your plan are needed. It's this review and the resulting need for revisions to the plan which brings the cycle full circle, back to the planning stage. Chapter 28 is designed to help Directors and managers ask the right questions to understand your organization's financial health during the monitoring stage.

Timing for the Financial Management Cycle

You'll want to establish some regular time frames for the cycle of financial management functions in your organization. First, develop the annual budget in time for the Board to discuss and adopt it before the beginning of the fiscal year covered by the budget.

Execution activities will be continuous throughout the year. Once you have a budget approved by your Board, you have authorization to organization to make the purchases covered by the budget, and keep working to get the resources and pay for them according to the plan. Of course, you'll only be able to make those purchases if you have obtained enough resources to pay for them.

Recording is also continuous. You'll need to keep written records of each check written, each bank deposit made, and all of your other financial transactions at the time the transactions occur.

Financial reports should be prepared at the end of each month. They are prepared directly from the accounting records and present the financial activity for the month just concluded and a summary of activity for the entire current fiscal year. Most nonprofits try to produce the financial reports for one month before the end of the next month, i.e. produce January's reports before the end of February. The more quickly you are able to produce the reports, the more useful they will be in your decision-making.

Monitoring is also a year-round activity. You'll want to review each month's financial statements as quickly as possible after the reports become available. Your review of the financial reports will help your decide whether your plans, embodied in your budget, are working. Many nonprofits do a mid-year budget revision process, formally revising the official organization budget to reflect revised plans for obtaining income and allocating resources.

Financial Management Check-up

The Financial Management Checklist below is designed to help you determine whether your nonprofit has established all the systems and processes you need to assure effective financial management. New organizations may want to review this checklist to get a comprehensive picture of all the steps involved in financial management. Of course, smaller and newer direct management nonprofits may not be dealing with all the complexity of larger, more well established groups. The Assessment Tool can serve as a development plan for your financial management efforts. You can develop the needed systems and processes in stages. The key is to get the needed system or process in place before you feel overwhelmed by the need for it. The Financial Controls Policies and Procedures for Small Nonprofit Organizations in the Forms section at the end of the book provides additional details on many of the key elements.

Financial Management Checklist
For Nonprofits with Delegated Management

1. FINANCIAL PLANNING/BUDGET SYSTEMS

    ☐ Organization has a comprehensive annual budget which includes all sources and uses of funds for all aspects of operations.

    ☐ All grant or contract budget agreements are incorporated into the comprehensive annual budget.

    ☐ All grant or contract budget proposals are reviewed by fiscal staff before submission to funders.

    ☐ Program managers play an active role in the development of budgets for programs under their direction.

    ☐ A board committee has a detailed understanding of the annual budget and plays a significant role in directing the use of unrestricted funds.

    ☐ The full board formally authorizes the annual budget and revisions to the budget.

    ☐ The organization has integrated meaningful consideration of financial issues into any strategic planning processes it undertakes.

    ☐ The organization has a capital budget and multi-year plans for major maintenance and replacement of facilities and equipment.

    ☐ The fiscal planning process includes continuous assessment of risks and identification of insurance coverage needs and appropriate risk management procedures.

2. EXECUTION

    ☐ The organization has written policies and procedures for fiscal operations including procedures for processing payroll, purchases, accounts payable, accounts receivable

    ☐ Policies and procedures are reviewed and revised regularly.

UNDERSTANDING FINANCIAL MANAGEMENT

☐ Actual processing activities are consistent with written policies and procedures.

☐ The concept of separation of duties is implemented to the greatest extent feasible within the limitations of the size of the organization staff.

☐ Authorization functions for purchasing, signing checks, adjusting accounts, and extending credit are not performed by individuals who also perform recording functions such as disbursements and/or receipts, maintaining accounts receivable records, or cash handling functions such as receiving and depositing funds or preparing checks.

☐ Review and verification functions such as reconciliation of the bank statement to the record of cash receipts and disbursements are not performed by individuals who also prepare checks, record checks, receive funds and prepare bank deposits, and/or record receipts.

☐ Payroll policies and procedures are clearly documented and consistently followed.

☐ Written authorization is required for all new hires and pay rate changes.

☐ Written timesheets are prepared by all employees, signed by the employee, and approved in writing by the employee's direct supervisor.

☐ Forms W-4 and I-9 are obtained and retained for each employee.

☐ Policies regarding overtime, vacation time, sick leave, holiday pay, and other leaves with or without pay are written clearly, and reviewed regularly for compliance with state and federal law.

☐ All fringe benefit plans are documented and in compliance with IRS and Department of Labor requirements. The proper tax treatment for all benefits and compensation arrangements has been determined and documented.

☐ Responsibility for maintaining fringe benefit records in accord with governmental requirements has been clearly assigned and records are reviewed regularly.

☐ Written purchasing policies clearly identify the purchasing authority of each staff position, and establish appropriate dollar limits for purchasing authority at each level.

☐ There are clear procedures for review of and authorization to pay all vendor invoices.

☐ Written policies and procedures for charging and collecting fees are followed consistently and reviewed regularly.

☐ Cash handling policies and procedures are well-documented and are tested periodically.

☐ All checks are restrictively endorsed upon receipt.

☐ Receipts are given for all cash transactions and donors/clients are informed that they should receive a receipt for all cash payments. Pre-numbered, multi-copy, customized receipts are used.

☐ A receipts log is maintained by the person responsible for opening the mail.

☐ Cash reconciliation sheets are maintained by all individuals responsible for accepting cash. All cash counts are initialed by the individual preparing the initial count and the individual receiving the cash for further processing.

☐ Post- dated checks are not generally accepted, and if accepted, are secured carefully.

☐ All disbursements are made by check except for small purchases made through a Petty Cash fund.

☐ All unused check stock is carefully secured.

☐ Bank reconciliation is performed by someone who neither makes bank deposits nor prepares checks.

3. RECORDING

☐ A complete written chart of accounts provides appropriate account titles and numbers for Assets, Liabilities, Net Assets, Revenues, and Expenses.

UNDERSTANDING FINANCIAL MANAGEMENT

☐ The Chart of Accounts clearly establishes the programs or functions which will be distinguished and the funding sources and/or distinct funds which will be tracked.

☐ The Chart of Accounts utilizes the same line item categories and the same program or function distinctions which are utilized in the comprehensive annual budget and the budgets for individual contracts or grants.

☐ Accounting policies and recording procedures are documented clearly.

☐ Appropriate computer software and hardware is utilized to perform recording functions.

☐ Appropriate electronic and physical security procedures are utilized to protect the integrity of computerized accounting records.

☐ All accounting records are backed up daily. Back-up media are stored in a secure area away from computer equipment.

☐ Back-ups of accounting data are stored off-site at least monthly.

☐ Detailed records of client fees and/or grants and contracts receivable are maintained and reconciled to the general ledger receivables balances.

☐ All contributions are recorded in the accounting records. If more detailed records are maintained by staff responsible for fund development, the fund development and accounting records of contributions are reconciled monthly.

☐ All general ledger balance sheet accounts are reconciled at least quarterly. All cash, payroll liabilities, and accounts receivable control accounts are reconciled monthly.

4. REPORTING

☐ Monthly financial statements are available no later than the end of the following month (i.e. April 30th statements are available no later than May 31st).

☐ Monthly financial statements include a Balance Sheet as well as a Statement of Activities and Changes in Net Assets.

☐ In organizations with multiple programs, statements of the expenses of each distinct program are prepared monthly.

☐ In organizations which receive restricted funds, separate statements of revenue and expenses are prepared for each funding source.

☐ Revenue and expense statements include the current month's activity, the fiscal year to date activity, and a comparison to the year to date or annual budget by line item.

☐ The excess (deficit) of support and revenue over expenses (net income) is reconciled to the change in fund balance between the beginning and ending of the accounting period.

5. MONITORING

☐ The executive director and the program managers review the monthly financial statements carefully.

☐ The fiscal manager highlights unusual items and identifies potential problems in notes to the financial statements shared with the executive director and board committee or full board.

☐ A board committee or the full board reviews the monthly financial statements carefully.

☐ The board or a board committee selects an independent CPA to conduct an annual audit or review. The board determines whether the organization should have an audit or a review, and whether or not the audit must conducted within the guidelines of OMB A-133 for organizations receiving funds which are federal in origin.

☐ The board or a board committee meets with the auditor and reviews the auditor's report, including any management letters, and reports on internal controls and compliance with governmental law and regulation.

☐ The board and executive director continually review the organization's financial statements to determine whether:

UNDERSTANDING FINANCIAL MANAGEMENT

☐ The use of the organization's resources is consistent with the organization's mission and priorities.

☐ The organization is solvent, i.e. has assets in excess of its liabilities.

☐ The organization has adequate cash and other liquid assets to meet its current obligations and assure its continuing ability to pay its employees, taxing authorities, and vendors on time.

☐ The organization is observing and documenting its observance of all restrictions imposed by funders and donors.

☐ The board and executive director are aware of the IRS requirements for maintaining tax exempt status and continually evaluate the organization's activities, use of funds, record keeping, and reporting to the IRS to assure compliance with all requirements.

With this overview of financial management, you are now ready to look at the nuts and bolts of how to handle the financial management of your nonprofit corporation. In the next chapter, we discuss budgeting—how to plan for your financial future.

24 MAKING A BUDGET

THIS CHAPTER COVERS

- Budget Terminology
- Why Have a Budget?
- Basic Budgeting Guidelines for Nonprofit Organizations
- Budget Development Steps
- Fixed and Variable Costs
- Functional Budgeting
- Budgets for Grants
- Budgeting for Restricted Funds
- Capital Budgets
- Cash Flow Projections
- Your Budget Process
- Boards and Budgets

Developing a budget for a nonprofit organization can be a relatively simple task or an extremely complex one, depending on the size of the organization, the variety of services it offers or activities it undertakes, and the number and nature of its funding sources.

This chapter presents the basics of budgeting for smaller, more single purpose organizations first, and then expands upon the basics to explore some more complex budget issues. If you or your organization are new to budgeting, the worksheet on page 440 may be particularly helpful.

If your organization receives grants from governmental entities or foundations which impose restrictions on the use of the funds, you will find the sections on functional budgeting, cost allocation, grant budgets and budgeting for restricted funds particularly important.

Most of this Chapter deals with budgets for operations, the income you will need to generate and the expenses you will incur to carry out your activities during the year. Some nonprofits will also develop capital budgets, plans for acquiring and maintaining facilities and equipment. Capital budgets may involve plans to borrow funds and plans to purchase assets (building and equipment). If your nonprofit owns or is planning to own land, buildings or a substantial amount of equipment, you will want to read the section on capital budgets and decide which approach will work best for you.

Budget Terminology

1. **Organization Budget**—Projected income and expenses for a defined period (usually the organization's fiscal year) for the operations of an entire organization.

2. **Fiscal Year**—A twelve-month period selected by an organization for financial management purposes. Typical fiscal years are: July 1 through June 30; January 1 through December 31; October 1 through September 30.

3. **Grant Budget**—Projected income and expenses for a particular project funded by a grant. The projected income and expenses are for a period defined by the grant contract or award letter. The grant period may or may not correspond to the organization's fiscal year. For example, an organization with a July 1–June 30 fiscal year may receive a grant for a twelve-month period beginning January and ending December.

4. **Cash Flow Projection**—A projection of anticipated cash receipts and cash disbursements for a defined period, such as three to six months. Cash Flow Projections are used internally to manage cash, in order to assure that sufficient cash will be on hand to meet demands and that excess cash is properly invested. Cash Flow Projections focus on timing—when during the year will funds be received and required—rather than on aggregate totals used in regular budgeting.

5. **Capital Budget**—Some nonprofits create separate budgets to reflect plans for purchase, rehabilitation or major improvement of facilities and equipment. A separate capital budget is essential for organizations planning a Capital Campaign to raise funds to purchase or complete a major rehabilitation of their facilities

Why Have a Budget?

While many folks think of budgets as some type of financial diet plan which focuses on "saying no" to needed expenses and doing without, in fact, budgets play two very positive roles in nonprofits.

First, the development of the annual operating budget provides an opportunity for your Board and staff to work together to identify the important work to be done by the nonprofit during the year; to agree upon specific strategies to do the work and the investment to be made in them; and to identify the sources from which resources will be obtained. The budget document provides a specific, written plan for the generation of income and the use of resources for salaries and other costs of operation.

In addition to serving as a plan for obtaining and using resources, your budget functions as an authorization document. When your Board of Directors adopts the annual budget, your Board is authorizing your Executive Director or those working under the Board in a direct management nonprofit to proceed to use the organization's resources in specified ways—to employ staff, rent facilities, purchase supplies, etc.

> *New nonprofits are often tempted to skip the creation of an annual budget because they feel everything is so uncertain. This approach frequently results in confusion and failure to cover all costs.*

New nonprofits are often tempted to skip the creation of an annual budget because they feel everything is so uncertain. Instead, they may create budgets for individual projects as part of a grants application process. This approach leads to a fragmented way of looking at the organization's activities and frequently results in confusion and failure to cover all costs. Even when funding is very uncertain, your nonprofit should develop a basic budget to guide the use of funds and direct efforts to obtain needed resources.

Basic Budgeting Guidelines for Nonprofit Organizations

Here are some basic guidelines for developing budgets for nonprofit organizations:

- Recognize that often there are not sufficient funds to do everything that you would like to do—be realistic in planning for how you are actually going operate with the limited funds available.

- Define your goals and objectives. Determine which activities are necessary to attain your objectives. Base your budget on the actual elements involved in each activity as they relate to the goals and objectives.

- Recognize that at the time the budget is developed (and possibly adopted) some funding may not yet be confirmed. Use realistic estimates based on specific fund-raising strategies, not wishful thinking or vague hopes.

- Recognize that annual operating budgets which rely heavily on grant funds:

    ◊ must reflect the budget items included in the grant budgets;

    ◊ must take into account the numerous, and perhaps conflicting or unclear, requirements on the use of grant funds;

◊ will have to integrate grant budget periods which do not coincide with the fiscal year of the nonprofit or with the budget periods of the other grants.

- Focus your expense budget planning efforts on the line items (expense categories) which will consume the largest share of your resources. In most nonprofits, salaries, payroll taxes, and fringe benefits will be 60% to 80% of the total expense budget. Concentrate on correctly projecting these personnel costs, and spend less time trying to be exact about relatively small costs.

- If your organization is trying to build up its net worth—trying to accumulate reserves—you will need to budget for a surplus rather than a break even budget. A budgeted "surplus" means that your planned income exceeds your planned total expenses. A break even budget is one in which projected income is exactly equal to the projected expenses. Some funders have encouraged nonprofits to use break even budgets. But planning only to break even will make it very difficult, maybe impossible, to build up your net worth. If you are dealing with a funder that emphasizes break even budgets, you may want to explore whether it may be acceptable to budget for that funder's grant on a break even basis, while projecting your overall organization budget on a surplus basis.

Be as realistic and as accurate as possible in developing a budget!!!

Budgeting for Funds from Prior Years

If you are planning to use funds that you raised in a prior year to support some of the costs your nonprofit will have in the current year, you will need to be careful to avoid a common budget mistake. Funds carried over from prior years are not a source of income and shouldn't be included in the list of income sources or total income line. If you will be using funds from a prior year to balance your budget, the total of the various types of income you anticipate receiving during the budget year will fall short of the total of all of the expenses you are anticipating for the year, resulting in a net loss. Right below the Net Loss line, you can enter a line titled "Planned Use of Net Assets" or "Use of Carry-Over Funds." This will communicate your plan clearly so that everyone has a realistic understanding of how much new income you plan to generate and how much of your savings you plan to use up.

FY 11/12 Budget	
Income	500,000
Expenses	550,000
Net Loss	(50,000)
Planned Use of Net Assets	50,000

Budget Development Steps

Here are some tips for preparing your budget. The Basic Budget Worksheet on page 529 suggests a format for your finished budget document. While you'll want the final document to be concise—hopefully a one page document—you'll need to do a lot of background work to get to this summarized version. Be sure you keep the detailed schedules of assumptions described below so that you can remember the basis for each of your projections.

Projecting Income

1. Government Grants and Contracts

Start with the grants and contracts which have already been committed to your organization. Be sure you include only the portion of the grant or contract amount which will be provided for the fiscal year for which you are budgeting. If your organization will have already begun receiving and using the grant before the beginning of your fiscal year, include only the portion of the grant which will still be available for use in the year for which you are budgeting. The Table below illustrates how you may need to analyze the portion of a grant that will be available in each fiscal year.

Award #1	FY 11/12 portion	FY 12/13 portion	Total Grant
	Oct. 1, 2011 - June 30, 2012	July 1, 2011 - Sept. 30, 2012	
Personnel	70,000	30,000	100,000
Occupancy	22,500	7,500	30,000
Supplies	3,000	2,000	5,000

After you have included the government grants and contracts for which you already have commitments, make a list of those that you believe you are likely to receive. Be specific about the source and the amount of each award that you anticipate receiving. Then evaluate how likely it is that you will receive each grant. Most nonprofits find that it works best to only include those grants that you are very likely to receive in the annual budget.

Special note: If you are projecting government grants which have restricted line item expense budgets—i.e. specify the categories of expenses for which grant funds are to be used—be sure you include those items in your expense projections.

Finally, government contracts for services often work differently from grants. Rather than restrict the specific expense line items for which funds can be used, contracts are often based on a payment per unit of service provided. For example, you may have a USDA Food and Nutrition program contract which specifies a reimbursement amount for every meal served to an eligible child. To project your income from a unit of service based contract, you will need to project the number of units of service you will provide and know the contract rates. Take care that the number of units of service you project providing matches the staffing and other expense levels you project in the expense section. You won't be able to collect the contract income unless you are able to provide the planned level of service.

2. Foundation Grants and Corporate Donations

Start by listing any foundation grants or corporate donations for which you have already received commitments. Then make a list of all the requests you plan to submit, including the name of the foundation or corporation, the purpose for which you will ask for funds, and the amount you plan to request.

Remember, asking is not the same as receiving, so estimate the percentage of all your requests which will be successful. It may help to group them into three categories: very likely, somewhat likely, and really a long shot. If your nonprofit has experience with corporate and foundation requests, use your past track record to estimate the amounts you will receive. If your organization does not have experience, or is making major changes in the way it approaches foundations and corporations, be conservative in your estimates.

Many foundations and corporations prefer funding new projects rather than general operations (see Chapter 22). If you will be submitting requests for specific projects or programs, remember to include the costs of doing those activities in your expense budget if you are including the grants for them in your income. It is fairly unlikely your organization will be able to obtain large amounts of unrestricted, general operating funding from foundations and corporations, so resist the urge to use this line item to plug, or to fill in "wishful thinking" amounts in the grant line item to balance your budget.

3. Contributions

First, make a list of all the different types of contributions you will be working to obtain. Your list might include gifts from individuals, from businesses, and from church or civic groups. You may want to break down the category of gifts from individuals down into sub-parts reflecting the ways you will attempt to obtain these gifts—i.e. direct mail, telephone solicitation, or in-person requests.

Once you have your list of types of contributions, go item by item and estimate the total amount you will receive from each type of donor and/or each major method of solicitation for the year. Rather than just picking a number out of the air, think specifically about the number of individuals or groups you believe will give and the average gift size you expect from them.

Or, if your organization already has experience with this type of contribution, consider the amounts you've received over the past few years and determine whether you can realistically anticipate receiving more or less this year. Be specific in your thinking, but remember the best you can do is make an educated guess—an estimate.

While your final budget will present contributions on a single line, your notes should include the assumptions you used to project that amount, both to help ensure that you are being realistic about the amount you will raise and to give you a tool to use to compare what actually happens to what you thought would happen.

In the sample below, the organization is grouping potential donors by the year the donor first responded. The chart reflects the number of donors in each group, the average size of gifts each group of donors has given and an estimate of the percentage of donors in each group who will respond to this year's appeal.

Yr End Appeal	# Donors	Aver. Gift Size	Est. % Response	Est. 11/12 Gifts
FY 10/11	300	$50	80%	$12,000
FY 09/10	250	$45	70%	7,875
FY 08/09	275	$60	60%	9,900
New Prospects	100	$25	25%	625
Total				$30,400

4. Special Events

Start with a list of all the special or fundraising events you are planning for the year (i.e. your spring auction, your summer car wash, and your fall wreath sale). For each item, estimate the total gross receipts. This means all the money you will receive without any reductions for expenses.

Next, predict the costs involved in producing each of these fundraising events. Make a detailed list, including the cost of any products you will purchase, promotional materials, mailings, hall rentals, etc.

On your final budget document you may choose to use the net income you expect from fundraising events. Compute the net income by subtracting the expenses of conducting the event from the projected gross receipts. However, it will be important to keep your more detailed projections of gross receipts and expenses for each event to compare against what actually happens. This comparison will help you in your future budget efforts by letting you know how realistic your estimates proved to be. The projections will also provide guidance to the fundraising committee or staff about how much your organization is prepared to invest in each event as well as what you expect the gross receipts and net proceeds to be.

5. Program Service Fees and Product Sales

Use this line to project income from charging fees for the services or activities your organization provides—i.e. admission charges, counseling fees, etc. To estimate your program's service fees, you'll need to be clear about the types of services you will provide, the way you will charge for services, and the amounts you will charge.

For example, a child care center may decide to have different charges for different types of service, like care for infants, preschoolers, and school age children. It may also decide to charge by the month for some services and by the hour for others. Finally, it may decide to vary the charges by the income level of the parents, using a sliding fee scale.

Write out the assumptions you are using to project fee income. For example, the child care center may plan on providing full time care for 20 preschool children at a charge of $700 per month per child. This would produce $14,000 per month (20 x $700) in program service fee income. If the center also planned to provide care for 30 school age children at $300 per child per month, it would project an additional $9,000 per month (30 x $300).

Whatever basis you use to project fee income, remember that you may not collect all that you charge. If you extend credit by allowing people to pay after rather than before they receive your services, you will need to either budget for an expense called "bad debt expense" or reduce your projected program service fee income by the amount you anticipate losing through non-collection. You can base this estimate of uncollectible amounts on your past history, or by contacting other organizations which provide a similar service and asking them what percentage of fees they find to be uncollectible.

If your nonprofit plans to sell products you will want to base your budget projection on the estimated number of units you will sell, your pricing structure, and the cost you will incur to either purchase or create the product, as well as any distribution costs. If you are already selling the product, you will be able to draw upon your past experience to predict both sales income and the cost of the products you will sell. If the sale of products will be a new activity, you will want to be sure that you have developed a realistic business plan which includes identification of the start-up investments you will need to make. Chapter ? includes a discussion of business plans.

6. Membership Fees

If your organization charges annual membership fees, you can project your membership fee income by multiplying the number of members you expect to have by the membership fee amount. If you are projecting a significantly greater number of members than the number who paid dues in previous years, be sure to include the cost of additional member solicitation efforts in your expense budget, and be sure there are specific plans to reach new people. If your group anticipates raising more membership fee income by raising the annual dues charge, be sure to consider the possibility that more members may choose not to renew than typically drop their membership in years without a fee increase.

7. Interest or Investment Income

Project your interest (or investment) income based on the amount of cash you will be able to invest in interest bearing or other income generating accounts. You will need to estimate how long your excess cash will remain invested and the rate of return you will receive. Your bank or investment manager can help you prepare this projection.

8. Other Income

Use this category for small amounts of income. Use past history or at least a list of the types of income you are considering. If you have another type of income which will contribute significantly to your overall income, be sure to list it as a separate named line item.

Projecting Expenses

1. Salaries

If your nonprofit employs staff, salaries will probably be the largest expense in your budget. Consequently, it's very important to project salary expense accurately. Be particularly careful to have the salary expense you project match the assumptions you've made in the income portion of the budget. If you projected income from a government grant which will fund four positions, be sure those four positions are included in your salary expense projection.

Create a schedule of all the positions your nonprofit will employ. List each position title, the rate of gross pay, and the number of such positions you will have. You can project the rate of pay on either a monthly or hourly basis. If you use monthly salaries, list the salary rate for full time work, and then show the percentage of full time you will use for this position. This percentage of full time is referred to as FTE or Full Time Equivalent. 1 FTE means one full time position. A half time position is shown as .5 FTE.

If your nonprofit has paid staff, salaries will probably be the largest expense in your budget. Consequently, it's very important to project it accurately.

If you want to use hourly pay rates, predict the number of hours for each position, either by week, month, or year. To predict salary expense on an hourly basis, you'll need to know your organization's policies about paying for holidays, vacations, and sick leave. If your nonprofit will pay hourly wage employees for holidays, vacations, and sick leave, you can estimate hours based on 260 work days per year (52 weeks x 5 days). If your organization does not offer these paid non-working days, estimate the days that full time employees actually work, and then adjust it for the percentage of full time equivalent you will use for each position.

If your nonprofit pays regular employees for holidays, vacations, and sick leave, and some or all of the positions require the hiring of substitutes when the regular employee is absent, be sure to include a projection for the number of hours of substitute time you will need. Base your estimate of substitute hours on the total paid absences permitted for positions for which substitutes will be required.

Remember, all salary expense projections should be stated as gross wages—i.e., before withholding of any taxes. Do not include the cost of employer taxes or fringe benefits in your salary expense line item. These items are listed separately, as shown below. You'll find more information to help project payroll costs in Chapter 27.

2. Employer Taxes

Employer taxes are taxes which your nonprofit must pay in addition to the gross wages which you included in the salary expense line item in your budget. Even if your organization has tax-exempt status, you will be responsible for the employer's portion of social security and Medicare taxes (referred to as FICA for Federal Insurance Contribution Act), Unemployment, and Workers Compensation coverage. Details about these taxes are discussed in Chapter 27.

> *Even if your organization has tax-exempt status, you will be responsible for the employer's portion of social security and Medicare taxes*

To project employer taxes in your budget, you will need to know both the maximum dollars in wages per employee subject to each tax and the tax rate for your particular organization. FICA rates are the same for all employers, but the rates are periodically adjusted. Check IRS Circular E to be sure you are using current rates.

As noted in Chapter 27, certain tax-exempt organizations have some choices about how to provide unemployment coverage for their employees. Determine which method your nonprofit will use and project the cost of that method. Most nonprofits will choose to pay the state unemployment insurance premium which functions like a tax on a portion of the gross wages paid to each employee. If you are participating in state unemployment insurance, the Employment Division will notify your organization of the rate percentage and of the maximum amount of each employee's wages subject to the tax.

As discussed in Chapter 27, Oregon employers have choices in how to obtain workers compensation insurance coverage. All employers, including nonprofits, are required to provide workers compensation coverage. To project this line item, determine the rates and requirements of your nonprofit's worker compensation coverage.

3. Fringe Benefits

Use the Fringe Benefits line item for amounts your nonprofit will pay as the employer's share of benefits.

Project the fringe benefit line item based on the cost of each of the benefits your nonprofit provides. Determine which positions are entitled to which benefits and the cost per year of each of those benefits. Include only the "employer paid" benefit items (typically health and dental insurance, disability insurance, retirement, etc.).

Some nonprofits have flexible benefit plans which permit their employees to pay certain costs with pre-tax dollars withheld from their paychecks. Don't include these employee withholding amounts in the fringe benefit line item. These amounts will already be included in the gross wages line of the budget.

4. Professional Service Contracts

Base this item on a list of the professional services you plan to purchase. Common professional services include audits, legal counsel, computer consultation, Board training, etc.

> *Some nonprofits are tempted to use professional service contracts to pay individuals who are actually functioning as employees. This practice can get you into a great deal of trouble.*

Some nonprofits are tempted to use professional service contracts to pay individuals who are actually functioning as employees. This practice can get you into a great deal of trouble. Check Chapter 20 to be certain that any of the payments you are considering to be professional service contracts meet the legal definitions for independent contractors. If they don't, and the folks performing these services should be considered employees, put the costs of their work in the Salaries, Employer Taxes, and Fringe Benefits line items.

5. Non-Personnel Costs

See the Basic Budget Worksheet on the next page for suggestions for the types of costs to be included in your budget. Base your projections on specific assumptions. For example, your rent line item should be based on the number of months you will rent the facilities and the monthly rent or lease amount. Include a separate line item for each significant type of cost.

If you have government or foundation grants or contracts which include specific line item budgets, be sure you use the same categories to project expenses in your annual budget as are used in your grant budgets.

MAKING A BUDGET 24

Basic Budget Worksheet

Date proposed _____ Date adopted _____ Budget period: From _____ to _____

SUPPORT AND REVENUE:

Government Grants or Contracts	$ _____
Foundation Grants	$ _____
Corporate Donations	$ _____
Special Events (net profit)	$ _____
Individual Contributions	$ _____
Program Service Fees	$ _____
Membership Fees	$ _____
Interest Income	$ _____
Other Income	$ _____
TOTAL SUPPORT & REVENUE	$ _____

EXPENSES:

Personnel

Position Title	FTE Salary	% of FTE	# of positions	Total $
_____	_____	_____	_____	$_____
_____	_____	_____	_____	$_____
_____	_____	_____	_____	$_____
TOTAL SALARIES				$_____

Employer Taxes

FICA rate _____ % x taxable wage _____ = $_____
Unemployment rate _____ % x taxable wage _____ = $_____
Workers' Comp rate _____ % x taxable wage _____ = $_____
TOTAL EMPLOYER TAX $_____

Fringe Benefits (employer share)

Health Insurance	$_____
Dental Insurance	$_____
Other	$_____
TOTAL FRINGE BENEFITS	$_____

Professional Service Contracts $_____
TOTAL PERSONNEL COST $_____

Non-Personnel Cost

Supplies	$_____
Printing	$_____
Postage	$_____
Telephone	$_____
Occupancy (rent, utilities, etc.)	$_____
Insurance	$_____
Travel Training/Conference Other	$_____
TOTAL NON-PERSONNEL	$_____
TOTAL EXPENSES	$_____

PROJECTED EXCESS OF SUPPORT AND REVENUE OVER EXPENSES $_____

Fixed and Variable Costs

The Effect of Volume of Services and Activities on Costs

Efforts to budget accurately may be helped by differentiating fixed and variable costs:

> **Fixed Costs** are those required to keep the organization open and offer even one unit of service. Fixed costs do not vary with the volume of service provided. For example, at least one telephone line is required to provide any telephone information and referral services.
>
> **Variable Costs** are those expenses which increase as the volume of service provided increases and decrease as the volume decreases. For example, an additional set of materials is required for each additional participant in a workshop.
>
> **Semi-Fixed or Step Variable Costs** are costs which are fixed over relatively short ranges of volume of service. For example, supervisors' salaries, if one supervisor is required for every ten direct service workers. Or, additional telephone lines if one new line is required for every additional hundred calls handled per day.

In general, increasing the volume of service will reduce the unit cost. If the program is limited in the amount which it can charge or receive for each unit of service, increasing the number of units of service provided, and consequently reducing the cost per unit, may be an effective budget balancing technique. If fixed costs form a large part of the cost of the unit of service, and if the program has unused capacity, even a small increase in volume of service will significantly reduce unit cost.

Functional Budgeting

Organizations providing more than one type of service or activity may find it helpful to do functional budgeting. This approach distinguishes between costs projected for the different types of services and costs projected for the management and fundraising of the organization. A sample functional budget is shown on page 533.

Functional budgeting allows your nonprofit to determine the cost of each program and the cost of each unit of service. For example, the cost for one day of preschool for a child could be determined by dividing the total cost of the preschool program by the number of days of preschool times the number of children attending per day. The unit cost information would be useful for setting fees for clients and for comparing the cost to operate this preschool program to the costs incurred by other preschool programs. This functional budget approach would also be useful when presenting budget information to a funder interested in funding only one or several of the programs.

MAKING A BUDGET 24

Functional budgeting distinguishes between costs projected for the different types of services and costs projected for the management and fundraising of the organization.

The functional cost center budget is best visualized as a matrix (like a spreadsheet) in which the rows are used to list income and expense categories (line items) such as contributions, program fees, salaries, telephone, and the columns are used to identify the distinct program, management, and fundraising purposes your organization will undertake. The matrix is completed by determining the portion of each income or expense line item that will be associated with each cost center.

	Total	Management	Fund raising	Prog A	Prog B	Prog C
Income						
Grants						
Contracts						
Prog. Fees						
Contributions						
Total Income						
Expenses						
Personnel						
Occupancy						
Other Expen.						
Total Expen.						

Management Costs

To do functional budgeting, you will need to know which of your costs are considered management or administrative costs. We're using the terms management and administrative interchangeably for this discussion even though some larger nonprofits may make a distinction between these two terms.

While there are some differences in how the IRS, the accounting profession and the federal government define management costs, they share in common the view that management costs include:

- Accounting and audit functions
- Board support
- Organization-wide strategic planning
- Human resources management

- Organization-wide technology (as opposed to software for specific program or fund raising purposes).

Fundraising Costs

Fundraising costs include the cost of make any unsolicited requests for contributions. This includes the cost of sending out requests for contributions, organizing volunteers to make phone calls for gifts, or making in-person requests. Fundraising costs include the cost of staff time to solicit gifts as well as the costs of printing, postage, list management, etc. Fundraising costs also include any payments to outside fundraising firms working to help your nonprofit raise money.

While the cost of researching foundation funding opportunities and preparing grant applications are generally considered fundraising expenses, the cost of completing Requests for Proposals to continue receiving contract dollars from governmental entities are generally considered to be management costs, not fundraising costs. Chapter 12 provides more guidance on how the IRS looks at fundraising and how you will be required to report fundraising costs on the Form 990.

Cost Allocation

If your organization decides to try functional budgeting, you will need to develop a cost allocation plan to allocate certain costs among the functions. While some costs are directly related to one program element, other costs provide benefit to more than one element. For example, in an organization providing a preschool program, a senior program and emergency services, the cost of a preschool teacher's salary is clearly a cost of the preschool. But, if all these programs and the organization's administrative staff share the same facility, a method must be devised to allocate or divide the cost of the facility (rent, utilities, etc.) among the programs and the administration.

If your organization decides to try functional budgeting, you will need to develop a cost allocation plan to allocate certain costs among the functions.

In addition to allocating shared costs like facilities expense, organizations with multiple programs may also allocate administrative costs among the programs to compute a "full cost" for each program. This approach recognizes that a program, such as the preschool, couldn't function alone without some administrative back-up (bookkeeping, a Board of Directors, fundraising, etc.). The allocation formula for administrative costs is designed to give each program a fair share.

Some nonprofits will include both "management" and "fundraising" costs in the "administrative" costs to be allocated. Others, particularly those receiving federal funds, will keep management and fundraising costs separated because most federal grants and contracts cannot be used for fundraising expenses.

MAKING A BUDGET 24

Sample Functional Budget

EXPENSES					TOTAL	ADMIN	F.R.	PROG A.	PROG B.	PROG C. GENERAL	PROG C. GRANT 1
Salaries: Positions	# Positions	% FTE	Monthly Salary	# Months							
Executive Director	1	1	3,000	12	36,000	27,000	9,000	0	0	0	0
Fiscal Manager	1	1	2,300	12	27,600	27,600	0	0	0	0	0
Progam Director	1	1	2,500	12	30,000	0	0	7,500	7,500	7,500	7,500
Prog A & B Supervisor	1	1	2,000	12	24,000	0	0	12,000	12,000	0	0
Prog C Coordinator	1	0.75	2,100	12	18,900	0	0	0	0	9,450	9,450
Case Manager	4	1	1,800	12	86,400	0	0	43,200	21,600	0	21,600
Specialist	3	1	1,500	9	40,500	0	0	0	13,500	13,500	13,500
Clerical Assistant	2	0.5	1,300	9	11,700	2,925	2,925	0	0	0	5,850
Subtotal: Salaries					275,100	57,525	11,925	62,700	54,600	30,450	57,900
Payroll Taxes (13%)					35,763	7,478	1,550	8,151	7,098	3,959	7,527
Fringe Benefits (15%)					41,265	8,629	1,789	9,405	8,190	4,568	8,685
Subtotal: Personnel					352,128	73,632	15,264	80,256	69,888	38,976	74,112
Professional Services					16,000	4,000	8,000	1,000	500	500	2,000
Occupancy					40,000	8,364	1,734	9,117	7,939	4,427	8,419
Supplies					15,000	1,000	5,000	4,000	2,000	1,000	2,000
Transportation					4,000	500	600	0	1,200	800	900
Other Expenses					20,000	2,000	4,000	2,000	3,000	4,000	5,000
TOTAL EXPENSES					447,128	89,496	34,598	96,373	84,527	49,703	92,431
Allocation of Admin					0	-89,496	8,658	24,117	21,153	12,438	23,129
EXPS W/ ALLOCATED ADMIN					447,128	0	43,256	120,490	105,680	62,142	115,560

SUPPORT AND REVENUE	TOTAL	UNDESIGNATED	PROG A	PROG B	PROG C GENERAL	PROG C GRANT 1
Government Grants/Contracts	160,560	0	20,000	25,000	0	115,560
Foundations	40,000	0	5,000	20,000	15,000	0
Individual Donations	85,000	77,000	5,000	1,000	2,000	0
Special Events	50,000	50,000	0	0	0	0
Program Service Fees	115,000	0	70,000	40,000	5,000	0
Investment Income	4,000	4,000	0	0	0	0
SUBTOTAL: SUPPORT & REVENUE	454,560	131,000	100,000	86,000	22,000	115,560
REVENUE - EXPENSES	7,432	87,744	-20,490	-19,680	-40,142	0
Allocated Undesignated Amounts	0	-80,312	20,490	19,680	40,142	0
NET INCOME	7,432	7,432	0	0	0	0

533

Cost allocation systems are designed to:

- Allocate shared costs—those costs not readily identifiable as belonging to a particular function or allocate management costs among all the program functions
- Provide information for management on the full cost of providing a service—i.e., program cost plus a share of management cost
- Satisfy restrictive funders that funds have been used exclusively to meet the costs of the specific program or service the funder wishes to fund

Direct Costs

Some types of costs can be easily classified by function. For example, if your organization operates a preschool and a senior center program, you can easily determine that the cost of employing a preschool teacher belongs in the preschool cost center (function) and the cost of a senior center staff person belongs in the senior center cost center. Similarly, the cost of supplies for the preschoolers belong in the preschool cost center while the cost of food for the seniors belong in the senior cost center. Costs which are easily attributed to a single cost center are referred to as direct costs, meaning that they can be directly associated with the purpose they are fulfilling.

Shared Costs

But not all costs can be assigned to a cost center so easily. Many costs actually benefit more than one program or benefit all the major functions—management, fund raising and programs. For example, if you rent one facility to house your entire operation, the rent expense provides space for management, fund raising, and all program functions. We think of costs which benefit more than one function (cost center) as shared costs.

In order to prepare a complete functional budget, you will need to develop a method to divide the shared costs among the functions (cost centers) that benefit from the shared cost line items. The method of dividing shared costs among cost centers is described as cost allocation. The goal of cost allocation is to identify and use a consistent and fair method to allocate shared costs. There are several common approaches to cost allocation.

Allocate Based on Staff Time

It is relatively easy to allocate costs which can be related to the number of staff working in a particular program or function by the percentage of FTE (full time equivalent) method. This method involves creating a percentage by dividing the number of FTE positions assigned to a particular cost center by the total number of FTE positions in the entire budget. For example, if 4 of your total of 8 FTE positions are assigned to the preschool program, you would allocate 50% (4 divided by 8) of the shared costs to the preschool program.

Allocate Based on Dollars

Other organizations may choose to allocate shared costs based on the amount of direct cost dollars being spent in each cost center. For example, if the total of all costs which can be directly attributed to all cost centers is $300,000 and the costs which can be directly attributed to the preschool cost center is $100,000, you could create a percentage by dividing $100,000 by $300,000 and determine that the percentage of shared costs which should be allocated to the preschool cost center should be 33%.

Allocate Based on Square Feet

Another approach would be to measure the space utilized by each function (cost center) and create a percentage based on the square feet used by one cost center divided by the total of all square feet. So, if the whole facility you are using for all functions has 6000 square feet, and the preschool program occupies 4000 square feet, you could divide 4000 by 6000 and determine that 66.6% of the cost of the facility should be allocated to the preschool.

Choosing a Cost Allocation Method

You can see from the examples above that the different methods we've described each produce a different percentage to be used to allocate the shared costs. How will your organization know which is the best method to use? Two principles should guide your choice. First—logical association. You want to choose a method which makes sense. This will be a method that divides cost in a way that seems reasonable in relation to what actually gives rise to the expense. So, while the square feet method makes sense for allocating the cost of renting a facility, it doesn't make much sense for allocating the cost of having a receptionist answer the nonprofit's phones. In the case of the receptionist, the number of people working in each function may be a more logical basis for allocating costs.

Next—simplicity. You will want to choose a method that is not unnecessarily complex and that you are certain you can do accurately. While larger nonprofits may use several different methods to allocate several different types of expenses, a small organization may want to choose just one method and use it consistently.

Allocating Management (Administration) Costs

Distinguishing program, fund raising and management costs lies at the heart of the functional approach to budgeting. In fact, both the IRS and the accounting profession want nonprofits to distinguish these three primary cost centers in their financial reporting, so budgeting in this format makes sense for organizations which want to compare what actually happens to their plan.

If you have made this key distinction in your budget, establishing cost centers for management, fund raising and one or more programs, you may want to go one step further in order to understand the full cost of each of your services. The concept of full cost or fully loaded costs involves assigning a portion of your total management costs to each of your program cost centers and to your fund raising cost center. By doing this allocation of management costs and adding the allocated share to each program's total cost, you are computing the full cost of operating each program, and the full cost of fund raising.

This concept of full cost reflects the fact that you would not be able to operate your preschool program if you didn't have a Board of Directors and an accounting system which are considered management or administrative costs. Once you have added the fair share of administrative costs to each program and to the fund raising cost center, you will be able to compute your cost per unit of service. For example, if you want to know how much it costs you to serve one child in preschool for one year, divide the full cost of the preschool program (including the preschool programs share of the administrative cost, its share of your shared costs, and its direct costs), by the number of children in the preschool. This information will be useful both for setting the fees you must charge to cover your costs and for comparing the cost of operating your preschool program to the costs experienced in other preschool programs.

You will need to choose a method to allocate administrative costs. The percentage of FTE positions and the percentage of program dollars described above are the two most common approaches.

Cost Allocation Plans

You can see by this point in the discussion that cost allocation can get a bit complicated. That's why nonprofit organizations that use this approach to preparing their budget (and then use it again in accounting and financial reporting) need to prepare a written cost allocation plan. The cost allocation plan provides a list of the cost allocation methods you have decided to use to allocate various costs and explains why you have chosen those methods. You will need to review your cost allocation plan regularly, at least once a year, to be sure that you are still satisfied with the approaches you have chosen.

Cost allocation can get complicated.
That's why nonprofit organizations that use this approach
need to prepare a written cost allocation plan.

Nonprofits receiving funding from governmental entities are often required to have written cost allocation plans. Organizations that receive large amounts of federal funding may also use a different method, obtaining a federally negotiated indirect cost rate. A detailed discussion of this approach is too complex to include in this book. Start building your understanding of the basic rules for dealing with the allocation of management and other indirect costs in federal funding agreement by reviewing OMB Circular A-122, now incorporated into the Code of Federal Regulations as 2 CFR. Part 230, Appendix A, Sections C and D at *http://www.whitehouse.gov/omb/circulars_a122_2004#ae*. Next, determine which federal agency will serve as your cognizant agency and obtain their procedures for submitting a proposal for establishing federally negotiated indirect cost rates.

MAKING A BUDGET 24

Budgets for Grants

Most foundation grant applications and requests for government support require submission of a budget proposal. Some funders provide forms or lists of budget categories, but most expect the nonprofit asking for the money to develop the format for the budget proposal. Some funders specifically exclude funding for certain types of items such as equipment or conference costs. So, before you begin preparing your grant budget proposal, you'll want to read the funder's guidelines carefully.

Start with Your Annual Operating Budget:

If you have prepared your nonprofit's annual operating budget in the functional format discussed earlier in this chapter, you may be able to use the portion of your annual budget which describes the program for which you are seeking grant funding as the basis for your grant proposal budget.

> *Example:* Safe Families, a nonprofit which serves victims of domestic violence, prepares its annual budget in a functional format, showing three program components, as well as management and fund raising. The three program components are "shelter services," "non-residential counseling," and "children's program." When Safe Families is applying for a foundation grant to support components of its children's program, it will use the line item expenses shown in the children's program column of its annual budget as a starting point for its grant budget.
>
> If Safe Families is applying to a foundation for a small amount of money in relation to the cost of the total children's program, perhaps requesting $5000 while the total cost of the children's program is $100,000, they may be able to simply show the whole plan for the children's program, including both the expenses and the other sources of revenue which will be used to support the program.

Of course some foundation and government funders will want to see more detail. In the Safe Families example above these funders would want to know which of the $100,000 in total operating expenses for the Children's Program would be paid for with the dollars which they would provide. To meet this requirement, Safe Families would set up a budget worksheet which showed the total budget for the Children's Program in the first column, and displayed to additional columns, one showing the costs that this grant funder is being asked to support, and the other showing costs of the Children's Program which will be met through support from other sources. It will be helpful to include a section for Income as well as Expenses, so that the specific sources supporting the "other costs" can be displayed. In this approach, Safe Families would label the first column "Total Children's Program Budget," the second column "Proposed XYZ Foundation Support," and the third column "Other Sources," and show both Income and Expense line items for all three columns.

Budgets When Funders Support Only New Projects

Some funders have an explicit requirement that their funds be used only for new services or expansions or enhancements of current services. Unless you are very certain that such a funder will be awarding funds to your organization, you probably will not have included the new program or program expansion/enhancement in your annual budget. In this situation, you're probably thinking that if your get the funds from this funding source you will add elements to your current program and if you don't receive the funding from this source you won't add those costs. Larger organizations may refer to this type of thinking as an "add-pack" approach to budgeting, meaning that they will add additional "packages" of expenses depending on the availability of funding.

Even if the funder you are approaching has an explicit requirement that funds will be awarded only for new services or expansion/enhancement of existing services, you will still want to develop a budget presentation which shows the whole cost of delivering the service. You'll want to be sure that you include a fair share of the shared costs which will be needed to make this new program or program expansion possible.

> *Example*: Let's return to Safe Families to illustrate this. Suppose Safe Families is preparing an application to a foundation which will support only new services or expansion/ enhancement of existing services. Perhaps Safe Families has seen a great increase in the number of Spanish speaking families using the shelter. While they currently operate a children's program, they would like to enhance that program to do a better job serving Spanish speaking families. To do this, they will need to get training from a consultant who knows more about parenting issues in Latino communities, purchase new supplies and books, offer current staff the opportunity to master basic conversational Spanish, and hire an additional staff person who is bilingual and comfortable with both parents and children.
>
> Of course their grant budget will show the cost of the training, consultation, supplies, and new staff position, but Safe Families also recognizes that the enhanced children's program can't operate without heat, lights, access to a telephone, accounting records, and supervision. These are all costs which Safe Families will have even if they do not succeed in enhancing the children's program to better serve Spanish speaking families. But, they are also costs which must be met in order to have a children's program for Spanish speaking families. So Safe Families will include the full cost of the children's program for Spanish speaking families in its grant budget—both the new costs and the continuing costs which can be directly related to the program they are describing.

Grant Budget Notes

Most funders really appreciate a "budget narrative" in addition to the budget document which shows line item categories with dollar amounts. Your budget narrative, on a separate page from the budget itself, will explain the basis for including each line item shown in the grant budget.

MAKING A BUDGET 24

In the example above, Safe Families would describe the type of consultation on working with Spanish speaking families they would purchase, the number of hours and the cost per hour of such consultation and provide a brief summary of the goals of working with such a consultant. For the supplies line item, Safe Families would describe how much of money would be spent on books, games, room décor, etc. They would not provide a list of every book or game to be purchased—this would be much more info than the funder would want.

Most funders really appreciate a "budget narrative" in addition to the budget document which shows line item categories with dollar amounts.

Example: If Safe Families had decided to include 10% of the cost of their Executive Director's salary, taxes and benefits in the grant budget, they would want to explain that 10% of the Executive Director's time would be needed to coordinate, supervise, and evaluate the new services for Spanish speaking families, including making certain that systems are in place and working to track the work accomplished and outcomes achieved in the new program. If they included a portion of the total telephone bill, they would explain that staff in the children's program must have immediate access to a phone in case of emergency and the basis for this line item is only a small portion of Safe Families total phone costs.

One final tip: When you have completed the budget component for your grant proposal, including both the numbers page and the narrative page, show both of them to someone who knows nothing about your organization. The budget itself plus the budget narrative should tell the story of what you are trying to do so well that the person does not need to read the whole proposal narrative to understand how the funds will be used. If they can't understand what you are asking the funder to support and why, you will need to revise your budget and the budget narrative until another "uninformed" person can tell what you are proposing to do.

Budgeting for Restricted Funds

The term restricted funds is used to describe funds that your nonprofit receives from an outside party, like a donor, a foundation or a government program, that limits or restricts how you can use their dollars. Typically the outside party puts the restrictions on the use of their funds in a letter or contract which directs your organization to limit the use of the funds to a specific program, a specific time period or in some cases to specific types of costs.

It's important to distinguish the situation in which the donor/funder is restricting the use of funds to specific line items within specific programs from one in which the restriction is only about what program the funds may used to support. If the restrictions merely direct that the funds be spent on specific program, without limiting the line item expenses, you will be able to handle budgeting for this source within the basic functional budget approach. Just consider the funding source to be an income source for the program function that the donor/funder wishes to support. For example, if XYZ foundation awards $5000 to support your preschool program, you will show the $5000 in both the total income column and in the column for the preschool program cost center. This will show that you are free to use the XYZ grant to meet any legitimate cost of the preschool program.

But, in situations in which the donor/funder restricts the use of their funds on both a program and line item basis, you will need to take some additional steps. For example, if the ABC foundation awards a line-item restricted grant to the preschool program, you will need to determine which line expenses of the preschool program may be met with funds from the ABC foundation. Once you are clear on the donor's restrictions, you may decide to create a separate column on your budget for just the ABC grant. This column will show the ABC grant as income and then show only the expense line items which the ABC grant may be used to pay. If you take this approach, you will want to remember that in order to know the full cost of the preschool program, you will need to combine the column for the preschool cost center (which won't include the ABC grant revenues or expenses) with the column for the ABC grant expenses. You can see an example of this approach in the Sample Functional Budget on page 533 in which Program C is broken into two columns, one for the portion of the costs supported through Grant 1 and the other for costs supported through multiple general sources. You will find more discussion of the challenge of planning for and tracking restricted funds in Chapter 26 which deals with accounting issues.

Capital Budgets

The use of the word "capital" when nonprofits talk about budgets or fund raising campaign, refers to the costs of acquiring or rehabilitating land, buildings, and equipment. These are referred to as "capital" costs. Larger nonprofits with substantial investment in land, buildings and equipment frequently prepare capital budgets as well as operating budgets. This means that they separate their plans for purchasing or rehabilitating their facilities and equipment from their plans for routine operating costs. Even when capital budgets are used, the cost of regular ongoing maintenance, like janitorial services or routine plumbing repairs, usually appear in the operating budget.

Does your nonprofit need to prepare a separate capital budget? In most cases smaller nonprofits will simply include plans to purchase new computers or furniture in the annual operating budget. But, if you are working towards the goal of purchasing new facilities or completing major rehabilitation on property your nonprofit already owns, you may find a capital budget is very helpful for communicating with potential donors, funders, and lenders for your capital projects. Of course potential donors and lenders will also want to see your operating budget to be sure that you have reasonable plans to meet the costs of operating your new facility or equipment.

Capital budgets may include an element that would not normally appear in an operating budget—the use of debt. Of course borrowing money is not a type of income (just like taking cash advances on a credit card is not a source of income for your family). But borrowing may be a legitimate strategy for nonprofits to acquire capital items, particularly buildings. In order to use debt as part of your plan to acquire facilities or equipment, you must show potential lenders that you will be able to repay the debt. If you plan to use debt as part of your capital budget, you will want to get help from an accountant or business consultant who is familiar with the preparation of pro forma style budgets. Your pro forma budget will demonstrate how cash obtained through the operation of the facilities you acquire with debt will be sufficient to meet the debt repayment requirements of lenders.

Budgeting for technology poses a particular challenge. Most foundation and government funders now expect to see line items in operating budgets for acquisition and replacement of computer hardware and software. Increasingly they also expect to see that budgets include the cost of staffing or consultants to make sure that the technology that is purchased operates dependably and is used fully. Of course, if your nonprofit has fallen far behind in meeting its technology needs, you may have to plan a special fundraising initiative to catch up. In this situation, it can be very useful to work with consultants who are knowledgeable about nonprofit technology needs to develop a comprehensive technology plan. Your plan will assure potential funders that you have thought through the needs of your nonprofit carefully and prioritized your needs in relation to your resources.

Cash Flow Projections

Your annual operating budget is a tool to project where you will obtain the funds needed for operations for the coming year and how you will use those funds. It is designed to help with big picture thinking, focusing on your overall plans for raising funds and earning income and operating your organization. Most annual budgets focus on what will happen over the course of a year not what will happen in any specific month.

Your nonprofit may need to use another budgeting tool in order to be certain that you will have cash available when you need it. The Cash Flow Projection is a budget tool designed to predict when cash will come in and when cash must go out of your nonprofit.

You can prepare a cash flow projection for any period of time, but most organizations will find that a six to twelve month period is most useful. First, you will need to estimate the amount of cash which will be available in your bank account at the starting point of your projection. Next, you will project how much additional cash will be deposited into your bank account during the first month of your projection period. When you add the additional cash you are expecting to take in to the cash you had at the beginning of the month, you will know the total cash available to your nonprofit in that month.

Next you will predict the amount of cash which will be needed to meet all your obligations that must be paid during that month. You'll subtract the total cash needed to be paid out from the total cash available to predict how much cash will be left at the end of the month. This projection of cash at the end of the month then becomes your projection of cash available at the beginning of the next month. You'll repeat these projection steps for each of the months to be included in your cash flow projection period.

If you see months in which the cash required to be paid out exceeds the cash you are projecting to be available, you will be able to predict that unless you alter your strategies, you will overdraw your bank account in those months. Doing the cash flow projection six months in advance will give you time to change strategies and avoid running out of cash.

Cash flow projections are generally prepared with spreadsheet software so they may be easily updated. While you will initially project out six to twelve months of cash coming in and going out of your bank account, you will need to update the projection each month to reflect the actual cash available at the beginning of each month and to revise your estimates of cash that will come in and need to go out based on what has actually happened.

Cash Flow Projection Worksheet
7-01-09 to 12-31-09

	July	Aug	Sept	Oct	Nov	Dec
Opening Cash	7,000	29,350	6,100	200	(5,250)	(23,350)
Expected Receipts						
Client fees	8,000	8,200	6,000	4,000	4,000	3,500
Gov Contract #1	10,000	10,000	10,000	10,000	10,000	10,000
Gov Contract #2	22,500	0	0	22,500		0
Donations	500	200	200	500	800	15,000
Foundation grants	20,000	0	20,000	0	0	30,000
Subtotal Receipts	61,000	18,400	36,200	37,000	14,800	58,500
Loans Received						
Total Cash Available	68,000	47,750	42,300	37,200	9,550	35,150
Expected Disbursements						
Payroll	28,000	28,000	28,000	23,000	23,000	23,000
Employer taxes	2,800	2,800	2,800	2,300	2,300	2,300
Fringe benefits	3,000	3,000	3,000	2,400	2,400	2,400
Professional services	500	4,000	4,500	500	2,000	200
Rent	2,000	2,000	2,000	1,500	1,500	1,500
Utilities	400	400	400	300	400	600
Office supplies	200	100	200	100	200	100
Program supplies	1,000	800	500	100	100	100
Insurance	0	0	0	12,000	0	0
Printing	200	100	200	100	600	100
Postage	50	50	50	50	300	50
Transportation	400	400	350	100	100	100
Other	100	0	100	0	0	100
Loan repayments	0					
Subtotal Disbursements	38,650	41,650	42,100	42,450	32,900	30,550
Ending Cash	29,350	6,100	200	(5,250)	(23,350)	4,600

Cash flow projections are very helpful for both nonprofits that tend to be short of cash and face periods in which they may not have the cash needed to meet obligations, and for nonprofits that actually have excess cash, more than is needed immediately. If your cash flow projection shows that you will have much more cash than is required to meet your operating cash demands, you will want to explore opportunities to invest the excess cash. Your Board is responsible for setting policies on the types of investments that can be used to invest excess cash.

Your Budget Process

There are many different approaches to developing the annual budget. In small non-profits, the Executive Director or a Board member is usually asked to prepare the first draft of the budget. That person's job is to organize all the information about both income and expenses into a document. It's very helpful if they also prepare budget notes that explain the assumptions they have made to create the document. The Board discusses this first draft budget, questions the assumptions and either adopts it if the budget seems reasonable or asks the budget preparer to make revisions and bring the revised version back for further discussion.

As organizations grow larger and involve more paid staff, the Executive Director and/or fiscal manager begin to include the staff who will be doing the programs and fund raising in the budget planning process. Sometimes this is as simple having a discussion at a staff meeting in which each staff member is asked to identify needs for the coming year and to predict how much income will be generated through their efforts. For example, the staff involved in the preschool would be asked to predict how many children will be served and whether fees should be raised. The Executive Director and fiscal manager then use the information generated by the staff to create the draft budget document for Board discussion.

Once the organization is large enough to have program managers and a fund development Director, the Executive Director and fiscal manager may ask these managers to prepare the first draft of their own program or fund raising budget. Then the fiscal manager combines the various first drafts, raises questions, and ultimately creates a draft budget for Board action. In this approach, the fiscal manager will typically take responsibility for estimating the shared costs and provide spreadsheet worksheet tools to help the program managers prepare their budget proposals.

No matter how small your nonprofit is, you will want to be very careful about how you project the income you will generate through fund raising and grant writing. You'll want to resist the temptation to do the whole expense budget first, and then just fill in numbers in the income section to cover the expenses. This can lead to serious overestimation of the amount of support your nonprofit will be able to raise. Instead, ask the person(s) responsible for each type of income generation—individual gifts, special events, program fees, etc.—to prepare a description of what they will do during the year to raise funds, including both the gross amount they think will be generated and the costs of raising that level of gross support. Only include in the income section amounts that you have good reason to believe your nonprofit will be able to raise.

Boards and Budgets

Most nonprofits will try several budget process methods as they develop. Your Directors will be most likely to feel fully committed to supporting your organization if they have played an active role in setting priorities for the use of resources. Your staff are most likely to feel fully committed to working for your organization if their direct knowledge of needs has been considered in planning. Organizations which set priorities by funder preferences often find that Board and staff have little commitment to the organization if funds are no longer available.

A strong, inclusive budget process provides a good opportunity for your Board and staff to work together to identify priorities for the organization and create effective strategies to obtain and utilize resources.

For many nonprofit Boards, the annual budget process is a vaguely unpleasant period in which trees are sacrificed to produce an endless flow of number filled pages presented by harried staff to tired Board volunteers grieved by being able to fully meet community needs and frustrated by funder limitations. Whether the response is passive rubber stamp or randomly targeted nit-picking designed to assure someone that the Board "did its job," or conscientious and careful review of all the data, many Directors find little satisfaction in their role in the budget process.

For nonprofits funded extensively with restricted governmental or foundation dollars, the budget process may strike Directors as closer to taking orders than making significant decisions. Once the various restricted funders have directed who may be served, what methods must be used, what records must be maintained, and what reports must be submitted, the approval of the budget may seem more like hopping aboard a carefully guided tour bus than charting a course for the nonprofit.

Directors who have participated in strategic planning may feel particularly disillusioned. What happened to that clear mission statement, those values and priorities the Board struggled to agree upon? What about the commitment to improve staff pay and benefits across the organization? What about the commitment to reach those who fall through the cracks with innovative programs?

Directors may find it difficult to connect the excitement of the strategic planning process and the passionate commitment they feel to the organization's mission with the grim sheets of numbers placed in front of them for approval. Not surprisingly, staff can find the budget process mechanical and disheartening, too.

You can help your Board members have a much more meaningful budget discussion if you prepare your budget proposal in the functional format discussed in this chapter and illustrated on page 533. This will allow Board members to see the income and costs associated with each of your programs as well as your administrative functions and the cost of fund raising itself.

Using the functional budget approach can facilitate discussion of the truly important questions. It will let your Board members understand which programs are fully supported or close to fully supported by grants, contracts and fees, and which ones depend upon your nonprofit's efforts to raise contributed dollars from individuals.

Then the Board can decide whether they are making the best use of the dollars which contributors give without restriction.

Board members will also realize that simply cutting expenses will not always solve financial problems since some grant and contract programs require that if you don't spend the money as directed by the funding contract, you must repay it to the funder. In these situations, cutting back on spending will result in cutting back on income, with no net gain to the organization and a clear loss to the people depending on your services.

On the other hand, Board members may realize that the organization is being weakened by continuing to try to support a program that does not have enough support through fees, grants and contracts. They may decide that the organization would be better off to drop the program and put its energy into developing new services or more fully sustaining existing services.

The key question for Board and management is: "Does the use of discretionary dollars reflect the nonprofit's priorities?" If not, what can be done to shift the use of discretionary dollars to support activities which reflect the Board and management's highest priorities? You may want to challenge your finance committee to draw a pie chart on the use of discretionary dollars without getting out calculators and the current year's budget sheets. If they have no immediate sense of what consumes your discretionary dollars, try the format in the Sample Functional Budget on page 533 for budget presentations to open a discussion of the relationship between priorities and use of funds under the Board's control.

Consult Appendix 1 if you would like information about source material related to this Chapter.

Budgeting allows you to project your future financial picture.
Once you have done this, you need to ensure that you have controls
in place to protect funds you receive from fraud and errors.
The next chapter describes how to do this.

25 PROTECTING YOUR NONPROFIT FROM FRAUD AND ERRORS

THIS CHAPTER COVERS

- Financial Policies and Procedures
- Key Banking Issues
- Petty Cash Funds
- Processing Payments
- Handling Cash Receipts
- Accepting Credit Card Payments for Donations or Purchases
- In-Kind Contributions
- Risk Management & Insurance
- What your Board Must do to Protect your Nonprofit
- Checklist of Key Controls

Once your Board has adopted the annual budget and you have raised funds, you're ready to start doing business.

This chapter focuses on the basic steps you'll need to take to be sure you're handling funds properly. The precautions described here are designed to protect both the organization and the individuals working with its funds. You want to have systems, policies, and procedures which prevent errors from happening and make it likely that those mistakes which do slip through will be found and corrected.

If you are a new nonprofit, this chapter will provide a step by step guide to putting your protections and systems in place. If your nonprofit has been operating for a while, this chapter will help you check out the systems and controls you have already put in place to be sure you are managing the risks and benefiting from the opportunities of electronic processing including online banking, remote deposit, credit cards, and data security.

25
PROTECTING YOUR NONPROFIT FROM FRAUD AND ERRORS

Who Should Do What? Developing Financial Policies and Procedures

To protect your organization and the people working with it, you'll want to establish clear, consistent policies and procedures to guide every aspect of accepting and using funds. Your most basic protection is an absolute policy of putting all funds given to the corporation into a corporate bank account, and paying all—or almost all—of the corporation's obligations by check from the corporate bank account. Of course, there are occasional situations in which small amounts must be paid in cash. The section of this chapter on Petty Cash Funds will help with protections for these unusual situations. We'll also explore the pros and cons of obtaining a corporate credit card or debit card and whether paying bills electronically makes sense for your nonprofit.

We've included a sample Table of Contents for a Fiscal Policies and Procedures Manual in Exhibit 25-1. Your organization should draft the simplest version for itself as soon as you know you will be receiving funds or incurring expenses. Your manual doesn't need to be long or fancy. In fact, the simpler you can make it the better. The important thing is that the Board, the staff, and any volunteers working with money know that you have established specific ways to handle the organization's business matters and that they are expected to follow them.

> *Avoid the common situation in which one person handles all receipts, makes all bank deposits, writes all the checks, keeps the bookkeeping records, reconciles the bank statement, and prepares the financial reports.*

As you work out the details of who will do what with money for your organization, remember to focus on protecting individuals and the corporation by separating the responsibilities for fiscal functions among several different individuals whenever possible. Specifically, you want to avoid the common situation in which one person handles all receipts, makes all bank deposits, writes all the checks, keeps the bookkeeping records, reconciles the bank statement, and prepares the financial reports.

What's wrong with this picture? The problem is that one individual is totally responsible for not only doing the work without making errors, but also finding any errors which did slip through. In general, it is much easier to detect errors made by others than the ones we make ourselves. Also, this approach leaves the organization totally dependent on that one person's skill and honesty.

What can you do to protect the individual and your organization? We know you won't have a huge staff of trained accountants (at least not in the early days), but you can be sure that you separate responsibility for making bank deposits and preparing checks from responsibility for doing bookkeeping—and most importantly, from responsibility for reconciling the bank account.

Exhibit 25-1

Sample Table of Contents for Fiscal Policies and Procedures Manual

I. Purpose of the Fiscal Policies & Procedures Manual 1

II. Fiscal Management Policies 1

- A. GAAP
- B. Accrual Accounting
- C. Deferred Revenue
- D. Equipment, Furnishings, and Real Property
- E. Donated Materials, Equipment, and Services
- F. Inventory
- G. Classification of Contributions
- H. Treatment of Restricted Funds
- I. Exchange Transactions
- J. Functional Expenses
- K. Cost Allocation
- L. General Ledger
- M. Budget
- N. Financial Statements
- O. Audit
- N. Interest Bearing Accounts
- O. Bonding
- P. Line of Credit/Borrowing
- Q. Petty Cash Fund

III. Purchases and Disbursement Procedures 4

- A. Purchases
- B. Processing Invoices
- C. Check Preparation
- D. Check Signatures

PROTECTING YOUR NONPROFIT FROM FRAUD AND ERRORS

    E.   Distribution of Checks

    F.   Filing Paid Invoices

    G.   Employee Travel Expense Procedures

    H.   Board Travel Expense Procedures

    I.   Credit Card purchases

IV. Procedures for Receipt & Deposits for Cash, Checks, and Credit Card Payments   4

    A.   Funds Received at the Office

    B.   Cash and Checks Received Outside the Office

    C.   Reconciliation of Receipts with Donor/Member Database

    D.   Credit Card Payments received

    D.   Bank Deposits

V. Procedures for Accounts Receivable 8

    A.   Approving credit

    B.   Recording new receivables

    C.   Recording payments on accounts receivable

    D.   Preparation of billings and statements

    E.   End of Month Accounts Receivable Reconciliation

VI. Billings and Fiscal Reports to Funders   10

VII. Payroll Procedures 11

    A.   Outside Payroll Service

    B.   Pay Periods

    C.   Processing of Monthly Timesheets

    D.   Review and Distribution of Paychecks

    E.   Payroll Tax Deposits

    F.   Recording the Payroll Checks in the Checkbook

    G.   Payroll Records

    H.   Benefit and Miscellaneous Payroll Payments

    I.   Allocation of staff time

    J.   Workers Compensation Reports

VIII. Bank Reconciliation   13

THE OREGON NONPROFIT CORPORATION HANDBOOK

IX. General Ledger   13

        A.   Monthly General Ledger Preparation

        B.   General Ledger Entry Procedures

        C.   Review of the General Ledger and Financial Statements

X. Financial Statements 17

XI. Budget Preparation and Revision Procedures   17

The bank reconciliation process is probably the most important control in a small organization.

Your bank reconciliation is the process by which you make sure that your organization's records of what's been put into your account, taken out, and what's left agree with the bank's records. The bank reconciliation process is probably the most important control in a small organization. Be sure you assign responsibility for the bank reconciliation to someone other than the person who makes deposits or has access to blank checks (including either preparing checks or signing checks). There are details on how to do bank reconciliations later in this chapter. The key issue is separating this responsibility from other financial functions and finding a careful, responsible person to perform it.

You can create the controls you need by asking yourself the following question about each step of handling funds for your organization: How can we be sure that more than one person verifies that this step has been done correctly without bogging down our work?

Read the section on Key Banking Issues to learn about other specific controls you can establish. You can create the controls you need by asking yourself the following question about each step of handling funds for your organization: How can we be sure that more than one person verifies that this step has been done correctly without bogging down our work? Remember, no system is fool proof. You may decide that rather than slow everything down to an unacceptable pace or expend a large portion of the organization's resources on bookkeeping activities, you will accept some risk of error or dishonesty. But be sure you have considered whether there may be other, simpler ways to obtain the same protection. If you can't think of any, check with other nonprofit organizations or consult a professional accountant.

25 PROTECTING YOUR NONPROFIT FROM FRAUD AND ERRORS

Key Banking Issues

Proper set-up and use of bank accounts is an extremely important part of good financial management. Hopefully, you have already established an iron-clad rule that all funds which your nonprofit receives (whether in cash or by check) should be deposited intact (with nothing removed or added) into your organization's bank account, and that your nonprofit uses checks to make payments for absolutely everything it possible can. Later on in this chapter we'll discuss Petty Cash Funds and corporate credit cards which can be used when paying by check simply won't work.

But beyond providing the mechanism for meeting this basic requirement, your banking relationship can help your nonprofit create and maintain some important controls and protections. To get the maximum benefit from your banking relationship, you'll need to think through some issues, establish some key policies, and build a positive relationship with your bank.

Opening Your Checking Account

Start your banking relationship by being certain that the bank staff person you are working with has experience opening accounts for nonprofit corporations. You should be asked to provide the Federal Employer Identification Number (EIN) that the IRS has assigned your nonprofit (discussed on page 47) and to provide evidence of a Board resolution directing the opening of the account at this particular bank.

Most banks can provide you with text for the corporate resolution to open the account which your board should adopt. Be sure your board adopts the resolution as stated and that the text of resolution is in your Board's minutes. Many banks will also provide the text of a second resolution through which your Board will identify the individuals entitled to serve as signers on the account. Regardless of whom your Board selects to act as signers, your Board President/Chair and Secretary will be required to sign as evidence that your Board approved both opening an account at this bank and approved specific individuals as signers for the account.

Many banks now require that nonprofit corporations submit copies of their Articles of Incorporation. Some also require copies of your IRS determination of tax-exempt status, if you are asking for various fee waivers the bank provides for charitable organizations.

Common Bank Account Set-up Mistakes

Unfortunately, not all banks train staff thoroughly about working with nonprofits. You will need to take care that you are not misled by a staff person who does not understand that your nonprofit corporation will be operating like a business and will require the types of services provided to business customers. Some important tips:

- Never agree to use your social security number as the tax identification number on the account. Even if means you must delay opening your account, wait until you have the federal EIN (Employer Identification Number) for your nonprofit corporation. See page 47 for how to get your nonprofit its own EIN.

- Do not use the federal EIN of another nonprofit corporation unless you have their explicit written permission to do so. You will need to present authorization to open the bank account which has been adopted by the Board of that corporation. But, even if the other corporation has approved your use of their EIN, you will want to think carefully about doing this. The effect of giving the other corporation's EIN is to inform the bank that the other corporation, not your nonprofit, owns the assets that will be in the account. If you are using another nonprofit's EIN, you should consult Chapter 10 on Fiscal Sponsorships to determine if you need to follow the rules described in that chapter.

- Discuss the question of requiring dual signatures on checks with the bank. Since all check processing is automated, many banks have adopted policies stating that they will not accept responsibility for monitoring checks to be certain that two authorized signatures are provided and that they will honor any check which has at least one authorized signature. If your bank has such a policy, you can still adopt a requirement that all checks have two signatures, but it will be up to your board to monitor whether the policy is being followed. The bank will not be calling your attention to checks with only one signature. See the discussion below for the pros and cons of requiring two signatures on your checks.

- Insist on a month end "cut-off" date for your statements. This will make reconciling your bank statements to your month end general ledger cash account balances much easier. Do not be put off by bank employees who insist this is a courtesy reserved for business customers. Your nonprofit is a business customer.

- Most banks offer online access to corporate bank accounts, allowing authorized persons to view the activity recorded in the corporation's account and in some cases, to authorize payments and/or transfers electronically. If you decided that you want to allow the persons authorized to sign checks to authorize payments or transfers online, you will need to establish procedures to document their activity. It is very important that the person you have selected to do your bank reconciliation be able to view the account activity but not be authorized to make payments or transfers.

Check Choices

In order to know what type of checks to order for your new account, you will need to know whether your nonprofit will be preparing checks by computer or by hand (manually). Whichever approach you will use, be sure you use only pre-numbered checks.

Checks for Manual Check Writing

The simplest approach to preparing manual checks is to use the three-on-a-page check format which provides a check stub for each check directly to the left of the check. This format provides enough room for the person writing the check to describe the purpose of the check as well as the payee, and date. While in the past bookkeepers frequently prepared checks using typewriters with multiple carbons, this approach has pretty much disappeared. If you happen to be using typed checks, you'll want to be sure that you have established a good system to file the check copies in check number sequence.

If you will also be preparing your payroll manually, request the version of the three-on-a-page format which provides a double stub—one part containing the payroll information which is given to the employee attached to the check, and the second part which remains in the checkbook for recordkeeping purposes. But, we strongly recommend using a payroll service or payroll software to avoid errors, so hopefully you won't be writing out paychecks manually. See Chapter 27 for more discussion of payroll issues.

Checks for Computerized Check Preparation

Today, most nonprofits prepare checks through using accounting software on a computer. The software program you are using will provide specifications for purchasing or directly printing the check stock needed to prepare checks. Some programs are designed to use with pre-numbered check stock. Other programs create the check number to be printed on each check as part of the process of printing the completed checks.

While you will want to prepare as many checks as possible using your computer software, most nonprofits find that at certain times they will need to be able to prepare checks manually as well. This typically occurs when the person who ordinarily prepares checks on the computer is not available or when you will need to prepare a check away from your office. If your computer software uses pre-numbered checks, you can use these same checks to prepare the occasional manual check. If your computer software does not work with pre-numbered check stock, you may want to consider having a separate set of pre-numbered manual checks printed in addition to the computer checks so that you can be certain that any manual checks are prepared on pre-numbered checks.

Keep Unused Check Stock Under Control

Regardless of what type of checks you are using, you will need to be sure that no one other than the person authorized to prepare checks has access to the unused check stock. Don't leave blank checks out where unauthorized people can have access to them. Lock them in a drawer or filing cabinet and make sure that information about how to access them is kept confidential. This is an important control because anyone who obtains your checks can create -and quite likely cash -checks against your account.

Protect Your Account from Unauthorized Checks

Banks process checks almost entirely electronically. They do not compare the signatures on the checks submitted for payment to the signature cards you have had authorized signers sign. You, the account holder, are responsible for examining the checks which are cashed against your account and protesting any checks which you believe do not have the correct signatures. Your rights to protest are time limited, so examining the checks returned with your bank statement or the checks posted on your bank's website quickly is an important control.

Nonprofit organizations can be the victims of identity theft. To protect your nonprofit from identity theft, you will need to monitor your account activity regularly. Thieves can gain access to the bank routing number for your account simply by looking at a legitimate check that your organization has issued. They create checks with the nonprofit's bank routing number and an individual name and address which matches fake ID that they will use to cash the checks. A great benefit of online access to review the transactions in your bank account is that you can check regularly to be sure that no improper checks are clearing through your account and alert your bank to any unauthorized activity.

> *Nonprofit organizations can be the victims of identity theft. To protect your nonprofit from identity theft, you will need to monitor your account activity regularly.*

Never Permit Blank Checks to Be Signed

You must never allow your nonprofit's check signers to sign blank checks. If a check that is signed while blank is later used for improper purposes, your nonprofit will not be able to protest it to the bank. Each check signer needs to understand that their signature should only be applied after they have examined evidence that the check has been prepared properly and is for a legitimate purchase by your nonprofit.

Should We Require Two Signatures on Each Check?

In the past, many nonprofits considered requiring two signatures on each check to be a very important control. Dual signatures protect each check signer by providing evidence that another responsible person agreed with them that the check was for a legitimate corporate purpose. Nonprofits frequently allow the Executive Director to serve as one of the signers and ask a Board member to serve as the second signer. Unfortunately, most banks no longer will accept responsibility for determining that your two signature requirement has been met before honoring your checks.

Today, many nonprofits have decided that they can obtain sufficient protection with a single signature system for most checks. These organizations also ask both the Executive Director and one or more Board members to be check signers. Each signer must be committed to examining documentation justifying each check that they will sign. This approach is based on the idea that one person carefully reviewing each check is a more effective control than two people carelessly signing, each believing that the other will do a more careful review. You will still need someone to have more than one authorized check signer to be sure that no one ever signs a check that is made out to them, whether it is a paycheck or a reimbursement for documented expenses.

Even if your nonprofit decides to use just one signature on most checks, you may want to establish a threshold amount which requires two signatures. For example, you may decide that any check over $5,000 must be signed by two signers. Remember, in most instances, your bank won't enforce this dual signature requirement and you will not be able to protest checks over the threshold amount because they carry only one signature. Instead, the person who examines your cancelled checks as part of the bank reconciliation process must be trained to alert the board if the two signature requirement is violated.

Should We Use On-line Payment Features?

Of course many banks now offer opportunities to pay bills on-line without the use of paper checks. Using on-line payment safely will require setting up some specific procedures to be sure that you are still keeping the function of preparing a payment separate from the function of authorizing the payment. In the typical check payment system, one person prepares the check and a second person reviews the documentation and the check itself before signing the check, giving their authorization that this is a legitimate use of corporate funds.

In an on-line payment system, one person can get all of the payments set up for review by the "check-signer" who holds the password to authorize the payments. For many organizations, this is just as time consuming as preparing physical checks. Some organizations use electronic payment only for specific recurring expenses, for example, a copier rental agreement. The person responsible for preparing payments must still review the invoice and record the payment. And, the person reconciling the bank account will need to pay special attention to be sure that the actual amount deducted each month is the expected standard amount.

The big question for smaller organizations to consider is whether electronic bill paying saves enough time to make it worth the increased control risks. Larger organizations may realize more significant time savings but will need to be certain that they have established controls that ensure effective review both before and after authorization of electronic payments.

Bank Deposits

If you are doing your books manually, you will need to order a business-style bank deposit book from your bank. Be sure you make a carbon copy of each deposit ticket as you prepare it. You will list each check and the total amount of cash included in the deposit. You can use the carbon copy provided in the bank deposit book to note the source of each amount, including each check and a list of the receipt numbers you have given for cash amounts. If you have a copier readily available, you may decide to photo copy each check in each deposit to avoid making a detailed listing of the checks. Of course, you'll still need to make a list of the sources of cash included in the deposit. If you take this approach, you will want to staple the photocopy of the checks to a copy of the deposit ticket. There is no need to photo copy cash. You will keep track of the cash in the deposit through your pre-numbered receipt system.

If you are using computer software to handle your accounting and check writing, your program will provide a system for preparing bank deposits. Many programs include a feature which prints out a listing of checks and cash which can be used as a deposit ticket for the bank. Be sure that your system allows you to create a record of the source of every item included in each deposit. Most nonprofits find that it is still helpful to photocopy the checks being deposited so that you can always be sure you know the source of all the funds that were included in each deposit.

However you prepare the deposit ticket, you will want to be sure that the person who takes the deposit to the bank receives a deposit receipt which should be filed with your copy of the deposit ticket. This is your verification that the deposit has actually been received by the bank.

Many banks now offer remote deposit devices that allow the user to deposit checks without actually taking them to the bank. The devices are used to scan each check the nonprofit wishes to deposit and transmit the information electronically to the bank. Remote deposit can provide an opportunity to improve controls in larger organizations by allowing the entire process of opening the mail, recording payments received, and preparing the bank deposit to be completed at a specific time by two employees working together. Some remote deposit devices also create a record of all of the information contained on the checks which can be transferred electronically into the nonprofit's donor tracking or accounting system without requiring detailed data entry.

Banks generally charge a fee for the remote deposit device and then a monthly processing fee. While these fees are dropping, they will still be too high for many smaller nonprofits, especially those with relatively few items to be deposited.

Do We Need to Get Our Processed Checks Returned with Our Bank Statement?

Many banks no longer return cancelled checks with bank statements or do so only if the account holder pays a fee for this extra service. This change raises questions for nonprofit organizations which have previously relied on examining cancelled checks for agreement with accounting records as a key control.

If your organization has decided to continue receiving cancelled checks with your bank statement, you will want to make arrangements to have the unopened bank statement examined by an individual other than the person with responsibility for either preparing or signing checks. In small nonprofits, the Board Treasurer will often be asked to fulfill this role of examining the cancelled checks. As nonprofits grow larger and have more checks, this job may become burdensome to a volunteer Treasurer. At that point, someone other than the person responsible for preparing checks or signing checks may be asked to take on the bank reconciliation function, including examining cancelled checks or reviewing the check images online. If you have your cancelled checks returned with your bank statement, this person should receive the statement unopened.

The person responsible for examining the cancelled checks and bank statement will need to compare the checks to the accounting record of checks written. The goal of this examination is to determine whether the accounting records have correctly recorded the payee and amount of each check and whether the bank has honored any checks that don't have valid signatures.

If you decide not to request the return of cancelled checks, your nonprofit will still be able to examine the checks which the bank has honored. Instead of receiving the actual cancelled checks, you will need to have the bank give the person responsible for examining the checks a password to access an electronic display of the checks which have cleared your account. The person examining the checks will be able to examine both the front and back of each check. The person given this responsibility for reviewing the checks and comparing the bank records to your accounting records should be given a password which limits their access to the account to review only. They should not be authorized to initiate or modify any transactions through their online access. You will want to develop a procedure that requires this person to check off or in some way indicate that they have reviewed each check just as they would have reviewed each physical check returned with your bank statement.

In addition to this independent review by a person who does not prepare or sign checks, it is also helpful to have the person responsible for preparing the checks and maintaining the books have online access to the bank account information as well to be able to check their own work in recording checks and deposits. But their review cannot substitute for the independent review of the person who provides the bank reconciliation.

Should We Use Positive Pay?

Larger nonprofits may be offered Positive Pay services by their banks as a fraud prevention tool. Organizations using Positive Pay electronically transmit to the bank a list of all checks issued, including the check number and amount of each check, and in some cases, the name of the payee. The bank will only honor checks which appear on this electronic list, thus avoiding cashing fraudulent checks. Banks charge fees for Positive Pay, so your nonprofit will need to decide if this increased protection is worth the cost.

Bank Reconciliations Are Essential

The bank reconciliation is one of the simplest and most powerful controls your nonprofit can implement. You can use the simple format for bank reconciliation which your bank provides on its bank statements or ask a trained accountant to help you design a format which will work better for you.

There are several very important aspects of doing bank reconciliations:

- The person who does the bank reconciliation should not be the same person who prepares the checks or signs checks. If possible, they should also not be the same person who makes bank deposits.

- The person doing the bank reconciliation should be given the bank statement unopened, just as it comes from the bank and have online access to view the bank account but no access to authorize transactions.

- Bank reconciliations should be done within the first 7 days after your bank statement arrives or immediately after the end of each month if you are using on-line access. Do not put off bank reconciliations.

- The person doing the bank reconciliation must examine each cancelled check (or electronic image of a cancelled check as described above) to determine that the name of the payee, the amount of the check, and the date of the check agree with your accounting records and that all checks have valid signatures.

- The bank reconciliation person must also verify that each deposit recorded in your accounting records agrees with the bank record of deposits.

- The bank reconciliation must prove that the ending balance in your general ledger cash account is in agreement with the reconciled bank balance for that month end.

- Bank reconciliation requires listing all outstanding checks—checks that have been prepared but have not yet cleared the bank.

- Reconciliation also requires listing deposits-in-transit—all deposits that are shown in your accounting records but that have not yet been recorded by the bank.

It is absolutely essential that you are able to match the cash balance that is in your accounting records to the balance on your bank statement. If you cannot complete the reconciliation, go to the bank and ask for help immediately.

With online access to bank account information, it is often very helpful to have the person doing the bookkeeping prepare a bank reconciliation report following all of the steps described above. In fact, most accounting software, provides an automated tool to use for bank reconciliation. But, the most important step will occur when the independent person chosen to do the formal bank reconciliation reviews the actual bank account records and compares them to the reconciliation prepared by the bookkeeper. The independent bank reconciliation person must take care to avoid assuming that because a "bank reconciliation" report is prepared through the accounting software, their review is unnecessary. Their careful review is an essential control.

Dealing with Multiple Bank Accounts

Nonprofits that will have cash in excess of their immediate needs at any time during the month should consider use of interest bearing accounts. With telephone transfer services or on-line banking, you can make use of separate savings and checking accounts quite convenient. However, you will need to establish special controls for telephone transfers or on-line banking, including requiring that the person who authorizes these transactions make a detailed record of the date, amount, and purpose of each transfer.

Organizations with substantial excess cash which is not required for periods of 30 days or more should consider Certificates of Deposit and other time deposit plans. In general, the larger the amount of cash available and the longer the period of time it can remain on deposit, the higher the interest rate will be. Boards of Directors must establish their own policies for investing funds. See page 497-98 for a discussion of Board investment policies.

While it may be helpful to very small organizations to establish a separate bank account to hold funds that have been restricted by a funder for a specific future use, in most cases it will work much better to track restricted funds in the accounting system rather than by opening multiple bank accounts. Each bank account that your nonprofit opens will require careful controls and bank reconciliation procedures.

> *Be sure to read contracts with your funding sources carefully. Some federal programs specifically forbid placing federal funds in interest bearing accounts. Other contracts require that funds be placed in interest bearing accounts.*

Be sure to read contracts with your funding sources carefully. Some federal programs specifically forbid placing federal funds in interest bearing accounts. Other contracts require that funds be placed in interest bearing accounts. Even if your funding agreements do not specify the use of interest bearing accounts, your board has a responsibility to see that funds earn interest whenever possible. Because the opportunities for investing surplus cash are complex, and the responsibility of managing the corporation's funds is great, it may be helpful to identify a regular investment adviser, either a Director or other community supporter with particular knowledge of sound cash management and investment strategy.

Petty Cash Funds

Many small purchases are easier to transact with cash (postage due requests from your mail carrier, taxi fare for an emergency, etc.). New programs are often tempted to pay these expenses with cash received from clients or with an employee's own funds. Both these methods will eventually cause bookkeeping messes. Always deposit in the bank all cash received by the program. Otherwise there will not be a complete record of program earnings. *Avoid having employees use personal funds for program expenses.* Too many checks to employees for reimbursement of purchases may appear to be disguised wages or possible misuse of program funds.

One way to deal with cash purchases is through creation of a Petty Cash Fund. One person should be responsible for administration of the Petty Cash Fund. To set up the fund initially, write a check for the full amount of the fund (usually $25 or $50 is adequate for small to medium-sized programs). Make the first check out to "Petty Cash— name of custodian" and record it in the Petty Cash Fund account. The "custodian" is the person who will be responsible for the Petty Cash Fund. He or she will cash the initial check establishing the fund and then provide cash to individuals who need to use cash to make small purchases. The Petty Cash Custodian will require receipts for all purchases and may ask the staff or volunteers who use the funds to sign for the cash she gives them.

As cash purchases are made, the custodian will record them in a journal or notebook. Save all receipts. When the fund is getting low, or at the end of the month, the check writer will prepare a check to reimburse the fund for the total amount expended (add up all receipts and prepare a check for this exact amount.) The total of this check plus the cash left in the fund should equal the original fund amount. When recording this check in the accounting records, distribute the expense to the appropriate accounts according to what was purchased. Do not distribute any of the total to the Petty Cash Fund account in the accounting records after the initial check to set up the fund. Instead, divide up the amount of the check to reimburse the fund into the categories of expense it was used for, such as office supplies, transportation, etc. The balance of the Petty Cash Fund account remains fixed at the original level you selected.

Always deposit in the bank all cash received by the program. Avoid having employees use personal funds for program expenses.

If after establishing and using a Petty Cash Fund for a while, it seems to require reimbursing too frequently for convenience, the fund can be increased by a fixed amount. This check is entered into the Petty Cash Fund account in the accounting records, and permanently increases the balance of the fund. The regular reimbursement of the fund for expenses continues as described above except that the amount of cash available for expenditures before reimbursement is necessarily larger.

Processing Payments

Your organization needs to develop clear procedures for authorizing purchases, authorizing payment of invoices, preparing and signing checks, cancelling invoices when paid, and filing paid invoices. In small nonprofits, the authorization of purchases is usually handled verbally. The Director or other designated staff member merely orders or purchases the necessary supplies and services in accord with the Board approved budget.

In larger organizations, procedures for purchasing can involve either check request forms or purchase orders. The check request form requires that anyone who wishes to have a check prepared to make a purchase or pay a bill fill in specific information. Typically check request forms require the name of the vendor, the purpose of the purchase, the program or funding source the purchase should be charged to, the date the check is needed by, and the signature of a supervisor or other person authorized to make purchasing decisions.

Purchase order systems are even more structured. They require getting approval to purchase before the actual purchase is made. The purchase order forms contain information similar to the check request forms. When the accounting department receives an invoice requesting payment, it matches the invoice to a purchase order to document that the purchase was approved properly. Purchase order systems are usually unnecessary and somewhat cumbersome in small organizations.

Your organization will need to identify individuals empowered to authorize payment of bills. These people need to have knowledge of whether the invoices are legitimate. Did the organization receive the items for which it is being billed? You'll want the person authorizing payment to initial each invoice as evidence as their authorization.

The next step in the payment cycle is actual preparation of the check to pay approved bills. Prepared checks should be attached to authorized invoices when they are given to the authorized check signer. The signer should review the authorization and check carefully. At the time the checks are signed, the invoice should be cancelled (marked "Paid" with the date of payment and the number of the check used for payment).

Finally, the paid invoices should be filed in an organized system. Two filing methods are commonly used. Some small organizations file paid invoices by the month of payment. Other organizations file paid invoices by vendor name (name of the firm or individual paid), with the most recently paid invoice at the front of the pile.

Reimbursing Expenses

Board members, staff, or volunteers may occasionally spend their personal funds or use their personal credit cards to purchase items for the organization or travel on behalf of your group. Your organization will need to establish clear policies and procedures to deal with whether and how you will reimburse these individuals for their purchases or costs.

In general, your organization will want to limit the number of purchases that are made using the reimbursement approach and establish a process for making purchases directly with corporate funds.

The big questions in this area involve whether your nonprofit will reimburse individuals for such purchases. Your policy will need to identify the persons within your organization who can authorize such purchases, i.e. give permission to an individual to make a purchase with personal funds which the organization will reimburse. The policy should also make it clear that even when a purchase has been authorized, the purchaser will be reimbursed only if they submit clear documentation showing what was purchased and how much it cost. Your policy should require that documentation for purchases include a specific description of what was purchased. This means that a credit card receipt simply showing the total amount charged to the card is not sufficient. Instead, the purchaser will need a receipt that shows what the charge was for—e.g., paper, toner, and markers.

Your procedures for handling reimbursements for purchases made with personal funds or credit cards should include use of a Request for Reimbursement form which details what was purchased, the vendor name, the amount of the purchase, the person who authorized the purchase, and the person who is requesting reimbursement. Most organizations will require the purchaser to attach the original receipt, although in some circumstances, a copy may be acceptable.

In general, your organization will want to limit the number of purchases that are made using this reimbursement approach and establish a process for making purchases directly with corporate funds. You may be able to open accounts with your most frequent vendors or obtain a corporate credit card which may be used by authorized persons. You'll want to review the corporate credit card issues discussed later in the this chapter before deciding to obtain credit cards for your nonprofit.

Travel Expense Reimbursements:

If your nonprofit has decided to pay for some or all of the expenses that staff or volunteers incur in order to travel to activities on behalf of your group, you'll need to establish policies and procedures to clarify what costs your organization will cover and how you will pay them.

Your travel policy will need to address both local travel and out-of-town travel costs. The big question for local travel is whether you will reimburse staff or volunteers for mileage costs for driving they do on behalf of the organization. The policy will also address reimbursement for other incidental costs related to local travel—parking fees, taxi fares, etc. Most nonprofits that reimburse for local travel establish a per mile reimbursement rate. Many utilize the rate established by the IRS as the allowable rate for businesses to use to support tax deductions for travel expense. The IRS updates the rate annually. You can find it by searching for Business Mileage Rate at *www.IRS.gov.*

Typically, nonprofits utilize mileage reimbursement request forms that identify the date, destination (and purpose if it is not clear from the destination), and mileage for each trip, and the total number of miles for which reimbursement is sought. While some organizations require the entry of an odometer reading at the beginning and end of each trip, this may not be necessary if you are prepared to occasionally spot check the mileage reports using MapQuest or other internet mapping tool.

For out-of-town travel, your policy should identify who has authority to decide which travel is to be paid for by the organization. You will also need to establish limits on the amount of travel expense that you will reimburse. For example, it is unlikely that a small nonprofit will agree to reimburse travelers for first class airfare, luxury hotel stays, or expensive gourmet meals.

As a starting point, you should decide whether your nonprofit will reimburse actual travel costs or use a per diem system. Most smaller nonprofits use the actual cost approach because they are encouraging travelers to spend as little as possible to limit the cost to the organization. In this approach, the traveler must submit receipts for all costs for which reimbursement is sought. As noted above, the receipts must specify what was purchased, the vendor, the date, and the amount.

In the per diem approach, the organization establishes an amount that will be paid for food, lodging, and other expenses for each day of out of town travel. You could decide to use rates established by your state government or the federal government. The traveler is then paid the per diem amount for each day of travel regardless of what the actual costs were. Some organizations prefer the per diem approach for simplicity and clarity. Others find the government published rates exceed what their organization can afford and don't want to spend time trying to define and update their own rates.

PROTECTING YOUR NONPROFIT FROM FRAUD AND ERRORS

Corporate Credit Cards

Some nonprofits open and manage corporate credit card accounts in order to avoid having staff or volunteers charge expenses for the nonprofit onto their personal credit cards. While having a corporate credit card can be convenient, it opens the organization to some risks and will require both clear policies and careful oversight.

In opening a corporate credit card account, your nonprofit is agreeing to be responsible for the charges made on the card by any person you have authorized to use it. This means that if one of the persons you have authorized to use the card makes purchases which are not appropriate for your organization, your nonprofit will still be required to pay for them. Most credit card companies require that a separate corporate credit card number be established for each person authorized to use the card. The physical card will display the authorized user's name as well as the nonprofit's name.

Your nonprofit will want to establish a very clear policy that any person who is given a corporate credit card must accept full responsibility for the security of the card and should not allow others to use their card. You may require individuals being issued a card to sign an agreement promising to reimburse your nonprofit of any expense charged to corporate credit card which is not approved by the nonprofit. The users must also be required to submit original receipts for all purchases made with the card.

Sound management of corporate credit cards requires that someone other than the person authorized to use the card must compare the charges made to the card to the receipts submitted by the user each month. Failure to submit complete receipts should result in cancelation of the credit card.

While having a corporate credit card can be convenient, it opens the organization to some risks and will require both clear policies and careful oversight.

Your nonprofit will want to be very clear about the types of expenses that should and should not be charged to corporate credit cards. Whenever possible, you will want to have regular suppliers bill your organization directly rather than using the corporate credit card to make the purchase. Increasingly, nonprofits are purchasing supplies, software, and other necessary items through the internet. You will want to establish very clear procedures for authorizing such purchases and printing and saving receipts that can be matched to the credit card billings.

If your nonprofit is running on a very tight budget and often has difficulties having enough cash to meet its immediate obligations, you will want to require any corporate credit card users to submit receipts for purchases as they are made rather than waiting until month end. Your accountant can use these receipts and also go online to check your credit card account frequently in order to be aware of the expenses that have been charged to the cards so that you will not have surprises when the monthly statement arrives.

Debit Cards

The Oregon Attorney General's office reports many problems with nonprofits that use debit cards and generally recommends against their use. Most small nonprofits will want to avoid obtaining and using debit cards even if your bank suggests providing them. In most cases the risk of misuse and difficulties documenting the purposes for which the cards are used will make using debit cards truly more trouble than they are worth. Even if your organization does decide to use a debit card for certain types of purchases, you will want to adopt a clear policy that prohibits use of the debit card to withdraw cash from your accounts. If cash will be needed for a change fund at an event, prepare a check to the person who will be responsible for managing the cash, have them cash it, and require them to see that the cash is redeposited into the account with correct identification of its source.

Handling Cash Receipts

The term "cash receipts" is used to describe all funds received by the corporation, whether they are received as checks or in actual cash. Your goal is to be certain that all cash receipts are deposited in the organization's bank account as quickly as possible. For funds which come to your organization by mail, you can establish a check log procedure for the person opening the mail. A check log is a list of each check received which notes the date received, the amount of the check, and who the check is from. The person opening the mail should prepare the log each time she or he opens the mail, compute a total of all funds received, and initial the log.

Ideally, you will have two people present to open the mail and verify the log. About the only way to make such a system work is to have all mail sent to a post office box and establish a time when two people can retrieve and process the mail together. You may decide that you can't afford to have two people spend time on this as a regular thing but that you could use this approach at times when your organization has done a special mail appeal and is anticipating receipt of a number of contributions. If you consistently have a high volume of contributions or other payments arriving by mail, you may want to consider the remote deposit system described earlier in this chapter.

Your goal is to be certain that all cash receipts are deposited in the organization's bank account as quickly as possible.

A separate person should prepare the actual bank deposit. This person will capture more information about each check received, including notes about the purpose for which the payment was made. Some organizations simply cannot find a separate person from the person opening the mail to prepare the bank deposits. If this is true for your organization, consider having the one person handling both functions make photocopies of all the checks received. This will at least allow others to review the judgments about the intended purpose of the payment made by the person doing the deposit.

Situations in which actual cash is involved are more challenging. If people bring cash to your office, be sure that the person accepting the cash provides a written receipt at the time of taking the cash. The receipt should state the person's name, the date, the amount of cash, and the purpose of the payment. Use a pre-printed (with your organization's name), pre-numbered receipt book which produces automatic duplicate copies of all receipts given. Control access to unused receipt books just like you would unused check stock.

If you accept cash at parties, special events, or other large informal gatherings, it may not be possible to give receipts to each person providing money. In a "pass the hat" situation, donors don't want to wait around for receipts and it is generally impossible to tell who gave what. In these situations, have two individuals from your organization count the money and have both initial the count when it is completed. Make arrangements for immediate bank deposit for the cash collections. If the gatherings where you collect cash are held outside business hours, you may need to make an immediate deposit at your bank and arrange protection for the person making the deposit.

Should We Accept Credit Card Payment for Donations or Purchases?

Many donors and customers strongly prefer to make contributions or pay for services or products by credit card. They are often willing to give more generously or make more purchases if credit card payment is available. Credit card payment is the primary way that donors contribute through the internet.

If you decide to offer this option for donations and purchases made directly to you (not through your website), you will need to establish a merchant account with your bank and include reconciliation of credit card payments received in your monthly bank reconciliation process. You may need to seek outside help to set up your system for recording payments by credit card because the reconciliation can be quite challenging without good internal systems. If you will accept credit card payments by phone, fax, or paper submission of account information without in-person examination of the credit card, you will need to work with your credit card processing firm to establish the controls needed to verify each charge. In order to accept credit card payments through your website, you will need to enter into an agreement with a secured online payment system like Network for Good or Paypal. Do not allow donors or customers to email their credit card information to you.

If you decide to accept credit card payments, be sure you have procedures that will protect your donors/customers credit card information. Lock up all credit card info and do not allow credit card info to be stored in your donor tracking system. Check with your credit card processing firm to learn how long you are required to keep physical evidence of the donor/customer's authorization for the charge. You will want to destroy credit card information that is no longer needed.

In-Kind Contributions

Your organization may receive goods or services as contributions as well as cash. These non-cash contributions are referred to as in-kind. As we will discuss in Chapter 26 on accounting and reporting, these in-kind contributions pose some special problems for accounting. But regardless of how your organization handles the accounting for in-kind contributions, you'll want to be sure you keep records of the important in-kind gifts you receive.

These basic records of in-kind contributions are needed both to help you thank donors and to allow your organization to take credit for the actual level of support from the community which you have generated. In some organizations, the value of in-kind contributions of labor and goods may equal or exceed the total amounts received from all other sources.

You can create a simple form to track each in-kind contribution, with space to record the date of the contribution, description of the goods or services received, and donor's name and address. Tracking in-kind gifts is an important fraud prevention step—allowing you to know what has been given to your organization. You may want to use time sheets to track the number of hours contributed by volunteers providing substantial services to your organization.

Risk Management and Insurance

Your nonprofit will be working very hard to get the resources you need to achieve your mission. So it's extremely important that your Board thinks through the various risks which could threaten your ability to continue your efforts. You'll want to think about both the risks that could cause the greatest potential harm and the ones that are most likely to occur. Once you've identified the most important risks, you'll want to develop strategies to avoid the possible harm, either by preventing the damaging event from happening or providing resources that will help your nonprofit bounce back from any damage you weren't able to prevent.

Start by making a list of the risks that are likely to impact organizations that do work similar to yours. Your list will probably include risks that are related to physical damage to your property—fire, flood, etc.—and then move on to risks to the people who are involved in your activities—falls, car accidents, etc. You'll also consider risks that arise when things you don't intend to have happen do—for example, a staff member or volunteer abuses a vulnerable client. Although most nonprofits don't like thinking about it, you will also confront the risk that someone will embezzle

PROTECTING YOUR NONPROFIT FROM FRAUD AND ERRORS 25

your funds or make inappropriate use of your nonprofit's assets. And, if you will have employees, your nonprofit will confront a complex web of risks related to employment law and worker safety.

> *It's extremely important that your Board thinks through the various risks which could threaten your ability to continue your efforts.*

As you think through these risks, your first question should be "how can we prevent these damaging things from happening?" In many cases, you will be able to identify a policy which you could establish which would eliminate or minimize the chances of something going wrong. For example, to eliminate the risk for your clients being injured in an automobile accident while being transported by your staff, you could decide to never transport anyone. However, that decision might make it impossible to achieve some of your key goals. So, you might choose a strategy to reduce the risk by establishing a policy that your will review the driving records of any staff or volunteers who will be driving clients for your program and prohibit anyone with moving violations or DUII charges from driving for your organization.

Insurance

It just isn't possible to eliminate all risks, so you will want to purchase insurance to provide resources to recover from the damages that arise when unintended things do happen. Talk with other nonprofits in your community to identify an independent insurance broker who has experience working with nonprofit organizations to select the types of insurance policies you most need and help you obtain policies at favorable prices.

The types of insurance most commonly used by nonprofit corporations, and the risks covered, are as follows:

- **Bonding**—Protects the corporation against losses from fraud or theft by covered employees, Directors, or volunteers.

- **General Liability**—"Trip and Fall" insurance protects the corporation from claims of bodily injury to clients or others who are injured accidentally at the corporation's facilities or in programs conducted at facilities owned by others. It may or may not cover volunteers. It may or may not include "Product Liability" coverage for food served, goods sold, etc.

- **Professional Malpractice**—Protects the corporation against claims arising from the professional services of the named professional. It's available primarily for recognized professions (doctors, nurses, social workers). It may or may not cover claims arising from actions of those supervised by the named professional.

- **Errors and Omissions**—This is coverage for mistakes which arise from errors and omissions in carrying out the work of the corporation. It should cover personal injury (economic harm, slander, etc.), as well as bodily injury. It may cover actions by employees only or include volunteers, Directors, etc. It may or may not provide for defense of staff, if they are named in a suit in addition to the corporation.

- **Directors and Officers**—This is insurance coverage for members of the Board for claims arising from their service on the Board. It may or may not include the Executive Director (who is a staff member) as well as the Board. (See pp. 362-63).

- **Volunteer Liability**—This is coverage for volunteers and for your organization for actions by the volunteers that may give rise to lawsuits. It should provide for the legal and other costs of defense of the volunteers and of the organization. (See pp. 463-65).

- **Vehicle Liability**—This protects the corporation from claims arising from the operation of motor vehicles by the corporation (bodily injury and property damage). It's required by law for any corporation-owned vehicle. It may or may not cover vehicles not owned by the corporation but used to do the work of the corporation (for example, those owned by staff or volunteers). The corporation may be liable for damages done by staff or volunteers driving their own vehicles on behalf of the corporation, so non-owned vehicle coverage will be essential if your nonprofit allows volunteers or staff to drive as part of their work for your organization.

- **Worker Compensation Insurance**—Oregon law requires all employers to carry worker compensation insurance. It protects the corporation from claims arising from an employee's on-the-job injury. It can be purchased from SAIF (a public state agency) or a private insurance carrier. It may or may not cover volunteers.

It just isn't possible to eliminate all risks, so you will want to purchase insurance to provide resources to recover from the damages that arise when unintended things do happen.

Your Board may want to obtain legal advice about the adequacy of your insurance coverage. Additional professional advice is available through an annual audit by a CPA. Standard audit procedures require the CPA to examine your insurance coverage and alert you to problems. This provides great assistance on risk management issues.

Ultimately, the Board is responsible for protecting the assets of your nonprofit, so attention to risk management is an important Board responsibility. In organizations in which the Board has delegated management to an Executive Director, the Board will want to ensure that the Executive Director or staff is handling risk management effectively.

25 PROTECTING YOUR NONPROFIT FROM FRAUD AND ERRORS

What Your Board Must Do to Protect Your Nonprofit

Whether your organization will have a large staff or be managed entirely by volunteers, the Board's commitment to integrity and willingness to invest time, effort, and resources to ensure effective controls will be the most important element for protecting the assets of your nonprofit. It is essential that the Board requires everyone involved in the organization, including Board members themselves, to follow the policies and procedures that have been established to protect the organization.

If your Board delegates management, it must evaluate the performance of each person who has been given authority and responsibility for managing the resources of the organization. A key part of the Board's annual evaluation of the Executive Director must be considering whether this individual has followed fiscal policies and consistently implemented control procedures, including educating the staff about expectations and insisting on honesty and compliance with policies and procedures.

The Checklists of Key Controls described below identifies specific control strategies for the Board to use in fulfilling its role. But beyond any specific procedure or task, the most important protection for your nonprofit will be the Board's consistent commitment to understanding and monitoring the finances of your organization.

Checklists of Key Controls

We have included two checklists to help you make sure your nonprofit has developed the systems and controls needed to protect your resources and reputation. At the end of Chapter 23 you will find a comprehensive Nonprofit Financial Management Checklist that identifies key controls throughout your financial management cycle. In the Forms section at the end of the book, you'll find Financial Control Policies and Procedures for Small Nonprofit Organizations, a detailed list of controls for smaller organizations. While this list of common control strategies may also be helpful to larger organizations with more professional financial management staff, the Policies may need to be modified to more accurately reflect the delegation of responsibility for some controls to management.

In addition to establishing key controls, you should also consider creating a culture and systems that encourage employees and volunteers to report to your organization any concerns they have about what appear to be improper practices. Studies have shown that fraud and embezzlement are committed by the most trusted person in the organization, usually someone who has been with the organization an average of about three years. Tips from whistleblowers are the most common method for learning about fraud and embezzlement in nonprofits. Your Board or Executive Director should consider adopting a whistleblower policy and ensuring that employees and volunteers understand how to follow it in the event they observe practices that could suggest fraud or embezzlement.

One final note, protecting your nonprofit from error and fraud is a never-ending story. Controls that were perfectly designed and beautifully implemented at one stage in your organization's development will need to be reviewed regularly and may need to be revised to be sure that they meet your needs as your organization grows and adds new programs and funding sources.

Consult Appendix 1 if you would like information about source material related to this Chapter.

Now that you have systems and procedures in place for handling funds, you are ready to move to the next steps of the financial management cycle: recording and reporting your financial activities.

26 KEEPING BOOKS AND PREPARING FINANCIAL REPORTS

THIS CHAPTER COVERS

- What is Accounting?
- Big Choices for Your Accounting System
- More Than Tracking Revenues and Expenses
- Double-Entry Accounting
- Basics for Very Small Nonprofits
- Dealing with Carry-over Funds
- How Is Nonprofit Accounting Different from Business Accounting
- Government Funds Accounting Requirements
- Fund Accounting
- Financial Statements
- Tips for Useful Financial Reports
- Accounting Software Choices
- Tips for QuickBooks® Users
- Who Should Do Your Accounting?

Once your organization has established its annual budget, put systems in place for handling funds, and begun to do the things you planned, you will need to keep records of everything that happens which has a financial impact on your organization.

In very small organizations, this financial recordkeeping can be little more than a checkbook—a simple record of all the money received and paid out by the nonprofit. Simple financial statements can be little more than a list of the sources of funds received and the nature of all payments made combined with a statement of the cash in the bank the organization had at the beginning and end of the month. Most individuals with no previous background in bookkeeping can learn to maintain these simple records and prepare these reports.

In larger organizations, more sophisticated records and reports will be needed. You will also most likely need to employ an individual trained in double-entry bookkeeping to keep the books and produce the financial statements.

This chapter discusses the major choices your nonprofit will need to make to set up the accounting system and financial reports that you will need. It provides sample financial reports and tips for choosing and using accounting software that will meet your needs.

Because payroll procedures are particularly demanding, that type of recordkeeping is described in the next chapter. Chapter 27 contains general information about the retention and inspection of records, including the financial records we discuss in this chapter

What is Accounting?

The goal of accounting is to maintain a usable record of every financial event your organization experiences. The art of good accounting is to design a system for keeping these records that allows you to produce useful financial reports.

A good accounting system will:

- Provide essential information about your nonprofit's financial health to guide your decisions
- Help your board and staff determine whether their budget plans are working
- Make it clear where your nonprofit gets its resources and how it uses them
- Allow your nonprofit to produce required reports easily for the IRS and your funders

At its heart, your accounting system is a giant set of lists of things that happened in your organization: checks that were written, deposits that were made, buildings that were purchased, goods and services which were given to you. But to be useful, your accounting system must provide a structure to categorize all the items in the lists so that they can be grouped and summarized into meaningful reports. All organizations, businesses as well as nonprofits, share some common elements in the structure they use for accounting. But before you can design the specific structure you will need for your nonprofit's accounting system, you will need to make some choices.

> *The goal of accounting is to maintain a usable record of every financial event your organization experiences.*

Once you have made those choices, you will create a Chart of Accounts (see Exhibit 26-1 on next page) for your nonprofit.

The Chart of Accounts is a list of the categories you will use to classify all financial transactions. To be useful, your Chart of Accounts needs to reflect your decisions about the big accounting choices and the types of reports your board and management will need to make decisions and the information your funders and the IRS will expect you to have.

Exhibit 26-1

Sample Chart of Accounts

Assets:

1010 Cash –checking
1040 Petty Cash
1050 Cash-savings

1110 Accounts receivable
1190 Allowance for doubtful accounts

1210 Pledges receivable
1220 Allowance for doubtful pledges
1240 Grants receivable
1250 Discounts for long term pledges
1270 Other receivables

1310 Inventories for sale
1320 Inventories for use
1350 Prepaid expenses
1360 Refundable deposits

1410 Marketable securities

1510 Land
1520 Buildings
1530 Accumulated depreciation
1540 Leasehold improvements
1550 Accumulated amortization
1560 Furniture, fixtures, equipment
1570 Accumulated Deprec on Acct

Liabilities:

2010 Accounts payable
2110 Accrued expenses –payroll
2120 Accrued expenses –vacation
2150 Other accrued expenses

2200 Grants payable
2250 Loans payable
2730 Mortgages payable

2900 Funds held on behalf of others

Net Assets:

3000 Unrestricted net assets
3300 Temporarily restricted net assets
3900 Permanently restricted net assets

Support and Revenue:

4010 Contributions –individuals
4050 Gift portion of event income
4070 Legacies/bequests

4110 In-kind contributions-services
4130 In-kind contributions-other

4210 Corporate gifts
4230 Foundation grants

4420 Federated fund raising org.
4510 Government grants
5010 Government contracts

5110 Program related sales
5210 Program service fees

5310 Membership dues

5410 Interest & dividend income
5610 Investment income
5810 Unrealized gains and losses

6310 Unrelated sales income

Expenses:

7210 Salaries of officers
7220 Other salaries
7310 Pension contributions
7320 Other benefits
7410 Employer payroll taxes

7510 Professional fund raising fees
7520 Professional services
7580 In kind –donated services

7710 Supplies
7720 In-kind -other expenses
7810 Telephone
7910 Postage & shipping

8010 Rent
8020 Utilities
8030 Real estate taxes
8050 Mortgage interest
8110 Equipment rental & maintenance

Expenses -continued:

8210 Printing
8220 Publications
8310 Travel
8510 Conferences
8610 Interest – general
8710 Insurance
8810 Membership dues
8820 Staff development
9100 Bad debt expenses
9250 Advertising

9300 Other expenses

9420 Grants to other orgs
9430 Allocations to affiliated orgs
9440 Awards to individuals
9450 Specific assistance to individuals

9910 Payments to affiliates

Note: A more complete chart of accounts is available in Unified Chart of Accounts for non-profit organizations at *http://nccs.urban.org/projects/ucoa.cfm.*

Functional Cost Centers:

In addition to the line item accounts described in the Sample Table of Contents, many non-profits assign codes to indicate the function or purpose of all expenses. Some also use the same functional cost center codes to identify income sources associated with each function. Function cost centers typically include:

Programs:
    Program A
    Program B
    Program C

Management

Lobbying

Fund Raising

Funding Source Cost Center:

In addition to line item accounts and functional cost center codes, nonprofits receiving restricted contributions assign codes to income sources to indicate whether the source is unrestricted or restricted and if restricted, to identify the source of the restrictions. Many nonprofits also use these funding source cost center codes to identify the specific expense transactions which will be attributed to each restricted funding source. Typical fund source cost centers include:

Unrestricted

Temporarily Restricted
    Grant 1
    Grant 2
    Individual donor A
    Individual donor B

Permanently Restricted
    Endowment 1
    Endowment 2

Big Choices for Your Accounting System

Should You Use the Cash or the Accrual Method?

Your nonprofit will need to choose between two quite different methods of maintaining financial records. The Cash method involves recording transactions at the time when cash changes hands. At its most basic, the Cash method focuses on recording everything that happens in your bank accounts—deposits, checks, etc.

In contrast, the Accrual method of accounting focuses on recording income when it is earned and expenses when they are incurred, regardless of when payment is received or made. In the Accrual method, you record transactions that result in your organization owing money to an outside party. Similarly, you record transactions that result in your organization being owed money for goods or services by an outside party. These obligations to outside parties are "payables" and the amounts owed to your nonprofit are "receivables".

Exhibit 26-2 on the next page provides more comparison between the Cash and Accrual methods of accounting.

A good general rule is: it is better to have accurately maintained cash basis records than inaccurately maintained accrual basis records.

The Accrual method of accounting allows you to make a more accurate comparison of revenues and expenses. For example, if you are operating a child care center, you want to know whether the income the center earned this month is sufficient to cover the costs incurred to provide the child care. In the Cash method of accounting, you will only re- cord as income the payments you received during the month, and record as expenses, the payments you actually made this month. If some parents don't pay for the child care until the next month or if you were unable to pay some of the center's bills this month, your Cash basis financial records will not include this information. If you use the Accrual method of accounting, you will include this information and record Accounts Receivable (for the fees the parents owe at the end of the month) and Accounts Payable (for the bills you didn't pay during the month).

While the Accrual method produces a more complete picture of what has happened financially in your nonprofit, it also requires that the person doing the record keeping have some basic bookkeeping training. They will have to understand enough about formal accounting to be able to create journal entries to record transactions that don't involve your bank account. A good general rule is: it is better to have accurately maintained cash basis records than inaccurately maintained accrual basis records.

Exhibit 26-2 **Comparison of Cash and Accrual Accounting**

	CASH	**ACCRUAL**
What is it?	A system which records income only when it is ***received*** and expenses only when they are ***paid out***	A system which records income when it is *earned*, and expenses when the *obligation to pay arises*, regardless of when payment is made
An Example: Your program charges client fees and bills monthly	In a cash system, you record client fees only *when payments are received*	In an accrual system, you record client fee income *when you have given the service* for which the fee is charged, regardless of then payment comes.
Advantages	• Simple to record • Easy to understand • Requires only a little more training than maintaining a checkbook	• Provides a more accurate picture of where the program really stands — What you are owed — What you owe others — What it really costs you to provide services • Standard system which is easily understood by all trained consultants.
Disadvantages	• Can be misleading • Doesn't provide a systematic way to track what you are owed	• Need trained bookkeeper or individual able to spend time learning • Need training to understand what the statements mean • Takes more time

Note: A modified accrual system is used by many nonprofit organizations. When financial statements are prepared, a system is used to take into account what is owed by and owing to the organization.

One factor to consider as you evaluate Cash versus Accrual accounting: Generally Accepted Accounting Principles (GAAP), the standards which professional accountants use to determine how nonprofit financial information should be presented, call for nonprofits to use Accrual accounting. This doesn't mean you have to choose Accrual accounting for your nonprofit. It does mean that if your nonprofit is audited and doesn't choose to present its financial statements using the accrual method, your auditor will have to comment on the fact that your statements are not presented in accordance with GAAP. This may not matter to you or it may be a serious problem if you have entered into any funding agreements which require your nonprofit to use GAAP accounting.

Do You Need to Track Multiple Programs or Multiple Funding Sources?

If your nonprofit will operate multiple distinct programs, use multiple locations or receive multiple grants which require reporting about the specific use of the grant dollars, you will want to structure your Chart of Accounts to distinguish not only line-item character of your expenses (like salaries, supplies, etc.), but also the program or functional character. We discussed this concept of purpose or function in Chapter 24 on budgets. The chart on page 533 may help you visualize this concept.

The term "line-item" refers to the type of expense. Exhibit 26-2 provides a sample nonprofit Chart of Accounts which includes multiple "line items". For example, salaries, benefits, rent, and supplies are all typical line-item types of expenses. The term "program or functional character" refers to the purpose for which these expenses were incurred. For example, if your nonprofit operates both an preschool program and an after-school child care program, and you want to be able to understand how much each of these two programs costs to operate, you would structure your Chart of Accounts to create program or functional categories for "preschool" and "after-school child care." Of course, you would also have line item categories like salaries, benefits, rent, and supplies, but you would characterize each expense you recorded by both its line-item description (supplies) and its program description (preschool). As you will see in the next section, the IRS requires charities to use a version of this functional approach. Specifically, the IRS requires that you report what portion of each line-item expense was used for program, management and fundraising.

This same functional or program character distinction can be used to deal with the need to track the expenses which you paid for with restricted grant funds. Let's look at a really simple situation in which you had only one program—for example, you only had a preschool—but you needed to track the use of two different grant sources of funds. You could use the concept of "functional character" of expenses to create functional categories to track the two grants. This would mean that when you recorded an expense for sup- plies in the supplies line item, you would also use a functional character category to track which grant source you used to purchase these supplies.

While the examples we've used so far have dealt with expenses, you can use the same approach to deal with income items. First, you will need to decide on the line-item categories you will use to track income. Typically these will include: individual donations, foundations, government, program fees, etc. If you were interested in knowing which program or function each income transaction was intended to support, you could use the same approach we described above to record not only the line-item nature of a transaction (for example, program fees) but also the program or functional character (for example, program fees for preschool).

Some organizations want to track both the program character and the source of funding which is being used to meet each line-item expense. To do this, your Chart of Accounts will need to allow characterizing each income or expense transaction on three levels: line item (for example: supplies); program (for example: preschool); and funding source (for example: xyz foundation grant).

If you are considering setting up a two or three level Chart of Accounts, it may be helpful to read over the functional budgeting section in Chapter 24. If you have created a functional budget (p. 533), you will want to also use the functional approach in your accounting. This will require setting up a multi-level Chart of Accounts.

If you are receiving funds from sources which restrict how you can use them, and especially from sources which will require a line-item accounting of how you have used their funds, you will want to read the next sections carefully. You may decide that you really need to go beyond the basic approach to accounting described in this section to set up your system in full compliance with Generally Accepted Accounting Principles.

How Will You Meet IRS Reporting Requirements?

Form 990 requires nonprofits to distinguish three types of expenses: program, management, and fund raising. In order to complete Form 990, your nonprofit will have to be able to provide a line-item schedule which shows what portion of each line-item expense (like salaries, supplies, etc.) was spent on program, management, and fund raising costs. The instructions to Form 990 provide definitions for these terms.

Smaller nonprofits are often able to meet the requirements of the Form 990 by estimating the percentage of each line item expense which was used for program, management, and fund raising. But larger organizations may find that it is easier to do the type of functional tracking described above, characterizing expenses by function as well as by line-item. Using this approach requires that you structure your Chart of Accounts to distinguish "management" and "fund raising" costs as well as the costs of distinct "programs". To do this, you will need the two-level Chart of Accounts described above, with one level used to categorize line items and the second level used to distinguish "function" with categories for management, fund raising, and each of your distinct program. The discussion of functional budgets in Chapter 24 will help you understand the issues involved.

Do You Want or Need to Use Generally Accepted Accounting Principles (GAAP)?

Does your organization want to follow Generally Accepted Accounting Principles (GAAP)? GAAP refers to a set of standards and practices which professional accountants (CPAs) consider to be the preferred methods. Many funding source contracts contain a requirement that your accounting records be maintained in accord with GAAP. If you are audited, your CPA will express an opinion about whether your financial statements present the financial condition and activities of your nonprofit fairly in accordance with GAAP. If you have chosen methods of accounting which are not consistent with GAAP, your auditor will note that as part of the opinion letter. (See pages

KEEPING BOOKS AND PREPARING FINANCIAL REPORTS 26

642-45 for discussion of whether your nonprofit should have an audit). You may find that some or all of your board members feel that following GAAP accounting standards is an important part of your organization's credibility and accountability to donors.

> *You may find that some or all of your board members feel that following GAAP accounting standards is an important part of your organization's credibility and accountability to donors.*

If you decide that your nonprofit should set up its accounting and reporting systems to be follow GAAP, you will probably need to get some help from an experienced nonprofit accountant. Later on in this chapter, we'll highlight some of the major requirements contained in GAAP for nonprofits.

You can get more in-depth information GAAP for nonprofits in the Accounting Standards Codification (ASC) published online by the Financial Standards Accounting Board. The good news is that these standards are available for free online `To access the free version go to *https://asc.fasb.org/* and follow the steps to log in to the free Basic View. The bad news is that even people with substantial experience with business accounting and reporting frequently find some of GAAP standards for nonprofits perplexing. You may also want to consider purchasing the AICPA accounting guide for Not-for-Profit Entities available at *http://www.cpa2biz.com*.

If you decide to set up your accounting system in accord with GAAP, you will need create a structure in your Chart of Accounts to track a further set of distinctions beyond the ones we discussed above for line-items, functions, and sources. This additional set of categories or levels in your Chart of Accounts will allow you to characterize income items by whether your nonprofit has received the funds without restrictions from the donor (Unrestricted), with restrictions which will be met by your doing certain things or by the passage of time (Temporarily Restricted) or with permanent restrictions such as those that require that funds contributed as an Endowment must never be used and always invested in order to produce income to support your organization (Permanently Restricted).

You may want to read the rest of this chapter before you make these big choices for your approach to accounting. You will need to consider both the size and the complexity of your nonprofit's financial activities, both now and in the immediate future.

THE OREGON NONPROFIT CORPORATION HANDBOOK

Nonprofit Accounting Requires More Than Tracking Revenues and Expenses

One of the most common misunderstandings that non-accountants have about accounting and financial reporting is thinking that all that nonprofits need to do is to track revenues and expenses. This misunderstanding probably arises from all the effort nonprofits go through to develop an annual budget, which of course focuses on revenues and expenses.

Accurate accounting requires that your nonprofit maintain financial records about five types of accounts: Assets, Liabilities, Net Assets, Revenues and Expenses.

But accurate accounting requires that your nonprofit maintain financial records about five types of accounts: Assets, Liabilities, Net Assets, Revenues and Expenses. On a mechanical level, this means that your Chart of Accounts (See Exhibit 26-2) will need to include line-item categories in each of these five major sections. The previous section discussed some of the major choices you must make about tracking revenues and expenses. Now we need to talk about Assets, Liabilities, and Net Assets.

First, some definitions:

Assets: things of value that your nonprofit owns.

Examples: cash, equipment, buildings, land, and accounts receivable

Liabilities: obligations your nonprofit have to outside parties.

Examples: accounts payable, mortgages payable

Net Assets: the equivalent of net worth for nonprofits, computed by subtracting your total Liabilities from your total Assets. Nonprofits following GAAP will have three potential types of Net Assets: Unrestricted, Temporarily Restricted, and Permanently Restricted.

Your decision about Cash versus Accrual accounting will make a big difference in how you record your Assets and Liabilities. If you are using Accrual accounting, you will have Asset accounts like Accounts Receivable and Prepaid Expenses and Liabilities accounts like Taxes Payable and Accounts Payable. If you are using Cash accounting you will not have these receivable and payable

KEEPING BOOKS AND PREPARING FINANCIAL REPORTS 26

accounts. In fact, in Cash basis accounting you don't record any Liabilities except for Mortgages Payable on real property (it's an exception to the rule).

Double-Entry Accounting Is Essential

An important distinction between list making and accounting lies in the fact that sound accounting uses an approach called "double entry" to prevent and detect mistakes. While its very tempting to assume that when you create records using a computer it's not possible to make mistakes, in fact, human error does continue to plague us despite great technological advances.

Double-entry accounting is a system which has been used for centuries to create important cross-checks to the accuracy of financial records. It also provides a framework to think about the impact of financial events on your nonprofit. The principles of double-entry accounting are in use in all General Ledger accounting software. These important principles are often not in effect when people decide to use spreadsheets (like Excel or Quicken) to maintain their accounting records.

The term General Ledger describes a complete set of records of all types of transactions including those which impact the Assets, Liabilities, Net Assets, Revenues, and Expenses. Unless your nonprofit is extremely small—like an all-volunteer club—you will want to maintain a complete double-entry General Ledger. Computer software is readily available to maintain a complete General Ledger. We'll discuss selection of software later in this chapter. And even today, some very small nonprofits may still choose to maintain their general ledger manually.

Double entry accounting is essential in both the Cash and the Accrual methods of accounting.

In double-entry accounting, we recognize that every financial event has two impacts. For example, if we write a check for $50 to purchase supplies, we have increased our Supplies expense by $50 and reduced our Cash in Bank by $50. Similarly, if we deposit a contribution of $100 into our bank account, we have both increased Contribution income by $100 and increased our Cash in Bank by $100. The double impact is usually easy to see when cash is involved, and sometimes more difficult to understand when events (called "transactions") don't involve cash. For example, if we use the accrual method of accounting and provide a month of child care to a family with the agreement that they will pay us in the following month, we need to record both the fact that we earned Program Fee income of $400 and that we increased the amount of our Accounts Receivable by $400.

Double entry accounting is essential in both the Cash and the Accrual methods of accounting. Recording the double impact of each transaction allows you to check the accuracy of your work through use of a mathematical equation (debits = credits). This equation lies at the heart of bookkeeping training but lies outside the scope of this book. On a practical level, recording the double impact of each transaction ensures that we keep an accurate record of our Assets, Liabilities, and Net Assets as well as of our Revenues and Expenses.

Very Small Nonprofits: Basic Accounting and Reporting

Clubs, associations, and very small organizations (under $50,000 in annual expenses) will probably want to use a very simple approach to accounting and reporting. Unless they have trained accountants keeping the books, they will want to use the Cash basis of accounting. They will classify income and expenses by line-items (donations, fees, salaries, supplies, etc.) but may not try to track the functional character of their expenses.

Each month, these very small organizations will complete these steps:

1. Deposit all funds received into the nonprofit's bank account.

2. Make a record of each deposit which lists the source of each item and the category of income. For example: a check from a donor will be categorized as "donation" income.

3. Make a record of each check prepared, noting the date, the payee, the amount, and the purpose of the check. The purpose will tell you what category this check should be attributed to.

4. Record checks that are voided too. List the amount as zero and the payee as void. You want void checks in your records so that you can be sure that you have listed all checks in numerical order.

5. Reconcile your bank statement (see page 557).

6. Produce a simple financial report each month like the one shown in the Exhibit 26-3. Prepare reports for full calendar months, showing the last day of the month as the ending date for your report.

These steps may be completed in a manual system—writing checks by hand and using a check register available from office supply stores to record deposits, checks, and bank balances. Or, you could use a spreadsheet or a simple general ledger accounting program. If you will do your bookkeeping on a computer, be sure to read the section on selecting software.

Exhibit 26-3 on the next page is a sample financial report for a very small nonprofit organization. Importantly it includes information about the organization's bank balance at the beginning and end of the period being reported, as well as information about cash received and disbursed. It is extremely important that someone other than the person who prepares this report reconciles the

Exhibit 26-3

Small Nonprofit Financial Report
for the month ending **September 30, 2005**
and the year-to-date July 1, 2005- September 30, 2005

	Current month Sept. 05	Year to Date 7/1/05-9/30/05	Annual Budget	Yr-to-date % of budget
Cash Received				
Individual donations	500	2,000	10,000	0.20
Jones Foundation grant	0	3,000	15,000	0.20
Program Fees	800	3,000	4,000	0.75
Total Cash Received	1,300	8,000	29,000	0.28
Cash Disbursed				
Salaries	1,000	3,000	16,000	0.19
Employer taxes	150	300	1,600	0.19
Contract services	300	1,000	6,000	0.17
Supplies	100	300	500	0.60
Telephone	40	120	480	0.25
Other expenses	50	100	500	0.20
	1,640	4,820	25,080	0.19
Increase (decrease) in cash	-340	3,180	3,920	0.81
Cash at beginning of month (9/1/05)	6,520			
Cash at end of month (9/30/05)	6,180			
Cash at beginning of year (7/1/05)		3,000	3,000	
Cash at end of year to date (9/30/05)		6,180	6,920	0.89

organization's bank account and makes certain that the info on the report is supported by the bank's records.

Dealing with Carry-over Funds

Many nonprofits plan to use funds accumulated in one year to meet costs for operating in a subsequent year. It's similar to a family that saves up money in one year to take care of purchases in the next year. But figuring out how to show this plan, and the actual use of the funds from the prior year can been challenging.

While using funds received in a prior year is a source of cash to meet current expenses, it is not a source of income from an accounting viewpoint. A basic accounting rule is that you can't count the same income twice. So just like a family would understand that they shouldn't include the use of their savings as a source of income on their tax return, a nonprofit will not want to show the use of its savings(carry-over funds) in its reports of income for the current year.

Probably the best way to handle this situation is to add a line to your budget called "planned use of funds received in prior years". Place this category at the very bottom of your budget, after showing all the income and expense categories and the net income that is projected when you subtract the expenses projected for the year from the projected new income for the year. This will make it possible to compare your plan for the use of prior year funds with the net income that results when you subtract the actual expenses you record during the year from the new income your record during the year. This will help everyone understand your plan to use funds from the prior year and to evaluate whether you have followed that plan.

How is Nonprofit Accounting Different from Business Accounting?

Once your nonprofit moves beyond the "very small" category, you'll probably need to know a bit more about Generally Accepted Accounting Principles (GAAP) for nonprofits. Even if you don't plan to follow all the rules of GAAP, your funders and the IRS will be expecting you to use some of the major concepts and will wonder if you really know how to manage your finances if you don't.

GAAP consists of a series of pronouncements contained in the Accounting Standards Codification published by Financial Standards Accounting Board (FASB). In addition to GAAP standards, nonprofits also have to pay attention to requirements of the Internal Revenue Service and, if they receive federal funds, to requirements for managing federal funds originally included in a variety of circulars published by the Office of Management and Budget (OMB) and now included in the Code of Federal Regulations along with requirements for specific federal programs. Details for finding the appropriate regulations are included in Appendix 1.

> *Once your nonprofit moves beyond the "very small" category, you'll probably need to know a bit more about Generally Accepted Accounting Principles (GAAP) for nonprofits.*

We'll discuss IRS and OMB issues later in this chapter. For now, we'll be discussing some major tenets in nonprofit accounting found in the Accounting Standards Codification (ASC). Check Appendix 1 for specific references to ASC sections relating to each topic.

The Financial Standards Accounting Board (FASB) really shook up the world of nonprofit accounting back in the mid-1990s by issuing dramatically new guidelines for nonprofit accounting and reporting. FASB was responding to concerns that many readers of nonprofit financial statements had a hard time understanding what, if any, restrictions had been placed on funds given to nonprofits and whether or not nonprofits had fulfilled those restrictions.

As a result, some of the ways nonprofits do accounting are fairly different from the ways that business entities do their accounting. This can puzzle nonprofit board members and require that even highly skilled business accountants get some additional training in order to meet the nonprofit standards.

KEEPING BOOKS AND PREPARING FINANCIAL REPORTS 26

In the next sections we'll explores of some of the key requirements for nonprofit accounting, including:

- Classification of Contributions
- Distinguishing Contributions from Purchases of Services or Goods
- Fulfilling Restrictions
- Unrestricted Expenses
- Three Classes of Net Assets
- Board Directions are Designations, not Restrictions
- Recording Promises to Give
- Multi-year Grant Commitments
- Program Fees Received in Advance
- Government Grants and Contracts
- Cost Allocation
- Accounting for Fundraising Costs
- Accounting for In-Kind Contributions
- Accounting for Land, Building, and Equipment

Classification of Contributions

To comply with GAAP, nonprofits must classify any contributions they receive as either unrestricted, temporarily restricted, or permanently restricted. The donor's direction is the determining factor in how the gift is classified. Donors are considered to have made a restricted gift if they state requirements for the use of the funds (purpose restriction) or the timing of the use of the funds (time restriction). If the donor does not state any restrictions, the contribution is considered to be unrestricted whether or not the nonprofit organization makes any specific plans for its use.

Contributions to endowments are the most common type of permanently restricted gift. They are considered *permanently restricted* if the terms of the gift require that the gift be permanently invested to generate income for the organization. Most other donor restrictions are temporary, meaning that the nonprofit will eventually fulfill the restriction by either carrying out the activities for which the gift was given or by operating during the time period specified for the use of the gift.

The sample financial statements at the end of this chapter illustrate several different ways to display the classification of contributions as unrestricted, temporarily restricted or permanently restricted on the Statement of Activities.

Distinguishing Contributions from Purchases of Services or Goods

Nonprofits must determine whether funds that they receive are being provided as contributions or as payments for services or goods which the nonprofit provides. In general, funds are considered contributions when the donor receives no significant benefit in return for making the gift. In contrast, funds received in exchange for the provision of services or goods are considered fees or sales.

Here's an example. If a parent pays a fee for child care provided for their child at a nonprofit child care center, the amount is considered fee income and the nature of the relationship between the child care center and the parent is considered to be an exchange transaction. In contrast, if an individual makes a gift to that child care center to help it achieve its mission but does not receive child care or any other service in return, the income is considered to be a contribution and the nature of the transaction is a gift relationship.

The distinction between contributions and exchange transactions is important in guiding the ways that the nonprofit will record the event, especially if the exchange payment is received before the service is provided or the contribution is provided before the nonprofit carries out the activities which the contribution is intended to support. In GAAP accounting, exchange transactions are always classified as unrestricted while contributions may be unrestricted, temporarily restricted, or permanently restricted. The distinction between contributions and exchange transactions is also important for completing the Form 990.

Three Classes of Net Assets

First recall that Net Assets represent the net worth of the nonprofit. If you subtract your nonprofit's total liabilities from your total assets, you will have computed your nonprofit's net assets or net worth.

GAAP requires that nonprofits break their total Net Assets down into three categories—Unrestricted Net Assets, Temporarily Restricted Net Assets, and Permanently Restricted Net Assets. The purpose of this breakdown is to let readers of the financial statements know which of the nonprofit's Net Assets the Board has freedom to use as it pleases (Unrestricted Net Assets) and which of the Net Assets can be used only for purposes specified by donors or at time periods specified by donors (Temporarily Restricted Net Assets), and which Net Assets may never be used (Permanently Restricted Net Assets).

Your nonprofit will strive to build its Unrestricted Net Assets in order to have something to fall back on in years in which it is difficult to raise funds or in which unexpected expenses occur. If your organization receives grants, you will also want to build up your Temporarily Restricted Net Assets in order to be sure you have funding to available to launch each new year's activities

Board Directions Are Designations, Not Restrictions

While Boards may talk about setting aside certain funds for specific purposes or may even pass resolutions directing that specific funds should be treated as endowments, under GAAP rules, these amounts are considered to be board designations and not treated as either temporary or permanent restrictions. This treatment reflects the fact that unlike the situation when a donor makes a gift with restrictions, Boards have the right to change their minds about the use of funds which they have previously designated for specific purposes.

Board designated funds are considered to be part of the nonprofit's Unrestricted Net Assets. In order to make it clear that your Board has designated funds for a specific purpose, you'll want to create a separate line item within the Unrestricted Net Assets category—for example, Board Designated Funds for Scholarships. This Board Designated line item will be included in your total Unrestricted Net Assets, but breaking it out as a separate line item reminds the Board and readers of the financial statements of the Board's direction.

Fulfilling Restrictions

When the nonprofit carries out activities or incurs costs that fulfill a purpose restriction or enters the time period specified in a time restriction, it records the fulfillment of the restrictions by releasing amounts previously classified as Temporarily Restricted into the Unrestricted Class. You can see an example of the recording of this release in the Statement of Activities on Exhibits 26-5 on page 600. (Note that to keep things simple, Exhibit 26-5 involves only Unrestricted and Temporarily Restricted funds—the organization depicted doesn't have Permanently Restricted funds). The release from restrictions is shown as a line item at the bottom of the list of income line-items. You'll notice that the release is shown in brackets in the column headed Temporarily Restricted and as a positive number in the column headed Unrestricted. This means this amount has been taken out of the Temporarily Restricted classification (released) and added into the Unrestricted classification.

A nonprofit's Unrestricted Net Assets increase when its Unrestricted Income exceeds its Unrestricted Expenses and decrease when its Unrestricted Expenses exceed its Unrestricted Income. Temporarily Restricted Net Assets increase when a nonprofit receives Temporarily Restricted Contributions and decrease when it releases amounts from restrictions by fulfilling the purposes or the time restrictions required by the donor.

Unrestricted Expenses

One of the most puzzling components of GAAP for nonprofits is the use of the words unrestricted and restricted in describing expenses. Nonprofits are required to pay close attention to the restrictions that donors attach to their contributions. We are required to classify all contributions as either unrestricted, temporarily restricted or permanently restricted. When we meet the donors' restrictions for the use of their gifts, we record an entry to note the release from restrictions. So with all this attention to recording restrictions and documenting our compliance with them, it may seem very surprising that formal nonprofit financial statements label all of the expenses as *unrestricted*.

The GAAP view on this subject is that since the act of incurring the expense fulfills the restriction, the expense itself should be considered unrestricted.

It will probably help to know that nonprofits regardless of this GAAP presentation approach, nonprofits are still diligent in tracking the expenses paid with restricted funds. Nonprofits that have multiple restricted sources of funds set up their Chart of Accounts to track line item expenses by the source of funds used to pay for them as well as by the functional character of the expense (management, fund raising, program) and by line item. Using this three level system (line item, function, and source), they have a detailed record of exactly which expenses are considered to be met by each restricted funding source. These detailed records of the expenses that qualify to meet each funding source's restrictions are the basis for the entry to record the release from restrictions.

Many funding sources will refer to the expenses met through use of restricted funds as restricted expenses. But when nonprofits prepare the highly summarized Statement of Activities following GAAP, they list all the expense line-items as Unrestricted Expenses. But remember, in order to maintain the records needed to document your compliance with funder restrictions, your accounting system will need to track the use of restricted funds. You may need help from a skilled nonprofit accountant to be sure your system will meet this test.

Recording Promises to Give

When donors make promises to give contributions in future years, GAAP requires the nonprofit to record the promised amount as a Temporarily Restricted contribution on the date the promise is made, and as a Pledge Receivable. It is considered a time restriction that will be fulfilled when the donor honors the pledge and actually transfers the funds to the nonprofit. When the donor sends in a payment on this pledged contribution, the nonprofit reduces Pledge Receivable and releases the amount of the payment from the time restriction. If the donor's pledge did not contain any purpose restrictions, fulfillment of the time restriction will be recorded as a release from the Temporarily Restricted category into the Unrestricted income category. If the donor imposed a purpose restriction when they made the pledge, receipt of the payment on the pledge will result in fulfillment of the time restriction, but you will need to wait to release the funds from the Temporarily Restricted class until you have fulfilled the purpose restriction. If your organization is planning a capital campaign or using multi-year pledges as part of your fund raising, be sure to check out the detailed requirements for recording pledges, including adjusting amounts to reflect the net present value.

One catch on recording promises to give. You'll use the treatment above only if the promise is unconditional, meaning the donor is not conditioning fulfilling the pledge based on circumstances or conditions that lie outside the direct control of the nonprofit. For example, a donor who promises to give $1 million if he wins the lottery has set a condition over which the nonprofit has no control and which is quite unlikely to occur. When a pledge is conditional, the nonprofit does not record it as either income or as a receivable. In order to meet the test to be recorded as a Temporarily Restricted gift, the pledge must have a reasonable likelihood of being fulfilled.

Multi-year Grant Commitments

GAAP also requires nonprofits receiving multi-year grant commitments to record the entire grant commitment as temporarily restricted grant income in the year the commitment is received. This means that even if your nonprofit doesn't receive any payments in the year in which you receive the award letter, you will still record the whole multi-year committed amount as Temporarily Restricted Grant Income and Grants Receivable. As you collect payments from the funder over the life of the grant, you will reduce Grants Receivable.

You will determine when you may record a Release from Temporary Restrictions for a portion of the multi-year grant based on two criteria. First, you must have entered the time period for which the grantor has awarded the funds, and secondly, you must also have either completed the activities for which funding was supplied or incurred the expenses that the funder had approved as valid uses for the grant funds.

This treatment can be confusing to the readers of your financial statements. In the year in which you receive the multi-year award, it will appear that your nonprofit has operated with a large surplus. In other words, your total income (Unrestricted and Temporarily Restricted) will be much larger than your total expenses, because your income will include funds awarded for future periods.

In the following years, your financial statements may appear to show that you have been operating at a loss, because you will incur the expenses the grant was intended to cover, but you will not be recording an additional grant income because you recorded the entire amount in the year you received the award.

Readers who understand GAAP will recognize that the release of Temporarily Restricted funds is providing support to meet your expenses and that actually you are operating your nonprofit on a sound basis. But you may need to educate both your Board and potential funders to prepare them to understand your financial reports.

Program Fees Received in Advance

After all this discussion about restricted contributions, we need to return to thinking about program service fees. Fees for goods or services are considered Unrestricted. If your participants pay as they go for your services, the accounting will be quite simple. If you extend credit, allowing your participants to pay after they receive goods and services, you will probably want to use the accrual basis of accounting and record Accounts Receivable as well as program service fee income.

On the other hand, if participants pay you in advance of receiving services, you will need to create an account called Deferred Revenue (or Fees Received in Advance) in the liabilities section of your Chart of Accounts. You will record the whole amount of the advance payment in this Deferred Revenue account (recording no part of the amount as income at the time your receive the payment). Then each month as you provide the services for which you have been paid in advance, you will reduce the Deferred Revenue account and increase your Program Fee income account. When you have provided all the services for which you were paid in advance, your Deferred Revenue account will have a zero balance and your Program Fee income account will include the whole amount paid.

Using Deferred Revenue to Track Grant Income

Some nonprofits will use the same Deferred Revenue method described above for exchange transactions to record grants received in advance. This approach is not consistent with GAAP. In this approach, you would record the amount of a check you receive from for a restricted grant as Deferred Revenue, a liability on your Balance Sheet. Then as you incur costs that meet the funder's restrictions, you would record a journal entry to reduce the Deferred Revenue and increase Grant income. When you had used all of the funds for the purposes the funder permitted, you would have a zero balance in the Deferred Revenue account, and the whole amount of the grant would be reported in the Grant income account.

While this would not be GAAP accounting, it could work quite well as a way to keep clear about what portion of each grant remains available for your use. But, if your audited financial statements will be presented in accordance with GAAP, using this Deferred Revenue method to handle grants may result in some significant audit adjustments. This means that you and your Board may have relied on financial statements during the year that report a significantly different net income than what you will see on your audited statements.

Government Grants and Contracts

If your nonprofit receives government funding, you will face a choice about how to record the income. Sometimes government grants and contracts should be considered as contributions. In other situations, government grants and contracts should be considered as exchange transactions and treated like program service fee income. How can you tell the difference?

If a government is paying your nonprofit to provide services to the government itself, you will record the income as an exchange transaction like program fees. This would be true if your nonprofit provided training for government employees and received payment from the government for providing the training. In exchange relationships, your agreement with the government will probably identity your nonprofit as *vendor*.

If the government is purchasing your services for specific groups of people but not for the government itself, it may be harder to determine whether this is an exchange transaction or a contribution. Health care providers receiving Medicare payments are definitely involved in exchange transactions. But Head Start grantees receiving a grant to operate a program for children who meet certain eligibility requirements are probably receiving a grant which will be treated like a contribution.

You can start sorting out the correct treatment of governmental dollars by talking with the funding source and reading your funding agreement. If the funds originated with the federal government you will probably see references in your contract which characterize the relationship as either a "sub-recipient" relationship which will generally mean you should treat the grant as contributed income, or as a "vendor" relationship which will mean you should treat the relationship as a purchase of service or exchange transaction.

One further complication in accounting for government grants arises when the agreement requires that your nonprofit incur the costs to deliver the services and then submit a request for reimbursement. Frequently such agreements involve awards that are clearly restricted to specific purposes. But, the reality that you will only receive reimbursement for costs actually incurred results in the government award being treated as "unrestricted" for GAAP accounting purposes. This reflects the fact that you will have already fulfilled the restrictions before you ever get the payment from government. Of course, you will still need to observe the restrictions contained in the grant agreement as you operate the program and use the funds.

If your nonprofit is audited, you'll want to discuss these issues with your auditor who will help you determine how it to present your government awards on your financial statements.

Cost Allocation

Nonprofit organizations that need to track the use of restricted funds and/or to distinguish expenses by function (management, fund raising, programs) will frequently need to allocate certain costs. We discussed the concept of cost allocation in Chapter 24. If your organization has prepared its budget using cost allocation techniques, you will want to do your accounting using those same techniques. If so, you will want to prepare a written cost allocation plan each year to document how you will allocate costs which cannot be directly attributed to specific funding source or functional cost centers.

Once you have created a cost allocation plan, be sure to follow it. If your organization is audited, your auditor will test whether the allocations you record are consistent with your cost allocation plan. If you obtain new grants and contracts during your fiscal year or experience major cut-backs or shifts in programs, you may need to revise your cost allocation plan to reflect the reality of how costs are actually incurring in your organization.

Most government funding agreements will require preparation of a written cost allocation plan to document the basis for attributing costs to their grant or contract. Larger nonprofits which receive substantial support through federal awards and contracts may choose to negotiate an indirect cost rate with the federal government. Federally negotiated indirect cost rates lie outside the scope of this book, but you can learn more federal rules for cost allocation and negotiation of indirect cost rates in OMB Circular A-122 Appendix A. at *http://ecfr.gpoaccess.gov*.

Accounting for Fundraising Costs

Charities are under enormous pressure to minimize the costs they attribute to fundraising. Numerous charity rating efforts have emphasized that "high" fundraising costs are a sign that a charity is either not legitimate or poorly managed. While this is true in a limited number of abusive organizations, it is also true that, just as in business, it costs money to make money. Substantial investment is often required in order to identify, cultivate, and mobilize donors to support important charities.

The IRS requires charities to report their expenses for fund raising on a line-item basis. The details of these requirements are discussed in Chapter 12 that deals with the Form 990.

GAAP accounting for nonprofits imposes more specific, and in some cases, confusing requirements for recording fundraising costs. If your nonprofit is audited, your auditor is expected to determine whether you have met GAAP standards for recording fundraising costs. Even if you are not audited, you will have to meet the IRS requirements and your fundraising expenses will be open to public scrutiny as part of the requirement to make your 990 available for public inspection.

Both the IRS and GAAP agree that the cost of making unsolicited requests for contributions are fundraising costs. This includes costs like printing, postage, and staff time to prepare direct mail appeals for contributions. It also includes the cost of renting a hall, paying for food, and paying an auctioneer for a fund raising auction. Recording these direct costs of fund raising should be pretty straightforward if you have set up your chart of accounts to include a functional level and established a functional cost center for fund raising.

GAAP has specific rules for dealing with costs for expenses that combine a fundraising purpose with a program or management purpose, including items like newsletters that include program information while also appealing for contributions. FASB ASC 958-720-45-28 through 55 describes the GAAP rules for determining whether such joint costs may be allocated between fund raising and the other purpose or must be attributed totally to fundraising even though another purpose is also addressed.

Under the GAAP rules, to determine whether you must attribute the entire cost of a joint effort to fund raising, you must apply three tests regarding the purpose of the communication, the audience it is sent to, and content of the communication. If any of the tests are failed, the entire cost of the activity is considered fundraising expense. If all three of the tests are met, you may allocate a portion of the costs to fundraising and the remaining costs to program or administration.

If your nonprofit does a significant amount of fundraising you will want to review ASC 958-720 and be certain that your fund development staff are aware of its requirements and communicate clearly with your accountant.

Accounting for In-Kind Contributions

"In-kind" is a term used to describe what happens when a donor contributes goods or services rather than contributing cash. GAAP requires that nonprofits report certain types of in-kind contributions on their financial statements. Even if this weren't a GAAP requirement, many nonprofits would want to record in-kind contributions in order to show the true extent of the support they receive from their communities. They would also want to record the value of the in-kind goods or services in their expenses to demonstrate what it would cost to operate their services if they didn't have in-kind help.

GAAP divides in-kind contributions into two basic categories. In-kind contributions that provide goods or services that are essential to the operation of the nonprofit and are provided by an individual with a recognized skill or credential should be recorded in the financial records as in-kind income and in-kind expense. In-kind contributions that are not essential to the operations or are provided by a volunteer without a recognized skill or credential may be disclosed in notes to the financial statements, but are not recorded as in-kind income or in-kind expense on the financial statements.

Even when GAAP will not permit recording the value of an in-kind gift in your accounting records, you will want to keep a record of it and tally up the value of all such contributions and acknowledge them in a note to your formal financial statements or when you are describing support for your program in annual reports and proposals. Some grant funding requires that the recipient organization demonstrate community support by tracking both types of in-kind contributions.

The definition of a recognized skill or credential can be challenging. Any service provided by a person who must be licensed to do the service will qualify—for example doctors, nurses, plumbers, electricians, etc. What about office skills like reception or data entry? Some accountants would say that if the volunteer has sufficient skill in these areas to be hired for paid work requiring training or experience, the requirement is met. Others prefer a more narrow definition and look for advanced degrees or certifications as evidence. This can be a good subject to discuss with your auditor.

Board members' contribution of their time to carry out board responsibilities cannot be recorded as an in-kind contribution on the financial statements according to GAAP. Similarly, GAAP excludes the value of volunteer time spent on fund raising, whether the volunteers are board members or non-board members.

In most cases, you will be able to record in-kind contribution income and in-kind expenses at exactly the same amount and the recording of in-kind will not impact your net income (i.e. both income and expenses will have been increased by the same amount, resulting in zero net income). One important exception to this occurs when you receive an in-kind contribution of equipment or land and buildings. These items are considered assets, so you will record their fair market value at the date you receive them in asset accounts which will appear on your Statement of Financial Position (Balance Sheet). However, you will also record the fair market value of these items as in-kind contribution income. The result will be an apparent profit caused by adding the in-kind contribution to your income but not offsetting it with an expense (since the value of the items was recorded as an asset).

How do you know the value of in-kind services or labor? Determine what the "going rate" for the same type of labor or services is. For example, if a trained accountant volunteers to do your accounting, value this contribution at the price an accountant with similar training and skills would charge to do similar work for another organization. To determine the value of in-kind labor used to make improvements to real property (for example putting a new roof on your building), determine the difference in the fair market value of the property before and after the work is done.

Gains and Losses on Investments

GAAP requires that nonprofits, like for-profits, report the fair market value of their investments. Investments in mutual funds or other stocks and bonds are recorded as assets when they are originally purchased or received as contributions. You will record any interest or dividends you receive as income. If you sell your investments, you will record the gain or loss on investments that results from the sale. The gain or loss is computed by subtracting your basis (what you paid for the stock or its value when you received it by donation) from the sales price after sales expenses. These gains and losses are referred to as Realized Gains or Losses on Investments.

GAAP requires that nonprofits also record Unrealized Gains or Losses on Investments. Remember that every transaction always has two impacts in your double-entry accounting system. The recording of Unrealized Gains and Losses will impact both your revenue account Unrealized Gains and Losses on Investments and your asset account Investments on your Balance Sheet. To determine the Unrealized Gains and Losses on Investments, you'll compare the published stock price at the date of your financial statements to your basis in the stock.

Accounting for Land, Building, and Equipment

Land, buildings, and equipment are assets. If your nonprofit purchases them, you will record the purchases in the assets section, not in the expense section of your Chart of Accounts. Your investment in land, building and equipment will be displayed on your Statement of Financial Position (Balance Sheet) in the assets section. These items are referred to as "fixed assets" or "capital assets".

While this sounds simple enough, there are several additional steps used in accrual accounting which can be confusing to non-accountants. If you purchase buildings and equipment you will also need to set up an asset account called "accumulated depreciation" and an expense account called "depreciation expense". Each year, you will record a portion of what you paid for the buildings or equipment as an entry to depreciation expense and accumulated depreciation. This is another example of double-entry accounting discussed earlier in this chapter.

Most nonprofits determine what portion of the cost of buildings and equipment will be used to compute the annual depreciation expense by establishing standard "lives" for the fixed assets. Typically, vehicles, computers, and other equipment will be given a standard life of 5 years and buildings will be given a standard life of 25 or 30 years. You will want to be sure that the standard life you assign a fixed asset is at least as long as any debt which uses the asset as collateral. You determine the amount of the annual entry to depreciation expense and accumulated depreciation by dividing the purchase price of the asset by the number of years in the standard life. For example, if you purchased a used van for $10,000 and your policies called for a standard life of 5 years for vehicles, you would divide $10,000 by 5 years to determine that the annual entry to depreciation expense and accumulated depreciation would be $2,000.

The accumulated depreciation account is often referred to as a contra-asset. This means it goes against (contra) or offsets/reduces the value of an asset account. It will be shown in brackets (meaning it has a credit balance for readers who are familiar with debits and credits in accounting). Any time you see a number in brackets on financial statements, you know that it is a negative number which must be subtracted when totaling a column of numbers.

Let's return to the van example to illustrate how this works. When you purchased the van you recorded it in the asset account called "equipment" for $10,000. At the end of the first year, you created an entry to record $2,000 into the depreciation expense category and balanced it with $2,000 in the accumulated depreciation account. When you produce your year-end Statement of Financial Position (Balance Sheet), you will see the $10,000 amount in the equipment line of the assets section, and right below it you will see the ($2,000) in the accumulated depreciation line item. You will subtract the accumulated depreciation amount from the equipment line to compute the net book value of the van at $8,000.

Quite likely this net book value of $8,000 will not be the same thing as the fair market value of the van. Fair market value is a term used to describe the price at which a willing buyer will purchase an item from a willing seller. This illustrates a key concept. In accounting, you are recording fixed assets at their historical cost (what you paid to purchase them) and then accumulating depreciation (through the posting of the annual depreciation entry described above). You are not trying to present the fixed asset at its fair market value.

Following the example of the van a bit further, you will post a depreciation expense/accumulated depreciation entry each year for five years (the standard life of the vehicle). At that point, your accumulated depreciation account balance will be ($10,000) and the vehicle will be said to be fully depreciated. This means that the net book value (what you get when you subtract accumulated depreciation from the initial purchase price of the van) will be zero. Since the van is fully depreciated, you won't make any more entries to depreciation expense/accumulated depreciation for it in subsequent years. You will continue to include the investment in the van and the related accumulated depreciation amount in the asset section of your financial statements to let readers know that you own a vehicle.

The basic accounting process described above for dealing with fixed assets is the same for businesses as for nonprofits, so board members or others familiar with business accounting will be able to help you understand it. One key difference between nonprofit and business accounting is that businesses typically use more complex methods to determine what portion of their investment in fixed assets will be recorded as depreciation each year. This is because businesses are permitted to consider depreciation expense as a tax deductible item and they will reduce their taxable income by claiming their deductions for depreciation expense as quickly as possible.

Some business-oriented board members will question why tax-exempt nonprofits should bother with recording depreciation since they do not need to generate deductible expenses for tax purposes. A short answer might be, GAAP requires nonprofits to record depreciation. But a more meaningful reason is that by recording a portion of what your nonprofit has invested in a fixed asset as depreciation expense each year, you are taking into account what it is really costing you to run your nonprofit.

Taking the van example a bit further to illustrate this point, let's assume that your nonprofit uses the van to transport children as part of your program. You have made a choice to purchase a van rather than lease it. If you had leased the van, the cost of the lease would clearly be an expense of your program. Once you decided to purchase the van, you had a further choice. If you decided to follow standard accounting practices, you recorded the purchase of the van in an equipment account in the assets section of your chart of accounts. You didn't record the whole $10,000 purchase as an expense in the year you bought it. If you have determined that you will get at least 5 years use out of the van, the process of recording an annual depreciation expense/accumulated depreciation entry will allow you to consider 1/5 of the cost of the van as an expense each year. This approach lets you spread the cost of the van over the 5 year period in which you will benefit from having the van.

If you chose not to follow standard accounting practices, you would have recorded the whole $10,000 purchase price as an expense in the year in which you bought the van. This is probably the treatment most cash basis organizations would use. It has the advantage of having expenses mirror the use of your cash, and of simplicity (you wouldn't have to create the annual entry to depreciation expense and accumulated depreciation). But, this approach will mean that after the first year in which you purchase the van, there will be no record on your financial statements that you own a van. It will not appear as an asset because you already recorded it as an expense in the year you purchased it.

While this might be a reasonable choice for handling a van purchase, it would not be reasonable to use this approach if you bought a building. Even in cash basis accounting, the purchase of a building is recorded and reported as an asset. And, if the nonprofit takes out a mortgage in order to purchase the building, the mortgage debt is recorded as a liability even in cash basis accounting.

The purchase of land is also considered the purchase of an asset, not an expense. But, land cannot be depreciated. So if you purchase a building and the land under it, you will have to determine what portion of the purchase price should be attributed to the building and what portion to the land. Then compute the annual depreciation expense/ accumulated depreciation expense as a portion of the building purchase cost, not of the land purchase cost.

> *Nonprofits record receipt of donated assets as in-kind contribution income and an increase to fixed assets.*

What about donated equipment, land and buildings? As noted above in the discussion of in-kind contributions, nonprofits record receipt of donated assets as in-kind contribution income and an increase to fixed assets. You will need to determine the fair market value of the asset you receive at the time you receive it. Donors of valuable fixed assets will generally obtain an independent appraisal of the value of the item to document the value of their contribution for tax purposes. You can use that appraisal as the basis for recording the fair market value of the asset or you can obtain your own independent appraisal. For smaller items, it is probably useful to think of fair market value as garage sale prices.

Government Funds Accounting Requirements

If your nonprofit will receive funds from federal, state, or local government entities, you need to become familiar with accounting and financial management requirements that are referenced in your grant or contract agreement. The federal Office of Management and Budget (OMB) publishes circulars which detail the requirements for recipients of federal dollars.

KEEPING BOOKS AND PREPARING FINANCIAL REPORTS 26

Unfortunately, it's not always easy to determine whether the dollars you receive through government grants/contracts are federal. Anytime you accept government funding, you will need to find out whether it is federal in origin. In other words, did the funds your local or state government is giving your nonprofit come from a federal source? It may be helpful to think of federal funds as being like a sexually transmitted disease. You must always know where your money has been before it comes to your nonprofit.

If you will be receiving federal dollars you will want to obtain OMB Circulars A-110, A-122, and A-133. You can download them for free from the OMB website at *www.white- house.gov/omb/circulars*. Circulars A-110 and A-122 are now also included in the Code of Federal Regulations as 2 CFR 215 and 230 respectively. These circulars explain what types of costs are allowable and unallowable uses of federal funds; what type of records you must maintain; and how you must allocate costs. Chapter 24 of this book provides some basic guidance on cost allocation that may help you understand the circulars. Chapter 25 provides help in establishing financial controls like those required by the circulars.

Whatever Happened to Fund Accounting?

Some readers may be wondering about *fund accounting*. This approach to accounting which is similar to methods used in governmental entities was used widely in nonprofits before the big change in nonprofit GAAP in the mid-1990s.

Some nonprofits continue to use many of the tools of fund accounting. This is especially important for organizations which receive funding directly from the federal government. Tracking the receipt and use of federal cash is a key requirement for direct recipients of federal funds. Federal rules limit the amount of time a recipient organization can keep federal cash on hand without disbursing it. In order to meet such requirements, a nonprofit has to be able to characterize its cash as federal or non-federal.

In fund accounting, the organization maintains a complete set of accounts (assets, liabilities, fund balances/net assets, revenues and expenses) for each of several different types of funds—typically an unrestricted fund, one or more restricted funds, a capital or property, plant and equipment fund, and an endowment fund. While these distinctions among types of funds are somewhat similar to the distinctions we now make between classes of Net Assets (Unrestricted, Temporarily Restricted, and Permanently Restricted), fund accounting differs from the approaches we've been discussing in this chapter by requiring that Assets and Liabilities as well as Net Assets (then called Fund Balances) be tracked for each distinct fund.

Nonprofits that receive restricted grants will need to structure their Charts of Accounts to distinguish the source of funds used to support specific expenses. However, systems to do this type of tracking typically focus on revenues and expenses only rather than on creating total separate self-balancing sets of Assets, Liabilities, Net Assets, Revenues, and Expenses which is the defining characteristic of fund accounting. Nonprofits that are required to distinguish assets and liabilities as well as net assets by fund typically purchase nonprofit specific accounting software. See the discussion of software selection issues at the end of this chapter for more information on these products.

Financial Statements

Your nonprofit needs monthly financial statements to understand your financial condition and determine whether the plans and strategies you included in your annual budget are working. By convention, financial statements report on complete calendar months. For example, you will prepare financial statements to report on all of the revenues and expenses incurred from June 1 through June 30th, not on revenues and expenses from May 14th to June 14th or any other period than a calendar month.

It is frustrating but true that nonprofit organizations use many different terms to describe reports which contain essentially the same information. We will be discussing four important types of monthly financial reports and explaining the various names which these reports may be called by various nonprofits. Each of the four has a distinct purpose and two of the four are absolute "must haves" for any nonprofit organization. We'll start by using the names which are recommended by Generally Accepted Accounting Principles (GAAP).

Statement of Financial Position

The Statement of Financial Position in Exhibit 26-4 on the next page presents the Assets, Liabilities, and Net Assets at a specific point in time or compares them at two points in time (for example: September 30, 2011 and June 30, 2011). This report is frequently called the Balance Sheet.

Statement of Activities

The Statement of Activities is also called a Profit and Loss Statement, an Income Statement, a Statement of Revenues and Expenses, or unfortunately misnamed a Budget Report. Referring to the Statement of Activities as the Budget Report may lead to confusion about the distinction between accounting and financial reporting and budgets. Budgets are plans for the future. Accounting records what actually happens. Financial statements present information about what has actually happened which is taken from the accounting records. Of course, many financial statements report what has actually happened (Revenues and Expenses) in comparison to the budget plan.

We've included two sample formats for the Statement of Activities in Exhibits 26-5 and 26-6. Both versions presents Revenues and Expenses and Changes in Net Assets (Net Income) for the first quarter of the organization's fiscal year, from July 1, 2011 through September 30, 2011. Either of these formats may be used to present a monthly report or a report that presents both the most recently completed month and the year to date. We'll discuss the differences between the formats and pros and cons for using them in the Tips for Useful Financial Reports section later in this chapter.

Exhibit 26-4

All Good Things
Statement of Financial Position
September 30, 2011

with comparative totals as of June 30, 2011

	9-30-11	6-30-11
Assets		
Cash	$160,000	$300,000
Receivables	401,100	81,100
Land, buildings, equipment, net	1,500,000	1,510,000
Total assets	**2,061,100**	**1,891,100**
Liabilities and Net Assets		
Liabilities		
Accounts payable	180,000	170,000
Mortgage payable	500,000	500,000
Total liabilities	**680,000**	**670,000**
Unrestricted Net Assets		
Avaialbe for operations	31,100	11,100
Invested in fixed assets	1,000,000	1,010,000
Board designated reserves	100,000	100,000
Sub-total - Unrestricted net assets	**1,131,100**	**1,121,100**
Temporarily restricted net assets	250,000	100,000
Total Net Assets	1,381,100	1,221,100
Total liabilities & net assets	**$2,061,100**	**$1,891,100**

Exhibit 26-5

Columnar Format

All Good Things
Statement of Activities
Quarter Ending 9-30-11

	Unrestricted	Temporarily Restricted	Total
SUPPORT AND REVENUE			
Foundation and corporate grants	$5,000	$290,000	$295,000
Governmental grants & contracts	140,000	-	140,000
Contributions from individuals	15,000	-	15,000
Events net of expenses	5,000	-	5,000
Investment income	1,300	-	1,300
Total suport and revenue	166,300	290,000	456,300
Net assets released from restrictions	140,000	(140,000)	-
Total support and revenue	306,300	150,000	456,300
EXPENSES			
Program services:			
Program X	25,630	-	25,630
Program Y	75,325	-	75,325
Program Z	101,455	-	101,455
Total program services	202,410	-	202,410
Administration	65,760	-	65,760
Fund Development	28,130	-	28,130
Total expenses	296,300	-	296,300
INCREASE IN NET ASSETS	**10,000**	**150,000**	**160,000**
NET ASSETS, Beginning of Year	1,121,100	100,000	1,221,100
NET ASSETS, End of Year	$1,131,100	$250,000	$1,381,100

All Good Things
Statement of Activities
Quarter Ending 9-30-11

Exhibit 26-6
Stacked Format

	1rst Quarter	Annual Budget	% Budget Realized	Projected Year End
Unrestricted Support & Revenues				
Foundation and corporate grants	$5,000	$30,000	$0	$20,000
Governmental grants & contracts	140,000	630,000	0.22	620,000
Contributions from individuals	15,000	60,000	0.25	50,000
Events net of expenses	5,000	50,000	0.10	50,000
Investment income	1,300	5,000	0.26	3,000
	166,300	775,000	1.00	743,000
Net assets released from restrictions	140,000	225,000	0.62	225,000
Total support and revenue	**306,300**	**1,000,000**	**0.31**	**968,000**
Unrestricted Expenses				
Personnel	200,000	720,000	0.28	700,000
Prof Services	35,000	40,000	0.88	40,000
Occupancy	11,300	45,000	0.25	45,000
Other expenses	50,000	170,000	0.29	165,000
Total unrestricted expenses	**296,300**	**975,000**	**0.30**	**950,000**
Increase in Unrestricted Net Assets	**10,000**	**25,000**	**0.40**	**18,000**
Temporarily Restricted Support				
New TR Grants Received	290,000	360,000	0.81	325,000
Released from Temp Restrict	(140,000)	(225,000)	0.62	(225,000)
Increase in TR Net Assets	**150,000**	**135,000**	**1.11**	**100,000**
Increase in Total Net Assets	**$160,000**	**$160,000**	**1.0**	**$118,000**

Most nonprofits that track expenses or both revenues and expenses by program will produce also produce a report in the same format as the Statement of Activities for each program or department as well as a report that combines all the departments. Nonprofits that are tracking restricted grants by line-item will often use this format to produce separate reports for each grant.

Statement of Functional Expenses

The report shown in Exhibit 26-7 on the next page presents the line-item expenses for the first quarter of the organization's fiscal year in columns for Management, Fund Raising, and the different Program expenses, as well as the total of all the functional expenses. Some nonprofits call this a Program Report. Some nonprofits use this same format with columns for Management, Fund Raising, and Programs to report revenues as well as expenses (see Exhibit 26-8). This format makes it easy to see which programs are generating enough income to meet their expenses and which require subsidy. Presenting both revenues and expenses in this report makes it easy to compare to the functional budget discussed in Chapter 24.

THE OREGON NONPROFIT CORPORATION HANDBOOK

Exhibit 26-7

All Good things
Statement of Functional Expenses
for the Quarter July 1, 2011 through September 30.2011

	7/1/11 thru 9/30/11	Admin	Fund Raising	Prog X	Prog Y	Prog Z
Personnel	$200,000	$40,000	$20,000	$20,000	$50,000	$70,000
Prof Services	35,000	15,000			10,000	10,000
Supplies	11,300	2,030	1,000	4,500	2,325	1,445
Other expense	50,000	8,740	7,130	1,130	13,000	20,000
Total Expenses	$296,300	$65,770	$28,130	$25,630	$75,325	$101,445

Exhibit 26-8

	A	B	C	D	E	F	G
1	All Good things						
2	Statement of Unrestricted Revenues and Expenses by Function						
3	for the Quarter July 1, 2011 through September 30.2011						
4		7/1/11 thru 9/30/11	Admin	Fund Raising	Prog X	Prog Y	Prog Z
5	Unrestricted Support and Revenues						
6	Foundation grants	5,000			5,000		
7	Government contracts	140,000				60,000	80,000
8	Individual gifts	15,000		15,000			
9	Events net of expenses	5,000		5,000			
10	Investment Income	1,300		1,300			
11	Released from Temp Restrictions	140,000		40,000	28,000	40,000	32,000
12	Total unrestricted support and revenue	306,300	0	61,300	33,000	100,000	112,000
13							
14	Direct Expenses		0.20	0.10	0.10	0.25	0.35
15	Personnel	200,000	40,000	20,000	20,000	50,000	70,000
16	Prof Services	35,000	15,000			10,000	10,000
17	Supplies	5,000	500	1,000	500	2,000	1,000
18	Other expense	15,000	2,000	3,000	1,000	3,000	6,000
19	Sub-total direct expenses	255,000	57,500	24,000	21,500	65,000	87,000
20							
21	Excess support & revenue over direct expenses	51,300	-57,500	37,300	11,500	35,000	25,000
22							
23	Allocated Expenses						
24	Occupancy	11,300	2,260	1,130	1,130	2,825	3,955
25	Depreciation	30,000	6,000	3,000	3,000	7,500	10,500
26	Sub-total allocated expenses	41,300	8,260	4,130	4,130	10,325	14,455
27	Direct and allocated expenses	296,300	65,760	28,130	25,630	75,325	101,455
28							
30	Allocation of administrative expenses	0	-65,760	8,024	7,311	21,486	28,939
31							
32	Expenses after allocation of administrative expenses	296,300	0	36,154	32,941	96,811	130,394
33							
34	Excess (deficit) of support & rev over total expenses	$10,000	$0	$25,146	$59	$3,189	-$18,394

Statement of Cash Flows

The report shown in Exhibit 26-9 on the next page explains how operating, investing, and financing activities have either increased or decreased the organization's cash during the first quarter of the fiscal year. Many small to mid-sized nonprofits do not produce the Statement of Cash Flows as a monthly financial statement mostly because it can be somewhat difficult to prepare (frequently the version automatically prepared by accounting software is not helpful). But the Statement of Cash Flows is one of the required statements for in audited financial statements.

Exhibit 26-9

All Good Things
STATEMENT OF CASH FLOWS
Quarter ended September 30, 2011

	9-30-11
Cash Flows from Operating Activities	
Increase in net assets	$160,000
Adjustments to reconcile increase in net assets to net cash provided by operating activities:	
Depreciation	30,000
(Increase) decrease in:	
Accounts receivable	(320,000)
Increase (decrease) in:	
Accounts payable	10,000
Net cash provided by operating activities	(120,000)
Cash Flows from Investing Activities	
Purchase of equipment	(20,000)
Net cash used in investing activities	(20,000)
Cash Flows from Financing Activities	
Repayments of loan payable	-
Net cash used in financing activities	-
Net Increase (Decrease) in Cash and Equivalents	(140,000)
Cash and Equivalents, Beginning of Quarter	300,000
Cash and Equivalents, End of Quarter	$160,000

This statement is useful for nonprofits using the accrual method of accounting to explain why cash may have increased despite having experienced an accrual basis loss (expenses greater than income) or cash may have decreased despite having experienced an accrual basis profit (income greater than expenses). Take care to avoid confusing the Statement of Cash Flows with a Cash Flow Projection (discussed in Chapter 24). The Statement of Cash Flows is a report of what actually happened to cash. The Cash Flow Projection is an estimate of when cash will be received and used.

Key Connection Between Financial Statements

The financial statements described above should be prepared each month and presented as a set together. If your records are being properly maintained and your statements are accurately prepared, you will see a very important connection between the Statement of Financial Position (Balance Sheet) and the Statement of Activities (Profit and Loss Statement). Here's how it works.

Each month, your Net Assets (on the Statement of Financial Position) will increase or decrease by the exact amount as the Increase or Decrease in Net Assets that appears at the bottom of the Statement of Activities, and is the equivalent to Net Income on for-profit financial statements. In fact, a GAAP format Statement of Activities will include a reconciliation section at the bottom that shows the impact of the Increase/Decrease in Net Assets by adding it to the Net Assets at the beginning of the accounting period and computing the Net Assets at the end of the accounting period. This final Net Assets amount at the end of the accounting period must equal the Net Assets amount reported on the Statement of Financial Position. If it doesn't, the books are out of balance and you will need to get help to get them corrected.

> *Nonprofits increase their Net Assets (net worth) by having income exceed expenses. Similarly, nonprofits decrease their Net Assets when expenses exceed income.*

While doing this reconciliation is a great way to make sure your books are in balance, it has a more important meaning. Nonprofits increase their Net Assets (net worth) by having income exceed expenses. Similarly, nonprofits decrease their Net Assets when expenses exceed income. Looking at this connection will help you stay clear about your overall financial strength and your progress (or lack of progress) towards growing stronger.

> *Budgets are plans for the future. Accounting records what actually happens. Financial statements present information about what has actually happened which is taken from the accounting records.*

There is also a key connection to observe between the Statement of Cash Flows, the Statement of Financial Position, and the Statement of Activities. The Statement of Cash Flows will report on the same period as is covered in the Statement of Activities. In the Exhibits in this chapter, both the Statement of Activities and the Statement of Cash Flows are covering the quarter from July through September. The Statement of Financial Position in Exhibit 26-4 is for the final date in that quarter, September 30th. The Statement of Cash Flows explains what caused the cash balance reported on the Statement of Financial Position to either increase or decrease during the quarter.

Tips for Useful Financial Reports

Nonprofit organizations are free to design the financial reports they use for internal purposes to meet their own preferences and needs. GAAP provides guidance for the format to be used in formal audited statements and requires the use of the three financial statements described above

KEEPING BOOKS AND PREPARING FINANCIAL REPORTS 26

(Statement of Financial Position, Statement of Activities, and Statement of Cash Flows). GAAP requires a fourth statement for voluntary health and welfare organizations, the Statement of Functional Expenses.

> *Be sure your monthly financial statements include both the Statement of Financial Position (Balance Sheet) and the Statement of Activities.*

Once your nonprofit grows beyond the "very small" category, or at any size if you are using accrual accounting, you will want to be sure your monthly financial statements include both the Statement of Financial Position (Balance Sheet) and the Statement of Activities. Both statements are needed to really understand the financial health of your nonprofit and to identify problems which must be addressed in order to assure continued success.

Most nonprofits find it helpful to present the Statement of Financial Position in two columns, comparing the Assets, Liabilities, and Net Assets at the end of the current period with the balances in these accounts at the end of the previous period. See Exhibit 26-4 This comparison may be made between two consecutive months, or between the end of the current month and the end of the previous fiscal year, or the end of the current month and the end of that same month in the prior fiscal year.

While GAAP requirements for the Statement of Activities do not include presenting a comparison of actual revenues and expenses to budget, your internal use statements will need to compare actual year-to-date revenues and expenses to your budget so that you can determine whether your budget plan is working. Unfortunately the multi-column format for the Statement of Activities (see Exhibit 26-5) can make it difficult to present the budget comparison without ending up with too many columns for the report to be read easily. This is because the multi-column format uses separate columns for Unrestricted and Temporarily Restricted activity and then a third column for the total of the two classes together. Adding a budget column and budget percentage realized column (as in Exhibit 26-6) would just be too much information for most readers.

The stacked format for the Statement of Activities in Exhibits 26-6 facilitates making the comparison between actual revenues and expenses for the period and the budget. In the stacked format approach, the Unrestricted activity (revenues and expenses) is shown at the top of the report and the Temporarily Restricted activity is shown underneath it. The grand total combining the Increase/Decrease in Net Assets (the Net Income) for both Unrestricted and Temporarily Restricted activity is at the bottom of the report.

This stacked sample in Exhibit 26-6 also includes a column for the Projected Year End total in each line item. This projection column allows Board members to see how management believes the year will turn out and can stimulate useful discussions about potential alternative strategies.

Regardless of whether you choose the multi-column approach (Exhibit 26-5) or the stacked approach (26-6), you will find that it is much easier for readers to understand your statements if you limit each financial report to one page. You can use subtotals of groups of similar line items to reduce the total number of lines on your reports. The detailed line item information will remain readily accessible in your general ledger, so you will be able to answer any detailed questions that arise. One great advantage of this approach is that it will help your Board stay focused on the most important issues rather than encouraging detailed discussions of budget variances of very small line item amounts.

> *It is much easier for readers to understand your statements if you limit each financial report to one page.*

The key to presenting useful financial information is understanding who will use the statements and what it is important for them to know. Chapter 28 on Evaluating Your Organization's Financial Health explores what Board members really need to understanding about their nonprofit. In presenting financial information it is often true that "less is more"—that is using fewer lines and more white space actually conveys more meaningful information. So, while your underlying accounting records will need to have many categories and reflect close attention to tracking distinctions in both the sources and uses of funds, your financial reports will probably work better if you combine smaller line items to help readers focus on the most significant issues and choices.

Some nonprofits also find it helpful to produce a different multi-column report of revenues and expenses that displays each month's activity in each revenue and expense line item. By reading this report across the columns, you can spot big variations in both income and expense accounts from month to month. This can be helpful for spotting errors or possible problems in accounts which you would expect to be roughly the same each month. It can also alert you to both positive and negative trends in key accounts like individual contributions or client fees. The challenge in using this report format lies in spending too much time worrying about small variations and losing track of the overall outcomes of your activities. This format is probably most useful for managers in an organization with professional staff or for the Treasurer in an all-volunteer organization but shouldn't substitute for the summarized Statement of Activities as a report for the Board.

Equally important is recognizing that for many users of your reports, words and graphics will always be more understandable than columns of numbers. The best financial reports include a short bullet-point narrative summary and a limited number of graphs depicting trends and ratios.

Accounting Software Choices

Your nonprofit will find a wide variety of accounting software that can meet your needs. There is absolutely no need to create your own software or adapt database or spreadsheet programs to do your accounting. This approach will almost certainly prove more costly and less helpful than purchasing a well-documented and supported product.

26 KEEPING BOOKS AND PREPARING FINANCIAL REPORTS

Start by understanding what your nonprofit needs most. All but the very smallest nonprofits will need general ledger software. These are the programs which allow you to maintain complete records of Assets, Liabilities, Net Assets, Revenues and Expenses.

Your choices will fall into two broad categories: products which have been designed for business use but can be successfully adapted to meet nonprofit needs; and products which are designed explicitly for nonprofit users. In our experience, both types of products can work well for nonprofits.

Almost all accounting software on the market today is capable of performing your accounting functions. The key questions in your selection process should be:

- How easily can the product be set up to meet your needs?
- How strong is the support provided by the software company?
- How easy or difficult will it be to find local consulting support for the product?
- How strong are the protections from error and fraud built into the product?
- How useful are the reports the product is designed to produce or how easily and safely can data be exported from the general ledger into a spreadsheet to produce the reports you need?

Beware of false price comparisons. The full cost of acquiring and using any product will include:

- Purchase price and any annual support or maintenance fee;
- Cost of any hardware upgrades needed to make the product run well (the minimum hardware requirements stated by the software maker are often insufficient to allow the product to run efficiently);
- Cost for help in setting up the chart of accounts and financial report design to meet your needs;
- Training for your staff—both the cost of the training and the cost of their time while participating in the training;
- Staff time to use the product to fully meet your accounting and reporting needs (this must include the cost of any off-the-books side efforts to create special reports that can't be drawn directly from the software);
- Cost of down-time and reconstruction if the product crashes frequently;
- Audit cost relating to ease or difficulty of tracking entries within the system;
- Cost associated with detecting and correcting errors or discovering and documenting fraud.

Once you consider all the cost factors, the actual purchase price of the accounting software will probably prove to be less than one third of the total actual cost. Beware of penny wise and pound foolish decisions like choosing the "cheapest" product and then spending large amounts of staff time (and consultant or auditor time) dealing with its limitations.

Business oriented accounting software can work very well for nonprofits if it includes the capacity to track cost centers. Business products often refer to this capacity as "departmental and division" tracking. Refer to the discussion of your Chart of Accounts earlier in this chapter to think through how many levels you will need. If you will need to categorize expenses (and potentially revenues too) by line-item, by function, and by source, you will need three levels. This can be accomplished with business software designed to handle both departments and divisions or both departments and multiple cost centers.

If you have decided that you want to produce internal financial statements that follow the GAAP format for displaying Unrestricted, Temporarily Restricted and Permanently Restricted income and the release from Temporarily Restricted into Unrestricted, like Statement of Activities in Exhibits 26-5 and 26-6 in this Chapter, you may want to look at products designed specifically for nonprofits which provide this format as a standard report. You can also accomplish this format with business software but it will require some careful set-up and will often require exporting data from your general ledger into spreadsheet software.

If you will be dealing with grants and contracts that overlap your fiscal year or funding that requires sophisticated cost allocations, you may want to seriously consider products designed specifically for nonprofits. You will need features that support cost allocation and preparing reports on grants that combine data from multiple fiscal years.

Tips for QuickBooks® Users

QuickBooks® has become the most widely used accounting software for nonprofits as well as for small businesses. It is inexpensive to purchase and quite easy to use, at least at a very basic level. It is also very flexible, allowing the user to define account titles and to easily export data into spreadsheet software in which attractive reports can be designed and prepared.

QuickBooks® has multiple versions designed for users dealing with differing levels of complexity. Nonprofits needing to track expenses by function and source as well as by line items will want to purchase QuickBooks® Pro, QuickBooks® Premium or QuickBooks® Enterprise. Starting in 2012, QuickBooks® Premium for Nonprofits will offer some new functions that may make it easier to handle the need to track increases and releases from Temporarily Restricted Net Assets. However, many small nonprofits find that QuickBooks® Pro is sufficient to meet their needs with the understanding that while it will allow you to track both functions and the use of restricted grants, it will not automatically handle full nonprofit GAAP presentation of the financial statements.

The key to using QuickBooks® to track functions (management, fundraising, and your different programs) and the use of funding sources for restricted purposes lies in making good use of the "class" and "customer/job" features. Nonprofits general use the "classes" to indicate functions (management, fund raising, and programs) and use the "customer/jobs" feature to track both income and expenses by funding source.

But QuickBooks® users need to be aware of some serious risks involved in using some of the older versions of the program. To protect your organization, you must use a version which offers the option of making it impossible to turn-off the "audit trail" feature. This feature is an essential control because it creates a record every time a change is made to any account. Even with the audit trail feature you will still need to adopt and actually carry out some additional control policies to prevent your records from being altered. The ease with which every entry to QuickBooks® can be changed can be an invitation to dishonest acts and/or a source of confusion and error for honest people who don't understand some key accounting controls.

> *Like messages written in sand on a beach,*
> *your records can disappear or change in QuickBooks®.*

Your policies must make it clear that data entered into QuickBooks® should not be altered after financial reports have been produced. Corrections to errors should be entered as journal entries in subsequent months.

Why does this matter? Because if data can be altered after reports are issued, you may find that the information you reviewed in one month's financial statements no longer exists at a later point in the year. Like messages written in sand on a beach, your records can disappear or change. Dishonest people can use this weakness to cover or hide improper disbursements or create confusion that will mask dishonest acts. Honest but untrained users, may use this feature to try to correct mistakes discovered later in the year, but in doing so, destroy the integrity of your records.

There are user controls that can be implemented to reduce these risks. Purchase a version with multi-level password control and you will be able to adopt a procedure in which only the person designated System Administrator can lock the records (preventing further alteration) at the end of a period. Of course this approach works only if you find a System Administrator other than your primary bookkeeper/accountant or other persons with access to your check stock and bank accounts. Some nonprofits are contracting with outside accounting services to play the System Administrator role and handle bank reconciliations. This approach substantially increases the controls in a QuickBooks® system.

Another approach involves adopting written policies which require that the audit trail feature be left on at all times and preclude altering data after financial reports are issued (requiring corrections to be posted when errors are detected in subsequent months). For this approach to work, your nonprofit will need to find someone (other than the primary accountant) to monitor whether the policies are being followed.

Who Should Do Your Nonprofit's Accounting?

Some readers may have already answered this question by throwing up their hands and shouting "anyone but me." It's important to pause and remember that size and complexity do make a difference.

Small Organizations

If your organization is small enough to use simple cash basis accounting and get all the information you need from a basic small organization financial report, your accounting can be done by a person with little or no accounting/bookkeeping training. The person you choose does need to be accurate and detail-oriented. They need to be committed to checking the accuracy of their work against bank records. They also need to be open and willing to show the details of your records to anyone in your organization and not be defensive about mistakes if others point them out.

If you will be using a volunteer bookkeeper or a staff person without formal training in bookkeeping, get help setting up your chart of accounts and financial report format. You will also want to support your bookkeeper by arranging to have a board member or other person review their work regularly.

Mid-sized or Small Nonprofits with Multiple Programs or Multiple Restricted Funding Sources

Start by investing time or money in getting your accounting system and financial reports designed correctly to do the tracking and reporting you will need. Seek help from skilled accountants who have worked with nonprofit organizations similar to yours. You may be able to obtain volunteer assistance from local CPAs or from experienced nonprofit fiscal managers. If you cannot find free assistance, it is probably worth paying for a limited amount of consultation from someone who is highly experienced with your type of funding and programs.

> *Many small and mid-sized nonprofits find that they can get better accounting and financial reporting done by using a skilled accounting service than they can by trying to hire a skilled accountant into a staff position.*

But even a well-designed system will require some expertise to operate properly. At a minimum, you will need a person who has experience as a full-charge bookkeeper. This is a term that describes a person who holds responsibility for seeing that all necessary accounting entries are recorded each month, closing the books and preparing standard financial statements. A full-charge bookkeeper has considerably more responsibility than an accounts payable or payroll clerk or assistant. These "clerk" positions are useful in larger organizations. They utilize less fully skilled individuals who work under the supervision of a more highly skilled accountant. But in your mid-sized nonprofit, there will probably not be anyone with the technical skills needed to supervise a clerk-level employee.

As your organization grows, you will want to employ a person who is experienced as a fiscal manager or business manager. In addition to the technical skills of a full charge bookkeeper, this person will be able to develop budget options and help your Executive Director and board evaluate your financial condition and explore alternative financial strategies.

Many small and mid-sized nonprofits find that they can get better accounting and financial reporting done by using a skilled accounting service than they can by trying to hire a skilled accountant into a staff position. There are some accounting services which specialize in nonprofit accounting and bring great expertise to their work. In smaller communities, you may need to look first for the "best" small business accounting firm. Ask local CPAs for their recommendations about which accounting services maintain the highest standards and are most dependable.

Remember that while the hourly rates quoted by an accounting service may seem quite high compared to the hourly wages of your staff, skilled accountants can do the work much faster (and probably better) than inexperienced staff could in your organization. Typically, the use of an accounting service turns out to cost about the same as the full cost of trying to do the work yourself, and sometimes it's actually cheaper. If your nonprofit will be audited, use of a skilled accounting service may result in lower audit cost. Check out this issue with your auditor before making a decision.

In considering whether to do your accounting work in-house with staff or contract out with an accounting service, you will want to consider the concept of "opportunity cost". If it turns out that in order to do the work in-house, your Executive Director must spend significant time overseeing, directing, and correcting the work of an unskilled staff person, your organization is incurring an opportunity cost by not having that time available to the Executive Director to work on community relationships, funding, and program direction.

Larger or Complex Nonprofits

While it's not possible to make a hard and fast rule, most organizations with annual expenses over $1 million per year will find that they need to employ a skilled fiscal manager. Typically the fiscal manager will be responsible for all accounting (including supervising assistants as the volume grows), financial reporting, compliance with financial management requirements of funding agreements and providing tools for board and staff to prepare the annual budget. In many nonprofits, the fiscal manager also provides oversight for technology, risk management and human resources functions as well.

Complexity is the driving force in compensation level. Very large or complex nonprofits will often decide they need a fiscal manager or chief financial officer with formal educational preparation, as well as strong on-the-job experience. Typically, they will prefer individuals who are CPAs or have MBA degrees. The most successful nonprofit fiscal managers combine formal training with substantial on-the-job experience and passionate commitment to the mission of the nonprofits they serve.

Consult Appendix 1 if you would like information about source material related to this Chapter. Appendix 1 has references of interest to all readers, not just professionals.

Chapter 27 details one very important part of financial recordkeeping—payroll and fringe benefits. If you have employees, you should turn there now.

If not, skip to Chapter 28 to learn how your Board and managers can use the financial reports you produce to monitor your financial systems and to ensure that they are working properly.

27 PAYROLL AND FRINGE BENEFITS

THIS CHAPTER COVERS

- Payroll Terms
- Payroll Basics
- Employer Taxes
- Preparing Your Own Payroll
- Payroll Tax Deposit Requirements
- Payroll Tax Reporting Requirements
- Fringe Benefit Basics

Since wages, taxes, and benefits can account for up to 65% to 85% of the cost of running many nonprofit corporations, payroll is a very important part of financial record keeping. And while offering fringe benefits such as health insurance and retirement is not required, many nonprofit employers choose to provide them.

This chapter offers a brief outline of the major requirements for processing payroll, depositing payroll taxes, and submitting required reports and a brief discussion of fringe benefits which focuses on understanding whether the benefits you choose will be considered taxable income to your employees. It is designed to help you make an important choice for your nonprofit—whether you will process payroll on your own or utilize a payroll service or outside accounting firm to handle the critical function. It will also help you understand how to report the fringe benefits you provide for employees.

Payroll tax and fringe benefit regulations have the force of the law behind them. This guide is not a substitute for instructions from the IRS or other taxing authorities. Those instructions, which are regularly revised, are essential for any sound payroll system. Mistakes can be costly since tax authorities can charge interest and penalties for late payments and—in crisis situations—can pursue individual Directors to personally pay for penalties equal to the nonprofit organization's unpaid payroll taxes.

Websites for all the payroll taxing agencies discussed in this chapter are listed in Appendix 2.

Payroll Terms

If you have not been responsible for processing payroll, making payroll tax deposits, and preparing payroll tax reports, one of your biggest challenges may be mastering the terms used in payroll discussions. Here's a brief description of payroll terms and concepts you'll need to help your nonprofit avoid time consuming and potentially costly mistakes.

Federal Employer Identification Number (EIN)

The Employer Identification Number is the unique number that the IRS utilizes to identify each corporation. Most nonprofits obtain an EIN before submitting their application for tax-exempt status to the IRS. Pages 47-49 include a discussion of how to complete the SS 4 form which is used to request an EIN from the IRS. If your organization has already obtained tax-exempt status, your EIN will appear at the top of your tax-exempt status determination letter from the IRS.

It's important to be sure that your nonprofit does not end up with more than one EIN, which will cause considerable confusion. This mistake generally occurs because newer leaders are unaware of a previous application for an EIN. You can research whether your nonprofit already has an EIN by reviewing correspondence from the IRS, and forms that have been submitted to other governmental agencies or to foundations.

State of Oregon Employer Identification Number

If your nonprofit will have employees, you will need to obtain an Oregon Business Identification Number (BIN) online through the Central Business Registry *https://secure.sos.state.or.us/ABNWeb* or on paper by downloading and completing the Combined Employer's Registration You will use your Business Identification Number for communications with both the Oregon Department of Revenue and the Oregon Employment Division If you filed your Articles of Incorporation using the online procedure, you should already have a BIN.

Gross Wages

Gross wages are the total amount of salary or wages the employee has earned during a pay period before any deductions are made.

Employer Taxes

These are taxes that employers are required to pay in addition to the gross wages of your employees. Requirements to pay employer taxes mean that it will actually cost your nonprofit more to employ an individual than the gross wages you agree to pay them. Employer taxes include: Employer's share of Social Security and Medicare, also referred to as FICA (Federal Insurance Contribution Act) Federal and State Unemployment Insurance (note that 501 (c)(3) organizations are exempt from Federal Unemployment Insurance Tax) and Transit District taxes in the Portland Metro Area and Lane County

Mandatory Payroll Withholdings

As an employer, you must withhold certain taxes from your employees' pay. These are taxes that the employee is required to pay. The law requires the employer to withhold these amounts and pay them over to the government. Both the IRS and the State of Oregon publish tables which establish the amounts which must be withheld based on the amount of pay, and the filing status of each employee.

In Oregon, employers are required to compute and withhold from employees' pay the following taxes:

- Employee's share of Social Security and Medicare, also referred to as FICA
- Federal individual income tax
- State individual income tax

Note: Oregon employers are required to withhold Oregon income tax from all employees performing work in Oregon, even if the employee lives in another state.

Workers Compensation Insurance:

Oregon law requires all employers to provide workers compensation insurance coverage for their employees. Employers may choose to purchase workers compensation insurance either from the State Accident Insurance Fund (SAIF), a state chartered not-for-profit entity or from approved private insurance carriers. In addition to purchasing workers compensation insurance, all employers also must contribute to the Oregon Workers' Benefit Fund for all employees.

The Workers' Benefit Fund assessment is computed on the days each employee works. Oregon employers are permitted but not required to withhold a portion of the Workers' Benefit Fund daily assessment. If you do not withhold this amount from your workers' pay, your nonprofit will be required to pay the entire assessment amount itself.

Voluntary Payroll Deductions

In addition to the mandatory deductions that employers must withhold from employees' pay, you may, but do not have to, offer your employees the opportunity to voluntarily instruct you to withhold additional amounts. If you do allow employees to have voluntary payroll deductions, you must be sure that you pay over the amounts withheld from your employees' pay to the proper recipients. You are legally obligated to pay all amounts you withhold from the employees' pay.

Common types of voluntary payroll deductions include:

- Charitable contributions
- Employee contributions to health insurance costs

- Employee retirement contributions
- Dependent Care Assistance Plan contributions
- Flex Plans or Cafeteria Plans

You may only permit voluntary deductions for retirement, Dependent Care Assistance Plans, or Flex or Cafeteria Plans if you have adopted the correct plan documents. You will need help from an attorney or a person knowledgeable about fringe benefit tax issues to review your plan documents to be certain they meet IRS requirements (as well as Department of Labor requirements for certain retirement plans).

Net Pay

Net Pay is the amount you will actually pay directly to the employee, either by issuing a paycheck or by making a direct deposit into the employee's bank account. You will compute the Net Pay amount by calculating the employee's gross wages and subtracting the mandatory withholding and voluntary payroll deductions which the employee has authorized you to make.

Draws or Payroll Advances

The term draw or payroll advance describes a partial payment of wages to an employee prior to the normal payday. Each organization is free to establish its own policy regarding whether and in what circumstances employees will be permitted to receive draws or payroll advances. Sound policies will limit the amount of any draw to an amount no greater than the wages the employee has already earned. If you decide to permit draws, you will need to be sure you have good systems in place to record the amount of the draw payment and be certain to deduct that amount from the employee's net pay on the first regular payday after the draw is given. You'll also want to be sure that any employee requesting a draw or advance puts the request in writing and signs an agreement acknowledging that repayment of the draw will be withheld from the next regular paycheck.

Payroll Direct Deposits

Many employees prefer to have their employers deposit their net pay directly into their bank account rather than receiving a paycheck. In order to offer employees direct deposit your nonprofit will need to have an account with a bank or credit union which offers this service and must be able to provide the deposit data in the format required by the financial institution. If you decide to offer direct deposit, be sure you review the controls for electronic payments discussed in Chapter 25.

Payroll Tax Deposits

Employers are required to deposit (pay to the government) both employer taxes and the employee taxes which the employer has withheld from the employees. Both the IRS and the State of Oregon impose significant penalties for failing to make deposits on time.

PAYROLL AND FRINGE BENEFITS 27

Payroll Tax Reports

Employers are required to prepare and submit reports of all wages paid and amounts withheld and deposited. Each taxing authority specifies what report must be prepared and when it must be submitted. Penalties for late filing or failing to file payroll reports are substantial.

Payroll Software

Many accounting software programs include a Payroll function. This is the portion of the program that is used to calculate each employee's wages and amounts to be withheld and to prepare paychecks. The software also maintains the records each employer is required to have and calculates the tax deposits the employer must make. In some cases, the software will also facilitate preparation of required payroll reports.

Payroll Services

These are businesses which contract to handle the entire payroll function for their clients. In most communities they are available at very low prices. A good payroll service will:

- calculate each employee's wages,
- calculate both mandatory and voluntary withholding,
- create all needed payroll records,
- compute payroll tax deposits and process electronic payment of the deposits,
- process direct deposit of pay and/or produce paychecks,
- produce all required payroll reports, both quarterly and annual
- produce W-2 year end payroll records needed by the employees for their taxes and your nonprofit for its reporting.

Many payroll services are extremely inexpensive. Before you set up a new payroll system, review the Section on Payroll Services and at least consider using a payroll service.

Fringe Benefits

The subject of fringe benefits is filled with endless complexities and choices. Common fringe benefits include:

- Paid time off for sick leave, vacation, or other purposes
- Health, dental, and disability insurance plans
- Plans to help employees meet certain expenses with pre-tax dollars
- Retirement plans

The section later in this Chapter on Fringe Benefits is designed to help you understand the basic choices your nonprofit will need to make and to give you tools to make sure that you are complying with governmental requirements for reporting about the benefits you provide.

Payroll Basics

Each organization must establish its own pay period and pay procedures. Most nonprofit organizations opt for a monthly or semi-monthly pay period. From a bookkeeping standpoint, a monthly system is the least time consuming. If employees have difficulty managing money when paid once a month, a system of mid-month salary advances can be developed. More frequent pay periods (such as weekly) result in extra effort and extra opportunity for error.

The rate of pay for the Executive Director should be established by the Board of Directors. In small nonprofits, the Board may also set pay rates for other positions. In larger nonprofits, the Board frequently delegates setting pay rates for staff to the Executive Director. The person responsible for actually preparing your payroll should have written authorization for adding new employees to the payroll or changing rates of pay. Procedures for authorizing pay rates should be clear and uniform.

Even small organizations should require timesheets or personnel activity reports from both salaried and hourly employees, recording days and hours worked in the pay period.

Even small organizations should require timesheets or personnel activity reports from both salaried and hourly employees, recording days and hours worked in the pay period. Both the employee and the supervisor, or other person authorizing payment, should sign the timesheet. Timesheets should be retained for at least one year. These simple steps can prevent time-consuming disputes about pay, vacation, sick leave and holiday time. They also can protect the organization from wage and hour complaints from disgruntled employees. They are essential for organizations that will be managing federal funds, whether they receive the federal dollars directly from a federal program or through a contract with state or local government or another nonprofit.

The pay system should clearly identify which positions are compensated by monthly salary and which are paid an hourly rate. Uniform procedures are needed for pro-rating monthly salaries for unpaid leave and partial months worked. Your organization must also clearly assign responsibility for maintaining records of vacation, sick and holiday time earned and used. Clear procedures and forms are required.

If your nonprofit will have employees, you will need to commit to understanding the wage and hour laws that apply to your situation. Some Oregon nonprofits are covered by federal wage and hour laws (Fair Labor Standards Act), while others are covered solely under Oregon law. To determine whether your organization must follow federal versus state rules, call or email the Oregon Bureau of Labor, Wage and Hour Division.

Both federal wage and hour laws and state laws impose requirements for overtime pay (time and a half) for employees working more than forty hours in a seven day work week. Exceptions are made for supervisory and professional employees. See pages 394-397 for a more extensive discussion of these requirements.

Good timesheets are essential for employees covered by overtime pay requirements. Pay special attention to the laws addressing "comp time." Many nonprofits have erroneously used compensatory time as a way of avoiding overtime.

Review pages 394-397 to be sure your nonprofit avoids the costly claims and penalties which can result from this mistake.

Employer Taxes

Each employer is required to pay certain taxes in addition to the gross wages paid to employees. Unlike the employee's federal and state income taxes which are withheld through payroll deduction, employer taxes are not withheld from employee wages. Employer taxes are paid entirely by the employer.

Employer taxes are not withheld from employee wages; they are paid entirely by the employer.

Employers' Share of Social Security and Medicare Taxes (FICA)

The most significant employer tax is the employer's share of Social Security and Medicare which when combined is often referred to as FICA (Federal Insurance Contributions Act). The Social Security and the Medicare taxes are each computed separately as a specified percentage of each employee's gross wages. The Social Security tax is applied to all wages up to a maximum amount each calendar year. The Medicare tax is applied to all wages without any maximum amount limitation. Certain religious organizations which object to FICA on religious grounds can elect to be exempt from FICA and Ministers may also be exempt from FICA, but beyond these exceptional situations, virtually all nonprofits must pay FICA taxes on wages paid to employees.

IRS Publication 15 *http://www.irs.gov/pub/irs-pdf/p15.pdf* provides guidance in for employers regarding both the current FICA tax rates and the maximum level of wages on which Social Security tax must be computed. Both the rate and the maximum level of wages covered are subject to change so employers must be sure that they are using current information.

Unemployment

All employers must provide for unemployment compensation coverage for their employees. Unemployment is not a payroll deduction. The full cost of unemployment is paid by the employer.

Federal Unemployment

If your nonprofit is tax-exempt under §501(c)(3), it is exempt from federal unemployment tax (FUTA). If it is nonprofit but not tax-exempt under §501(c)(3), you are liable for FUTA and must file Form 940 annually and deposit quarterly with Form 8109.

State Unemployment

If your organization is tax-exempt, it may choose between two plans for meeting State Unemployment requirements. It can pay a percentage of gross wages (currently around 3% of gross wages up to $33,000 per employee but subject to change, so be sure you have current information); or, it can be "self-insured," paying no tax, but remaining completely responsible for payment of unemployment claims of former employees.

For organizations required or choosing to use the percentage tax plan (called the insurance plan), the percentage is determined for each organization by the Employment Division based on an experience rating system (for example, the more claims filed by employees you have laid off, the higher your rate). State unemployment taxes are generally due quarterly. Oregon now combines reporting and payment of unemployment taxes with reporting and payment of state income tax withholding. Both the report and the combined payments are submitted to the Department of Revenue. Most employers will be required to deposit both state income tax withholding and Unemployment taxes electronically.

Self-Insurance

Tax-exempt organizations considering the "self-insure" approach may want to investigate the unemployment trusts available only to 501(c)(3) organizations. Organizations joining the trust make quarterly payments to the trust to build up a deposit. The deposit is invested by the trust with its earnings added to the specific organization's deposit. When the deposit reaches the level the trust determines to be adequate to cover potential unemployment claims, the organization stops making quarterly payments. The trust pays unemployment claims with the funds in the organization's account. The trust provides insurance against extremely high claims amounts and some financing (with interest) to assure that cash is available when needed if the organization's deposit is not sufficient to pay claims. You can get contact information to reach the unemployment trusts serving Oregon by contacting the Nonprofit Association of Oregon Helpline at 503.239.4001. The trust approach offers greater security than simply being a self-insured employer, but is still represents an element of risk. If the organization suffers funding cutbacks and must lay off a substantial portion of its staff, their unemployment claims will surely exceed the premium the organization would have paid under the insurance program, and will come at the time when the organization is least able to pay them.

Tax-exempt organizations considering the "self-insure" approach may want to investigate the unemployment trusts available only to 501(c)(3) organizations.

SAIF or Workers' Compensation

All Oregon employers are required to provide workers' compensation insurance coverage for their employees.

Most Oregon employers provide for workers' compensation for on-the-job injury through the State Accident Insurance Fund (SAIF), a state chartered not-for-profit corporation. You may choose a private carrier instead or be self-insured. In some cases, premiums paid to a private carrier may be lower than those charged by SAIF, particularly if that carrier also underwrites your property or liability insurance. Talk to your insurance agent.

You can learn about SAIF and register to participate at *http://www.saif.com/employer/learn_about_coverage/obtainingcoverage.aspx*. Employers covered through SAIF must submit quarterly reports and pay premiums quarterly. Both reports and payments may be submitted electronically through the SAIF website. The SAIF premium is computed by multiplying a percentage times gross wages paid. The percentage is determined by the type of work each employee does. For example, the percentage for janitors is much higher than for office workers or teachers because janitors are more likely to be injured. To prepare the form, the employer groups the wages of employees in the same percentage categories and applies the percentage to their gross wages. The totals for each rate group are added together with the total SAIF payment.

Wages for employees who perform two or more different types of work (for example, drive a day care center bus and work with the children as a teacher) must be divided to reflect the portion of their day expended in each activity. The employer must document that the time distribution is correct or else the higher premium rate may be assigned to all hours worked. If you will have employees performing multiple functions, be sure to discuss recordkeeping requirements with your insurer.

In addition to the insurance premium described above, employers must pay an assessment into the Workers Benefit Fund maintained by the state. The assessment is a daily charge for each employee. The employer may deduct a percentage of the daily charge from each employee's wages, or may choose to pay the entire amount per employee per day worked directly.

Employers pay their Workers Benefit Fund assessment directly to the state (not to their insurance carrier) through the Combined Payroll Tax Reporting System as part of their state payroll tax payment. Even if you do decide to use a private insurer rather than SAIF for workers' compensation coverage, you will still be required to pay the daily assessment into the Workers Benefit Fund.

Local Governmental Unit Employer Taxes

Employers located or doing business within certain geographical areas of Oregon are subject to special taxes. Usually the tax is based upon the wages paid. The amount of business conducted in the district is another basis for taxation. A partial list of such agencies includes:

- Tri-County Metropolitan Transportation District
- Lane County Mass Transit District

If your organization has tax-exempt status from the IRS, it may also be exempt from these local taxes. Request exemption through the local tax authority. See Chapter 11.

Preparing Your Own Payroll

Setting Up Your Payroll System

If your nonprofit will have employees, you must set up a payroll system. This is an excellent time to think about using a Payroll Service. A good payroll service can handle all the set-up steps described in this section.

If you're determined to do payroll on your own, you will need to complete several major steps:

- Inform the IRS that you will begin having employees.
- Register with the State of Oregon Department of Revenue and Employment Department.
- Determine whether your local area has an employer transit tax and whether you will be considered exempt. If not, register as an employer with your transit district.
- Obtain workers compensation insurance coverage.

Next you will need to require your employees to complete several forms, including:

- **IRS Form W-4**: each employee is required to provide their social security number and the number of exemptions they will claim on their tax return. You need this information in order to deduct the right amount of federal and state income tax from their pay. The form is available at *http://www.irs.gov/pub/irs-pdf/fw4.pdf*
- **Form I-9**: Each employee must complete the form and allow you to make a photocopy of their social security card or other proof of the fact that they can work legally in the United States. You must require all employees to complete Form I-9,

not just those you think may be from other countries. Form I-9 is available at *http://www.uscis.gov/files/form/i-9.pdf*.

- **Your Own Form Authorizing Voluntary Payroll Deductions**. To make voluntary payroll deductions (see above), you will need to create a form through which employees direct you to make voluntary deductions from their pay. You must get each employee who wishes to have voluntary deductions taken to complete and sign the form. In signing the form, employees will give you legal permission to withhold the amounts specified by the employee from their pay.

Payroll Withholding Tax Tables

In order to meet your legal responsibility to withhold federal and state income tax from employees' paychecks, you will need to obtain payroll withholding tables from the IRS *http://www.irs.gov/pub/irs-pdf/p15.pdf* and the State of Oregon Department of Revenue *http://www.oregon.gov/DOR*.

If you decide to use payroll software to do your payroll processing, your software should contain current payroll withholding tables. Be sure to check that the version of the software you are using contains the most current payroll withholding tables. Most payroll software providers supply regular updates to registered users. But if you are using an unregistered copy of the program or you have failed to load the newest version into your system, you may make serious errors in preparing your payroll.

Payroll Records

Once you have all the information described above, you are ready to begin creating your payroll records and processing payroll. While your employees are probably most interested in your ability to produce paychecks, as the employer you have many more responsibilities beyond simply issuing paychecks.

Each employer is required to maintain a complete record of every employee, including their signed forms W-4 and I-9. You must also maintain a complete record of all gross wages each employee earned, the amounts you have withheld from their gross pay, the net pay you have given the employees and any employer taxes you are required to pay.

To meet your employer responsibilities, you will need both a payroll journal that contains the records of all your payroll calculations and payments and individual payroll records that contain the record of the earnings, withholding and net pay of each individual employee.

Your payroll journal will contain the following information for all your employees:

- Dates included in each pay period
- List of each employee you had during each pay period
- Gross wages of each employee for the pay period
- Amount withheld for federal income tax

- Amount withheld for state income tax
- Amount withheld for the employees' share of Social Security and Medicare
- Workers Comp withholding amount (optional)
- Each employee's voluntary deductions
- Total deductions from each employee
- Net pay for each employee
- Any payroll advances given to each employee
- Paycheck number or direct deposit record number, date, and amount

Your payroll journal will not only contain an accurate list of this information for each employee, it will total the amounts in each category so that you will know the total gross wages you had for the pay period, the total amount you withheld for federal income tax, etc.

Payroll Processing Procedures

Since the cost of wages and employer taxes will comprise a very large portion of your total expenses (nonprofits typically spend at least 70% of the annual budget on these costs), you will want to think through your payroll processing procedures very carefully to be sure you handle this function correctly. Here are a few key procedures you should consider. Most of them are essential whether you will process payroll yourself or use a payroll service.

Timesheets

Require your employees to maintain a daily record of the time they work for your nonprofit. At the end of the pay period, have each employee sign their timesheet and have a supervisor review the timesheet and sign it to indicate that they believe it is a correct record of the time the employee worked.

Prepare and Approve the Payroll Journal

Enter each employee's timesheet information into your payroll system. Print out a report of all the information you have put into the system. The report will show the gross wages, withholding, advances and net pay for each employee. Have a responsible person review this report carefully to be sure it is accurate. Once they have approved the report, go ahead and produce the paychecks. Payroll services ask their clients to review this information and authorize the service to move forward to issue the paychecks. Be sure a responsible person reviews the report before authorizing the payroll service to move forward.

PAYROLL AND FRINGE BENEFITS 27

Signing Paychecks or Authorizing Direct Deposit Payments

If you will be paying your employees the "old fashioned way" with actual paychecks, be sure the person responsible for signing paychecks compares each paycheck to the Payroll Journal and considers whether the pay amount seems reasonable. Investigate any concerns. Signing the check represents your authorization that the payroll is correct.

Increasingly, employees prefer to be paid through direct deposit into their bank accounts. Most payroll services offer this feature as part of their service (one more reason for really thinking about using a payroll service). If you are not using a payroll service but want to offer direct deposit you will have to work with a bank that offers this service and may be asked to pay a small fee for using it.

Using direct deposits means that you will have to have a responsible person review the final proposed deposits before authorizing the bank to make the direct deposits. Be sure that this step doesn't get lost in the mechanics of handling the direct deposit transfers—it is just as important that you do a careful final review in direct deposit payroll systems as those in which actual paychecks are issued.

Payroll Tax Deposits and Payroll Tax Report Submission

Be sure you have a clear understanding about who is responsible for making the payroll tax deposits and for preparing the payroll tax reports. Make sure the person responsible knows when your deposits and reports are due and that at least one other person understands the due dates and will check to be sure you have met the deadline.

Payroll Tax Deposit Requirements

It is essential that you learn and meet the requirements for depositing payroll taxes. Late penalties and interest on undeposited taxes can easily equal or exceed the total tax due. Directors may have personal liability for penalties on undeposited payroll taxes. The IRS and other taxing authorities can literally shut down and padlock the premises of organizations that do not pay their payroll taxes.

The IRS and state and local taxing authorities all have different requirements concerning when withheld employee taxes and employer taxes must be paid. Get the instructions from each taxing authority and construct a calendar of when each tax deposit is due. Be extremely careful to set aside enough cash to pay quarterly taxes such as unemployment. Be sure that more than more than one person in the organization understands the deposit requirements and that someone other than the person with primary responsibility for making the deposits and filing the reports is aware that the requirements are being met.

Payroll services can be very helpful in relation to these requirements. Your payroll service will prepare the required reports, compute the amount of tax due and either deposit the payment directly for you or instruct you on the preparation of a check to make payment and the due date for submission.

> *Directors may have personal liability for penalties on undeposited payroll taxes. The IRS and other taxing authorities can literally shut down and padlock the premises of organizations that do not pay their payroll taxes.*

Warning!! Taxes withheld from employees' wages do not belong to the employer. You are acting as an agent for your employees, holding their money for deposit to the IRS or State of Oregon, so you cannot decide to spend their money for other purposes. The IRS and the State will impose severe penalties if you fail to pay over the money you have withheld from your employees' paychecks.

Payroll Tax Reporting Requirements

Employers are required to prepare both quarterly and year end reports of gross wages, federal income tax withholding, Social Security and Medicare withholding and state income tax withholding.

Each quarter, employers must complete Form 941 to report on gross wages, federal and Social Security and Medicare withholding, and employer Social Security and Medicare taxes to the IRS.

The State Department of Revenue for Oregon also requires quarterly reports of wages paid and state tax withheld on Form OQ. The Oregon Employment Division requires quarterly reporting of the wages paid to each employee and to all employees for the quarter on Form OQ. If you are part of the unemployment insurance program, you will compute the tax due on Form 132 and be required to submit the payment either through electronically or through attaching a check to your report. If you have chosen to be "self-insured" for unemployment purposes (see discussion above), you must still submit Form O to inform the Employment Division about the wages you have paid. Download the Oregon Employer's Guide *http://www.filinginoregon.com/pages/forms/business/guides/2011EmployerGuide.pdf* for information on both state withholding requirements and reporting for the Employment Division.

For tax purposes, the year is divided into four quarters:

- January, February and March
- April, May and June
- July, August and September
- October, November, and December

Payroll is always reported on a calendar year, regardless of your organization's fiscal year. So the Annual Reports required by the IRS and the State of Oregon require you to report on wages paid, withholding, and employer taxes for the calendar year, from January through December.

By January 31st, each employer must have completed its annual payroll reports and given each of its employees IRS Form W-2 which details the total wages paid to the employee, total amounts of federal and state income tax withheld as well as the employee's share of FICA (Social Security and Medicare) which has been withheld. The W-2 also provides information about retirement and other fringe benefits with the employer has paid and other amounts which the employer has withheld from the employee's pay.

The employer provides the employee with three copies of the W-2, one of which the employee will use with their federal tax return, one for use with the employee's state tax return, and one for the employee's records. Most payroll software actually prints the completed forms quite easily. Employers may still order forms W-2 and other tax forms from the IRS and from the Oregon Department of Revenue or purchase them through office supplies stores.

Employers also prepare IRS Form W-3 to summarize the information contained on all of the employees' W-2 forms, and Oregon Form WR to summarize information on state withholding.

One final note on payroll tax reports: Accuracy matters. Be sure you compare the total wages and withheld amounts shown on your Form W-3 to the total of all the W-2s you are issuing to employees and that you compare the W-2s to your underlying payroll records. Even with computers doing most of the processing, errors can and do occur. The IRS and the Oregon Revenue Department will eventually identify errors and resolving them will be time-consuming and costly.

If all this has begun to seem overwhelming, remember that payroll services not only prepare your paychecks and payroll records, they also prepare all the payroll tax reports. You may want to consider using a payroll service even if your organization is very small.

Fringe Benefit Basics

Nonprofits, like all employers, are free to choose whether to offer fringe benefits to some or all of their employees. Common fringe benefits include a hugely diverse array of possible arrangements for:

- Paid time off for sick leave, vacation, or other purposes

- Health, dental, and disability insurance plans
- Plans to help employees meet certain expenses with pre-tax dollars
- Retirement arrangements

Some types of fringe benefits may be provided to employees without increasing their taxable income (and resulting income tax), while others are considered taxable income under IRS regulations. Employers are required to maintain records and submit reports regarding fringe benefits to both employees and the IRS. Employers offering certain types of retirement benefits may also have to comply with regulations from the U.S. Department of Labor under the provisions of ERISA (Employee Retirement Income Security Act), submit special tax returns to both the IRS and the Department of Labor and have certain types of retirement plans audited by independent auditors.

So as your nonprofit begins evaluating fringe benefit options, you may want to focus on keeping things simple or plan to get professional advice to guide your decisions and ensure your compliance with myriad regulations. We'll discuss the most common fringe benefits here with the understanding that in many cases, like health insurance, federal regulations may change dramatically.

Paid Time Off

Many nonprofits provide employees with a specified number of days paid time off, including time off for personal illness and/or illness of an immediate family member, paid vacation, and in some cases opportunities for paid time off to pursue educational activities. The compensation that employees receive under such paid time off arrangements is considered part of their taxable wages and is subject to payroll withholding and being including in the wages upon which the employer tax liability will be computed.

Your nonprofit will want to establish clear policies regarding how much paid time off employees in various positions may utilize, how they are to submit requests to use paid time off, and any limitations regarding the time period in which they must use the paid time off or "lose it." In Oregon, employers who offer employees paid time off for vacation are generally required to compensate employees for unused vacation when they leave employment unless they have clearly stated that they will not do so. In contrast, Oregon employers are not required to compensate employees for unused sick leave upon termination unless they have specifically stated that they will do so. Of course, employers may always choose to adopt provisions that are more generous to employees.

Health, Dental and Disability Insurance

Many nonprofits find it very helpful to work with an expert health insurance broker to explore the various opportunities that are open to them for providing health, dental and disability insurance. This is an area in which the only constant appears to be change as public policy around health care grows ever more controversial.

Currently, Oregon insurance regulations require that all group health insurance plans sold in Oregon make employer group coverage available to any employer with 2 or more employees. Group health plans are permitted to set rates for an individual employer based on the age and gender of the employer's workforce. Most health plans offer multiple options to employers including some with relatively high monthly premiums and low co-pays or deductibles and others with lower monthly premiums with higher co-pays and deductibles.

Once you have gathered current information from health plans that offer coverage in your part of the state, you will need to determine whether your nonprofit can afford to pay the full cost of each employee's health insurance coverage as well as whether you can afford to pay the cost of insuring the employee's family members. If you determine that your employees must pay a portion of the health insurance premium, you will be able to handle the collection of the employee share of the premiums through payroll deductions. If you decide to use this approach, you will need to have each employee who will be paying their share of the insurance premium through payroll deduction complete an authorization form allowing you as the employer to withhold their share.

As health insurance premiums continue to rise, many employers are exploring options to combine plans with quite high deductibles and co-pays (that have lower premiums) with reimbursement plans through which the employer reimburses the employee for all or part of the deductible and co-pay. Check with your health insurance broker to learn if this approach could work for you. Many employers are also rethinking dental insurance plans which while not terribly expensive in terms of monthly premiums frequently limit the amount of coverage available for the more expensive services.

Many nonprofits also provide some form of disability insurance to provide income for employees who are either temporarily or permanently unable to work. Long term disability policies are quite reasonably priced but require employees to be unable to work for longer periods than the more expensive short term disability policies which begin providing income to the employee more quickly after a disability occurs.

Help for Nonprofits with Cost of Health Insurance

The Affordable Care Act of 2010 created the Small Business Health Care Tax Credit, an opportunity for smaller employers to get some help with the cost of health insurance premiums. While the provisions that have been most widely publicized deal with potential tax credits for for-profit businesses, the law also creates help for qualifying tax-exempt organizations. The basic requirement for participation is that the employer have no more than 25 employees and that average compensation for employees is not greater than $50,000 per year. You can learn more about the requirements by reviewing the information on the Small Business Health Care Tax Credit at *www.IRS.gov* . Of course, like all aspects of the health insurance issue, be sure to check for changes.

Common Pitfalls in Health Insurance

All of the approaches we've described above are designed to be sure that the contribution the employer makes to help the employee obtain health insurance is not considered to be taxable income to the employee. One common pitfall is for the employer to either directly pay or reimburse employees for the cost of health insurance that the employee has purchased outside the employer's group health plan. The desire to make such payments arises in organizations that have not yet obtained a group health plan or situations in which an employee prefers a health insurance plan other than the one the employer is offering. Such payments or reimbursements will be considered taxable income to the employee unless they are made through a properly designed medical expense reimbursement plan discussed in the next section.

Other Plans to Help Employees Meet Expenses with Pre-Tax Dollars

The Internal Revenue Code permits the use of a variety of plans to allow employees to cover specific costs with pre-tax dollars. Such plans must be carefully drafted and professionally administered to be certain that the tax code requirements are met. A growing number of nonprofits offer employees the opportunity to participate in qualifying plans for medical expenses, child care, and the care of elderly or disabled relatives who are dependent upon the employee. Establishing a medical expense reimbursement plan may allow employees to shelter from tax the dollars they wish to expend to purchase health insurance other than the plan that your nonprofit provides or to meet medical costs which are not covered by your health plan. Many of these plans create little or no cost for the employer and offer significant tax benefits for the employees.

In addition to plans that are designed for a specific purpose like medical expense reimbursement or dependent care expenses, employers may also establish flexible benefit plans sometimes referred to as cafeteria plans under IRC Section 125. Flexible benefit plans allow employees to make choices among multiple benefit categories. Some plans involve only the employee's own funds (voluntary salary reduction) while others involve employer contributions as well.

Qualified fringe benefit brokers or consultants can help you find plan administrators to work to establish and manage plans which meet tax code requirements.

Retirement Plans

The legal issues surrounding retirement plans could truly take a lifetime to master and are clearly beyond the scope of this guide. Two primary regulatory systems will impact your choices. IRS regulations define which retirement approaches will result in taxable income to the employee and which will permit sheltering of income from tax. In addition to IRS rules on taxability and requirements for reporting by employers, the US Department of Labor administers ERISA which establishes allowable pension practices and includes reporting (Form 5500) and in some cases auditing requirements. A few key points may help you begin exploring the choices that make sense for your organization.

Employee Contribution Only Retirement Plans

Many smaller nonprofits limit the help provide employees with retirement to participating in plans that are funded solely through the employee's own contributions. The primary benefit to employees in these plans is the ability to shelter the income contributed to such plans from income tax. Charitable organizations may offer most of the retirement options that are permissible for business employers. Additionally, 501 (c) (3) organizations may offer 403 (b) plans. Your nonprofit will need to work with an established retirement plan provider to be sure that any plan you offer meets all the IRS requirements to ensure that employee contributions will not be subject to income tax.

Employer Contributions to Retirement

You will also find a number of choices available if your nonprofit decides to make contributions to retirement for the employees. Some plans involve both employee and employer contributions while others are limited to employer only contributions. All plans must meet complex IRS and ERISA requirements so you will want to get professional advice before deciding which type of plan will work best for your organization.

Common Pitfall in Retirement Contributions

While there are many retirement plan options that can work well for your nonprofit, one common mistake is to believe that your nonprofit can handle retirement by making contributions into an employee's individual IRA (Individual Retirement Account). Any funds that an employer contributes to an employee's IRA account will be considered taxable income to the employee and should be included in the employer's calculations of taxable wages. You can avoid this pitfall easily by establishing a qualified retirement plan for your organization through a bank, insurance company, or other financial institution.

Your Board and managers need to be able to use the financial reports you develop to evaluate your organization's financial health. The next chapter offers specific suggestions for how they can do this.

28 EVALUATING YOUR ORGANIZATION'S FINANCIAL HEALTH

THIS CHAPTER COVERS

- How to Ask the Right Questions About Your Financial Statements
- The Manager's Role in Monitoring Financial Performance
- Should Your Nonprofit Have an Independent Audit or Review
- Understanding and Preparing for Audits and Fiscal Monitoring
- Will Your Organization Need an A-133 Audit

Each of us wants to be able to say that the nonprofit we are building is sustainable. We want our organizations to be around to achieve their long term goals, and to be able withstand the ups and downs of the economy, the challenges of changing funder preferences, and the stress of leadership transition. We want our organizations to be financially healthy and to have confidence that they are well managed financially.

While most Board members, managers and staff would quickly agree with these goals, many of us are a bit unsure how we would know if our organizations are making progress toward financial health and sustainability. This chapter focuses on the questions that every nonprofit leader should ask to understand their nonprofit's current financial position and chart a course to increase its sustainability.

This chapter also explores some practical steps Boards and managers can take to be sure that the financial information they are using is reliable, including evaluating the costs and benefits of having an independent audit by a CPA. We'll also look at how Boards and managers of nonprofits managing substantial amounts of federal funding can get the maximum benefit from the A-133 audits they may be required to have by their funders.

How to Ask the Right Questions about Your Financial Statements

Here are the eight basic questions you'll want to ask as you review your nonprofit's financial statements. You can find more information about the information contained in each statement in Chapter 26.

How Financially Strong is This Organization?

Start with the *Balance Sheet* or *Statement of Financial Position*. This statement presents the assets, liabilities and net assets of the organization on a specific date. It may also present a comparison of assets, liabilities and net assets at two different dates, for example, the end of the last year, and the end of the most recently completed month.

Look first at the *total net assets* line. Net assets represent the net worth of the organization at the date specified on the statement. It's helpful to think of net worth as what would be left if the organization gathered in everything it owns of value (cash, investments, land, buildings, etc.) and collected all that is owed to it (receivables), and then paid off everything it owes to others (wages, payroll taxes, payables, mortgages, etc). The *net assets* are roughly equivalent to *Owner's Equity* in business financial statements. The *net assets* provide a cushion to fall back on in hard times and can give your organization the foundation it needs to be able to take risks in undertaking new activities.

If the *net assets* amount is shown in <brackets>, the organization has a negative net worth, owing more than it owns. If it's not shown in brackets, the organization has a positive net worth—at least on paper. Like businesses, nonprofits report their land, building, and equipment at the amount they cost when purchased, less accumulated depreciation. This "book value" can be far from market value, that is, what the land, building or equipment could be sold for today. If the market value is much higher than the book value, the net assets will understate your organization's actual net worth. If the market value is much lower than the book value, the net assets will overstate your actual net worth.

Looking at the *net assets* is a first step. To really evaluate your organization's financial strength, you'll have to ask a few more questions.

Can the Organization Meet Its Obligations on Time?

Simply having a positive net worth doesn't guarantee that the organization can pay its employees, its payroll taxes, and its vendors on time. That depends upon its cash position or liquidity. Look again at the Balance Sheet (Statement of Financial Position). Create a subtotal of all the cash accounts and any receivables or investments which can be readily turned into cash. Next, look at the liabilities. Create a subtotal for wages, taxes, and other accounts payable that must be paid within

12 months—this subtotal constitutes your current liabilities. Then compare your cash and cash equivalents subtotal to your current liabilities subtotal.

Does the organization have more cash or items which can readily be turned into cash than current liabilities, or at least as much? If so, it will probably be able to meet its obligations on time. If not, it will have difficulty paying everything on time. If it has significantly more cash than is required to meet current liabilities, it is in a good position to take on additional obligations through expansion or taking reasonable risks. Or, it may be time to invest some excess cash in longer term investments.

> *Simply having a positive net worth doesn't guarantee that the organization can pay its employees, its payroll taxes, and its vendors on time.*

If the Balance Sheet (Statement of Financial Position) provides information about two points in time—the end of the current month and the end of the previous month or previous fiscal year—you can evaluate whether the cash position (i.e. cash available to meet obligations or invest) is improving or worsening. Compare the cash balances, the accounts receivable, and the accounts payable. If the accounts receivable are increasing, find out why. Does the increase simply reflect a higher volume of service and higher amounts being billed, or does the increase reflect difficulty collecting what is owed to the organization? If the accounts payable are increasing, ask for an "aging,"—i.e., a list which shows which of the amounts have been owed for 30, 60, 90, or more days. Then determine why payments have not been made and what will be the consequence of further delays.

Are There Limitations on What the Organization Can Do With Its Resources?

While having a positive net worth is clearly better than having a negative net worth, simply noting that the net assets line on the balance sheet is positive doesn't tell the whole story. Ask a few more questions.

Are there restrictions on any portion of your nonprofit's assets? If your financial statements are being prepared in accordance with formal GAAP accounting standards, you will see your *net assets* broken down into three groupings: *unrestricted net assets, temporarily restricted net assets,* and *permanently restricted net assets.*

The term "restricted" refers to a restriction (limitation) placed on the use of a gift by a donor or funding source. For example, a donor may say "use my contribution only for the children's program" or a foundation award may state that the funds may be used only "to meet the costs of the mental health services expansion project" described in your proposal to the foundation.

The term "temporarily restricted" is used to refer to restrictions which will be met through, the use of funds for the specified purpose, the passage of time, or some other action. The term "permanently restricted" refers to gifts which will have restrictions on their use forever, i.e., a permanently restricted endowment.

EVALUATING YOUR ORGANIZATION'S FINANCIAL HEALTH

Your evaluation of overall financial strength should include recognition that restricted funds may be used only for their restricted purposes, and are not available for other purposes. Thus, *temporarily restricted net assets* represent gifts that have been received with donor restrictions which your nonprofit has not yet fulfilled. The resulting *temporarily restricted net assets* will be available to carry out restricted purposes in the future, but are not available for general, unrestricted purposes.

In contrast, permanently restricted net assets represent gifts that have been received with donor restrictions requiring that the gift be held by the organization permanently. Most commonly, the donor intends that the organization will invest the funds and use the income generated through investment either for specific purposes or for general support of the organization's activities. Such gifts are frequently referred to as endowment gifts.

> *If your financial statements are being prepared fully in accordance with formal accounting standards, you will see net assets broken down into three groupings: unrestricted net assets, temporarily restricted net assets, and permanently restricted net assets.*

To fully understand your nonprofit's financial health, you'll need to understand both the extent to which your Board has full or limited ability to direct the use of the net assets. If the net assets are unrestricted, the Board has full authority to direct their use. If the net assets are temporarily restricted, the Board may direct their use only in accord with the restrictions. If the net assets are permanently restricted, the Board must focus on its responsibility to invest the resources wisely with the understanding that the nonprofit must retain the permanently restricted net assets in perpetuity.

Once you are clear about this major distinction between unrestricted, temporarily restricted, and permanently restricted net assets, you will want to focus your attention on the unrestricted net assets to consider the extent to which they are available to meet the organization's operating costs.

To understand the availability of the unrestricted net assets, start by looking for the portion of unrestricted net assets which represents investment in fixed assets. Some organizations will show this as a separate line in the net assets section called *net assets invested in property, plant and equipment*, or *capital net assets*. Others will include it in the total *unrestricted net assets* and you will have to do some analysis to figure it out.

To determine the portion of the organization's net assets which represents investment in fixed assets, find all the asset accounts which include land, buildings, equipment, leasehold improvements, etc. Next, find all the liability accounts which are related to these fixed assets—typically, mortgages payable used to finance the purchase of property and buildings, or notes payable associated with major equipment purchases. To compute the portion of total net assets invested in fixed assets, subtract the liabilities you identified from the assets you identified.

Remember that the portion of the net assets invested in fixed assets won't be immediately available to support operations. The organization would have to sell its fixed assets, or borrow against them, in order to obtain cash for operations use. As you look at the organization's investment in fixed assets, think about how essential these assets are to the organization's ability to conduct its operation. Does owning them reduce operating costs or does it tend to increase operating costs by requiring constant maintenance expenses?

Next consider whether any portion of the unrestricted net assets have been set aside by the Board for specific purposes. For example, some Boards decide to set aside a specific portion of the unrestricted net assets to function very much like an endowment. The Board wants to invest these funds so that investment earnings may be used to support ongoing operations, or in some cases, support specific programs or costs. Such funds are described as Board Designated Quasi-endowment funds but they are considered to be part of the organization's Unrestricted Net Assets. Because the fund has been created through the action of the Board, its use may be changed by action of the Board. This contrasts sharply with the Permanently Restricted endowment funds discussed above. The restrictions on the Permanently Restricted funds were created through the action of a donor and may not be changed through Board action.

To fully understand your nonprofit's financial health, you'll need to understand both the extent to which your Board has full or limited ability to direct the use of the net assets.

If your Board has designated a portion of the unrestricted net assets as a Board Designated Quasi-endowment, these funds will not be immediately available for operations. Instead, your Board will need to give very serious consideration to changing the designation and using up these resources for current operations.

As you think about the organization's overall sustainability, the unrestricted, temporarily restricted, and permanently restricted net assets represent different types of financial strengths. The Unrestricted Net Assets represents a cushion that your Board has full authority to direct. Parts of it may be immediately available, while other parts are invested in fixed assets or have been designated by the Board to function as reserves.

The Temporary Restricted Net Assets represent resources that will be available for use in future periods, but donor restrictions will limit how and/or when your organization may use them. The Permanently Restricted Net Assets will never be available to meet immediate needs. But, permanently restricted net assets do contribute to overall financial strength by representing a future source of resources to support your work through the income generated by investing the endowment.

Less formally presented financial statements may not separate net assets into unrestricted, temporarily restricted, or permanently restricted groupings. If yours have no breakdown, you'll need to ask whether any of the funds the organization has received have been restricted by the donor. If so, you will want to get help to modify your statements so these restrictions are presented clearly.

How Can I Tell if the Organization is Complying with Restrictions on the Use of Funds?

In some organizations, a substantial part of the resources received carry restrictions attached by donors or grant funders. The restrictions may be either fairly general (use this money only for the children's program) or very specific (use this money only to buy art supplies for the children's program). The Statement of Support, Revenue, and Expenses (Statement of Activities) should let you see that restrictions have been established by the donor/funder, and that the spending of these funds has been in accord with the restrictions.

If your nonprofit uses the standard GAAP reporting format, you'll see a distinction made between unrestricted and temporarily restricted gifts and grants on the statement reporting revenues and expenses. The gifts or grants that your organization received with donor restrictions will be presented in a column titled "temporarily restricted" (or "permanently restricted" if the gifts were to an endowment), or in separate section of the statement, clearly labeled as temporarily restricted gifts and grants. In both approaches, you'll also see a line at the bottom of the income section which reports on amounts "released" from temporarily restrictions and added to unrestricted income. This line indicates that you have complied with the donors' restrictions and used their funds according to their wishes.

Some nonprofits choose not to use the GAAP format. You can read more about this choice in Chapter 26. If your nonprofit is not using the GAAP format, you should still be able to see evidence that you are tracking donor restrictions by looking at the Balance Sheet. There you will see a line item labeled "deferred revenue—grants received in advance" in the Liabilities section. This line item reports on funds which the nonprofit has received with restrictions which it has not yet used for the restricted purposes. When the nonprofit does use the funds for the purposes directed by the donor/grantor, the "deferred revenue" line item in the Liabilities section will be reduced and the grant income line item on the Statement of Activities (income statement) will be increased by the same amount. This entry reflects the fact that the nonprofit has earned the right to use the restricted funds by incurring costs which meet the donor's restrictions.

Understanding how nonprofits report on receiving and using restricted funds can be challenging, in part because different nonprofits use different methods for presenting this information. If you are not clear how you can see the receipt and use of restricted funds on your nonprofit's financial statements, it will be worthwhile asking an accountant to explain your current system and help you think through whether a different method would work better for your organization.

Is the Organization "Breaking Even"?

To answer this question you'll have to see the Statement of Activities (Statement of Support, Revenue, and Expenses). This statement reports on revenues and expenses over a period of time—a month, a quarter, or a year. Expect to see both revenues and expenses broken down into separate line item categories describing the type of revenue (grants, contributions, fees, interest, etc.) and the types of expenses (salaries, taxes, rent, supplies, etc.).

There are two important ways to look at this information. First, look at the bottom line—the net income which may also be called the Excess (Deficit) of Revenues over Expenses or the Increase (Decrease) in Net Assets. If revenues exceed expenses, the net income will be positive. If expenses exceed revenues, the net income will be negative and shown in brackets. This positive or negative net income for the period you are looking at is really the explanation of whether the net worth (net assets) of the organization is growing or shrinking. A positive net income will result in an increase in the net assets (net worth). A negative net income will result in a decrease in the net assets (net worth).

Another important way to look at revenue and expense information is in comparison to the organization's budget for the time period. Hopefully, the organization has a complete annual budget which shows all the planned sources of income and all the planned types of expenses. (Chapter 24 illustrates some common budget approaches.) You can compare the actual revenues and expenses reported on the Statement of Activity to the planned revenues and expenses presented in the budget. Your questions will be, "Are things going as we had planned? Are we generating the income we thought we would? Are we controlling costs within the limits set in the budget?"

You will also want to look at your revenues and expenses in comparison to prior years. This can be particularly helpful when you have some revenues or expenses which do not occur evenly throughout the year. For example, if you have major fund raising activities every year in December, simply comparing your fund raising income and expense to your annual budget in October won't really tell you whether you're on track. It will be more helpful to compare your current year to past years, and especially helpful to think about what percentage of fund raising income was generated by October in previous years compared to the percentage of your annual budget for fund raising income which has been generated by October this year.

This approach of comparing the current year revenues and expenses to past years allows you to look at trends. Over the past three years, has the percentage of your total income coming from individual donors or program fees increased or decreased? Has the percentage of fund raising income consumed by fund raising expenses increased or decreased? Hopefully you have already thought through what your goals are in these areas as you worked on preparing your annual budget. If you have set a goal of increasing the percentage of your total income which comes from individual donors, you can evaluate whether you are achieving that goal by looking at trend information.

Is the Organization Using Its Resources Wisely?

This is perhaps the most important question of all. To answer it, you must know what the mission of the organization is, and the financial statements must give you enough information to be able tell the purpose of the expenses as well as their descriptive character. For example, looking at a report which shows that the organization spent x dollars in salaries for the year, tells us the character of the expenses (i.e. salaries) but doesn't tell us the purpose (i.e. were the salaries spent for programs for children, seniors, or for administrators?).

EVALUATING YOUR ORGANIZATION'S FINANCIAL HEALTH 28

We can get some information about the purpose of expenses through a functional presentation on the Statement of Activities or through a separate Statement of Functional Expenses. The functional presentation will distinguish expenses for program, administrative, and fundraising purposes, and if the organization has several different programs, distinguish the costs associated with each.

With functional expense data you can consider whether the organization seems to be spending its resources in accord with its mission and in a way which reflects its priorities. You may want to ask whether the organization can also convert this functional expense information into a cost per unit of service (this requires defining units of service and tracking them). The unit of service cost will allow you to compare the cost to provide a service at your organization with the cost at another similar organization. Of course, such a comparison requires that both organizations have reliable data and have defined things similarly.

The concept of combining some key financial information with some other key program or fund raising indicators is frequently referred to as a "dashboard."

You may want to ask to have some supplemental information included on your financial reports to help you keep tabs on key indicators of both program and financial performance. For example, you may ask to see the number of clients served each month in comparison to your capacity, i.e. an average attendance of 200 in a child care facility licensed for 250 could be a sign that the organization needs to enroll children more rapidly or may have customer satisfaction problems. Average client census of nine in a residential care facility with sixteen slots would indicate potentially serious problems. This type of service utilization information is very important for organizations depending on payments per service provided.

The concept of combining some key financial information with some other key program or fund raising indicators is frequently referred to as a dashboard. To develop a useful dashboard you'll have to identify the variables that make the most difference in your financial outcomes. For many nonprofits these will include the number of donors, donor retention rate, and average gift size as key indicators for fund raising and number of clients served and/or units of service as key program indicators. Effective dashboards pick the info to be included very carefully in order to avoid distracting readers with too many variables.

Are the Books In Balance?

While most readers of financial statements will have to rely on someone with greater accounting knowledge to evaluate the quality of the accounting in the organization, there is one simple test you can do to alert yourself to very obvious problems with the accounting.

To do the test, you must have the financial statements for two consecutive periods, i.e. for January and February. Take the total net assets from the first of the two periods, and add the net income (change in net assets) reported for the second period to it. The answer should be the same number as is shown for the total net assets at the end of the second of the two periods. If it's not, seek help from someone knowledgeable about accounting. This could be an indication that the books are not in balance.

How Do We Know the Financial Statements Are "Right"?

An audit completed by an independent CPA will give you the greatest assurance that the information presented on the financial statements presents the organization's financial position and activity fairly and should be relied upon. However, audits are generally done only once a year, and in small organizations, the cost of an audit may simply be too great to consider.

However, there are a number of simple procedures and cross checks which the accountant or Executive Director can perform each month to test the reliability of the statements. Be sure the organization has written fiscal policies and procedures and that they include the basic tests of accuracy. You could also ask a Director with a business background to review the financial records in detail at least once a year. You may also want to ask the Treasurer to complete the checklist of simple tests in the following section to verify the financial statements and include the checklist with the financial report.

The Manager's Role in Monitoring Financial Performance

Beyond the financial health questions discussed above, organizations with paid staff will need to rely on their managers to examine the financial reports in much greater detail. Be sure you have given specific managers responsibility for performing each of the monitoring steps discussed below. And be sure all those taking on parts of these responsibilities are communicating regularly with each other, and that one person has ultimate responsibility for resolving the problems you identify.

Steps to Be Sure the Reports Are Accurate:

- Verify that bank reconciliations have been completed for all cash accounts each month and that the balances shown on the financial statements agree with the reconciled balances.

- If you have accounts payable and accounts receivable, be certain that there are lists of all the individual amounts owed or owing which add up to the totals shown on the financial statements.

EVALUATING YOUR ORGANIZATION'S FINANCIAL HEALTH

- If you have acquired equipment, land or buildings, be sure these items are reflected in the assets section of your Balance Sheet.

- Perform the test of the connection between the Statement of Activities and the Balance Sheet described in the previous section. The *change in net assets (net income)* shown on the Statement of Activities should be the same as the *change in net assets* which can be computed by comparing the net assets at the beginning and end of the period reported on the Statement of Financial Position (Balance Sheet).

- Review the revenue and expense line items carefully. First compare them to the budget and be sure any significant differences between the actual revenues and expenses and the budget make sense to you. If they don't, ask the accountant to show you the detailed listing of transactions posted to the accounts which have unexpected balances. Review the transactions to see if something has been listed in an improper category.

- Review the revenue and expense line items to be sure that expenses have been correctly categorized in relation to different projects or funding sources.

Steps to Determine Whether Action is Needed to Protect the Organization's Financial Health:

- Review the revenue line items which have fallen short of the planned level.

- Consider whether it is realistic to think that the shortfall can be made up in the remaining portions of the year. Avoid wishful thinking. Base your evaluation on specific plans with specific estimates.

- If part of your funding is dependent upon the number of people served or the volume of service provided, check the numbers in these areas carefully. If you are not achieving your targets, figure out what is preventing it.

- Review all expense items which are significantly greater than the projected level. Determine whether your annual estimate will still prove correct (e.g., you have just expended amounts in this category at a more rapid rate than planned, but the annual estimate is correct).

- Based on your analysis, consider whether you will need to pursue additional strategies to generate the revenue you need or whether you should make reductions in your spending level.

- Review all financial reports you are preparing for funders that have provided restricted grants with great care. Be sure they are based on the numbers in your General Ledger and those numbers are correct.

- Be sure you are familiar with the requirements of your contracts with restricted funders. Do you have to obtain their permission to move amounts from one line item to another? If so, your analysis of the reports should focus on identifying any requests for changes you will need to submit to the funder.

- Are any of your grants or contracts "use it or lose it" agreements in which your organization is not entitled to receive funds unless you expend them on specified items? In a "use it or lose it" contract, controlling costs so that you underspend the contract is not helpful to your organization. Instead, if it appears that you are underspending, consider what additional resources the project needs, or whether you can make a case to include more of your overall operating costs into the contract budget. Once you've developed a strategy, then you will have seek approval from the funder.

- Write down the major assumptions you've made in your analysis of the financial statements. Compare these assumptions to your next month's financial statements. This will provide rapid feedback about how realistic you are being.

- Consider preparing a year-end projection of revenues and expenses. Create the projection by starting with your year-to-date revenue and expenses in each line item and then estimating what additional income will be generated and expense incurred during the remaining months in the fiscal year. Combine the actual year to date information in each line item with your best estimate of what will happen in the remaining months of the fiscal year to create the total year-end projection.

- Remember, the longer you wait to make revisions in your plan, the more dramatic the revisions may need to be because you will have less time to benefit from their effect.

Should Your Nonprofit Have an Independent Audit or Review?

One of the best ways to be sure that your financial reports are telling the real story about your organization's financial activity and health is to have an independent audit or review. Audits and reviews are specific procedures performed by Certified Public Accountants. In both audits and reviews, the CPA uses her or his professional training to examine your records and financial reports. Both audits and reviews result in the CPA preparing a report which includes your financial statements presented in the formally correct way for non- profit organizations.

Neither standard audits nor reviews are designed to detect fraud! Review Chapter 25 to learn more about how you can protect your organization from fraud and steps you can take if you believe that your organization may have been the victim of fraud.

Audits

In an audit, the CPA does enough examination and analytic procedures to feel comfortable writing an "opinion letter." The opinion letter tells readers whether they should rely on the financial statements as fairly presenting your organization's financial position. The opinion letter may be unqualified—i.e. the auditor says that readers can rely on the financial statements as a fair presentation of your financial position and your financial activities—or it may be qualified. In a qualified opinion, the auditor tells readers that they can rely on the statements except for certain areas in which the organization has not used standard methods or where it has not been possible for the auditor to verify the reliability of a part of the statements. It's also possible that the auditor will issue an adverse opinion, telling readers that the statements do not fairly present your nonprofit's financial position, or a disclaimer of opinion, stating that it wasn't possible to determine whether the statements do or don't present your position fairly or that the auditor was not independent of your organization.

In addition to providing your Board—and funders—with assurances that your financial statements present your position fairly, the audit process should help your organization identify needed improvements in your financial management systems. You should also receive a management letter, describing any significant problems in the system discovered during the audit. It is very important for your Board of Directors to play an active role in relation to the audit. You will want to give a Board committee responsibility for selecting the audit firm for your nonprofit and make sure that the auditor you select stays in good communication with the chair of that committee. At a minimum, you will want the auditor to meet with the committee at the conclusion of the audit to discuss what was learned during the audit.

> *You will also want to arrange an exit interview—an opportunity for the finance or audit committee or the whole Board to discuss the audit findings with the auditor. Boards lose an important part of the value of an audit if they delegate to staff the responsibility for communicating with the auditor.*

Larger nonprofits may want to follow the guidelines of the Sarbanes Oxley Act (which does not actually apply to nonprofits but provides some useful guidance on the relationship between Boards and auditors). Voluntary compliance with Sarbanes Oxley would require that your Board appoint an Audit Committee with explicit responsibility for auditor selection and communication. The Audit Committee would have at least one financial expert, a person knowledgeable about nonprofit accounting practices and able to have a professional level conversation with the auditor.

Smaller nonprofits may decide to have the finance committee of the Board serve as the audit committee. While smaller nonprofits may not have a financial expert to appoint to the finance committee, the other members of the committee should be willing to insist that the auditor meets with the committee and presents the information in a way that committee members can understand.

The full Board needs to be able to rely on the committee that has hired and met with the auditor to report back accurately about the soundness of your financial systems and any issues about your financial health which the auditor has identified.

Your Board will find useful resources for working effectively with the auditor available without charge through the American Institute of CPAs Not-for-Profit Audit Committee Toolkit at *http://www.aicpa.org/interestareas/businessindustryandgovernment/resources/notforprofitresourcecenter/pages/aicpanot-for-profitauditcommitteetoolkitdownloads.aspx.*

Reviews

When a CPA conducts a review rather than an audit, she or he performs fewer procedures and does not seek evidence from outside the organization to corroborate the information recorded in the organization's books. The review report does not include an opinion letter. This means that the CPA is not telling readers whether or not she or he believes that the financial statements fairly present the organization's financial position. Reviews are less expensive because they require less time from the CPA and expose the CPA to less potential liability. Your organization may decide that a review is adequate for your needs, particularly if you are small and have little or no restricted money. Although the review does not provide the assurance of an opinion, it does require the CPA to look closely at your records, and will frequently result in the identification of significant errors and suggestions for improving your system.

Choosing Your Auditor

If you decide that you want to have either a review or an audit, you will need to select a CPA firm to conduct it. Start by asking other nonprofits about their auditors. You will want to identify CPA firms which are experienced with nonprofit organizations, and hopefully somewhat familiar with your type of nonprofit. If you will need a federal funds audit (discussed later in this chapter), you will need to find CPA firms which do these specialized procedures.

Once you have identified several CPA firms which appear qualified, ask to meet with each of them to discuss your needs. Most CPAs will want to ask you some questions about your organization and your accounting and may possibly take a look at your system before making a proposal to do your audit or review. You will want to ask them to tell you about their firm, specifically who in the firm will do what portions of the audit. In larger CPA firms, the actual field work of the audit or review—the part done in your office—is usually assigned to very junior staff who may have very little knowledge of common bookkeeping practices and may require a great deal of assistance from your staff. While their work will always be reviewed by someone in the firm with more experience, you may find dealing with these junior staff very time consuming and frustrating.

Some nonprofits prefer working with smaller CPA firms in which more senior staff are available to work on your audit year after year. If you are considering a smaller firm, be sure to ask about timing. How quickly can they complete the audit?

Whether you are considering small, medium, or large CPA firms, always ask for a list of all their nonprofit audit clients and make calls to check out the experiences these organizations have had with the audit firm. Scan the list first for organizations you know and for those which seem similar in size or focus.

Once you've made your selection, the auditor will prepare an engagement letter which serves as a contract for the work. Be sure every service you are expecting to receive is described in the letter. For example, if you would like the auditor to also prepare your Form 990, that service should be included in the engagement letter.

The audit business is quite competitive. Most auditors are eager to have satisfied clients. So as the audit progresses, if there are things you don't understand or that you are dissatisfied with, let the auditor know so that problems can be worked out. It is usually advantageous for a nonprofit to keep the same auditor for several years. This allows the auditor to become familiar with your system and staff, and work more efficiently. It also saves your staff time by not requiring them to orient a new person each year.

Understanding and Preparing for Audits and Fiscal Monitoring

Types of Audits

Not all audits are performed by CPA's or upon the request of the nonprofit itself. The four major types of audits performed on the records of nonprofit organizations are:

Independent Audit by a Certified Public Accountant (CPA)

The Board of Directors of the corporation requests and pays for an audit by a CPA firm to provide assurances for the Board, and for outside funding sources, that the records are being kept according to Generally Accepted Accounting Principles and that the financial statements fairly state the organization's financial activities and position.

Funding Source Audit or Fiscal Monitoring

Almost all contracts to receive government funds require the recipient organization to allow the funding agency to examine the recipient's books. The purpose of these audits is to determine whether the recipient organization has complied with the requirements in the contract for the management and use of the government funds. There is usually no charge to the recipient organization, although your staff time required to answer the auditor's questions represents a significant cost. The funding source auditor/monitor may issue a written report of their findings, including requirements for changes in your system or revision of your reports or may simply conduct an exit interview. Fiscal monitoring can have serious impact on future funding so you will want to be sure your Executive Director is involved in the exit interview and reviews the written report.

Payroll Tax Audit

The IRS, State Department of Revenue, Employment Division, and all other payroll tax authorities have the right to examine any employer's financial records to determine whether all wages have been reported and taxes properly computed and paid. There is no charge for these audits, but they may result in requirements to pay back taxes, interest, and penalties if errors or omissions are found.

990 or CT-12 Audit

Both the IRS and the State of Oregon Attorney General have the right to audit the books of nonprofit corporations. These audits focus on verifying the information which the nonprofit reported on Form 990 (the IRS) or Form CT-12 (State of Oregon). If you have had an independent audit, the 990 or CT-12 auditors will often do little more than com- pare your 990 or CT-12 to your independent audit. If you have not had an independent audit, the IRS or State auditors may spend a considerable amount of checking to see if the reports you filed agree with your books. The IRS will also be interested in looking for specific activities which are limited or prohibited for §501(c)(3) organizations, i.e. political activity, lobbying, unrelated business income, or private inurement. These "no-nos" are discussed in Chapters 5, 8, and 9. In most cases, there will be no consequences to an IRS or State of Oregon audit. However, both the IRS and the State can charge penalties for filing substantially incorrect returns. The IRS can assess specific taxes and penalties for Unrelated Business Income, excess lobbying, or political activity. And, the IRS may threaten to revoke your tax-exempt status if your improper actions play too significant a role in your organization.

Preparing for an Audit

All four types of audits involve a process of checking, reviewing, and verifying the accounting and financial reporting of the organization. The auditor reviews the internal financial records (including records of transactions, journals, and ledgers) and in addition seeks supporting evidence from outside. You may be asked to provide:

- Financial Statements, Trial Balance, General Ledger
- All journals, subsidiary ledgers, records of receipts and disbursements
- Bank statements and cancelled checks or access to electronic banking records, including detail on electronic payments, etc.
- Invoices, bills, petty cash records, receipts
- All payroll records—regular wages, overtime wages, vacation pay, bonuses, commissions, profit sharing; all records of other than cash remuneration to employees—value of room and Board, free rent, labor exchange, etc.; all timesheets
- All contracts, purchase of service agreements, notes, mortgages

EVALUATING YOUR ORGANIZATION'S FINANCIAL HEALTH 28

- Your governing instruments (Articles of Incorporation, Bylaws); minutes of the Board of Directors meetings; approved budgets; personnel policies, financial policies, etc.

Will Your Organization Need an A-133 Federal Funds Audit?

An "A-133 Audit" is an audit of financial statements done in accordance with requirements of Office of Management and Budget (OMB) Circular A-133, which is required for nonprofit organizations expending $500,000 or more in federal funds during their fiscal year. Federal funds may come directly from a federal agency or may pass through a state or local government or another nonprofit.

Generally, A-133 audits will be done by independent CPA's. OMB Circular A-110 (now also referred to as 2 CFR 215, reflecting its inclusion in the Code of Federal Regulations) explains the standards which recipients of federal funds must meet for procurement—i.e. selecting and engaging an auditor and making other significant purchases.

A nonprofit is subject to the A-133 requirements only if it is considered a "recipient" or "sub-recipient" of federal grants or contracts. This includes federal funds received through state or local governments, or through agreements with other nonprofits. The amount of federal funds received for purposes of determining A-133 audit requirements does not include amounts nonprofits receive when acting as vendors of goods or services under purchase of service agreements. However, this is a highly confusing area. There is substantial disagreement about what constitutes a true vendor agreement. You will want to discuss all of your sources of funds that may include federal dollars with your auditor and seek their advice about which sources must be included as federal for purposes of determining whether an A-133 audit is required.

One caution—even if you do not meet the $500,000 in federal expenditures threshold that requires an A-133 audit, you must still meet the same requirements for managing federal funds that lie at the heart of the A-133.

An A-133 audit looks different than a "regular" audit. The A-133 audit will include the standard financial statements and a separate Schedule of Federal Fund Expenditures, each with an auditor's opinion. The auditor's opinion letter will reference Government Auditing Standards and OMB A-133. Additionally, the auditor will prepare reports on her or his review of the nonprofit's internal control structure and on her or his review of compliance with law and regulation. The auditor's reports on the reviews of internal control structure and compliance will include any findings of material weaknesses or significant deficiencies. The report on compliance must contain the auditor's opinion on whether federal funds were administered in accordance with applicable law and regulation. The report may also include a schedule of "findings" that presents detailed descriptions

647

of the problems the auditor identified and requires the recipient organization (your nonprofit) to describe how you will be addressing the problems described in the findings.

The Nonprofit Organization's Responsibilities

If your nonprofit is subject to an A-133 audit, you must:

- Determine which funds received are federal in origin
- Obtain the CFDA (Catalog of Federal Domestic Assistance) number for all funds received
- Engage a qualified auditor to perform an audit under A-133 requirements
- Establish and maintain controls which will prevent or detect material non- compliance, and ensure that direct and indirect costs are computed and billed in accordance with A-133 requirements
- Maintain records which document the use of federal funds for allowable purposes
- Be certain that all reports to funders are supported by the organization's accounting records (primarily the General Ledger)
- Be familiar with all laws and regulations compliance with which is required by contracts for federal dollars and document compliance
- Document the eligibility for services of all clients served with federal dollars
- Prepare responses to all findings in the audit reports
- Submit the completed A-133 audit to the appropriate federal, state, or local entity
- Resolve any concerns of funders regarding "substandard" audit reports.

The Auditor's Responsibilities

The auditor in an A-133 audit must:

- Be fully trained and prepared to meet A-133 requirements
- Obtain a thorough understanding of the nature of the nonprofit's activities, sources of funds, and requirements of funding sources
- Conduct the audit in accordance with *Government Auditing Standards* and
- OMB Circular A-133
- Prepare required reports, including opinions on the financial statements, the Schedule of Federal Funds, and the compliance with law and regulation for major Federal programs; reports on the reviews of internal control and compliance; and material findings such as weaknesses in internal controls, questioned costs, and noncompliance with law or regulation
- Be certain that reports and audit work papers meet A-133 standards
- Work with the nonprofit to resolve any concerns by funders regarding "substandard" audit reports, procedures, etc.

EVALUATING YOUR ORGANIZATION'S FINANCIAL HEALTH

The Focus of the A-133 Audit

A-133 audits focus on controls over the use of federal funds. The A-133 audit seeks to answer three important questions:

- Are financial statements *presented fairly* under GAAP?
- Does the organization's control structure provide reasonable assurance of *compliance with federal regulations*?
- Has the *recipient complied with applicable laws* and regulations?

The auditor examines your policies and procedures to determine whether they assure that:

- Resource use is consistent with laws, regulations, and award terms;
- Resources are safeguarded against waste, theft, misuse, or loss;
- Reliable data is obtained, maintained, and fairly reported. The A-133 auditor will test transactions to determine if:
- Expenditures were for allowable services;
- Records show benefits went to eligible participants;
- Matching requirements and level of effort requirements were met;
- Federal reports and claims are supported by books and records from which financial statements were prepared;
- Amounts claimed for matching or cost sharing comply with appropriate cost principles.

The A-133 audit will focus heavily on your compliance with specific federal laws, regulations and requirements such as:

- Political Activity
- Davis Bacon Act
- Civil Rights Act
- Cash Management
- Federal Financial Reports
- Allowable Costs
- Indirect Costs
- Other Cost Allocation
- Drug Free Workplace Requirements
- Administrative Requirements
    - ◊ interest earned
    - ◊ program income
    - ◊ period of funds availability
    - ◊ real property

- ◊ equipment
- ◊ supplies
- ◊ procurement
- ◊ subgrants
- ◊ revolving loan payments

Steps to Prepare for A-133 Audits

Your nonprofit will need to take the following steps to prepare for an A-133 audit:

- Select an auditor;
- Get lists of schedules and documents needed;
- Discuss review of contracts;
- Get CFDA numbers;
- Test your reports—tie to Financial Statements, General Ledger, underlying documents;
- Test your compliance—eligibility, match, allowable costs;
- Reflect on the internal controls you did have—informal as well as formal—prepare policies and procedures manual;

One final tip: Don't over-prepare—check with your auditor to be sure you are ready to provide the information the auditor most needs.

Consult Appendix 1 if you would like information about source material related to this Chapter. Appendix 1 has references of interest to all readers, not just professionals.

So far, Part V has focused on financial systems and records. However, your nonprofit also has to observe other types of recordkeeping and reporting and is subject to some laws governing your operations not covered elsewhere in this book. We cover the federal and state electioneering and lobbying rules that apply to all nonprofit corporations in Chapter 29 and other compliance requirements in Chapter 30.

29 ELECTIONEERING AND LOBBYING RULES FOR ALL NONPROFIT CORPORATIONS

THIS CHAPTER COVERS

- Spaghetti Rules
- Federal Election Rules
- Federal Lobbying Rules
- Oregon Rules Governing Political Campaigns
- Oregon Lobbying Rules
- Local Political and Lobbying Rules
- Use of Federal Funds for Political and Lobbying Activities
- Political Expenditure Tax

Chapter 8 described restrictions imposed by the IRS on political activities and lobbying that apply to tax-exempt organizations, primarily those exempt under §501(c)(3). The federal government, and to a lesser extent, the state, also regulates campaign finance, electioneering, and lobbying by all nonprofit corporations and unions, as well as business corporations, in order to encourage fair elections and to limit back room lobbying. The definitions of what constitutes political activity and lobbying under federal and state election and lobbying laws are different than the definitions that the IRS uses, so exempt organizations need to be aware that federal and state election and lobbying laws may cover activities that the IRS does not regulate.

This chapter discusses the federal and state campaign and lobbying rules that apply to all nonprofit corporations. Organizations that are tax-exempt and that engage in electioneering or lobbying must read Chapter 8 and this chapter and comply with the rules in both chapters that apply to them. Other nonprofit corporations must follow the rules in this chapter but do not have to observe the rules in Chapter 8. We cannot provide complete coverage of these complex rules in this chapter, but we try to provide enough information so that you can determine if you need professional advice.

Spaghetti Rules

All nonprofit corporations that are involved in electioneering or that lobby need to be aware of federal and state election and lobbying regulations. The plethora of regulations make this a mess that is much less tasty than but about as tangled as spaghetti. You should start by sorting out which rules might apply to you.

- The IRS regulations on political activity and lobbying discussed in Chapter 8 apply *only to certain groups exempt from federal income taxation*. They cover political activities and lobbying at the federal, state, and local levels. Groups exempt from federal taxation whose political activities or lobbying are regulated as described in Chapter 8 must follow the rules in Chapter 8 *and* the rules in this chapter. Non-exempt nonprofits and exempt corporations that are not subject to regulation in Chapter 8 follow only the rules in this chapter.

- *Groups exempt under §501(c)(3)* cannot engage in any activities to influence the election of candidates and are restricted in how much lobbying they can do. The meaning and limitations of the campaigning and lobbying restrictions are described in Chapter 8. If your organization is exempt under §501(c)(3), you cannot engage in any campaigning in connection with federal, state, or local candidate elections nor can you contribute to PACs that support or oppose candidates or parties. The only political activities described in this chapter in which you can engage are to sponsor candidate debates (subject to the rules in Chapter 8 and to the rules in this chapter), to support or oppose nominations for *appointed*, not elected, positions, to support issue-only PACs, and to support or oppose state ballot measures (but not recall petitions). Be aware that state ballot measures are treated as *lobbying* under IRS rules but are treated as *electoral activities* under Oregon law, so you will need to read the sections on Oregon rules governing political campaigns if you support or oppose ballot measures. Keep these limitations in mind as you read the federal and state rules on political activities in this chapter.

- Any group *exempt under any subsection of §501(c)* that tries to influence elections or appointed positions at the federal, state, or local level should read the section on the political expenditure tax on pages 673-674. You may be required to pay this tax. If you are registered as a PAC, you can skip this section.

- The *federal* regulations (except for the IRS rules) discussed in this chapter apply only to political activity and lobbying *at the federal level*. If you do not try to influence federal elective or appointed positions or to lobby at the federal level, you can skip that material.

- *State* regulations on political activity apply to *federal, state, and local* activity, so you will need to read that section if you support or oppose a candidate, political party, or ballot measure at any governmental level.

- *State* lobbying rules apply only to lobbying done *in connection with state government*. If you don't lobby the state legislature, these rules do not apply to you.

- Any nonprofit *that receives federal funds* should read the section on federal funds on pages 672-73. Your funding may contain restrictions on your political or lobbying activities at the federal, state, or local levels.

Not all political activity and lobbying is regulated. If you are not tax exempt, you may engage in an activity that you think of as a political activity or lobbying that is not regulated. For example, the state of Oregon does not regulate get-out-the vote efforts for ballot measure campaigns and federal law does not apply to state ballot measures. If you do not get federal funds, you can engage in this activity without any regulation under these laws. As long as you are not violating some other law, you can engage in political and lobbying activities that are unregulated.

You're probably getting the inkling that the rules governing federal and state electioneering and lobbying are quite complex. We give you an overview here so that you can determine if you need to be concerned about these rules. All of these rules have penalties if you fail to follow them that we don't try to cover here. If you are engaging in political campaigning or lobbying that may be covered by these rules, get legal advice.

Federal Election Rules

Federal election rules are campaign finance reform laws designed to regulate how money is spent to influence federal elections. The *Citizens United* case in 2010 eviscerated a great deal of federal election law, creating considerable uncertainty about much of federal election regulation. Current federal laws attempt to regulate election spending by controlling the source and amount of contributions made directly to federal candidates, by restricting contributions to and spending by political action committees (PACs) that coordinate their messages with candidates, and by requiring public disclosure of some contributions and electioneering. The federal election rules described in this section are in a great state of flux as a result of the *Citizens United* case and may change, so be sure you have current advice on this issue.

> *The federal election rules described in this section are in a great state of flux as a result of the* Citizens United *case and may change, so be sure you have current advice on this issue.*

Nonprofit organizations may become involved in electioneering in several ways. A nonprofit may want:

- to *endorse or oppose* a candidate or political party,

THE OREGON NONPROFIT CORPORATION HANDBOOK

- to *contribute* to a candidate or party,
- to *advocate for* a candidate or party,
- to *engage in voter registration and education activities*.

Each of these activities is subject to regulation.

> *If you are exempt under §501(c)(3), you are prohibited from all electioneering. You cannot engage in any of the activities in this section nor contribute to PACs, except to support or oppose nominees for appointed positions and issue-only PACs and to sponsor candidate debates subject to strict limitations.*

The federal laws do not restrict nonprofit involvement in state or local races. State laws may. (See pages 664-70.) In addition, you have to file all reports required under the federal election laws with the Oregon Secretary of State. If you are exempt under §501(c)(3), you are prohibited from all electioneering (see pp. 173-80). You cannot engage in any of the activities in this section nor contribute to PACs, except to support or oppose nominees for appointed positions and issue-only PACs as discussed on pp. 669-70 and to sponsor candidate debates subject to the strict limitations described on page 662.

> *The federal laws do not restrict nonprofit involvement in state or local races. State laws may.*

Endorsing or Opposing Candidates

Organizations exempt under §501(c)(3) cannot endorse or oppose candidates. All other nonprofits can endorse or oppose a candidate for office.

Contributions to Federal Candidates and Political Parties by Nonprofit Corporations

Federal candidates raise and spend money through candidate or party political committees. Federal candidates cannot receive money or in-kind contributions from nonprofit (and business) corporations or unions and therefore your nonprofit corporation cannot give directly to a federal candidate or party. The ban on contributions includes in-kind contributions and anything of value, not just cash contributions. For example, you cannot offer your mailing list, the use of your staff to canvas or your phones for phone-banking to federal candidates. You may sell your mailing list or rent your phones as long as you get a fair price paid in advance for the sale or rental. The federal election law restrictions do not apply to state and local candidates.

Your nonprofit corporation or union can set up a separate segregated fund which can make some contributions to a candidate. You will almost always be required to register the fund as a political action committee (PAC). Your corporation can pay the administrative expenses of the PAC and can encourage certain people connected with your corporation to contribute to the PAC. Other than paying the administrative expenses, your corporation or union cannot contribute to this type of PAC. The PAC can make limited contributions to a candidate. These separate segregated fund PACs are described below.

Federal candidates cannot receive money or in-kind contributions from nonprofit (and business) corporations or unions and therefore your nonprofit corporation cannot give directly to a federal candidate or party.

Advocating for Candidates or Political Parties by Nonprofit Corporations

Direct contributions to a federal candidate are only one way to support a candidate or party. A corporation or union can also support or oppose a candidate or party by urging voters to vote for or against a candidate through its newsletters, mailings, media advertisements, and its website.

Prior to the *Citizens United* case, sixty years of election law allowed Congress to place restrictions on the ability of corporations and unions to spend money on expressly advocating for a candidate or party in a federal election. Corporations and unions could not place ads or otherwise spend funds to directly endorse or oppose a candidate or party and could not give funds to other groups that endorsed or opposed candidates or parties. Corporations and unions could only influence elections by giving to their own political action committees (PACs), which were subject to limitations on giving and subject to reporting and disclosure requirements that provided transparency about the sources of money for candidates. They could also implicitly but not explicitly endorse candidates in their advertising and publications.

If you are a (c)(3), you cannot engage in any advocacy of the type described here.

The *Citizens United* case in 2010 struck down much of federal election law in the area of advocacy. As you review the changes and now permissible activities, remember that if you are a (c)(3), you cannot engage in any advocacy of the type described here. *Citizens United* hasn't changed that because it addressed Federal election law. But the Internal Revenue Code prohibition on political activity as a condition of your (c)(3) exemption remains in force regardless of *Citizens United*.

If your nonprofit corporation (and for-profit corporation) or union is not exempt under §501(c)(3), it can now directly spend unlimited funds on advocating for or against a candidate as long as you do so *independently* of the candidate or party you support. Your expenditures are independent expenditures if you do not coordinate your activities or your communications with a federal candidate or party. For your communication to remain uncoordinated, the candidate and the candidate's campaign staff or party cannot share financial responsibility for your activity or communication. The campaign cannot be involved in decisions about your activity or communication, including what you say in your message, when you publicize it, which media you use, or who you try to reach. If you do coordinate with a candidate, your expenditure will be considered a contribution to the candidate, which you cannot do.

> *Your nonprofit corporation (and for-profit corporation) or union that is not exempt under §501(c)(3) can now directly spend unlimited funds on advocating for or against a candidate as long as you do so independently of the candidate or party you support.*

You can make unlimited independent expenditures in several ways:

- You can spend directly to promote your candidate or party. For example, you can run a newspaper ad under your corporation or union's name that urges voters to vote for a particular Presidential candidate. This is the simplest way for your nonprofit corporation or union to promote its views, and the one many nonprofit corporations and unions will probably use. If your political activity becomes your primary activity, however, this may threaten your tax-exempt status. To avoid this, you may need to fund a PAC to conduct your activities.

- You can give money to another organization exempt under §501(c)(4) or (c)(6) and that organization can use the funds to support or oppose a candidate or party. While (c)(4)s and (c)(6)s can engage in a limited amount of campaigning, political activity cannot be their primary purpose. These organizations do not have to disclose their donors unless the donor specifically designated the contributions for election ads, so your identity can remain confidential if you avoid a specific designation for the use of the funds. If the other organization spends a substantial part of its funds on electioneering, it will lose its exempt status as a (c)(4) or (c)(6) and will have to disclose its donors.

- You can give funds to a PAC. (See the discussion below.) The PAC can use the funds for campaigning but will be required to file disclosure reports about its donors.

You cannot give funds directly to the candidates as discussed above.

> *Example*: Advocates for Family Farmers, an Oregon nonprofit corporation exempt under §501(c)(4), wants to support a candidate for the U.S. Senate. Its Board wants to endorse the candidate as an organization, contribute $1,000 to the candidate, allow the candidate to use its offices for phone-banking, urge its newsletter subscribers to vote for the candidate, and place an ad in the local newspaper urging the community to vote for her. Can AFF do all these things?
>
> AFF as a (c)(4) can endorse the candidate and can urge voters to vote for the candidate in its newsletter and in the newspaper, as long as it does not coordinate its messages with the candidate. It cannot contribute directly to the candidate but it can pay to set up a separate segregated fund PAC as described below. It can allow the candidate to phone-bank if it gets a fair rental price paid in advance. (Otherwise, the use of the phone bank would be an impermissible contribution to the candidate.)

Remember that if you are a (c)(3), you cannot engage in any advocacy of the type described here. Federal election law does not prohibit it, but the Internal Revenue Code does as a condition of your (c)(3) exemption.

Federal Political Committees

At the federal level, nonprofits that are organized and operated primarily to influence the selection of candidates to federal, state, and local elected or appointed office or to an office in a political party are commonly called political committees. Their activities to influence these elections or appointments are called their exempt functions. There are several types of political committees. The most common are political parties, candidate committees, and political action committees (PACs).

PACs are formed by individuals and organizations, including nonprofit corporations, to support candidates, political parties, or issues that the PAC seeks to advance. Political committees, including PACs, are exempt from federal income taxation except taxation on their investment income under §527 of the Internal Revenue Code. To take advantage of the exemption, almost all of them register with the IRS.

Political committees, including PACs, are also subject to the federal election rules, except for four types of political committees:

- Those that focus only on state or local elections.
- Those that operate only to influence appointed positions and not elected positions—for example, Cabinet positions or federal judgeships.
- Those that receive and spend no more than $1,000 per year in federal electioneering and are not segregated funds of nonprofit corporations or unions.
- Those that only sponsor uncoordinated communications or engage in partisan voter registration drives.

THE OREGON NONPROFIT CORPORATION HANDBOOK

Remember that PACs that are not subject to federal election rules may be subject to Oregon state rules. See pp. 664-70.

We discuss PACs that are formed by nonprofit corporations or unions and PACs that are set up independently, because these are the political committees of most interest to nonprofit corporations. Political committees set up by candidates or political parties have different rules than the ones we describe in this book.

Political Action Committees (PACs)

For purposes of federal electioneering, PACs are formed in one of three ways:

- Corporations, including nonprofit corporations, and unions can set up *separate segregated funds,* also called *connected PACs,* to make contributions to candidates or parties. Corporations and unions behind connected PACs can use their general funds to set up and administer these PACS and to solicit for money.

- Anyone may set up a *nonconnected PACs*. Individuals, corporations, and unions can contribute to these PACs, though the PAC must observe certain restrictions with respect to monies from corporations and unions. These PACs may contribute to candidates, with restrictions that prohibit union and corporate money from going to candidates, and can make unlimited expenditures to advocate for or against a candidate or party. The PACs must pay the fees for setting up, administering, and soliciting funds from the funds that they solicit. If your PAC coordinates with a candidate, much more restrictive rules apply.

- Anyone, including a corporation or union, can set up a *Super PAC*. Super PACs do not contribute directly to campaigns and do not coordinate with candidates. They can endorse or oppose candidates. Super PACs can raise and spend unlimited sums of money.

§501(c)(3) organizations cannot form or contribute to PACs, except those whose sole activity is to support or oppose a candidate for appointed, not elected, office.

SEPARATE SEGREGATED FUND PACS

The federal PAC rules are designed in part to restrict corporations and unions from raising and contributing substantial amounts of their own funds directly to candidates. Separate segregated fund PACs are the method by which corporations and unions can contribute to some degree to candidates and parties. A corporations or union cannot make unlimited contributions to its separate segregated fund PAC but it can pay the set-up, administrative, and fundraising expenses of the PAC. Your corporation or union can only raise money from a restricted class of people—your members, executive, and administrative employees and their families that are connected with your corporation or union. There are rules governing how you conduct your solicitations.

Your separate segregated fund PAC can contribute up to $2,500 per election cycle to each federal candidate, $5,000 a year to other PACs, and $38,500 a year to a national political party.

NONCONNECTED PACS

If you are a nonconnected PAC—that is, a PAC that was not set up by a corporation or union—you can solicit contributions from anyone, including unions or for-profit or nonprofit corporations. You can spend your funds by making contributions to candidates, with certain restrictions. You can also advocate for or against a candidate in the media, through the mail, and other methods. How you handle your funds depends on whether you receive funds from unions or corporations.

NO CORPORATE OR UNION FUNDS

If you do not accept funds from unions or corporations, you can deposit all of your funds into one account. You can accept contributions of any amount, as long as your PAC does not coordinate with a political campaign.

> *Your PAC may spend money by contributing directly to a candidate or political committee or you may engage in express or issue advocacy.*

Your PAC may spend money by contributing directly to a candidate or political committee or you may engage in your own advocacy for the candidate or party. If you contribute directly to a candidate, political party, or other PAC, the amount that you can contribute depends on whether you are a multi-candidate PAC. If you are not a multi-candidate PAC, you can contribute up to $2,500 to each federal candidate per election, $5,000 to any other PAC per year, $10,000 combined limit to state and local parties per year, and $30,800 to a national political party per year.

You are a multi-candidate PAC if you have been registered with the FEC for at least six months, have contributed to at least five federal candidates and have more than 50 contributors. As a multi-candidate political committee, you can contribute up to $5,000 per election to each federal candidate, $5,000 a year to other PACs, $5,000 a year combined limit to local political parties, and $15,000 a year to a national party.

If your PAC wants to engage in its own direct advocacy for a candidate or party, there are no limits on how much you can spend as long as you do not coordinate your activities with a candidate. (See page 599 for a discussion of coordination.) This means that you can spend as much as you want on independent ads supporting or attacking candidates. If you coordinate your communications with a candidate, your expenditure is a contribution to the candidate and is subject to the contribution limits described above.

CORPORATE OR UNION FUNDS

If you receive corporate or union funds, you must put these funds in a separate segregated account. Corporations and unions can make unlimited contributions to your PAC as long as you do not coordinate with a campaign and as long as you use the corporate and union funds only for your advocacy work, not for contributions to candidates or parties. To ensure that you do not contribute these funds to candidates or parties, you must keep these funds in a separate account, called a non-contribution account. You cannot accept funds from foreign nationals, government contractors, national banks, and corporations organized by Congress. You can use these funds for your advocacy work but you cannot make contributions to a candidate or party from this account. You must allocate to the non-contribution account the percentage of administrative expenses that corresponds to the percentage of activity for that account.

SUPER PACS

The *Citizens United* case and subsequent cases led to the creation of a third kind of PAC, dubbed the Super PAC. If you don't donate funds to candidates but do engage in advocating for or against a candidate, you can be a Super PAC. You can't coordinate with a candidate or party. You can raise unlimited sums of money and can spend unlimited sums of money. You must report your donors to the Federal Election Commission. These PACs are called Super PACs because they can raise and spend unlimited amounts of money.

Coordination with a Campaign

PACs who coordinate with a campaign are treated like they are making a contribution to the candidate. Their expenditures are treated as a contribution to a candidate and the PAC is subject to the rules for contributions to a candidate discussed above.

§501(c)(3)s and PACs

§501(c)(3) organizations cannot form or contribute to federal PACs, except:

- PACs whose sole activity is to support or oppose a candidate for *appointed* (such as a candidate for the U.S. Supreme Court), not elected, office; or

- PACs that are restricted to advocating for issues only and cannot contribute to candidates or political parties.

§501(c)(3)s can set up a §501(c)(4) organization and the (c)(4) can set up a PAC that supports or opposes a candidate for elected office, but the (c)(3) money and resources cannot be used for the PAC unless the PAC' falls within one of the rare exceptions above. See pp. 200-02.

Registration and Disclosure Requirements

If your PAC is subject to federal election rules, you must have a treasurer who keeps track of the contributions and expenditures and complies with the disclosure regulations. Separate segregated fund PACs must file a statement of organization with the Federal Election Commission (FEC) within ten days after becoming a political committee and non-connected PACs must file within 10 days of raising or spending $1,000. This filing is in addition to the notice of status that §527 PACs file with the IRS.

If your political committee is covered by federal electioneering rules, you must follow the Federal Elections Commission's rules on reporting. Check the FEC's website at *www.fec.gov*. If your PAC is exempt under §527, you also have to comply with IRS reporting requirements.

Voter Activities

Your nonprofit corporation or union can spend your general funds on certain types of voter activities that are directed to the general public rather than to your restricted class described on pp. 658-59. To avoid partisanship, you must follow special rules.

Voter Registration

- You have to conduct your activities in a neutral manner and you cannot expressly advocate for a candidate for federal office or for a party.

- You can engage in voter registration and get-out-the-vote programs aimed at the general public but you cannot advocate for or against a candidate or party and you cannot coordinate your project with a candidate or party. (Coordination is discussed above.)

- You cannot conduct your registration and get-out-the-vote drives by directing the drives primarily to individuals previously registered with or intending to register with the party you favor.

- Any services, including rides to the polls, that you offer must be made available to all regardless of party affiliation. You have to give written notice of this to everyone to whom you offer services or rides.

- Individuals who conduct your drives cannot be paid based on the number of individuals registered or transported who support a particular party.

§501(c) (3) organizations as well as other nonprofits may engage in certain voter activities, but they must also comply with the stricter get-out-the-vote rules described in Chapter 8.

As long as you observe these rules, you can conduct your drives among populations of unregistered voters that you generally believe will support your candidate or party. §501(c) (3) organizations as well as other nonprofits may engage in certain voter activities, but they must also comply with the stricter get-out-the-vote rules described on page 163.

Voter Guides

In addition to getting citizens to vote, you can educate voters. You can distribute voting records of the federal candidates but you cannot advocate in favor of or against a candidate or party, nor can you coordinate the production or distribution of the candidate's records with a candidate or party. You can also distribute voter guides that explain the candidates' positions on the issues as long as you don't coordinate with a candidate or party. In the case of voter guides, you must either avoid express advocacy or meet a more detailed list of criteria designed to ensure fairness. §501(c)(3) organizations must also comply with the more stringent voter education rules described on page 174.

Candidate Debates

Nonprofit corporations exempt under §501(c)(3) may host federal candidate debates. §501(c)(4) organizations that do not support or oppose a candidate for federal office or a party can also host candidate debates. Other nonprofit corporations cannot sponsor federal candidate debates.

> *Nonprofit corporations exempt under §501(c)(3) may host federal candidate debates. §501(c)(4) organizations that do not support or oppose a candidate for federal office or a party can also host candidate debates.*

Here are the rules you need to follow:

- These (c)(3) and (c)(4) nonprofits may use their own funds and may accept funds donated by corporations and unions to cover the costs of the debate.

- The debate must include at least two candidates and cannot be structured to promote one candidate over the other.

- Your nonprofit must use preestablished criteria to determine whether to include a candidate. For example, you may require that candidates have at least 10% of the vote in independent polls in order to be included.

- For debates before a primary, you can restrict the candidates to those from one party but you may not use party as the sole criteria to determine who is in a debate before the general election.

If your organization is exempt under §501(c)(3), you must follow the somewhat more detailed criteria on page 174 as well as the rules here if you sponsor candidate debates.

ELECTIONEERING AND LOBBYING 29

Federal Lobbying Rules

The federal Lobbying Disclosure Act requires some organizations to disclose how much lobbying of Congress and federal agencies that they do. Most churches and religious orders are exempt from the law. The law accomplishes disclosure by requiring registration and reporting of lobbying. It does not limit *how much* lobbying that you do. This is a complicated area. In our brief description here, we will alert you about whether you are lobbying through one of your employees or volunteers. If so, you need to get professional advice about what is allowed and how to register and report properly. If you are hiring an outside lobbyist or a lobbying firm, they should deal with the registration and reporting discussed here.

The Lobbying Disclosure Act defines lobbying as written and oral communications directed to certain legislative and executive branch officials in the federal government. The law covers communications made in regard to federal legislation, rules, regulations, Executive Orders, the administration of a federal program or policy, or the nomination or confirmation of a person whose position is subject to confirmation by the Senate. There are numerous exceptions to the definition of a lobbying contact, including the provision of information in response to a request from an executive or legislative branch employee, responses to notices in the Federal Register for public comment, and testimony before Congress and congressional committees.

> *The federal Lobbying Disclosure Act requires some organizations to disclose how much federal lobbying that they do.*

The lobbying law divides the year into four quarterly periods—beginning in January, April, July, and October. Your organization is required to register and file reports if you meet two requirements:

- You must have at least one lobbyist who is your employee, who makes more than one lobbying contact, and who spends 20% or more of his or her time engaged in lobbying over a three-month period. You do not have to comply with the lobbying law if you hire only outside lobbyists, if your lobbyist is a volunteer who receives no compensation, if your lobbying employee only makes one lobbying contact, or if your lobbying employee spends less than 20% of his or her time lobbying during a semi-annual period.

- Your total lobbying expenses must exceed, or be expected to exceed, $11,500 in a quarterly period. (This sum is adjusted each year, so get updated information from *http://clerk.house.gov*.)

If your organization is required to register under the federal lobbying law, you must register within 45 days of making your first lobbying contact. You can obtain the form to register as a Sen-

663

ate lobbyist by going to the Senate website at *www.senate.gov*. House lobbyists should go to *http://clerk.house.gov*.

As a registered lobbyist, you must file two types of reports:

- You must file quarterly reports on your lobbying contacts that are due 20 days after the end of each quarter. In these reports, you must list, among other things, the issues and bills targeted by your lobbying; the houses of Congress and federal agencies that you lobbied, and your lobbying expenses. In addition, associations and coalitions that receive more than $5,000 per quarter from an organization for "lobbying activities" must disclose that organization's name if that organization participates actively in the planning, supervision, or control of the lobbying.

- You have to file a semi-annual report on any political contributions you make. These reports include any aggregate political contribution your organization made of $200 or more to a federal candidate or party. Your aggregate political contribution includes contributions made by a PAC that you established, finance, maintain, or control. You will also certify that you understand the House and Senate rules about gifts and travel provided to members of Congress and did not violate them.

You can get more information about the Lobbying Disclosure Act, including examples, at *http://lobbyingdisclosure.house.gov/amended_lda_guide.html*.

Lobbying by (c)(3) Organizations

The definition of lobbying under the federal lobbying law is quite different than the definition of lobbying used by the IRS for tax-exempt purposes that we discussed in Chapter 8. The Lobbying Disclosure Act's definition is broader in that it includes lobbying of administrative agencies. It is narrower in that it includes only lobbying of the federal government and does not include any grassroots lobbying. Organizations exempt under §501(c)(3) can face complex bookkeeping requirements to meet both the IRS and Lobbying Disclosure Act lobbying rules. To alleviate this burden, the Lobbying Disclosure Act allows (c)(3)s that have made the lobbying election under subsection (h) (see pages 193-94) to choose to use the definition of lobbying under the subsection (h) rules rather than the definition under the federal lobbying law to determine if they meet the threshold for registration and to report lobbying expenses if they are required to register. You should get an accountant's assistance with this.

Oregon Rules Governing Political Campaigns

Oregon laws that govern political involvement have several distinct features. They cover federal, state, and local political candidates. The laws apply both to candidate races and to ballot measures and establish rules, registration, and reporting requirements. Nonprofits that are involved in political campaigns and in ballot measure advocacy need to familiarize themselves with all of these rules. You may be liable for penalties if you fail to follow Oregon campaign finance rules. The Oregon Secretary of State publishes an excellent and readable book, the *Campaign Finance Manual*, that explains Oregon's rules and electioneering and contains the forms required by the state. You can obtain this from the Secretary of State at the address or on the website listed in Appendix 2.

> *(c)(3)s involved in Oregon ballot measures need to be familiar with the election rules described in this section.*

Organizations exempt under §501(c)(3) will generally not be concerned with this section, since (c)(3)s cannot be involved in electoral activity. However, an important exception is ballot measures. The IRS treats involvement in ballot measures (except recall petitions) as lobbying and not political activity and allows (c)(3)s to do a limited amount of lobbying. (See Chapter 8.) However, the state of Oregon covers ballot measures under its election laws. Consequently, (c)(3)s involved with Oregon ballot measures need to be familiar with the election rules described in this section.

Oregon law recognizes a variety of political committees—candidate committees that run election campaigns, measure committees that start and run ballot measure campaigns, political party committees, and political committees that take positions on both elections and ballot measures. Candidate, ballot measure, and political party committees are formed for specifically electioneering purposes and we do not attempt to cover those groups in this chapter.

> *The Oregon election rules may classify your nonprofit as a political committee even if you don't think of yourself as a political committee.*

In this section, we focus on the political committees and on nonprofits with broader missions that want to support or oppose a candidate or ballot measure. The important news for nonprofits is that the Oregon election rules may classify your nonprofit as a political committee even if you don't think of yourself as a political committee—and it's easier than you might think! Your nonprofit may be covered by these regulations:

- if you make *independent expenditures* to support or oppose a candidate or ballot measure,
- if you are *classified as a political committee by the state,* or
- if you *form a separate political committee.*

Independent Expenditures

Oregon law regulates nonprofits (and others) that support or oppose a candidate, party, or ballot measure by recognizing two levels of involvement. On one level are nonprofits that use their own funds to make a very few expenditures in a campaign. If you engage in very limited campaigning and do not make your expenditure with the cooperation of the candidate or political committee, you may be making an *independent expenditure*. An independent expenditure is an expenditure for a communication that expressly advocates the election or defeat of a clearly identified candidate or ballot measure and that was not made with the consent of, in consultation with or at the request or suggestion of a candidate, agent or political committee of the candidate or measure. For example, you may make an independent expenditure by paying for a voter pamphlet argument or for an advertisement without the knowledge of a candidate or committee connected with a ballot measure.

> *If you make an independent expenditure of more than $100 to support or oppose a candidate, political committee or ballot measure, you must file a Statement of Independent Expenditures (PC 10) with the appropriate elections office.*

The state does not regulate independent expenditures as heavily as it does those made by political committees. If you make an independent expenditure of more than $100 to support or oppose a candidate, political committee or ballot measure, you must file a Statement of Independent Expenditures (PC 10) with the appropriate elections office. If you report your expenditure as a contribution to a political committee and your contribution is reported by the committee, you do not have to report it again.

If you make an expenditure that you coordinate with a candidate, a political committee, or a ballot measure, your expenditure is no longer independent and will be treated as a *contribution* to that candidate, political committee, or ballot measure. If you engage in more than a few independent expenditures that support or oppose one candidate, party, or ballot measure so that you have "taken up the cause," you may also move outside the classification of independent expenditure and may be classified as a political committee.

Political Committees

Nonprofits that solicit funds for election or ballot measure campaigns or that make more than a few expenditures for a campaign have a greater level of involvement in the electoral process and are subject to more state regulation. The law defines those groups with this greater level of involvement as political committees. Your nonprofit may be classified as a political committee without your knowledge or consent or by your choice.

Involuntary Classification as a Political Committee

Your nonprofit may be classified as a political committee even though you did not intend this result. You will become a political committee under Oregon law if you solicit and receive contributions for the purpose of supporting or opposing a ballot measure, candidate, or political party. This means that if your organization receives contributions that are designated for your political activity, the state will treat you as a political committee and you must report as one. If the contributions are designated for a candidate or political committee who is required to report them and you turn them over within 7 days, you are not a political committee.

Two common questions come up in determining whether the state can classify your nonprofit as a political committee:

- Do funds that come to you for your general purposes count as political if one of your purposes is political but others are not?

- Does "support or oppose" mean that you have to take a clear position in favor of or against a candidate or ballot measure, or will other more indirect actions force you into the political committee category?

Your nonprofit may be classified as a political committee even though you did not intend this result.

Many nonprofits, especially (c)(4) social welfare organizations that are set up for social welfare purposes, have several purposes, one of which is to take positions on political issues and other purposes that may relate to education, charitable activities, or civic improvement. When donors contribute to the general fund of these organization, their funds may be used for any or all of these purposes. Some part will have to be used for political purposes. Even so, the state generally takes the position that these types of contributions that are not earmarked for political activities do not make these organizations political committees subject to reporting under the state election laws.

Example: Latino Empowerment is a (c)(4) that assists immigrants from Mexico and Central and South America find jobs and housing and that engages in political advocacy to support candidates that favor improved laws for undocumented workers. It receives considerable funds from donations for its work. As long as these funds are not restricted to use on political issues, Latino Empowerment does not have to report as a political committee.

The second question is what kinds of actions "support or oppose" candidates, parties, or ballot measures, so that the state calls you a political committee. Explicit language that urges a voter to elect or vote against a candidate or measure clearly supports or opposes that candidate or ballot measure. However, your activities may support or oppose a candidate or ballot measure even if you do not use explicit language of support or opposition. You have engaged in express advocacy that will make you a political committee under Oregon law if your message, taken in context, clearly urges the election or defeat of a candidate and seeks action rather than simply gives information. You should get legal advice if you are drafting messages that you don't want to be interpreted as an endorsement or opposition to a candidate or measure.

Example: Clean Government runs an ad just before the election complaining about the corruption of union bosses with the words UNION BOSSES appearing in large print. CG runs the pictures of a dozen candidates with the words PUBLIC EMPLOYEE FINANCED stamped on each photo. CG doesn't explicitly urge its readers to vote against these candidates. It has nonetheless engaged in explicit advocacy, since the context of its message implies more than an argument on the issues about union corruption. By presenting candidate photos as it did, it has exhorted its readers to vote against them.

If you do engage in soliciting money to support or oppose a candidate, party, or ballot measure, your nonprofit becomes a political committee and will have to comply with the registration and reporting requirements of political committees described below. One significant consequence of being a political committee is that your complete list of contributors who gave more than $100 becomes a public record whether or not each donor's contribution was used for your political purposes. Other nonprofits can generally keep their list of contributors private.

Choosing to Form a Separate Political Committee

Many nonprofits that engage in electioneering do not want to be classified as a political committee because they do not want to disclose their donors and do not want to meet the reporting requirements for all of their operations. If your nonprofit wants to engage in supporting or opposing a ballot measure, candidate, or party but does not want to be classified as a political committee, you can set up a separate political committee to handle your political activities.

> *If your nonprofit wants to engage in supporting or opposing a ballot measure, candidate, or party but does not want to be classified as a political committee, you can set up a separate political committee to handle your political activities.*

You organize a political committee by naming a treasurer and your Directors and by registering with the state. All your contributions and expenditures to the committee go through a separate bank account set up by your treasurer. Treasurers are personally liable if they fail to carry out the duties required by the law. The state fines vary but can be substantial for each late or insufficient filing of contribution and expenditure reports, so you should exercise care in naming a treasurer. Anyone who directly and substantially participates in the decision-making concerning the solicitation or expenditure of funds and the support or opposition to a candidate or ballot measure is a Director and should be named. You must have at least one other Director in addition to your treasurer.

Example: Coalition for Responsible Taxation is a §501(c)(3) organization that seeks to educate the public about the Oregon tax system. The Coalition decides to support a ballot measure to improve Oregon's tax structure. Some of its contributors do not want the Coalition to set up a separate political committee to receive contributions and to make expenditures because the contributors wish to remain anonymous. In spite of their wishes, CRT must establish a separate political committee or the (c)(3) becomes a political committee, requiring disclosure of all its contributors over $100.

ELECTIONEERING AND LOBBYING

You must register your political committee within three business days of receiving your first contribution or making your first expenditure. The location for registration varies. Check with the Secretary of State's office (see Appendix 2) to determine where you register.

All reporting is done by computer. In most cases, you must file periodic reports of your contributions and expenditures. In these reports, you must list the name, address and occupation of your donors who contribute more than $100. You cannot receive contributions from anonymous donors or from foreign nationals nor can you accept contributions that you know to be in a false name.

The Oregon Secretary of State's *Campaign Finance Manual* (see Appendix 2) explains the rules for and the forms to be filed by political committees.

Contributions to Political Committees

Federal campaign laws described above contain complex regulations to limit the size and source of contributions to the political committees of federal candidates and parties. Oregon law does not limit the amount of money that an individual, corporation, union, or other entity can contribute to candidates, except that a political committee cannot accept anonymous contributions, contributions in a false name, or contributions from foreign nationals. Oregon also does not restrict contributions by corporations or unions.

Electioneering Conduct

In addition to registration and reporting requirements, Oregon law also restricts certain conduct related to elections and ballot measures. You cannot write, publish, or place an advertisement that contains false statements relating to a candidate, political committee, or ballot measure. If you assist in circulating petitions for a ballot measure, you cannot obtain signatures by lying about the contents or the effect of the petition. You also cannot knowingly accept false or unqualified signatures and you cannot of course pay people to sign a petition or threaten them to get them to sign.

Your nonprofit cannot attempt to unduly influence an election. Most common violations include giving something of value to voters—for example, hats, frisbees, or toys—or providing refreshments beyond what is normally provided to induce people to attend a political gathering. For example, offering soft drinks and coffee is common, while a free spaghetti feed is illegal.

(c)(3) Organizations

Generally, if you are exempt under §501(c)(3), you cannot engage in any of the activities described in this section and cannot contribute to PACs. The exception is for ballot measures, other than recall petitions. Oregon's use of political campaign laws to cover ballot measures creates an exception to these rules because ballot measures are legislative in nature and are therefore treated by the IRS as lobbying, not political activity. (See page 183.)

One important consequence of the inclusion of ballot measures as part of Oregon's political campaign laws is that organizations exempt under §501(c)(3) may be involved in supporting or opposing a ballot measure. (c)(3)s may contribute to political committees whose only function is to support or oppose ballot measures and whose funds can never be used for other purposes as long as the (c)(3) does not exceed its lobbying limits described in Chapter 8. (c)(3)s cannot contribute to political committees that support or oppose candidates or parties. (See Chapter 8.) Oregon's definition of political activity is different than the definition under federal election laws in this chapter, since there are state but no federal ballot measures.

If you are exempt under §501(c)(3), you cannot engage in any of the activities described in this section and cannot contribute to PACs. The exception is for ballot measures, other than recall petitions.

Oregon Lobbying Rules

The Oregon lobbying law is a *disclosure* statute with registration and reporting requirements and a *regulatory* law restraining the conduct of lobbyists. The definition of who is a lobbyist and the registration and reporting requirements in Oregon are different from the federal lobbying rules.

Under Oregon law, a lobbyist is an individual or entity who, for compensation or as a representative of a group, attempts to influence legislative action:

- by communicating with a legislator,
- by encouraging executive officials or others to communicate with a legislator, or
- by attempting to obtain the good will of a legislator.

There are a few surprises buried in this law. One surprise is that your volunteers may be lobbyists. A second is that a lobbyist is a person who attempts to influence legislation by encouraging "others" to communicate with a legislator. This means that organizations that engage in grassroots lobbying by communicating with their members or the public about legislation and encouraging contact with a legislator are engaging in lobbying. Many groups put out action alerts that are this kind of lobbying. If your employee or volunteer sends out this kind of communication, you need to determine if they need to register as a lobbyist. (See below.)

Attempting to obtain the good will of a legislator can also be a surprise. This can occur if an organization offers inducements to a legislator designed to incur favor—for example, takes a legislator to dinner, gives tickets to a sporting event, or invites a legislator to a convention and pays all the expenses. This is an attempt to obtain good will even if the lobbyist does not talk to the legislator about a matter before the legislature.

The Oregon definition of lobbying is quite broad. Lobbying covers direct and indirect contacts with legislators as well as attempts to obtain good will. Like IRS law, Oregon law covers grassroots lobbying but the definition is much looser and more inclusive than the IRS definition. Unlike the federal lobbying law, Oregon lobbyists can be volunteers who lobby as a representative of your group as well as your paid employees.

In some respects, the federal rules are broader than Oregon's. Unlike the federal lobbying law, Oregon's lobbying statute applies only to lobbying the legislature. Oregon law does not include lobbying administrative agencies, except to the extent that the lobbyist tries to persuade the executive official to influence legislation rather than an administrative action. Unlike IRS law for (c)(3) organizations (discussed in Chapter 8), time spent on research does not count toward lobbying time. Time spent creating testimony or waiting at the hearing to testify also does not count toward lobbying time. Unlike IRS law, ballot measures are not considered legislative action. However, advocating for ballot measures may subject you to Oregon's political campaign rules discussed above.

> *Lobbyists can be volunteers who lobby as a representative of your group as well as your paid employees.*

The law requires most lobbyists to register with the Oregon Government Standards and Practices Commission. Your lobbyist is not required to register if he or she:

- receives no compensation or reimbursement of expenses for lobbying, limits her or his lobbying activities to testifying before public committee sessions in the legislature or public hearings of state agencies, *and* registers in the records of those committees or agencies;

- does not spend more than a total of 24 hours nor more than a total of $100 lobbying during the calendar quarter.

    Example: Oregon for Veterans is a (c)(4) organization that advocates for Oregon veterans. It sends out action alerts to its members about legislation that affects veterans and encourages its members to contact state legislators on issues of interest to veterans. One quarter an employee spent 50 hours researching issues and 30 hours writing and sending numerous alerts. The state does not count research toward the lobbying hours but does count writing and sending the alert toward the lobbying calculation. This employee needs to register because her time writing and sending the alerts exceeds the 24 hour limit. Because the time is calculated by what time "individuals" spend, Oregon for Veterans could have two employees divide the job and, if each employee spent less than 24 hours writing and sending the alerts, no registration is required.

If your lobbyist must register, she or he must do so within three business days after spending more than 24 hours or more than $100 lobbying during any calendar quarter. All lobbyists who must register must report on their lobbying expenditures to the Oregon Government Standards and Practices Commission. You can obtain registration and reporting forms from the Commission at the address in Appendix 2. Your statement will be a public record.

In addition to registration and disclosure regulations, the Oregon lobbying law prohibits certain lobbying conduct. Your lobbyist cannot attempt to influence a legislator's vote by promising financial support for the legislator's candidacy or by threatening to finance the legislator's opponent. You cannot pay your lobbyist based on whether or not the lobbyist is successful. Your lobbyist cannot make false statements to legislative or executive officials or supply them with documents that the lobbyist knows are false.

Local Political and Lobbying Rules

Cities and counties may have their own political and lobbying rules. The City of Portland has lobbying rules that require registration and reporting by lobbyists who lobby city officials. "Lobbying" is attempting to influence the official actions of city officials. The rules cover only direct and not grassroots lobbying. City officials include any elected official or their staff, city Directors in charge of bureaus and the Portland Development Commission, and appointees to several named commissions and the Fire and Police Disability and Retirement Board. The city rules are quite detailed and can be found in the city code at Chapter 2.12.

You will need to check with your own locality for lobbying rules if you want to lobby a city or county official or body.

Use of Federal Funds for Political and Lobbying Activities

The federal government has put several restrictions on the use of federal funds for lobbying and political activities at the federal, state, and local levels. The restrictions vary, depending on what kinds of funds you receive, what activities you pursue and whether you are exempt under §501(c)(4). If you receive any monies from the federal government pursuant to a federal *contract, grant, loan or cooperative agreement*, you cannot use those funds to lobby *federal* legislative or administrative officials covered by the Lobbying Disclosure Act. (See pages 663-64 for more discussion of this Act.)

Most nonprofits, except for colleges and universities, also cannot use federal funds from *grants, cooperative agreements and certain cost contracts* to lobby *federal or state* legislators either directly or by urging the public to get involved (including organizing demonstrations, marches and rallies). You are also restricted from using these monies for certain kinds of legislative liaison efforts. You can lobby *local* officials without restrictions. These nonprofits are also prohibited from using these federal monies to attempt to influence *federal, state, and local elections* or to contribute to political committees. You may use most federal *awards* and other non-federal monies to engage in your lobbying and political activities.

If you are tax-exempt under §501(c)(4), you are subject to the above restrictions as well as some additional ones. If you receive *awards, grants or loans* from the federal government, you cannot do any *federal* lobbying as that term is defined in the Lobbying Disclosure Act with *any* of your funds, *even those you obtained from other sources*. This prohibition for (c)(4)s does not apply if the money you received from the federal government was part of a federal *contract*. If your (c)(4) received an *award or loan*, you can use this money for *state and local* lobbying if this activity is otherwise permissible under the terms of your award or loan. *Grants* are subject to the restrictions described above that forbid lobbying *state* legislators either directly or by urging public involvement and forbid engaging in legislative liaison efforts. You can use grants for local lobbying.

> *Most nonprofits cannot use federal funds from grants, cooperative agreements and certain cost contracts to lobby federal or state legislators either directly or by urging the public to get involved (including by organizing demonstrations, marches and rallies).*

Although the government's rules distinguish between the types of funding you receive and what activities you can pursue, the federal government in practice sometimes fails to make the distinctions and enforces the lobbying bans more broadly than its rules require. If you receive federal monies and plan to engage in lobbying or political activities, talk to your funder or get legal advice.

Political Expenditure Tax

The IRS grants tax exemption under §527 of the Internal Revenue Code to political committees (political parties and PACs) that are organized primarily for the purpose of collecting contributions and making expenditures to influence the election or appointment of individuals for federal, state, or local public office. These purposes are called their exempt function. Groups exempt under §527 are subject to considerable public disclosure about their contributors and finances. Some organizations that are exempt under §501(c) may also attempt to influence the election or appointment of individuals to federal, state or local office. These organizations are not §527 organization because their political activities are not their primary purpose. But they are engaging in a function (political activity) that is the same as the exempt function for §527 groups.

The IRS imposes a tax (called a political expenditure tax or exempt functions expenditure tax) on groups that engage in §527-type political activity but that are not registered as §527 groups. The tax is an effort to discourage an end-run around the §527 disclosure rules. §501(c) organizations can make a choice about how they handle their political activities. Your §501(c) organization can use your own general funds for your §527 political activities or you can establish a separate, segregated fund under §527. If you use your funds from your general account, your §501(c) group does not have to comply with the notice and reporting requirements of §527 but you have to pay a tax on the lesser of your investment income (normally exempt from taxation under an exception to the unrelated business income tax rules as described on p. 214) or the amount of the exempt function expenditure. If your organization has no investment income, you do not need to be concerned with this tax and can avoid disclosure of your donors by failing to register as a §527 organization.

If your organization establishes a §527 separate segregated fund, that fund in most cases must give notice and report on its contributions and expenditures but avoids the tax. Although it is rare that §501(c)(3) organizations would be concerned with this tax (because they should not be electioneering at all), you do need to be concerned about this tax if your (c)(3) attempts to influence the *appointment* of individuals to public office.

When is an expenditure for a political activity by a §501(c) organization subject to the political expenditure tax? The obvious case is when you *expressly advocate* for or against the election or appointment of an individual to public office. The IRS lists other factors that may show that an advocacy communication is for a taxable political activity even though you do not explicitly endorse or oppose a candidate. These factors include the identification of a candidate for public office, publication during an electoral campaign, targeting voters in a particular district, identification of the candidate's position on a policy issue, distinguishing the candidate's position from that of other candidates, and the lack of an ongoing series of such communications by the organization.

> *Example*: Tobacco Free America, a (c)(4) organization, advocates for smoke-free workplaces. A month before the Senate elections, TFA published a full page ad in the largest newspaper in Senator Jones' district stating the Senator Jones, up for re-election, had voted consistently in favor of tobacco interests and had opposed efforts to create smoke-free workplaces. The ad ended with the statement "Let Senator Jones know how you feel about smoke-free workplaces." This was the first time that TFA had run an ad. TFA's ad is probably for taxable political activity and TFA will have to pay the political expenditure tax even though TFA did not expressly urge voters to vote against Senator Jones.

It is easy to confuse the rules that trigger the political expenditure tax with federal and state rules about express and issue advocacy under the election laws. Express and issue advocacy rules arise under the federal election laws and are enforced by the Federal Election Commission for federal candidates. Express advocacy rules that are more broadly defined also arise under Oregon election law and are enforced by the Elections Division of the Secretary of State's office for federal, state and local candidates. The political expenditure tax is part of the Internal Revenue Code and is enforced by the Internal Revenue Service for federal, state, and local candidates. All three agencies have rules that apply if you *expressly endorse or oppose* a candidate (and you fall within their jurisdiction). But the rules about less clear-cut advocacy are different for each agency. You need to carefully think through which agencies are regulating you and how your expenditures will be classified under their rules.

ELECTIONEERING AND LOBBYING 29

Consult Appendix 1 if you would like information about source material related to this Chapter. Appendix 1 has references of interest to all readers, not just professionals.

Chapter 30 describes other compliance issues—record-keeping, reporting, and legal requirements—applicable to all nonprofit corporations.

30

COMPLIANCE: ONGOING MAINTENANCE OF YOUR NONPROFIT

THIS CHAPTER COVERS

- Books and Records
- Reports and Registrations
- Confidential Information
- Notices
- Releases
- Terrorism Laws
- Tax-Exempt Groups: Operational Rules

Previous chapters have described the financial systems that your nonprofit corporation needs to have in place and the special lobbying and campaigning rules you must follow. This chapter considers other rules that your nonprofit should follow in order to comply with various state and federal laws related to nonprofits—books and recordkeeping, reports, registrations, proper notice, and releases. We cover the terrorism laws, since the consequences of non-compliance are draconian. The chapter also discusses rules that pertain specifically to tax-exempt organizations. We do not attempt to cover every rule for every nonprofit, but we do alert you to and discuss some of the regulations that apply to most nonprofits

The consequences of failing to comply with nonprofit and tax-exempt regulations range from the annoying to the disastrous—you may have to pay a fine, you may lose your corporate or even your tax-exempt status, or you may end up in jail.

COMPLIANCE: ONGOING MAINTENANCE OF YOUR NONPROFIT 30

Books and Records

What Books and Records Should You Keep?

You need to keep those books and records that will facilitate your operations and allow you to comply with a variety of laws. This will vary from organization to organization. We list the books and records most nonprofits will need. Some of these may not apply to your group and some nonprofits will need to keep additional records.

Books: Financial Records

- Board-approved annual budget
- Financial statements
- If you have audited financial statements, keep all of them
- Bank statements for all accounts
- Chart of Accounts
- Cash Receipts and Disbursements Journal
- General Ledger
- Payroll timecards, record and reports
- Forms 990 and CT-12
- Personnel records
- Account payable invoices and cash payment vouchers
- Fixed assets schedules
- Inventory schedules
- Accounts receivable detailed records
- Receipt and use of restricted donations and endowment use (sufficient information to determine historic dollar value and specific information about what the restriction is)
- Donor records

Records

- Articles of Incorporation and amendments
- Bylaws and amendments
- Department of Justice registration
- IRS exemption application, attachments, and all correspondence with the IRS about the application
- IRS exemption letter

- Resolutions (decisions) of Board
- Minutes of Board, committee, and membership meetings
- Other records of Board, committee, and membership actions
- Written communications required to be made by Oregon law and those regarding general membership matters made to members
- List of the names and business or home addresses of your Directors and officers
- Annual reports delivered to Secretary of State
- Membership list with name, address, and membership date of each member in alphabetical order by class showing the number of votes each member has
- All documentation showing proper handling of conflicts of interest
- All documentation showing proper handling of suspicious circumstances
- All documentation on any matter that may become a subject of a lawsuit or claim
- Employee related matters—payroll records discussed in Chapter 27 and employee tax records
- Contracts, leases, property, insurance documentation
- All significant operational policies—e.g., personnel policies
- Client files

How Long Should You Keep Them?

Your attorney, accountant, and archivist would probably be happiest if you simply kept all your books and records forever. However, most groups don't have the space for this. We have compiled this list to help you keep documents for as long as they are reasonably likely to be needed.

If you receive government funding, government rules may require you to keep additional records or keep records for longer periods then is listed here. Be sure to consult your funding agreement and government regulations on this. If you have agreed with private funders or others to keep records, you will need to honor those agreements as well.

As you work out archiving your records, don't forget electronic records and emails. If you are a smaller organization and can save all of your electronic records, that may be the simplest solution. If you are larger and your electronic data and emails exceeds your capacity to save all of it, you may need to get professional help with archiving this data.

Federal and state laws prohibit you from destroying records that are the subject of a governmental investigation. An organization of any significant size should consider a document retention and destruction policy that establishes a schedule for when documents are destroyed and that freezes destruction of any documents that may be relevant to any current government investigation. Although the Board may want to delegate the specifics of the policy to the staff, the Board should consider a policy that requires such a staff policy. For a sample policy, see the Records Retention and Destruction policy in the Forms section.

COMPLIANCE: ONGOING MAINTENANCE OF YOUR NONPROFIT

Permanently

- Articles of Incorporation and Amendments and Bylaws
- IRS exemption documents
- Resolutions of Board
- Minutes of Board, committee, and membership meetings
- Other records of Board, committee, and membership actions
- Financial statements
- Real estate documents
- Fixed assets and accumulated depreciation schedules
- Audited financial statements
- Restricted gift information

At Least Ten Years

- All documentation showing proper handling of conflicts of interest
- All documentation showing proper handling of suspicious circumstances
- Insurance information
- All documentation on any matter that may become a subject of a lawsuit or claim (including contracts, leases, etc.)
- General ledgers
- Bank statements
- Client files (you should check with any applicable governmental agencies for longer requirements on these)

At Least Seven Years

- Canceled checks or electronic records of disbursements
- Chart of Accounts
- Cash Receipts and Disbursements Journal
- Payroll timecards, records, and reports and personnel records
- Forms 990 and CT 12 and all tax records
- Accounts payable invoices and cash payment vouchers
- Inventory schedules

Accounts receivables detailed records

- Government reports

At Least Four Years (after Tax is Paid or Due)

- Employment tax records

At Least Three Years

- Written communications required to be made by Oregon law and those regarding general membership matters made to members within the past three years

Other Periods

For books and records not mentioned above, consider carefully the purpose of the book or record and how it might be useful to you in the future. Be sure you have reviewed governmental funding agreements and the regulations referenced in them to determine if you have agreed to specific record retention requirements.

You are balancing possible future need against the expense and inefficiency of maintaining records you don't need.

Other future uses might include financial documentation, evidence in a lawsuit, contacting previous donors, archives about your organization, etc. You are balancing possible future need against the expense and inefficiency of maintaining records you don't need. For some organizations, converting records to electronic formats and utilizing internet based records storage services may be a cost effective strategy. It is generally wise to err on the side of keeping rather than throwing away.

Who Can See or Copy Your Books and Records

Oregon law is not entirely clear on who can inspect and copy your records and books.

Members

Oregon has extensive rules about records that must be made available for inspection and copying by members. See pages 384-387.

Nonmembers' Rights to Inspect and Copy Books and Records

DIRECTORS

Directors should have access to all records necessary to carry out their Board functions. Probably the only circumstance in which a Director could be denied access to records would be if the Director wanted them for an improper purpose. The Board would need to make that final decision.

STAFF MEMBERS

Staff members should have access to all records necessary to carry out their jobs. As employees, staff members are entitled to see their personnel records (see page 421).

GENERAL PUBLIC

The Oregon statute is somewhat unclear as to what access the general public has to the records of an Oregon nonprofit corporation. It is quite likely that there is no right to access, except for the tax-exempt and public benefit corporations described below. If your organization has sufficient government connections, it is possible you may be subject to the federal Freedom of Information Act or public records laws of the state of Oregon. You may also be required to allow certain types of public inspection as a condition of certain government funding agreements.

TAX-EXEMPT ORGANIZATIONS

If your nonprofit is a tax-exempt organization, the public can inspect your tax-exempt application, its supporting documentation (which includes your Articles and Bylaws, at least as of the time of filing) and your correspondence with the IRS about your application. The public can also inspect documents or letters issued by the IRS relating to your approved application. Your annual return (usually, Form 990 or 990 EZ) is also subject to public inspection. However, the following information can be withheld: the names and addresses of contributors to tax-exempts, other than private foundations, and the amount of that contributor's contribution, if it could reasonably be expected to identify the contributor; and the names, addresses, and amounts of contributions from persons who are not U.S. citizens made to a foreign organization. This is discussed in more detail on pages 630-632.

PUBLIC BENEFIT CORPORATIONS

If your nonprofit is a public benefit corporation, you are required to register with the Oregon Department of Justice. That registration includes some information about what you do, who your Board and officers are, and a copy of your Articles and Bylaws. (See page 47). That information is a public record.

OPEN RECORDS LAWS

Public bodies in Oregon must make their public records open for inspection by everyone, with certain exceptions. The issue for Oregon nonprofit corporations is "Are nonprofit corporations public bodies?" In most cases, the answer is "no." However, if your group exercises significant governmental functions, you may be subject to the Open (Public) Records Law. See pp. 29-30.

What Records Can and Must Be Protected

It is beyond the scope of this book to describe all the rules concerning confidentiality and record-keeping. To a large degree, this will vary from organization to organization. As a starting point, see the discussion below on confidentiality before you disclose records.

Reports and Registrations

Your nonprofit is responsible for submitting certain reports and registration renewals on an annual basis in addition to the tax reporting discussed in Chapter 12. In many cases the agency to which you submit the report will send you an annual notice. However, you must submit the reports or registrations even if you don't receive a notice.

> *Because your failure to file an annual report can trigger the dissolution of your corporation, it is extremely important that you check to ensure that your annual report is filed each year.*

Secretary of State (Corporation Commissioner)

Every year your corporation must submit an annual report to the Secretary of State (Corporation Commissioner's office). The Secretary of State will mail or email a form to the address that they have for the corporation. You need to fill out the form and mail it back or file it electronically along with a fee. If they fail to send it to you, it is your obligation to obtain a copy and deliver it to them in a timely fashion. If the annual report is not completely and properly filled out, the Secretary of State will notify you in writing and return the report for correction. You have 45 days to correct the errors.

If the corporation fails to file the annual report or fails to make the necessary corrections within 45 days, the Secretary of State will administratively dissolve the corporation. This has serious repercussions for your organization and potentially for the Board members. (See 753-56 for what this means and what you must do if this happens to you.) Because your failure to file an annual report can trigger the dissolution of your corporation, it is extremely important that you check to ensure that your annual report is filed each year. Consider linking this task with another annual event, such as the filing of your tax forms. You can check whether the report was filed by going to the Secretary of State's Name Registry on its website at the address in Appendix 2. If your Entity Status is "ACT," then your corporation is current (active) in its filings. If it is "INA," then you need to check the detailed listing on the website to see why you are listed as "inactive."

If information provided in the annual report changes before you file your next annual report and the change does *not* require an amendment to the Articles of Incorporation, you are required to file an amendment to the annual report with the Secretary of State. The amendment must state the name of the corporation and the information that is changed. An example of such a change would be a change in the President or Secretary of the corporation or a change in your federal employer ID number.

> *A scam surfaces from time to time in which a business sends an official looking form to Oregon nonprofit corporations made to look like it comes from the Secretary of State's Corporation Division. Watch out for this imposter.*

One word of caution: A scam surfaces from time to time in which a business sends an official looking form to Oregon nonprofit corporations made to look like it comes from the Secretary of State's Corporation Division. The form notifies the nonprofit that it needs to renew its annual registration and indicates that the fee to renew is, say, $238. It requests your renewal information and has a line at the bottom for you to sign. When you sign, you are actually signing a form that allows the for-profit who sent the form to file your annual report (which costs $50) for you. For the same amount of work and a lot less money, you can fill out and sign the annual report that the state sends. Watch out for this imposter!

Department of Justice (Attorney General)

If you are a Public Benefit Corporation, you should register with the Department of Justice. You may already have done so. If you have registered, the Department will send you an annual reporting form, the Form CT-12. See Chapter 12. If they fail to send it, you must contact them to get it and file it. They do charge a fairly small fee each year, based on the amount of your gross receipts. You may also need to register with the Department of Justice if you engage in bingo or other gaming. See pp. 487-89.

Other State and Local Licenses and Filings

If your nonprofit engages in activities in another state, you will probably need to register to do business in that state. You will need to consult the laws of that state to see what the threshold is for registration. You should check with the local governments in Oregon (or elsewhere) where you are located to see if there are any additional licenses that you need. If you operate any type of business, it is likely that you will need a business license. (See Chapter 11 for a discussion of exemptions from licensing for nonprofits.) If your operations invoke any sort of state licensing requirements—for example, nursing homes, child care centers, adoption agencies—you will need to comply with those as well.

Confidential Information

If you have the following kinds of records, your organization should become familiar with all applicable rules about confidentiality and disclosure and take steps to safeguard the confidentiality of the records:

- Financial records (see below);
- Confidential client records, such as medical, mental health, or legal files;
- Personnel records (see p. 421);
- Records pertaining to HIV status;
- Criminal records;
- Trade secrets.

Identity Theft

Nonprofits that possess personal information about individuals must be aware of their responsibilities to protect the data and their obligations if the security of the data is compromised. Personal information means that you have an individual's first name or first initial and last name in combination with one or more of the following:

- social security number;
- driver license number or state ID card;
- passport number of U.S. issued identification number; or
- financial account number, credit or debit card number in combination with any required security code, access code, or password that would access the individual's financial account.

Personal information may also include not having the person's name but having one or more of the items described above if the information would be enough to allow identity theft.

Remember that you also need to protect your corporation from identity theft as well. Members or others who request to see your records should not be allowed to see your bank account numbers, credit card information, or other financial information that might endanger your nonprofit. If that information is on documents that the member of other party is allowed to see, cover it before disclosing a copy of the document.

If you collect the personal data described above, you are required to develop safeguards to protect the security and confidentiality of the data. If you have a breach of security (such as a stolen laptop) that may result in an unauthorized person obtaining computerized personal information, the law provides that you must give notice to the affected individuals. You need to set up systems to protect your personal data. This protection should be in place before someone makes a request to inspect or copy your records. Get professional advice if you collect personal data from your clients, volunteers, employees, customers, or others.

COMPLIANCE: ONGOING MAINTENANCE OF YOUR NONPROFIT 30

Medical Information

The privacy of medical information, whether collected from your staff, volunteers, clients, or others, is protected by federal and state laws. If you are not aware of your obligations in this area, get professional advice.

Notices

In a variety of circumstances, your corporation must give or be given notices. Generally, notices are required for Board meetings and membership meetings, as discussed on pages 325, 373-75. The following (admittedly boring) rules apply to notices that the Oregon law requires that you give or be given. In some cases the law provides different notice requirements than above. We cover those elsewhere in this book.

Oregon law is unclear about whether you may use email, email lists, websites or other electronic methods to give notice.

Personal and Newspaper Notice

Notice may be verbal or written (unless otherwise specified for a particular kind of notice). Notice may be communicated in person, by telephone, telegraph, teletype, or other form of wire or wireless communication, or by mail or private carrier, including publication in a newspaper or similar document mailed to a member's or Director's address. If these forms of personal notice are impractical, notice may be communicated by a newspaper of general circulation in the area where the meeting is to be held or by radio, television, or other form of public broadcast communication.

Notice by Email

Oregon law is unclear about whether you may use email, email lists, websites, or other electronic methods to give notice. Until the law is clarified, you take a risk that you have not provided proper notice if you use these venues for notice. If you use an electronic method, you can eliminate your risk if you have *everyone who is entitled to notice* sign a waiver of notice whether or not they attend the meeting for which the notice is issued. The Forms section in the back of the book includes sample forms entitled Waiver of Notice of Meeting of Directors and Waiver of Notice of Meeting of Members. Obviously, in many cases, especially with respect to membership meetings, this will not be practical.

If you cannot get signed Waivers from everyone, you can further minimize your risk if you have everyone who is notified by electronic means sign a consent to this method of notice. The individual should include their email address in the consent and agree to notify you if their address changes. If you get a notice that an email is undeliverable, you should send notice to that individual using one of the clearly permissible methods.

Effective Date of Notice

Verbal notice is effective when it is communicated if it is communicated in a comprehensible manner. Written notice given by a corporation *to its members*, if comprehensible, is effective when it is mailed, if it is mailed postage paid and it is correctly addressed to the member's address shown in the corporation's current records. Other personal written notice, if comprehensible, is effective at the earliest of the following:

- When received;
- Five days after its postmark, if mailed by the United States mail, if correctly addressed and with first class postage affixed;
- On the date shown on the return receipt, if sent by registered or certified mail, return receipt requested, and the receipt is signed by or on behalf of the addressee;
- Thirty days after its deposit in the United States mail if mailed correctly addressed and with other than first class, registered, or certified postage affixed; or
- The date specified by the Articles or Bylaws with respect to notice to Directors.

Address for Notice

Written notice is correctly addressed to a member of your corporation if addressed to the member's address shown in the corporation's current list of members. A written notice or report delivered as part of a newsletter, magazine or other publication sent to members will constitute a written notice or report if addressed or delivered to the member's address shown in the corporation's current list of members, (or in the case of members who are residents of the same household and who have the same address in the corporation's current list of members, if addressed or delivered to one of them, at the address appearing on the current list of members). Written notice is correctly addressed to another corporation (other than in its capacity as a member of your corporation) if addressed to its registered agent or, if it has none, to its principal office shown in its most recent annual report or, if none, in the Articles of Incorporation or its application for authority to do business.

Releases

Your organization can get written releases from the people you serve or deal with in which those people agree not to sue you or your agents, employees, and volunteers in the event that an injury occurs. These releases are often not upheld by the courts, particularly if the activity involved is an essential service or a dangerous activity or it the release is signed by someone who is a member of a vulnerable population. However, in some cases, they are upheld.

Example: Your nonprofit community center operates a program that teaches adults how to swim. You require each adult to sign a release in which she or he releases you from all liability for injuries to her or him that occur in connection with the swimming lessons. One of the adults drowns during a lesson and his family sues your nonprofit for damages. In a very similar case, the Oregon appellate court upheld the release.

In the Forms section, you will find a very simple "Complete Release" that you might include as part of an application for services or other document. The Forms section also includes a more thorough "Complete Release and Hold Harmless Agreement by Client" that is drafted for the situation in which you provide services for a reduced fee to your client. On page 463, we discussed releases by volunteers in exchange for your providing worker compensation insurance. There are many possibilities in addition to these. Your choices about whether to have a release and how thorough you should make it will be governed by many other considerations in addition to legal ones—you'll want to assess how much risk you have, whether you are covered by insurance, how offensive the release will be to your clients or those you serve, how likely it is that the release will be enforced, etc. You should have any release you draft checked by an attorney.

Terrorism Laws

After the September 11, 2001 terrorist attacks, the federal government responded with new laws and amendments to existing laws designed to prevent terrorism. These laws apply to nonprofits as well as to individuals and businesses. Although nonprofits who are grant-makers or who work internationally are most affected by these laws, many of them apply to other nonprofits as well. You may be aiding a suspected domestic or international terrorist if you supply financial assistance, technical assistance, in-kind support, or humanitarian aid. The laws apply to domestic nonprofits as well as those who make grants or provide aid abroad. Perhaps most difficult to swallow is that, in some cases, the government can apply sanctions to your nonprofit even though you did not realize you were assisting suspected terrorists.

In many cases, the laws are very vague and open to numerous interpretations. The various laws are worded somewhat differently and so may not impact all nonprofits in the same way. Although you may feel sure that you don't deal with terrorists, your conviction (even if correct) does not shield you from paying attention to this area of law. The terrorism laws are quite complex and eliminate or modify some of the protections and limitations that Americans had come to expect in our laws. We can't give you a detailed picture here but we alert you to what kinds of actions constitute aid to suspected terrorists and to the major consequences of aiding a suspected terrorist or terrorist organization. We discuss your alternatives and direct you to the government website that list suspected terrorists. If you need help in this area, you should consult a knowledgeable attorney.

Actions that Aid Suspected Terrorists

Your nonprofit does not have to supply guns or money in order to aid suspected terrorists under current law. Although each law is different, generally if you offer grants, financial assistance, technical assistance, in-kind support, or humanitarian aid to suspected terrorists or terrorist organizations, you have aided terrorists. More troubling, some of the laws are written broadly enough to include an American organization that gives money to a foreign non-governmental organization that then provides humanitarian aid (for example, food or medical help) to a suspected terrorist.

Although you may feel sure that you don't deal with terrorists, your conviction (even if correct) does not shield you from paying attention to this area of law.

Sanctions for Aiding Suspected Terrorists

Your nonprofit faces four major types of penalties if you aid suspected terrorists—the federal government can freeze your assets without a hearing, the government can impose criminal penalties (fines and imprisonment) on your organization and its responsible individuals, private parties may bring a civil suit against those who support terrorism, and the IRS may revoke your tax-exempt status.

Freezing Your Assets

Executive Order 13224 issued by President Bush shortly after the September 11 attacks prohibits all U.S. persons, including nonprofits, from engaging in transactions with individuals and organizations suspected of being terrorists. The Order is so broad in scope that it can cover people and groups not on any government list. If the government believes that your organization has violated this Order, *whether or not you know it*, it can freeze your assets even as it investigates. The government froze the assets of several U.S. charities, including one in Ashland, Oregon.

Criminal Penalties

The Patriot Act and subsequent legislation contains criminal sanctions against any entity that provides material support, resources, or financing knowing or intending that this support will be used in terrorist acts or by foreign terrorist organizations. Since suspected terrorists may live in the United States, the Act applies to domestic nonprofits although nonprofits engaged in international work have the greatest potential liability.

The law has long contained a variety of trade sanctions and embargoes that restrict activities by nonprofits with particular foreign countries. The Treasury Department and the Commerce Department administer these embargoes. The restrictions usually apply to nonprofits, even to those providing humanitarian aid. Violators are subject to criminal and civil penalties.

Civil Lawsuits

The Patriot Act authorizes private parties to bring civil lawsuits against those who materially support terrorism. Since September 11, victims of terrorist attacks have brought civil suits against a variety of foundations and nonprofits linked to Al Qaeda, including at least two United States foundations.

Revocation of Tax-Exempt Status

The Internal Revenue Code has always provided for revocation of tax-exempt status for an organization that failed to operate for exempt purposes. Using assets to support terrorism will obviously subject an exempt organization to revocation. In 2003, Congress amended the Code to suspend the tax-exempt status of an organization that is designated by other governmental agencies as a terrorist organization. The suspension occurs automatically and, most troubling for innocent donors, is retroactive to the date that the government first published the name of the organization on one of its lists of suspected terrorists.

Treasury Department's Voluntary Guidelines

The Treasury Department has released revised Guidelines to assist nonprofits to comply with Executive Order 13224 and the Patriot Act. The Guidelines are called "U.S. Department of the Treasury Anti-Terrorist Financing Guidelines: Voluntary Best Practices for U.S.-Based Charities" and can be found on the Department of Treasury's website. You are not required by law to follow the Guidelines and compliance with them does not assure your nonprofit that you have not violated the law. Even so, the nonprofit community has been concerned that the courts might assume that these Guidelines are best practices.

Organizations that conduct foreign operations, particularly grant-making, are at the greatest risk.

The Guidelines suggest that nonprofits with international operations exercise extensive efforts to check out individuals and nongovernmental organizations to whom they make grants and also check the nonprofit's own key employees. The Guidelines contain details about the information the nonprofit should obtain and suggestions for lists of terrorists the nonprofit can consult. Conducting a search can be challenging because it may be difficult or impossible for the nonprofit to obtain the information it needs about the individuals and organizations it funds and because it can be difficult to match names on the terrorist lists. A nonprofit may conduct the searches itself and many small nonprofits do this. If this is a significant issue for your nonprofit and you have the resources, you should get professional help. There are internet software products and professional companies that can help you with these investigations.

The Guidelines have caused some concern in the international charitable community. The Guidelines ask nonprofits to collect information that is often impossible or prohibitively costly to collect.

Even where the information can be obtained, collecting information about locals may compromise the local community's belief in the nonprofit's independence and neutrality. If a nonprofit is perceived as dependent on the U.S. government, this may damage the nonprofit's ability to deliver effective programs. In some countries, a nonprofit that is seen as an arm of the U.S. government also can create safety risks to the nonprofit's personnel.

What Should You Do?

You have to make your own assessment of how vulnerable you might be to aiding terrorists, how risk averse you are, how extensive an investigation will be required for your group, how much money and resources you can devote to this issue, and how following the Guidelines might impact the effectiveness of your organization's work and the safety of your personnel. Organizations that conduct foreign operations, particularly grant-making, are at the greatest risk. Remember that the terrorism laws apply to terrorist activities anywhere, not just groups associated with the 911 attacks. Members of violent drug cartels in Mexico, for example, may be terrorists. The larger the number of gifts you make, the greater your risk and the greater your expense in investigating the risk.

You have to make your own assessment of how vulnerable you might be to aiding terrorists, how risk averse you are, how extensive an investigation will be required for your group, and how much money and resources you can devote to this issue. Organizations that conduct foreign operations, particularly grant-making, are at the greatest risk.

If you don't consult a professional, you should consider several strategies to reduce your risk. You will need to balance these strategies with the risk that they may damage your local relationships:

- Collect basic information about the individuals associated with your grantees and your own key employees. You will want to have their names in English and in their language of origin, and any other names used. You'll need their nationality, citizenship, address, and date and place of birth.

- For grantees, you need information about the organization, including where it was incorporated, who formed and operates it, what it does and where it operates. Obtain a translated copy of the governing documents of your foreign grantee organizations and a translated copy of their foreign charity status. Review them to see if they raise any red flags.

- Consult the government-generated lists of suspected terrorists listed below to see whether your grantees or key employees are listed. As you will see when you view the lists, the search can be quite daunting, particularly the OFAC list. Because

COMPLIANCE: ONGOING MAINTENANCE OF YOUR NONPROFIT

the government can place individuals on the lists without any kind of hearing, it is quite likely that there are innocent people on the lists. In addition, many individuals have the same name and organizations using the lists obtain a significant number of false positives. These lists change frequently and may contain names spelled differently than those being checked by your nonprofit. The lists also contain names that are very difficult to eliminate. In addition to the lists below, some countries maintain their own lists. Check to see if the country in which you operate has its own list of suspect terrorists.

- Investigate your grantees. Make regular visits to their programs and make efforts to obtain information about them from reliable local sources, including churches, newspapers, business connections, nongovernmental organizations, and governmental officials.

- Include anti-terrorism language in your grant agreements. If you are particularly vulnerable to aiding terrorists, you might include anti-terrorism language in your Bylaws.

- Direct your giving through another (c)(3) public charity that does extensive due diligence compliance.

- Document carefully all the efforts you make to comply with the terrorism laws. Include in your documentation the list searches that you do and other background checks you conduct, even if they are informal inquiries.

Government Lists of Suspected Terrorists

Here are the major lists of suspected terrorists:

• Treasury Department's Office of Foreign Assets Control (OFAC) maintains the Specially Designated Nationals (SDN) list at *www.treas.gov* and search for "Specially Designated Nationals."

• The United Nations maintains an Al Qaida Sanctions List at *www.un.org*. Type "Al Qaida Sanctions List" into the search engine.

Tax-Exempt Groups: Operational Rules

If you have been recognized as tax-exempt under §501(c), you must also comply with certain federal requirements concerning your records and your procedures in addition to the on-going legal requirements described above that you must meet as a nonprofit corporation.

Public Inspection and Copying of Papers

You need to make certain of your public records available for inspection and copying.

What Can be Inspected and Copied

APPLICATION

You must make available for public inspection a copy of your application for exemption (Form 1023), all papers submitted in support of the application, and any determination letter or other document the IRS issued on the application. These requirements apply to organizations whose applications were submitted to the IRS after July 15, 1987 or before that date if the organization had a copy of the application on July 15, 1987. If your application contains trade secrets or other apparatus you want withheld from the public, you can request written permission from the IRS to withhold it. You can withhold the names and addresses of your contributors unless you are a private foundation or a political action committee. Failure to comply with these requirements will subject you to penalties, unless you can show reasonable cause for noncompliance.

> *To avoid disclosing the names of your contributors or of these forms that you do not have to disclose, set up a special disclosure file that contains only the forms that you must disclose.*

ANNUAL INFORMATION RETURN

You must make available for public inspection a copy of each annual information return (Form 990 for most groups and certain additional forms for trusts and pooled-income funds), for the three most recent annual returns. You do not have to disclose the names or addresses of contributors unless you are a private foundation or political action committee, so you will want to avoid filing a copy of your Schedule B when you file your Form 990 with the Oregon Department of Justice. You must allow inspection of Form 990-T (Exempt Organization Business Income Tax Return), relating to unrelated business income, although you do not have to disclose some of the schedules attached to that Form. (See the IRS website for exceptions.). You also have to allow inspection of Form 8872, relating to contributions and expenditures of political organizations.

COMPLIANCE: ONGOING MAINTENANCE OF YOUR NONPROFIT 30

You are not required to allow inspection of Form 1120-POL (the U.S. Income Tax Return for Certain Political Organizations), Schedule A of Form 990-BL or Schedule K-1 of Form 1065. If you are a subordinate organization that receives a request for inspection, you must acquire a copy of the material from your parent organization and make it available within a reasonable time.

To avoid disclosing the names of your contributors or of the forms that you do not have to disclose, set up a special disclosure file that contains only the forms that you must disclose. Be sure your staff is instructed to respond to disclosure requests using this file and not the corporate master file. You can also avoid these disclosure problems by using a website posting as described below.

Inspection Rules

You may have an employee present during inspection. The requestor can take notes or can request copies. These documents must be available for inspection during regular business hours at your principal office. If you maintain regional or district offices with three or more employees, these documents must also be available at those offices. If you post your documents on a website, this satisfies your obligations under the copying rules but does not satisfy the requirement that you make them available for inspection. If someone wants to personally inspect them, you must allow them to do so as described above.

In lieu of providing copies, you can make your documents widely available by posting them on your own website.

Copying Rules

You must also provide copies of the documents that are available for inspection upon request. If someone makes the request for copies in person, you must supply them that day. If you receive a request in writing, by fax, by private delivery or by email for copies, you have 30 days from the date received to fill it. If you require payment in advance for the copies, you have 30 days from the time you received payment. Check the IRS website for the current fee list for what you can charge for copies.

In lieu of providing copies, you can make your documents widely available by posting them on your own website or as part of a database that provides the required information for a number of tax-exempt organizations. The IRS currently supplies Form 990 information for public inspection at *www.guidestar.org*. The Internet posting must allow the user to download your information at no cost and to view and print it in a manner which exactly reproduces the IRS document. Your Internet posting can't require the use of special hardware or software unless the software is readily available to the public free of charge. One format that meets this criteria is Portable Document Format (.pdf). And if you choose the Internet approach, you must tell those who request your information where it can be found on the Internet.

Charitable Contributions

Organizations exempt under §501(c)(3) often receive donations in a variety of forms from donors who want to deduct these expenses as charitable contributions on their tax returns. While donors should get tax advice about the deductibility of a specific gift from their own tax professional and not from your organization, your nonprofit must understand key IRS requirements and comply with important requirements for gift acknowledgement and disclosure.

Basic IRS Rules for Charitable Contributions:

Nonprofits quickly learn that donors want and expect to receive acknowledgement of every gift they provide. Maintaining records about your donors is essential to fundraising success since individuals who have given once are more likely to give again than individuals who have never given to your organization. Acknowledging each gift is also an important financial control, providing an easy way to determine whether all the gifts you receive have actually been deposited into your accounts.

> *The IRS requires that in order for a taxpayer to claim the charitable tax deduction for any single contribution that is equal to or greater than $250, the donor must obtain a written receipt from the charitable organization that received the gift.*

But beyond these internal motivations for acknowledging contributions, your nonprofit will need to become familiar with some key IRS requirements for tax-exempt organizations and additional requirements for individuals who want to claim charitable tax deductions on the personal income tax returns.

PURE GIFTS

Let's start with the requirements for donors to *substantiate* (document) their gifts in order to be able to treat them as tax deductible charitable contributions. The IRS requires that in order for a taxpayer to claim the charitable tax deduction for any single contribution that is equal to or greater than $250, the donor must obtain a written receipt from the charitable organization that received the gift. The IRS refers to the requirement that the donor have this documentation as "substantiation." Canceled checks are not enough to "substantiate" individual gifts that are equal to or greater than $250.

Some donors will make a series of gifts throughout the year. While each gift is under $250, the total of the gifts may equal or exceed $250. The IRS does not require such donors to obtain acknowledgements from the charity for each of these gifts, but your organization will want to acknowledge every gift and keep records about all the gifts each donor makes each year. Donors may contact you to ask for an annual summary of their gifts to your organization, so you will want to have a system in place that makes responding to such requests easy.

Example: Your church member pledges and pays $200/month, for a total of $2,400/year. Because no single payment is $250 or more, you do not have to provide an acknowledgement letter for the donor to take the deduction. (The donor will need to save her cancelled checks for proof.) If the church member paid the pledge in full in one payment, you would have to provide a letter. Your donor, of course, is more likely to give next year if you acknowledge her gift and thank her.

Your written acknowledgment of contribution can be by receipt, letter, fax, or email. The IRS requires that the acknowledgement of any of these contributions must be "contemporaneous," which actually means that it must be given to the donor "at the time the donor's tax return is filed or is due, whichever comes first." While your organization could meet this deadline by providing the acknowledgements on or before January 31 of the tax year when the filing is due, successful nonprofits learn that donors really appreciate an immediate acknowledgement of each gift.

There is an important exception to the requirement that the donor obtain an acknowledgement letter from the organization for donors who make gifts through payroll deduction plans. The donor does not need an acknowledgement letter if the donor has a pay stub, Form W-2 or other document from the employer showing the amount withheld and the payment to the your organization.

WHEN DONORS RECEIVE GOODS OR SERVICES IN RETURN FOR GIFTS

The requirements for communicating with donors about gifts get a bit more complicated when your organization is providing the donor with something of value in return for their "gift." The IRS describes the situation in which the donor receives something of value for her/his contribution as a *quid pro quo* contribution. If the donor pays your nonprofit more than $75 and gets something in return, you must provide a written disclosure statement that states the value of what the donor received for his/her payment and the amount of the donor's payment to you that is deductible.

If the donor pays your nonprofit more than $75 and gets something in return, you must provide a written disclosure statement.

You organization is required to provide a written disclosure statement at the time you solicit the gift or when you receive the contribution. The statement must be provided in a manner likely to come to the donor's attention (a disclosure in small print within a larger document might not meet this requirement) Many organizations include the information about the *quid pro quo* value of what the donor receives and the portion of the payment which qualifies as a charitable contribution in both the solicitation and in the acknowledgement of the gift.

Example: If you will ask donors to pay $100 for a ticket to attend your annual fund raising dinner, and the meal provided would typically cost $30, the donor will have received something of value for his $100 payment, so the $100 payment will not be entirely a contribution. The IRS requires that you provide a written disclosure statement in the invitation to attend the dinner or when you receive the check which states the value of what the donor will receive ($30) and the portion of the total payment which she or he can deduct as a charitable contribution ($70).

To meet the IRS requirements for disclosure your organization will need to determine the fair market value of the goods or services which you will be providing to donors. A good approach is to use the price that is usually charged for the items you will provide rather than the price your organization has actually paid for the items.

Example: If you will be providing a 4 course dinner with wine, your statement of the value of goods and services the donors received will be based on the price typically charged for such a meal, not the actual cost to your organization which may be considerably lower if you have obtained donated food and wine or if a corporate sponsor has agreed to pay the cost of the food and wine.

You must provide a written disclosure statement to any donor who makes a *quid pro quo* payment to you of more than $75, even though the contribution amount is less than $75.

Example: If a donor pays $100 for a dinner worth $30, you must provide a disclosure statement, because the payment was more than $75, even though the actual value of the contribution was only $70.

As with gifts that don't include a *quid pro quo* element, you do not have to add together separate payments at different times under the *quid pro quo* rules.

Example: If you hold spring and fall dinners and a donor attends both and pays $50 at each event for a meal worth $20, you do not have to provide a written disclosure statement to the donor (whose total payment was $100), since the donor paid less than $75 at each event.

If you have a donor who has contributed more than $250 at a single event, you will need to provide both a disclosure statement and an acknowledgement letter (substantiation) of the contribution.

IRS Publication 1171, *Charitable Contributions: Substantiation and Disclosure Requirements*, contains a good summary of the IRS rules and particularly useful suggested wording for your acknowledgement and disclosure letters. Publication 1171 is available on the IRS website (*www.irs.gov*)—be sure to check the website periodically to keep track of changes and updates as IRS requirements evolve. Better yet, sign up on the IRS website to receive the Exempt Organization Update, the IRS free electronic newsletter for charitable organizations.

While the IRS sample wording will ensure that you meet the substantiation and disclosure requirements, it is far from warm and fuzzy and doesn't express much gratitude. Many charities craft a more personal, gracious message and then include the specific wording recommended by the IRS at the bottom with a caption indicating this is the documentation required by the IRS.

Your gift acknowledgement letter should include your organization's name, the amount of the contribution, and a statement regarding whether you did or did not provide goods or services to the donor in return for the gift. If you did provide goods and services, you are required to state the estimated fair market value of the items. If you are a religious organization, you should include a statement that any goods or services provided in return consisted entirely of intangible religious benefits (if true).

EXCEPTIONS TO DISCLOSURE RULES

There are several important exceptions to the *quid pro quo* disclosure rule. The IRS considers items with limited value that are provided to donors to thank them for their support to meet a token *exception*. You are not required to disclose the value of these *token* items and the entire amount of the donor's gift will be considered a charitable contribution.

In addition to the *token exception*, another exception allows *members* of an organization to receive certain benefits without triggering a disclosure letter. A third exception relates to intangible religious benefits. See IRS Publication 1771 for more details about these exceptions.

As noted above, you are not required to acknowledge gifts from donors using payroll deductions systems. In payroll deduction systems, the requirement to disclose whether or not the donor received goods or services in return for their gift is taken care of through wording on the donor's pledge card or withholding authorization that states that the donor has not received goods or services in return for their gift.

PENALTIES

The IRS imposes a penalty on organizations that fail to provide the written disclosures described above, either in the solicitation for the gift or in the acknowledgement, or both. The penalty is $10 per contribution, not to exceed $5,000 per fundraising event or mailing. You can avoid the penalty if you can show that you had reasonable cause to fail to meet the disclosure requirements.

Non-Cash Contributions

If donors contribute property rather than cash or a check, you must provide a written acknowledgement if the value of the property is $250 or more. As with cash/check contributions, you do not have to add up all contributions throughout the year, but do need to estimate the value of the property at each donation. Your organization does not have to (and should not) provide a valuation of the property.

Like acknowledgement letters for gifts of cash or check, your acknowledgement letter for gifts of property should include your organization's name, and a statement of whether or not you provided goods or services to the donor in return for the gift. The key difference is that for gifts of property your acknowledgement letter will include a description of the non-cash property but not an estimate of its value. It is not your responsibility to determine the fair market value of a donor's gift of property.

If the value of the non-cash property a donor contributes to your organization is over $500, the donor must submit to the IRS a Form 8283, which a representative of your organization must sign, if the donor plans to deduct the donation. If the donor claims that the value of the donated property was over $5,000 and the gift is not stock or bonds, the donor must obtain an independent appraisal from a qualified appraiser as part of the Form 8283. Your organization's signature on Form 8283 acknowledges receipt of the donated property but does not require that you agree with the value the donor is asserting. If your organization sells or otherwise transfers donated property worth more than $5,000 within three years, you are required then to file Form 8282 with the IRS and give a copy to the donor.

> *For gifts of property your acknowledgement letter will include a description of the non-cash property but not an estimate of its value. It is not your responsibility to determine the fair market value of a donor's gift of property.*

There are special rules for donated cars, boats and planes worth more than $500. Consult the IRS instructions for Form 4302, *A Charity's Guide to Vehicle Donations*, for how to handle these items.

Unreimbursed Expenses as Donations

Individuals (usually volunteers) who incur expenses while doing something for your organization for which you do not reimburse them may be able to claim these expenses as charitable deductions on their tax returns. The volunteer/donor's payment of an expense incurred to help your organization fulfill its charitable mission without reimbursement is a form of a donation to your nonprofit.

If the expense is less than $250, the individual will need to save receipts for the costs incurred but does not need anything from your organization. If your donor incurs a single unreimbursed expense of $250 or more on behalf of your nonprofit, the donor will need an acknowledgement letter from your organization as well as their receipts for the expense in order to claim the charitable tax deduction.

Your acknowledgement letter for such unreimbursed expenses needs to describe the services the donor performed and whether your organization provided anything in return.

> *Example*: The President of your Board paid the $300 restaurant bill to take the volunteers out for a thank-you dinner and does not want reimbursement from your agency. If the President wants to deduct this contribution on her tax return, she will need an acknowledgement letter from your corporation.

Generally, a nonprofit does not provide goods or services to a donor who donates unreimbursed expenses, but if the nonprofit does, it will need to follow the rules described above for disclosing the value of goods and services provided by your organization in return for the gift.

Solicitations by Exempt Organizations Other Than §501(c)(3)

Some groups who are exempt under any section other than §501(c)(3) must include certain language when they solicit charitable contributions. See pages 505-06.

Member Notification Regarding Lobbying

Some groups exempt under §501(c)(4), (5) and (6) that engage in lobbying must either notify their members about what portion of their dues are deductible or pay a tax. This is discussed on page 199.

Changes in Activities

Tax-exempt organizations are required to notify the IRS if they change their purposes or activities in ways that might affect their tax-exempt status. If you contact the IRS *before* you make the change in order to get assurances from the IRS that the change is acceptable, the IRS will require that you request a private letter ruling. This is a very expensive process and you will need professional help. If you make the change and then contact the IRS to notify them of the change, the IRS may respond with questions but does not assess a new fee. Be sure if you take this route that your change does not affect your tax exemption. If there is some doubt, consider timing your change so that you can notify the IRS as soon as possible after the change and be prepared to make adjustments if the IRS insists. You notify the IRS about the change when you file your Form 990 or 990-EZ. (See Chapter 12.) If you do not file these forms, you will need to contact the IRS at the number listed in Appendix 2 to find out where to send your notification.

Group Exemptions

If you are a central organization that has a group exemption for your subordinates (see page 117), you must file an annual report with the IRS. Check the IRS website for the information you must supply.

Special Requirements for Schools

If you received recognition under §501(c)(3) as a school, you must do the following to keep your status:

- Your authorized official must certify annually with Form 5578 that you are following racially nondiscriminatory policies.

- You must publish an annual notice in the newspaper advertising your non-discriminatory policy during the period in which you solicit for students or, if the school does not solicit, during registration. There are exceptions. Check the IRS Publication 557 for details.

- You must keep records for three years after getting your exemption showing the racial composition of your student body, faculty, and staff, of the financial assistance awarded to students, of all published materials relating to students admissions, programs, and scholarships, and of all materials used to solicit contributions on behalf of the school. There are exceptions. See IRS Publication 557.

Excess Benefits Transactions

If you are exempt as a public charity under §501(c)(3) or you are exempt under §501(c)(4), the IRS scrutinizes transactions with your insiders (called "disqualified persons") to make sure that your corporation is not providing unfair benefits to these people. In spite of the harsh sound to the term "disqualified persons," the IRS rules do not forbid transactions with disqualified persons but attempts to ensure that transactions with these insiders are fair to the corporation. Much of the scrutiny is around salaries but the regulations include any financial transaction with a disqualified person, such as leasing property from a Board member or hiring a Board member as a consultant or employee of the corporation.

*Your goal is to act **in advance** of a transaction with a disqualified person to take advantage of IRS rules that create an assumption that your transaction is reasonable.*

If you engage in an excess benefits transaction, your organization is not fined although the IRS could revoke the tax exemption of a group that seriously violated the law. Instead, the statute imposes a heavy tax on the disqualified persons and on any organization manager (including Board members) who participated in the excess benefit transaction, knowing that it was such a transaction. The IRS currently places a priority on monitoring these transactions and the Form 990 inquires extensively about them.

Many exempt organizations have overlooked these regulations, believing that they do not pay anyone enough money to fall under the regulations or that the use of comparability studies for their top executives satisfies the requirements of the regulations. Both assumptions are false. The sanctions for engaging in excess benefits transactions may be assessed on Board members and insiders in smaller organizations and in organizations that perform comparability studies. In order to protect your personnel against excess benefit sanctions (sometimes called intermediate sanctions), you should identify disqualified persons and their compensation. You next need to identify what transactions are subject to the rules. Your goal is to act *in advance* of a transaction with a disqualified person to take advantage of IRS rules that create an assumption that your transaction is reasonable.

Identify Disqualified Persons

Every organization has disqualified persons. A disqualified person is any person or entity (such as a business, foundation, or trust) who exercises substantial influence over your corporation. In

COMPLIANCE: ONGOING MAINTENANCE OF YOUR NONPROFIT 30

lay terms, these people are insiders. Your Board needs to identify disqualified persons so that it can act properly in relationship to them. An individual or entity may be a disqualified person by virtue of his or her position in your organization, influence on your organization or relationship with another disqualified person.

Voting members of your Board, officers, and any person who has ultimate responsibility for implementing the decisions of your Board or for supervising the management of your organization are always disqualified persons. The latter category will commonly include the President, chief executive officer (if you have one), Executive Director (even if not highly paid), chief operating officer, chief financial officer and Treasurer.

Any other individual who exerts substantial influence on the organization is also a disqualified person. This is a deliberately vague category and generally includes the founders, substantial contributors, those compensated by revenue from organizational activities that they control, persons controlling capital expenditures or employee compensation, and those who manage large programs for the organization.

The law further provides that disqualified persons remain disqualified for five years after their influence in your organization ends. This means that if you engage in a transaction with someone who, within the last five years, was a disqualified person, you have to follow the excess benefit rules. For example, if you hire the person who was your Executive Director four years ago to do some contract work for your organization, this transaction is a transaction subject to the excess benefits rules.

Family members and business interests of disqualified persons are disqualified persons. Family members include the spouse, children, grandchildren, great grandchildren, whole and half-blooded brothers and sisters, and the spouses of any of these people, and any ancestors (parents, grandparents, etc). Corporations in which a disqualified person owns more than 35% of the voting power, partnerships in which the disqualified person owns more than 35% of the profit or capital interest, and trusts or estates in which the disqualified person owns more than 35 %of the beneficial interest are also disqualified persons.

Identify and Report Compensation

In most cases, the compensation will be clear. For example, if your corporation leases space from a Board member, the compensation will be the amount of the rent and any other costs that the corporation pays.

However, there are some cases where compensation is not so clear. This often comes up with respect to employee compensation. Compensation includes salary, fees, bonuses, severance payments, and benefits, whether or not the benefits were included in gross income for tax purposes. It also includes items like gym memberships, cell phones, and vehicle use, to the extent that the employee uses these items for personal purposes.

Economic benefits given to employees are not treated as excess benefits if they are given as reasonable compensation for services. However, economic benefits are only treated as compensation if your corporation treats them as compensation *when they are paid.* You must provide contemporaneous written substantiation that this is the case. If you cannot do this, the IRS will treat the economic benefit as an *automatic* excess benefit transaction without regard to whether the economic benefit was reasonable. For example, your employee's use of a car is an automatic excess benefit transaction if your organization failed to report it as compensation at the time it was provided to your employee.

> *Compensation includes salary, fees, bonuses, severance payments, and benefits, whether or not the benefits were included in gross income for tax purposes.*

One method of providing contemporaneous written substantiation is by timely reporting the benefits as compensation on an original Form 990, W-2, or Form 1099 or on the Form 1040. Your organization can also use an approved written employment contract executed on or before the transfer of the benefit, appropriate documentation in your minutes showing timely approval of the transfer as compensation by your authorized body, and certain other written evidence.

If you cannot provide contemporaneous written substantiation, you and the individual receiving the payments may be subject to the intermediate sanction penalties described below.

Identify Transactions Subject to the IRS Rules

Generally all transactions between your group and a disqualified person in which you provide the disqualified person with an economic benefit are subject to the excess benefits transactions rules. There are a few important exceptions.

One significant exception to the excess benefits law exempts most newly-hired employees from its provisions. The law does not apply to a person you hire from outside the organization for a position that would otherwise make them a disqualified person (for example, Executive Director, CFO, COO, etc.) unless they were already a disqualified person. The logic behind this exception is that the organization is contracting with an unrelated individual in a marketplace setting and the competition of the marketplace should ensure that the organization does not pay excess compensation.

In order to qualify for the new-hire exception, you must hire your new employee under a binding written contract and the new employee must substantially perform his or her obligations under the contract. Your compensation arrangements with your employee must be in the form of a fixed payment. A fixed payment is an amount of cash or other property that is specified in the contract or is determined by a fixed formula in the contract that is paid in exchange for your employee's services. A fixed formula may incorporate amounts dependent on future contingencies as long as no person exercises discretion about the amount of the payment or whether to make it. The IRS considers qualified pension, profit-sharing, and stock bonus plans to be fixed payments. If you are considering compensation that is not clearly a fixed payment, you should get professional advice.

> *Example*: A written agreement to employ a person who is not a disqualified person prior to the employment contract as Executive Director of an arts organization for

COMPLIANCE: ONGOING MAINTENANCE OF YOUR NONPROFIT 30

$200,000 per year is not subject to the excess benefit sanctions. This is a fixed payment. The same result applies if the organization also offers the Executive Director the $200,000 salary plus a bonus equal to 2% of the total season subscription sales that exceed $100,000. The bonus is a fixed payment pursuant to an initial contract, because the salary is fixed and the bonus is fixed according to a formula over which no one has discretion.

When your new hire into an insider position is promoted or when you change the terms of the employment contract in more than insignificant ways (such as by raising the salary), that person is now an insider and will be subject to the disqualified person rules.

> *One significant exception to the excess benefits law exempts most newly-hired employees from its provisions.*

The IRS also allows your organization to provide economic benefits to disqualified persons in the following circumstances without complying with the excess benefit rules:

- You can reimburse disqualified persons for their reasonable expenses incurred on behalf of your organization pursuant to an expense reimbursement plan that meets the IRS requirements for such plans which generally include requiring reimbursement for expenses actually incurred rather than awarding a fixed expense allowance. You probably already have an expense reimbursement plan. Check with your accountant to be sure it complies with the IRS rules.

- You can give the same economic benefits to your members and donors who are disqualified persons as those you give to non-disqualified members and donors. You must have a significant number of such non-disqualified members and donors.

- You can give economic benefits to a disqualified person because that person is a charitable beneficiary and the gift carries out your mission. For example, Mental Health Consumers seeks to empower individuals with mental health needs and includes several such people on its Board. This exception means that these Board members of Mental Health Consumers can use its services without triggering a requirement that Mental Health Consumers follow the excess benefits transactions rules before it provides these services.

- You can give disqualified persons who volunteer for your organization the same economic benefits you give to members of the general public in exchange for a membership fee or contributions of less than $75 per year. This provision allows disqualified persons who volunteer to get the kind of small gratuities that others get for minimal contributions to your organization.

- You can give disqualified persons who are employees non-taxable fringe benefits.

- You can give economic benefits to governmental units as long as they are for public purposes. A governmental unit is most likely to become a disqualified person because it appoints a representative to your Board. This exception allows your group to make gifts to the government for public purposes. This is clearly not the kind of transaction that the excess benefit rules are trying to discourage.

Create a Rebuttable Presumption of Reasonableness

The IRS may scrutinize any transaction other than those listed above between your corporation and your disqualified persons. The IRS assumes that your compensation arrangements for a disqualified person are *not* reasonable and that any transfer of property to a disqualified person is *not* at fair market value *unless* you meet a reasonableness test. To meet this test, you must follow the three steps described below to properly document that your Board or an authorized committee used appropriate data in your transaction with a disqualified person. If you meet the reasonableness test, the IRS assumes that your transaction is reasonable unless there is strong evidence to persuade them otherwise.

> *The IRS assumes that your compensation arrangements for a disqualified person are **not** reasonable and that any transfer of property to a disqualified person is **not** at fair market value **unless** you meet a reasonableness test.*

We have included a Form entitled "Conflicts of Interest and Executive Compensation Policy" in the Forms section that will help your organization create the rebuttable presumption of reasonableness and comply with these rules. Our policy is complex because it combines both IRS excess benefits transactions rules and Oregon conflicts of interest rules, which overlap in places but do not track each other precisely. To be a little more understandable to your Board, the policy refers to disqualified persons and others covered by the policy as insiders. You should consider adopting this or a similar policy to protect your Board members and disqualified persons.

1. THE DECISION-MAKING BODY MUST BE NEUTRAL

An authorized body of your exempt organization must approve the arrangement with your disqualified person before it is finalized. The authorized body may be your Board or a Board committee given the power to engage in the transaction. Your authorized body must be composed entirely of individuals who do not have a conflict of interest when it is considering the transaction.

A Director has a conflict of interest if he or she has a material financial interest affected by the transaction, is in an employment relationship subject to the direction or control of such a disqualified person or receives compensation or other payments subject to their approval, has a family relationship with the disqualified person, or agrees with a disqualified person to approve a transaction providing economic benefits in exchange for the approval by the disqualified person of a transaction providing benefits to the Director. For example, if the Board is considering hiring or buying property from one of its Directors, that disqualified person cannot sit on the committee that is empowered to approve the transaction.

The Director with a conflict of interest can meet with the body only to answer questions and must not be present for the debate and voting on the compensation arrangement or property transfer. Note that these conflict of interest rules disqualify more people than the rules under Oregon law and that the Director with a conflict has more restrictions on participation in the meeting than under Oregon law. See pages 299-303 for Oregon's rules.

2. THE BOARD MUST USE APPROPRIATE COMPARABLE DATA TO DETERMINE IF THE TRANSACTION IS FAIR TO THE CORPORATION

The approval by your Board or committee must be based on appropriate financial data. Your Board or committee has appropriate data if, given the knowledge and expertise of your Directors, your Board or committee has sufficient information to determine that compensation is reasonable or that the property transfer is at fair market value. Relevant information for compensation includes:

- ◊ compensation levels maintained by similarly situated organizations for comparable positions,

- ◊ current compensation surveys by independent firms, and

- ◊ actual written offers from similar institutions competing for the services of the disqualified person.

If your organization has gross annual receipts of less than one million dollars, appropriate data can be data on compensation paid by three comparable organizations in the same or similar communities for similar services. Such smaller organizations may also meet the requirement of appropriate data in other ways. You can obtain information about nonprofit salaries at *www.guidestar.org* or, if you are a private foundation, at the Council on Foundations' website at *www.cof.org*. You should get professional advice if you need help determining what is appropriate data.

3. THE BOARD MUST PROPERLY DOCUMENT THE TRANSACTION

Your authorized body must document its decision contemporaneously with the transaction. To do this, you must keep written or electronic records that state:

- ◊ the terms of the transaction and the date it is approved,
- ◊ the members present and who voted on it,
- ◊ the comparability data and how the data was obtained, and
- ◊ any actions taken with respect to any member of the authorizing body who had a conflict of interest.

If you determine that the financial arrangement of the transaction was higher or lower than the range of comparability data, you must record the basis for your determination.

---

*If the written substantiation requirement is not satisfied, the IRS will treat the economic benefit as an **automatic** excess benefit transaction without regard to whether the economic benefit was reasonable.*

Your Board should approve the payment of all elements of the compensation before it is actually paid to the disqualified person. For your decision to be contemporaneous, your records must be prepared before the later of the next meeting or 60 days after the final action is taken. The records must be reviewed and approved by your Board or authorized committee within a reasonable time.

Intermediate Sanction Penalties

The Internal Revenue Code imposes substantial penalties on both the disqualified person and on any organization manager who participates in the excess benefit transaction, knowing it is such a transaction. The Code taxes the disqualified person who participates in an excess benefit transaction an initial tax equal to 25% of the excess benefit. If the disqualified person does not correct the transaction within the taxable period, the Code imposes a tax on the noncompliant party of 200% of the excess benefit involved. This tax cannot be paid by the exempt organization.

The statute imposes on any organization manager that participated in the excess benefit transaction, knowing that it was such a transaction, a tax equal to 10% of the excess benefit to a maximum of $10,000. An organization manager is any officer, Director or trustee of the tax-exempt organization or any individual having powers similar to those of the officers, Directors or trustees of the organization. Consequently, your Directors and officers that participated in the transaction may also personally pay taxes.

Consult Appendix 1 if you would like information about source material related to this Chapter. Appendix 1 has references of interest to all readers, not just professionals.

COMPLIANCE: ONGOING MAINTENANCE OF YOUR NONPROFIT 30

Part V is concerned with situations in which your corporation has changed or is changing in significant ways. Chapter 31 discusses when and how to review and amend your Articles and Bylaws. Chapter 32 focuses on the situations in which you sell virtually all of your assets or plan to merge with another corporation, and Chapter 33 covers dissolutions.

PART VI

CHANGING YOUR CORPORATION

31

REVIEWING AND CHANGING YOUR ARTICLES AND BYLAWS

THIS CHAPTER COVERS

- Reviewing Your Articles of Incorporation
- Changing Your Registered Agent or Registered Office
- Amending Your Articles of Incorporation
- Restating Your Articles of Incorporation
- Reviewing Your Bylaws
- Amending Your Bylaws

Every Oregon nonprofit corporation should review its Articles and Bylaws every few years to be sure that these documents comply with Oregon law and conform to the procedures you are actually using. This chapter describes in detail how to review your Articles and Bylaws and how to amend your Articles and Bylaws if they need changing for any reason.

Reviewing Your Articles of Incorporation

Many organizations never look at their Articles of Incorporation after they are filed. In fact, some don't know where they are. You should keep your Articles of Incorporation with your important corporate documents. If you can't find them, get a copy from the Secretary of State. (See Appendix 2 for contact information.)

> *You should keep your Articles of Incorporation with your important corporate documents.*

It is a good idea to review your Articles of Incorporation periodically. You want to be sure that the provisions in your Articles about your corporation are still accurate. You should also review your Bylaws at the same time to be sure that your Bylaws don't contradict anything in your Articles and that you are following your Bylaws. If your Articles listed the names of your Board members, you don't need to notify the Secretary of State when your Board changes. If your registered agent or corporate address changed, you don't need to amend your Articles to reflect these changes. Follow the procedure described below to provide the correct information. The state might already have the new information from your latest annual report. To find out, you can go to the Secretary of State's website (Appendix 2) and look at your corporate information available through their name registry.

Changing Your Registered Agent or Registered Office

At the time you filed your Articles, you listed a registered agent and an address for your registered agent. It is very important for you to keep the state notified of any changes in either. You may change your registered agent or registered office by sending to the Office of the Secretary of State a statement that gives the name of the corporation and, if the current registered office is to be changed, the address, including the street and number, of the new registered office, or, if the current registered agent is to be changed, the name of the new registered agent along with:

- A statement that the new agent has consented to the appointment; and

- A statement that after the change or changes are made, the street addresses of the registered office and the office or residence address of the registered agent will be identical.

REVIEWING AND CHANGING YOUR ARTICLES AND BYLAWS

The Secretary of State has a form that you can use for this purpose on their website. See Appendix 2 for information on how to contact them.

If your registered agent changes the street address of the agent's designated office or residence, she or he must notify the corporation in writing of the change and also send to the Office of the Secretary of State a statement as described above. That statement must recite that the corporation has been notified of the change.

Your registered agent may resign upon delivering a signed statement to the Secretary of State. If the registered office is also discontinued, the registered agent should inform the Secretary of State. After this statement is filed, the Secretary of State will immediately mail a copy to your corporation at its principal office (at the address shown in the most recent annual report or, if none, the address noted in the Articles of Incorporation). The authority of the registered agent is terminated and the registered office is discontinued, on the 31st day after the date on which the statement was filed by the Secretary of State, unless the corporation sooner appoints a successor registered agent. You do need to appoint another registered agent.

If you don't file the forms described above to record a change of registered agent or corporate address, you will be providing this information in your next annual report and the Secretary of State will update your information then. However, the better practice is not to wait until then. The state generally sends its notice of the annual report to your registered agent or corporate address. If this information has changed and you don't get the notice of renewal, you will probably not remember to file your annual report and the state will dissolve your corporation.

Amending Your Articles of Incorporation

If information in your Articles (other than a change in the Board members, the registered agent, or your address) has changed, you need to amend your Articles. Your corporation may make lawful amendments to your Articles at any time.

The procedure you follow to amend your Articles differs depending on whether or not you have members who are entitled to vote on the amendment and whether or not anyone else's consent is required to amend your Articles. In order to determine this, you need to read your Articles and any Restatement or Amendments to the Articles and review your Bylaws.

Amendment by Corporations with No Members or No Members with Voting Rights on Amendments

If your corporation has no members entitled to vote on Articles, the incorporators, until Directors have been chosen, and after that, the Directors, may adopt amendments to the corporation's

Articles. If the Articles require that an amendment to the Articles must be approved in writing by a specified person other than the Board, then that approval must be obtained.

The corporation must give notice as discussed on pages 64 or 81 (for special meetings) of any meeting at which an amendment is to be voted upon. The notice must also state that the purpose (or one of the purposes) of the meeting is to consider the proposed amendment to the Articles and it must contain a copy of it or state its general nature. The amendment must be approved by a majority of the Directors *in office* (and not just a majority present at the meeting) when the amendment is adopted, unless the Articles or Bylaws or the Board requires a greater vote.

Corporations With Voting Members

If your corporation has members, you need to determine what voting rights your members have to see if members have the right to vote on amendments to the Articles. Check your Articles and Bylaws to see if the voting rights of members are explained. Many organizations fail to describe the voting rights of their members. If that is your case, your safest assumption is to proceed as though your members have all the voting rights of members and thus the right to vote to amend the Articles. If your Articles or Bylaws say that members have the right to vote on amendments to Articles or the right to vote on all matters that the law allows, then your members must vote to amend the Articles. If your Articles or Bylaws list some issues on which members vote but do not include voting for Amendments to Articles, then a membership vote on your Articles is probably not required. (The law is a bit unclear on this.)

If your corporation has members, you need to determine what voting rights your members have to see if members have the right to vote on amendments to the Articles.

If you have members entitled to vote on the Articles, the procedure for amending your Articles varies depending on the nature of the amendment. Some amendments can be adopted by the Board without member approval. Most amendments will require the approval of both the Board and the members.

By the Board Without Member Approval

Unless the Articles provide otherwise, your Board of Directors has the authority to adopt certain types of amendments without the approval of members with voting rights:

- To delete the names and addresses of the initial Directors and incorporators;
- To delete the name and address of the initial registered agent or registered office, if a statement of change is on file with the Secretary of State;
- To delete the mailing address if an annual report has been filed with the Secretary of State;

REVIEWING AND CHANGING YOUR ARTICLES AND BYLAWS

- To change the corporate name by adding, changing, or deleting the word "incorporated," "company," "corporation," "limited," or abbreviations for these words;

- To change the corporate name by adding, deleting, or changing a geographical attribution to the name; and

- To include a statement of whether the corporation is a Public Benefit, Mutual Benefit, or Religious Corporation.

By the Board, Members, and Others

If your corporation has members with rights to vote on the Articles, amendments to the Articles must be approved by the Board (in some cases), by the members (in some cases), and by anyone whose approval is required in writing by your Articles.

- *By the Board*—If your corporation is a Public Benefit or Religious Corporation and the amendment does not relate to the number of Directors, the composition of the Board, the term of office of Directors or the way in which Directors are selected, then Board approval is required. The corporation must give notice as discussed on pp. 64 or 81 (for special meetings) of any meeting at which an amendment to the Articles will be voted on. The notice must state that one of the purposes of the meeting is to vote on a proposed amendment to the Articles and must contain a copy or summary of it.

    The law is a little unclear about how many Directors must support the amendment, so the safest course is that the Directors approve the amendment by a majority of Directors in office, unless your Articles or Bylaws require a greater vote. Member approval may also be required (see below).

- *By the Members*—Except for those matters which can be decided by the Board without member approval (described above), voting members must approve changes in the Articles. Your corporation must give the voting members notice of the meeting at which the amendments to the Articles are to be adopted in the same manner in which the members receive notice of membership meetings (see pages 373-74). The notice must also state that the purpose or one of the purposes of the meeting is to consider the proposed amendment and must contain a copy or summary of the amendment. If the vote is to be done by written consent or written ballot, the material soliciting the approval of the amendment must be accompanied by a copy or summary of the amendment.

    The voting members must approve the amendments to the Articles by at least two-thirds of the votes cast or a majority of the voting power, whichever is *less*. This means that if you have 100 voting members (so that 51 is a majority) and 60 cast votes (two-thirds of which is 40), then 40 votes are needed to amend the Articles.

- *By Designated Individuals*—If your corporation is one whose Articles require that specific people must give approval in order to amend the Articles, that approval must be given in writing. This provision of the Articles may not be amended without the approval in writing of the designated individual.

In some circumstances, the Board or members may increase the number of votes that is needed for approval of an amendment to the Articles. If the Board initiates an amendment to the Articles or the corporation is a Public Benefit or Religious Corporation and the amendment does not relate to the number of Directors, the composition of the Board, the term of office of Directors, or the method or way in which Directors are selected, the Board may increase the number of votes or percentage of votes that are required to adopt the amendment. Where the Board initiates the amendment, the Board must adopt a resolution stating the proposed amendment and directing that it be submitted to a vote at a meeting of members (which may be either an annual or special meeting).

Members entitled to vote on the amendments may also increase the percentage or number of votes that are required to adopt the amendment.

Class Voting by Members on Amendments

Some nonprofit corporations have different classes of members with each class having different rights or privileges. For example, a mutual benefit yacht club may have one class of members who own very large boats, pay dues at the highest level, and each have multiple votes based on the size of their moorage space and another class of smaller boat owners paying lower dues with one vote per member. The law requires a vote by class in certain circumstances for these corporations. These rules are generally aimed at protecting the voting rights of the class.

RELIGIOUS CORPORATIONS

If your organization has members who vote as a class and is a Religious Corporation, the members of the class entitled to vote on the Articles are entitled to vote as a class on a proposed amendment to the Articles only if the class vote is provided for in the Articles or Bylaws. Your Religious Corporation may also provide in its Articles or Bylaws for the number of votes necessary to pass amendments to the Articles; if your do not do so, the amendment must be approved by a two-thirds vote of the votes cast by the class or a majority of the voting power of the class, whichever is less.

PUBLIC BENEFIT CORPORATIONS

In a Public Benefit Corporation, the members of a class entitled to vote on the Articles are entitled to vote as a class on a proposed amendment to the Articles if the amendment would affect the rights of that class as to voting in a manner different than how the amendment would affect another class or members of another class.

MUTUAL BENEFIT CORPORATIONS

In a Mutual Benefit Corporation, the members of a class entitled to vote on the Articles are entitled to vote as a class on a proposed amendment to the Articles if the amendment would:

- Affect the rights, privileges, preferences, restrictions, or conditions of that class as to voting, dissolution, redemption, or transfer of memberships in a manner different than such amendment would affect another class;

REVIEWING AND CHANGING YOUR ARTICLES AND BYLAWS

- Change the rights, privileges, preferences, restrictions, or conditions of that class as to voting, dissolution, redemption, or transfer by changing the rights, privileges, preferences, restrictions, or conditions of another class;
- Increase or decrease the number of memberships authorized for that class;
- Increase the number of memberships authorized for another class;
- Effect an exchange, reclassification, or termination of the memberships of that class; or
- Authorize a new class of memberships.

In a Public Benefit or Mutual Benefit Corporation, if a class is to be divided into two or more classes as a result of an amendment to the Articles, the amendment must be approved by the members of each class entitled to vote on Articles that would be created by the amendment. In a Public Benefit or Mutual Benefit Corporation, a class of members is entitled to the voting rights specified here, even though the Articles and Bylaws provide that the class may not vote on the proposed amendment.

Filing of Amendment

Once you have adopted an amendment, you need to prepare the Secretary of State's form for "Articles of Amendment." (You can get this from the Secretary of State's website in Appendix 2). One copy of the Articles of Amendment form to which you attach a copy of the actual amendment must be signed by your President or one of your officers. The original must be delivered to the office of the Secretary of State for filing along with a filing fee. For a small additional fee, the state will send one copy back to you with the date filed stamped on it. The amendments are effective on that date unless your document specifies a *later* effective date. The delayed effective date must be within ninety days of the filing date. The unchanged part of the original Articles (and other amendments to them) are still effective; the new amendments simply change some part of them or add to them.

If you are a Public Benefit or Religious Corporation, you can amend your Articles to become a Mutual Benefit Corporation only if notice, including a copy of the proposed amendment, has been delivered to the Attorney General at least 20 days before you complete the amendment.

Tax-Exempt Organizations

If you are tax-exempt and the amendments to your Articles substantially change the purpose, character, name, method of operation, or kind of activities of your corporation, you must notify the IRS of the change and send a copy of your amended Articles to the IRS. If you file the Form 990 or 990EZ (see Chapter 12), you can accomplish this when you file your Form 990.

Restating Your Articles of Incorporation

Your corporation may choose to restate your Articles rather than to amend them. Your restated Articles replace the original Articles of Incorporation and any amendments to them and your original Articles and amendments are no longer valid. Contrast this with amendments to Articles which are used together with the original Articles as the organizational documents for a nonprofit corporation. Organizations commonly restate their Articles when they have had several previous amendments to their Articles, because it gets confusing reading original Articles and numerous Amendments.

The restated Articles must include all statements required to be in the original articles, except that you don't need to restate the names and addresses of the incorporators, the initial or present registered office or agent, or the mailing address of the corporation if an annual report has been filed with the Secretary of State.

> *Your restated Articles replace the original Articles of Incorporation and any amendments to them and your original Articles and amendments are no longer valid.*

Your Board can restate your Articles at any time with or without approval of members or any other person. If the restatement includes any amendments that would otherwise require approval by the members entitled to vote, it must be adopted using the same procedure as an amendment. The same notice must also be given and the voting requirements are the same. Once you have adopted Restated Articles, you will need to attach them to a cover sheet with information needed by the Corporation Division for filing. Complete and use the "Restated Articles of Incorporation" (filling in the section for nonprofit corporations) on the Corporation Division's website section as your cover sheet. The Secretary of State Corporation Division's website is listed in Appendix 2.

If your corporation is a Public Benefit or Religious Corporation, and you are restating your Articles so that you can become a Mutual Benefit Corporation, you must give notice, including a copy of the proposed restatement, to the Attorney General at least twenty days before you finalize the restatement.

Reviewing Your Bylaws

Your Bylaws provide the rules for how your nonprofit corporation is governed. It is critical that your corporation has a set of Bylaws that is current and that complies with the law. Unfortunately, many Oregon nonprofit corporations don't have a current and accurate set of Bylaws. This has come about for two reasons. Oregon nonprofit law is quite detailed and contains some pitfalls that most nonprofits would not expect in terms of how nonprofit corporations are to be governed and so they have Bylaws that don't comply with the statute.

The second factor that contributes to inaccurate Bylaws is the way that many corporations assemble their Bylaws. Many groups that don't get legal help put together their Bylaws by the cut-and-paste method. The group assembles the Bylaws by getting sample copies of Bylaws from several different groups or from the Internet. The group picks and chooses the provisions that it wants in its own Bylaws. These provisions are then cut and pasted into a new set of Bylaws.

> *Unfortunately, many Oregon nonprofit corporations do not have a current and accurate set of Bylaws.*

This method is probably a good way to get some idea of what items you might consider putting into your Bylaws but is a terrible way to assemble a final product. There are several reasons for this. Often, you have no way of knowing whether the Bylaws you are using comply with Oregon law. They may have come from another state (and no state has a law exactly like Oregon's); they may have been written before 1989 under Oregon's old statute; or they may have been drafted by someone who did not know what they were doing. Even if the samples you are using are completely in compliance with Oregon law, in the process of cutting and pasting you may build in inconsistencies and ambiguities without realizing it.

Consequently, unless you have had your Bylaws reviewed by someone who is familiar with Oregon law, you should review them now. The process of reviewing Bylaws is somewhat different from drafting them when you start a new corporation, because you have existing Articles and Bylaws with which you must work. If at all possible, you should have an attorney review your Bylaws for you after you have followed the suggestions of this chapter and come up with your best product.

Understanding the Hierarchy

The legal workings of your nonprofit corporation are governed by a variety of sources—the law, your Articles of Incorporation, your Bylaws, and your Board policies. These sources exist as a hierarchy—those above in the hierarchy control those below. In this hierarchy, the law controls all of your organizational documents and actions (Articles, Bylaws, Board policies). In many situations, state law allows your Articles and Bylaws to control the governance of your corporation and only steps in if you do not provide differently in your Articles or Bylaws. Your Articles then control your Bylaws and your Bylaws control any policies of your Board.

Articles of Incorporation

The most important corporate document you have is your Articles of Incorporation (and amendments or restatements to it). Your Articles are typically very short and establish basic items like your name, offices, whether you have members, and distribution of assets upon dissolution and may include other provisions you add. Your Articles and its amendments are like your corporation's constitution. If your other organizational documents conflict with your Articles, your Articles prevail. This means that you must read your Articles and amendments along with your Bylaws when you review your Bylaws because your Bylaws cannot contradict your Articles.

Many groups that do not get legal help put together their Bylaws by the "cut-and-paste" method. This method is a terrible way to assemble a final product.

Bylaws

Your next most important corporate document is your Bylaws. The purpose of Bylaws is to provide for how your Board governs itself. The Bylaws should contain provisions about your Board, members, officers, and committees and should include a provision for amending the Bylaws. As described in Chapter 13, the Board governs both itself and the corporation. Generally, provisions for how the Board governs the corporation are best not covered in the Bylaws but are enacted as Board policies. This gives the Board greater flexibility to manage corporate governance, since these policies are easier to amend.

Board Policies

The Board may establish policies from time to time as long as the policies do not conflict with the Articles or Bylaws. These policies may concern both how the Board manages or oversees the management of the corporation and its management of the Board itself. Chapter 16 described in detail the types of Board policies related to the management of the corporation. As noted in Chapter 16, the Board may also enact policies to supplement the provisions in the Bylaws about how it governs itself.

Tips for Reviewing Bylaws

As you review your Bylaws, keep these guidelines in mind:

Consistent with Laws

Your Bylaws must be consistent with the law. The discussion below will cover some of the most common pitfalls in the law.

REVIEWING AND CHANGING YOUR ARTICLES AND BYLAWS

Consistent with Your Articles

Your Bylaws must be consistent with your Articles. Begin your review of your Bylaws by reading your Articles of Incorporation and all of its amendments or its latest restatement and all of its amendments after the restatement. If your Bylaws conflict with any of these documents, your Articles prevail. For example, if your Articles say that your Board is composed of 7 people and your Bylaws say your Board has 9 members, then your Board can only be composed of 7 members. If you need to change your Articles, see the discussion earlier in this Chapter on that topic.

> *Begin your review of your Bylaws by reading your Articles of Incorporation and all of its amendments.*

There are a few matters that the law requires that you place in your Articles. These provisions are not valid if you put them only in your Bylaws. See pages 39-41. For example, if some group other than your Board of Directors or a committee composed only of Directors makes Board level decisions for your corporation, you must include this in your Articles. If you have these provisions in your Bylaws and not in your Articles, these provisions are very likely not valid.

Internally Consistent

Each provision in your Bylaws must be consistent with the other provisions in your Bylaws. Read your Bylaws carefully to see if there are inconsistencies. For example, if your Bylaws provide in one section that your officers are a President and Secretary and in another provide duties for a Treasurer, you need to harmonize these sections.

Focus on Governance, Not Management

In a sense, the Board has two jobs—to manage corporate governance and to manage corporate operations. We recommend that Bylaws focus on the governance responsibilities and leave management of the corporation to Board and administrative policies. In most corporations, this means that the Bylaws will be concerned with how the Board functions—how it is selected, how it makes valid decisions, etc. In membership corporations, since members elect at least one Board member and may make other governance decisions, the Board needs to be concerned with who is a voting member, how members make proper decisions, and what voting rights members have. Items related to corporate management, like the fiscal year and who has authority to sign contracts, are best handled as policies. This allows managers more flexibility, since Bylaws are harder to change, and safeguards the corporation, since future managers are unlikely to think about consulting the Bylaws for management matters and may inadvertently operate in violation of the Bylaws.

Readability and Utility

Your Bylaws should be written so they are easily understandable. They should strike a balance between being detailed enough so that your organization knows how you are run but not so detailed that they stifle whatever flexibility you need. Your Bylaws should not contain references to other documents like *Robert's Rules of Order* unless you are prepared to become familiar with these documents and use their procedures. See p. 329.

Completeness

Be sure in reviewing your Bylaws that you notice what is not in them as well as what is there. Have you covered items about voting, quorums, meetings, and notice? Compare your Bylaws to the Bylaws in the Forms section of this book for Nonmembership Corporations or Membership Corporations to be sure everything that should be covered is covered. For example, it is not uncommon for Bylaws to fail to provide for how they are to be amended.

There are some common traps and pitfalls in the law that the Bylaws of many groups inadvertently violate.

Common Pitfalls in Bylaws

After you have completed your review of your Bylaws to be sure they comply with the basic rules described above, you need to determine if your Bylaws comply with Oregon law. The most thorough way to do this would be to review Chapter 4 with your Bylaws in hand, section by section, to see if your Bylaws satisfy the legal requirements. If your organization is a homeowners' association formed on or after July 1, 1982, you will need to consult an attorney, since special laws apply to the Bylaws for homeowners' associations.

There are some common traps and pitfalls in the law that the Bylaws of many groups inadvertently violate. At a minimum, you should look at your Bylaws to see if they have avoided these traps. If you find that your Bylaws have not avoided all of these traps, this should be a signal to you that you should do the more thorough review recommended above.

The common traps and pitfalls are listed below, divided into three categories. The first category includes pitfalls that apply to all Oregon nonprofit corporations; the second refers to pitfalls for membership corporations only; and the third category applies to nonmembership corporations only.

All Oregon Nonprofit Corporations

UPDATING THE CORPORATE PURPOSE

If you decide to add to or change your corporate purpose, be sure that you do not have assets that are committed to the old purpose. If you held fundraisers or otherwise promised donors a particular use for the assets, you have to honor those commitments.

REVIEWING AND CHANGING YOUR ARTICLES AND BYLAWS 31

WHO RUNS THE CORPORATION

The Board manages the affairs of the corporation. If done properly, the Board can delegate some of its decision-making authority to a Board committee (see below). Except for these Board committees, no one other than your Board can have the ultimate authority to manage your corporate affairs, unless your Articles provide for a different authority. For example, if your Bylaws provide that your members (or some other group) hire your Executive Director or adopt the budget, this is illegal if the provision is not also in the Articles.

The delegation of the Board's authority to make decisions is different from the delegation that the Board makes to an Executive Director to administer the corporation. Although the Board has delegated to the Executive Director the authority to make management decisions, the Board retains the right to oversee and override any decision that the Executive Director makes. The Executive Director works for and under the Board. Because the Board retains the final authority, this kind of delegation does not require a provision allowing it in your Articles.

> *If your Bylaws provide that your members (or some other group) hire your Executive Director or adopt the budget, this is illegal if the provision is not also in the Articles.*

TERM OF DIRECTORS

The term for each elected Director cannot exceed 5 years (but they can be re-elected without limit). This may be violated if your Bylaws say that an elected Director serves until replaced. The law does not set term limits for appointed and designated Directors.

QUORUM

The quorum needed for a Board meeting must be at least one-third of the number of Directors fixed by your Bylaws. If you have a variable-sized Board, the quorum must be at least one-third of the number of Directors set by the Board or, if the Board has not set a number, one-third of the number of Directors in office immediately before the meeting began. Be sure that your Bylaws recognize both possibilities so that the Board understands that its quorum count depends on which method it used to determine the number of Board members. See pages 62 or 74-75 for a discussion about variable sized Boards.

Another pitfall is found in Bylaws that have a fixed number of Directors and that say "A quorum is a majority of Directors in office." If the organization has allowed the number of Directors to fall below the number fixed in the Bylaws, as frequently happens, this can lead to invalid meetings and decisions.

> *Example*: The Bylaws of the Latino Federation fix the number of Directors at 16 and provide that a quorum is a majority of Directors in office. For the last year, there have only been 9 Directors. A majority of 9 is 5. However, the law uses the fixed number in the Bylaws for the quorum calculation, so that a majority of 16 is 9. If the organization has Board meetings attended by only 5 Directors, it does not have a

quorum. Any business transacted is invalid even though it is complying with the language of its Bylaws.

MAJORITY VOTE

The Board can take action only if the action taken gets at least a majority vote of the Directors *present* (and not of Directors *voting*). This can create a problem if Directors abstain from voting. For example, if 7 Directors are present and 5 vote, the majority needed to decide the issue is 4 Directors and not 3. Bylaws that provide for a majority vote for Board action without specifying that it is a majority of Directors *present* or Bylaws that state that a majority of Directors *present and voting* can pass an action should be amended to clarify that an action can pass only if it receives a majority vote of the Directors *present*.

Votes by email or telephone poll are not a meeting and are not valid.

VOTE BY EMAIL OR TELEPHONE POLL

Many Bylaws contain provisions that allow the Board to vote by email or by a telephone poll. Boards can only vote when they are in a meeting (whether in person or by telephone or computer conference settings) in which all of the participants can hear or communicate simultaneously with each other. This allows dissenters or those with questions a chance to influence the decision. Votes by email or telephone poll are not a meeting and are not valid. If 100% of the Directors favor an action, the Board can make this decision by a consent vote. See the discussion on page 330 on these issues.

COMMITTEES

If you have committees that can make Board-level decisions, each such committee must have at least two Directors on it. The statute is somewhat ambiguous but it appears that all of the voting members of the Committee must be on the Board. Many Bylaws place the Executive Director or some other non-Director as a voting member on the Executive Committee that has the power to make Board-level decisions. This is probably improper.

The creation of a Board-level committee and the appointment of Directors to the committee (or the designation of the method of selecting committee members) must be approved by the greater of:

- a majority of all the Directors in office when the action is taken; *or*
- the number of Directors required by the Articles or Bylaws to take action in voting matters (which is usually a majority of those present).

How is this for complicated? Usually this means that your Board appoints committee members by a majority vote of all Directors in office, and not by a majority of Directors present at the meeting. Your Bylaws should have some provision that ensures that the Board understands how many votes are needed in this situation. (See the language on this point on pages 66 or 83.)

OFFICERS

Some Bylaws fail to name the corporate officers. Your Bylaws should provide for at least two officers: President and Secretary. You can call these officers by other names and one person can hold both offices.

SUPERMAJORITY VOTE

Certain actions that substantially affect the structure or functioning of the corporation—such as certain amendments to your Articles of Incorporation, the sale of your assets other than in the regular course of business, mergers, and dissolution—cannot be taken by a majority vote of the Directors at the meeting. These actions require at least a vote of the majority of Directors in office. Your Bylaws cannot permit a lesser vote. If your Bylaws simply provide that action is taken by a majority of Directors present at the meeting and do not provide for a greater vote in the above circumstances, your Board may be misled in the future. See the language on this point on pages 67 or 84.

Membership Corporations

The common understanding about membership corporations is that they are corporations that have members who support the corporation's goals and pay dues. However, the law does not define membership corporations in this way. Membership corporations are those in which the members elect at least one member of the Board of Directors. If your members do not elect at least Director on your Board, you are not a membership corporation as that term is defined by Oregon law. Review the discussion on pages 25-26 and in Chapter 19.

If your members do not elect your Board, you are not a membership corporation as that term is defined by Oregon law.

If you are not a membership corporation as the law defines it, you should review your Articles to see if you have filed as a membership corporation. If so, you need to amend your Articles and file as a nonmembership corporation. You should also review your Bylaws to see if you refer to your corporation as a membership corporation. If you do, you also need to amend your Bylaws. See page 58 for suggestions on how to handle this if you have supporters that you have been referring to as members. Since you are not a membership corporation, you do not have to comply with the remaining items in this section that pertain to membership corporations.

If you truly are a membership corporation with members who elect at least one member of your Board, you should review this next section carefully. Oregon law contains a number of provisions governing membership corporations that you might not expect.

CONSENT OF MEMBERS

Members must consent to be members. Your Bylaws cannot make someone a member without their consent. This is often violated by incorporated neighborhood associations that provide that everyone within a given geographical boundary is a member. Page 370 discusses this along with some suggestions for how to handle this situation if it is a problem for you.

ANNUAL MEETINGS

You have to hold at least an annual meeting of the members. You must give notice to all your members of the meeting. The notice has to be given in a "fair and reasonable" manner. Notice is fair and reasonable if you notify your members of the place, date, and time of the meeting by first class mail at least 7 days before the meeting or by other than first class mail from 30-60 days before the meeting. See pages 373-74. Although you don't have to put these provisions in your Bylaws, it is a good idea to do this so that future Boards and officers are reminded of these requirements.

VOTING BY PROXY

Your members are entitled to vote by proxy; that is, to give someone else the right to vote for them. Page 380 describes proxy voting. If you don't want your members to be able to do this, your Bylaws (or Articles) must forbid it. If it is not in one of these documents, you must add it, or allow proxy voting. See page 75 for suggested language to ban proxy voting.

EXPULSION OF MEMBERS

You may not expel, terminate, or suspend a member of a public benefit or mutual benefit corporation unless you do so by a fair and reasonable procedure carried out in good faith. It is a good idea to put this procedure in your Bylaws. The law considers the following to be a fair and reasonable procedure:

> *Membership may be terminated by the Board of Directors after giving the member at least 15 days written notice by first class or certified mail of the termination and the reasons for the termination, and an opportunity for the member to be heard by the Board, orally or in writing, not less than five days before the effective date of the termination.*

You may not expel, terminate, or suspend a member of a public benefit or mutual benefit corporation unless you do so by a fair and reasonable procedure.

See pages 387-88 for more discussion about this.

REMOVAL OF BOARD OF DIRECTORS

Some or all of the Board must be elected by the members. Those Directors elected by members can only be removed in one of two ways:

REVIEWING AND CHANGING YOUR ARTICLES AND BYLAWS

- By the members, if the number of votes to remove would be sufficient to elect the Director at a meeting to elect Directors; or

- By the Board, if the Articles or Bylaws provide reasons for removal and the Director is removed by a majority of Directors then in office. (See pages 383-84 for a fuller discussion.)

A common pitfall in membership organizations is a Bylaws provision that Directors are elected by the members but can be removed by the Board without specifying reasons for removal.

INSPECTION OF MEMBERSHIP LIST AND CORPORATE RECORDS

Your corporation must make available many of its corporate records and its membership list for inspection by its members, if the inspection if in good faith for a proper purpose. Some corporations want to limit the members' rights to inspect. If you are a Religious Corporation, your Articles or Bylaws can limit or abolish your members rights to inspect. If you are a Public Benefit Corporation organized primarily for political or social action, your Articles may limit or abolish the right of your members to inspect the membership list and to obtain information about your contributors. If your Public Benefit Corporation tries to restrict access to its records through your Bylaws (without having this provision in your Articles), it is not effective. See pages 384-87 for more information about inspection of records.

A Director elected by the Board in a nonmembership corporation can only be removed by a vote of two-thirds of the Directors then in office (or a greater number set by the Articles or Bylaws). You cannot remove a Director with a lesser vote.

Nonmembership Corporations

REMOVAL OF BOARD

A Director elected by the Board in a nonmembership corporation can only be removed by a vote of two-thirds of the Directors then in office (or a greater number set by the Articles or Bylaws). You cannot remove a Director with a lesser vote. Many Bylaws provide for removal by a majority vote. Some provide for removal without discussing the vote needed, which frequently leaves the impression that a majority vote is sufficient. Your Bylaws should establish the two-thirds vote and should also say "of the Directors then in office."

Amending Your Bylaws

Consult your Bylaws (and Articles) to see if they contain a procedure for amending your Bylaws. If they do have a procedure, check the procedure against the law as described below. If it is legal, follow the procedure in your Bylaws. If it is not, you need to amend your Bylaws as described here.

Amendment by Corporations with No Members or No Members with Voting Rights on Amendments

In order to amend your Bylaws, you need to determine if you are a nonmembership or membership corporation. If your corporation has members, you need to determine what voting rights your members have. Check your Articles and Bylaws to see if the voting rights of members are explained. Many organizations fail to describe the voting rights of their voting members. If that is your case, your safest assumption is to proceed as though your members have all the voting rights of members and thus the right to vote to amend the Bylaws. If your Articles or Bylaws say that members have the right to vote on amendments to Bylaws or the right to vote on all matters that the law allows, then your members must vote to amend the Bylaws. If your Articles or Bylaws list some issues on which members vote but do not include voting for Amendments to Bylaws, then a membership vote on your Bylaws is not required.

Corporations With No Members Who Vote on the Bylaws

If you conclude that you are a nonmembership corporation or you are a membership corporation in which the members do not vote on amending the Bylaws, then your Board has the sole power to amend the Bylaws. Your corporation must provide notice (see pages 64 or 81 for special meetings) of any meeting of Directors at which an amendment of the Bylaws is to be approved. That notice must also state that one of the purposes of the meeting is to consider a proposed amendment of the Bylaws and must contain a copy or summary of the proposed amendment.

> *Many organizations fail to describe the voting rights of their voting members. If that is your case, your safest assumption is to proceed as though your members have all the voting rights of members and thus the right to vote to amend the Bylaws.*

Corporations With Voting Members on the Bylaws

If your Bylaws give members the right to vote on Bylaws, then members may amend the Bylaws even though the Board may also do so. If your members have the right to amend the Bylaws, you

REVIEWING AND CHANGING YOUR ARTICLES AND BYLAWS 31

must provide notice of the members' meeting to the members. Follow the provisions for notice for a special or annual meeting (pp. 376-79), depending on which type of meeting the members will vote on the amendment. That notice must state that one of the purposes of the meeting is to consider a proposed amendment of the Bylaws and must contain a copy or summary of the proposed amendment.

The Board also has the right to amend the Bylaws for most matters unless the *Articles* reserve the power to amend exclusively to the members. Note that this provision must be in the Articles; putting it in the Bylaws alone is not enough. However, the Board cannot amend the Bylaws to increase the quorum required for any member action or to add to, change or delete the vote required for any member action that must be approved by the members.

If your members entitled to vote on Bylaws amend or repeal a particular Bylaw, the members can expressly provide that the Board may not amend or repeal that Bylaw. The members' action is then final.

Approval by a Third Party

If your Articles require written approval of the Bylaws or a provision of the Bylaws by a third person, that provision may not be amended without the approval in writing by that person.

Tax-Exempt Organizations

If you are tax-exempt and the amendments to your Bylaws substantially change the purpose, character, name, method of operation, or kind of activities of your corporation, you must notify the IRS of the change and send a copy of your new Bylaws to the IRS. If you file the Form 990 or 990EZ (see Chapter 12), you can accomplish this when you file your Form 990.

Consult Appendix 1 if you would like information about source material related to this Chapter.

32
MERGING WITH ANOTHER CORPORATION OR SELLING YOUR ASSETS

THIS CHAPTER COVERS

- Mergers
- Sale of Most of the Assets of Your Corporation

A merger occurs when one or more corporations combine with another corporation. This chapter discusses the unique set of issues that the merging corporations must solve. We also discuss the procedure that you follow to move from being two or more corporations into becoming one.

For a variety of reasons, your corporation may decide to sell, lease, exchange or otherwise dispose of all, or substantially all, of your assets. If you decide to do this, you must follow certain legal rules described in this chapter.

MERGING WITH ANOTHER CORPORATION OR SELLING YOUR ASSETS **32**

Mergers

A merger occurs when two or more corporations decide to become one corporation. A merger is a complicated process that includes legal, financial, managerial, cultural, and psychological components. Mergers commonly bring up many feelings in both organizations. Each group is looking at some significant changes and some personnel may be displaced by the merger. It is critical that the groups recognize and plan for this in advance. In virtually every merger, you will need to involve an attorney and an accountant. Some nonprofits retain other consultants to assist them in negotiating the emotional terrain of restructuring missions, jobs, and organizational cultures. If you decide that you are serious about the merger, you should retain professionals early to assist you in the process. This chapter will prepare you for some of the common issues you will need to consider and guide you through the legal process.

> *Mergers commonly bring up many feelings in both organizations. Each group is looking at some significant changes and some personnel may be displaced by the merger. It is critical that the groups recognize and plan for this in advance.*

Why Nonprofits Decide to Merge

Nonprofits decide to merge for several reasons. Often the merging organizations are providing similar services and believe that they can provide those services more efficiently if they do so as one organization. Sometimes a funder requires the two organizations to merge so that the funder does not duplicate funding efforts. Nonprofits may merge because they are providing different but related services and believe that their merger will allow the delivery of those services in a package that is more beneficial to the clients. Sometimes nonprofits merge because each group has a strength that the other needs: for example, one group may have a strong fundraiser and the other may have an established reputation in the community. Occasionally the Board of a nonprofit that is struggling financially will determine that merging with a stronger nonprofit will provide the greatest benefit to the community.

Some Merger Terminology

Mergers are a legal mirror trick in which two or more corporations become one. The new corporation that will continue after the merger is referred to as the *surviving corporation*. The other corporation is called the *disappearing corporation*. Don't be too disturbed by the legal terminology. The fact that one survives and one disappears is a result of the legal recognition that there will only be one corporation where before there were two (or more). In fact, the new corporation is the result of discussions and agreements by both corporations. The one that is chosen as the surviving corporation is often chosen for practical reasons and not necessarily because it was the stronger or better of the two. The surviving corporation is in reality the new, merged corporation.

Limitations on Mergers by Public Benefit or Religious Corporations

A nonprofit corporation may merge with another nonprofit corporation or with a business corporation. Oregon law places some restrictions on the mergers for Public Benefit and Religious Corporations, because both are formed for a public purpose and often attract donations, grants and volunteer services because they have held themselves out as serving the public. The legislature wants to ensure that the merger does not result in a misuse of the assets of these corporations.

A Public Benefit or Religious Corporation can merge with the following:

- Another Public Benefit or Religious Corporation;
- A corporation from another state which, in Oregon, would qualify as a Public Benefit or Religious Corporation;
- A wholly-owned business or Mutual Benefit corporation, provided the Public Benefit or Religious Corporation is the surviving corporation and continues to be a Public Benefit or Religious Corporation after the merger;
- A business or Mutual Benefit corporation, provided that certain conditions are met; *or*
- Any other corporation (including business corporations), as long as the Public Benefit or Religious Corporation has received prior written consent of the Attorney General or prior approval by the court in a proceeding in which the Attorney General has been given written notice. The Attorney General will closely scrutinize these mergers. You should consult an attorney *before* you enter into serious negotiations for this type of merger.

Unless there has been prior written consent by the Attorney General or prior approval by the court, no *member* of a Public Benefit or Religious Corporation may receive or keep anything as a result of the merger other than a membership in the surviving Public Benefit or Religious Corporation.

Alternatives to Mergers

Before we get more deeply into how the merger process works, you should consider some alternatives to merger. One alternative is to decide whether your goals would better be served by entering into some kind of collaboration with the other organization than it would be by an actual merger. Collaborations are generally contractual relationships in which both organizations continue intact as organizations but operate some programs, operations, or events jointly. A collaboration could allow you to avoid duplicating services and to deliver services to more clients. If you are considering a merger but you each have resources that the other needs, a collaborative agreement would allow you to share resources without closing one organization.

If a collaborative relationship will not address the reasons for the merger, another option is to dissolve one corporation and have the other carry out some or all of the organization's activities. The dissolving corporation will first use its assets to pay off its creditors' claims and then transfer any remaining assets to the second, continuing corporation. Many smaller organizations considering

MERGING WITH ANOTHER CORPORATION OR SELLING YOUR ASSETS 32

mergers opt for this choice. The primary reason is that it gives the surviving organization more assurance that it is not taking on unanticipated obligations of the dissolving organization. Organizations that choose this route will typically go through much of the merger process below to ensure that the ultimate outcome is what both parties want and that there are no major surprises, but at the end the corporation that would otherwise disappear in the merger instead dissolves.

> *You should consider alternatives to merger.*

The major difference between the merger and dissolution process is that, as the disappearing corporation goes through a dissolution process, it notifies all potential creditors of the dissolution and gives them a chance to file claims. If none are filed, or those filed are paid, the corporation can then distribute its assets after payment of claims to the other corporation. Generally, the distribution will be pursuant to an agreement or a restricted gift acceptance in which the other corporation agrees to honor certain terms the parties agreed to. For examples of the terms, see the discussion below on Issues to Deal With in a Merger.

What happens if a creditor emerges who was not known or taken care of at the time of the merger/dissolution? In a merger situation, the surviving corporation takes the assets of the dissolving corporation subject to any liabilities, known or unknown, of the dissolving corporation. Although the surviving corporation will exercise due diligence to uncover all liabilities, sometimes something slips through the cracks. All of the survivor's assets can be at risk to cover the claim. In a dissolution, a claim may also slip through the cracks or, in the case of claims not known to the dissolving corporation, may surface later, but at worst the claimant can generally only make a claim against the assets that the dissolving corporation transferred to the surviving corporation, not all of the survivor's assets.

The drawback with the dissolution process is that it takes longer and adds to the expense. Once the parties agree on terms, the parties can vote on the merger and the merger can happen fairly quickly. On the other hand, the dissolution will take longer, since the dissolving corporation must then vote on the dissolution, notify known and potential creditors, publish a newspaper ad, and wait a period of time for claimants to come forward. Another drawback is that many organizations will not have cash to liquidate all of their claims, so the organizations will need to negotiate with the creditors to arrange delayed payment or, if the creditors refuse, be forced into the merger.

An Overview of the Merger Process

The merger process begins when a nonprofit considers the possibility of aligning with another corporation. Usually the suggestion originates with the Executive Director or a Board member, often because it has been suggested by a funder. Once the corporation decides on a merger partner, the parties form a planning committee to work through the numerous issues raised by the merger. At the same time, they begin a due diligence search in which each party discloses extensive information to the other so that each party can determine whether it wants to finalize the merger. Once the parties settle the issues and decide to merge, they then agree upon the plan for merger. The plan formalizes the decisions that the parties made in a binding agreement. Each organization must then take the plan to their Board and to their members eligible to vote on mergers, if any. When the plan is approved, the surviving corporation files Articles of Merger with the Secretary of State's office to notify the state about the merger. The surviving corporation will also notify other appropriate officials. It will handle practical matters that arise after the merger: for example, ensuring that all property is transferred from the disappearing to the surviving corporation, complying with the terms of the plan of merger, and notifying outside parties about the finalization of the merger.

The Steps of the Merger

Formation of a Planning Committee

When your nonprofit has located a likely merger partner, the two corporations start discussions with each other about the possibility of merger. At this stage the parties are considering the advantages and disadvantages of the merger. Generally, the organizations appoint about a half dozen leaders from each group to form a planning committee. In smaller and midsize nonprofits, this committee considers all the details of the merger. The planning committee in larger nonprofits may delegate much of their work to subcommittees that deal with specific issues, like the selection of the Executive Director or the kinds of financial systems to be used by the surviving organization. Regardless of the size of your organization, you should develop a timeline for the merger and keep each other apprised as to what progress is made toward the merger. Keep in mind that the timeline is very flexible. Each merger is unique and you will almost certainly find yourself revising your timeline on numerous occasions.

Keep in mind that the timeline is very flexible. Each merger is unique and you will almost certainly find yourself revising your timeline on numerous occasions.

Letter of Understanding

With the formation of a planning committee, the parties will often sign a letter of intent that fleshes out the parties' decision to explore the possibility of merger. Generally, the letter is not a binding commitment to finalize the merger but a good faith statement to proceed with the process. It may contain some binding promises. For example, the parties may agree to hold in confidence information each gets from the other. Each nonprofit may promise that it won't exploit donors or funders of the other side that it discovers in the process. The letter may contain agreed-upon damages that a party that breaks the contract must pay. An attorney should draft this letter.

The Due Diligence Investigation

Each corporation needs to become thoroughly informed about the other corporation in order to make a reasonable decision about whether to approve the merger and to avoid unwelcome surprises after the merger is complete. The process by which this occurs is often referred to as the *due diligence* process and involves a very extensive exchange of documents and information. Among other items, each organization should attend to these items:

> *Each corporation needs to become thoroughly informed about the other corporation in order to make a reasonable decision about whether to approve the merger and to avoid unwelcome surprises after the merger is complete.*

- Review the legal status of the other by examining the other organization's Articles of Incorporation and amendments, Bylaws, policies, and Board, committee ,and member minutes.

- Give serious attention to the other party's financial information. You need to obtain documentation like the audits and management letters, the unaudited financial statements, budgets, insurance, fundraising material and any information on taxes. You should verify the ownership and value of the major assets.

- Pay particular attention to the liabilities of the other corporation because these liabilities will become the liabilities of the merged organization. You need to exercise special care to investigate potential liabilities that may not be apparent on financial statements. These include potential claims by employees, deferred maintenance on facilities and potential lawsuits against the other corporation.

Much of the information you need to gather will be specific to the type and size of nonprofits that are involved. Your own attorney and accountant can advise you more specifically.

> *In the process of the due diligence search, the parties often disclose sensitive and confidential financial and managerial information to each other.*

Each corporation should understand the potential consequences of this exchange of information. In the process of the due diligence search, the parties often disclose sensitive and confidential financial and managerial information to each other. Each nonprofit may be revealing the names of donors or trade secrets that the other could use to their benefit if merger talks fail. Key personnel in one corporation will interact with decision-makers in the other and may be approached to switch ships if the merger does not succeed. Each party will learn important details about how the other runs its programs. You need to be willing to live with this possibility.

At the same time that the parties pursue their due diligence search, they discuss in detail and reach resolutions about a variety of issues that must be resolved in order for the merger to occur.

Issues to Deal With in a Merger

Regardless of the reasons for the merger, all nonprofits need to deal with some common issues raised by the merger. Here are some of the most important.

> *You will need to determine who will be on the Board of Directors and who the Executive Director of the surviving corporation will be.*

PURPOSE AND STRUCTURE OF THE SURVIVING ORGANIZATION

The organizations will commonly develop a mission statement or a philosophical direction for the surviving organization. You will need to decide on the name for the surviving corporation—it may keep its own name, it may take the name of the disappearing corporation or it may take a new name. You should agree on the governance and structure for the new organization and you should draft the Articles and Bylaws for the surviving corporation. You will need to determine who will be on the Board of Directors and who the Executive Director of the surviving corporation will be.

ASSETS AND LIABILITIES

Each organization will want full disclosure about the other's assets, liabilities, net assets, and other items pertinent to making an informed decision about the merger. You will exchange this kind of information in the due diligence process described above. The organizations should consider how to handle the transition of assets from the disappearing corporation to the surviving corporation. Is there property that needs to be deeded? Are there stocks or investment portfolios that will be transferred? How should you handle the timing on this? How do you arrange for the transfer of bank accounts?

The organizations will need to consider how to handle their indebtedness. You need to determine whether the consent of any creditors of either corporation is needed to the merger. You also need to explore whether either corporation has potential liabilities that do not appear on the balance sheet and how to handle them.

MEMBERSHIP

If either of the organizations is a membership organization, the organizations will have to deal with how to handle membership issues. Will the new organization have members and, if so, who are they? If the merger involves a Mutual Benefit Corporation or a business corporation, the organizations may need to convert the memberships or stock into cash or other property.

EMPLOYEE ISSUES

As part of your merger planning you will determine the terms of employment that will be offered by the surviving corporation, including the compensation and benefits the surviving corporation will provide. You will need to determine whether you will transfer all of the accrued vacation and sick leave of employees moving from the disappearing corporation to the surviving corporation or make some other provision such as cashing them out or requiring them to "use it or lose it." This may be a particularly challenging question if the two merging corporations have very different approaches to providing benefits. If the surviving corporation plans to change any of its benefits or personnel practices immediately upon merger, it should provide notice to the current employees and make transition plans. Consult an attorney familiar with employment issues to ensure that your plans are legal.

The surviving corporation will also need to discuss the merger plan with its fringe benefit providers to assure smooth transition for the employees moving from the disappearing corporation into the coverage of the surviving corporation.

LEASES AND CONTRACTS

Both corporations need to review their lease and contracts to be sure that they will remain in compliance with them after the merger. Many leases require renegotiation in the event of a significant change in corporate status, such as a merger.

You will need to inform your funders of your merger plans and get their consent if it is needed.

AUDITS

You want to discuss your plans to merge with the auditor of both the surviving and disappearing corporations. There are several options for completing the audits and presenting the financial statements of both corporations. Your auditor can explain the options and make recommendations. You will want to take particular care in planning to meet audit requirements for government funds.

FUNDERS

You need to inform your funders of your merger plans and get their consent if it is needed. You may need to make some adjustments to your grants if the merger is occurring mid-cycle. Many organizations attempt to time their mergers to avoid mid-cycle mergers if possible. Special attention is needed for government funding agreements since there may be legal restrictions in the governmental entity's ability to enter into agreements with the merged organization.

You should ask your funders to prepare any contract amendments or new contracts which will be required to maintain the funder's relationship with the surviving corporation. While many funders encourage mergers, you cannot assume that they have an understanding of the legal issues involved and will take care of contracts on their own. You will also want to seek whatever assurances you can get that your funder will continue to provide the combined amounts of funds currently available to the two corporations rather than reducing the amount once there is only one corporation.

REMEDIES IF THE SURVIVING CORPORATION VIOLATES THE MERGER AGREEMENT

One issue of concern for some disappearing nonprofits is what they can do if the surviving corporation does not honor the merger plan. The problem with enforcing the plan of merger is that the disappearing corporation has, well, disappeared. Although Board members associated with the merger survive, the legal entity that was the corporation did not. The surest way to achieve compliance is to ensure that the disappearing corporation has a controlling voice on the new Board but this rarely happens. If this is an important issue for you, you need to talk to your attorney.

One issue of concern for some disappearing nonprofits is what they can do if the surviving corporation does not honor the merger plan.

Creating the Plan of Merger

Once the due diligence search is complete and the details of the merger have been agreed upon, the organizations are then ready to initiate the legal steps to effect the merger. The next step from the legal point of view is to create a legal plan of merger. The plan must state:

- the name of each business or nonprofit corporation planning to merge and the name of the surviving corporation into which each of the others plans to merge;

- the terms and conditions of the merger, including the agreements that the two corporation worked out in response to the issues raised above and details about how and when the merger will occur;

- the manner and basis of converting memberships of each Public Benefit or Religious Corporation into memberships of the surviving corporation; and

- if the merger involves a Mutual Benefit or business corporation, the manner and basis of converting the memberships or shares of each merging corporation into memberships, obligations, shares or other securities of the surviving corporation (or any other corporation) or into cash or other property.

The plan of merger may contain amendments to the Articles of Incorporation and Bylaws of the surviving corporation and other provisions relating to the merger.

Adopting the Plan of Merger

Unless the Articles, Bylaws, Board of Directors, or members provide differently, the plan of merger must be adopted:

- by the Board; and

MERGING WITH ANOTHER CORPORATION OR SELLING YOUR ASSETS 32

- by the members entitled to vote on the merger ; and
- in writing by anyone whose approval is required for an amendment to the Articles or Bylaws.

If your corporation has members, you need to determine whether your members have the right to vote on mergers. Check your Articles and Bylaws to see if the voting rights of members are explained. Many organizations fail to describe the voting rights of their members. If that is your case, your safest assumption is to proceed as though your members have all the voting rights of members and thus the right to vote on mergers. If your Articles or Bylaws say that members have the right to vote on mergers or the right to vote on all matters that the law allows, then your members must vote on mergers. If your Articles or Bylaws list some issues on which members vote but do not include voting for mergers, then a membership vote on your merger is not required.

ADOPTION BY THE BOARD

Whether or not your corporation has members entitled to vote on the merger, the merger must be approved by the Board. Each Director must get notice of the Directors' meeting at which such approval is to be obtained (as explained on page 325). The notice needs to state that the purpose (or one of the purposes) of the meeting is to consider the proposed merger. At the meeting, a majority of Directors *in office* at the time the merger must approve the merger. If the corporation has members entitled to vote on the merger, the Directors should then agree to send the plan to the members for a vote.

ADOPTION BY THE MEMBERS

If your corporation has members entitled to vote on the merger, your Board should submit the plan to the members after the Board approves the merger. If the Board seeks to have the plan approved by the members at a membership meeting, the corporation must give notice as described on pages 373-75. To meet this requirement, you must have a complete, updated list of members. For some groups that have not been consistent in maintaining membership records, this may mean figuring out the best strategy to determine who the members are for purposes of meeting the notice requirement. The notice must state that the purpose (or one of the purposes) of the meeting is to consider the plan of merger, and must provide a copy or summary of the plan which includes:

- for members of the *surviving* corporation, any provision that, if contained in a proposed amendment to the Articles of Incorporation or Bylaws, would entitle members to vote for the provision; and

- for members of the *disappearing* corporation, a copy or summary of the Articles and Bylaws which will be in effect immediately after the merger takes place.

Unless your Articles, Bylaws, Board, or members require a greater vote, the members at the meeting must approve the merger by at least 2/3 of the votes cast or a majority of the voting power, whichever is less.

> *Example*: A corporation has 100 members entitled to vote on the merger and 60 actually vote. 45 vote in favor of the merger. The merger is approved by the lesser of 51

votes (the majority of 100) or 40 votes (⅔ of 60). In this case, 40 votes is the minimum required and the merger is approved.

If the Board wants to have the plan approved by the members *by written consent or written ballot*, the material soliciting the approval needs to include the same information required to be sent out with the notice to members as described above.

As discussed on page 371, some membership corporations have more than one class of member. If one of the merging corporations has classes of members, the members must vote by class if the plan contains a provision that, if contained in a proposed amendment to the Articles, would entitle the class of members to vote as a class. The plan is approved by each class if it receives 2/3 of the votes cast by the class or a majority of the voting power of the class, whichever is less.

APPROVAL BY A THIRD PARTY

A merger in effect amends the Articles and Bylaws. If your Articles or Bylaws require approval by a third party or parties for amendments to the Articles or Bylaws, you must obtain that approval in writing.

Abandonment

After the merger is adopted, and at any time before Articles of Merger are filed, the plan of merger may be abandoned in accordance with the procedure given in the plan or, if none is given, in a manner determined by the Board.

Filing the Articles of Merger

After a plan of merger is approved by the Board and, if required, by the members and any others, the surviving corporation must deliver to the Secretary of State for filing an original copy of the Articles of Merger and a filing fee. You can find Articles of Merger on the Secretary of State's website. (See Appendix 2). The merger takes effect when the Articles of Merger are filed, unless the plan names a delayed date. The delayed date must be within ninety days of the filing date. You cannot name a merger date *before* the plan is filed. If a particular merger date is important to you, be sure to plan so that the Articles are filed by that date.

The effect of the merger is that the corporations that participate merge into the surviving corporation and the disappearing corporations cease to exist.

The Effect of a Merger

The effect of the merger is that the corporations that participate merge into the surviving corporation and the disappearing corporation or corporations cease to exist. Title to all property owned by each corporation is vested in the surviving corporation. If the disappearing corporation owned real property or held other property, it should transfer these properties to the surviving corporation. You may need to involve an attorney to prepare new deeds or other evidence of title. The surviving corporation also has all the liabilities and obligations of each disappearing corporation. The Articles and Bylaws of the surviving corporation are amended as provided by the plan of merger.

If the plan called for memberships or shares of the disappearing corporations to be converted into memberships, obligations, shares, or other securities of the surviving corporation (or any other corporation) or into cash or other property, the surviving corporation must do this, and the former holders of the memberships or shares are entitled only to the rights provided in the Articles of Merger. The surviving corporation typically handles these details.

Accounting for Mergers and Take-Overs

Accounting requirements for dealing with mergers and other strategies that result in one nonprofit carrying out the work previously done by two separate organizations are presented in the Statement of Financial Accounting Standards (SFAS) 164 issued by the Financial Accounting Standards Board (FASB) in 2009. SFAS 164 spells out some significant differences between nonprofit and for-profit accounting for mergers and other combining strategies. The technical accounting issues involved are beyond the scope of this book.

The standards characterize the alternatives to mergers as "acquisitions," a term which may not fit well with the way nonprofits discuss the strategies they will use to combine efforts. A key part of your planning process should involve accountants with a clear understanding of SFAS 164 who can help the planning committee understand the financial statement implications of some of the legal choices they are considering. You'll want to "begin with the end in mind" in order to select the legal strategies that will result in the continuing organization being able to present its financial condition in ways that are readily understandable and add credibility to your efforts.

Special Note for Tax-Exempt Corporations

If you have a §501(c) tax exemption, you must notify the IRS on your annual information return about your merger. Be sure to follow the instructions on the return.

Sale of Most of the Assets of Your Corporation

Your organization may find itself in the position of selling or disposing of all or substantially all of your property, even though you are not dissolving. This is a very unusual event but it can happen. If your organization decides to sell, lease, exchange, or otherwise dispose of all, or substantially all, of your property and assets, you may do so with the following restrictions.

In the Usual Course of Your Activities

If the sale or other disposal of all or substantially all of your properties is in the usual or regular course of your activities, you may do so without approval of members or any other person, unless your Articles provide differently. You may mortgage and incur indebtedness whether or not it is in the usual or regular course of your activities without the approval of members or any other person, unless the Articles provide differently. For example, if your nonprofit sells religious books and sells virtually all of them, this disposal of virtually all of its property is in the usual course of its activities.

Not in the Usual Course of Your Activities

Sometimes an organization will sell or dispose of all of its property for reasons that are not related to engaging in its usual nonprofit purpose. Since the purpose of the nonprofit is to use its assets for its mission, the law wants to be sure that there is some corporate oversight of this unusual transaction. If you want to sell or otherwise dispose of all or substantially all of your corporation's property *other* than in the usual or regular course of your activities, the corporation must obtain approval for the transaction by the Board, by the members entitled to vote on the transaction, and in writing by anyone whose approval is required for an amendment of Articles or Bylaws. The Articles, Bylaws, Board or members may require a greater vote or voting by class in order to approve the transaction.

You must decide whether you have members entitled to vote on this transaction and whether anyone else's approval is required for this transaction. In order to determine this, you need to read your Articles and any Restatement or Amendments and Bylaws. If your corporation has members, you need to determine whether your members have the right to vote on the sale of your assets. Check your Articles and Bylaws to see if the voting rights of members are explained. Many organizations fail to describe the voting rights of their members. If that is your case, your safest assumption is to proceed as though your members have all the voting rights of members and thus the right to vote on the sale of assets. If your Articles or Bylaws say that members have the right to vote on the sale of assets or the right to vote on all matters that the law allows, then your members must vote on the sale. If your Articles or Bylaws list some issues on which members vote but do not include voting for the sale of assets, then a membership vote on the sale is not required.

Adoption by the Board

Whether or not the corporation has members entitled to vote on the transaction, it must be approved by a majority of the Directors in office at the time the transaction is approved. Notice of the Directors' meeting must be given as provided on page 325 for special meetings, and the notice must state that one of the purposes of the meeting is to consider the sale or other disposition of all or substantially all of the property of the corporation, and must contain a description of the transaction.

MERGING WITH ANOTHER CORPORATION OR SELLING YOUR ASSETS

Adoption by the Members

If your corporation has members entitled to vote on the sale, your Board (after approving the sale) must submit the issue to the members for a vote. If the Board seeks to have the transaction approved by the members *at a membership meeting*, the corporation must give notice as explained on pages 373-75. The notice must also state that one of the purposes of the meeting is to consider the sale or the disposition of all or substantially all of the property of the corporation and include a description of the transaction. If the Board wants to have the transaction approved by the members *by written consent or written ballot*, the material soliciting the approval has to contain a description of the transaction.

The Board may condition its submission of the proposed transaction to a vote of the members, and the members entitled to vote on the transaction may condition their approval on a receipt of a higher percentage of affirmative votes or any other basis. Unless your Articles, Bylaws, Board, or members require a greater vote, the members must approve the merger by at least 2/3 of the votes cast or a majority of the voting power, whichever is less.

Approval by a Third Party

If your Articles or Bylaws require approval by a third party to the sale of all or substantially all of your assets, you will need to obtain this approval in writing.

Finalizing the Sale

A Public Benefit or Religious Corporation must give written notice to the Attorney General twenty days before it sells or otherwise disposes of all or substantially all of its property, unless the transaction is in the usual or regular course of its activities or the Attorney General has given the corporation a written waiver of this notice requirement. After the sale or other disposition of property is authorized, the transaction may be abandoned without further action by the members or any other person in accordance with a procedure stated in the resolution proposing the transaction or, if none is stated, in the manner determined by the Board.

§501(c)(3) Groups

If your group has a §501(c)(3) tax exemption, you must notify the IRS on your annual information return if there is a full or partial liquidation or a major disposition of your assets. A major disposition occurs if you dispose of at least 25% of the fair market value of your assets. However, if you *sell* your assets for a fair price you do not need to report this separately on the return. You do need to report the income from the sale of your assets on Form 990. Follow the instructions on your return.

Creditors

Your creditors may have rights that are impacted by your decision to dispose of your property. You should get some legal advice for your own particular situation.

Consult Appendix 1 if you would like information about source material related to this Chapter. Appendix 1 has references of interest to all readers, not just professionals.

33

DISSOLVING YOUR NONPROFIT CORPORATION

THIS CHAPTER COVERS

- Voluntary Dissolution
- Involuntary Dissolution
- Activities After Dissolution
- Special Note for Tax-Exempt Corporations that are Voluntarily or Involuntarily Dissolved

"Dissolution" is the legal term for what happens when a corporation ends its existence. A dissolution of your corporation may be either voluntary (of your own choice) or involuntary (when you are forced to do so by others).

Voluntary Dissolution

A nonprofit corporation may choose to dissolve for several reasons. There may not be enough people with the energy to continue its work. The group may not be able to attract sufficient funding to survive. Occasionally, the corporation may feel it has fulfilled its mission or there are other groups working to accomplish the same purposes. Sometimes divisions in the group make it impossible to continue. Sometimes a corporation dissolves because it has acquired more debt than it can pay and prefers this alternative to bankruptcy.

Issues to Consider

If your corporation has decided on dissolution, you need to consider a number of issues concerning how the dissolution will occur. We list here some of the most common:

- You should develop a plan to liquidate or dispose of your assets.

- You will need to determine if you have sufficient assets to pay all your creditors, whether there are any claims against the corporation, and what will be the expenses of closing down. This Chapter discusses how to identify and pay these claims and expenses.

- You will need to consider whether you have leases, contracts, grants, or other legal relationships that will be impacted by your dissolution and deal with them. If you are vacating property before a lease has expired, for example, the lessor becomes a claimant/creditor and will need to be dealt with as such.

- If you have employees, you will need to consult your personnel manual and should also consider talking to an attorney about employment law, in order to determine what your duties and potential liabilities are. You may need to set aside a reserve for potential claims by your employees.

- If your employees have a pension plan, you need to consult with a professional experienced in pension issues. Your Plan Administrator may have personal liability for the plan.

- Be sure that any tax issues have been taken care of before you distribute your assets.

- You need to review all current contracts with funders to determine whether they include audit and record inspection requirements. Make plans to comply with these requirements or get legal advice about the consequences of violating the agreements.

- If you are going to have assets remaining after all creditors, claims, and expenses are paid, you must determine what happens to these assets. You should consult

DISSOLVING YOUR NONPROFIT CORPORATION 33

your Articles of Incorporation and possibly your Bylaws to see what these documents state should happen to your assets on dissolution. If the documents provide that the Board is to decide, your Board needs to make this determination.

> *Most Board members will drift away during the process, so be sure that the Board names and, if necessary, pays an agent to handle the winding up process.*

- If your corporation is a Public Benefit or Religious Corporation and no provision has been made in the Articles or Bylaws for distribution of assets on dissolution, you must transfer your assets after payment of your debts to an organization organized for a public or charitable purpose, a religious corporation, the United States, a state, a person, or an entity that is exempt under §501(c)(3) of the Internal Revenue Code.

- If your corporation is a Mutual Benefit corporation and no provision has been made in the Articles or Bylaws for distribution of assets on dissolution, you must transfer your assets after payment of your debts to your members or, if you have no members, to those people whom you holds yourself out as benefiting or serving.

- You should develop a timeline for the dissolution. The timeline should include when the dissolution is effective. The dissolution can be effective on the date you file the Articles of Dissolution with the Corporation Division or within 90 days after that. As described later in this Chapter, you can wind up the affairs of the corporation after the dissolution is effective.

- You will need to make provision for the storage of the corporate records for a period of years, generally at least seven years.

- You need to decide who has authority to act for the corporation during what may be a lengthy dissolution process. Most Board members will drift away during the process, so be sure that the Board names and, if necessary, pays an agent to handle the winding up process.

After you make decisions about these and other issues, you should formulate them into a written plan of dissolution. At a minimum, your plan should include:

- A statement that the organization is dissolving, will liquidate its assets and pay its creditors;
- A timeline for the dissolution, including a statement of the date that the dissolution is final;
- A statement of who gets any assets after creditors are paid;

- The name of the agent who is authorized to wind up the affairs of the corporation after dissolution;
- Provisions for storage of your documents;
- Any other issue to consider described above that applies to your corporation.

> *If the corporation dissolves and there is a dissatisfied creditor or if you give assets to someone who should not be receiving them and the Attorney General's office investigates, the Board may be held personally accountable.*

If your organization has assets of any substantial value or any potential claim that you cannot pay or make provision for, you should seriously consider getting some legal advice. If the corporation dissolves and there is a dissatisfied creditor or if you give assets to someone who should not be receiving them and the Attorney General's office investigates, the Board may be held personally accountable.

Overview of the Dissolution Procedure

Voluntary dissolution is legally accomplished when dissolution is voted on by the corporation, the Attorney General is notified in certain cases, Articles of Dissolution are prepared, and the Articles of Dissolution are filed with the State. After dissolution, the corporation can wind up its affairs (liquidate its property, pay its creditors, etc.) as described below but cannot continue its programs or engage in new business.

Dissolution by Incorporators

If a corporation has no members and doesn't yet have an initial Board of Directors, the incorporators may dissolve the corporation by delivering Articles of Dissolution to the Secretary of State for filing. This happens very rarely. The incorporators have to get any approvals for dissolution required by the Articles or Bylaws. The corporation must give the incorporators notice equivalent to that required for special meetings of the Board discussed on page 325, of any meeting at which dissolution will be considered. The notice must also state that one of the purposes of the meeting is to consider dissolution. In approving the dissolution, the incorporators will need to adopt a plan of dissolution indicating who will get the assets owned or held by the corporation after all creditors have been paid.

Dissolution by the Board, Members and Third Parties

Once the corporation has a Board or has members who have voting rights on dissolution, the incorporator is no longer empowered to dissolve the corporation. Unless your Articles, Bylaws, Board, or members provide differently, your corporation is dissolved:

DISSOLVING YOUR NONPROFIT CORPORATION

- by the Board; and
- by the members entitled to vote on dissolution, and
- in writing by anyone whose approval is required for an amendment to the Articles or Bylaws.

If your corporation has members, you need to determine whether your members have the right to vote on dissolution. Check your Articles and Bylaws to see if the voting rights of members are explained. Many organizations fail to describe the voting rights of their members. If that is your case, your safest assumption is to proceed as though your members have all the voting rights of members and thus the right to vote on dissolution. If your Articles or Bylaws say that members have the right to vote on dissolution or the right to vote on all matters that the law allows, then your members must vote on dissolution. If your Articles or Bylaws list some issues on which members vote but do not include voting for dissolution, then a membership vote on your dissolution is not required.

You must also check to see if anyone else must approve. If you cannot easily determine these things, you need to have an attorney answer these questions for you.

ADOPTION BY THE BOARD

Whether or not the corporation has members entitled to vote on dissolution, dissolution must be approved by a vote of the majority of Directors *in office* at the time the transaction is approved. The corporation must provide notice of the meeting at which the dissolution is to be considered, equivalent to that required for special meetings of the Board discussed on page 325. The notice must state that one of the purposes of the meeting is to consider dissolution of the corporation and must include a copy or summary of the plan of dissolution.

ADOPTION BY THE MEMBERS

If your corporation has members entitled to vote on the dissolution, your Board (after adopting the plan) must submit the plan of dissolution to your members for approval. If the Board wants to have the dissolution approved by the members at a membership meeting, the corporation has to give the members notice as discussed on pages 373-75 which states that one of the purposes of the meeting is to consider dissolving the corporation. It must include a copy or summary of the plan of dissolution. Unless the Articles, Bylaws, Board of Directors or members require a greater vote, or voting is by class, dissolution is authorized if it is approved by the members entitled to vote on dissolution by at least two-thirds of the votes cast, or a majority of the voting power, whichever is less.

If the Board wants to have dissolution approved by the members *by written consent or written ballot*, the material soliciting the approval must include a copy or summary of the plan of dissolution.

The Board may condition its submission of the proposed dissolution to a vote of members or the members may condition their approval of the dissolution on receipt of a higher percentage of votes or on any other basis.

Notice to the Attorney General

Your Public Benefit or Religious Corporation must give the Attorney General written notice that it intends to dissolve at or before it delivers its Articles of Dissolution to the Secretary of State. The notice has to include a copy or a summary of the plan of dissolution. Your corporation cannot transfer assets as part of the dissolution process until twenty days after it has given a written notice to the Attorney General or until the Attorney General has consented in writing or indicated in writing that the state will take no action with respect to the transfer or conveyance, whichever is earlier.

When all or substantially all of the assets of the Public Benefit Corporation have been transferred or conveyed following approval of dissolution, the Board needs to deliver to the Attorney General a list showing those, other than creditors, to whom the assets were transferred or conveyed. The list must indicate the address of each person, other than creditors, who received assets and indicate what assets each received.

> *A Public Benefit or Religious Corporation must give the Attorney General written notice that it intends to dissolve at or before it delivers its Articles of Dissolution to the Secretary of State.*

Articles of Dissolution

After the dissolution is authorized, the corporation completes the dissolution by delivering to the Secretary of State for filing an original copy of the Articles of Dissolution along with a filing fee. (See the Secretary of State for "Articles of Dissolution.") The dissolution is effective on the date it is filed by the Secretary of State unless the document specifies a delayed effective date. However, the delayed effective date may not be later than ninety days after the document is filed.

Revocation of Dissolution

A corporation may revoke its dissolution within 120 days of its effective date. The revocation must be authorized in the same manner as the dissolution was authorized unless the authorization of dissolution permitted revocation by the Board of Directors alone. After the revocation of dissolution is authorized, the corporation revokes the dissolution by delivering Articles of Revocation of Dissolution to the Secretary of State for filing. You can get these forms from the Secretary of State. Unless a delayed effective date is specified, the revocation of dissolution is effective when the Articles of Revocation of Dissolution are filed. When the revocation of dissolution is effective, it takes effect as of the effective date of dissolution and the corporation resumes carrying on its activities as if a dissolution had never occurred.

DISSOLVING YOUR NONPROFIT CORPORATION 33

Claims Against a Dissolved Corporation

If your corporation is dissolving, it is very important for you to establish who your creditors are. These people must be paid before your remaining assets are distributed. Although it is not mandatory, Oregon law provides a procedure by which you can determine who your creditors are. It is a very good idea to follow this procedure because, if you do not, and a creditor does not get paid, it is possible that the individual Directors may be liable for the claim.

You should begin by identifying those claims that you know about. Obvious claims would be suppliers and those who have loaned you money or extended credit. However, consider also:

- employees who may have claims for unpaid benefits, unemployment claims, or other claims;
- your landlord, if you lease space;
- funders who have restricted the use of assets purchased with funds provided by the funder;
- any taxing authorities; and
- whoever holds your mortgage, if you own your building.

If your corporation is dissolving, it is very important for you to establish who your creditors are. These people must be paid before your remaining assets are distributed.

In the case of claims that are known to you, you should notify those claimants in writing about the dissolution at any time after its effective date. The purpose of your notice is to give your potential creditors the opportunity to notify you that they have a claim and how much they believe that you owe them. Your written notice to the claimants must describe the information you want the claimant to include in the claim, provide a mailing address where the claim can be sent, state a deadline (which may not be fewer than 120 days from the effective date of the written notice) by which the dissolved corporation must receive the claim, and state that the claim will be barred if not received by that deadline. It is a good idea to send your notices by certified mail, return receipt requested, so that you can prove that your claimants received their notices. For purposes of this procedure, a claim does not include a contingent liability (one which is not now fixed but will become definite in the future) nor does it include a claim based on an event that occurred after the effective date of dissolution.

If you follow the above procedure, claimants who you wrote to and who don't deliver a claim to you by the deadline cannot bring a claim against your corporation. If a claimant submits a claim and you dispute its validity or the amount of the claim, you can respond with a written rejection of the claim in full or a partial rejection that states what you believe you owe and rejects the remainder of the claim. Claimants who do file a claim with you within the deadline but whose claims you reject have ninety days from the date of the rejection notice to file a proceeding to enforce the claim; otherwise, they also lose their claim.

It is possible that, at the time of dissolution, there may be potential claims against the corporation that are not known to you. In order to protect against these claims, you may publish notice of your dissolution and request that people with claims against the corporation present them in accordance with the notice. The notice must be published at least one time in a newspaper of general circulation in the county where your principal office is located. It must describe the information to be included in the claim, provide a mailing address where the claim can be sent, and state that the claim against the corporation will be barred unless the proceeding to enforce the claim is begun within five years after publication of the notice.

If the dissolved corporation publishes this notice, the following claims are barred unless the claimant begins a proceeding to enforce the claim within five years after the publication:

- A claimant who did not receive written notice that was directed to the known claimants;

- A claimant whose claim was sent in a timely manner to the dissolved corporation but was not acted on; *and*

- A claimant whose claim is contingent or based on an event occurring after the effective date of dissolution.

You cannot continue your program activities after dissolution.

If someone has a claim against your corporation, it may be enforced against the dissolved corporation to the extent of its undistributed assets or against any entity (other than the creditor) to whom the corporation distributed its property upon liquidation. If the entity received a *pro rata* share of a distribution, the entity's liability will not exceed the same *pro rata* share of the claim. The entity's total liability for all claims may not exceed the total amount of assets distributed to that person, less any liability of the corporation paid on behalf of the corporation by that entity after the date of distribution.

If the corporation is required to transfer assets to a creditor, claimant, or member who cannot be found or who is not competent to receive them, the corporation must sell the assets for cash (unless the asset is subject to a trust restriction) and deposit this with the Division of State Lands. The corporation's agent handling this must prepare under oath duplicate copies of a statement containing the names and last-known addresses of the people entitled to the funds. One of the statements must be delivered to the Secretary of State and the other to the Division of State Lands.

DISSOLVING YOUR NONPROFIT CORPORATION

Effect of a Dissolution/Winding Up Affairs

A dissolved corporation continues its corporate existence but may not carry on activities except those necessary to wind up its affairs. This means that you cannot continue your program activities after dissolution. Winding up activities include:

- Protecting its assets and minimizing its liabilities;
- Paying its indebtedness;
- Liquidating its properties that will not be distributed as they are;
- Returning assets held by the corporation upon conditions requiring a return;
- Transferring its assets as provided in the Articles or Bylaws or by law;
- Sending the Attorney General the list showing who received its assets as described on page 681; *and*
- Doing other necessary acts to wind up its affairs.

See pages 755-56 for a discussion of the consequences if you continue to operate your corporation after it has dissolved.

Involuntary Dissolution

In some cases, your corporation may be dissolved by someone other than you.

> *The most common cause of administrative dissolution is when a corporation fails to pay its annual fee to the Secretary of State.*

Administrative Dissolution

The Secretary of State may administratively dissolve a corporation if:

- The corporation fails to pay when due any fees owed by it;
- The corporation fails to deliver its annual report to the Secretary of State when due;
- The corporation fails to have a registered agent or registered office in Oregon;
- The corporation fails to notify the Secretary of State that its registered agent has resigned or been changed or that its registered office has been discontinued or changed; *or*
- If the period of duration stated in the Articles of Incorporation expires.

The most common cause of administrative dissolution is when a corporation fails to pay its annual fee to the Secretary of State (see page 682).

If the Secretary of State decides to dissolve your corporation, the Secretary's office will give your corporation written notice that grounds exist to dissolve the corporation. If you do not correct each problem or demonstrate to their reasonable satisfaction within 45 days after notice is given that the grounds for dissolution do not exist, the Secretary of State will administratively dissolve your corporation and give the corporation notice of dissolution. If the corporation is a Public Benefit Corporation, the Secretary of State will notify the Attorney General in writing.

An administrative dissolution is a very serious matter if your corporation does not want to be dissolved. As with a voluntary dissolution, your corporation is not allowed to continue to do business other than winding up your affairs. If you do engage in business, such as buying or selling property, incurring indebtedness, or making commitments to engage in programs, you are now doing so as an unincorporated association and not as a corporation. This creates potential personal liability for all of the decision-makers and may cloud the title on the property you hold or sell. It is very important that you deal with this promptly. If you were exempt from taxation under any subsection of §501(c), your exemption, which was issued to your corporation, no longer covers your unincorporated association. Among other things, this means that contributions by donors to §501(c)(3) organizations are not deductible. Your remedy is reinstatement.

> *An administrative dissolution is a very serious matter if your corporation does not want to be dissolved. This creates potential personal liability for all of the decision-makers and may cloud the title on the property you hold...Contributions by donors to §501(c)(3) organizations are not deductible.*

Reinstatement

A corporation that has been administratively dissolved may apply to the Secretary of State for reinstatement within five years from the date of dissolution. The application must state the name of the corporation and the effective date of its administrative dissolution and state that the grounds for dissolution either did not exist or have been eliminated. If the Secretary of State determines that the application contains the necessary information, that the information is correct and that the corporation's name is still available, the Secretary of State will reinstate the corporation. You will be required to pay the filing fees for all the years during which you were dissolved.

If the administrative dissolution occurred more than five years ago, you can request that the Secretary of State waive (overlook) the five-year rule. You will need to provide evidence that the corporation continued its existence as an active concern during the period of the dissolution. Contact the Secretary of State's Corporation Division (see Appendix 2) for forms and information on the reinstatement and waiver.

The reinstatement takes effect as of the effective date of the administrative dissolution and the corporation resumes carrying on its activities as if the dissolution had never occurred. This probably means that your tax exemption classification is also reinstated. If the Secretary of State denies a corporation's application for reinstatement, the Secretary of State must give written notice to the corporation explaining the reasons.

Filing for a New Corporation

Some corporations that have been administratively dissolved bypass the reinstatement process (especially if a corporation owes substantial fees for the years it was dissolved) and file a new corporation using the same name of the old corporation. In most cases, these corporations continue to use the old EIN (employer identification number). If you are tempted to do this, think again. Even though the new corporation has the same name as the old corporation, it is not the same legal entity as the old corporation. (To the law, this would be like assuming a living person named Maria Smith is the same person as a deceased person named Maria Smith.) If the old corporation was recognized as tax-exempt, its exemption does not apply to the new corporation. In addition, creating a new corporation does not resolve any of the problems that may have arisen when your organization operated as an unincorporated entity.

Many organizations do not realize that the new corporation does not have tax exemption and mislead their donors and funders into believing that the corporation is tax-exempt. The IRS will have the old corporation and its EIN on its list of exempt organizations because no one has reported that the old corporation was dissolved. However, if the IRS were to audit a donor's return and learned of the dissolution, the donor's contribution to the new corporation would be disallowed. Foundations relying on the organization's tax-exempt status could also encounter problems with the IRS.

In almost all cases, the better procedure to follow if your corporation is involuntarily dissolved is to apply for reinstatement. If you have questions, you should get professional help.

Judicial Dissolution

In a variety of circumstances, the courts may act to dissolve the corporation. In cases where the Attorney General suspects fraud or other types of mismanagement, the Attorney General can apply for a judicial dissolution. In other circumstances, members, a Director, or people specified in the Articles may apply for dissolution. Creditors in some cases also have the right to apply for dissolution, as does the corporation itself. You should see an attorney if a judicial dissolution is involved.

Activities After Dissolution

A corporation that has been voluntarily or involuntarily dissolved continues its corporate existence but may not carry on any activities except those necessary to wind up its affairs and notify its claimants. There can be quite serious consequences if your corporation continues to carry on activities after dissolution other than winding up. *You carry on these activities not as a corporation but as an unincorporated association even if you are unaware that your corporation was dissolved.* If you acquire or dispose of property in the name of the corporation, the purchases or sales may not be valid. It is likely that the Board and possibly the managers will be personally liable for any debts and liabilities that your group incurs that it cannot pay. If your corporation was tax-exempt under §501(c)(3), that status does not apply to the unincorporated association. Donors who give you money believing that you are tax-exempt probably cannot take a charitable deduction. Funders who give you grants relying on your (c)(3) status may also encounter problems.

> *There can be quite serious consequences if your corporation continues to carry on activities after dissolution other than winding up. It is likely that the Board and possibly the managers will be personally liable for any debts.*

Special Note for Tax-Exempt Corporations That Are Voluntarily or Involuntarily Dissolved

If you have a §501(c) tax exemption, you must notify the IRS on your Form 990 annual information return about your dissolution, whether it was voluntary or involuntary. See the instructions for the return for more information.

Consult Appendix 1 if you would like information about source material related to this Chapter.

APPENDICES

1. Source Material

2. List of Tax and Regulatory Agencies

Appendix 1. Source Material

We have designed this Appendix primarily for attorneys, accountants and similar professionals who want to pursue the issues raised in this book in more depth. We also include some materials written for professionals within nonprofit organizations and for a wider audience. We've labelled these materials "Non-technical materials," and we list them at the beginning of each Chapter or section heading below so that they are easy for non-specialists to locate. Attorneys and accountants may also want to consult these sources. Because this Appendix is designed primarily for attorneys and accountants, we use citation shorthand familiar to them. We don't attempt to explain this to other readers because this kind of research really requires a certain kind of expertise. Please be aware that this Appendix does not attempt to provide a complete listing of legal or accounting sources pertaining to each topic. Obviously, such a project would be its own volume. We point you to a starting place and to sources that support the material in the chapters to which they refer.

General works on nonprofit organizations: Marilyn E. Phelan, Nonprofit Enterprises: Corporations, Trusts and Associations (Westlaw, updated Sept. 2011). General works on tax exempt organizations: Frances R. Hill and Douglas M. Mancino, Taxation of Exempt Organizations (2011), with Supplements.

Chapter 1

Should Your Organization Be a Nonprofit Corporation?

For a more detailed discussion of most of the legal structures discussed in this chapter, see ADVISING OREGON BUSINESSES Chapters 1-4, 7, 9 (Oregon State Bar: Rev. 2001 and 2007 Supp.). ORS Chapter 62 governs cooperatives. For unincorporated associations and trusts, see MARILYN E. PHELAN, NONPROFIT ORGANIZATIONS: LAW AND TAXATION, §1.3-1.9; Leslie v. Bendl, 92 Or App 519, 759 P2d 301 (1988), rev den 307 Or 245 (officers and directors of political committee have common law personal liability for acts that they authorize).

Chapter 2

The Structure and Types of Oregon Nonprofit Corporations

General: *Official Commentary to the Revised Oregon Nonprofit Corporation Act*, Special Issue OR L REV (1992).

Statutes: See ORS Chapter 65, especially:

65.301-.369—Board of Directors

65.371-.384—Officers

65.001(28) and (29)—Definitions of member and membership

65.131-.254—Members

65.774-.784—Inspection of records and reports to members

65.001(30), (37), and (39)—Types of nonprofit corporations.

Quasi-governmental nonprofits: Cynthia Cumfer, *Quasi-Governmental Nonprofit Organizations*, in ADVISING NONPROFIT ORGANIZATIONS, Chapter 6B (Oregon State Bar: 2002).

Public meeting and records laws. On the question of whether nonprofit corporations may be treated as public bodies for purposes of the public meeting and record laws, see ORS 192.410-.505 (public records inspection) and ORS 192.610-.710 (public meetings law). Prior to 1994, most nonprofits were guided by an Attorney General opinion that stated that "public bodies" subject to the public records and meeting laws did not include private nonprofits and cooperatives, including those set up to carry out public purposes. "Attorney General's Public Records and Meetings Manual," 44 AG 239 (September 1984). The Manual did indicate that the public meeting law applied to private groups that furnished advice to public bodies and to nonprofits that the state set up and controlled (for example, local alcoholism planning commissions). The Attorney General has since suggested that a public charter school may be subject to the public records law, depending on the scope of its contract. Opinion #8273, 49 AG 254 (September 13, 2000).

Oregon courts have established a functional equivalent analysis to determine if a nonprofit entity is subject to the rules governing public bodies. The Oregon Supreme Court characterized the Oregon State Bar, a private nonprofit corporation, as a public body subject to the public *records* law. State ex rel Frohnmayer v. Oregon State Bar, 307 Or 304, 767 P2d 893 (1989). Five years later, the court held that a private nonprofit organization that was engaged to handle a school district personnel matter did not exercise sufficient governmental functions to be classified as a public body for public records purposes. The court articulated criteria for determining when a private nonprofit became a public body. The Marks court cited with approval cases in other jurisdictions that held that, under a "functional equivalent" analysis, a charter school, an alumni federation of a state university and an incorporated county hospital were public bodies subject to public records laws. Marks v. McKenzie High School Fact-Finding Team, 319 Or 451, 878 P2d 417 (1994). A year later the Court of Appeals found that the Rockaway Beach fire department, although operating somewhat independently under its own bylaws, obtained most of its funding from the city and was subject to enough city control that it was a city agency and thus was a public body subject to the public records law. Laine v. City of Rockaway Beach, Oregon, 134 Or App 655, 896 P2d 1219 (1995).

The public *meetings* law is more complex and applies to meetings of the "governing body" of a "public body." In Independent Contractors Research Institute v. Department of Administrative Services, 207 Or App 78, 139 P3d 995 (2006), the Chief Procurement Officer of the state Department of Administrative Services (DAS) set up a volunteer advisory council to make recommendations to him about making purchases under a particular program. The court held that DAS was a public body but that the Superintendent was an individual and not a governing body. Therefore, the meetings were not public meetings. The court noted in dicta that, unlike public meetings laws, the public records laws do not refer to a governing body and so do cover situations where records are kept by individual state officers.

Chapter 3

Setting Up Your Oregon Nonprofit Corporation

General: David E. Atkin, *Setting Up a Nonprofit Organization and Getting the Tax Exemption*, in Advising Nonprofit Organizations, Chapter 1 (Oregon State Bar, 2001); Cynthia Cumfer, *Governance and Maintenance of Oregon Nonprofit Organizations*, in Advising Nonprofit Organizations, *id*, Chapter 2; Ross L. Laybourn, Jr., *The Oregon Attorney General's Role*, in Nonprofits in the Headlines, Chapter 3 (Oregon State Bar, 2004).

Name: ORS 65.094 (choosing name); ORS 65.097 (reserving name); ORS 56.023 and 705.635 (using "bank" or "trust" in name).

Corporations Sole: Rev Rul 2004-27, IRB 2004-12 (IRS warning about fraudulent use of corporations sole); US v. Gardner, 2008 WL 906696 (D Ariz 2008) (court issued permanent injunction against Bethel Am Ministries for promoting corporate sole tax scams).

Trademarks: Stuart E. Foster and Timothy L. Jackle, *Sole Proprietors*, Advising Oregon Businesses §1.25-1.31 (Oregon State Bar: Rev. 2001 and 2007 Supp.).

Articles: ORS 65.047 (provisions); ORS 65.051 (filing); ORS 65.111 (registered office and agent); ORS 65.044 (incorporators); ORS 65.301(3) (limitations of Board powers); ORS 65.241 (quorum), 65.244 (voting), 65.464 (amendments to Bylaws in membership corporations); ORS 65.307(2) (size of Board in membership corporations); ORS 65.324 (removal of Directors for cause in membership corporations); ORS 65.774(5)(b) (members' rights to records).

Bylaws: ORS 65.061.

Organizational meeting: ORS 65.057.

Department of Justice: ORS 128.650-.660; OAR 137-010-0005 through 0055 (regulation of public benefit corporations).

Doing business in another name: ORS Chapter 648.

Postal benefits: United States Postal Service Publication 417 (available on the USPS website at *www.usps.com*).

Chapter 4

Writing Bylaws

Members: ORS 65.001(28) and (29); ORS 65.131-.254.

Board of Directors: ORS 65.301-.369.

Committees: ORS 65.354.

Officers: ORS 65.371-.384.

Indemnity: ORS 65.387-.414.

Amendments to Bylaws: ORS 65.461-.467.

Email Notice: For a discussion of using electronic means for notice, see the discussion under Chapter 27 in this Appendix.

Discrimination: We are not aware of cases that consider the issue of discrimination in choosing Board members. Courts have considered the issue of discrimination in admitting members in cases brought under the public accommodations laws. Roberts v. U.S. Jaycees, 468 US 609 (1984) (Jaycees violated Minnesota's public accommodations laws by refusing to admit women); New York State Club Assn v. City of New York, 487 US 1 (1988) (club violated city's public accommodation ordinance by refusing to admit women); Boy Scouts of America v. Dale, 530 US 640 (2000) (Boy Scouts did not violate New Jersey's public accommodation law by refusing to allow gay man to be scoutmaster).

Chapter 5

Federal Tax-Exempt Status

Non-technical materials: The IRS has some materials that you may want to consult: Publication 557, *Tax Exempt Status for Your Organization*; Publication 4220, *Applying for 501(c)(3) Tax-Exempt Status*, and Publication 4221-PC, *Compliance Guide for 501(c)(3) Tax-Exempt Organizations*. All are available free on the IRS website at *www.irs.gov*. You may also want to consult the IRS article, *Life Cycle of a Public Charity*, at http://www.irs.gov/charities/charitable/article/0,,id=122670,00.html. Private foundations may want to consult IRS Publication 578, *Tax Information for Private Foundations and Foundation Managers*. After you have obtained your exemption, be sure to check out the IRS advice on staying exempt at *www.stayexempt.irs.gov/VirtualWorkshop.aspx*.

General: FRANCES R. HILL AND DOUGLAS M. MANCINO, TAXATION OF EXEMPT ORGANIZATIONS, Chapters 2, 3, 4, 7, 32.

Who Qualifies for (c)(3) Status

General: William S. Manne, *Private Inurement*, in Advising Nonprofit Organizations, Chapter 6C (Oregon State Bar, 2001).

Statutes: 26 USC §§501(c)(3); 26 USC §504 (excess lobbying by (c)(3) results in denial of (c)(4) status).

Regulations: 26 CFR §1.501(c)(3)-1; §1.504-1 and 504-2.

Cases: Church of Scientology of California v. Commissioner, 823 F2d 1310 (9th cir 1987) (private inurement to founder); United Cancer Council, Inc. v. Commissioner, 165 F3d 1173 (7th cir 1999) (professional fundraising firm was not insider to whom inurement rules apply).

Private Foundations and Public Charities

General: William S. Manne, *Private Foundations,* in Advanced Nonprofit Law: Beyond the Basics, Chapter 2 (Oregon State Bar, 2002).

Statutes: 26 USC §507 (termination of private foundation status); §508 (private foundation rules); §509 (private foundation defined); §§4940-4948 (private foundation taxes); §§4958, 4961-4963 (excess benefits taxes).

Regulations: 26 CFR §§1.507-1 through 1.507-8; §§1.508-1 through 1.508-4; §§1.509(a)-1 through 1.509(e)-1, especially §1.509(a)-3 (what this book calls PSOs and FASOs); 26 CFR §1.509(a)-4 (supporting organizations); §§53.4940-1 through 4948-1; §§53.4958-0 through 4958-8; §§53.4961-1 through 4963-1.

Procedures

General: Hill and Mancino, Taxation of Exempt Organizations, ¶32.01-32.03 (general).

Statutes: 26 USC §508 (who must file Form 1023 and presumption about private foundation status).

Regulations: 26 CFR §1.508-1 (15 month and retroactivity rules); Rev Rul 67-390, 1967-2 CB 179; Gen Couns Mem 38740 (June 3, 1981) (incorporation of (c)(3) unincorporated association creates a new entity that must file a new Form 1023 for exemption); Rev Proc 92-85, 1992-2 CB 490 (extensions of time for filing Form 1023 to 27 months), modified by Rev Proc 93-28, 1993-2 CB 344.

(c)(4) Social Welfare Organizations

General: Hill and Mancino, Taxation of Exempt Organizations, Chapter 13.

Statutes: 26 USC §501(c)(4).

Regulations: 26 CFR §1.501(c)(4)-1.

(c)(5) Labor and Agricultural Organizations

Statute: 26 USC §501(c)(5)-1.

Regulations: 26 CFR §1.501(c)(5)-1.

(c)(6) Business Leagues

General: Hill and Mancino, Taxation of Exempt Organizations, Chapter 14.

Statute: 26 USC §501(c)(6)

Regulations: 26 CFR §1.501(c)(6)-1.

Cases: Guide International Corporation v. United States, 948 F2d 360 (7th cir 1991) (line of business requirement for business leagues); Associated Master Barbers & Beauticians of America v. Commissioner, 69 TC 53 (1977) (insurance is a profit-making business that cannot be conducted as a substantial activity by (c)(6) organizations).

(c)(7), (8) and (10) Social Clubs and Fraternities

General: Hill and Mancino, Taxation of Exempt Organizations, Chapter 16.

Statutes: 26 USC §§501(c)(7), (8), and (10); 26 USC §501(i).

Regulations: 26 CFR §1.501(c)(7)-1 (social clubs); Rev Rul 69-635, 1969-2 CB 126 (members in social club must commingle); Rev Rul 74-30, 1974-1 CB 137 (members of social club must have identity of purpose); 26 CFR §1.501(c)(8)-1 and (c)(10)-1 (fraternities)

Cases: Zeta Beta Tau Fraternity, Inc. v. Commissioner, 87 TC 421 (1986) (college fraternity exempt under (c)(7) is not entitled to more favorable tax treatment granted to fraternal organizations under (c)(10)).

(c)(19) Veterans Organizations

Statutes: 26 USC §501(c)(19)

Regulations: 26 CFR §1.501(c)(19)-1.

General Information for Tax-Exempt Groups:

Group Exemption

General: Hill and Mancino, Taxation of Exempt Organizations, §32.04.

Regulations: 26 CFR §601.201(n)(8); Rev Proc 80-27, 1980-1 CB 677, modified by Rev Proc 96-40, 1996-32 IRB 8.

User Fees

General: Hill and Mancino, Taxation of Exempt Organizations, §32.07.

Regulations: Rev Proc 2011-8.

Chapter 6

Filling Out the Tax-Exempt Applications

Special Topics

Below cost rules: Rev Rul 71-529, 1071-2 CB 234 (substantially below cost); Rev Rul 72-369, 1972-2 CB 245 (donative element); *IRC 501(c)(3)-Substantially Below Cost* (IRS CPE for FY 1986); Airlie Foundation v. Internal Revenue Service, 283 F Supp2d 58 (DDC 2003) (court denied exemption to educational conference center because it operated center in commercial manner and did not provide enough services at substantially below cost).

Gaming: Hill and Mancino, Taxation of Exempt Organizations, ¶22.11[3]; OAR 137-025-0030 (Oregon nonprofit must have its tax-exempt status for at least one year to get bingo license).

Economic Development: An economic development program may be charitable under several rationales. It may lessen the burden of government. Monterey Public Parking Corp. v. US, 321 F Supp 972 (ND Cal 1970), *aff'd on other grounds*, 481 F2d 175 (9th cir 1973) (construction of public parking facility lessened burden of government); PLR 199932052 (May 14, 1999) ((c)(3) that promoted model Maglev transportation project that included the construction and operation of a parking garage lessened the burden of government). Economic development may also combat community deterioration. 26 CFR §1.501(c)(3)-1(d)(2) (combatting community deterioration is charitable); Rev Rul 74-587, 1974-2 CB 162 (organization designed to stimulate economic development in low income areas is exempt); Rev Rul 76-147, 1976-1 CB 151 (community improvement organization in high income community combats community deterioration and is exempt). The IRS will challenge economic development programs that permit inurement or improper private benefit. Rev Rul 78-86, 1978-1 CB 151 (IRS refused to follow holding of Monterey Public Parking Corp. *supra*, because of private benefit).

Development and Management of Facilities: Hill and Mancino, Taxation of Exempt Organizations, Chapter 4 (private benefit).

Joint Ventures: Hill and Mancino, Taxation of Exempt Organizations, Chapter 29.

Childcare: Hill and Mancino, Taxation of Exempt Organizations, ¶3.03[5].

Intellectual Property: Hill and Mancino, Taxation of Exempt Organizations, ¶3.04 (scientific research).

Contributions: Joseph P. Toce, Jr. et. al., Tax Economics of Charitable Giving, Chapter 25 (2003).

International Nonprofits: Frances R. Hill and Douglas M. Mancino, Taxation of Exempt Organizations, Chapters 35 and 36.

Grants and Loans to Other Organizations: Rev Rul 68-489, 1968-2 CB 210 (accountability regulations).

Linked Organizations: Hill and Mancino, Taxation of Exempt Organizations, Chapter 27.

Schedules

Schedule A (Churches): Hill and Mancino, Taxation of Exempt Organizations, ¶8.05[1].

Schedule B (Schools): Hill and Mancino, Taxation of Exempt Organizations, ¶8.05[2].

Schedule C (Hospitals): Hill and Mancino, Taxation of Exempt Organizations, ¶8.05[3] and [4].

Schedule D (Supporting Organizations): Hill and Mancino, Taxation of Exempt Organizations, ¶8.07.

Schedule E (Retroactivity): Hill and Mancino, Taxation of Exempt Organizations, ¶32.02[1][b]-[d].

Schedule F (Homes for Elderly and Low Income): Rev Rul 72-124, 1972-1 CB 145 (elderly); PLR 9438039 (June 29, 1994) (elderly); Elizabeth C. Kastenberg and Joseph Chasin, *Elderly Housing* (IRS CPE for FY 2004); Rev Proc 96-32, 1996-20 IRB 14 (safe harbor guidelines for low income housing).

Schedule G (Successors): Rev Rul 67-390, 1967-2 CB 179.

Schedule H (Scholarships): Hill and Mancino, Taxation of Exempt Organizations, ¶¶7.04[5], 9.02[2][a], 10.09[3][b], 11.03[4].

Chapter 7

Publicly Supported Organizations and Fee/Activity Supported Organizations

General: David Ross Gray, Nonprofit Foundations: A Tax Guide for Charitable Organizations (1978) and Supplements; Frances R. Hill and and Douglas M. Mancino, Taxation of Exempt Organizations, Chapter 8.

Statutes: 26 USC §509(a) (listing (c)(3)s that are not private foundations); 26 USC §170(b) (referred to in §509(a)).

Regulations: 26 CFR §1.509(a)-2 (general); 26 CFR §1.170A-9 (on publicly-supported organizations); 26 CFR §1.509(a)-3 (on what this book calls fee-activity supported organizations); 26 CFR §1.509(a)-6 (status assigned to organizations that are both PSO and FASO); 26 CFR §1.509(d) (definition of support); 26 CFR §1.509(e) (definition of gross investment income); 26 CFR §1.507-6 (substantial contributors); 26 USC §507(d)(2)(C) (substantial contributor 10 year exceptions); 26 CFR §53.4946-1(f) (foundation managers); (26 CFR §1.509(a)-7 (reliance by contributors on definitive rulings on public charity status).

Chapter 8

Political Activity and Lobbying by Tax-Exempt Organization

Non-technical materials: The Alliance for Justice has some excellent materials available at a very low cost on political activities and lobbying. Their easy-to-read publications cover the IRS lobbying rules, federal tax and election laws, ballot measures, linked organizations, use of the Internet for lobbying and political activities and foundations that want to support advocacy. Some of the publications are older, so be sure that you update any information you rely on. You can reach them at Alliance for Justice, 11 Dupont Circle, NW, 2d floor, Washington, D.C. 20036; telephone 202.822.6070, or go to their website at *www.allianceforjustice.org* and follow the link to Publications.

General: FRANCES R. HILL AND DOUGLAS M. MANCINO, TAXATION OF EXEMPT ORGANIZATIONS, Chapters 5, 6; David E. Atkin, *State and Federal Law*, in NONPROFITS IN THE HEADLINES, Chapter 4 (Oregon State Bar, 2004).

Political Activity

General: HILL AND MANCINO, TAXATION OF EXEMPT ORGANIZATIONS, Chapter 6.

Statutes: 26 USC §501(c)(3); §4955 (political expenditures tax).

(c)(3) Regulations: 26 CFR §1.501(c)(3)-1(c)(3) (on political activity); 26 CFR §53.4955-1 (tax penalties); Rev Rul 78-248, 1978-1 CB 154 (candidate questionnaires, voting records and scorecards), *amplified by* Rev Rul 80-282, 1980-2 CB 178 (voting records and scorecards); Rev Rul 86-95, 1986-2 CB 73 (candidate forums and debates); Rev Rul 2007-41, 2007-25 IRB 1421 (political campaigns including website issues); TAM 91-17-001 (Sept. 5, 1990) (issue advocacy); TAM 1999-07-021 (May 20, 1998) (issue advocacy).

Cases: Branch Ministries, Inc. v. Rossotti, 40 F Supp2d 15 (DDC 1999) (IRS revoked exemption of church that opposed candidacy of Bill Clinton in 1992).

(c)(4), (5) and (6) Regulations: HILL AND MANCINO, TAXATION OF EXEMPT ORGANIZATIONS, ¶¶13.04, 14.04[2], 15.04, 16.02[7], 16.03[6]; 26 CFR §1.501(c)(4)-1(a)(2)(ii); Rev Rul 81-95, 1981-1 CB 332 ((c)(4)'s primary activities promote social welfare and its less than primary participation in political campaigns does not make it non-exempt); GCM 34233 (Dec. 30, 1969) (involvement in political campaigns is not an exempt purpose of (c)(5) and (6) groups).

Internet

Rev Rul 2007-41, 2007-25 IRB 1421, Situations 18-21.

Lobbying

General: HILL AND MANCINO, TAXATION OF EXEMPT ORGANIZATIONS, Chapter 5.

Statute: 26 USC §501(c)(3); §4911 and 4912 (lobbying taxes).

Substantial Parts Test

Statutes: 26 USC §501(c)(3); 26 USC §504; 26 USC §4912.

Regulations: 26 CFR §1.501(c)(3)-1(b)(3)(i) (insubstantial parts test); 26 CFR 1.501(c)(3)-1(c)(3)(ii); Rev Rul 70-449, 1970-2 CB 111 (testimony before Congressional committee at committee's request is not lobbying).

Cases: Seasongood v. Commissioner, 227 F 2d 907 (6th cir 1955) (less than 5% of time and efforts is insubstantial); Haswell v. United States, 500 F 2d 1133 (Ct.Cl. 1974), cert den. 419 US 1107, 95 SCt 779 (1975) (subjective balancing test of all facts and circumstances); Christian Echoes National Ministry, Inc. v. United States, 470 F2d 849 (10th cir 1972) (upheld IRS revocation of exemption of religious organization that engaged in substantial lobbying and intervened in political campaigns).

Lobbying Election

Statutes: 26 USC §501(h) (subsection h election).

(c)(3) Regulations: 26 CFR §1.501(c)(3)-1(c)(3)(ii); 26 CFR §1.501(h)-1 to 3; 26 CFR §56.4911-0 through 10 (lobbying election and computation rules).

(c)(4) and Affiliated Groups

General: HILL AND MANCINO, TAXATION OF EXEMPT ORGANIZATIONS, ¶¶13.03, 14.04[1], 15.04, 16.03[6].

Cases: Federal Election Commission v. Massachusetts Citizens for Life, 479 US 238 (1986) (unconstitutional to restrict electioneering activities of (c)(4) advocacy group).

Statutes: 2 USC §1611 (Lobbying Disclosure Act provision that (c)(4)s that lobby cannot get federal grants or loans); 31 USC §1352 (prohibits all recipients of federal grants, loans and contracts from using those funds to lobbying federal legislative and executive officials).

(c)(4), (5) and (6) Regulations: TAM 200908050, 2009 WL 421204 (February 20, 2009) (website rules for linked organizations); Rev Rul 61-177, 1961-2 CB 117 ((c)(6) (business league can have lobbying as sole activity); Rev Rul 71-530, 1971-2 CB 237 (organization whose only activity is lobbying can qualify as exempt under (c)(4)).

Deductibility of Dues/Lobbying Tax

General: Hill and Mancino, Taxation of Exempt Organizations, ¶14.05.

Statutes: 26 USC §6033(e).

Regulations: 26 CFR §1.162-20; Rev Proc 98-19, 1998-1 CB 547 (deductibility rules).

Chapter 9

Business Activities by Tax-Exempt Organizations

General: Frances R. Hill and Douglas M. Mancino, Taxation of Exempt Organizations, Chapters 21-22; Sean Barnett.

Statutes: 26 USC §§511 (unrelated business income tax), 512 (unrelated business income and exceptions), 513 (unrelated trade or business) and 514 (debt-financed property).

Regulations: 26 CFR §1.511-1 to 1.514(g), especially §1.513-1 (definition of UBI). On web links and other UBI issues: PLR 200303062 (October 2, 2002). When an exempt organization carries on a business, this activity can implicate IRS positions on commerciality and partnerships with business: Rul 67-4, 1967-1 CB 121 (commerciality doctrine); Rev Rul 98-15, 1998-12 IRB 6 ((c)(3) hospital can form LLC with for-profit hospital management company); Rev Rul 2004-51, 2004-22 IRB 974 (joint ventures).

Cases: Goldsboro Art League v. Commissioner, 75 TC 337 (1980) (commerciality doctrine); Presbyterian and Reformed Publishing Co. v. Commissioner, 743 F2d 148 (3rd cir 1984) (commerciality doctrine); Plumstead Theatre Society, Inc. v. Commissioner, 74 TC 1324 (1980) (joint venture with business); St. David's Health Care System v. U.S., 349 F3d 232 (5th cir 2003).

Trade or Business

Regulations: 26 CFR §1.513-1(b)

Regularly Carried On

Regulations: 26 CFR §1.513-1(c)

Cases: National Collegiate Athletic Ass'n v. Commissioner, 914 F2d 1417 (10th cir 1990) (revenue received by NCAA, an exempt organization, from program advertising in men's championship tournament is not revenue from an activity that is regularly carried on and is therefore not taxable).

Substantially Related To

Regulations: 26 CFR §1.513-1(d)(4)(iv) (when ads are unrelated business income); 26 CFR §1.512(a)-1(f)(2) (computation of advertising income); 26 CFR §1.513-1(d) (substantially related); 26 CFR §1.513-3 (conventions and trade shows); 26 CFR §1.513-4 (corporate sponsorship); 26 CFR §1.513-4(f), Examples 11 and 12 (corporate sponsorship and websites); 26 CFR §1.513-7 (travel and tours); Rev Rul 73-105, 1973-1 CB 264 (sales of merchandise in folk art museum related to its exempt purpose are not taxable but sales from scientific books and souvenir items unrelated to its exempt purpose are taxable); Rev Rul 80-296, 1980-2 CB 195 (sale of broadcast rights to college game is related to educational purpose of college and does not produce taxable income).

Cases: United States v. American College of Physicians, 475 US 834 (1986) (ads in AMA Journal are not substantially related to AMA's exempt purpose and are taxable).

Calculations

General: HILL AND MANCINO, TAXATION OF EXEMPT ORGANIZATIONS, Chapter 25.

Regulations: 26 CFR §1.513-1(d)(4)(iii) (dual use of facilities or personnel); 26 CFR §1.513-1(d)(4)(iv) (allocation rules for UBI activity that "exploits" exempt activity.

Exceptions

General: HILL AND MANCINO, TAXATION OF EXEMPT ORGANIZATIONS, Chapters 23, 24 and 26.

Statutes: 26 USC §§512, 513, 514.

Regulations: 26 CFR §1.512(b)-1 (special rules and exclusions); 26 CFR §1.514(a)-(1) (unrelated debt-financed income); §1.513-5 (bingo); 26 CFR §1.514(a)-(g) (exclusions from unrelated business income). The adjustments for inflation for low cost items are provided each year by the Treasury Department in Revenue Procedures.

Royalty Cases: Sierra Club, Inc. v. Commissioner, 86 F3d 1526 (9th cir 1996) (sale of mailing list yields passive royalty income that is not taxable); Oregon State University Alumni Ass'n v. Commissioner, 193 F3d 1098 (9th cir 1999) (affinity card income is royalty income); Arkansas State Police Assn v. Commissioner, 282 F3d 556 (8th cir 2002) (money paid by publisher to (c)(5) labor union to publish union's official publication is not royalty because union maintained control over publication).

Protecting Your Exempt Status

General: BRUCE HOPKINS, THE LAW OF TAX-EXEMPT ORGANIZATIONS, Chapters 28 and 31 and Supplement (8th ed., 2003) (on structures to avoid loss of exemption for excess unrelated business income).

Chapter 10

Fiscal Sponsorship

Non-technical materials: *Fiscal Sponsorship: 6 Ways to Do It Right* (Study Center Press: 2005), by Gregory L. Colvin. This book can be obtained from Study Center Press, 1095 Market St., Suite 602, San Francisco, CA 94103, 1.888.281.3757, www.info@studycenter.org.

Regulations: Rev-Rul 67-149, 1967-1 CB 133 ((c)(3) providing financial assistance to other (c)(3)s is exempt); Rev Rul 68-489, 1968-2 CB 210 (accountability requirements for grants made by (c)(3)s to non-(c)(3) groups).

Chapter 11

State and Local Tax Exemptions

State and District

State Income Tax: ORS 317.080(1) (§501(c) and (d) organizations are exempt); ORS 317.080(9) (certain old age homes are exempt); ORS 748.414 (fraternal benefit societies are exempt); ORS 748.414 (fraternal benefit societes).

Tri-Met and Lane Transit: ORS 267.380(2)(b) ((c)(3)s except hospitals excluded from Mass Transit District taxation).

County Property Tax:

Statutes: General charitable exemptions are found at ORS 307.130-.150.

Other nonprofit exemptions:

> ORS 307.166–leasing by one exempt organization to another.
>> ORS 307.115–nonprofit holding property for park or public recreation.
>> ORS 307.157–nonprofit cemeteries.
>> ORS 307.160–public libraries.
>> ORS 307.195–nonprofit student housing.

ORS 307.210–nonprofit water associations.

ORS 307.220–nonprofit telephone associations.

ORS 307.241-.245, .370-.385–nonprofit housing for elderly.

ORS 307.471–school-rented student housing.

ORS 307.515-.548–low income housing.

ORS 748.414–fraternal benefit societies, except for real estate and office equipment.

Procedures for Most Nonprofits: ORS 307.162.

Leased Property by Exempt Organizations: ORS 307.112.

Regulations: OAR 150-307, especially 150-307.130 and 150-307.162.

Cases: Cascade Raptor Center v. Lane County Assessor, 2011 WL 4021408 (September 12, 2011) (nature education and wildlife center was exempt under Southwest Oregon Public Defender criteria in part because it could show an element of gift-giving in that its volunteers and contributions reduced the cost of its services for which it charged); Theatre West of Lincoln City v. Dept. of Revenue, 319 Or 114, 873 P2d 1083 (1994) ("literary" includes theatres); YMCA v. Dept. of Revenue, 308 Or 644, 784 P2d 1086 (1989) (YWCA's gym is not used exclusively for charity since charity requires an element of giving); Southwest Oregon Public Defender Services, Inc. v. Dept. of Revenue, 312 Or 82, 817 P2d 1292 (1991) (public defender services funded by the state are charitable, since the organization has charity as its primary object; its services further its charitable object; and the performance of its service includes an element of giving when evaluated from perspective of recipient).

Chapter 12

Tax Returns for Tax-Exempt Organizations

Federal

General: Frances R. Hill and Douglas M. Mancino, Taxation of Exempt Organizations, ¶33.03.

State

Regulations: OAR 137-010-0015 and 10-0020 (form and contents of this annual report); OAR 137-010-0030 (payment of the required filing fees).

Chapters 13-17

Successful Functioning: Board of Directors

Non-technical materials: Oregon Department of Justice, Guide to Non-Profit Board Service (available at *http://www.doj.state.or.us/charigroup/pdf/nonprofit.pdf* or by telephone listed in Appendix 2); Financial Stewardship Resources, Important Documents: A Directors and Officers Workbook (available at *http://financialsteward.org*).

Duties and Responsibilities of Board

General: Marilyn E. Phelan, Nonprofit Enterprises: Corporations, Trusts and Associations, Chapter 4.

Statutes: ORS 65.301 and 65.357 (duties and standards)

Cases: Stern v. Lucy Webb Hayes National Training School for Deaconesses, 381 F Supp 1003 (DDC 1974) (rejects older standard that directors act as trustees and establishes a corporate standard); American Baptist Churches of Metropolitan New York v. Galloway, 710 NYS 2d 12 (2000) (employee and consultant of Baptist Church who set up "rival" nonprofit and used connections made while employed by Baptist Church to secure funding breached their duty of loyalty to Baptist Church); Northeast Harbor Golf Club v. Harris, 725 A 2d 1018 (Me 1999) (director of golf club usurped corporate opportunity when she used information acquired as director to engage in private speculative opportunities rather than promote those opportunities on behalf of the golf club).

Board Committees

Statute: ORS 65.354.

Officers

Statute: ORS 65.371-.384.

Replacing Directors and Officers

Statute: ORS 65.321 (resignation), .324-.331 (removal of directors), .334 (vacancies on board), .381 (resignation and removal of officers).

Personal Liability of Directors and Officers

General: Debra Kawecki and Leonard Henzke, *Employment Tax Update--Review of Current Litigation*, D-26 (IRS CPE for FY 2003) (IRS authors reminded exempt organizations examiners that they should assess §6672 penalties against the responsible parties in an exempt organization that wilfully fail to collect and pay employee withholding taxes).

Statute: 26 USC §6672 (liability for failure to withhold federal taxes).

Cases: Hirsovescu v. Shangri-La Corp., 113 Or App 145, 831 P2d 73 (1992) (nonprofit directors were not shielded from personal liability under ORS 65.369(1) for wrongful discharge, since it is an intentional tort).

Protection of Board and Officers

Statutes: ORS 65.369 (limited liability); ORS 65.407 (indemnification).

Chapter 18

Members and Membership Corporations

Statutes: ORS 65.131-.134 (admission of members); ORS 65.144 and ORS 65.151-.154 (rights and obligations); ORS 65.177 (delegates); ORS 65.214-.221 (notice of meetings); ORS 65.201-.204 (meetings); ORS 65.211 (action without meeting); ORS 65.222 (ballots); ORS 65.227-.254 (voting); ORS 65.437 and .464 (amendments of Articles and Bylaws); ORS 65.224 (members list and inspection by members); ORS 65.771-.782 (records and inspection by members); ORS 65.164-.167 (resignation and termination).

Cases: The rights of members and of membership corporations are a fairly fertile ground of litigation although Oregon appellate courts have not addressed these issues under the current statutes. Courts give considerable deference to the right of private associations to handle membership matters. Even so, holdings on when a nonprofit can expel its members vary depending on the property interest implicated in the membership and the type of nonprofit: Bernstein v. Alameda-Costra Medical Assn, 139 Cal App 2d 241, 293 P2d 862 (1956) (standard is whether medical association acts in good faith in expelling member); Bernstein v. The Players, 120 Misc 2d 998, 466 NYS 2d 897 (1983) (court upheld expulsion of member of social club who questioned financial transactions of the club); Guinn v. Church of Christ of Collinsville, 775 P2d 766 (Okla 1989) (court limits church's ability to discipline member after member left). Courts have considered whether the admission of members to nonprofit organizations falls under the public accommodations laws with uneven results: Roberts v. U.S. Jaycees, 468 US 609 (1984) (Jaycees violated Minnesota's public accommodations laws by refusing to admit women); New York State Club Assn v. City of New York, 487 US 1 (1988) (club violated city's public accommodation ordinance by refusing to admit women); Boy Scouts of America v. Dale, 530 US 640 (2000) (Boy Scouts had constitutionally protected freedom of association that permitted them to discriminate based on sexual orientation in spite of New Jersey public accommodation statute that forbade it).

Chapter 19

Employees

Wage and Hour Laws

General: Lainie Dillon Decker, Christine Hammond, and Edward J. Reeves, *Wages and Hours: Fundamentals,* and Carol J. Bernick and Christine S. Totten, *Enforcement of Wage Statutes*, in Labor and Employment Law: Private Sector, Chapters 3 and 4 (Oregon State Bar: 2012)

Statutes: 29 USC §201, *et. seq.*; ORS Chapters 652 and 653.

Regulations: 29 CFR §778 (overtime); 29 CFR §785 (hours worked); OAR 839-020-0030 to 0051 (wage and hour).

Discrimination Issues

Statute: ORS 659A.309 (illegal to refuse to hire family members in some circumstances)

Personnel Policies

General: J. Michael Porter and Donald B. Potter, *Employment Actions in Contract*, Labor and Employment Law: Private Sector, Chapter 2 (Oregon State Bar: 2011).

Statutes: ORS 652.750 (employee has right to inspect and obtain copy of personnel records); ORS 659A.315 (restrictions on employer's right to restrict off-duty use of tobacco).

Family Leave

General: Eve L. Logsdon and Karen L. O'Connor, *Family Leave Laws*, Labor and Employment Law: Private Sector Chapter 21 (Oregon State Bar: 2011).

Statutes: 29 USC §2601, *et. seq.*; ORS 659A.150-.186.

Regulations: 29 CFR §825.100-.800; OAR 839-009-0200 *et. seq.*

Chapter 20

Independent Contractors

Federal Income Tax Withholding

General: Clay D. Creps and Krista N. Hardwick, *Independent Contractors*, in Labor and Employment Law: Private Sector §16.2(c)(1) (Oregon State Bar: Rev. 2011) and cases cited therein; IRS Publication 1779, *Independent Contractor or Employee* (2011). The IRS material is available on the IRS website at *www.irs.gov*.

Regulations: Rev Rul 87-41, 1987-1 CB 296 (20 factor test).

Oregon Income Tax Withholding

General: Creps, *Independent Contractors*, in Labor and Employment Law: Private Sector, §16.2-2(a)(2) and (2)(d).

Statutes: ORS 316.162(2)(j) (withholding for independent contractors as defined in ORS 670.600); ORS 670.600 (definition of independent contractor).

State Unemployment

General: Creps, *Independent Contractors*, in Labor and Employment Law: Private Sector, §16.2–2(i).

Statutes: ORS 657.015 (definition of employee); ORS 657.025 (definition of employer); ORS 657.030 (exclusions from coverage); ORS 657.040(1) (independent contractor exceptions); ORS 657.072 (exclusions for certain religious organizations); ORS 657.092 (exclusions for events with gratuities, prizes, scholarships, or reimbursement of expenses).

Regulations: OAR 471-031-0005 *et. seq.*

Cases: Petersen v. Employment Division, 135 Or App 344, 898 P2d 210 (1995) (interprets independent contractor and independently established business tests of ORS 657.040(1)); Employment Division v. Surata Soy Foods, Inc., 63 Or App 221, 662 P2d 810 (1983) (cooperative members who receive patronage dividends for their work are employees subject to unemployment tax withholding).

On churches: ORS 657.072(1) purports to distinguish between churches and other religious organizations for purposes of unemployment taxation. The statute exempts ministers of churches from unemployment coverage. Oregon cases have held that both ORS 657.072(1)(a) and (1)(b) unconstitutionally favor churches over other religious organizations. In both situations, Oregon courts have required unemployment coverage by all religious organizations, including churches, in order to comply with the federal unemployment insurance law so that Oregon can retain federal dollars. Salem College and Academy v. Employment Division, 298 Or 471, 695 P2d 25 (1985) (ORS 657.072(1)(a) is unconstitutional); Employment Division v. Rogue Valley Youth for Christ, 307 Or 490, 770 P2d 588 (1989) (same); Newport Church of Nazarene v. Hensley, 335 Or 1, 56 P2d 386 (2002) (ORS 657.072(1)(b) is unconstitutional). The Court of Appeals has rejected a Free Exercise challenge to the unemployment tax statute. Church at 295 S. 18th St., St. Helens v. Employment Division, 175 Or App 114, 28 P3d 1185 (2001), rev den 333 Or 73, 36 P3d 974 (requiring church to acknowledge that it, not God, was evangelist's employer did not violate church's free exercise rights and evangelist was subject to tax, even though he was paid by tithe, not wage or salary).

Worker Compensation

General: Creps, *Independent Contractors*, in Labor and Employment Law: Private Sector, §16.2-2(j).

Statutes: ORS 656.005(13) defines employer and 656.005(30) defines worker. ORS 656.027 provides that all workers are exempt with exceptions.

Cases: S.W. Floor Cover Shop v. National Council on Comp. Ins., 318 Or 614, 872 P2d 1 (1994) (reconciled statutory definition of worker with statutory definition of independent contractor in work compensation cases); Rubalcaba v. Nagaki Farms, Inc., 333 Or 614, 43 P2d 1106 (2002) (clarified S.W. Floor Cover Shop's holding).

Four factor right to control test: Woody v. Waibel, 276 Or 189, 554 P2d 492 (1976) (recognizes importance of control test); Castle Home, Inc. v. Whaite, 95 Or App 269, 769 P2d 215 (1989) (states four factors); Cy Investment, Inc. v. National Council on Comp. Ins., 128 Or App 579, 876 P2d 805 (1994); Trabosh v. Washington Co., 140 Or App 159, 915 P2d 1011 (1996); Stamp v. DCBS, 169 Or App 354, 9 P3d 729 (2000).

Two elements of relative nature of work test: Woody v. Waibel, *supra* (defines test); Cy Investment, Inc. v. National Council on Comp. Ins., *supra*; Trabosh v. Washington Co., *supra*; Stamp v. DCBS, *supra*.

Federal Wage and Hour

General: Creps, *Independent Contractors*, in Labor and Employment Law: Private Sector, §§16.2-2(k)(1).

Cases: Brock v. Superior Care, Inc., 840 F2d 1054 (2d cir 1988) (five factors of independent contractor economic realities test under Fair Labor Standards Act); Martin v. Selker Bros., Inc., 949 F2d 1286 (3rd cir 1991) (six factor economic realities test); Mathis v. Housing Authority of Umatilla County, 242 F Supp2d 777 (D Or 2002) (court uses Martin's six factor economic realities test to determine that Section 8 Coordinator of nonprofit organization was not independent contractor in overtime wage case); Crossley v. Elliott, 2011 WL 1107868 (D.C. Virgin Islands, 2011) (court uses general factors pointing to economic reality).

State Wage and Hour

General: Creps, *Independent Contractors*, in LABOR AND EMPLOYMENT LAW: PRIVATE SECTOR, §16.2-2(k)(2).

Wage and hour statutes: ORS 653.010(2) (defines employee but excludes certain services performed for nonprofits); ORS 653.010(3) (defines employer).

Other types of wage claims: ORS 652.310(1) (defines employer); ORS 652.310(2) (defines employee).

Cases: State ex rel Roberts v. Bomareto Ent., 153 Or App 183, 956 P2d 254 (1998) (definition of employee in ORS 652.310 does not apply to ORS 653.010 which has a very expansive definition of employee); Northwest Advancement v. BOL, 96 Or App 133, 772 P2d 943 (1989), rev den 308 Or 315, U.S. cert den 495 US 932 (1990) (court used federal law and common law control test to find that door-to-door sales people were employees).

Chapter 21

Volunteers

Volunteers as Employees

Non-technical materials: Check the websites for SOLV (*www.solv.org*), Hands on Portland (*www.handsonportland.org*), and Community Nonprofit Resource Group (*www.cnrg.org*).

Federal Wage and Hour Law

Statutes: 29 USC §201 *et. seq.* (Federal Labor Standards Act). 29 USC §203(s)(1)(A)(ii) establishes that FLSA applies to employers that gross at least $500,000 annually and (B) describes organizations subject to coverage although they gross less than $500,000.

Regulations: 29 CFR §778.316 (parties cannot agree not to pay for overtime).

Cases: The cases considering when volunteers become employees are not entirely reconcilable. Some courts look at the economic realities and classify volunteers as workers if the nonprofit receives commercial benefits from their services. Tony and Susan Alamo Foundation v. Secretary of Labor, 471 US 290 (1985) (court used economic realities test to hold that former drug addicts, derelicts and criminals who staffed commercial operations for long periods and expected in-kind benefits were workers for purposes of FLSA because they were not working solely for personal purposes); Archie v. Grand Central Partnership, 997 F Supp 504 (SDNY 1998) (former homeless and jobless who worked at various jobs in clerical, food-service and similar positions were workers since the nonprofit received direct economic benefit from their services). New DOL rules have mitigated the Alamo holding in some situations. Purdham v. Fairfax County School Board, 637 F3d 421 (4th cir 2010) (school board assistant was a volunteer golf coach under a DOL guidance letter issued after the *Alamo* case that allowed employees to serve as volunteers if the volunteer work was different in kind from the work for which the employee was paid).

Other cases take the position that the volunteers are not workers if the volunteer is the main beneficiary of a job program, even if the nonprofit also benefits. Isaacson v. Penn Community Services, 450 F2d 1306 (4th cir 1971) (volunteers for nonprofit that developed positions to help conscientious objectors satisfy the national service requirement were not workers); Williams v. Strickland, 87 F3d 1064 (9th cir 1996) (participants in Salvation Army's work therapy programs served their own interests and were not employees where the rehabilitation program included counseling, church services and work therapy on a fulltime basis, including refinishing furniture and sorting donations for the thrift shop); Solis v. Laurelbrook Sanitarium and School, 642 F3d 518 (6th cir. 2011) (board school students who worked as part of vocational training and in accordance with religious school's beliefs about morality were not employees, since the students and not the school were the primary beneficiaries of the relationship).

State Wage and Hour Law

Statutes: ORS Chapters 652 and 653 (wage and hours laws).

Regulations: OAR 839-020-0030(2)(a) (each work week stands alone for purposes of overtime); OAR 839-020-0046(3) (time spent in work for charitable purposes at employer's request or under its direction or control is work time but time spent voluntarily outside of normal work hours is not work time); OAR 839-020-0115(3) (if FLSA and state standards are different, employers must comply with those most favorable to worker). Oregon has special wage and hour regulations for certain types of nonprofits. OAR 839-020-0125(2)(e) (hospitals and institutions for care of aged, sick or mentally ill) and (2)(f) (nonprofit amusement or recreational establishments); OAR 839-020-0150(1) (adult foster care) and (3) (soccer referees).

State Unemployment

Cases: Oregon Festival of American Music v. Employment Department, 204 Or App 479, 130 P3d 795 (2006) (nonprofit music festival was employer and contracting musicians were employees under the unemployment statutes).

Worker Compensation

Statutes: ORS 656.018(1)(a) (liability of employer for worker comp benefits is exclusive remedy for all injuries by subject workers); ORS 656.027 (subject workers and exceptions). ORS 656.039(1) allows employers to elect to cover nonsubject workers and make them subject workers. Various subsections of ORS 656.027 describe many nonprofit volunteers as nonsubject workers. See ORS 656.027(11), (14), (17) and (20). Read together, ORS 656.018, 656.027 and 656.039 seem to provide that volunteers listed in ORS 656.027 that become covered workers must use worker compensation as their exclusive remedy. However, ORS 656.005(30) defines "worker" as a person who engages to furnish services for remuneration. It is difficult to reconcile this definition with volunteers who receive nothing for their services.

Cases: Smith v. State Accident Industrial Commission, 144 Or 480, 23 P2d 904, 25 P2d 1119 (1933) (Grange member who donated labor was not a worker); Oregon Country Fair v. National Council on Compensation Insurance, 129 Or App 73, 877 P2d 1207 (1989) (Fair had to provide worker compensation coverage to individuals who were paid per diem for one month to prepare fair site because they were workers but volunteers at fair who worked 3 days for vouchers were not workers under ORS 656.027(10) exemption for those who provided services for room and board); Hopkins v. Kobos Co., 186 Or App 273, 62 P3d 870 (2003) (resident of religious recovery home donated his labor to a private business that made a donation to the charity and was not a worker entitled to worker compensation coverage from the business because the resident did not expect to be paid).

Volunteer Liability

Cases: Dunn v. Garcia, 95 Or App 150, 768 P2d 419 (1989), rev den 307 Or 719 (abused boy scout did not have cause of action under *respondeat superior* against scoutmaster whose wife abused him for failure to counsel him, since scoutmaster's acts toward him were not motivated, even in part, by a purpose to serve the Scouts); Erickson v. Christenson, 99 Or App 104, 781 P2d 383 (1989), *appeal dism'd*, 311 Or 266, 817 P2d 758 (1991) (court reversed the trial court that dismissed *respondeat superior* claim by women who sued pastor and church for pastor's sexual relationship with her, since pastor established a confidential relationship with her that was within the scope of the pastor's employment); Lourim v. Swenson, 328 Or 380, 997 P2d 1157 (1999) (Boy Scouts may be liable under *respondeat superior* for sexual abuse by volunteer scout leader if part of leader's job was to gain trust of boys).

Protection for Volunteers

Statutes: 42 USC §14,501 *et. seq.* (Volunteer Protection Act); ORS 30.475-.492 (protection from liability for volunteers who transport elderly/people with disabilities and who clean-up hazardous waste).

Cases: Armendarez v. Glendate Youth Center, 265 F Supp 2d 1136 (D Ariz 2003) (volunteer director of nonprofit could not be personally sued under FLSA for unpaid wages because Volunteer Protection Act applied against any claims for harm).

Chapter 22

Funding: Obtaining Resources for Your Organization

Non-technical materials: CRAIG MCPHERSON, OREGON FOUNDATION DATABOOK, $100, available from C&D Publishing at *www.foundationdatabook.com/ororder. html*; REBECCA PEATOW, ED., GUIDE TO OREGON FOUNDATIONS, 12th edition. $46, available from 211 info, 621 SW Alder, #810, Portland, OR 97205, 503.226.3099. The IRS explanation of its rules about acknowledging donations can be found at *http://www.irs.gov/charities/article/0,,id=96102,00.html*. For information on social enterprise, go to *http://www.redf.org/publications-intro.htm*. The address for the Oregon Community Foundation for management of endowment funds is 1221 SW Yamhill, #100, Portland, OR 97205, 503.227.6846. Contact information for organizations of fundraising professionals:

> Association of Fund Raising Professionals of Oregon
>
> P.O. Box 55512
>
> Portland, OR 97238
>
> 503.715.3100
>
> *http://www.afporegon.org/contact.aspx*
>
> email: *afp-oregon@comcast.net*
>
> Emerald Valley Development Officers
>
> 2852 Willamette Street
>
> PMB OR #157
>
> Eugene, OR 97405-8200
>
> 541.607.4062 (voicemail)
>
> email: Laura Purkey at *lpurkey@comcast.net*

Solicitations

General: Cheryl Chasin, Susan Ruth and Robert Harper, *Tax Exempt Organizations and World Wide Web Fundraising and Advertising on the Internet* (IRS CPE for FY 2000) (available at IRS website at *www.irs.gov)*; Ross Laybourn, Jr. *The Attorney General's Office: Internet Solicitation, Gaming, and Fundraising Issues*, in ADVISING NONPROFIT ORGANIZATIONS, Chapter 3 (Oregon State Bar, 2001).

Statutes: 18 USC §1037 (CAN-SPAM Act of 2003); 26 USC §6113 (solicitation disclosures by non (c)(3) organizations); ORS 128.801-.995 (Charitable Solicitation Act, including professional and commercial fundraisers).

Regulations: Notice 88-120, 1988-2 CB 454 (safe harbors for non-(c)(3) solicitations); OAR 137-010-0045 through 0055 (charitable solicitations act, including professional and commercial fundraisers, and charitable trust act).

Cases: For some important cases on the First Amendment restrictions on governmental regulation of charitable solicitations, see Riley v. National Federation of the Blind of North Carolina, Inc., 487 US 781 (1988); American Charities v. Pinellas County, 189 F Supp 2d 1319 (MD Fla 2001); Public Citizens, Inc. v. Pinellas County, 321 F Supp 2d 1275 (MD Fla 2004).

Bingo and Gambling

Statutes: ORS 167.108-.166 (criminal gambling offenses); ORS Chapter 464 (state administrative regulation of legalized gambling).

Regulations: OAR 137-025-0020 through 137-025-0530.

Cases: Evans v. Attorney General, 148 Or App 133, 939 P2d 111 (1997) (state fined independent contractor who managed bingo for nonprofits and who was paid in excess of state administrative rules).

Chapter 24

Making a Budget

Regulations: OMB Circulars A-110, A-122 and A-133, available from *www.whitehouse.gov/omb/circulars*.

Chapter 26

Keeping Books and Preparing Financial Reports

Non-technical material: CHRISTINE MANOR, QUICKBOOKS FOR NOT-FOR-PROFITS (look for the latest version published by Sleeter Store and available at *http://sleeter.store.yahoo.com* by following the links for "Not-for-Profit"). For assistance in choosing accounting software, go to *http://www.aicpa.org/pubs/jofa/sep2003/johnston.htm*.

Accessing the Accounting Standards Codification:

Authoritative guidance on GAAP (Generally Accepted Accounting Principles) for nonprofits is found in the Accounting Standards Codification (ASC) published online by the Financial Standards Accounting Board. Access to ASC is free online. Go to https://asc.fasb.org/ and follow the steps to log in to the free Basic View. You may also want to consider purchasing the AICPA accounting guide for Not-for-Profit Entities available at http://www.cpa2biz.com. Sources are identified here by ASC section and subsection number.

- Should You Use the Cash or Accrual Accounting Method -235-10-50-1
- Classification of Contributions 958-605-45, 958-605-30-4,
- Distinguishing Contributions from Purchases of Services or Goods ASC Glossary "exchange transactions", 958-605-55-8,
- Unrestricted Expenses 958-225-45-7
- Three Classes of Net Assets-958-205-50-1B
- Recording Promises to Give 958-605-45-5, 958-605-30-4, 958-605-25
- Cost Allocation 958-720-45
- Accounting for Fundraising Costs 958-720-50, 985-720-45-29, Allocation of Joint Costs of Fundraising 958-720-50-2

- Accounting for In-Kind Contributions – Property and Equipment 958-605-25-2, 958-605-30-2, Services 958-605-50-1, Materials and Facilities 958-605-25
- Gains and Losses on Investments 958-320-35-11
- Accounting for Land, building , and equipment 988-360-10-50-1, 840-30-50-1, 958-360-50-1,
- Statement of Financial Position, ASC 958-45-1, ASC 958-210-55-4
- Statement of Activities, 958-225-45
- Statement of Cash Flows, 230-10-15-3, 230-10-45-24
- Statement of Functional Expenses: ASC 958-205-45-4
- Government Funds Accounting Requirements 958-606-45-4 (addressing governmental sources using cost reimbursement contracts)

Regulations: OMB Circular A-122, available at *http://www.whitehouse.gov/omb/circulars/a122*.

Chapter 28

Evaluating Your Organization's Financial Health

Non-technical material: KATHERINE DEYOUNG, HOW TO CONDUCT AN INTERNAL AUDIT (A GUIDE FOR SMALL NONPROFIT ORGANIZATIONS), to be published by Financial Stewardship Resources (*www.financialstewards.org*) in 2012. This is a notebook that walks you through an overview of how you handle your finances. It offers tools to help you evaluate the strength of your internal controls, verify your financial figures, and examine the processes by which your finances are handled.

Chapter 29

Electioneering and Lobbying Rules for All Nonprofit Corporations

Federal Campaign Rules

Non-technical material: A GUIDE TO THE CURRENT RULES FOR FEDERAL ELECTION (2011), published by the Campaign Legal Center (available free online at *www.campaignlegalcenter.org*). This is a summary of the Citizens United case and the effect that it has had on campaign spending. It is an overview and is not written from the perspective of nonprofit organizations.

Statutes: 2 USC §§431-455 (Federal Election Campaign Act); 116 Stat 81 (Bipartisan Campaign Reform Act of 2002, aka McCain-Feingold Law).

Cases: Citizens United v. FEC, 558 US 8 (2010) (unlimited expenditures by independent PACs); SpeechNow.org v. FEC, 599 F3d 686 (DC Cir 2010) (unlimited contributions by individuals to independent PACs); Club for Growth, 2010 WL 3184267 (FEC 2010); Commonsense Ten, 2010 WL 3184269 (FEC 2010) (unlimited contributions by corporations, unions, and individuals to independent PAC).

Regulations: 11 CFR Parts 100, 102, 104-106, 108-111, 114; Rev Rul 2004-6, 2004-4 IRB 328 (describes when public advocacy expenditures by §501(c) organizations may be expenditures for an exempt function subjecting the organization to tax under §527(f)).

Federal Lobbying Rules

Statutes: 2 USC §1601-1612 (Federal Lobbying Disclosure Act).

Cases: National Association of Manufacturers v. Taylor, 582 F3d 1 (DC cir 2009) (federal lobbying rules are constitutional).

State Campaign Rules

Non-technical material: ELECTIONS DIVISION, CAMPAIGN FINANCE MANUAL (Oregon Secretary of State, 2010) (available free online at *www.oregonvotes.org/doc/publications/campaign_finance*).

Statutes: ORS Chapter 260.

Regulations: OAR 165-012, especially 165-012-0005 (the provisions of the CAMPAIGN FINANCE MANUAL are part of the administrative regulations for ORS Chapter 260).

Cases: State ex rel Crumpton v. Keisling, 160 Or App 406, 982 P2d 3 (1999), rev den, 329 Or 650 (2000) (definition of express advocacy for expenditures in support of or opposition to candidate involving usage of "union bosses").

State Lobbying Rules

Statutes: ORS 171.725-.785.

Regulations: OAR 199-010-0005 through 199-010-0150.

Federal Funds for Lobbying

Statutes: 2 USC §1611 ((c)(4)s that lobby cannot get federal grants or loans); 31 USC §1352 (restrictions on using federal funds to lobby federal officials).

Regulations: 48 CFR §3.801 et. seq.; 70 FR 57455-01; OMB Circular A-122, Cost Principles for Non-profit Organizations, May 10, 2004 (restrictions on using federal funds for lobbying and political activities).

Political Expenditures Tax

Statutes: 26 USC §527.

Regulations: 26 CFR §1.527-1 through 1.527-9; Rev Rul 2003-49, 2003-20 IRB 903 (question and answer format on how to comply with the notice and reporting requirements for §527 organizations); Rev Rul 2004-6, 2004-4 IRB 328.

Chapter 30

Compliance: Ongoing Maintenance of Your Nonprofit

Access to Books and Records

Statutes: ORS 65.224 (membership list and inspection); ORS 65.771-.782 (recordkeeping requirements and inspection by members)

Reports and Registrations

Statutes: ORS 65.647-.657, 65.787 (administrative dissolution and annual report); ORS 128.650-.660 (Attorney General requirements).

Regulations: OAR 137-010-0005 through 0055.

E-Mail Notices

Statutes: One big issue for nonprofits is whether notice that is required at various places in ORS Chapter 65 can be sent by email. ORS 65.034(2) states that notice may be communicated in various forms, including "teletype or other form of wire or wireless communication..." The statute was written in 1989 before email was widely used and it is not clear whether wireless communication includes email. Washington enacted a special statute to authorize email, but the statute includes some restrictions to mitigate the changeability of email addresses. RCW 24.03.009 and 24.03.080. The Oregon legislature has amended ORS Chapter 65 to recognize the use of the Internet by nonprofits but has not amended ORS 65.034(2) to add email to the list of ways notice can be communicated. ORS 65.337(3)(b); ORS 65.341.

The federal Electronic Signatures in Global and National Commerce Act (E-SIGN) provides that records relating to any transaction that affects interstate or foreign commerce may be in electronic form. 15 USC §7001. The law allows a state to supersede §7001 by adopting the Uniform Electronic Transactions Act. Oregon has done this in ORS Chapter 84. ORS 84.061 states that Chapter 84 supersedes E-SIGN. ORS 84.004(16) defines a transaction as an action to conduct business, commerce or governmental affairs. If a law requires a person (which includes a legal entity) to send information in writing, the sender may satisfy the law by using an electronic means if both parties have consented and the sender does not inhibit the ability of the recipient to print or store the electronic record. ORS 84.022(1).

One big question for nonprofits is whether nonprofits are conducting "business, commercial or governmental affairs" in their "transactions." The Oregon law provides no additional guidance nor does the Uniform Laws Annotated. The commentary to the Uniform Laws describes "transactions" but does not provide any nonprofit examples. It does note that a "transaction" must be between two or more people and does not encompass unilateral signatures. For example, signing a health care power of attorney is not a transaction. Uniform Laws Annotated, Uniform Electronic Transactions Act, §2 (West: 2002).

If your nonprofit engages in commercial operations, those operations are almost certainly covered. However, Oregon law is much less clear about whether a nonprofit's use of e-mail to deliver notice of meetings, for example, is a transaction that is covered. The cautious approach is to use the statutory methods of delivery. If a nonprofit uses e-mail, it may want to comply with ORS 84.022(1) above by getting the consent of the recipients, if possible.

Releases

Cases: Mann v. Wetter, 100 Or App 184, 785 P2d 1064 (1990), rev den 309 Or 645, 789 P2d 1387 (agreement releasing scuba diving school from liability upheld); Silva v. Mt. Bachelor, Inc., 2008 WL 2889656 (D Or 2008) (ski release upheld).

Terrorism

Non-technical material: *Handbook on Counter-Terrorism Measures: What U.S. Nonprofits and Grantmakers Need to Know* (Council on Foundations and others, 2004) (an older but very readable summary that is available for free at *www.cof.org*); U.S. Department of the Treasury Anti-Terrorist Financing Guidelines: Voluntary Best Practices for U.S.-Based Charities (undated, circa 2006) (available from the U.S. Department of Treasury website).

General: Hill and Mancino, Taxation of Exempt Organizations, Chapter 32.04.

Statutes and Executive Orders: USA Patriot Act of 2001, Pub L No. 107-56, 115 Stat 272 (2001); 26 USC §501(p) (authorizes IRS to suspend exemption of organization listed as terrorist); Exec Order No. 13,224, 66 Fed Reg 49,079 (September 25, 2001), amended by Exec Order No. 13,258, 67 Fed Reg 44,751 (July 3, 2002) and Exec Order No. 13, 284, 68 Fed Reg 4,075 (January 28, 2003).

Regulations: Rev Proc 2008-9, 2008-2, IRS 258.

Cases: Global Relief Foundation, Inc. v O'Neill, 315 F3d 748 (7th cir), cert den, 540 US 1003 (2003) (court denied GRF's injunction and upheld freezing of assets); Holy Land Foundation for Relief & Dev. v. Ashcroft, 333 F3d 156 (DC cir 2003), cert den 540 US 1218 (2004) (court upheld government designation of HLF as a terrorist organization); Boim v. Holy Land Foundation, 549 F3d 685 (7th cir 2008) (organization that donates to terrorists may be civilly liable for damages caused by terrorists); Al Haramain Islamic Foundation, Inc., v. U.S. Department of Treasury, 660 F3d 1019 (9th cir

2011) (government froze assets of Oregon charity and declared it a terrorist organization; the court held that the government's classification was reasonable, that the government had violated due process in making the classification but that the violations were harmless; that the government's failure to get a warrant was unreasonable; and that another nonprofit that wanted to coordinate its advocacy with the organization had the free speech right to do so).

Guidelines: U.S. Department of the Treasury, *Anti-Terrorist Financing Guidelines: Voluntary Best Practices for U.S.-Based Charities* 6 (undated, circa 2006).

Special Rules for Tax-Exempt Groups

General: HILL AND MANCINO, TAXATION OF EXEMPT ORGANIZATIONS, Chapter 33.

Inspection and Copying

Statutes: 26 USC §6104(d); 2.

Regulations: 26 CFR §301.6104 (public inspection and web rules); T.D. 8818, 1999-17 IRB 3 (April 26, 1999) (inspection and copying rules); Notice 2008-49, 2008-20 IRB 979 (Form 990-T forms that are not public).

Acknowledging Donations

Statutes: 26 USC§170(f)(8) (substantiation of gift over $250),

Regulations: 26 CFR §6115 (disclosure of quid pro quo contributions over $75); 26 CFR 1.170A-13(f), 1.6115-1; Rev Pro 66-49, 1966-2 CB 1257 (donations); Rev Rul 67-246, 1967-2 CB 104 (*quid pro quo* rules), *amplified by* Rev Proc 90-12, 1990-1 CB 471 (*quid pro quo* rules).

The IRS explanation of its rules about acknowledging donations can be found at *http://www.irs.gov/charities/article/0,,id=96102,00.html*.

Change in Activities

General: HILL AND MANCINO, TAXATION OF EXEMPT ORGANIZATIONS, ¶32.13.

Group Exemptions

Regulations: Rev Proc 80-27, 1980-1 CB 490, §6 (annual information); 26 CFR §601.201(n)(8)(iv) (annual information).

Schools

Regulations: Rev Proc 75-50, 1975-2 CB 587 (racial nondiscrimination rules).

Excess Benefits Transactions

General: Cynthia Cumfer, *Structure and Governance*, Nonprofits in the Headlines Chapter 1 (Oregon State Bar, 2004); Laura Kalick, *The IRS Focuses on Automatic Excess Benefit Transactions and Compensation*, Taxation of Exempts 3 (July/August 2004); Frances R. Hill and Douglas M. Mancino, Taxation of Exempt Organizations ¶4.04 (2002); Lawrence M. Brauer and Leonard J. Henzke, Jr., *'Automatic' Excess Benefit Transactions Under IRC 4958* (IRS CPE for FY 2004), at *http:www.irs.gov/charities/article/0,,id=119768,00.html*.

Statutes: 26 USC §4958.

Regulations: 26 CFR §53.4958-0 through 53.4958-8.

Chapter 31

Reviewing and Changing Your Articles and Bylaws

Statutes: ORS 65.431-.467.

Chapter 32

Merging With Another Corporation or Selling Your Assets

Non-technical: Thomas A. McLaughlin, Nonprofit Mergers and Alliances: A Strategic Planning Guide (2010) (a very readable book with good information).

Statutes: ORS 65.481-.534.

Chapter 33

Dissolving Your Nonprofit Corporation

Statutes: ORS 65.621-.674.

Appendix 2. List of Tax and Regulatory Agencies

State

Attorney General/Oregon Department of Justice
Charitable Activities Section
1515 SW 5th, #410
Portland, OR 97201
www.doj.state.or.us
971.673.1882
503.229.5120 — fax
503.378.5938 — TDD

This is the place to file your registration with the Attorney General is you incorporate as a public benefit nonprofit and to file the Form CT-12. For gaming rules (bingo and the like, not soccer), go to *www.doj.state.or.us/ChariGroup/Howtoraffle.htm* and type "gaming" into the search box.

Bureau of Labor and Industry (BOLI)
Technical Assistance for Employers
800 NE Oregon, Suite 1045
Portland, OR 97232
www.boli.state.or.us
971.673.0761
971.673.0762 — fax

BOLI is the source for information about state employment laws, regulations and seminars for employers.

Oregon Department of Revenue
955 Center St. NE
Salem, Oregon 97301-2555
www.gov/DOR
503.378.4988
800.356.4222
503.945.8738 — fax
503.945.8100–transit tax exemptions

This is the address for estimated tax payments. Check website for addresses for other payments.

Oregon Government Standards and Practices Commission
3218 Pringle Rd SE, Suite 220
Salem, OR 97302-1544
www.gspc.state.or.us
503.378.5105
503.373.1456 — fax
This agency regulates state legislative lobbying.

Oregon Secretary of State
Corporations Division and Elections Division
255 Capitol Street NE, #151 (corporations) and #501 (elections)
Salem, OR 97310-1327
www.sos.state.or.us
503.986.2200–corporations
503.373.7414–elections
The Secretary of State's Corporations Division is where you file your incorporation papers as a nonprofit corporation and your annual report. The Elections Division regulates political activity. For the state *Campaign Finance Manual*, go to *www.oregonvotes.org/doc/publications/campaign_finance*.

You can get free copies of recent corporate filings online from the Corporations Division. Go to the Business Names menu, type in the name of the corporation, click on the corporation's name in the next menu, and go to the Summary History of corporate filings at the bottom of the page. If there is an image next to the name of a document that was filed, you can click on the image and the document will appear. You can copy it for free. Otherwise, you will need to pay a small filing fee to get it from the Corporations Division.

State of Oregon Employment Department
875 Union Street NE
Salem, Oregon 97311
www.emp.state.or.us
800.237.3710
877.517.5627
503.947.1472 — fax
The Employment Department offers job fairs and recruitment and handles the unemployment tax and benefit audits.

Federal

Federal Election Commission
999 E Street NW
Washington, D.C. 20463
www.fec.gov
800.424.9530
202.219.3336 — TTY
The FEC regulates broadcast communications in political campaigns.

Department of Treasury
Internal Revenue Service Center
Kansas City, MO 64999
This is where you file Form 1099 and Transmittal Form 1096 and Form 941, the Quarterly Tax Report when no payment is made.

Department of the Treasury
Internal Revenue Service
Ogden, UT 84201-0027
This is the address to file Form 990, the Annual Tax Return, and Form 2758, the Extension of Time to File Annual Return.

The Internal Revenue Service is online at *www.irs.gov*. To get IRS Publications online, go to *www.irs.gov* and type in "Publication" and its number in the Search box. The IRS has different offices for different purposes. For those most likely to be of interest to users of this book:

Internal Revenue Service
P. O. Box 12192
Covington, KY 41012-0192
1.877.829.5500 for filing assistance
This is the office where you file the Form 1023 and Form 1024, the Applications for Tax-exempt Status.

Internal Revenue Service
P.O. Box 105083
Atlanta, GA 30348-5083
Here you file Form 941, the Quarterly Tax Report when you are making a payment.

Internal Revenue Service
Attn: EIN Operation
Cincinnati, OH 45999
This is where you file Form SS-4 — Application for Employer ID Number (EIN).
To get your EIN by fax, fax Form SS-4 to 859.669.5760
To get your EIN by phone, call 800.829.4933
To get your EIN online, go to *www.irs.gov/businesses/* and search for "EIN." At the EIN screen, look for "Apply for an EIN Online."

Small Business Administration
www.sba.gov
To get information about making a business pland (under small business").

Social Security Administration
Data Operations Center
Wilkes-Barre, Pennsylvania 18769-0001
www.ssa.gov
File Forms W-2 and W-3 here.

U.S. Department of Labor
Frances Perkins Bldg.
200 Constitution Avenue NW
Washington, D.C. 20210
www.dol.gov
1.866.487.2365
TTY: 1.877.889.5627
For information on wage and hour and employment law.

U.S. Equal Employment Opportunity Commission
1801 L Street NW
Washington, D.C. 20507
www.eeoc.gov
1.800.669.4000
TTY: 1.800.669.6820
For information on civil rights laws.

U.S. Senate
Office of Public Records
232 Hart Senate Office Building
Washington, D.C. 20510-7116
www.senate.gov
202.224.3121

For registration for federal lobbyists, go to *www.senate.gov* and follow links to Legislation and Records and Lobbying Disclosure.

FORMS

Forms

- Ballot for Election of Directors
- Ballot for Proposed Action
- Board and Committee Minutes Policy
- Bylaws of a Membership Corporation
- Bylaws of a Nonmembership Corporation
- Complete Release
- Complete Release and Hold Harmless Agreement by Client
- Complete Release and Hold Harmless Agreement by Volunteers
- Conflicts of Interest and Executive Compensation Policy
- Consent to Corporate Action Without a Meeting by the Board of Directors
- Consent to Corporate Action Without a Meeting by the Members
- Financial Controls Policies and Procedures for Small Nonprofit Organizations
- Form 990 Review Policy
- Joint Venture Policy
- Minutes of First Meeting of Board of Directors
- Minutes of Meeting of the Board of Directors
- Minutes of Meeting of the Members
- Promissory Note
- Proxy Vote
- Records Retention and Destruction Policy
- Transparency Policy
- Waiver of Notice of Meeting of the Board of Directors
- Waiver of Notice of Meeting of Members
- Whistleblower Policy

BALLOT FOR ELECTION OF DIRECTORS

NAME OF CORPORATION: _____

This written ballot is a ballot for you to vote for your choices for of the Board of Directors of this corporation. Vote for no more than ____ of the choices below by placing an "X" or check mark on the line to the left of your choices or by filling in a blank space. Blank spaces are for other nominees. If you vote for more candidates than indicated above, your ballot will be disregarded. You may cast fewer votes than indicated. If you attempt to cast more than one vote for a single candidate, we will count only one vote for that candidate.

  ____ NAME OF CANDIDATE

  ____ NAME OF CANDIDATE

  ____ NAME OF CANDIDATE

  ____ NAME OF CANDIDATE

  ____ NAME OF CANDIDATE

  ____ _____

In order to meet quorum requirements, the corporation must receive ___ valid ballots. [or, "The number of ballots received is sufficient to meet the quorum requirements of this corporation."]

Place this ballot in the small envelope and sign and date the small envelope on the outside on the line indicated. Place the small envelope in the return envelope and mail or deliver it to the corporation. Your ballot must be received by 5:00 p.m. on _____, 20___ in order to be counted.

BALLOT FOR PROPOSED ACTION

NAME OF CORPORATION: _____

This written ballot is a ballot for you to vote for or against the proposed action below. In order to meet quorum requirements, the corporation must receive ___ valid ballots. [or, "The number of ballots received is sufficient to meet the quorum requirements of this corporation."]

__% of affirmative votes on these ballots is necessary in order to approve this proposed action [or, "A majority of affirmative votes on these ballots is necessary in order to approve this proposed action."]

PROPOSED ACTION:

I vote   _____ FOR this action.

           _____ AGAINST this action.

Please place an "X" or check mark by the choice above that reflects your vote. Place this ballot in the small envelope and sign and date the small envelope on the outside on the line indicated. Place the small envelope in the return envelope and mail or deliver it to the corporation. Your ballot must be received by 5:00 p.m. on _____, 20___ in order to be counted.

BOARD AND COMMITTEE MINUTES POLICY

The Secretary shall perform, or cause to be performed, the official recording of the written consent actions and minutes of all proceedings of the Board of Directors meetings and of all actions and proceedings of any committee that exercises board authority. The Secretary shall ensure that these records are kept in a permanent file whose location is known to the Secretary. The Secretary may delegate performance of some or all of these duties but shall oversee the performance to ensure that it is satisfactory.

BYLAWS OF A MEMBERSHIP CORPORATION

NAME OF CORPORATION: _____

ARTICLE I: PURPOSE

This corporation shall be organized and operated exclusively for charitable, scientific, literary, religious, and educational purposes. Subject to the limitations stated in the Articles of Incorporation, the purposes of this corporation shall be to engage in any lawful activities, none of which are for profit, for which corporations may be organized under Chapter 65 of the Oregon Revised Statutes (or its corresponding future provisions) and Section 501(c)(3) of the Internal Revenue Code (or its corresponding future provisions).

This corporation's primary purpose shall be _____
_____.

ARTICLE II: MEMBERS

Section 1. *Classes and Voting*. There shall be one class of members of this corporation. Each member shall be entitled to one vote on all matters for which a membership vote is permitted by law, the Articles of Incorporation, or the Bylaws of this corporation.

Section 2. *Qualifications*. A person shall become a member of the corporation by _____
_____.

Section 3. *Termination of Membership*. Membership may be terminated by the Board of Directors after giving the member at least 15 days written notice by first class or certified mail of the termination and the reasons for the termination, and an opportunity for the member to be heard by the Board, orally or in writing, not less than five days before the effective date of the termination. The decision of the Board shall be final and shall not be reviewable by any court.

Section 4. *Annual Meeting*. The annual meeting of the members shall be held on _____ at a place to be determined by the Board of Directors.

Section 5. *Special Meetings*. Special meetings of the members shall be held at the call of the Board of Directors, or by the call of the holders of at least five percent of the voting power of the corporation by a demand signed, dated, and delivered to the corporation's Secretary. Such demand by the members shall describe the purpose for the meeting.

Section 6. *Notice of Meeting*. Notice of all meetings of the members shall be given to each member at the last address of record, by first class mail at least 7 days before the meeting, or by means other than first class mail at least 30 but not more than 60 days before the meeting. The notice shall include the date, time, place, and purposes of the meeting.

Section 7. *Quorum and Voting*. Those votes represented at a meeting of members shall constitute a quorum. A majority vote of the members voting is the act of the members, unless these Bylaws or the law provide differently.

Section 8. *Proxy Voting*. There shall be no voting by proxy.

Section 9. *Action by Consent*. Any action required by law to be taken at a meeting of the members may be taken without a meeting if a consent in writing, setting forth the action to be taken or so taken, shall be signed by all the members.

ARTICLE III: BOARD OF DIRECTORS

Section 1. *Duties*. The affairs of the corporation shall be managed by the Board of Directors.

Section 2. *Number*. The number of Directors may vary between a minimum of three and a maximum of fifteen.

Section 3. *Term and Election*. The term of office for Directors shall be one year. A Director may be reelected without limitation on the number of terms s/he may serve. The Board shall be elected by the majority of the members at the annual meeting of the members.

Section 4. *Removal*. Any Director may be removed, with or without cause, at a meeting called for that purpose, by a vote of a majority of the members entitled to vote at an election of Directors.

Section 5. *Vacancies*. Vacancies on the Board of Directors and newly created Board positions will be filled by a majority vote of the Directors then on the Board of Directors.

Section 6. *Quorum and Action*. A quorum at a Board meeting shall be a majority of the number of Directors prescribed by the Board, or if no number is prescribed, a majority of the number in office immediately before the meeting begins. If a quorum is present, action is taken by a majority vote of Directors present. Where the law requires a majority vote of Directors in office to establish committees that exercise Board functions, to amend the Articles of Incorporation, to sell assets not in the regular course of business, to merge, to dissolve, or for other matters, such action is taken by that majority as required by law.

Section 7. *Regular Meetings*. Regular meetings of the Board of Directors shall be held at the time and place to be determined by the Board of Directors. No other notice of the date, time, place, or purpose of these meetings is required, except as otherwise provided in these Bylaws.

Section 8. *Special Meetings*. Special meetings of the Board of Directors shall be held at the time and place to be determined by the Board of Directors. Notice of such meetings, describing the date, time, place, and purpose of the meeting, shall be delivered to each Director personally or by telephone or by mail not less than two days prior to the special meeting. Written notice, if mailed postpaid and correctly addressed to the Director at the address shown in the corporate records, is effective when mailed.

Section 9. *Meeting by Telecommunication or Computer.* Any regular or special meeting of the Board of Directors may be held by telephone, telecommunications or electronic means, as long as all Directors can hear or read each other's communications during the meeting or all communications during the meeting are immediately transmitted to each participating Director, and each participating Director is able to immediately send messages to all other participating Directors. All participating Directors shall be informed that a meeting is taking place at which official business may be transacted.

Section 10. *Action by Consent.* Any action required or permitted by law to be taken at a meeting of the Board may be taken without a meeting if a consent in writing, setting forth the action to be taken or so taken, shall be signed by all the Directors. A written communication includes a communication that is transmitted or received by electronic means. Signing includes an electronic signature that is executed or adopted by a Director with the intent to sign.

ARTICLE IV: COMMITTEES

Section 1. *Executive Committee.* The Board of Directors may elect an Executive Committee. The Executive Committee shall have the authority to make on-going decisions between Board meetings and shall have the authority to make financial and budgetary decisions.

Section 2. *Other Committees.* The Board of Directors may establish such other committees as it deems necessary and desirable. Such committees may exercise the authority of the Board of Directors or may be advisory committees.

Section 3. *Composition of Committees Exercising Board Functions.* Any committee that exercises any authority of the Board of Directors shall be composed of two or more Directors, elected by the Board of Directors by a majority vote of the number of Directors prescribed by the Board, or if no number is prescribed, by a majority vote of all Directors in office at that time.

Section 4. *Quorum and Action.* A quorum at a Committee meeting exercising Board authority shall be a majority of all Committee members in office immediately before the meeting begins. If a quorum is present, action is taken by a majority vote of Directors present.

Section 5. *Limitations on the Authority of Committees.* No committee may authorize payment of a dividend or any part of the income or profit of the corporation to its Directors or officers; may approve dissolution, merger, or the sale, pledge, or transfer of all or substantially all of the corporation's assets; may elect, appoint, or remove Directors or fill vacancies on the Board or on any of its committees; nor may adopt, amend, or repeal the Articles, Bylaws, or any resolution by the Board of Directors.

ARTICLE V: OFFICERS

Section 1. *Titles.* The officers of this corporation shall be the President, Secretary and Treasurer.

Section 2. *Election.* The Board of Directors shall elect the officers to serve one year terms. An officer may be reelected without limitation on the number of terms s/he may serve.

Section 3. *Vacancy*. A vacancy of any office shall be filled not later than the first regular meeting of the Board of Directors following the vacancy.

Section 4. *Other Officers*. The Board of Directors may elect or appoint other officers, agents and employees as it shall deem necessary and desirable. They shall hold their offices for such terms and have such authority and perform such duties as shall be determined by the Board of Directors.

Section 5. *President*. The President shall be the chief officer of the corporation and shall act as the Chair of the Board. The President shall have any other powers and duties as may be prescribed by the Board of Directors.

Section 6. *Secretary*. The Secretary shall have overall responsibility for all recordkeeping. The Secretary shall perform, or cause to be performed, the following duties: (a) official recording of the minutes of all proceedings of the Board of Directors and members' meetings and actions; (b) provision for notice of all meetings of the Board of Directors and members; (c) authentication of the records of the corporation; (d) maintenance of current and accurate membership lists; and (e) any other duties as may be prescribed by the Board of Directors.

Section 7. *Treasurer*. The Treasurer shall have the overall responsibility for all corporate funds. The Treasurer shall perform, or cause to be performed, the following duties: (a) maintenance of full and accurate accounts of all financial records of the corporation; (b) deposit of all monies and other valuable effects in the name and to the credit of the corporation in such depositories as may be designated by the Board of Directors; (c) disbursement of all funds when proper to do so; (d) presentation of financial reports as to the financial condition of the corporation to the Board of Directors; and (e) any other duties as may be prescribed by the Board of Directors.

ARTICLE VI: CORPORATE INDEMNITY

This corporation will indemnify to the fullest extent not prohibited by law any person who is made, or threatened to be made, a party to an action, suit, or other proceeding, by reason of the fact that the person is or was a Director, officer, employee, volunteer, or agent of the corporation or a fiduciary within the meaning of the Employee Retirement Income Security Act of 1974 (or its corresponding future provisions) with respect to any employee benefit plan of the corporation. No amendment to this Article that limits the corporation's obligation to indemnify any person shall have any effect on such obligation for any act or omission that occurs prior to the later of the effective date of the amendment or the date notice of the amendment is given to the person. The corporation shall interpret this indemnification provision to extend to all persons covered by its provisions the most liberal possible indemnification--substantively, procedurally, and otherwise.

ARTICLE VII: AMENDMENTS TO BYLAWS

The Board of Directors may vote to amend or repeal these Bylaws or to adopt new ones by a majority vote of Directors present, if a quorum is present. Any amendment to the Bylaws to increase the quorum required for any member action or to add to, change or delete the vote required for any member action must be approved by the members. Prior to the adoption of the amendment, each Director shall be given at least two days notice of the date, time, and place of the meeting at which the proposed amendment is to be considered, and the notice shall state that one of the purposes of the meeting is to consider a proposed amendment to the Bylaws and shall contain a copy of the proposed amendment.

DATE ADOPTED: _____

I certify that these Bylaws are a true copy of the Bylaws of this corporation.

SIGNATURE BY CORPORATE OFFICER: _____

BYLAWS OF A NONMEMBERSHIP CORPORATION

NAME OF CORPORATION: _____

ARTICLE I: PURPOSE

This corporation shall be organized and operated exclusively for charitable, scientific, literary, religious, and educational purposes. Subject to the limitations stated in the Articles of Incorporation, the purposes of this corporation shall be to engage in any lawful activities, none of which are for profit, for which corporations may be organized under Chapter 65 of the Oregon Revised Statutes (or its corresponding future provisions) and Section 501(c)(3) of the Internal Revenue Code (or its corresponding future provisions).

This corporation's primary purpose shall be

ARTICLE II: NONMEMBERSHIP

This corporation shall have no members.

ARTICLE III: BOARD OF DIRECTORS

Section 1. *Duties*. The affairs of the corporation shall be managed by the Board of Directors.

Section 2. *Number*. The number of Directors may vary between a minimum of three and a maximum of fifteen.

Section 3. *Term and Election*. The term of office for Directors shall be one year. A Director may be reelected without limitation on the number of terms s/he may serve. The Board shall elect its own members, except that a Director shall not vote on that member's own position.

Section 4. *Removal*. Any Director may be removed, with or without cause, by a vote of two-thirds of the Directors then in office.

Section 5. *Vacancies*. Vacancies on the Board of Directors and newly created Board positions will be filled by a majority vote of the Directors then on the Board of Directors.

Section 6. *Quorum and Action*. A quorum at a Board meeting shall be a majority of the number of Directors prescribed by the Board, or if no number is prescribed, a majority of the number in office immediately before the meeting begins. If a quorum is present, action is taken by a majority vote of the Directors present, except as otherwise provided by these Bylaws. Where the law requires a majority vote of the Directors in office to establish committees to exercise Board functions, to amend the Articles of Incorporation, to sell assets not in the regular course of business, to merge, or to dissolve, or for other matters, such action is taken by that majority as required by law.

Section 7. **Regular Meetings**. Regular meetings of the Board of Directors shall be held at the time and place to be determined by the Board of Directors. No other notice of the date, time, place, or purpose of these meetings is required, except as otherwise provided in these Bylaws.

Section 8. *Special Meetings*. Special meetings of the Board of Directors shall be held at the time and place to be determined by the Board of Directors. Notice of such meetings, describing the date, time, place, and purpose of the meeting, shall be delivered to each Director personally or by telephone or by mail not less than two days prior to the special meeting. Written notice, if mailed postpaid and correctly addressed to the Director at the address shown in the corporate records, is effective when mailed.

Section 9. *Meeting by Telecommunication or Computer*. Any regular or special meeting of the Board of Directors may be held by telephone, telecommunications or electronic means, as long as all Directors can hear or read each other's communications during the meeting or all communications during the meeting are immediately transmitted to each participating Director, and each participating Director is able to immediately send messages to all other participating Directors. All participating Directors shall be informed that a meeting is taking place at which official business may be transacted.

Section 10. *Action by Consent*. Any action required or permitted by law to be taken at a meeting of the Board may be taken without a meeting if a consent in writing, setting forth the action to be taken or so taken, shall be signed by all the Directors. A written communication includes a communication that is transmitted or received by electronic means. Signing includes an electronic signature that is executed or adopted by a Director with the intent to sign.

ARTICLE IV: COMMITTEES

Section 1. *Executive Committee*. The Board of Directors may elect an Executive Committee. The Executive Committee shall have the authority to make on-going decisions between Board meetings and shall have the authority to make financial and budgetary decisions.

Section 2. *Other Committees*. The Board of Directors may establish such other committees as it deems necessary and desirable. Such committees may exercise the authority of the Board of Directors or may be advisory committees.

Section 3. *Composition of Committees Exercising Board Functions*. Any committee that exercises any authority of the Board of Directors shall be composed of two or more Directors, elected by the Board of Directors by a majority vote of the number of Directors prescribed by the Board, or if no number is prescribed, by a majority vote of all Directors in office at that time.

Section 4. *Quorum and Action*. A quorum at a Committee meeting exercising Board authority shall be a majority of all Committee members in office immediately before the meeting begins. If a quorum is present, action is taken by a majority vote of Directors present.

Section 5. *Limitations on the Authority of Committees*. No committee may authorize payment of a dividend or any part of the income or profit of the corporation to its Directors or officers; may approve dissolution, merger, or the sale, pledge, or transfer of all or substantially all of the corporation's assets; may elect, appoint, or remove Directors or fill vacancies on the Board or on any of its committees; nor may adopt, amend, or repeal the Articles, Bylaws, or any resolution by the Board of Directors.

ARTICLE V: OFFICERS

Section 1. *Titles*. The officers of this corporation shall be the President, Secretary and Treasurer.

Section 2. *Election*. The Board of Directors shall elect the officers to serve one year terms. An officer may be reelected without limitation on the number of terms s/he may serve.

Section 3. *Vacancy*. A vacancy in any office shall be filled not later than the first regular meeting of the Board of Directors following the vacancy.

Section 4. *Other Officers*. The Board of Directors may elect or appoint other officers, agents and employees as it shall deem necessary and desirable. They shall hold their offices for such terms and have such authority and perform such duties as shall be determined by the Board of Directors.

Section 5. *President*. The President shall be the chief officer of the corporation and shall act as the Chair of the Board. The President shall have any other powers and duties as may be prescribed by the Board of Directors.

Section 6. *Secretary*. The Secretary shall have overall responsibility for all recordkeeping. The Secretary shall perform, or cause to be performed, the following duties: (a) official recording of the minutes of all proceedings of the Board of Directors meetings and actions; (b) provision for notice of all meetings of the Board of Directors; (c) authentication of the records of the corporation; and (d) any other duties as may be prescribed by the Board of Directors.

Section 7. *Treasurer*. The Treasurer shall have the overall responsibility for all corporate funds. The Treasurer shall perform, or cause to be performed, the following duties: (a) maintenance of full and accurate accounts of all financial records of the corporation; (b) deposit of all monies and other valuable effects in the name and to the credit of the corporation in such depositories as may be designated by the Board of Directors; (c) disbursement of all funds when proper to do so; (d) presentation of financial reports as to the financial condition of the corporation to the Board of Directors; and (e) any other duties as may be prescribed by the Board of Directors.

ARTICLE VI: CORPORATE INDEMNITY

This corporation will indemnify to the fullest extent not prohibited by law any person who is made, or threatened to be made, a party to an action, suit, or other proceeding, by reason of the fact that the person is or was a Director, officer, employee, volunteer, or agent of the corporation or a fiduciary within the meaning of the Employee Retirement Income Security Act of 1974 (or its corresponding future provisions) with respect to any employee benefit plan of the corporation. No amendment to this Article that limits the corporation's obligation to indemnify any person shall have any effect on such obligation for any act or omission that occurs prior to the later of the effective date of the amendment or the date notice of the amendment is given to the person. The corporation shall interpret this indemnification provision to extend to all persons covered by its provisions the most liberal possible indemnification--substantively, procedurally, and otherwise.

ARTICLE VII: AMENDMENTS TO BYLAWS

These Bylaws may be amended or repealed, and new Bylaws adopted, by the Board of Directors by a majority vote of Directors present, if a quorum is present. Prior to the adoption of the amendment, each Director shall be given at least two days notice of the date, time, and place of the meeting at which the proposed amendment is to be considered, and the notice shall state that one of the purposes of the meeting is to consider a proposed amendment to the Bylaws and shall contain a copy of the proposed amendment.

DATE ADOPTED: _____

I certify that these Bylaws are a true copy of the Bylaws of this corporation.

SIGNATURE BY CORPORATE OFFICER:

_____

COMPLETE RELEASE

I assume all liability from any cause whatsoever in connection with _____ _____ [hereinafter called "this nonprofit organization"], and I release this nonprofit organization, and its directors, officers, employees, agents, and volunteers from all liability from any cause whatsoever, whether such claims are for negligence or any other theory of recovery, except for intentional misconduct, in connection with this nonprofit organization.

DATED: _____

SIGNED: _____

COMPLETE RELEASE AND HOLD HARMLESS AGREEMENT BY CLIENT

By my signature on this document, I assume all liability from any cause whatsoever that may arise out of, in connection with, or during the time of my receiving services from _____ [hereinafter called "this nonprofit organization"], including but not limited to all liability from any cause whatsoever for personal injury or property damage, whether such claims are for negligence or any other theory of recovery, except for intentional misconduct.

I release and hold harmless this nonprofit organization and its directors, officers, employees, agents, volunteers, assigns, and successors [hereinafter, "the protected parties"] from all liability from any cause whatsoever, whether such claims are for negligence or any other theory of recovery, except for intentional misconduct, as described above.

By this document, I assume all liability as described above that existed at the time of the execution of this document, whether such claims are for negligence or any other theory of recovery, except for intentional misconduct; and all liability from that time forward into the future until such time as this nonprofit organization shall execute in writing a document revoking this document.

By this document, I release and hold harmless the protected parties from all liability from any cause whatsoever as described above, whether such claims are for negligence or any other theory of recovery, except for intentional misconduct, that existed at the time of the execution of this document and all liability from that time forward into the future until such time as this nonprofit organization shall execute in writing a document revoking this document.

The consideration for this document is the services that this nonprofit organization is providing to me at a reduced cost.

This document shall be given a liberal construction, with all ambiguities resolved in favor of the protected parties. If any provision of this document is deemed to be partially void, invalid, or unenforceable, the remainder of that provision shall continue in full force and effect to the maximum extent permitted by law and all remaining provisions of this document shall continue in full force and effect. To the extent that any provision of this document is deemed to be completely void, invalid or unenforceable, that provision shall be severed from the remainder of this document and all remaining provisions of this document shall continue in full force and effect.

DATED: _____

SIGNED: _____

COMPLETE RELEASE AND HOLD HARMLESS AGREEMENT BY VOLUNTEERS

By my signature on this document, I assume all liability from any cause whatsoever that may arise out of, in connection with, or during the time of my volunteering to provide services for or in connection with _____ [hereinafter called "this nonprofit organization"], whether such claims are for negligence or any other theory of recovery, except for intentional misconduct; except that I shall be entitled to any and all worker compensation benefits that are available to me as a volunteer under the coverage of the worker compensation policy held by this nonprofit organization.

I release and hold harmless this nonprofit organization, its directors, officers, employees, agents, volunteers, assigns, and successors [hereinafter, "the protected parties"] from all liability from any cause whatsoever, whether such claims are for negligence or any other theory of recovery, except for intentional misconduct, as described above.

By this document, I assume all liability as described above that existed at the time of the execution of this document and all liability from that time forward into the future until such time as this nonprofit organization shall execute in writing a document revoking this document.

By this document, I release and hold harmless the protected parties from all liability from any cause whatsoever, whether such claims are for negligence or any other theory of recovery, except for intentional misconduct, as described above that existed at the time of the execution of this document and all liability from that time forward into the future until such time as this nonprofit organization shall execute in writing a document revoking this document.

The consideration for this document is the provision by this nonprofit organization of worker compensation insurance coverage to me as a volunteer.

This document shall be given a liberal construction, with all ambiguities resolved in favor of the protected parties. If any provision of this document is deemed to be partially void, invalid, or unenforceable, the remainder of that provision shall continue in full force and effect to the maximum extent permitted by law and all remaining provisions of this document shall continue in full force and effect. To the extent that any provision of this document is deemed to be completely void, invalid or unenforceable, that provision shall be severed from the remainder of this document and all remaining provisions of this document shall continue in full force and effect.

DATED: _____

SIGNED: _____

CONFLICTS OF INTEREST AND EXECUTIVE COMPENSATION POLICY

PURPOSE

The Board of Directors shall monitor the transactions between the corporation and insiders to ensure that any transaction between the corporation and an insider that is a conflict of interest is fair to the corporation and does not grant excessive benefit to the insider. The purposes of this policy are to ensure that directors and officers act loyally to the corporation and that directors, officers and those who exercise substantial influence over the corporation do not use their influence to obtain benefits in excess of fair market value in transactions with the corporation. This policy seeks to ensure that the corporation maintains high ethical standards and observes state and federal taxation concerning conflicts and excess benefits transactions.

SECTION 1: DEFINITION OF CONFLICTS OF INTEREST

Definition of Conflict. A conflict of interest arises when an insider described below may benefit financially from a decision he or she could make in his or her capacity as an insider, including indirect benefits to family members or businesses with which the insider is closely associated. A conflict of interest arises in any such transaction between the corporation and an insider, except for:

- transactions in the normal course of operations that are available to the general public under similar terms and circumstances, and

- expense reimbursements to an insider made pursuant to an accountable plan under IRS Reg. 1.62-2(c)(2).

Consequences of Conflicts. Some conflicts of interest are prohibited and our organization cannot engage in them. Others are permitted but are subject to special procedures set out below to ensure that the transaction is fair to our organization and complies with applicable law, regulations and funder agreements.

Conflicts that Fall Outside of Definition. The board recognizes that this policy may not describe all of the transactions or matters in which an insider or an individual or business closely connected with an insider may engage in a transaction or other matter with the corporation that creates divided loyalties or the possibility or perception of a conflict of interest or of unfair advantage to the other party. In such case, the board shall determine whether the transaction should be treated as a conflict of interest under this policy or should otherwise be scrutinized.

SECTION 2: DEFINITION OF INSIDER

An insider is any of the following persons, family members or entities:

Insider. An insider is any person who is in a position of authority over the corporation or who exerts substantial influence over the corporation, including directors, officers, the top management official, the top financial official, other key employees, the founders and major donors. An insider described in this section remains an insider for five years after his or her influence over this corporation ends.

Family Members. Family members of insiders are also insiders. Family members include the spouse or partner in a civil union recognized by state law; children, grandchildren, great-grandchildren, whole and half-blooded brothers and sisters, and spouses of any of these people; and any ancestors (parents, grandparents, etc.)

Entities. An entity in which a director is a general partner, director, officer, top management official, top financial official or other key employee is an insider. Corporations and limited liability companies in which an insider owns more than 5% of the voting power, partnerships in which the insider owns more than 5% of the profits and trusts or estates in which the insider owns more than 5% of the beneficial interest are insiders.

Other Nonprofits and For-Profits. Another nonprofit or for-profit entity is an insider if:

- one of our directors is also a director or officer of the other entity, and

- we and the other entity are engaged in a transaction that is significant enough that the transaction is or should be approved by the boards of both organizations.

SECTION 3: PROHIBITED CONFLICTS

Loans to Directors or Officers. Our organization cannot make a loan or guarantee an obligation to or for the benefit of any of its directors or officers.

SECTION 4: PROCEDURE FOR PERMISSIBLE CONFLICTS

In order to ensure that permissible transactions with insiders are fair to the corporation and comply with state and federal laws:

1. *Full Disclosure.* All insiders must promptly and fully disclose all material facts of every actual or potential conflict of interest to the Board of Directors at the time such conflict arises.

2. *Determination of Fairness.* When the corporation engages in a transaction with an insider that constitutes a conflict of interest, the Board shall handle the transaction as follows:

> *a. Impartial Board.* The Board shall exclude any insider that has a conflict of interest with respect to the transaction from all discussion and from voting on the transaction. The Board may ask questions of the insider prior to beginning its discussion.

b. *Comparable Data.* The Board shall gather appropriate data to ensure that the compensation for each insider is reasonable. In the case of employee compensation packages, the Board shall utilize reliable surveys of compensation for comparable positions or shall utilize data for at least three similarly situated employees in comparable positions. The Board shall not use the employee whose compensation is under consideration to collect comparability data.

c. *Documentation.* The Board shall document its decision by keeping written records that state the terms of the transaction and date approved, the directors present and who voted on it, the comparability data and how the data was obtained, and any actions taken with respect to directors who had a conflict of interest with respect to the transaction. The records must be prepared before the latter of the next Board meeting or 60 days after the final action is taken. Once prepared, the records must be reviewed and approved by the Board within a reasonable time.

3. *Identification of Employee Insiders.* When employee compensation packages are established each year, the Board shall identify those employees who are insiders. The Board shall monitor the compensation packages of insiders in accordance with the procedure in this section above.

4. *Reporting Benefits.* When the corporation provides an economic benefit to an insider for the insider's services as an employee or an independent contractor, the corporation shall contemporaneously document the transaction as required by the IRS (generally on an original Form W-2, Form 990, or Form 1099 or with a written employment contract).

SECTION 5: COMPLIANCE WITH THIS POLICY

In order to ensure compliance with this policy:

1. *Annual Disclosure Statement.* The officers, directors and key employees shall each year disclose interests that could give rise to a conflict of interest under this policy. Such disclosure shall be made on the Disclosure and Acknowledgment attached to this policy and shall be filed with the Secretary or the Secretary's designee.

2. *List of Potential Insiders.* On an annual basis, the Secretary of the corporation or the Secretary's designee shall develop and maintain a list of insiders who engage in or are reasonably likely to engage in transactions that constitute conflicts of interest with the corporation during the year.

3. *Ongoing Disclosure Obligation.* Officers, directors and key employees shall have an ongoing obligation to notify the Board promptly of interests that subsequently arise that could give rise to a conflict of interest under this policy.

4. *Monitoring by Secretary.* The Secretary or the Secretary's designee shall monitor and enforce compliance with this policy by reviewing the list of insiders and the Disclosure and Acknowledgment forms each year and by bringing potential or actual conflicts to the attention of the President of the Board. The President shall disclose conflicts to the Board as they arise and ensure that the procedures in this policy are followed.

5. *Conveyance to Executive Director.* The Secretary or the Secretary's designee shall convey the list of insiders identified above to the Executive Director and shall instruct the Executive Director to notify the Board if the Executive Director or any employee plans to engage in a transaction with an insider that constitutes a conflict of interest, including payment or reimbursement for business or travel expenses of the insider and/or members of the insider's family not made pursuant to an accountable plan under IRS Reg. 1.62-2(c)(2). If so, the Board shall monitor the transaction to ensure that it complies with the procedure in Section 4 above.

SECTION 6: DELEGATION TO COMMITTEE

The Board may delegate its responsibilities under this policy to a committee of the Board. The committee shall comply with this policy and shall report its decision to the Board in a timely fashion.

Signature:_____   Printed Name:_____

Title: _____   Date Adopted: _____

ANNUAL QUESTIONNAIRE

CONFLICTS OF INTEREST AND EXECUTIVE COMPENSATION POLICY DISCLOSURE AND ACKNOWLEDGMENT STATEMENT

[Each Director, Officer and Key Employee should sign and submit this form annually.]

DISCLOSURE

Please report below any conflicts of interest or potential conflicts of interest between the corporation and you, a family member or a business or corporation with which you are connected within the meaning of the Conflicts of Interest and Executive Compensation Policy.

You have an ongoing obligation to notify the Board promptly of any such conflicts of interest that subsequently arise.

LIST OF CONFLICTS OR POTENTIAL CONFLICTS

Please list and explain any conflicts here:

ACKNOWLEDGMENT

I have received, read, understand and will comply with the Conflicts of Interest and Executive Compensation Policy of the corporation. I affirm that, other than the interests reported, I am aware of no conflicts of interest that I have or may have within the meaning of the Conflicts of Interest and Executive Compensation Policy.

Signature: _____

Title: _____

Print Name: _____

DATE: _____

Please submit this form to the Secretary of the corporation and retain a copy for your records.

CONSENT TO CORPORATE ACTION WITHOUT A MEETING BY THE BOARD OF DIRECTORS

NAME OF CORPORATION: _____

We, the undersigned, being all the Directors of this corporation, an Oregon nonprofit corporation, do consent to the following corporate action as if such action had been taken at a duly held meeting of the Board of Directors of the corporation:

ACTION:

This action is to be effective as of this _____ day of _____, 20___.

_____   Date Signed: _____
Signature

_____   Date Signed: _____
Signature

_____   Date Signed: _____
Signature

_____   Date Signed: _____
Signature

_____   Date Signed: _____
Signature

CONSENT TO CORPORATE ACTION WITHOUT A MEETING BY THE MEMBERS

NAME OF CORPORATION: _____

We, the undersigned, being all the members of this corporation, an Oregon nonprofit corporation, do consent to the following corporate action as if such action had been taken at a duly held meeting of the members of the corporation:

ACTION:

This action is to be effective as of this _____ day of _____, 20___.

_____   Date Signed: _____
Signature

_____   Date Signed: _____
Signature

_____   Date Signed: _____
Signature

_____   Date Signed: _____
Signature

_____   Date Signed: _____
Signature

FINANCIAL CONTROLS POLICIES AND PROCEDURES FOR SMALL NONPROFIT ORGANIZATIONS

NOTE: *These policies and procedures are designed for small nonprofits that do not have an administrator with financial expertise. They are set up to divide the fiscal control roles between two people, the Secretary and Treasurer. You can use any two competent, unrelated people. As you grow in capacity, you should increase the number of people involved to improve the segregation of the roles. When you can afford to do so, you should have these reviewed by an accountant who can tailor financial controls to your organization.*

The policies describe the risks that each policy is designed to address. The Board or whoever develops and adapts your control policies and procedures should design them with the risks in your particular situation in mind. You can find a schematic guide to these policies and procedures that may make them easier to follow attached to the Financial Controls Policies at www.cumfer.net under the Resources tab.

Purpose. We are a nonprofit organization committed to protecting and using our assets for our non-profit mission. Proper financial practices are very important in doing this, since proper practices help to prevent and detect errors and fraud. Good financial practices also assure our donors that we use their gifts for the purposes for which they were intended.

I. GENERAL PRACTICES

Review of Risks. These policies were drafted after consideration of the risks associated with the various aspects of our financial operations to enact policies and procedures designed to minimize those risks. The Board will review these policies each year to consider whether the risks have changed. Such changes may include receipt of grant monies for the first time or receipt of grants with restrictions, a change in the laws regulating our nonprofit, hiring of employees or a major change in our programs. If so, the Board needs to identify any new risks and adopt appropriate procedures to minimize those risks. The Board shall consult with a professional if necessary to ensure that it is properly addressing the risks.

Segregation of Roles. There are several fiscal "roles" in our organization—custody, authorization, execution, and monitoring. For example, the person who has authority to sign checks is acting in the custodial role. The person who approves payment of a bill is authorizing. The Board as a whole acts in an authorizing role when it approves the annual budget of makes a decision to purchase a major item like a copier. The person who prepares the checks for signature by an authorized check signer is acting in the execution role, executing an action that has been authorized by the Board through the annual budget or by the individual responsible for approving payment of the bill. The person who reconciles the bank statement acts in the monitoring role. The Board also acts in a monitoring role when it reviews the monthly financial reports to be sure that its plan—the budget—is being executed properly.

As much as possible, the Board seeks to separate the responsibilities for fiscal roles so that at least two and preferably more individuals fulfill these roles. It is particularly important that the same person does not authorize, execute and monitor any transaction. At each step of handling funds, the organization shall ensure that more than one person verifies that the step is done correctly.

II. RECEIPT OF FUNDS

RISKS

Our organization faces the risk that funds that we receive may be stolen or lost or that someone may be falsely accused of stealing funds. We also face the risk that we may fail to record a restriction that a donor has placed on our use of funds.

POLICY

All funds, whether cash or check, which the organization receives will be deposited intact into the bank account, with no monies removed to make payments or for other purposes. All cash receipts should be deposited into the bank as soon as possible. This allows for a complete accounting and independent verification of what happens to our funds. Communications from donors that establish restrictions on the use of their contributions will be saved. If we believe that a donor has restricted the use of funds in a conversation, we will follow up and get written confirmation of the donor's intent.

PROCEDURES

1. *Receipt of Checks in the Office*. The Secretary opens all mail addressed to the organization. The Secretary makes a photocopy of all checks received and provides the photocopies to the Treasurer. This allows the Treasurer to verify that all checks received are deposited.

The Secretary will endorse all checks by an endorsement stamp that provides that the check is "For Deposit Only" and will be paid to the order of the corporate bank and lists the organization's name and account number. This lessens the risk that a check may be stolen and cashed.

2. *Receipt of Cash in the Office*. Cash is easily stolen or miscounted and must be handled carefully:

- If cash comes into the office, the person accepting the cash must provide a written receipt when taking the cash:

- The receipt should state the person's name, the date, the amount of the cash and the purpose of the payment.

- Use a pre-numbered receipt book with an automatic duplicate copy with the organization's name printed on it.

- No pages may be removed from the receipt book.

- The person with access to the receipt book shall keep it in a locked drawer and shall lock cash in a secured location until the Secretary can retrieve it.

- If possible, when the Secretary opens the location with the cash, one other person will accompany the Secretary so that they can count the cash together.

The Secretary or the Secretary's designee shall train all office volunteers in these procedures.

The Treasurer will compare the receipt book and the bank's list of cash deposits when making the Bank Reconciliation described below.

3. *Deposit Slips.* The Secretary will deposit corporate funds as follows:

- Prepare a deposit slip in duplicate.

- Photocopy the checks and staple the photocopies to the copy of the deposit ticket that we keep.

- If cash will be included in the deposit, the Secretary will attach a list to the duplicate deposit ticket which includes the sources of the cash and the receipt #s in the duplicate receipt book for each source of cash.

- File this documentation chronologically in a locked cabinet to prevent theft.

- The Treasurer will consult the deposit ticket and attached photocopies when making the Bank Reconciliation described below.

4. *Bank Deposit.* If no cash is present, the deposit may be mailed to the bank. If cash is present, a second person (if available) shall verify deposited funds prior to the Secretary sealing the envelope and making the deposit in person. The person verifying the cash shall initial the cash on the copy of the deposit slip retained by the organization.

5. *Receipt of Checks and Cash Outside the Office.* If checks and/or cash come in outside the office (such as at a fundraising event), we need to take special precautions to protect these receipts from theft and to ensure that no one is falsely accused of stealing funds:

- Two people need to prepare the deposit slip for the funds in duplicate.

- Both must count the cash and initial the cash count on the copy of the duplicate deposit slip kept by the organization.

- If the individuals accepting the contributions at the event know the names of the individuals making gifts in cash, they will provide a receipt using the pre-numbered receipt book. If the funds are received through a "pass the hat" style collection in which it is not possible to know who gave what amount, the individuals accepting the contributions will note that no receipts were provided to donors on the duplicate deposit slip.

- It is not necessary to write out a receipt for contributions made by check unless the donor requests a receipt. However, the individuals accepting the contributions should make a list of all checks received at the event, including the name of the donor and the amount of the contribution. They will compare this list to the deposit to be sure all checks have been included in the deposit.

- If no cash is received at the event, the individuals accepting the contributions by check will give the Secretary the list and the checks within 24 hours of the event.

- If there is cash in the deposit, one of the two individuals accepting contributions must deposit the funds immediately. If checks will be deposited with the cash, the individuals accepting the checks should be sure that the list of checks they prepare includes the donor's address as well as name.

- The duplicate receipt book and the list of checks received shall be given to the Secretary who will send acknowledgement letters.

The Secretary or the Secretary's designee shall train all volunteers in these procedures.

6. *Credit Card Contributions*. We do not accept contributions by credit card. If we decide to do that, we need to get accounting advice to make sure we have the proper controls in place.

7. *Acknowledging Donations*. While IRS rules require that we acknowledge all donations that are more than $75, our policy is to provide written acknowledgement for every gift we receive:

- The Secretary shall respond to each donation with a letter thanking the donor for their generosity:

- If the gift was cash (which includes a check), the letter should include the amount of the gift and state that the gift was cash.

- If the gift was donated property of some kind, the Secretary's letter does not need to and should not value the property. If the donor did receive something of value in return, the Secretary's letter must contain a description of the donation and a good faith estimate of the value of what we gave back to the donor.

- The letter should include the statement: "Thank you for your contribution of $_____, received on _____, 20__. [PICK ONE: "No goods or services were provided in exchange for your contribution" or "In exchange for your contribution, we gave you _____ whose fair market value was $__."]

In addition to thanking our donors and providing documentation the donor needs to deduct the contribution, the acknowledgment letter may alert donors whose amount is misstated to contact us to correct the error. Additionally, our records of the letters we send will help us keep an up-to-date record of how to contact all our donors.

8. *Posting Donor Names on Website*. The Secretary shall post the names of all donors (except those requesting anonymity) on our website. The website will indicate that we hope to acknowledge every donor. It will invite donors who are not listed to contact the Treasurer. In addition to publicly thanking all our donors, a donor whose check or cash was mis-reported, lost or stolen may alert us to the problem.

III. DISBURSEMENT OF FUNDS/ USE OF CORPORATE PROPERTY

A. PAYMENTS BY CHECK

RISKS

We face the risks that our funds will be spent on unauthorized items, that someone will steal our funds by taking blank checks or by writing checks to payees who are not our vendors, that someone will use corporate property for personal purposes or that payments we make will be improperly recorded.

POLICY

Make all disbursements from the organization's funds by check, with the exception of petty cash. This allows us to track how our funds are spent, who is spending them and who is authorizing expenditures.

PROCEDURES

1. *Opening Bank Accounts*. Bank accounts may be opened only upon authorization by the Board of Directors.

- All bank accounts must be opened with the organization's employer identification number (EIN).

- The Board shall approve the authorized signers on the organization's bank accounts.

- Because of the Treasurer's role in reconciling the bank statement, the Treasurer cannot be a check signer.

- If possible, the Secretary should not be a check signer because of his/her role in the custody and preparation of the checks.

2. *Custody of Checks*. The Secretary is the only person authorized to have access to unused check stock. The checks should be stored in a locked location and information about how to access them should be kept confidential from everyone but the President.

3. *Check Authorization*. All invoices will be forwarded immediately to the Treasurer for review and authorization to pay.

- The Treasurer will review all invoices for mathematical accuracy, agreement with a written invoice, conformity to budget or Board authorization and compliance with grant fund requirements.

- The Treasurer will ensure that all conditions and specifications on a contract or order have been satisfactorily fulfilled, including inventorying items received against packing slip counts.

- The Treasurer will code the invoice with the appropriate expense or chart of accounts line time number and other information as needed for accounting purposes.

- By approving an invoice, the Treasurer indicates that he/she has reviewed the invoice and authorizes a check.

- The Treasurer is responsible for timely follow-up on discrepancies and payment.

- The Treasurer will send approved invoices to the Secretary for payment.

4. *Expenses Not Invoiced.* In some cases, expenses may not be invoiced, such as rent. When such expenses are due, the Treasurer needs to ensure that the expense is in the budget and write a note authorizing payment of the expense and the amount of the expense and supply it to the Secretary.

4. *Payment by Checks.* Upon approval of the invoice and note by the Treasurer, the Secretary is authorized to prepare all checks and should do so.

If a check is voided, the check will have "VOID" written in large letters in ink on the face and have the signature portion of the check torn out. Voided checks will be kept on file.

In the event that it is necessary to issue a duplicate check for checks in an amount over $50, the Secretary will order a stop payment at the bank on the original check.

5. *Duties of Check Signers.* All checks will be signed by the signers designated by the Board of Directors. Prior to signing a check, a check signer will do the following:

- Compare the check to the original invoice or the Treasurer's note to pay the expense.

- Be sure that the Treasurer has initialed the invoice. This is to protect against the risk that you are paying based on a copy of the bill that has already been paid.

- Compare the amount on the check to the amount on the invoice or note.

- Compare the name of the payee on the check to the name on the invoice. Be sure that the names match exactly. This is to prevent an embezzler from using a legitimate invoice from, for example, Printing Company, to get a check payable to the embezzler's account at Printing LLC.

- Check the date on the invoice or the Treasurer's note against the date of signing the check. If the difference is more than 60 days, get written approval from the Treasurer before signing the check. This is to mitigate the risk that the organization is paying the same expense twice.

- Check to be sure that the amount of the check is not clearly unreasonable. For example, a $30,000 monthly payment for bookkeeping services would be unreasonable for most small nonprofits.

6. *Prohibited Practices.* In no event will:

- invoices be paid unless approved by the Treasurer;
- blank checks be signed in advance;
- a check signer sign a check made out to the signer;
- checks be made out to "cash," "bearer," etc.

Each check signer will be made aware that signing blank checks exposes our organization to theft since the bank is entitled to charge our account for any check that has a valid signature. A signed blank check is an invitation to theft.

7. *On-line Payments.* If we make online payments, we will make arrangements with the bank that allow the Treasurer to have online, read-only access to the account. We will also arrange with the bank to be sure that only the individuals the board has authorized as check signers will be permitted to authorize the payment of bills electronically. In addition to the monthly reconciliation, the Treasurer will periodically spot-check the account to compare the bank automatic payments with the vendor statements.

B. PETTY CASH FUNDS

RISKS

Payments by cash are not as completely documented and are not as easily monitored as payments by check and thus subject the organization to greater likelihood of errors and fraud.

POLICY

The Petty Cash Fund should only be used when payment by check is impracticable.

PROCEDURES

Administration of Petty Cash Fund. The Secretary is responsible for the administration of the Petty Cash Fund. The Fund shall be funded with checks made out to "Petty Cash—name of Secretary" and initially recorded in the Petty Cash Fund account. The Secretary will require receipts for all purchases and may ask those reimbursed to sign for money the Secretary provides as reimbursement.

The Secretary will record all cash purchases in a journal and save the receipts. When the fund gets low, the Secretary will apply to the Treasurer for authorization to reimburse the fund for the total amount expended. The check written to reimburse the Petty Cash Fund will be recorded in the appropriate expense accounts for the items that were purchased with Petty Cash, so that these expenditures made through the Petty Cash fund are properly classified by type—for example, postage, parking fees, etc.

C. EXPENSE REIMBURSEMENT

RISK

The organization does not have the same level of control over expenses incurred on behalf of the organization by those who pay with personal funds and seek reimbursement as it does for expenses paid directly by the corporation. The corporation is not in as good a position to determine whether the good or service purchased might have been obtained at a lower price elsewhere, whether there is a personal benefit to the person seeking reimbursement and how the expenditure fits in with the rest of the organization's budget.

POLICY

In proper circumstances, Board members, employees and volunteers are entitled to be reimbursed for expenses related to the organization that they incurred on behalf of the organization. To receive reimbursement, you must meet the following requirements:

- Your expense must have been authorized in advance by the Board or by the Secretary or later approved by the Board or the Secretary.

- Your expense must have been incurred for goods or services purchased for the organization.

- If your expense is for travel, the travel must be for work related to the organization. We will reimburse no more than the standard mileage rate for business use of a car as established by the IRS. The organization will reimburse meal expenses incurred in direct connection with the organization's business, or at the per diem rate established by the IRS.

PROCEDURES

To be reimbursed for expenses:

1. *Documentation*. You must provide reasonable documentation showing the date, amount and what the expense was for. Credit card receipts and store receipts that do not describe the purchase are not reasonable documentation. Your receipt must describe the purchase.

2. *Other Reimbursement*. Your voucher must reflect reimbursement from sources other than ours.

3. *Timely Submission*. You must submit your documentation with a request for payment within 60 days from the date the expense was incurred.

4. *Overpayment*. If we overpay you, you must return any excess reimbursement within a reasonable period of time.

D. PURCHASING

RISK

The corporation wants to ensure that all purchases on behalf of the corporation are authorized by the Board or by Board policies. Unauthorized purchases deplete the organization's resources and interfere with the Board's ability to govern properly.

POLICY

All purchases made on behalf of the organization must be made pursuant to the Board-approved budget or Board rules.

PROCEDURES

The Treasurer can authorize purchases of $_____ or less which conform to the Board's budget. The Board must approve purchases above that amount. The Board must authorize any purchase which does not conform to the Board's budget.

E. USE OF CORPORATE PROPERTY

RISKS

The corporation faces a risk that individuals will use corporate property without authorization for personal purposes. Usage reduces the life of property and eventually is an expense that the corporation assumes. It also betrays the trust of our donors who expect that the corporation will use its resources only for purposes that help us achieve our mission.

POLICY

Property and equipment owned by the corporation may only be used for corporate activities or activities approved by the corporation. They may not be used for personal purposes.

PROCEDURES

If a Board member, officer, employee, or volunteer wants to use corporate property or equipment for any purpose other than a corporate purpose, that individual must obtain permission from the Board of Directors.

IV. CREATION OF CORPORATE OBLIGATIONS

RISK

The corporation needs to ensure that any obligation undertaken in the corporate name is authorized by the corporation and is for a corporate and not a personal purpose.

A. CREDIT AND DEBIT CARDS

RISKS

Corporate credit or debit cards can be misused when people charge personal expenses on them, fail to obtain documentation showing that a purchase was for the corporation or put expenses on the corporate card for purchases that are embarrassing to the corporation.

POLICY

The corporation will not authorize the use of debit cards for any purposes. The Board will determine whether there is a compelling need for the corporation to obtain one or more credit cards. If the Board determines that credit cards are needed, the Board will authorize specific individuals to utilize a corporate credit card. A corporate cardholder may use the credit card only for official purposes directly related to the needs of the organization. The cardholder may not use a corporate credit card for personal purposes, even if he or she plans to reimburse the organization.

The following purchases are **not** allowed on the corporate credit card:

- Personal purchases
- Cash advances or loans
- Payroll advances
- Purchased for other organizations
- Alcohol
- Personal entertainment
- Fuel for personal vehicles
- Purchases from a business you own or operate unless pre-approved by the Board
- Any item inconsistent with the mission and values of the organization

An individual purchase shall not exceed $_____. Aggregate monthly purchases shall not exceed $_____.

PROCEDURES

In order to use the card, the cardholder must follow these procedures:

1. *Cardholder Agreement.* Upon issuing a corporate card to a cardholder, the cardholder must sign a statement that the cardholder has read and understands this Credit Card policy and will reimburse the corporation for any personal charges on the card.

2. *Advance Approval.* The Board must give advance written approval to make a purchase whenever practical. The cardholder's purchase request should describe the purchase and cost.

3. *Original Receipts.* The cardholder must keep the original receipt that describes each purchase made on the card. The credit card receipt is not sufficient.

4. *Notification of use of the credit card*: The cardholder will email the Treasurer after each use of the corporate credit card noting the date, vendor, and amount of each charge made. This is will allow the Treasurer to be aware of the cash that will be required to pay the credit card bill and alert the Treasure to potential unnecessary use of the credit card.

5. *Expense Form.* Within 5 days after the end of the billing cycle, the cardholder must prepare and sign an expense detail form and attach original receipts and a copy of the purchase request. In the case of meals, the statement must include the names of all persons at the meal and a brief description of the business purpose, in accordance with IRS regulations.

6. *Approval by Treasurer.* The cardholder must give the expense detail form to the Treasurer for approval. The Treasurer shall review each purchase to ensure that it was reasonable, necessary and the best value for the organization. The Treasurer will reconcile the expense detail form to the credit card billing statement, authorize payment and follow up on any inconsistencies.

7. *Notification of Loss/Theft.* The cardholder must notify the bank and the organization immediately in the event that the card is lost or stolen.

B. BORROWING AND LINES OF CREDIT

RISKS

The organization needs to ensure that borrowing in the corporate name is authorized.

POLICY

The Board must approve application for and acceptance of any Lines of Credit. Once the Line of Credit is authorized by the Board, the Treasurer can authorize borrowing within the limit of the line of credit up to $_____. The Board must approve all borrowing against the line of credit greater than that amount.

The full Board must approve any other borrowing of funds in the name of the corporation, including the use of any promissory notes. The Board must give very serious attention to be sure that the corporation will have sufficient funds available to repay any loans or lines of credit on time.

V. BANK RECONCILIATION AND ON-LINE MONITORING

RISKS

Even the most honest and attentive individual makes mistakes. Monitoring allows us to uncover errors. If our records and the bank records do not agree, it is likely that our records are wrong.

Monitoring also assists us in identifying discrepancies between our accounting records and our banking records that suggest theft or fraud, checks signed by unauthorized signers, and identity theft.

POLICY

The Treasurer will monitor the corporation's accounts regularly and will prepare a written reconciliation of all bank or investment accounts which proves that the balances presented on our financial reports agree with the records of the financial institution.

PROCEDURES

1. *Records to Treasurer*. The Secretary shall provide the Treasurer with a copy of all records of deposits, disbursements (checks written), and other bank transactions and of our accounting records for review.

2. *Bank Statement*. The corporation will direct the bank to send the bank statements to the Treasurer.

3. *Reconciliation*. The Treasurer will reconcile the bank statement monthly. The reconciliation should be done within 7 days of receiving the statement, as follows:

- Check all checks for correct signatures and number of signatures and protest to the bank any incorrect signatures.

- Review the checks in the bank records to ensure that:
    - ◊ the name of the payee, the amount of the check and the date of the check agree with the corporation's accounting records;
    - ◊ whoever the check was made out to was the depositor of the check; and
    - ◊ each check has a valid signature.

- Compare the bank deposit records with our accounting records to determine whether each deposit recorded in the accounting records agrees with the bank record.

- Check the cash entries in the receipt book against the bank record of deposits to ensure that all cash was deposited.

- Check whether the ending balance in the general ledger cash account agrees with the bank statement, after making the adjustments on the bank reconciliation form.

- List all outstanding checks. On all checks outstanding over 90 days, take appropriate action.

- List all deposits in accounting records not yet recorded by the bank.

- If the reconciliation is done electronically, the Treasurer must check off on a form to be given to the Board that he or she performed the review above.

4. *On-Line Banking*. Both the Secretary and Treasurer should have on-line, read-only access to the bank account. The Secretary should use the on-line access to check his/her work. The Secretary should review the account on-line on a weekly basis to check for identity theft that is diverting corporate funds. The Treasurer can reconcile the bank statements and spot-check the on-line payments as described above.

5. *Return of Cancelled Checks by the Bank.* The Board will determine whether it is necessary to direct the bank to return the cancelled checks with the bank statement. If the Board determines that it will not require return of the cancelled checks, it will establish procedures to ensure retention of the electronic images of the checks for at least 3 years.

FORM 990 REVIEW POLICY

Each board member shall be provided a copy of the Form 990 for review before it is filed and shall review it. The board may charge a committee of the board to conduct a more thorough review of the Form 990. The committee shall report to the board in a timely fashion the results of its review of the Form 990.

JOINT VENTURES POLICY

A joint venture is any joint ownership or contractual arrangement through which there is an agreement to jointly undertake a specific business enterprise, investment, or exempt-purpose activity. The board shall carefully consider any agreement under which the corporation plans to participate in a joint venture with another organization that is not exempt under §501(c)(3). The board shall arrange for legal review to evaluate the organization's participation in the joint venture and to ensure that the agreement does not violate the corporation's §501(c)(3) status.

MINUTES OF FIRST MEETING OF BOARD OF DIRECTORS

NAME OF CORPORATION: _____

The initial meeting of the Board of Directors of the above corporation, an Oregon corporation, was held at Portland, Oregon, on _____, 20___, at ___ .m., pursuant to a call for such meeting by _____, the incorporator.

Present were the following Directors, who constitute a quorum: _____
_____
_____.

By unanimous vote of the Board of Directors, _____
_____ was chosen chairperson of the meeting and
_____ was chosen to serve as Secretary of the meeting.

The Secretary presented to the meeting a Waiver of Notice of this meeting, signed by the initial Board of Directors of the corporation, and the Chairperson directed that such Waiver be attached to the minutes of the meeting.

Report on Articles. The incorporator reported that the Articles of Incorporation have been filed in the appropriate state office for the state of Oregon, and were stamped on _____, 20___.

Bylaws. The incorporator then submitted to the meeting a form of Bylaws for the regulation of the affairs of the corporation. These Bylaws were read, and after discussion, it was unanimously

DECIDED: that the Bylaws presented to this meeting are adopted as the Bylaws of this corporation, and that a copy of these Bylaws be placed in the records of the corporation.

Officers. The Board of Directors then proceeded to the election of officers. Nominations were made, and the following persons were duly elected to the following offices:

    President—

    Secretary—

Bank Account. The chairperson then stated that it was desirable to designate a depository for the funds of the corporation. It was unanimously

DECIDED: that _____ is selected as a depository for the funds of this corporation. The President of the Corporation is authorized to establish these accounts. Funds shall be withdrawn from this depository on checks of this corporation signed by one of the following:

    Signer—

    Signer—

and may be payable to bearer, or to the order of, and for the use and benefit of, the signers of the checks.

Borrowing Power. The Chairperson stated that the next order of business would be to discuss the necessity of the corporation borrowing funds from time to time for business purposes. After deliberation and discussion, it was unanimously

DECIDED: that the corporation is authorized to borrow such sums of money not to exceed a total amount of $_____ at any one time without further authorization; and

DECIDED: that the officers of the corporation are authorized to negotiate the terms of such borrowing on behalf of the corporation and to execute on behalf of the corporation any promissory notes, instruments, and other documents necessary or reasonable to evidence such borrowing from banks, institutions or other third persons.

Reimbursement of Expenses. It was then suggested that the Secretary of the corporation be authorized to pay all expenses and to reimburse any persons for expenses made in connection with the organization of the corporation. It was unanimously

DECIDED: that the Secretary of this corporation is authorized to pay all charges and expenses incident to or arising out of the organization of this corporation and to reimburse any person that has made any disbursements for this corporation.

Salary and Expenses of Officers. It was then suggested that the officers of the corporation be paid no salary but that the corporation should pay all reasonable and documented expenses incurred by the officers in the performance of their duties. It was unanimously

DECIDED: that the officers shall receive no salaries and that the corporation is to reimburse each officer for reasonable and documented business expenses.

Ratification of Incorporator's Actions. The Chairperson then stated that any acts of the incorporator, performed so far on behalf of this corporation, should be ratified and confirmed as the duly authorized acts of the corporation. The unanimous decision was as follows:

DECIDED: that any and all acts of the incorporator of this corporation are hereby ratified and approved as duly authorized acts of this corporation in all respects as if they had been done pursuant to specific authority granted by this corporation.

Fiscal Year. The Chairperson next proposed that the fiscal year of the corporation begin on the first day of _____ and end on the last day of _____. The Board unanimously

DECIDED: that the fiscal year of the corporation shall be as proposed above.

OPTIONAL ITEMS

Tax Exemption. It was proposed that the corporation apply for tax exemption under Section 501(c)(3) of the Internal Revenue Code and for all other applicable federal, state, regional and local tax exemptions and benefits. The unanimous decision was as follows:

DECIDED: that the President shall have the authority to apply on behalf of the corporation for tax exemption under Section 501(c)(3) of the Internal Revenue Code and for all other applicable federal, state, regional, and local tax exemptions and benefits.

Criteria for Members. It was suggested that the criteria for members be established. The Board unanimously

DECIDED: that the criteria for membership in this corporation shall be:

_____

_____

_____

READ AND APPROVED:

_____

Chairperson

MINUTES OF MEETING OF THE BOARD OF DIRECTORS

NAME OF CORPORATION: _____

Date:

Time:

Place:

Directors Attending:

Notice (if required): The Secretary reported that the attached notice of the meeting as required by the Bylaws was properly given to all members. [Attach Notice]

Quorum: A sufficient number of Directors were present to constitute a quorum.

Prior Minutes Approved. The minutes from the last meeting of the Board of Directors were presented by the Secretary. The minutes were adopted by a vote of _____ to _____.

Committee Reports:

Agenda Item:

Discussion:

Decision:

Agenda Item:

Discussion:

Decision:

Agenda Item:

Discussion:

Decision:

Agenda Item:

Discussion:

Decision:

There being no further business, the meeting was adjourned.

_____, Secretary

MINUTES OF MEETING OF THE MEMBERS

NAME OF CORPORATION: _____

Date:

Time:

Place:

Number of Votes Represented at the Meeting:

Quorum: A sufficient number of votes were present to constitute a quorum.

CONSENT ITEMS AND REPORTS

Notice [if required]: The Secretary reported that the attached notice of the meeting as required by the Bylaws was properly given to all members. [Attach Notice]

Other Consent Items and Reports:

ACTION ITEMS

Agenda Item:

Discussion:

DECISION:

Agenda Item:

Discussion:

DECISION:

Agenda Item:

Discussion:

DECISION:

Agenda Item:

Discussion:

DECISION:

ADJOURNMENT: There being no further business, the meeting was adjourned.

SIGNED: _____

        SECRETARY

PROMISSORY NOTE

Date: _____

Place: _____

For value received, _____ [hereinafter called Corporation] promises to pay to the order of _____ _____, whose address is _____ _____, the sum of _____ _____ ($_____), in monthly payments of $_____, with the first payment due on _____, 20___ and a like payment due on the _____ day of each month thereafter and continuing until paid in full, with interest thereon at the rate of _____ percent (____ %) per annum from the date of this note until paid, interest to be paid annually and being included in the minimum regular payments above required. If any of the above-described payments are not so paid, all principal and interest becomes immediately due and collectible at the option of the holder of this note. If this note is placed in the hands of an attorney for collection, I promise and agree to pay the holder's reasonable attorneys fees and collection costs, whether or not a suit or action is filed, and including any attorneys fees and costs incurred on appeal.

_____

Signature, as Agent for Corporation

PROXY VOTE

I, the undersigned, a member of _____, do hereby appoint ___ _____ as attorney and agent for me, and in my name, place, and stead, to vote as my proxy, at any regular or special membership meeting of the above-named corporation to be held between the date of this proxy and _____, 20___, unless sooner revoked, with full power to cast all votes that my membership in the above-named corporation entitles me to cast including but not limited to votes at meetings, votes by written ballot, consents to actions without meetings, and waivers of notices of meetings, as if I were personally present or otherwise voting.

I hereby revoke all proxies made before this by me.

IN WITNESS WHEREOF, I have executed this proxy on _____, 20___.

SIGNED: _____

RECORDS RETENTION AND DESTRUCTION POLICY

This corporation is committed to ensuring that records are retained as appropriate and as required by law and that unlawful destruction of documents does not occur.

A. SUPERVISION OF RECORD RETENTION EFFORT

The Executive Director [or, in a direct management nonprofit, the Board Secretary] or his/her designee shall serve as the Record Retention Supervisor. The Supervisor will manage records in accord with these guidelines as well as to ensure compliance with all local, state, and federal laws. The Supervisor may establish guidelines for additional records.

The Supervisor shall develop a policy for retention of electronic records, including emails. The electronic retention policy shall determine what files need to be kept and shall include backup procedures, archiving of documents, and regular check-ups of the reliability of the system.

B. OBSERVANCE OF RETENTION POLICY.

All employees and volunteers will follow records retention guidelines set out in these guidelines and by the Record Retention Supervisor. Records outlined in the Record Retention Schedule should be retained for the length of time provided on the schedule and destroyed at the end of the stated period.

C. DURATION/SPECIAL CIRCUMSTANCES

The Record Retention Supervisor may adjust the duration of retention as needed by the corporation, provided the term meets the minimum retention requirements of local, state, and federal laws.

D. DOCUMENT DESTRUCTION

No officer, director, employee, or volunteer of this corporation shall knowingly destroy a document with the intent to obstruct or influence the investigation or proper administration of any matter within the jurisdiction of any department or agency of the United States or any state or its subdivisions.

E. SUSPENSION OF RECORD DESTRUCTION SCHEDULE

In the event the corporation becomes involved in any governmental investigation, audit or litigation, the further disposal of documents shall be suspended until such time as the Record Retention Supervisor, with advice of an attorney, determines otherwise. All staff and volunteers shall be notified of the suspension of regular disposal procedures.

F. DISCIPLINE

Any employee found to have knowingly violated this policy and destroyed records shall be subject to appropriate disciplinary action up to and including discharge.

G. RETENTION OF DOCUMENTS

[This is a guide for smaller corporations. Larger corporations should develop their own schedule, which generally would not be part of this policy.]

The following documents shall be retained as described:

Type of Document	Minimum Requirement
Accounts payable ledgers and schedules	7 years
Audit reports	Permanently
Bank Reconciliations	2 years
Bank statements	3 years
Checks (for important payments and purchases)	Permanently
Contracts, mortgages, notes and leases (expired)	7 years
Contracts (still in effect)	Permanently
Correspondence (general)	2 years
Correspondence (legal and important matters)	Permanently
Correspondence (with customers and vendors)	2 years
Deeds, mortgages, and bills of sale	Permanently
Depreciation Schedules	Permanently
Duplicate deposit slips	2 years
Employment applications	3 years
Expense Analyses/expense distribution schedules	7 years
Year End Financial Statements	Permanently
Insurance Policies (expired)	3 years
Insurance policies, current accident reports, claims, etc.	Permanently
Internal audit reports	3 years
IRS application materials and exemption letter	Permanently
Articles of Incorporation, amendments, bylaws, minutes	Permanently
Patents and related Papers	Permanently
Payroll records and summaries	7 years
Personnel files (terminated employees)	7 years
Restricted donations and endowments	Permanently
Retirement and pension records	Permanently
Tax returns and worksheets	Permanently
Timesheets	7 years
Trademark registrations and copyrights	Permanently
Withholding tax statements	7 years

TRANSPARENCY POLICY

The corporation desires to be as transparent as possible consistent with good management and its obligations to protect the privacy of donors, employees, volunteers, clients, and other persons or entities. The corporation shall make its Articles of Incorporation, any amendments or restatements to the Articles, its bylaws, its Conflict of Interest policy, its Form 1023 and related correspondence with the IRS, its most recent three years of the Form 990, and recent financial statements available to the public for inspection and copying upon request.

The documents described above shall be available for inspection upon request at the corporation's office during regular business hours.

The corporation may comply with the requirement that it provide copies by posting these documents on the corporation's website in a .pdf format.

WAIVER OF NOTICE OF MEETING OF THE BOARD OF DIRECTORS

NAME OF CORPORATION: _____

We, the undersigned, the directors of this corporation, each waive notice of the date, time, place, and purposes of the meeting of board of directors on _____, 20___, at _____ __.m., at _____, Oregon. We consent to the transaction of any business which may properly come before this meeting.

_____ DATE: _____

_____ DATE: _____

_____ DATE: _____

WAIVER OF NOTICE OF MEETING OF MEMBERS

NAME OF CORPORATION: _____

We, the undersigned, the members of this corporation, each waive notice of the date, time, place, and purposes of the meeting of the members on _____, 20____, at _____ ____.m., at _____, Oregon. We consent to the transaction of any business which may properly come before this meeting.

_____ DATE: _____

_____ DATE: _____

_____ DATE: _____

WHISTLEBLOWER POLICY

This corporation seeks to conduct all of its activities in a responsible, legal, and ethical manner. All officers, directors, employees, and volunteers of this corporation must practice integrity and honesty in fulfilling their responsibilities and must comply with all applicable laws and regulations. The purpose of this Whistleblower Policy is to provide a mechanism to report irresponsible, illegal or unethical behavior.

WHISTLEBLOWER COMPLAINTS

If an officer, director, employee or volunteer should discover information leading him or her to believe that a serious wrongdoing or illegal or unethical behavior has occurred in this corporation, he or she shall report this information to the President of the Board. If the President of the Board is not available or is implicated in the wrongdoing, he or she shall report the information to another Board officer.

The President or Board officer shall conduct an investigation. Reports of violations will be kept confidential to the extent possible, consistent with the need to conduct an investigation. Appropriate corrective action will be taken if warranted by the investigation.

NO RETALIATION

1. The corporation's policy is to protect from retaliation and discrimination any person who in good faith:

> (a) refused to participate in any federal, state or local offense; reported to law enforcement or other officials any information that the person believed to be evidence relating to the commission or possible commission of any federal, state or local offense; or initiated, testified or aided in proceedings related to the above;

> (b) initiated or aided in civil proceedings;

> (c) refused to engage in a violation of a governmental administrative regulation; reported any information related to a violation of governmental administrative regulations; commenced, testified at , aided or participated in a governmental adjudicatory proceeding;

> (d) refused to engage in or attempted to stop fraud against, gross waste of or abuse of authority by the government; or

> (e) reported other information about wrongdoing, illegal or unethical behavior pursuant to this Policy.

An officer, director, employee, or volunteer of this corporation shall not, with intent to retaliate or discriminate, take any action harmful to any person described above, including interference with the lawful employment or livelihood of any person.

2. In the event that an officer, director, employee, or volunteer intends, for any reason, to take any action harmful to any person who has acted as described above, the officer, director, employee, or volunteer must obtain the approval for such action from the board of directors prior to taking action. Such approvals must be obtained even if the officer, director, employee, or volunteer believes that the person who provided information to the law enforcement officer or other official provided untruthful information.

Index

A

Accounting. *See* Financial management; Financial recordkeeping; Financial reports
Address. *See* Registered offices
Affiliated organizations   113, 200
  Form 1023   136
Agricultural organizations   112
  tax exemption   110
Amateur sports
  tax exemption   96
Annual meetings. *See* Board of directors: meetings: annual; *See also* Members: meetings: annual
Apostolic organizations   113
Articles of incorporation   4
  §501(c)(3) exemption
    organized for exempt purposes   96
    provision prohibiting political activity   98
    provision showing organized for exempt purposes   96
  affiliated organizations   191
  amendments   713
    approval by board   715
    approval by designated individuals   715
    approval by members   715
    by board without member approval   714
    by membership corporations   714
    by nonmembership corporations   713
    class voting   716–717
    filing amendments   717
    mutual benefit corporations   716
    public benefit corporations   716
    religious corporations   716
    tax exempt organizations   717
  described   34
  disposition of assets on dissolution   37, 747
  filing   34, 41
    online   35
  filling out   34, 35
  getting a copy   712
  indemnification   37
  limiting liability of directors   37, 39
  management by someone other than board   19
  naming Board optional   39
  optional provisions   39
  provision requiring cause for removal of directors   318
  provisions that must be in Articles   35–36
  relationship to bylaws   54
  restating   718
  reviewing   712
Associations   6. *See also* Homeowners associations
  advantages and disadvantages   13
  as incorporator   39
  as person   163
  as substantial contributors   154, 156
  bank account   13
  books and records   7
  control   7
  holding property   13
  liability   7
  neighborhood   726
  normalcy period   165
  registration   7
  tax consequences   7
  tax exemption   93
Attorney General   72. *See also* Department of Justice; Reports: Attorney General
  changing to mutual benefit corporation   717
  consent to mergers   732
  consent to sale of all assets   743
  dissolution investigation   748
  judicial dissolution   755
  notice of administrative dissolution   754
  notice of dissolution   750
Audits   643
  A-133 audit. *See herein* federal funds audit
  choosing an auditor   644–650
  CT-12 audit   646
  federal funds audit   647–650
    auditor's responsibilities   648–650
    focus   649–650
    nonprofit's responsibilities   648
    preparation   650
  Form 990 audit   646
  funding source audit   645
  independent audit by CPA   645
  payroll tax audit   646
  preparing for   646–650
  should you have one?   642–650
  types   645–650

B

Ballot measures

INDEX

communications with members 186, 196
direct lobbying 183
independent expenditures 665
not political activity to IRS 173
Oregon political committee 201, 665, 666
Oregon political restrictions 669
Oregon voter registration 653
political activity under Oregon law 652, 664
public as legislature 183
Ballots. *See* Board meetings: voting; Members: voting
Bank accounts. *See also* Handling funds
IRS seizure for nonpayment of taxes 250
need for tax identification number 47
Bingo, raffles or gaming. *See* Fundraising: bingo, raffles or gaming
Form 1023 133
licenses 487, 488
exceptions 488
Board. *See* Board of directors
Board committees 23, 24, 295, 336–340. *See also* Board duties: committees
advisory and task-oriented committees 340
audit committee 339
board and committee minutes policy 338
executive 724
executive compensation committee 339
exercising board authority 40, 66, 83, 336, 724
finance 283
finance committee 339
fundraising committees 339
inspection of records 386
investment committee 339
limitations on powers 67, 84
not exercising board authority 66, 83
personnel committee 339
quorum and action 66, 84
Board duties 265–287
actively manage 58
audits 281
check signing 282
community relations 275
corporate purpose 267–287
delegated management 272–287
choosing executive director 276
concerns of smaller corporations 285–287
definition 268
founder as executive director 277
limitations on delegation 275
oversight 278
terms of delegation 273
direct management

definition 267
founders 271
how to manage 269–287
independent contractors 271
members 272
protecting corporate status 271
recordkeeping 270
duty of due care 298
duty of loyalty 303
duty to follow corporate purpose 298
endowments 281
executive compensation 281, 282
finance committee 283
fundraising by board 275
how to manage
management tasks 269
illegal distributions 282
independent contractors 287
internal controls 285
investments 280
management 267–287
payment of taxes 287
personnel policies 278
records retention 278
restricted funds 280, 286
strategic planning 267
suspicious circumstances 284
Board meetings 322. *See also* Open meetings laws
action by majority vote 62–63, 80
action without 65, 82
agenda 328
annual 324
attendance 296
board packets 294
by computer 64, 297, 327
by email 64, 297
by teleconference 297, 327
by telephone 64, 81–82
call for meeting 324
conducting 327
conflicts of interest 299. *See also* Conflicts of interest
(c)(3) and (c)(4) organizations 301
consent by email 297
consent without a meeting 297
decision-making 297
decision-making process 328
defined 297
duty of due care 298
duty of loyalty 299
duty to follow corporate purpose 298
emergency 323

INDEX

executive director reports 295
executive sessions 326, 330
frequency 324
getting information 292–304
holding effective meetings 332
homeowner associations 299
location 326
minutes 330
  approval of 328
  waiver of notice 325
  where to store 332
notice 325. *See also* Notices
objection to action 329
organizational meeting 45
presiding officer 328
proxy voting prohibited 330
quorum 62, 79–80, 327, 328
  fixed number on board 327
  proxies 328
  variable number on board 327
regular 323
  63, 80–81
Roberts Rules of Order 56, 329
special 63, 81, 323
standard of conduct 297–304
valid meetings 297
voting
  ballot 330, 336
  email 297, 330, 336
  telephone poll 330, 336
waiver 325
who can attend 325–327
why have meetings? 322–323
Board of directors 4, 19, 289–304. *See also* Board meetings; *See also* Board duties; Board meetings
  access to records 681
  action without meeting 65
    telephone poll 330–333, 336
    vote by ballot 330, 336
    vote by email 330, 336
  advisory boards 357
  amendments to Articles of Incorporation by 713–714
  appointment of directors 21
  board member defined 19
  changes in board
    notification to Secretary of State not required 712
  clarifying board expectations 312–320
  committees. *See* Board committees
  community-based organizations 313
  composition of board 21, 305–320

conflicts of interest 299. *See also* Conflicts of interest
  (c)(3) and (c)(4) organizations 301
  proper handling 358
decisions 54, 322–351
delegated management 266
  members 285
  when to delegate 272
designation of directors 21
direct management 266
director defined 19
dissolution
  disposition of assets 747
  liability for improper disposition of assets 748
  role of board 749
diversity 308
duties 299
  actively manage 19, 723
  due care 298
  follow corporate purpose 298
  loyalty 299
election of directors 21
  by board 60
  by members 77
email 81
  consent by 335
  meetings 64
  notice of meetings 64
  voting by 330
evaluating effectiveness of board 350–351
ex officio directors 68, 77
expiration of term 316
Form 1023 listing of 128–129
homeowners association 299
how board operates 321–351
indemnification 360
  bylaws provisions 69, 86
institutional boards 315–320
limitations on powers 40
limited liability 359
  Articles of incorporation language 37
loans to directors and officers 303
majority vote 329
management. *See See* Board duties
  delegation to others 723
membership corporations
  election by members 367, 373, 377, 381
  limiting liability of directors 40
merger
  approval of 738, 739
  submission of plan to members 739–740
most vulnerable to lawsuits 356–357
multiple roles of directors 22

nonmembership corporations   58
  committees of board   65
  limiting liability of directors   40
number of directors   20
  fixed   59, 76
  setting the number   59, 76
  variable   59, 76
orientation   311
overlapping   260
perpetuating wisdom   351
personal liability   5, 353
  agreement to be liable   355
  breach of duty of loyalty   353
  clauses limiting   39–40
  excessive lobbying   180, 191
  failure to act with due care   353
  insurance   362
  misuse of fiscal sponsorship   225
  protection against   357, 441
    provision in Articles   360
policies   34, 54, 296, 345–351, 720
  board policy manual   46, 296, 350
  delegated management   347–351
  direct management   346–351
  Form 990 governance   346
  gift acceptance   280, 482
powers   5, 19
  to amend Articles of Incorporation   714, 715
powers exercised by other than Board   721
protection of directors   304
publicly supported organization
  representative governing body   160
qualifications of directors   20, 59, 76
recruiting   306
removal   316, 319–320
  appointed directors   318
  automatic   319
  by members with cause   41
  designated directors   318
  directors elected by directors   317
  directors elected by members   318
  in membership corporation   77
  in nonmembership corporation   60
  missing meetings   319
replacing   316
resignation   316
restatement of Articles of Incorporation   718
retaining   306
sale of assets   742
  submission of plan to members   743
spin-off organizations   315
staff sitting on board   310
staggered boards   22, 60, 76, 77

standard of conduct   23
terms of directors   22, 60, 76, 77
  staggered   22, 60, 77
transitions of boards   313–320
vacancy   319
  in membership corporation   78
  in nonmembership corporation   61
variable size   59, 76, 77
  quorum   79
  quorum issues   62
  staggered terms   60
who can sue directors   355
Board of trade   110
Board policy manual. *See* Board of directors: policies
Books. *See* Records; Financial recordkeeping; Financial reports
Budgets   518–545
  administrative costs   531
  basic budget worksheet   529
  board's role   544–545
  capital budgets   519, 540–545
  cash flow projections   519, 541–545
  cash flow projection worksheet   542
  contributions   523
  corporate donations   523
  cost allocation   532–545
    choosing method   535–545
    management costs   535–545
    plans   536–545
  cost center budget   531
  developmental steps   522
  direct costs   534–545
  employer taxes   527
  fiscal year   519
  foundation grants   523
  fringe benefits   527
  functional   530
  functional budget sample   536–537
  fundraising costs   532–545
  funds from prior years   521
  government grants and contracts   522
  grant analysis table   522
  grant budget   519
  grants
    narrative   538–545
    new projects   538–545
  guidelines   520
  interest   525
  investment fees   525
  membership fees   525
  notes   523
  organization budget   519

INDEX

process models   543–545
program service fees   524
projecting income   522
reasons for   519
restricted funds   539–545
salaries   526
shared costs   534–545
special events   485, 523
terminology   519
Business activities   203–218
  business plan   14, 205
  email
    unsolicited promotions   501
  investments   497
  joint ventures   218
  product sales   494
  program fees   492
  running a business   204
  social enterprise   495
  threat to exemption   496
Business identification number (BIN)   614
Business leagues   110
Business organizations
  §501(c)(6)   110
  cooperative   8
  general partnerships   9
  limited liability companies   10
  limited partnership   10
  profit corporations   9
  qualified directors   359
  sole proprietorship   11
  tax exemption   110
Business plan. *See* Business activities
Bylaws   52–88
  §501(c)(3) exemption
    organized for exempt purposes   96
  amending   70, 728–729
    approval by third party   729
    by membership corporations   41, 728
    by nonmembership corporations   728–729
    by tax-exempt organizations   729
  and board policies   720
  annual meetings   726
  committees   65, 82
    exercising board authority   724
  conflict management   57
  consent of members   726
  corporate indemnity   69
  cut and paste method   53
  described   34
  drafting tips   54
  expulsion of members   726
  focus on governance   55

indemnity provision   69
inspection of membership list   727
inspection of records   727
internal consistency   55
majority vote   724
membership corporations   70–88
  amendments   87–88
  board of directors   75
  corporate indemnity   86
  members provisions   71
  officers   84
nonmembership corporations   57
  amendments   70
  board of directors   58
  nonmembership provision   58
  officers   67
officers   67, 84
pitfalls   722
purpose   57, 71
  updating   722
quorum   723
record retention   679
relationship to Articles   55, 720
relationship to board resolutions   54
relationship to other rules   53
relationship to the law   55
removal of directors   726, 727, 60, 77
reviewing   718
  membership corporations   725
  nonmembership corporations   727
  tips   720
Roberts Rules   56
supermajority vote   725
term of directors   723
understandibility   56
voting by email   724
voting by proxy   726
voting by telephone poll   724
who runs corporation   723

C

Candidate appearances   176
Candidate debates   175
Cemetery associations   110, 113
Chamber of commerce   110
Charitable solicitations. *See* Solicitations
Charities
  public benefit corporations   28
  state tax exemptions   239–244
  tax exemption   93, 94
  tax returns   247–262
Childcare

INDEX

Form 1023   134
Churches   102
Classes of members. *See* Members
   obligations   371
Closing corporation. *See* Dissolution
Committees. *See* Board committees
Compliance   676–708
Condominiums
   bylaws   70
Confidential information   684–706
Conflicts of interest. *See* Board of directors; Board meetings
   approval by outsiders   303
   (c)(3) and (c)(4) organizations   301
   defined   299
   employees on the board   23
   excess benefits transactions   700–706
   Form 1023   128
   how to handle   358
   insiders   700–706
   membership corporations
      notice to members   73, 373, 374
   mutual benefit corporations   302
   occurrence among nonprofits   300
   permissible action in spite of conflicts   358
   proper handling   300–304
   public benefit corporations   301
   religious corporations   301
   responsibility of board   23
Connected organizations. *See* Affiliated organizations
Consolidations. *See* Mergers
Contributions. *See* Handling funds: acknowledgment letter to donors
   accounting   585–612
   (c)(4) notice   505
   donor acknowledgement   481
   donor acknowledgement letters   694–706
   Form 1023   135
   unreimbursed expenses
      before receiving exemption   108
   unreimbursed expenses as   698
Cooperatives   8, 112
   tax exemption denied   110
   use of word restricted   33
Corporate offices. *See* Registered offices
Corporate sponsorships. *See* Unrelated business income
Corporation sole   33
Crop financing corporations   113

D

Daycare. *See* Childcare
Department of Justice   681. *See also* Attorney General
   registration with   47–51
   restricted funds   228
Development foundation   106
Direct lobbying. *See* Lobbying election
Directors. *See* Board of directors; Executive director
Disqualified persons   163–164
   excess benefits transactions   700
      definition of disqualified persons   700
   fee/activity supported organizations
      definition of disqualified person   163–164
   Form 990   259
   Form 1023   128
   publicly supported organizations
      definition of disqualified person   153
      lumping together rules   153
      two percent limitation   153
   substantial contributor is owned by   156
   substantial contributor owns   156
   supporting organizations   105
Dissolution   745–756
   activities after   755
   administrative   753
   adoption by members   749
   approval by the board   749
   Articles of Dissolution   750
   creditors   751
   effect   753
   involuntary   753
   issues   746
   judicial   755
   notice to Attorney General   750
   plan   747, 748, 749, 750
   reinstatement   754–755
   revocation   750
   tax exempt corporations   756
   voluntary   746
      by board   748
      by incorporators   748
      members   748
      procedure   748
      third parties   748
   winding up affairs   753
Donations. *See* Contributions

E

Educational organizations
   tax exemption   94

INDEX

Email
  lobbying by employees   179
  meetings   64, 82
  notices   64, 81, 685
  unsolicited promotions   500
Employee handbook   399
  administration   423–426
  amendments to   420–426
  distribution   422–426
Employee insurance associations   112
Employees   393, 394–426. *See also* Payroll
  Affordable Care Act of 2010   629
  classified as independent contractors   426
  compensation of high-ranking employees   424
  comp time   396–426
  disability leave   414
  disciplinary action   417
  discrimination   398–426, 399–409
  dismissal   417–426, 423–426
  evaluation   416
  evaluation of the executive director   424–426
  family leave laws   412
  flexible benefits plans   630
  fringe benefits   627–631
  health and disability insurance   628
  jury duty   414
  medical records   420–426
  military leave   414
  on the board of directors   310
  optional leave   414
  paid time off   628
  personnel records   420–426
  pre-tax dollar plans   630
  retirement plans   630–631
  termination of employment   418–426
  unionization   399–426, 400–409
  volunteers who are paid   426
  wage and hour laws   394–426
    enforcement   397–426
    who must follow laws   394
  worker compensation laws   413
Employer identification number   47, 551, 614. *See also* Tax identification number
  online application   48
Endowments   281
Excess benefits transactions   700. *See also* Conflicts of interest: excess benefits transactions
Executive director
  as independent contractor   440
  as officer   68, 343, 85
  defined   19
  evaluation by board   424–426

  illegal authority
    making board-level decisions   724
  mergers   736
  personal liability
    excessive lobbying   180, 191
    political activities   180
  role   4
Executive sessions. *See* Board meetings: executive sessions
Expenditure responsibility   234

F

Federal election rules. *See* Political activity
Federal tax exemption   91–118
  §501(c)(3)   91, 93
    advance or definitive ruling   109
    commercial activity   97
    cost of applying   109
    criteria   93–118
    effective date of exemption   107
    lobbying   98. *See also* Lobbying; Lobbying election
    political activity   98. *See also* Political activity
    Who must apply?   107
  §501(c)(4)   91, 109
  agricultural organizations   110
  business leagues   110
  changes in activities   699
  civic leagues   109
  classifications   99
    public charities   99, 101
  compliance   692–706
  contributions. *See* Handling funds
    before receiving exemption   108
    unreimbursed expenses   698
  cost of applying   115
  donor acknowledgement letters   694
    contents of letter   696
    gifts   694
    non-cash contributions   697
    penalties   697
    quid pro quo contributions   695
      exceptions   697
    unreimbursed expenses   698
  do you want tax exemption?   92
  fraternal societies   111
  group exemptions   117, 699
  horticultural organizations   110
  inurement   97
  labor unions   110
  non (c)(3) exempt groups   110
  political organizations   112

INDEX

private benefit   97
public charities. *See* Public charities
public inspection of records   116
revocation of exemption   248
schools   699
social clubs   111
social welfare organizations   109
veterans organizations   112
Federal tax exemption application
  application for §501(c)(3)
    advance or definitive ruling   109
    articles of incorporation   36
    cost of applying   109
    effective date of exemption   107
    who must apply   107
  application for non-(c)(3) groups
    filling out Form 1024   143
  copy of another organization's application   120
  Form 990
    social security numbers   260
  questions back from IRS   144
  retroactivity   140
  time of IRS response   118
Federal tax returns   247
  accounting methods   251
    changing   252
  accounting period   250
  automatic revocation   248
    reinstatement   249
  changing your fiscal year   250
  common mistakes   255–262
  exemptions from filing   247
  failure to file   248–262
  Form 990   247
    governance questions   254
    independent contractors   256
    key employees   256
    where to file   249
  Form 990EZ   247
    where to file   249
  Form 990N   247
  Form 990 Schedule A
    described   249
    who files it   249
  functional accounting   256. *See also* Financial recordkeeping
  fundraising expenses   256
  how to complete forms   253
  loans   258
  lobbying   258
  penalties   249
  political activity   258
  private foundation status   259
  public inspection   252
  related organizations   260
  signatures   260–261
  unrelated business income   258
  waiver of penalties   249
  who must file   247
Fee/activity supported organizations   106
  definition   146
  disqualified persons   163–164
  gross investment income test   164
  normalcy period   165
  qualified support   162–164
  recordkeeping   165–171
  support base
    calculation   148
  support requirements   146
  support test   162
    calculation   162
  unusual grants   157–158, 163
Financial management   507–517
  accuracy of reports   640–650
  balanced books   639–650
  balance sheet   633
  breaking even   637
  checkup   511–517
  dashboard reports   639
  evaluating financial health   632–650
  financial health   641–650
  key elements   509
  monitoring   510
  planning   509
  recording   510
  restricted funds   634–635
    compliance with restrictions   637
  reviews   644–650
  risk management   566–570
  signs of good management   508
  timing   511
  wise use of resources   638–650
Financial recordkeeping   571–612
  accounting defined   572–580
  basic accounting for small nonprofits   582–612
  carryover funds   583–612
  cash vs. accrual accounting   580
  cash vs. accrual comparison   575
  classification of contributions   585
  computerized choices. *See herein* QuickBooks
  contributions
    distinguished from purchases   586
  cost allocation plan   591
  decisions to make   575–580
  deferred revenue   590
  differences from business accounting   584–612

INDEX

double entry   581
equipment   594
Form 990 reporting requirements   578
functional accounting   577
    used on Form 990   256
fund accounting   597–612
GAAP   578, 584
general ledger   581
government funds accounting requirements   596–612
government grants and contracts   590
in-kind contributions   592
investments   593
IRS reporting requirements   578
land and building   594
multiple programs or funding   577
multi-year grant commitments   589
net assets
    classes   588
OMB Circulars   597
program fees received in advance   589
promises to give   588
restrictions
    board designated funds   587
    unrestricted expenses   587
restrictions fulfilled   587
types of accounts   580
who does it   609–612
    larger nonprofits   611
    mid-sized nonprofits   610
    small nonprofits   610
    small nonprofits with complex funding   610
Financial reports   571–612. *See also* Financial management
    accounting software choices   606–612
    accuracy   640, 640–650
    balanced books   639–650
    basic accounting for small nonprofits   582–612
    connections between financial reports   603
    dashboard reports   639
    differences from business accounting   584–612
    financial statements   598–612
        types   598
    how to review   633
    preparing useful reports   604–612
    QuickBooks® tips   608–612
    sample statement of activities   598
    statement of cash flows   602
    statement of functional activities   601
Fiscal controls. *See* Handling funds
Fiscal sponsorship   219–237
    agreement   236
    alternatives   222

assistance to individuals
    improper   224
    permitted   222
avoidance of lobbying tax   225
avoidance of public support test   224
characterization of fund uses   225
conduit to non-exempt organization   224
contract for services   223
control   228
described   219
expenditure responsibility   234
fees   230
how to structure   232–237
independent contractor   235–236
    agreement   236
internal accounting for project funds   229
issues   225–236
liabilities   230
misuses   223
models   232–236
new projects   221
ongoing projects with major donor   221
ownership of property   230
pass-through donations or grants   223
payment to sponsor   230
penalties for misuse   225
program of sponsor   222
proper uses   220
protecting sponsor's funding sources   231
public relations   231
restricted fund   226, 233
special issues of sponsor   231
unrestricted funds   226
Fiscal year   121, 519
    setting your year   45
Foreign organizations   135
    Form 1023 questions   135
Form 990. *See* Federal tax returns
    governance policies   346
Foundations
    §501(c)(3) exempt organization   93
        exempt purposes   94
    development   102, 106, 146
    grants   473–506
        described   148
        unusual   157–158
    managers   105
        as disqualified persons   155, 156
    preference for funding §501(c)(3) organizations   109
    private
        contributors are public record   117
        described   99

INDEX

drawbacks   99
employees on board   310
Form 990   259
Form 990-PF   246
Form 1023   138
ineligibility for lobbying election   182
use of fiscal sponsorship   225
private operating   101
tipping problem   157
Fraternal societies
tax exemption   111
Fraud. *See* Handling funds: fraud protection
Functional accounting. *See* Financial recordkeeping
Fundraising   471–506. *See also* Contributions; Foundations
bingo, raffles or gaming   487
problems   489
corporate giving   477
corporate sponsorships   477
donor acknowledgment   481
ethical issues   502
events   482
Form 1023   133
foundation grants   473–506. *See also* Foundations: grants
funding preferences   475
funding priorities   475
personal relationships   476
fundraising firms   504
contracts with   502–506
gift acceptance policy   482
government contracts   491–506
government grants   490–506
grants. *See* Grants
how nonprofits are funded   472–506
individual contributions   478
in-kind contributions   499
internet fundraising   500
internet sales   495–506
investment income   497
membership fees   484–506
product sales   494
program service fees   492
religious organizations as funders   486
reporting expenses   256
social enterprise   495
social media   500
solicitation disclosures by non-(c)(3) groups   505–506
staff fundraiser   502
subsidies   493
third party payers   493

trainings   503
unethical   503–506
percentage of event   503
percentage of grants   503
percentage of solicitations   503

G

Garden clubs   112
General partnerships   9
Governmental nonprofits   29
issues   30
Government grants and contracts
role in public support test   106
Government unit   104
Grants. *See also* Foundations: grants
corporate   477
foreign
Form 1023 questions   135
Form 1023 questions   135
lobbying restrictions   672
public support test   148, 153, 157
terrorism laws   687
Grassroots lobbying. *See* Lobbying election
Group exemptions. *See* Federal tax exemption: group exemptions

H

Handling funds   546–570
bank deposits   555
banking   551–570
check choices   552–570
checks returned   556
check stock controls   553
common mistakes   551
computerized accounting software   553
online access   552
online payments   555
opening checking account   551
Positive Pay   557
reconciling bank statements   557–570
two signatures on checks   552, 554
unauthorized checks   553
Board's role   569–570
cash receipts   564
checklist of key controls   569–570
corporate credit card   563
credit card payments to you   565–570
developing policies and procedures   547–548
expense reimbursement   561
identity theft   554
in-kind contributions   566–570
insurance protection   567

key concepts   547–548
multiple bank accounts   558
petty cash funds   559–570
processing payments   560–570
risk management   566–570
signing blank checks   554
travel expense reimbursements   562
Homeowners associations
bylaws   70
protection for directors   359
state tax exemption   239
Horticultural organizations
tax exemption   110
Hospitals   103

I

Identity theft   554, 684–706
Incorporators
avoidance of organizational meeting   45
calling organizational meeting   42, 45
defined   38–39
in religious corporation sole   34
role in amendments to Articles   713
role in dissolution   748
role in incorporation   41
schools
names supplied to IRS   103
Indemnification   360, 69, 86
Independent contractors   427–443
agreement in writing   442–443
ask the IRS   441
assessing your exposure   441
danger signals   439
definition   428
expert opinion in writing   441
federal 20 factor test   430
federal income tax   429
federal wage and hour laws   438
fiscal sponsorship relationships   235
Form 990   256
Form SS-8   441
limiting your exposure   442
penalties for noncompliance   439
protections for your organization   440
state unemployment   434
state wage and hour laws   438
worker compensation   435
exceptions to worker test   436–437
subcontractors   437
test for worker   435–437
Initiatives. *See* Ballot measures
In-kind contributions

fundraising   499
Insiders. *See* Disqualified persons: excess benefits transactions; Conflicts of interest
Inspection of books and records. *See* Records: inspection
Insurance
directors and officers   362
errors and omissions insurance   363
personal coverage   363
protections   362
employees
workers compensation   435
fiscal sponsorship
coverage for project   230
retention of records   678
risk management   567
volunteer liability policy   465
volunteers   463–467
Intellectual property   134
Internal Revenue Service. *See* Federal tax exemption; Federal tax returns
International organizations. *See* Foreign organizations
Internet
lobbying   186
payment for weblinks   211
political activity   178
sale of goods or services   495–506
using for fundraising   500
Investment income
accounting for   593
managing   497
private foundations   100
private operating foundations   101
public support test   150, 164

J

Joint ventures   218
Form 1023   134
sample policy   218
Journal. *See* Payroll

L

Labor unions
tax exemption   110
Land trust   33
Licenses
state and local   50, 683
Limited liability companies   10, 94
Limited partnerships   10
use of word restricted   33
Linked organizations. *See* Affiliated organizations

INDEX

Literary organizations
  tax exemption   95
Loans
  by founders   46
  to directors or officers   303
Lobbying   172–202, 651–675
  §501(c)(3) organizations   180
    lobbying tests   181
      mathematical test   181–182
      substantial parts test   181
  §501(c)(4) organizations   198–202
  §501(c)(5) and (6) organizations   199
  administrative agencies   187
  compliance   194
    allocating employee and overhead expenses   195–202
    allocating expenses on communications   195
  deductibility of dues used for   199
  direct   183–187
  discussions of broad problems   188
  education and monitoring   198
  federal fund restrictions   672
  federal lobbying disclosure act   663
  Form 990   258
  Form 1023   133
  grassroots   183
  internet   186
  local rules   672–675
    city of Portland   672
  non-(c) 3 organizations   198–202
  non-deductibily of lobbying expenses by staff or volunteer   195
  nonpartisan analysis   187
  not lobbying   187–202
  recordkeeping   194
  self-defense communications   188
  state registration   670
  tax   199
  technical advice   188
  web link to (c)(4)   201
Lobbying election   182
  §501(h) election   181–182
  affiliated organizations   190
  communications with members   184–186
  compliance   194
  definition of lobbying   182
    what is not lobbying   184
  direct   183–187
  direct encouragement to action   184
  excessive lobbying
    penalties   191
  exempt purpose expenditures   189–194
  formula   188
  making the calculation   189–194
  grassroots   183
  indirect encouragement to action   184
  legislation   183
  lobbying expenditures   188–194
  mass media advertisements   186
  procedure to elect   194
  recordkeeping   195
  research expenses   196
  whether to elect   193
  who can make   182
  who cannot make   182
Local tax returns   262
Lodges   110

M

Medical information   685
Medical research organizations   103
Members. *See* Mutual benefit corporations: members
  admission
    criteria   369
  classes   71–72, 371
    rights and obligations   371
  consent   370–371
  defined   25, 367
  delegates   379
  dues   26, 373
  election of directors   25, 383
    annual meeting   377
  expulsion   387–392, 72
  inspection of records   384
    restrictions   387
    with a reason   386
    without a reason   385
  liabilities   371–392, 372
  meetings   376
    action without   378–379, 75
    annual   377, 73
    conduct   378
    minutes   378
    notice   373, 73–74
    quorum   74
    record date   375
    regular   377
    Roberts Rules of Order   378
    special   73
    waiver of notice   374
    who attends   376
  mutual benefit corporations
    conflicts of interest   389
    right to assets on dissolution   389

INDEX

special rights   389–392
obligations   371–392
qualifications   72
removal of directors   383–392
resignation   387
rights   371, 371–392
  management of corporation restricted   372
suspension   387–392, 72
termination   387–392, 72
vacancy on board   383–392
voting   71–72, 379
  amend bylaws   41
  ballot   74–75, 75, 381
  by mail   381
  corporate acceptance   382
  in person   380
  majority vote   74–75, 380
  proxy   75, 380
  quorum   379
  size of board   41
  vote splitting   381
Membership corporations   367–392
  change to nonmembership corporation   390–392
  considerations in setting up   26–27
  responsibilities to members   368
Mergers   730–744
  accounting rules   741–744
  adoption. *See herein* plan of merger
  alternatives   732
  assets   736–738
  audits   737–738
  contracts   737
  defined   731
  disappearing corporation
    definition   731
  due diligence investigation   734
  effect   740
  employees issues   736–738
  filing Articles of Merger   740
  funders   737–738
  issues   736–740
  leases   737
  letter of understanding   734
  liabilities   736–738
  limitations   732
  members   736
  planning committee   734
  plan of merger
    abandonment   740
    adoption   738
    adoption by board   739–740
    adoption by members   739–740
    creating plan   738–740

violation of plan   738
process   733–744
public benefit corporation
  limitations   732
reasons for   731
religious corporations
  limitations   732
steps   734–744
surviving corporation
  definition   731
  purpose   736–738
  structure   736–738
tax exempt organizations   741
terminology   731
Minutes. *See* Board meetings; Members: meetings
Mutual benefit corporations. *See* Members: mutual benefit corporations
  amendments to articles   716–719
  change from public benefit to   717, 718
  defined   27
  dissolution   747
  loans to directors   303
  major features   29
  members   73
    right to assets on dissolution   389
    termination   388, 726
    voting   382
  number of directors   20
  removal of directors   41
Mutual property and casualty companies   113

N

Name
  choosing   33
  doing business under another name   49
  reserving   33
  using "bank" in name   33
  using "trust" in name   33
Nonmembership corporations. *See* Board of directors
Nonprofit corporations   4
  amending articles of incorporation   713
  amending bylaws   728
  governmental connections   29
  operation
    governed by board of directors   19
  should you be one?   3–17
  structure and types   18–31
  types   27
Nonprofit organizations
  choosing which is best for you   13
  disadvantages   12

INDEX

postal rates   50
types   4. *See also* Types of nonprofit organizations
Notices   685. *See* Email
  address   686
  effective date   686

O

Office address.   *See* Registered offices
Officers   25, 67, 84. *See* President; Secretary; Treasurer
  duties   341
  election   67, 85
  executive director as   343
  indemnification   360
  limited liability   359
  most vulnerable to lawsuit   356–357
  names   341
  other   25, 68, 344, 85
  personal liability   353
    agreement to be liable   355
    breach of duty of loyalty   353
    failure to act with due care   353
    insurance   362
    misuse of fiscal sponsorship   225
    protections   357
  replacing   316
  resignation   319–320
  signers of Form 990   260
  standards of conduct   25, 344–345
  vacancy   68, 85
  who can sue officers   355
Open meetings laws
  board meetings   326
Open records laws   681
Oregon Department of Justice
  social media fundraising   501

P

Pass-through organizations.   *See* Fiscal sponsorships
Payroll   613–631
  cafeteria plans   616
  compensation rates   618
  definition of terms   614–631
  deposits
    direct   616
    tax   616
  direct deposit of paychecks   625
  draws   616
  employer taxes   614, 619
  FICA   619
  flex plans   616
  fringe benefits   617, 627–631
  journal   624
  local government taxes   622
  mandatory withholding   615
  net pay   616
  paychecks   625
  pay period   618
  procedures   618, 624
  records   623
  SAIF   621
  services   617
  setting up system   622
  Social Security and Medicare   619
  software   617
  steps to preparing   622–631
  tax deposits   625–631
  tax reporting requirements   625, 626–631
  tax reports   617
  tax tables   623
  timesheets   618, 624
  unemployment   620–631
    self-insurance   620
  voluntary deductions   615
  worker compensation   615, 621
Pension plans
  employee supported   113
Personnel policies   278, 399. *See also* Employee handbook
  administration   423–426
  amendments   420–426, 421–426
  approaches   401–426
  attendance   406
  behavior standards   407
  benefits   415
  bereavement leave   415
  conditions of employment   406–426
  confidentiality   408
  conflicts of interest   408
  developing   400–426
  disciplinary action   417
  dismissal   417
  drug and alcohol use   407
  educational leave   415
  emergency leave   414
  employee classifications   410
  employee evaluation   416
  employment categories   409–426
  exempt employees   409
  family leave   412
  grievance procedure   419
  harassment   405
  holidays   411

job reclassification   416
jury duty   414
leave policies   414
lobbying   408
no expectation of privacy   407
nondiscrimination policy   405
nonexempt employees   409
obeying all laws   406
outside employment   408
payroll procedures   410
philosophy of organization   404
political activities   408
reimbursements   416
salary increases   410
salary range   410
sick leave   412
termination of employment   418–426
time banks   415
trial period   409
vacation   411
what to include   403–426
work day   406
Personnel records   420–426
Policies. *See* Board of directors: policies; Personnel policies
Political action committees (PACs)
 federal political committees   657–661
 federal tax exemption   112
 state political committees   666
Political activity   172–202
 campaign rules   651–675
 candidate appearances   176
 candidate debates   662
 Citizens United case   653
 federal election rules   653
  advocacy for candidate   655
   §501(c)(3) prohibited   654
  Citizens United case   653
  contributions   654
  political action committees (PACs)   658
   §501(c)(3) restrictions   660
   registration and disclosure   660
   Super PACs   660
  political committees   657–661
 federal fund restrictions   672
 Form 990   258
 Form 1023   133
 internet   178
 legislative scorecards   180
 local rules   672–675
 political expenditure tax   657, 673
 state election rules   664
  §501(c)(3) organizations   669

  electioneering conduct   669
  independent expenditures   665–675
 tax exempt organizations   112, 173
  §501(c)(4)   198
  §501(c)(5) and (c)(6)   199
  candidate education   177
  candidate forums   175
  issue advocacy   176
  non-(c)(3)s   198–202
   limitations   199
  permissible activities for (c)(3)s   174
  prohibited activities   174
  voter education   175
  voter registration   176
Postal benefits   50–51
President   18, 67, 68, 86. *See also* Officers
 duties   25
 not prescribed by law   67
 power to call board meetings   64, 81
 report at annual meeting   376
 signing minutes   332
 usual duties   341
Prevention of cruelty to animals or children
 tax exemption   96
Private foundations. *See* Foundations: private
Profit corporations   9
Proxy voting. *See* Board meetings; Members: voting
Public benefit corporations
 access to records
  limitations   41
 amendments to articles   716–719
 defined   27
 directors
  removal   41
 expulsion of members   388
 Form CT-12   261
 loans to directors and officers   303
 major features   28
 mergers   732
 public access to records   681
 registration with Attorney General   47
Public charities   101
 described   99
 Form 990   259
 Form 1023   138, 139
Public disclosure of records. *See* Records
Publicly supported organizations   106, 145–166
 criteria to qualify   152
  mechanical test   152
 definition   146
 direct public support   153
 disqualified persons   153

facts and circumstances test   159–161
family members   156
foundation manager   155
indirect public support   158–159
normalcy period   165
recordkeeping   165–171
substantial contributor   154
support base calculation   148
support requirements   146
thirty-five percent disqualified person   156–157
twenty percent owner   156
two percent limitation   153
   amounts excluded   157–158
   unusual grants   157–158
Public safety organizations   106
   tax exemption   95
Purpose of corporation   57, 71

Q

Quasi-governmental nonprofits   29–31
QuickBooks®   608–612
Quorum. *See* Board meetings; Bylaws

R

Real estate board   111
Record date   375
   date for notice of membership meetings   373
   date for notice of special membership meetings   377
   how date is set   375
Records   677. *See also* Financial recordkeeping; Financial reports
   confidential records   682
   copying rules   693
   destruction   678
   group exemptions   699
   how long to keep   678
   inspection
     by directors   681
     by employees   681
     by funders   746
     by general public   681
     by members   384, 385, 680, 727
     by nonmembers   681
     Form 990   692
     of tax exempt organizations   116, 252, 692
     restrictions on members' rights   387
   open records laws   681
   public benefit corporations   681
   public records law   681
   record retention and destruction policy   349
   records retention and destruction policy   347

   retention   678
   schools   699–707
   tax exempt organizations   681
   transparency policy   347, 349
   what you should keep   677
   who can inspect   680
Referendum   174. *See also* Ballot measures
Registered agent
   address   36
   changing   712
   described   35
   director as   22
Registered offices   36
   changing   712
Registrations   682. *See also* See Department of Justice
   charitable solicitations in other states   500–506
   Department of Justice   47
   doing business in other states   49
   federal lobbyists   663
   federal political committees   657–661
   state lobbyists   670
   state political committees   666
Releases   463, 686
Religious corporations
   amendments to Articles   716–719
   defined   27
   directors   19
     conflicts of interest   358
   loans to directors and officers   303
   major features   28
   members
     termination   73
   mergers   732
   property tax exemption   242
   registration with Attorney General   47
   tax exemption   95
Reports   682
   Attorney General   683
   Corporation Commissioner   682
   Department of Justice   683
   Secretary of State   682
Resignations
   by Board members   345
   by officers   345
Restricted funds
   board designated funds   587
   board's obligation to observe restrictions   286–288, 637
   donor restricted funds   637
   financial planning   634–635
Risk management   566–570
   insurance   567

Roadmap to this book   50–51
Roberts Rules of Order   56, 378. *See also* Board meetings

S

Sale of assets   741–744
   creditors   743–744
   in usual course of activities   742
   notice to Attorney General   743
   notice to IRS by §501(c)(3) groups   743
   not in usual course of activities   742–744
Sarbanes-Oxley Act   643
Scholarships   136
Schools   103
   tax-exempt rules   699–707
Scientific organizations
   tax exemption   95
Secretary   25, 67, 69, 86. *See also* Officers
   call for meeting
     notice delivered to   377
   duties   25, 69
   membership meeting minutes   378
   proxy
     delivery to   380
   signing minutes   332
Section 501(c)(3). *See* Federal tax exemption: §501(c)(3)
Setting up a nonprofit corporation. *See* Starting a nonprofit corporation
Social clubs
   tax exemption   111
Social enterprise   495–506
   threat to exemption   496
Sole proprietorships   11
Solicitations. *See* Registrations: Department of Justice
   by non-§501(c)(3) groups   505–506, 699
   email   501
   individuals   478
   internet   500
     across state lines   500–506
     donate now buttons   500
   registration for charitable solicitation   500–506
Starting a nonprofit corporation   32
   articles of incorporation
     additional provisions   39
     filing   41–42
     filling out   35
   bylaws   42
   choosing a name   33
   licenses and permits   50
   organizational meeting   45
   registering in other states   49
   registering with the Department of Justice   47
   reserving a name   33
   tax identification number   47
   using another name   49
State and local tax exemption   238–244
   county business tax   240
   county property tax   240
     art museums   241
     cemeteries   243
     charitable   241
     day care centers   242
     fire departments   241
     fraternal organizations   243
     housing for elderly   243
     how to apply for exemption   243
     leases and lease options   244–245
     literary   241
     low income housing   243
     public parks and recreation   243
     religious groups   242
     schools and educational organizations   242
     scientific groups   241
     senior centers   243
     student housing   243
     whether to apply   241
     who is eligible   241
   homeowners associations   239
   local business license   244
   state income tax   239
     how to apply for exemption   239
     who is covered   239
   Tri-met tax   240
   unrelated business income tax   239
State and local tax exemptions
   Lane Transit District tax   615
   Tri-Met tax   615
State and local tax returns. *See* State tax returns; Local tax returns
State tax returns   261
   how to fill out   262
   when due   261
   who must file   261
Structure of nonprofit corporation   18
Successor organizations   141
Supporting organization   104

T

Tax exemption. *See* Federal tax exemption; State and local tax exemption
Tax identification number. *See* Employer identification number

INDEX

Tax returns   246–262. *See also* Federal tax returns; State tax returns; Local tax returns
Terrorism laws   687
  actions that aid terrorists   688
  sanctions for aiding terrorists   688
    civil lawsuits   689
    criminal penalties   688
    freezing assets   688
    revocation of tax-exempt status   689
    voluntary compliance guidelines   689
  what you should do   690
Timeshares
  bylaws   70
Treasurer   69, 86, 341
  duties   342
Trusts   5
  as direct public support   153
  black lung benefit   113
  books and records   6
  charitable
    registration with Attorney General   6
  control   6
  liability   6
  multi-employer benefit   113
  registration   6
  supplemental unemployment benefit   113
  using trust in name   33
Types of nonprofit corporations   27–29
  major features   28
  religious corporations. *See* Religious corporations
  which type are you?   27
Types of nonprofit organizations   4–17
  associations   6. *See* Associations
  charitable trusts   5
  nonprofit corporations   4

U

Umbrella organizations. *See* Fiscal sponsorships
Unemployment benefit trusts   113
Unionization   399–426
Unrelated business income   206–218
  advertising   209–212
  bingo   489
  corporate sponsorships   210–212
  denial of exemption   216
  exceptions   213–215
  Form 990   258
  internet sales   495
  mixed activities   209
  payment for weblinks   211
  protection of tax exemption   216
    forming new corporation   217
  regularly carried on   208–209
  revocation of exemption   216–218
  sale of goods   212
  services   212
  social venture enterprises   495–506
  substantially related to exempt purpose   208
  trade or business   207–209
Unrelated business income tax   215–218
  calculations   215
  payment   215
  state tax form   246
  who must pay   215
Unusual grants   157

V

Veterans organizations   110
  tax exemption   112
Volunteer fire organizations   110
Volunteers   444–468
  as disguised employees   426, 453
  assessing risk of harm by volunteers   456–457
  assessing risk of harm to volunteers   461
  evaluating   451–452
  injury to   460, 465
  insurance   463
  liability for volunteer's actions   458
  liability generally   456
  orienting   449
  personal liability of   457
  placing in right spot   448–449
  protections   461
    crisis management plan   467
    damage control   462
    good communication   467
    preventive actions   462
    releases   465
  recognizing and rewarding   452
  recordkeeping   463
  recruiting   445–467
  releases   463
  screening   447
  supervising   451
  training   450
  volunteer liability policy   465
  when volunteer is liable   457
  worker compensation   465
Voter guides   662
Voter registration   176, 661–664
Voting. *See* Board meetings; Members
Voting records   175, 662–664
Voting scorecards   175

W

Waivers. *See* Releases
Whistleblowers   569
  policy   349
Worker compensation. *See* Insurance: employees; Payrolls